# A Celebration of Literature and Response

## Children, Books, and Teachers in K–8 Classrooms

Marjorie R. Hancock

*Kansas State University*

Merrill,
an imprint of Prentice Hall
*Upper Saddle River, New Jersey*     *Columbus, Ohio*

**Library of Congress Cataloging-in-Publication Data**

Hancock, Marjorie R.

    A celebration of literature and response: children, books, and teachers in k-8 classrooms/ Marjorie R. Hancock.

      p.  cm.

    Includes bibliographical references and index.

    ISBN 0-13-740291-0

    1. Children's literature—Study and teaching (Elementary)

2. Reader-response criticism. 3. Children—Books and reading.

I. Title

LB1575.H36   2000

372.64'044—dc21

99-31123
CIP

Cover art: SuperStock, Inc. Fine Art
Editor: Bradley J. Potthoff
Editorial Assistant: Mary Evangelista
Production Editor: Mary M. Irvin
Design Coordinator: Diane C. Lorenzo
Text Designer: Carlisle Communications, Inc.
Cover Designer: Karrie Converse-Jones
Production Manager: Pamela D. Bennett
Director of Marketing: Kevin Flanagan
Marketing Manager: Megan Shepherd
Marketing Coordinator: Krista Groshong
Production Management and Editorial Supervision: Carlisle Publishers Services

This book was set in Garamond by Carlisle Communications, Ltd., and was printed and bound by R. R. Donnelley & Sons Company. The cover was printed by Phoenix Color Corp.

©2000 by Prentice-Hall, Inc.
Pearson Education
Upper Saddle River, New Jersey 07458

10 9 8 7 6 5 4 3 2

ISBN: 0-13-740291-0

Prentice-Hall International (UK) Limited, *London*
Prentice-Hall of Australia Pty. Limited, *Sydney*
Prentice-Hall of Canada, Inc., *Toronto*
Prentice-Hall Hispanoamericana, S. A., *Mexico*
Prentice-Hall of India Private Limited, *New Delhi*
Prentice-Hall of Japan, Inc., *Tokyo*
Prentice-Hall (Singapore) Pte. Ltd., *Singapore*
Editora Prentice-Hall do Brasil, Ltda., *Rio de Janeiro*

# Preface

*A* *Celebration of Literature and Response* is written for undergraduate and graduate courses in children's literature that blend an appreciation for children's books with an emphasis on the critical involvement of the reader with literature. Whether the course resides in education, English, or library science, the blended perspective on both literature and the reader should have wide appeal. This text effectively balances the importance of both the literature and the reader from an educational perspective. The blended perspective of this text—literary appreciation and response-based instruction in K–8 classrooms—also makes the text useful in language arts or reading methods courses. Adults who advocate children's literature and work with children will find interest in both the emphasis on literature and the reader.

The scholarship for this text is grounded in Louise Rosenblatt's transactional theory of reader response. Its practicality, however, is reinforced by reader response research and authentic classroom practice. *A Celebration of Literature and Response* adequately fulfills two purposes. First, it links the scholarship of reader response and a respect for quality children's literature with an appreciation for the response-based connections that involve the reader in that literature. Second, it provides both preservice and inservice teachers with an instructional perspective as they expand their knowledge of contemporary children's literature across literary genres while acquiring meaningful response-based strategies to include in literacy programs. The focus on both books and readers is a critical aspect of a response-based literature perspective and brings a unique quality to this text.

*A Celebration of Literature and Response* is organized around five main "celebrations" as a framework for building a bridge between reader response theory, quality children's literature, and exemplary literature-based practice. Part I, Celebrating Literature, Response, and Teaching, invites reflection on the meaningful connections between children's literature, children as readers, and the role of reader response in literature-based instruction. Louise Rosenblatt's transactional theory of reader response defined in understandable terms provides a framework for sharing the rich, developmental parameters of response. Part II, Celebrating Literature, has substantial chapters that invite readers to appreciate the major literary genres and formats of children's literature, including a chapter on multicultural literature. Rich bibliographies of current book titles interwoven with selected children's classics form a sound foundation for later classroom connections. Part III, Celebrating Response Connections, contains a blend of response-based strategies for eliciting a developmental range of reader response in K–8 children across oral, written, and artistic dimensions. In Part IV, Celebrating Interdisciplinary Connections, the integration of content area instruction through literature clusters and literature-based theme explorations is explored. Part V focuses on Celebrating Response Through Assessment by proposing authentic assessment for documenting growth in response and by aligning literature and response-based instruction to literacy standards.

The following list highlights some of the unique aspects of this text that make it stand out from others in the field:

- **Reader response focus.**   Reader response to literature is not only discussed in introductory chapters, but integrated throughout the entire text. Each genre chapter concludes with connections to response-based chapters. Part III focuses on a developmental perspective across the spectrum of response options.
- **Authentic voices of response.**   Examples of authentic responses of children, preservice teachers, and inservice teachers to literature are interspersed throughout the text to bring life to the ideal of reader response to literature.
- **Up-to-date literature.**   Although literary classics are woven throughout the chapters, the text emphasizes literature from the 1990s to add strength and excitement to the educator's repertoire of literature for classroom connections.
- **Developmental labeling of literature.**   Bibliographies throughout the text contain the designation of P (primary, K–2), I (intermediate, 3–5), and M (middle school, 6–8) to assist teachers in age-appropriate use of literature. These designations indicate the level(s) at which the literature will best elicit response.
- **Extended bibliographies.**   In addition to the children's books cited within and at the end of each chapter, many chapters contain extended lists of recent children's books that emphasize a certain aspect of literature or provide additional response models for classroom use.
- **Multicultural literature.**   Not only is multicultural children's literature woven throughout genre chapters and the entire text, but it is showcased in its own chapter emphasizing selection criteria, outstanding literature across cultures, and a framework for effective classroom inclusion.
- **Interdisciplinary instruction.**   Suggestions for selecting literature across genres for integrated instruction in multiage settings are shared. The process and procedures for creating literature clusters and literature-based theme explorations are effectively articulated in step-by-step format.
- **Assessment focus.**   The text addresses this key issue with a chapter that includes rubrics, checklists, response portfolios, and other response documentation strategies. The text addresses the important connections between assessment and response-based instruction while justifying the inclusion of literature in the classroom.
- **Appendixes.**   The extensive appendixes include lists of book awards, professional resources, and Internet sites of interest to educators. All information is current, well

organized, and presented in a manner useful to preservice and inservice teachers as well as researchers in children's literature.

- **Website.**   A Companion Website is available as a resource for both instructors and students. It can be accessed at www.prenhall.com/hancock (see p. vii and viii for more information.).

Those who select *A Celebration of Literature and Response* as a text for preservice or inservice teachers are encouraged to align course assignments and practicum or classroom-based activities with the reader response opportunities shared in the text. Although the genre focus suggests a traditional course, response connections to other chapters are predictably shared at the end of each chapter in Part II. This perspective allows a theory-into-practice approach and encourages meaningful connections between the text and authentic response in the college classroom. For example, a literature response journal with historical fiction, literature discussions on a work of realistic fiction, or dramatic reenactments of scenes from a traditional folktale replicate the response-based activities that inevitably will find their way into the K–8 classroom.

Although other highly respected, quality texts exist in the field of children's literature, *A Celebration of Literature and Response* merits consideration because of its dual focus on books and readers. Quality literature and a foundation of reader response theory build valid instructional possibilities for child-centered, response-based involvement through literature.

## Acknowledgments

This textbook is the culmination of 10 years of elementary teaching in Illinois and 8 years of undergraduate and graduate teaching, supervision, and research at Kansas State University. The enthusiastic children, dedicated teachers, demanding professors, and outstanding professionals I encountered during my career made this book possible. Louise Rosenblatt deserves recognition for her conceptualization of a theory of reading literature that melds children and books together in a democratic classroom environment, encouraging each individual to connect personal experiences and innermost feelings to quality literature. Exploring her theory at the doctoral level began to answer so many questions I had as a teacher, thus planting the seed for this text.

Authentic settings, real children, and dedicated teachers make this book believable. The preservice teachers of Kansas State University confirm my instructional philosophy as they confidently share successful response-based lessons in their practicum and student internship experiences. The teachers and children at Ogden Elementary School, my professional development site for six years, deserve thanks for supporting the infusion of countless literature-based lessons into their classrooms. My graduate students and inservice participants across the state of Kansas took children's literature and response-based ideas to their students and generously reported their enthusiastic results. Throughout the pages of this book are woven their reflections, their use of literature, and their own responses to children's books.

Special appreciation is due teacher researchers, graduate students, and practitioners for opening their classrooms to literature and reader response: Irene Barber, Valerie Coughlin, Grainne Dunbar, Linda Johnson, Joyce Heilman, Joanne Hoffman, Jennifer Hoss, Janet Kellogg, Ron Marstall, Linda Martin, Rene Maule, Debbie Mercer, Ruth Messer, Kelly

Mueller, Julie Rothwell, Charlotte Skinner, and Susan Thornberg. Thanks to these and many unmentioned educators are due for their contributions to responses and visions shared throughout the text.

I'd also like to thank the people at Merrill/Prentice Hall. From the day Brad Potthoff walked into my Kansas State University office in March 1996, he has helped set my professional agenda for a challenging, yet fulfilling experience. His editorial assistant, Mary Evangelista, had immediate answers to endless inquiries from a novice textbook author. Mary Irvin and the countless people who designed and put this book into production were instrumental to its outcome. Kelli Jauron and Kathy Davis, in particular, checked citations and polished my writing with their expert editing staff.

My sincere thanks go to the professional reviewers who provided informed perspectives and opinions: Sue Burgess, Framingham State College; Donna J. Camp, University of Central Florida; M. Jean Greenlaw, University of North Texas; Helen Doucet, McNeese State University; Colon K. Ducolon, Champlain College; Susan Garness, Minot State University; Constantine Georgiou, New York University; Mary Maness, Bartlesville Wesleyan College; Betty Jo McCarty-Roberts, Florida State University; Mary H. McNulty, Francis Marion University; Sam Sebesta, University of Washington; and Jennifer Smith, Northern Kentucky University. This book is far better through the incorporation of their expertise and sound suggestions.

I especially want to thank my children, Michael, Amy, and Patrick, for their understanding and encouragement during this project. Our mutual love of literature and respect for teaching have greatly influenced their personal and professional lives.

With my deepest love and respect, I dedicate this book to my late husband, Bill Hancock, who believed in me long before I believed in myself. His endearing love and constant support throughout our precious years together made this book possible.

# Discover Companion Websites: A Virtual Learning Environment

Technology is a constantly growing and changing aspect of our field that is creating a need for content and resources. To address this emerging need, we have developed an online learning environment for students and professors alike—Companion Websites—to support our textbooks.

In creating a Companion Website, our goal is to build on and enhance what the textbook already offers. For this reason, the content for each user-friendly website is organized by topic and provides the professor and student with a variety of meaningful resources. Common features of a Companion Website include:

## FOR THE PROFESSOR

Every Companion Website integrates **Syllabus Manager™,** an online syllabus creation and management utility.

- **Syllabus Manager™** provides you, the instructor, with an easy, step-by-step process to create and revise syllabi, with direct links into Companion Website and other online content without having to learn HTML.
- Students may logon to your syllabus during any study session. All they need to know is the web address for the Companion Website and the password you've assigned to your syllabus.

- After you have created a syllabus using **Syllabus Manager™,** students may enter the syllabus for their course section from any point in the Companion Website.
- Class dates are highlighted in white and assignment due dates appear in blue. Clicking on a date, the student is shown the list of activities for the assignment. The activities for each assignment are linked directly to actual content, saving time for students.
- Adding assignments consists of clicking on the desired due date, then filling in the details of the assignment—name of the assignment, instructions, and whether or not it is a one-time or repeating assignment.
- In addition, links to other activities can be created easily. If the activity is online, a URL can be entered in the space provided, and it will be linked automatically in the final syllabus.
- Your completed syllabus is hosted on our servers, allowing convenient updates from any computer on the Internet. Changes you make to your syllabus are immediately available to your students at their next logon.

# FOR THE STUDENT

- **Topic Overviews**—outline key concepts in topic areas
- **Electronic Blue Book**—send homework or essays directly to your instructor's email with this paperless form
- **Message Board**—serves as a virtual bulletin board to post—or respond to—questions or comments to/from a national audience
- **Web Destinations**—links to www sites that relate to each topic area
- **Professional Organizations**—links to organizations that relate to topic areas
- **Additional Resources**—access to topic specific content that enhances material found in the text

To take advantage of these resources, please visit the *A Celebration of Literature and Response: Children, Books, and Teachers in K–8 Classrooms* Companion Website at www.prenhall.com/hancock.

# Introduction:
# An Invitation to Celebrate

*If books could be more, could show more, could own more, this book would have smells. . . .*

*It would have the smells of old farms; the sweet smell of new-mown hay as it falls off the oiled sickle blade when the horses pull the mower through the field, and the sour smell of manure steaming in a winter barn. It would have the sticky-slick smell of birth when the calves come and they suck for the first time on the rich, new milk; the dusty smell of winter hay dried and stored in the loft waiting to be dropped down to the cattle; the pungent fermented smell of the chopped corn silage when it is brought into the manger on the silage fork. This book would have the smell of new potatoes sliced and frying in light pepper on a woodstove burning dry pine, the damp smell of leather mittens steaming on the back of the stovetop, and the acrid smell of the slop bucket by the door when the lid is lifted and the potato peelings are dumped in—but it can't.*

*Books can't have smells.*

*If books could be more and own more and give more, this book would have sound. . . .*

*It would have the high, keening sound of the six-foot bucksaws as the men pull them back and forth through the trees to cut pine for paper pulp; the grunting-gassy sounds of the work teams snorting and slapping as they hit the harness to jerk the stumps out of the ground. It would have the chewing sounds of cows in the barn working at their cuds on a long winter's night; the solid thunking sound of the ax coming down to split stovewood, and the piercing scream of the pigs when the knife cuts their throats and they know death is at hand—but it can't.*

*Books can't have sound.*

*And finally if books could be more, give more, show more, this book would have light. . . .*

*Oh, it would have the soft gold light—gold with bits of hay dust floating in it—that slips through the crack in the barn wall; the light of the Coleman lantern hissing flat-white in the kitchen; the silver-gray light of middle winter day, the splattered, white-night light of a full moon on snow, the new light of dawn at the eastern edge of the pasture behind the cows coming in to be milked on a summer morning—but it can't.*

   *Books can't have light.*

   *If books could have more, give more, be more, show more, they would still need readers, who bring to them sound and smell and light and all the rest that can't be in books.*

   *The book needs you.*

                                                                              G.P.

*From *The Winter Room* by Gary Paulsen. Copyright ©1989 by Gary Paulsen. Reprinted by permission of the publisher, Orchard Books, New York.

Gary Paulsen's prologue to *The Winter Room* exemplifies the critical role that a reader plays in a transaction with a book. A celebration of literature, in all its glory, cannot take place without the reader. A book is printed text brought to life only when the reader brings smell to "... *new potatoes sliced and frying in light pepper on a woodstove burning dry pine ...* "(pp. 1–2). The reader turns words on the page into the sound of "... *six-foot bucksaws as the men pull them back and forth through the trees to cut pine for paper pulp ...*" (p. 2). Only a reader can envision and bring life to "... *the new light of dawn at the eastern edge of the pasture behind the cows coming in to be milked on a summer morning ...*" (p. 3). Books need the reader to create the sensory and emotional experiences carried by printed words on a page. Without a reader, literature cannot reach its potential. Literature must invite the personal perspective of the reader if the celebration is to begin.

   The premise of this textbook on children's literature is built around the transactional theory of reader response of Louise Rosenblatt who supports the mutual interaction of the reader and the text during a literary event. This philosophy supports the belief that each reader forms a unique connection with a text *as* he or she reads. This perspective is a world apart from the traditional book reports I assigned during my early years of teaching or that you may have written in elementary school. Reader response theory encompasses a realm of response options that spontaneously and purposefully occur during and following the reading of a book. Therefore, this text not only surveys children's literature, but introduces those aesthetic options teachers can present to encourage the reader to bring the text to life through personal response in the classroom. This text is a blend of literature and reader, of book and response, of teachers guiding and students responding. This textbook serves as a motivating introduction to the world of children's literature and the realm of children's responses as readers.

   *A Celebration of Literature and Response* consists of five areas for celebrating children's books and readers.

   **Part I: Celebrating Literature, Response, and Teaching.** Chapter 1 invites teachers to embrace children's literature as an instrument of response-based instruction. Readers investigate the definition of children's literature and reader response while clarifying a response-based teaching philosophy. Reasons for blending children's books and children's responses in the classroom provide convincing justification for assuming a response-based approach to teaching. Simulated visits to classrooms assist in visualizing the blending of literature, readers, teaching, and response. Chapter 2 introduces Louise Rosenblatt's transactional theory of reader response to literature and its impact on the way educators view readers and literature. While her ideals have been available for more than 50 years, it is only recently that elementary teachers have conceptualized the natural connection between reading instruction and the potential of reader response to literature. Rosenblatt's legacy to literacy provides a foundational theory that encourages practitioners to open their classrooms to literature and to celebrate the natural responses of children to books. The second part of the chapter brings reader response to life as a developmental perspective on types of reader response to literature unfolds.

**Part II: Celebrating Literature.** Six substantive chapters invite readers to appreciate the major literary genres and gain an understanding of literary elements and book selection criteria. Chapter 3 guides us through the picture book format of children's literature building an awareness of the art and design of the picture book. Chapters 4, 5, 6, and 7 celebrate the genres of traditional literature/fantasy, poetry, realistic and historical fiction, and biography and informational nonfiction, respectively. Chapter 8 on multicultural literature across the genres provides a framework and numerous literary treasures that share ethnic cultures with children. Throughout each chapter, quality children's books are shared as illustrative examples. Special bibliographies in each chapter share additional quality book titles from the 1990s, and nostalgic classics that reflect the best aspects of each genre are interwoven throughout the text.

**Part III: Celebrating Response Connections.** These five chapters form the heart of the text and the practical links sought by preservice and inservice teachers. They enrich the classroom repertoire of response-based activities through literature. These chapters contain a blend of teaching strategies for eliciting a developmental range of reader response and suggested literature that assists in involving the reader in the literary experience. Concrete examples of activities with specific children's book titles abound. Chapter 9 begins with read-alouds and emerging response and builds toward literature conversations as children grow in their ability to talk about books. Chapter 10 employs a developmental approach toward written response through journals. Chapter 11 celebrates literature as a model for writing by focusing on literature that assists children as apprentices of the author's craft. Chapter 12 focuses on the expressive arts of drama, art, and music as outlets for reader response to literature. In Chapter 13, aesthetic response to nonfiction becomes a reality through planned informational responses.

**Part IV: Celebrating Interdisciplinary Connections.** The integration of content area instruction, particularly for multiage instruction, is facilitated by blending the fictional and factual aspects of children's literature. Chapter 14 discusses the possibilities for literature-based integrated thematic instruction through "literature clusters" and "theme explorations." Step-by-step procedures for creating classroom investigations through literature are illustrated. This chapter includes a process for conceptualizing themes, selecting literature, and planning related activities. Several model literature clusters and theme explorations geared to three multiage levels are shared through graphic organizers, annotated bibliographies, and related language-based activities.

**Part V: Celebrating Response Through Assessment.** Because authentic assessment is a key issue in the use of literature in the classroom, Chapter 15 directly addresses this issue with various assessment configurations. Included are a developmental response continuum, a rubric for literature response journals, checklists for literature discussions, and suggestions for portfolio documentation. Little mention has been given to assessment of reader response or response-based activities, yet the issue of assessment may be a pivotal factor that determines the ultimate future of literature-based literacy instruction.

*A Celebration of Literature and Response* features an abundance of current literature in its examples and bibliographies. Practitioners seem energized by an introduction to new literature and are likely to implement new ideas with recent titles. Yet the text also weaves in familiar classic titles so readers have their own past literature experiences from which to draw. The intention of the text is not to ignore the importance of quality literature through the years, but to update the reader to the best of the new influx of quality published books. Appendix A focuses on contemporary and classic award-winning literature, Appendix B shares an extensive annotated bibliography of professional resources related to children's books and authors, and Appendix C lists Internet Websites that deal with children's literature.

*A Celebration of Literature and Response* invites you to participate in a celebration of quality children's literature and a celebration of responding to that literature. As a reader, you are invited to respond to thoughts and ideas in this text as you read. Share your questions, concerns, literacy memories, or book reading experiences through discussion. Record your innermost reactions, classroom connections, and personal responses to ideas shared in this text in a response journal or the margins of the text. Then, seek out the quality children's literature titles shared in this text and respond to them at your own level. Most of the children's response activities shared in this text can be used with adults who are novices in reader response. Your instructor may choose to connect course assignments to the many response-based activities shared throughout the text.

I hope that you, as the reader of this book, will interact with the words on the page and bring them to life through your own experiences with literature, with children, with teaching, and with the world around you. *Only you can bring this book to life.* Only the reader can celebrate literature by bringing his or her own perspective to a book. I invite you to celebrate literature, not by merely reading about it, but by experiencing it in your own unique way. This book is an invitation to access some of the hundreds of quality titles shared within these chapters, to read and respond to them on a personal level, and to share them with children across the spectrum of suggested response-based activities. Only then will the celebration of literature, response, and lifelong reading truly begin—both for you as a teacher and for the children you teach.

—Marjorie Hancock

# Contents

Contents                                                                          xv

# Celebrating Literature, Response, & Teaching

The appeal of children's literature, the richness of reader response, and the satisfaction of quality teaching blend into a meaningful instructional philosophy in the K–8 classroom. Part I of *A Celebration of Literature and Response* challenges the reader to capture the very essence of the transaction between literature and response. Sam Sebesta (1997) promises this transaction is "a powerful potion, giving strength to the reader and the wish for more (p. 545)." As this celebration begins, elaborating the foundational knowledge that underlies this philosophy seems appropriate to fully appreciate the power of connecting readers, books, and teaching through reader response. Therefore, Part I of this text shares the theoretical and practical background needed to convey the innumerable benefits of teaching from a response-based perspective. Constantly linked to authentic literature, real classrooms, and energetic readers, these opening chapters provide the definitions, the theoretical perspective, and the practical connections necessary to proceed through this text with a flexible literary vision, a broadening response perspective, and a continuing celebration of the natural link between literature and readers.

Chapter 1 begins with a definition of children's literature and convincingly presents a rationale for its inclusion in K–8 classrooms. Clarifying the concept of reader response through the perspectives of the reader, the text, and the context for response further contributes to an understanding of the uniqueness of each child in his or her interactions with text. This chapter transports the reader to the world of a literature-based classroom as it paints a portrait of teaching. It blends quality literature, meaningful response-based activities, and a variety of response options across both literary genres and curricular areas.

The theoretical underpinnings of reader response to literature occupy the opening discussion of Chapter 2. The eloquent quotes and rich beliefs of Louise Rosenblatt (1978) convincingly capture the essence of aesthetic response. Practical connections to the world of real readers focus on modes of response to literature. They encourage developmentally appropriate responses across the language arts of reading, writing, listening, speaking, and visual representation. Children's book titles and related response modes weave their way throughout the text to constantly bring theory and practice together. At any age, readers' natural desire to share the literature with which they interact underlies the premise of reader response.

The introductory momentum of Part I provides the reader the information to most fully appreciate the philosophy, literature, and teaching connections of the remainder of the book. Part I provides basic background on literature and reader response, serves as the foundational link between theory, research, and practice, and highlights the natural link between literature, reader response, and teaching. Encouraging a celebration of both literature and reader response, these chapters issue an invitation to further investigate the unexplored boundaries of the interaction between books and readers in K–8 classrooms.

Rosenblatt, L. M. (1978). *The reader, the text, the poem: The transactional theory of a literary work.* Carbondale, IL: Southern Illinois University Press.

Sebesta, S. L. (1997). Having my say. *The Reading Teacher, 50,* 542–549.

## Chapter 1

# Literature, Teaching, and Reader Response:

## *Blending Books and Readers in the Classroom*

*W*hen I recall early encounters with literature and first stirrings of response in my own literacy past, I remember only a few books during my childhood. Books were stored in the unfinished attic of our small four-room home. Through the dim light of a single ceiling bulb, I remember the sight, smell, and touch of the yellowed, Scotch-taped pages of an incomplete set of Childcraft books—my first invitation to celebrate literature. I can still recall running my fingers along the black engravings on the orange textured covers as I longed to venture through three volumes containing ballads and poems, fairy tales, and animal stories—my first awakening to response to books. The desire to experience the richness of the words and the constant lure of story created a need to learn to read and uncover the magic between their covers.

My first years in elementary school turned me into a functional reader—a reader of basals, a master of worksheets. I learned to read through phonics, befriended Dick and Jane, and memorized sight word cards. I did what I was told, produced the right answers to comprehension questions, remained in the middle group, and gradually became a fluent reader. In fact, I was able to climb the stairs to the attic and unlock the key to the words in those tempting Childcraft books.

It wasn't until third grade, however, that I realized how literature, in stark contrast to instructional materials, would touch my own life and expand my view of reading. One special *teacher, Mrs. Dunne, made learning an adventure that year. In a classroom of fifty students, she managed to infuse the crowded environment with engaged activities and motivating teaching techniques. What I remember most is Mrs. Dunne's voice as she introduced a daily literature read-aloud. Her rich invitation to literature and her compelling enthusiasm for reading blended with the exciting plots and memorable characters. First and foremost, I remember Gertrude Chandler Warner's* The Box Car Children, *which ignited a response within me that has yet to be extinguished. Each day I anticipated the continuing adventures of Henry, Jessie, Violet, and Benny as they found treasures in the dump, shared creative meals on the blue tablecloth, and reunited with their loving grandfather. When Mrs. Dunne turned the final page of my first engagement with children's literature, she eagerly invited each of us to take a journey through those pages on our own. Not only did she permit me to take the book home, she told me about a wonderful place called the public library where similar journeys through literature awaited me.*

*That year in third grade I made a promise to myself. I pledged to become a teacher just like Mrs. Dunne with a passion for children and learning. I also vowed to cherish and read aloud literature in my own classroom with the same energy and fervor that Mrs. Dunne had read to me. My journey as a teacher at both elementary and college levels has provided me the privilege to take that journey and keep that promise while creating lovers of children's literature among both children and adults along the way.*

As you think back on your own personal reasons for becoming a teacher, you may discover that your career goal is linked to children's literature. As readers attempt to recall their earliest responses to literature, it is often the memory of the read-aloud voice of a teacher that invades their thoughts. Many of our fondest memories of school and reading include the read-alouds that marked our invitation to celebrate literature through response: E. B. White's *Charlotte's Web,* Laura Ingalls Wilder's *Little House in the Big Woods,* Roald Dahl's *James and the Giant Peach,* or C. S. Lewis's *The Lion, the Witch, and the Wardrobe.* Fondest memories of school often flow toward weekly visits to the school library, documenting numbers of literature books read, or dressing up as a book character. No matter what your literacy background, literature likely played a role in your decision to be a teacher.

The quality and role of children's literature in today's K–8 classrooms extend far beyond reading aloud, and reader responses far exceed mere record keeping. Literature currently pervades the curriculum as a resource for instruction, independent reading, and content area connections. Literature's richness is felt through narrative, expository, and poetic voices. It tugs on readers' heartstrings and whets their intellectual appetites as children naturally relate the relevancy of story and information to their own lives.

*A Celebration of Literature and Response* invites you as a teacher to embrace children's literature, to respond to it with both mind and heart, to make it an instrument of your teaching, and to share it with children in your classroom. What you take away from this textbook has the potential to touch children's lives, turn them into avid readers, and motivate them to continue their personal celebration of literature and response through a lifetime of reading. If your goal focuses on becoming a special teacher, including literature-based instruction in your classroom, and giving children the freedom to respond to literature in a personal way, then learning more about children's literature, children as readers, literature-based teaching, and reader response may be the most important step you take toward enriching your teaching prowess and clarifying your own educational philosophy.

This opening chapter serves as an invitation to preservice or inservice teachers to contemplate the connections between literature and teaching. Its purpose is to convince you that you need teaching, that teaching needs literature, and that literature needs children who respond to it and bring it to life. If our ultimate promise as educators is to create lifelong, passionate readers, then our means to achieve that goal must be children's books that transcend, transform, transport, and translate printed words and vivid illustrations into memorable experiences that lead to a lifetime of reading enjoyment.

What is children's literature? Why teach with children's literature? What is reader response to literature? Why incorporate response to literature as a basis of a literature-based philosophy? These are the four critical questions this chapter addresses as you begin your journey or reaffirm your promise to link readers and books through the power of response to literature.

# WHAT IS CHILDREN'S LITERATURE?

Children's literature can be defined as literature that appeals to the interests, needs, and reading preferences of children and captivates children as its major audience. Children's literature may be fictional, poetic, or factual, or a combination of any of these. The format that houses children's literature may be a picture book in which story blends with compelling illustrations or photographs for a visual and verbal adventure through story or factual content. Or the format may be a chapter book in which quality writing carries the story through a sequential unfolding of fictional plot or informational descriptions. Also referred to as trade books (in contrast to textbooks), children's literature provides appealing formats and motivating content to inspire children as they progress as emergent, novice, developing, and master readers.

Children's literature spans classic titles—Natalie Babbitt's *Tuck Everlasting,* Margaret Wise Brown's *Goodnight Moon,* and Robert McCloskey's *Make Way for Ducklings*—that have stood the test of time. Children's literature includes contemporary favorites—Peggy Rathmann's *Officer Buckle and Gloria,* Phyllis Reynolds Naylor's *Shiloh,* and Lois Lowry's *The Giver*—that currently capture the attention of children. Children's literature also includes the newest books that grace bookstore shelves and school libraries—Jon Scieszka and Lane Smith's *Squids Will Be Squids: Fresh Morals, Beastly Tales* and Jane Leslie Conly's *While No One Was Watching,* or Louis Sachar's Newbery recipient *Holes*—which still must undergo the careful scrutiny and approval of children. Children's books are honored on national award lists, receive children's choice awards, and reoccur in listings of notable books in language arts, social studies, and science. Children's literature has progressed in both quality and quantity during the last decade, and has found credible acceptance both as independent reading material and as an instructional resource for both children and teachers.

The content of children's literature focuses primarily on the domain of childhood and early adolescence while including a wide variety of experiences that appeal to readers from elementary through middle school. While content varies widely, it must appeal to the developmental level and natural interests of the individual reader. The following dimensions of content reflect a developmental approach to reading interests and evolving awareness of literature.

***Appreciating the wonder of language.***    Children's literature captures and shares the wonder of the written word and the appeal of well-chosen language. Rhyme, rhythm, and repetition are the hallmark of books with appeal for the very young. Typically captured in poetic voice, young children can celebrate familiar Mother Goose characters or identify with everyday experience through a language-based adventure. Poetry collections and poem picture books contain words that roll off the tongue, create visual interpretations, and applaud the sounds of language. Picture storybooks eloquently select words and phrases that hold the interest of the listener on an enjoyable adventure through a book. Older readers focus on the use of word choice and literary devices as authors weave their stories through creative use of language. *Children's literature crafts words, creates images, and describes everyday objects in special ways.*

***Sparking the imagination.***    Young children, in particular, enjoy books that whet their imaginative powers and allow them to venture into the realm of the impossible. Evil stepmothers, beautiful princesses, and talking lions transport a child into a special place where the unbelievable seems real. Traditional tales typically have strong appeal to young readers as versions of *Rapunzel* by Paul Zelinsky and *The Gingerbread Boy* by Richard Egielski become a part of early childhood literary experiences. Literary tales of fantasy spark the imagination of older readers as well and transport them to worlds of talking animals or to kingdoms like Prydain that stretch their beliefs beyond reality. *Children's literature challenges creativity and ignites inventiveness in children.*

***Reliving everyday experiences.***    From going to bed (Mercer Mayer's *There's a Nightmare in My Closet*) to going to school (Kevin Henkes's *Chrysanthemum*), from gaining an appreciation of family (Kimberly Willis Holt's *My Louisiana Sky*) to struggling to find acceptance (Katherine Paterson's *The Great Gilly Hopkins*), children's literature honestly portrays the lives of children and preadolescents during those important years of growing up. Realistic fiction reveals experiences common to childhood and impending adulthood including those that challenge and define the nature of an individual. *Children's literature affirms real life and offers vicarious experiences from authentic situations while fostering empathy for the human condition.*

***Revisiting the past.***    Children's literature transports readers to historical places and settings or introduces characters placed in historical contexts. Historical fiction reveals the realities of historical circumstances (Veronica Chambers' *Amistad Rising*), introduces flesh-and-blood characters (Alyse/Beetle in Karen Cushman's *The Midwife's Apprentice*), and shares unique perspectives about significant historical events (Jane Yolen's *Encounter*) that impact contemporary life. *Children's literature transports readers and transcends time while encouraging valid connections between the past and the present.*

***Sharing lives and information.*** Children's literature shares the lives of historical figures and the feats and triumphs of real everyday people through biography. From sports heroes (Katherine Krull's *Wilma Unlimited*) to leadership models (Russell Freedman's *Eleanor Roosevelt*), character and determination provide inspiration and direction in children's own lives. Nonfiction informational books extend the growing body of information about our world. Quality factual representations introduce the reader to the facts behind science (Walter Wick's *A Drop of Water*), a retrospective journey into an historical event (Jim Murphy's *The Boy's War*), or an introduction to the arts (Phillip Isaacson's *A Short Walk Around the Pyramids and Through the World of Art*). *Children's literature replays the triumphs and determination of reknown figures and shares an explosion of information and facts about the world in which we live.*

While the content of recent children's literature is impressive and at times overwhelming to the adult reader, the quality of children's literature varies widely and should be a selective factor in determining the appropriateness of literature for children. Using children's books for enjoyment or instruction implies recognition of evaluative criteria and making certain that the best of children's books make their way into the lives of readers. Children's literature has certainly blossomed in content and quality since the days of *The Boxcar Children*, but it still possesses the potential to motivate children to become readers, to cause readers to reflect on the human condition, and to expand their knowledge of and perspectives on the world.

# WHY TEACH WITH LITERATURE?

Teachers today are making countless instructional decisions daily based on the premise that children's books are effective instructional resources. Why are some teachers, districts, and schools committed to using children's literature in the classroom? When we look at the high-quality books published for children, the visual appeal of their illustrations, and the enjoyment their stories bring readers, we can understand the lure of literature as the basis of instruction. But the reasons go far beyond the appeal of the book. The support begins in the early literacy environment and progresses throughout the school years as literature effects language development, reading achievement, and writing in literature-rich classroom settings. Much research (Galda & Cullinan, 1991; McGee, 1992; Tunnell & Jacobs, 1989) affirms the benefits of using literature as a foundation of literacy instruction both in the home and in the classroom.

***Literature fosters home literacy.*** The convincing argument for the use of children's literature for literacy instruction and teaching curricular content begins with the early years in the home. For more than 25 years, studies of emergent literacy document the important role of literature in children's reading achievement, social interactions, and the rites of passage into a literate world (Teale & Sulzby, 1986). Children who are read to at home develop highly positive associations with books. Their perception of their parents' attitude toward reading is an important influence on their own attitudes toward reading. The pleasant bond developed between reader and listener provides memories of warm, loving experiences later associated with the reading act. Marie Clay (1979) attests that being read literature early and often develops familiarity with the conventions of print. Studies consistently point to positive relationships between the number of books in a home and a child's reading ability (Durkin, 1966; Lamme, 1985) and the relationship between being read to at an early age and success in reading at school (Durkin, 1974). All signs point to literature as a key to early literacy and continued literacy growth.

***Literature enhances language development.***    If literature can have such an impact in the home environment, it seems logical that immersion in literature can have similar positive influences in the early school environment. Reading and listening to a variety of books increase interest and motivation in learning to read (Mendoza, 1985). The language of literature assists in language development while children feed their "linguistic data pool" (Harste, Woodward, & Burke, 1984) from encounters with stories. Exposure to quality writing through literature leads to a wider oral and written vocabulary as a child matures.

***Literature aids comprehension.***    Stories provide a way for children to make sense of their world. As they connect their own lives to a story, children begin to sort out the complexities of daily life (Wells, 1986). Knowledge about narrative structure is a benefit to children acquainted with literature. Knowing that a story has a beginning, a problem, a resolution, and an end begins to provide a visual framework of how a story works. Most recently, research acknowledges that informational text also sets up early expository schema and that reading aloud and responding to nonfiction is also valid to a child's early sense of understanding how text works (Vardell, 1998). Because a meaning-centered approach to literacy must be supported by continued growth in understanding, literature provides the necessary support for that process.

***Literature provides a writing model.***    Reading literature as a model of quality writing is linked to success in writing proficiency. Exposure to narrative through the use of literature results in more elaborate language structure by those exposed to literature compared with those exposed to basal stories (Eckhoff, 1983). The sense of story developed during early reading provides the framework for the structure of story. Reading and discussing literature as the author's craft makes children more aware of their own authorship (Hansen, 1987).

***Literature inspires inquiry within and across disciplines.***    Literature can focus on subject matter associated with the traditional disciplines. Many teachers enhance instruction by including a related piece of children's literature as motivation for the prescribed curriculum. Literature not only has the potential to answer questions, but it can also incite learners to ask even more. Inquiry-based learning often begins with literature and exposure to a single title, but continues on an adventure of connections among books (Short, 1993). The natural connections between literature and the engagement of a curious reader begin the inquiry process that may evolve from a single discipline, but expand to an interdisciplinary study.

***Literature creates readers.***    Availability and choice of books, time spent with books, and a supportive, enthusiastic teacher are essential elements for creating readers. Children need time to look at books, to listen to books, to respond to books, to read independently, and to reflect on the reading experience. Observations of successful literature-based classrooms indicate that the teacher plays a key role in creating the literature-rich environment that supports literacy (Hepler, 1982; Hickman, 1981). The teacher is the orchestrator of a setting that provides books, choice, time, and support so that children are encouraged to connect with books. A teacher who supports literature as the basis of literacy and curricular instruction provides an effective entry into literacy and also puts children one step closer to becoming lifelong readers.

Why literature? Literature provides a passport to the world of reading by serving as a motivating means to acquire the strategies and fluency needed to comprehend text. Literature creates excitement and enjoyment about the reading process by transporting the child to worlds of fact and fantasy. Literature provides a model for writing both story and information by providing strong support for the author's craft. Literature simply creates readers. Bernice Cullinan (1992) claims teachers have the "joyful responsibility of handing these treasures on to children . . . we can fill children's baskets of memory with beautiful language and life experiences with the books we share with them. The memories will last a lifetime" (p. 430).

# WHAT IS READER RESPONSE?

Reader response to literature describes the unique interaction that occurs within the mind and heart of the individual reader throughout the literature event. While the theoretical foundation of reader response is grounded in the work of Louise Rosenblatt (see Chapter 2), this initial discussion will assist you in understanding the components of reader response within a literature-based teaching philosophy. The three components of reader response include (1) the reader, (2) the literature, and (3) the context for response (Galda, 1988). A visual model of the components contributing to response to literature (Figure 1.1) serves as a visual representation that links children's literature, the reader, and the response environment. Reader response to literature is affected by who we are as readers, the books we select to read, and the broad and narrower contexts that surround the reading event. As these components define the dynamic act of reading, they blend into the unique transaction of reader response to literature. Looking at each of these factors more closely emphasizes the complexity of reader response to literature and clarifies the many factors that contribute to the individuality of response.

## Reader Response: The Reader

Readers, young and old, actively engage with literature. Who we are and what we have experienced in our lives influence our responses to books. The places we've traveled, the people we've met, the books we've read, and the values we hold determine how we interact with the literature we read. Jane Yolen (1985) aptly focuses on the crucial role of the reader when she states:

> There is no real story on the page, only that which is created between the writer and the reader. Just as a writer brings a lifetime to the creation of a tale, so the reader carries a different lifetime with which to recreate it. (p. 590)

Several characteristics of the "reader" illustrate the variations among individual readers and lend credence to the individuality of reader response.

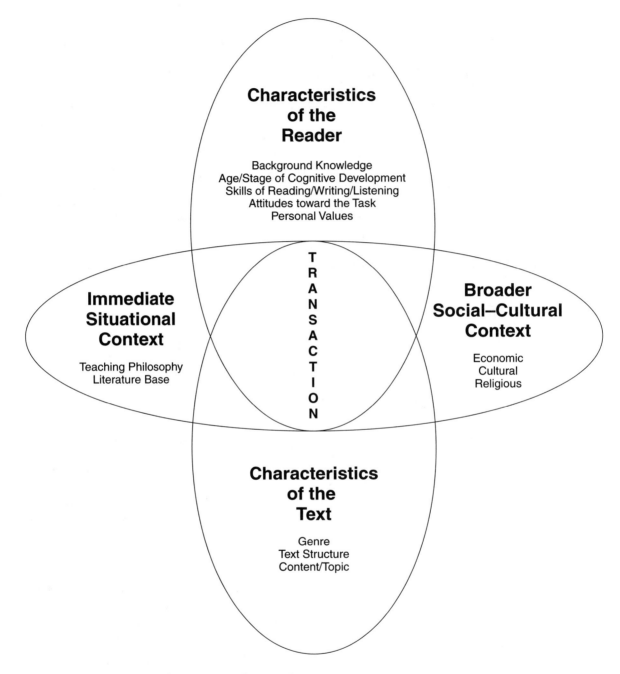

**FIGURE 1.1**  Components of Response: Reader, Text, Context

***Background knowledge.***    Readers bring a lifetime of experiences to the reading event. Whether that life span is 8 or 80 years, the reader is a product of a foundation of knowledge that aids in creating the individual imprint on the text. Knowledge obtained through academics, through travel, and through personal experience provide a schema for the reading event. Realizing that each reader is the product of a lifetime of varied experiences, it is understandable why reader response is so ideosyncratic in nature. Even elementary children's responses to literature are characterized by their brief but vital experiential backgrounds.

***Past literary experience.***    A more specific type of foundational experience impacting the reader is that which focuses on past literacy events. Being read to, the kinds of books read, the priority placed on reading in one's life, and memories of the reading act itself all influence how the reader will react to books. A wide range of positive experiences ultimately leads to positive views of books, whereas limited negative experiences may distort a reader's textual interaction. The reader's identity in terms of literacy history influences response to reading. This characteristic is influenced by both home experiences with books as well as the use of literature in the reader's academic setting. The greater the familiarity with literature and the greater the comfort zone of reading, the more fluid and spontaneous the response.

***Age or stage of cognitive development.***    Applebee (1978) pointed out the changes in children's responses to literature as they mature. Younger children undoubtedly respond differently than older readers as expressive response grows to interpretive response and the degree of abstract discussion and ability to infer character motivation increases with age. The child's concept of story also grows with maturity leading to a greater appreciation of reading different genres of literature for different purposes. As a child matures, he or she may define personal literary preferences while gradually indicating a willingness toward less preferred genres viewed in broader literary contexts. The same reader reading and responding to the same book at different ages evidences itself as two unique experiences.

***Literacy skills.***    Readers who possess the skills to read, write, listen, and speak are more likely to enjoy the reading event and share a willingness to respond. A child who is caught up in comprehension, decoding, and new vocabulary will likely concentrate on the mechanics of reading rather than personal engagement with the text. The degree of fluency in the art of reading does influence the intensity and depth of personal response to a book. Children who struggle with receptive and communication skills, however, are still quite capable of response to literature, although the depth and variety of their responses may be somewhat encumbered.

***Attitudes toward the task.***    Just as in any learning situation, motivation for both reading and responding can come from outside and within the reader. While a new book self-selected or chosen by a teacher creates a natural motivation for most children, a love of reading and a desire to share depends on intrinsic motivation. The natural desire to read and transact with a book leads to genuine response, while resistance may limit response, but does not prevent it from occurring.

***Personal morality and values.***    Readers are a reflection of their ethical backgrounds because their lives are grounded in varying concepts of acceptable and unacceptable behavior. Moral background becomes an influencial part of response to the actions and decisions of characters in literature. Readers measure the right and wrong of characters against their personal value systems. These comparisons typically find their way into the responses of all children and affirm or refute their internal belief systems.

These six reader characteristics illustrate the multiple factors that create the unique reader who is a critical part of the response process. As teachers realize the various components of the reader that affect response, they gain a deeper understanding of why the literary responses children share reflect such a diversity of thought.

## Reader Response: The Literature

Textual characteristics also impact the response of readers to literature. An examination of how text selection influences response allows teachers to value the importance of self-selected or teacher-selected texts in the response process. The following text characteristics impact reader response.

***Genre.***    The genre of the selected literature influences the content and intensity of the transactional response. All literary genres are capable of eliciting reader response, but some genres (and specific books within a genre) naturally influence intense aesthetic response. Realistic fiction, for example, is both a preferred genre for middle elementary readers and a genre that elicits intense response. If the genre is one preferred by the reader, response is likely to be more genuine, honest, and comfortable. Nevertheless, a variety of literary genres should be shared with readers in an attempt to develop reading tastes and their own response capabilities.

***Text structure.***    Narrative, expository, and poetic text structures each influence response in a unique way. Children often respond to a book with a particular structure in that writing mode. For example, responses to a book of poetry may actually be the writing of one's own poem modeled from the pattern, topic, or structure of the text. Narrative writing, on the other hand, often results in first-person responses. Straightforward expository writing may elicit efferent facts but is often tempered by narrative sharing of personal reactions to those facts.

***Literary elements.***    Various literary aspects of the text itself may influence response. An author's writing style can influence response as a story unfolds in a positive or negative framework. Characterization, particularly the age of the main character, can influence character identification and a reader's interest in the story. Point of view can influence the reader's emotional distance from the text. While first person draws the reader closer to the character and story outcome, third person may help the reader take a detached, objective stance toward story events. Even the lead-ins and endings of both entire books and individual chapters impact response in that they encourage readers to predict outcomes or extend the story in their own minds.

***Content/Topic.***    The story or informational content between the covers of a book strongly influences response. If the content is aesthetic and touches the reader's life in a personal way (divorce, sports competitions, friendship), the response is likely to be more spontaneous and genuine as children make connections between their own lives and that of the character. If the topic of an informational title is self-selected, the response is likely to build on the background knowledge or interest in the topic that initially led the reader to the book.

The nature and quality of response are dependent on the text to which the reader responds. If the teacher selects the text, issues of genre, text structure, literary quality, and topic interest must be considered. If the child chooses a text for independent reading and response, not just any title will do. There are indeed books whose inherent aesthetic nature leads to a richer, emotional response to literature. These are the titles that are recognized and highlighted throughout this entire text—books with special features that naturally cause them to elicit response through a variety of outlets.

## Reader Response: The Context

The context or setting for response to literature involves a dual perspective. First, the context for response includes the broad social–cultural context of a child's life, which forms the foundation of response. A child's family's socioeconomic status, cultural or ethnic background, or religious beliefs set the stage for the kinds of responses a child chooses to share. Connections between a book and one's own life become apparent in this broader context of response. The reader as a product of environmental surroundings brings a personal context to the reading event.

The second contextual perspective on response focuses exclusively on the immediate situational context of the classroom, which includes the philosophy of the teacher, the literature-based focus, and the valued, respected expression of individual response in the classroom setting.

The context in which reader response is generated influences the ways in which readers choose to respond. Teachers whose beliefs are grounded in holistic philosophy are likely to align literature-based instruction with their whole to part learning philosophy. They select instructional methodology that includes reading workshops containing a critical response component. These teachers value self-selection, independent thinking, and genuine response. Children need not seek the "right" answer, but are encouraged to bring original thoughts to their written responses or oral discussion groups as books are shared. The context surrounding the invitation to respond must genuinely support originality of thought, interpretation, and connections if an honest response is to occur. A context built on valued individualism and personal reaction allows the optimal context for reader response.

As the reader, the text, and the context overlap to form a personal response to literature, teachers recognize and appreciate the varying individual perspectives that blend into textual response. The most fulfilling aspect of response to a teacher is the variety of responses that cross his or her path during oral or written sharing. Unlike worksheets keyed to tallying specific correct answers, reader response encourages the individual to encounter the text in a one-on-one engagement and to share the spontaneous, distinctive reaction with the text. Nurturing the uniqueness of the reader, valuing the traits of the text, and acknowledging the importance of the context for response allows response to emerge and flourish over time.

What is reader response? Reader response implies the unique, individual connection between a reader and children's literature in the context of a teaching or learning environment. No two readers have the same response to the same text. Reader response to literature encourages the expression of independent thoughts, personal reflections, and emotional engagement during and following the reading event.

# WHY A READER RESPONSE VIEW OF LITERATURE AND TEACHING?

For the past decade, many elementary/middle-level teachers have incorporated a response-based view of children's literature in their classrooms. In these literature-based settings, children may write in journals as they read, talk about books with peers, or express personal meaning through the expressive arts. Enjoying reading is a hallmark of this approach, while becoming a fluent reader maintains its importance. In this approach to literacy instruction, several factors appear as priorities or characteristics.

- Instruction is *literature based* because it is accomplished through real children's books with more time spent on real reading and less time spent on reading instruction itself.
- Instruction is *child centered* with choice an honored aspect of the program. Topics and purposes are keyed to children's interests and needs and authenticity sparks motivation both for readers and lifelong learners.
- Instruction is *integrated* with the language arts as listening, speaking, writing, viewing, and visual representation become outlets for response to literature.

A response-based view of children's literature focuses on two major assumptions. First, the stance a child assumes as a reader fluctuates between aesthetic (pleasure/personal connections) and efferent (details/information). This premise assumes reading is a dynamic process featuring changing purposes as a reader interacts with the unfolding text. Second, individual meaning is personally constructed from an engaged, reflective encounter with literature. Because literature is absorbed by unique readers, multiple interpretations of texts are encouraged and honored as each literature experience is personalized. This view of reading stretches beyond testing personal recollections by answering a series of questions at the end of a story or attending to details as an indication of reading ability or prowess. Internalizing this theoretical perspective leads to an invigorating style of teaching and learning literacy in K–8 classrooms.

Reader response to literature evidences itself in many observable ways in real classroom settings. Even as a novice observer, the use of literature as the basis of literacy instruction provides an indication of a response-based program. Recognizing sustained silent reading, writing during reading, and periodic book discussions are first signs of the implementation of this approach. Looking beyond the literature, however, the more informed observer might recognize chanting, the shared book experience, dramatic reenactment, reading workshops, literature response journals, and literature circles as indicators of a response-based teaching philosophy.

Why would a teacher choose to adopt this philosophy in light of recurring "back-to-basics" outcries, increased accountability, and a move toward a more "balanced" approach to literacy? Dixie Spiegel's (1998) retrospective report on the implementation of reader response activities and the simultaneous growth of readers provides a framework for a discussion of the positive aspects of this type of instruction. The results of a decade of implementation of reader response in the elementary/middle-level classroom point to a number of reasons for its continued inclusion in literacy instruction. As you continue to read, place yourself in the role of the reader and recall your own instructional experiences, attitudes toward reading, and personal connections to literature during your own K–8 learning experience. At the same time, place yourself in the role of teacher and reflect on your own literacy goals and outcomes for your students.

***Experiencing reading success.***   Perhaps the most satisfying outcome of a response-based approach to literacy is the feeling of accomplishment children exhibit as readers. Self-confidence often lacking in more traditional classrooms abounds here. Even children who struggle with reading feel glimmers of success as their own growth is documented rather than being compared to the average reader at a designated grade level. As valued meaning makers, each child feels the importance of the unique viewpoint he or she brings to the literature. Increased success leads to growing contributions to literature circles and expansion of written responses. The confidence of believing in oneself as a reader and a learner may provide the greatest impetus to continuing learning outside the classroom.

***Meeting diverse needs.***   Because a response-based approach requires literature across all literary genres as a resource for teaching, there is "something for everybody" and the gap between quality literature, reading preferences, and reading ability is narrowed. Classrooms are filled with diverse readers with different abilities, tastes, and interests. Finding the right book for the right child at the right moment only becomes possible when selecting from thousands of fiction and nonfiction titles rather than being restricted by a single textbook or anthology as a resource for learning. The sheer numbers of quality books cry out for inclusion not only in the literacy program, but as a basis for instruction across curricular areas.

***Becoming risk takers.***   Because a response-based classroom includes sharing one's own interpretation of literature, readers become risk takers whose unique opinions are valued. Students utilize their own writing and speaking voices as they contribute to literature journals and discussions. Instead of responses matching those of a teacher or a teacher edition of a textbook, reader response broadens the scope of acceptance as a springboard for continuing conversations about literature. Students learn to validate their thinking, to support their contentions with details from literature, and to express themselves articulately without the threat of intimidation. The risk taking fostered in a response-based approach extends beyond the classroom as critical thinking and decision making become lifelong learning processes.

***Assuming responsibility for learning.***    Readers gain a sense of responsibility for selecting literature and for fulfilling the demands of a response-based agenda. Because their audience often includes peers, students seem even more responsible for reading books, constructing meaning, recording reflective responses, and explaining an interpretation. Children learn to value and share their own voice in response to the books they read. The small group aspects of response-based instruction, especially literature circles, promote responsibility in ways that are absent from traditional methodologies.

***Making personal connections.***    A response-based approach to teaching encourages the ownership of literature through personal connections to one's own life, other pieces of literature one has read, or to the world beyond one's own life. A reader becomes a part of a book and gains a vested interest in the reading process when he or she can connect to it in a personal way. For example, children can relate characters' feelings and experiences to occurrences in their own lives (loss of a pet, loss of a friend, personal struggles, personal successes). When that connection is made, the book forms a bond with the reader and the act of reading becomes a more satisfying experience. When students share their own personal connections to literature, they share a part of themselves, assume the role of expert, and bring credibility to their discussion. Readers can also connect to characters' situations, moral dilemmas, and decision making. Characters as role models help readers realize they are not alone in their personal situations. These opportunities are greatly minimized when instruction is limited to textbooks. Personal connections to literature create lifelong readers who feel the sense of kinsmanship, friendship, and identity with characters that face circumstances not unfamiliar to their own.

***Encouraging higher level thinking.***    Reader response to literature moves the reading process from a passive encounter to an active partnership in creating meaning throughout the entire reading encounter. Response-based activities often solicit a reader's response throughout the reading process instead of waiting for a retrospective view at the completion of the text as in the case of traditional book reports. This type of ongoing thinking, constant reflection, and monitoring of emotions serves as a model for a lifetime of reflective thinking during the reading process. While student response may be documented through response journals or periodic literature circles, the message of "read–reflect–respond" gradually becomes a natural part of the reading process, even when response is no longer required outside of the school setting. Students actually begin to think about the author's message rather than focusing only on the unfolding of events. Greater involvement with literature leads to a deeper interaction with story, characters, and theme. Internalizing the response process results in continued higher level considerations over time.

***Understanding reading as a process.***    A response-based approach implies active involvement with literature. Sharing responses with peers builds the realization that meaning making is individualized and an ongoing process throughout the entire literary encounter. Predicting, connecting, evaluating, identifying, and relating constitute active reading strategies that exhibit themselves throughout the response process. The constructive nature of meaning making also provides opportunities to weigh others' opinions against one's own viewpoint. Reader response fosters listening skills and makes room for altering one's own meaning as evidence and different viewpoints are shared.

***Appreciating literary quality.*** Literature as a basis of reader response affords readers the opportunity to expect quality in the books they read. Teachers who utilize a response-based approach to instruction bring familiarity with children's literature classics to their classrooms while keeping abreast of current, quality children's books. They read professional journals, collaborate with their library/media center specialist, and seek literature that matches skills, strategies, and topics taught in the curriculum. Because literary elements form a part of literary discussions, readers demand the high quality of many of the teacher-selected books introduced during read-aloud sessions. Sharing quality authors and illustrators with children provides a model for quality reading. If valuable time is to be spent reading, then reading the highest quality literature becomes an important lifelong consideration.

Why should a teacher want to incorporate a reader response approach in K–8 classrooms? Teachers who incorporate reader response approaches to literature issue lifelong invitations to children to engage in reading and researching through literature. Children acquire many admirable traits as readers, reflective thinkers, and decision makers through a steady diet of response. Their ability to share their own responses while accepting the opinions of others transcends the school setting. If your educational outcomes focus on creating readers that read outside the walls of your classroom and beyond the hours of the school day, then you have the opportunity to learn more about literature and response in the coming chapters. Learning more about literature, about readers, and about reader response can set the stage for the philosophy you share in your classroom.

# BLENDING LITERATURE, TEACHING, AND READER RESPONSE IN THE CLASSROOM

What does children's literature, literature-based instruction, and a reader response philosophy "look like" in a real classroom? Perhaps this evolving discussion of its multiple benefits has excited you about children's literature and the importance of designating reader response as the core of your teaching philosophy. Yet an observational "visit" to a first-grade, a third-grade and a sixth-grade classroom might more clearly visualize this philosophy in action. As you reflect on the following teaching/learning scenarios, picture the classroom arrangement, sense the immersion in literature, grasp the role of the teacher, and revel in the motivation of the students as they engage in literature-based reader response through quality teaching.

A first-grade teacher's journal entries provide an outstanding example of literature and reader response as the basis of instruction with young children. Read this primary teacher's reflective journal to begin to internalize the importance of literature, the freedom of children to respond, diverse opportunities for a variety of responses, the enthusiasm that fills this classroom, and the philosophy that drives this instruction.

*During the first week of school, one of the books I read to the children was* Five Little Monkeys Jumping on the Bed. *They knew the chant from kindergarten. Today as they were working on a math activity that had monkeys pictured in one section, they began chanting "Five little monkeys . . ." with rhythm and expression. The book is on our library table—they love to read it during their free time.*

*The children loved* Berlioz the Bear. *They started clapping when the bee stung the hindquarters of the mule. I also read* The Owl and the Pussycat *and* The Mitten. *They were so enthusiastic over Jan Brett's illustrations. The book fair didn't have* The Wild Christmas Reindeer, *but we can order it. . . . I did!*

*I used a lot of poetry today. After lunch as we were getting ready for storytime I taught the children the poem "I Eat My Peas with Honey" since we had peas for lunch. I also read a pizza poem by Ogden Nash—we had pizza, too! After school I wrote the poems on chart paper, but I have a problem. Where am I going to hang all these poems? We'll see how the children like them . . . maybe they will have an idea about where they should be displayed.*

*Today I introduced* Goldilocks and the Three Bears, *which lends itself to acting out so we plan to work on that aspect of response. This will be a different approach to responding for us. Some of the children volunteered to bring in items for the performance. I didn't remind them or write a note, but they remembered. What fun they had (me, too) as they acted out the story. I discussed with them that acting out, making a puppet play, etc., were ways to "respond" to the stories we read. This helps us understand the story better.*

First-Grade Teacher's Reflective Journal

Every journal entry is filled with the joys of literature and response. Children revel in literature-based opportunities. They have become risk takers whose choices are honored and whose ideas become the basis for instruction. With 20 years of teaching experience, this educator has turned her love of literature and her belief in the value of response into an active classroom philosophy. Literature, authors, language, and language arts surround the children with the motivation and materials to become readers. Books become familiar companions, language becomes an alliterative escapade, writing becomes a challenge, and the expressive arts are valued as a mode of response. This teacher is an artist, a crafter of language, and an orchestrator of response with her students. She believes in literature and response as a means of inviting her students into the world of reading.

As children progress in school, their eagerness for reading regretfully diminishes. Traditional programs may offer monotony and regimented schedules with little freedom for choice, self-expression, or variety. Peering into a third-grade response-based classroom, however, affords a view of an energetic approach to literacy.

*On entering Mr. Lowell's third grade, I am immediately awakened to a rich blend of books, readers, and response. Within four brightly painted walls lies a wealth of titles from all genres displayed in a variety of configurations. An author study table featuring Roald Dahl catches my eye, but I am quickly distracted by a thematic study displaying a myriad of titles related to "An Exploration of Change." My visual sense notes books across genres ranging from* A Circle of Seasons *by Myra Cohn Livingston, to* Many Thousand Gone *by Virginia Hamilton, to* Letting Swift River Go *by Jane Yolen. A huge mural sweeping the length of the back of the classroom contains a map of the United States with colored thumbtacks holding labels of book titles set in various venues of our country. I note* Night of the Twisters *in Nebraska,* Peppe the Lamplighter *in New York, and* Only Opal *in the Pacific Northwest.*

*Moving my focus from books to response, I find delight in the colorful mobiles hanging from the ceiling that depict all of the beloved characters of Beverly Cleary. Literature webs cover open wall spaces, while sculptures of dinosaurs next to a copy of* Time Flies *fill the shelf below the windows. Organized in plastic crates are response journals which include reading graphs of books of varied genres. A castle of cardboard is accompanied by David Macauley's* Castles *and homemade pig puppets compliment Stephen Kellogg's newest version of* The Three Little Pigs.

*My attention flows to the readers who quietly fill the open and isolated spaces of the room. While some children choose the solitude and familiarity of their desks, others seek the comfort of pillow-filled corners and a carpeted, wooden loft. Children read—some with piles of picture books at their sides, others with a single chapter book in their lap. Children read—many slowly digest captions and illustrations in nonfiction selections, while others cling to every word the author offers. I have entered the classroom at DEAR time (Drop Everything and Read). I mentally applaud the on-task behavior of children who are not reading because they have to, but because they want to and are given choice in their selections for twenty minutes of enjoyment tailored to their needs. I know that the literature-based philosophy I am witnessing is not confined to this part of the day, but woven throughout the entire curriculum. The evidence of response displayed indicates a full-time commitment to literature in the lives of children.*

Author Observational Notes

This classroom scenario exemplifies the phrase "littered with literacy" and evokes the principles of response-based instruction in an intermediate elementary classroom. Reading of authentic literature, freedom of choice, encouraged risk taking, and literature as the focus of cross-curricular instruction evidence itself in all directions. The room reflects active engagement in literature throughout the school day and provides motivation and access to literature throughout the school year.

By the time readers reach middle school, the configuration for response-based teaching through literature is typically implemented in reading workshop format. The three essential components of a reading workshop include the literature itself, response to literature through the language arts, and literature conversations. As independence thrives with approaching adolescence, group work becomes the hallmark of reader response and interactive discussions and collaborative response-based projects dominate the reading period. A scenario from a sixth-grade classroom sets the stage for the workings of this response-based approach at this level.

*Ms. Lopez has chosen a "survival" themeset of literature for her nineteen middle-level readers. With groups of six, six, and seven students, she has selected three titles from which they may choose: Paula Fox's* Monkey Island, *Felice Holman's* Slake's Limbo *and Gary Paulsen's* Brian's Winter. *After a brief, energetic booktalk about each on Friday, she allowed students to rank their choices for reading workshop. Satisfied students, most of whom receive their first choice this Monday morning, get to the business of reading. Typically, thirty minutes of the one-hour workshop is devoted to reading, fifteen minutes to recording response, and fifteen minutes to literature circles or whole class conversations. The students show familiarity with the schedule as little time is wasted on organization.*

*After reading for thirty minutes, Paul's group decides on an illustrated timeline to share their thoughts on* Brian's Winter. *Keith suggests a response journal in chronological order of the unfolding plot for* Slake's Limbo. *Meredith, on the other hand, encourages her group to choose sketches with captions for a single event from each chapter of* Monkey Island. *Obviously, this teacher encourages a variety of modes of response and provides for individual differences among groups. The last portion of class time today is spent as a whole class discussion focusing on the type of survival faced by each book's character. Before class closes, reading assignments for the following day are determined by the group with an agreement to share responses in literature circles the next day. Ms. Lopez reminds students that contractual forms for response are due on Wednesday.*

*While the reading workshop pattern will likely continue for almost two weeks, responsibility apparently lies with the readers and their sharing of thoughts, opinions, and reactions to daily reading through peer discussion. When the reading of the books is completed, individuals plan to share their response projects within the group and then more extensively with the entire class. On a daily basis, the momentum of the literature provides the impetus to read while the positive reaction to talking about books with peers sustains the discussion process.*

Author's Observational Notes

The independence, freedom, and responsibility of the reading workshop format makes it ideal for preadolescent readers who tend to thrive in its apparently unstructured nature. Yet daily routines actually keep this format quite structured while readers remain highly accountable for learning. The modeling of organization, talk about books, and high expectations maintained by the teacher as facilitator make the reading workshop highly effective when blending literature, written/oral/artistic response, and book discussion.

These classroom "visits" highlight the potential effectiveness of literature-based instruction across grade levels. As children's literature and reader response blend through the strong philosophy of literature-based teaching, children appreciate quality literature, express unique response to the books they read, and build a foundation for a lifetime of quality reading. These scenarios are indicative of the quality teaching and learning occurring in schools across the nation when literature, teaching, and reader response blend in a unified philosophy. These classrooms can serve as models for your own teaching environment in which a constant flow of quality literature, a variety of reader response options, and a teaching philosophy supporting literature blend into effective practice supporting the goal of creating lifelong readers.

# CLOSING THOUGHTS

The blending of quality children's literature, eager readers, and response to literature results in rich engagement in the act of reading. Children's literature comes to life only when books and readers interact. This textbook celebrates both the wonder of children's literature and the empowerment of the individual reader as they relate to the interconnections of children's literature, aesthetic teaching, and reader response. Connecting literature and reader response becomes the basis of literacy instruction both within and beyond the school. To gain a clearer understanding of the links between children's literature, teaching, and reader response, the reader of this text is enthusiastically invited to do the following:

- Seek out and respond to the quality children's literature presented between the covers of this text.
- Apply the connected response-based activities in a classroom setting, either at the elementary/middle level with children or in the college classroom.
- Explore and observe the full spectrum of response options across literary genres and curricular content areas.

The teacher who possesses and implements a response-based, literature-focused philosophy of teaching serves as a catalyst for authentic reader response and the creation of lifelong readers. You are invited to anticipate the continuing celebration of children's literature and reader response as they gently weave their way through the succeeding chapters of this text and into your teaching philosophy and current or future literature-based classroom.

# REFERENCES

Applebee, A. (1978). *The child's concept of story: Ages two to seventeen.* Chicago: University of Chicago Press.

Clay, M. M. (1979). *Reading: The patterning of complex behavior* (2nd ed.). Auckland, New Zealand: Heinemann.

Cullinan, B. E. (1992). Whole language and children's literature. *Language Arts, 69,* 426–430.

Durkin, D. (1966). *Children who read early.* New York: Teachers College Press.

Durkin, D. (1974). A six-year study of children who learned to read in school at the age of four. *Reading Research Quarterly, 10,* 9–61.

Eckhoff, B. (1983). How reading affects children's writing. *Language Arts, 60,* 607–616.

Galda, L. (1988). Readers, texts, and contexts: A response-based view of literature in the classroom. *The New Advocate, 1,* 92–102.

Galda, L., & Cullinan, B. E. (1991). Literature for literacy: What research says about the benefits of using trade books in the classroom. In J. Flood, J. M. Jensen, D. Lapp, & J. Squire, (Eds.), *Handbook of research on teaching the English language arts* (pp. 529–535). New York: Macmillan.

Hansen, J. (1987). *When writers read.* Portsmouth, NH: Heinemann.

Harste, J., Woodward, V., & Burke, C. (1984). *Language stories and literacy lessons.* Portsmouth, NH: Heinemann.

Hepler, S. (1982). *Patterns of response to literature: A one-year study of a fifth- and sixth-grade classroom.* Unpublished doctoral dissertation, The Ohio State University.

Hickman, J. (1981). A new perspective on response to literature: Research in a classroom setting. *Research in the Teaching of English, 15,* 343–354.

Lamme, L. (1985). *Growing up reading.* Washington, DC: Acropolis Books.

McGee, L. M. (1992). Focus on research: Exploring the literature-based reading revolution. *Language Arts, 69,* 529–537.

Mendoza, A. (1985). Reading to children: Their preferences. *The Reading Teacher, 38,* 522–527.

Short, K. G. (1993). Making connections across literature and life. In K. E. Holland, R. A. Hungerford, & S. B. Ernst (Eds.), *Journeying: Children responding to literature* (pp. 284–301). Portsmouth, NH: Heinemann.

Spiegel, D. L. (1998). Reader response approaches and the growth of readers. *Language Arts, 76,* 41–48.

Teale, W. H., & Sulzby, E. (1986). *Emergent literacy: Reading and writing.* Norwood, NJ: Ablex.

Tunnell, M. O., & Jacobs, J. S. (1989). Using "real" books: Research findings on literature-based reading instruction. *The Reading Teacher, 42,* 470–477.

Vardell, S. M. (1998). Using read-aloud to explore the layers of nonfiction. In R. Bamford, & J. Kristo (Eds.), *Making facts come alive: Choosing quality nonfiction literature K–8* (pp. 151–167). Norwood, MA: Christopher-Gordon.

Wells, G. (1986). *The meaning makers: Children learning language and using language to learn.* Portsmouth, NH: Heinemann.

Yolen, J. (1985). The story between. *Language Arts, 62,* 590–592.

# CHILDREN'S BOOKS CITED     [ P ] = K–2; [ I ] = 3–5; [ M ] = 6–8

Babbitt, Natalie (1975). *Tuck everlasting.* New York: Farrar, Straus & Giroux.[ I/M ]

Brown, Margaret W. (1947). *Goodnight moon.* Illus. by Clement Hurd. New York: Harper & Row.[ P ]

Chambers, Veronica (1998). *Amistad rising: A story of freedom.* Illus. by Paul Lee. San Diego: Harcourt Brace.[ I/M ]

Conly, Jane L. (1998). *While no one was watching.* New York: Henry Holt.[ I ]

Cushman, Karen (1995). *The midwife's apprentice.* New York: Clarion.[ M ]

Dahl, Roald (1961). *James and the giant peach.* Illus. by Nancy E. Burkert. New York: Knopf. [ I ]

Egielski, Richard (1997). *The gingerbread boy.* New York: HarperCollins.[ P ]

Freedman, Russell (1993). *Eleanor Roosevelt: A life of discovery.* New York: Clarion. [ M ]

Henkes, Kevin (1992). *Chrysanthemum.* New York: Greenwillow.[ P ]

Holt, Kimberly W. (1998). *My Louisiana sky.* New York: Henry Holt.[ I ]

Isaacson, Philip M. (1993). *A short walk around the pyramids and through the world of art.* New York: Knopf.[ I/M ]

Krull, Kathryn (1997). *Wilma unlimited: How Wilma Rudolph became the world's fastest woman.* Illus. by David Diaz. San Diego: Harcourt Brace.[ I ]

Lewis, C. S. (1961). *The lion, the witch, and the wardrobe.* New York: Macmillan. [ I ]

Lowry, Lois (1993). *The giver.* Boston: Houghton Mifflin. [ I/M ]

Mayer, Mercer (1969). *There's a nightmare in my closet.* New York: Dial. [ P ]

McCloskey, Robert (1941). *Make way for ducklings.* New York: Viking. [ P ]

Murphy, Jim (1990). *The boy's war: Confederate and Union soldiers talk about the Civil War.* New York: Clarion. [ I/M ]

Naylor, Phyllis R. (1991). *Shiloh.* New York: Atheneum. [ I ]

Paterson, Katherine (1978). *The great Gilly Hopkins.* New York: Crowell. [ I ]

Rathmann, Peggy (1995). *Officer Buckle and Gloria.* New York: Putnam. [ P ]

Sachar, Louis (1998). *Holes.* New York: Farrar, Straus & Giroux. [ I/M ]

Scieszka, Jon (1998). *Squids will be squids: Fresh morals, beastly tales.* Illus. by Lane Smith. New York: Viking. [ I ]

Warner, Gertrude Chandler (1942). *The boxcar children.* Morton Grove, IL: Albert Whitman.[ P/I ]

White, E. B. (1952). *Charlotte's web.* New York: Harper & Row. [ P/I ]

Wick, Walter (1997). *A drop of water: A book of science and wonder.* New York: Scholastic. [ I ]

Wilder, Laura I. (1932/1953). *Little house in the big woods.* New York: Harper & Row. [ P/I ]

Yolen, Jane (1992). *Encounter.* Illus. by David Shannon. San Diego: Harcourt Brace. [ I ]

Zelinsky, Paul (1997). *Rapunzel.* New York: Dial. [ I ]

## Chapter 2

# Reader Response to Literature
## *From Rosenblatt's Theory to Classroom Practice*

*On a stormy spring afternoon in Kansas, a first-grade teacher invites her 15 restless students to the read-aloud center to experience Patricia Polacco's* Thundercake. *While most children sit pretzel style on the multicolored ABC rug, others rim the fringes of the carpeted area by choice. One holds a book, one clutches a stuffed turtle, while others come unencumbered. As one child perches uncomfortably under a computer cart, another finds his way to his teacher's lap. As Mrs. Scott begins to read the compelling text with expression, eyes are glued to each page. Cross-legged positions are abandoned as Dione and Jessyca unconsciously approach the rocking chair. Other listeners stretch their necks to savor the illustrations, which capture the fear of an impending storm. Giggles arise as Old Nellie Peck Hen frightens Mary Ellen and as Old Kick Cow lets out an unexpected moo. Throughout the read-aloud, the children spontaneously join in as Mary Ellen and her Babushka count the distance between the thunder and the lightning. "One ... two ... three ... CRASH, BAM, BOOM" chant the first graders. Some children even snap their fingers as if to imitate the rainfall and enthusiastically clap their hands to replicate the thunder. The listeners edge ever closer to the teacher as real thunder, as if on cue, vibrates the classroom windows as skies darken. As the book concludes, even Rushida has abandoned the safety of the computer cart and is found perched at the edge of the story rug area. As Mary Ellen and Babushka settle down to a slice of thundercake at the conclusion of the story, the rain begins to pelt the class-*

*room windows. The hands of the children shoot skyward as their own tales of fear, thunderstorms, and grandmas wait to be heard. After sharing several accounts and feelings, Mrs. Scott guides students to the adjacent work area where ingredients for baking their own thundercake await. Busy hands measure, sift, and stir as chatter about storms, cakes, and Mary Ellen continues. Dawn monitors the recipe from the treasured copy of* Thundercake. *As the batter containing the "secret ingredient" is popped into the cafeteria oven, the children anticipate the read-aloud of a related informational book,* Storms, *by Seymour Simon, as a continuing part of their literature-based theme exploration on weather. Comparisons are made between the two books as explanations of thunder are discussed and confirmed. The rain continues outdoors as the children receive a fresh-baked slice of homemade thundercake and celebrate their thoughts from the afternoon's literature encounters in their journals.*

Observation by Author as University Supervisor
in Professional Development School Setting

In the past decade educators have simultaneously experienced a renaissance in the publication of children's literature and in emerging philosophical trends that enriched and expanded the role of trade books in the classroom setting. Holistic philosophy, the reading–writing connection, and literature-based instruction have provided momentum for the increased inclusion of children's literature during the entire school day. Not only is literature being read aloud, but, in cases like the scenario that opens this chapter, it has assumed the heartbeat of the curriculum. Literature has become the focus of both reading and writing programs and has ventured across curricular boundaries through interdisciplinary instruction.

The purpose of this chapter is to share Louise Rosenblatt's theory of reader response and to connect its reality to the authentic literature response modes of K–8 children. The first part of the chapter shares Rosenblatt's theoretical perspective in understandable terms, and the second part brings that theory to life through an examination of the seven patterns of response exhibited by children when they respond to literature. The link between theory and practice is a vital one for practitioners who seek a theoretical foundation to support quality literature-based activities in the K–8 classroom. The practical link to real books and real children ensures internalization of a response-based perspective by envisioning children's responses to literature.

# LOUISE ROSENBLATT'S THEORY OF READER RESPONSE

. . . there is in reality only the potential millions of individual readers of the potential millions of individual literary works. . . . The reading of any work of literature is, of necessity, an individual and unique occurrence, involving the mind and emotions of some particular reader. (Rosenblatt, 1938, p. 32)

Since its publication in 1938, Louise Rosenblatt's *Literature as Exploration* has provided the theoretical basis for research in the teaching and study of literature and has impacted the way literature is taught in school settings. Acknowledged as the first book to support a reader response theory of literature, this masterpiece considers the personal, social, and cultural contexts of the reading act while showcasing the dynamics of the individual reader and the individual text as unique forces in the personal response to literature. Although supported by some teachers of college and high school literature for years, it has only been during the past decade that children's literature advocates have discovered the words of Rosenblatt as support for the inclusion of children's literature as a natural part of the elementary/middle-level curriculum. In her eloquent discussion of the role of the reader in the literary transaction, Rosenblatt support teachers' desires to surround readers with quality children's literature experiences, resulting in the creation of lifelong readers whose emotions and empathy fostered by literature will reach beyond reading to influence their view of humanity.

For more than 60 years, the name of Louise Rosenblatt has been synonymous with the *transactional theory of reader response* to literature. The theory focuses on the reciprocal relationship between the reader and the literature that results in individual responses to the text during and following engaged reading of literature. The interaction of the reader with the text is central to this theory as "a person becomes a reader by virtue of his activity in relation to the text" and "the text, a set of marks on the page, becomes the text of a poem . . . by virtue of its relationship with the reader . . ." (Rosenblatt, 1978, p. 18). The resulting transaction occurs as the reader brings a wealth of life and literature experiences to the text and culminates in a response that evokes the literary work of art as a truly personal experience for the reader.

The pinnacle of reader response results when the reader focuses an awareness on the very personal meaning that he or she is shaping. Then, and only then, will the reader create the aesthetically based literary work of art which Rosenblatt refers to as "the poem." The poem symbolizes the literary work of art created by the unique intervention of the reader. The reader draws on his or her own literature, life, and cognitive experiences. Out of the interaction of the text and the reader's unique background, "the poem" is formed. The "evocation of the poem" refers to the lived-through process of creating a unique perspective on the work while being guided by the text. As the reader continuously responds to the work, a constant stream of attitudes, ideas, and feelings runs through the participant's mind. Previous reading of literature and past personal experiences strongly influence the ongoing responses to a book. A circular process occurs as the reader responds to the words on the page while at the same time drawing on unique experiences and knowledge to organize those thoughts. Out of this interaction, "the poem" is formed. As noted in the quote that opens this section, each reader thus evokes his or her own meaning from the same text, thereby prioritizing and encouraging the unique response to literature.

In *The Reader, the Text, the Poem* (1978), Rosenblatt artfully described the evolving balanced role of reader and text by likening the reading transaction to a play performed on a stage. Dr. Rosenblatt asks her readers to imagine a darkened stage with the author stage left, the reader stage right, and the book midway between them. The spotlight initially focuses on the author so that the reader and the text become almost invisible to the audience. In this scene, single meaning resides fully in the author's mind. Imagine the spotlight shifting next to the text with the reader and the author completely obscured. The reader remains in the shadow, his or her secondary role taken for granted while meaning lies solely in the printed word. After many years, however, the spotlight begins to move in the direction of the reader. The reader begins to gain importance as an active participant in the reading event. As the play ends, the spotlight focuses on all three characters—the reader, the author, the text. Rosenblatt's theory highlights the whole stage scenario as both the text and its creative author interact with the reader to create meaning.

Rosenblatt was the earliest scholar to stress the equality of the text and the reader in any literary transaction. Rosenblatt (1978) eloquently articulated this shared role between reader and text to create a vision in her readers' minds:

> Instead of a rigid stencil, a more valid image of the text seems to be something like an open-meshed woven curtain, a mesh of flexible strands that holds a certain relationship to one another, but whose total shape and pattern change as any one part is pulled or loosened. One can imagine the reader peering through the curtain, affecting its shape and the pattern of the mesh by the tension or looseness with which he is holding it, and filling in the openings from his own palette of colors. (p. 76)

This image portrays the reader as an interactive participant who synthesizes a personal response to literature. The dual nature of the text is also envisioned because it encourages personal responses by the reader while minimally limiting interactions within its own constraints.

Although other writers have attempted to crystallize the reader's role in the literary transaction through the years (Bleich, 1973; Holland, 1968; Iser, 1978; Probst, 1984; Richards, 1929), it was Louise Rosenblatt's passionate words that painted a vivid portrait of the transaction between the reader and the text in the minds of elementary practitioners. Teachers were able to grasp Rosenblatt's complex theory, translate its distinctive message into instructional methodology, and share the wonder of natural response with readers of children's literature.

# EFFERENT AND AESTHETIC RESPONSE

An awareness of the distinction between aesthetic and nonaesthetic reading is necessary if we are to understand transactional theory. Rosenblatt clearly differentiates between efferent and aesthetic reading, with the distinction lying in the primary direction or focus of the reader's attention.

In *efferent* reading, the reader's attention is focused primarily on acquiring information. This might be associated with the reading of an informational book on the desert, a close reading of Avi's *Beyond the Western Sea* to gain familiarity with the huge cast of characters, or a reading of Diane Stanley's *Leonardo da Vinci* to obtain specific facts about the artist's life. This type of reading is designated efferent because it involves what is carried away from the reading event. In this case, facts about the desert, the names and relationships of Avi's complex cast of characters, and the accomplishments of a great Renaissance man would become the product of the reading experience. Equate efferent reading with the type of comprehension that is often asked for during basal reader or textbook instruction. The questions evoke only right or wrong answers, thereby cueing the reader to view reading as an information gathering event.

In contrast, **aesthetic** reading is primarily concerned with the lived-through experience that occurs during interaction with the text. Aesthetic reading focuses on feelings and thoughts that flow through the reader's mind and heart as she or he reads. Aesthetic reading might be associated with repeated readings of Maya Angelou's poem *Life Doesn't Frighten Me,* vicariously experiencing the trials of wilderness survival in Gary Paulsen's *The Haymeadow,* or lingering over outspoken diary entries reflecting the culture of the Middle Ages in Karen Cushman's *Catherine, Called Birdy.* This type of reading focuses more on the ongoing process of reading, the personal interaction, rather than the product of comprehension. The enjoyment of reading, involvement with the characters, and the single reader's emerging thoughts take priority over secondary details. Equate this with literature-based reading in which personal interaction with texts is encouraged through open-ended response prompts, response journals, or literature conversations. All interactions with the text are encouraged and valued as a targeted outcome of the active art of reading.

The terms *efferent* and *aesthetic* apply to a selective stance the reader adopts toward the literary text. The efferent stance pays more attention to the cognitive, the factual, the public, and the quantitative aspects of textual meaning. The aesthetic stance focuses on the affective, the emotional, the private, and the qualitative aspects of personal meaning. Efferent and aesthetic reading, however, should not be considered mutually exclusive of one another.

Although one important aspect of the reading event is the selection of a predominantly efferent or a predominantly aesthetic stance toward the text, Rosenblatt attests that most reading incorporates a continuous, unconscious fluctuation between these two stances. An accurate view of reader response lies on a continuum between the efferent and the aesthetic extremes, not on a distinct line between the two. At any moment during the reading process, the reader's stance can lie anywhere along this efferent–aesthetic continuum. Rosenblatt attests that most reading resides near the middle of the continuum and indicates a constant fluctuation between both extremes as characteristic of most readers. "No two readings, even by the same person, are identical" (Rosenblatt, 1994). Readers are simultaneously moving back and forth along the continuum as they read, blending information and sentiment, knowledge and connections to one's own experience.

For example, while discovering that Leonardo da Vinci was born during the Renaissance in 1452 (efferent), the reader might also identify his inventiveness and determination as admirable traits (aesthetic). At the same time, while becoming emotionally involved in a fictional flash flood in Wyoming (aesthetic), the reader might actually discover what supplies must be packed for a summer of rigorous sheepherding (efferent). Readers are not consciously aware of adopting one stance or the other. The reading experience remains a unique event in that some readers take on the aesthetic stance intuitively while many, unfortunately, never learn to read aesthetically at all. Recognizing the differences between aesthetic and efferent reading while gaining an awareness of their interplay as part of the reading process serves as an important introduction to reader response theory and its connection to classroom practice. Teachers should clarify, model, and encourage both types of responses as readers interact with literature.

The shift in emphasis of reader response theory from the impact of the text alone to the dynamic interaction of the reader with it implies new priorities and procedures for the literature-based classroom. Rosenblatt's reader response theory suggests that students should not be subordinate to the literature, but active participants in the reading process, making personal meaning and significance from the literature they encounter (Probst, 1984). Although theoretical differences are dispersed in ideas regarding the reader–text relationship, there is generally some consensus of thought on the following assumptions:

(1)  Meaning is not "contained" in the text, but is derived from an interaction between the content and the structure of the author's message and the experience and the prior knowledge of the reader.

(2)  Readers comprehend differently because every reader is culturally and individually unique.

(3)  Examining readers' response to text is more valid than establishing one "correct" interpretation of text meaning.

(Chase & Hynd, 1987, p. 531)

Louise Rosenblatt's theory has cast aside the isolated dominance of the text and directed the spotlight to the vital role of the reader whose response brings life to literature and literature to life (Hynds, 1989). A quote from Holland (1975) encompasses the spirit of reader response and the value of the reader in the literary transaction through a fairy tale illusion:

A literary text . . . consists only of a certain configuration of specks of carbon black on dried wood pulp. When these marks become words, when those words become images or metaphors or characters or events, they do so because the reader plays the part of a prince to the sleeping beauty. He [she] gives them life out of his [her] own desires. (p. 12)

Rosenblatt's lead in establishing the stature of the reader in the reader–text interaction has meaningfully provided the theoretical foundation needed for response-based, literature-focused instruction in the elementary/middle-level classroom setting.

Rosenblatt's theory of reader response supplied the theoretical basis of meaningful research studies conducted during the past 35 years. The attempt to reveal what thoughtful responses to literature take place in the mind of the reader has led researchers to focus on several dimensions of the response process. The diverse dimensions of response have been examined through both oral and written modes, across a variety of age groups, within a variety of genre, and through varied categorical schemes. Research has resulted in response categorization schemes (Hancock, 1993; Purves & Rippere, 1968; Squire, 1964) and affirmed the developmental nature of response (Applebee, 1978; Cullinan, Harwood, & Galda, 1983; Sebesta, Monson, & Senn, 1995). Other studies have documented reader stance as a basis for response (Cox & Many, 1992a, 1992b; Langer, 1990) and the dynamic role of the reader during the reading process (Many, 1991; Many & Cox, 1992). Case studies focused on the idiosyncratic nature of response (Fry, 1985; Galda, 1982; Hancock, 1991). Research conducted in classroom settings described patterns of response to literature (Hepler, 1982; Hickman, 1981; Kiefer, 1983; Yocum, 1987), and more recent studies share collaborative or teacher action research that reflect the strengths of response-based classroom practices (Barone, 1990; Egawa, 1990; Hubbard, Winterbourne, & Ostrow, 1996; Kelly, 1990; Leal, 1993; Madura, 1995; Roller & Beed, 1994; Wollman-Bonilla & Werchadlo, 1995). The response-based ideas shared in this text are built from these quality research studies and provide a credible bridge between theory and practice for the teacher of literature and children.

# PATTERNS OF RESPONSE TO LITERATURE

An appreciation for response to literature begins with theory but continues with an awareness of the wide range of responses that children exhibit as they interact with books. Janet Hickman (1980, 1981) observed and described patterns in elementary children's responses to literature as they occurred in the natural context of a K–5 school environment. Modes of response to literature observed by Hickman included (1) listening behavior, (2) contact with books, (3) the impulse to share, (4) actions and drama, (5) making things, (6) oral response, and (7) written response.

Much of what occurs in response to literature is unplanned and unrehearsed, as illustrated by the spontaneous reaction to the read-aloud event that opened this chapter. On the other hand, many response-based activities are well conceived and planned by the teacher following the reading of a book (i.e., thundercake baking and journal writing). Teachers possess a great deal of power over children's response to literature (Hickman, 1983; Pantaleo, 1995). Through inclusion of teacher-selected books as read-alouds, effective incorporation of literature into the content areas, provision of easy access to literature, and management of opportunities for demonstrating these modes of response, teachers influence both the quantity and quality of the responses expressed by children. The teacher is indeed a powerful determiner of the response of children to the literature they read. That role can be nourished by an increasing awareness and knowledge of the possibilities and power of reader response. Learning to observe and encourage these variations in reader response opens a new view of literature in the classroom for both teacher and children.

The following discussion on modes of response to literature is based on the Hickman findings and further enhanced by professional observations of the interaction of children and books from kindergarten through eighth grade in real school settings. These patterns of response are presented in a gradual continuum moving from spontaneous response toward planned response activities initiated by the teacher. Acquiring an understanding of the potential of all varieties of response gains importance as teachers strive to build a strong response base and support a growing confidence in personal expression as they create lifelong readers. Much of this chapter serves as an overview to response topics that will be discussed in greater depth in Part III of this text.

## Listening Behavior

One of the most natural and observable modes of literature response is the behavior exhibited as literature is being read aloud to children. Listening behavior evidences itself in a child stretching to view an illustration, in the sound of spontaneous laughter, or in the chanting of a repetitive phrase. Listening behavior surrounds every library story hour, every home read-aloud event, and every classroom storytime. Since children learn to listen as they are learning to read (Lundsteen, 1990), listening behavior is developmentally the first mode of response to books. As parents, teachers, and caregivers, we often become too engaged in the act of reading aloud to actually notice this response. Awareness of its existence is the first step toward building an appreciation of response to literature.

Observe these rudimentary, but important behaviors during read-alouds because they provide a developmental foundation for other modes of response. Human response mandates physical, spontaneous, and participatory response in a listener during a read-aloud event. Children nudge closer to Kevin Henkes's books to examine the contents of *Lily's Purple Plastic Purse,* chuckle at her treatment of *Julius, the Baby of the World,* and applaud when Victoria forgets her lines in the school play in *Chrysanthemum.* Noting these natural occurrences in almost any uninhibited read-aloud setting convinces teachers of the importance of listening behaviors in establishing a groundwork for response.

***Physical response.***    Listening behavior evidences itself in where a child chooses to sit, the proximity of the child to the book, and listener movement during the read-aloud. Children stand, jump, and twirl without even planning these movements. Although physical response can be somewhat limited by adult direction and behavioral expectations, the importance of allowing for natural movement during a read-aloud is essential to capturing genuine response, particularly with younger children.

Pandell and Wolfe's *Animal Action ABC* energetically invites children to arch like a humpback whale, drink like a giraffe, march like a penguin, and unfold like a bat. Photographs of children imitating animal movements serve as an invitation for physical response. A group of kindergartners contorted, stretched, and reshaped their bodies as they responded to this book. It is hard to imagine any child sitting still during the sharing of this title. The same active invitation is extended by Laura Cauley's *Clap Your Hands,* which encourages listening participants to engage in active movements that range from touching your toes to doing a somersault to wiggling your nose. Listening is not always a quiet activity, but one which can welcome physical participation.

***Spontaneous response.***    This type of listening behavior includes the laughter, the tears, the facial expressions, the brief comments, and the applause that may interrupt or follow the read-aloud. Unplanned and unsolicited, these genuine reactions of listeners are worthy of recognition as a response to literature. Traditionally, the read-aloud was honored as a quiet episode, but an understanding of spontaneous response allows for individual reactions as they automatically occur within the listener.

A read-aloud of Gail Jorgensen's *Gotcha!* to young children results in sighs of disappointment with a bear's repeated attempts to catch a pesky fly. The final triumph of the fly brings giggles and smiles to engaged faces. Fifth graders, engrossed in a read-aloud of Karen Hesse's *Letters from Rifka,* begin scratching their heads as Rifka contracts ringworm. A sigh of relief and delight occurs as Rifka arrives in America and the tickling on her scalp is found to be the growth of new hair. The encouragement and valuing of spontaneous response make listening a more active process and the read-aloud an interactive event.

***Participatory response.***    So many read-aloud choices for young children are predictable books with repetitive phrases and refrains. Joining in, chanting, clapping, and repeating provide a natural mode of listening behavior. No invitation is needed to bring about the participatory nature of response. It is inherent in the text and draws from the natural instincts of a child to become an active participant in a piece of literature.

*To Market, To Market* by Anne Miranda engages readers with a classic rhyme: "To market, to market, to buy a fat pig. Home again, home again, jiggity jig!" But traditional similarity ends there. Predictable text follows a disgruntled shopper buying a red hen, a plump goose, a live trout, and several other purchases that turn into disasters when she brings them home. Colored print invites listeners to join in on the name of the animal and a repeated "Uh-oh!" on each page encourages further participation. Humorous illustrations by Janet Stevens turn a shopping melee into a participatory delight. While Mary Ann Hoberman's *The Seven Silly Eaters* can be read just for fun the first time, it brings natural participation on repeated readings. Built on rhyme and a cumulative display of a hungry brood of children, the story invites listeners to join in at the end of lines and become a part of predictable dialogue. Planned teacher read-aloud pauses allow for planned listener participation and rollicking classroom fun. Celebrating the natural invitations of books like these allows both teachers and children to appreciate the power of response that makes listening an active experience.

## Contact With Books

Readers initiate their own response to literature through the multiple ways in which they make direct contact with books. Whether browsing in the library/media center, reading in a comfortable chair, or attending to books in their desks, contact with books tells observers something of a reader's interest, intent, and immersion in books. Contact with books includes reader choice as a response to literature. The self-selection of a book from the vast holdings of a library must be considered a genuine, personal response to literature.

***Browsing and choosing.***    Observe children as they enter the inviting world of the library/media center or discover a fresh classroom display of themed book titles. Their wide-eyed faces light up at both brightly colored new books and at familiar favorites. Their fingers touch a shiny plastic cover, trace the words of the title, or fumble to turn a brightly illustrated page. Individual choice is a response to literature. In teachers minds, response and choice should be synonymous with expressions of interest—the most obvious of children's responses to literature (Hickman, 1985). The act of selecting books for reading over those left for other readers involves scanning, decision making, and selecting—natural responses to literature. Monson and Sebesta (1991) report the complexity of reading interests and their important relationship to reading preferences.

Children's book preferences form an important aspect of reader response. Children often seek books by favorite authors, in preferred genres, or former read-alouds by the classroom teacher. Remember how everyone wanted to read C. S. Lewis's Narnia Chronicles after the teacher read-aloud of *The Lion, the Witch, and the Wardrobe?* The more familiar children become with literature, the more impact their literature schema has on their choices. Choice is a response that expands with the assistance of a knowledgeable teacher who immerses his or her students in literature.

The selection process warrants teacher observation and documentation. A fourth-grade student held a chapter book in each hand as the dismissal bell rang for lunch. His eyes journeyed from one cover to the other and back again. Finally, he placed one book back on the shelf and hurried to the scanner to check out *Brian's Winter*. When asked why he made that choice, he admitted that his teacher had read aloud *Hatchet* and he couldn't wait to read another book by Gary Paulsen. When asked about the book he returned to the shelf, he stated it would have been easier to read, but that he had read it two times before and was ready for something new. Teachers can learn a great deal by asking children why they choose the books they do. As Hickman (1980) and Schlager (1978) discovered, teachers play a critical role in influencing reading choices. Their knowledge of and personal choices in literature can affect reader response exhibited through literature preferences of self-selected titles.

***Attention to books.*** Linger behind children as they leave the library or media center with their newly acquired selections. They hug them—*Verdi*; they clasp them to their bodies—*Rabbits & Raindrops*; they walk while reading them—*A Pizza the Size of the Sun*; and they treat them like best friends—*Some Smug Slug*. Books even find their way to the cafeteria and the playground for the most dedicated readers. The attention children pay to books provides another avenue for response. Some children become so absorbed in a book that they simply don't hear the teacher calling them for the next activity. Many children experience that same commitment to self-selected books, especially on first acquiring them. They can't seem to get enough of the illustrations, the printed words, or the warm invitation a book extends to them as readers. The act of reading them over and over again or returning to a bookmarked chapter provides indications of this mode of response. Observe and celebrate this attention to literature within the context of the school day.

***Proximity of books.*** The location of books in children's lives provides another indication of literature response. Some children immediately stash books in a backpack for carrying home, whereas others use their desktop for immediate access. For some children a day never passes without a pile of library books perched on the corner of their desks. Keeping books close at hand indicates the desire and anticipation of the independent reading event and supports the long-term goal of creating lifelong readers. Teachers who fill their classrooms with literature and make it available to their students make literature accessible for independent reading throughout the day. Books kept close at hand reflect their value and importance in our daily lives.

## The Impulse to Share

Although the reading event may be viewed as a personalized experience between the reader and the text, the act of reading dictates an almost instinctive need to share the textual event with others. The social aspects of response to literature surface as children exhibit an eagerness to share within their community of readers (Hepler & Hickman, 1982). Children, and even adults, cannot resist talking about books, making personal connections, rereading passages, or recommending a book to a friend. Reading was never meant to be an isolated incident in an elementary setting. Active minds and hearts demand opportunities to share unique characters, inspiring illustrations, and personal experiences related to books.

***Reading together.***   Whether reading with a book buddy, partner reading, or round-robin reading in a small group, reading together elicits natural moments for reflection and sharing. Spontaneous thoughts and comments automatically spill forth as readers pause between read-aloud passages to allow for personalized comments. These responses range from predictions and explanations to wishes and wonderings, and their strength lies in the progression of interactive meaning-making that occurs during the reading of a text. Response must be considered on-task reading behavior, modeled by the teacher, and encouraged as a natural part of the ongoing reading process.

***Telling about a book.***   Almost spontaneously, children begin to talk about the books they are reading. While some teachers have incorporated a short time slot at the beginning or end of reading workshop to share books, younger children often choose to bring favorite literature to share for show-and-tell. Whether "telling" encompasses reading aloud a special passage or recounting the story itself to encourage others to read the book, telling is an important element of response. Eve Bunting's *Fly Away Home* always elicits comments. Spreading the word about good reading material fulfills a natural impulse to share the excitement of a quality reading experience.

Teachers who realize the inherent need to share plan opportunities for book sharing as a part of their daily routine. A scheduled time following sustained silent reading is likely to overflow with descriptions of favorite parts, highlighted illustrations, and personal recommendations. Reading is social and the need to share its excitement and joy requires planned informal time in the course of the school day.

***Sharing discoveries.***   "Look at this!" "Listen to this!" "Look what I found!" Comments like these are vigorously expressed during and following independent reading time in elementary classrooms. Children can't wait to share a character, an incident, an exciting illustration, or a fact-filled passage with anyone who will listen. The strength of this type of response lies in its genuine, extemporaneous nature. The masterful spontaneity that is reader response is often supported by reading partners who serve as listeners and sharers during these highly explosive response moments. Once again, it is the informed, response-conscious teacher who allows children to share these spontaneous thoughts. As children mature, these personal reactions can be recorded in a journal for sharing at a later time. If children are inhibited from sharing these discoveries as they occur, however, they begin to realize that a teacher values only those responses shared at the end of a book. The rich interactive nature of the reading process as it unfolds throughout a text can be lost if only retrospective response is encouraged.

***Sharing connections.***   As children are exposed to more and more literature, they begin to connect each book to another title as they draw from their literature schema. For example, a second grader connected an independent reading of Lois Ehlert's *Eating the Alphabet* with a teacher read-aloud of Janet Stevens's *Tops and Bottoms*. When children make these higher level connections, they need to share their discovery with others for affirmation of their own response. Teachers who allow time for sharing as a natural response to reading provide the opportunity for this validation and expansion of thought. As this response phenomenon occurs foundationally in the primary grades, it builds into increasing self-confidence to discuss literature connections as the literary base expands across grade levels. Intertextual connections form an important response mode and are often indicators of those children who are destined to become lifelong readers.

Children also naturally connect books to their own lives. Teachers hardly close the back cover of a picture book before hands begin waving to share these natural connections. David, for example, couldn't wait to relate his story of hiding in a storm cellar during a tornado warning following the reading of *Thundercake.* Stories of fear brought up an intertextual connection to Emily Arnold McCully's *Mirette on the High Wire.* Allowing a reasonable amount of time for sharing personal connections builds a foundation and confidence for future response. Children learn that response is valued and unique to the individual and move away from the "right" answer to a personal response to a question. This response principle provides a springboard for expanding developmentally appropriate response activities as the reader grows and matures in exploring other response options.

## Actions and Drama

Being directly engaged and involved helps children identify with the literature they read. Besides focusing on vocabulary and aiding comprehension, action and drama include those children whose learning styles thrive on active immersion. Whether student initiated or teacher planned, puppet shows, improvisation, movement activities, and plays based on literature foster active comprehension and a deeper connection to literature.

***Echoing the action.*** Many books exist that invite children to become a part of the action of the story. In Nancy Van Laan's *Possum Come a-Knockin',* children take their cues from the dramatic actions of each perplexed family member as they whittle, knit, untangle, pound, hiss, and growl while a mischievous critter plays possum outside their door. Eric Carle's *From Head to Toe* encourages listeners to follow the movements of various animals. The question-and-answer format guarantees response as children proudly chant "I can do it!" as they replicate the movements. Listening skills cue children into applying their actions to accompany the active words of the literature texts.

***Dramatic play.*** Reenactment of fairy tales or folktales provides a means for dramatic play as response to literature. Acting out *Goldilocks and the Three Bears* reinforces sequencing as children develop a clearer sense of story in the fairy-tale genre. Dramatically reenacting Jan Brett's version of *The Mitten* allows for many characters to sequentially squeeze into a make-believe mitten and await a sneeze-induced explosion. Oral articulation and expressive talents are explored as this blend of language and drama expands the response capabilities of dramatic performers in the classroom.

***Readers' theater.*** Authentic literature that has been scripted into a readers' theater format is ideal for reading fluency, oral expression, and dramatic interpretation. The personalized expressive touch imposed on the original words of the text provide yet another dramatic response option. For example, Amy MacDonald's hilarious *Rachel Fister's Blister* readily translates into a readers' theater script. A multiplicity of characters allows for whole class participation in the hectic efforts of the Fister family attempt to relieve the hurt caused by the blister on Rachel's toe. Everyone's advice is enlisted until the wise Queen saves the day. Readers' theater scripts provide the words directly from literature while the readers' voices provide the dramatic response.

## Artistic, Musical, and Constructive Response

Teachers often plan extension activities related to the arts following the reading of literature. Whether these take the form of drawings, multimedia presentations, musical accompaniment, or constructed models, they provide a hands-on approach to response and reach the child who may be less comfortable with the oral or written response options. The variety and meaningful connectedness to literature inferred from this response option provide a wealth of ideas for classroom extensions.

*Visual representation.*   Drawing or visual replication of a story, a single scene from a story, or a sequence of scenes appeals to the visual learner as a mode of response. Visual representation can reflect comprehension, emotions, attention to story detail, and personal interpretation of text. Kindergarten and first-grade response journals are delightfully filled with visual representations of story characters and actions. These drawings often serve as a springboard to oral and written language as they provide clues for what to say and what to write. Visual representations may serve as a rehearsal for later development of oral and written responses.

*Constructions.*   Many books inspire hands-on activities that extend the story into the realm of artistic response. While Eleanor Coerr's *Sadako* inspires the folding of paper cranes, *Pink Paper Swans* requires more intricate origami folds. *Stephen Beisty's Cross-Sections: Castles* may inspire the construction of a medieval fortress complete with privy, dungeon, and towers. Literature that suggests artistic construction allows the less verbal, but manually talented, child to excel in expression of response in this unique mode.

*Tasting reading.*   Just as the children in a primary classroom became engaged in the baking of their thundercake in the opening scenario of this chapter, so too does literature often inspire the preparation and consumption of other culinary delights. While response takes on an active tone in this mode of response, literature provides a memorable experience through related cooking episodes. Lisa Campbell Ernst's fairy-tale variant of *Little Red Riding Hood: A Newfangled Prairie Tale* naturally leads to the baking of grandma's wheatberry muffin recipe imprinted on the endpapers. Marjorie Priceman's *How to Make an Apple Pie and See the World* takes the reader on a quest for the ultimate ingredients to put together the world's best apple pie. The gingerbread cookie recipe on Jim Aylesworth's *The Gingerbread Man* and Amanda's gooseberry pie in Sonia Levitin's *Boom Town* create literature memories through taste experiences and provide variety in sharing response to these special books.

*Musical response.*    Selecting haunting background music for a read-aloud of Jan Wahl's *Tailypo!* or making rhythmic sounds on washboards and spoons to accompany the reading of the Birdseyes' *She'll Be Comin' Round the Mountain* are two ways in which musical response can be incorporated into the literature-based classroom. Ysaye M. Barnwell's *No Mirrors in My Nana's House* is accompanied by a CD recording of the author reading the text and Sweet Honey in the Rock singing it. The stark, faceless, brilliantly colored artwork of Synthia Saint James seems to further enhance the lyrics and melody. The captivating rhythm will have children singing the story throughout the day. A musical connection to literature can be found in many titles that incorporate song lyrics including Nadine Westcott's *There's a Hole in the Bucket*. The music specialist can take an active part in extending this response mode into the classroom or the teacher can integrate the musical tones within the curriculum. Note how this response style reaches yet another mode of expression for musically talented children.

## Oral Response

As children listen to or read literature, their authentic responses may be conveyed through the oral response mode. This is typically the most common response mode as the voice of the reader longs to share and be valued for its individuality. While spontaneous comments are valued, the mode of oral response tends to be more directed by teacher-initiated configurations or prompts. While response still remains genuine, it takes on a more structured identity, allowing for a greater focus on the words of the reader.

*Retelling/storytelling.*    As teachers invite children to tell a story, their comprehension skills and attention to detail come into focus. Their sense of story, character, setting, and plot must organize their response, while their own creativity is fostered and valued in the individualized sharing of a tale. Folktales and fairy tales work well with this response option as sequence and simple characterization provide structure for oral response. Mirra Ginsburg's *Clay Boy* presents a simple, sequentially structured story with a series of characters and a focused plot reminiscent of many traditional fairy tales. Retelling or, in a more creative mode, storytelling this tale from Russia provides children an opportunity to bring their own voices to a somewhat structured presentation. Steve Sanfield's *Bit by Bit* is simply sequenced and told by a storyteller as it relates how Zundel the tailor's winter coat becomes, in turn, a jacket, a vest, a cap, a pocket, a button, and finally a few colored threads. Yet the threads reinvite the continued retelling of the tale by the reader. Although oral response may be somewhat limited by the constraints of the tale, the words and emotions of the reteller provide much room for personalized response to the story.

*Prompted response.*    To assist children in moving beyond spontaneous comments about literature, teachers construct response prompts to provide a more structured and directed approach to the oral response process. Response prompts can be defined as open-ended questions that elicit unique and individual response. Rather than limiting a child to a right or wrong answer, they are posed in an effort to encourage individual interpretation and discussion. Here are three formidable prompts designed by Bleich (1978): What did you notice? How did this book make you feel? What does this book remind you of from your own life? As limiting as these three prompts may seem to be, they actually allow for freedom of expressive thought and foster developmental growth over time and across grade levels. Their power lies in their open endedness, which allows each reader to bring personal interpretation to literature. When these prompts are applied to a poignant picture book text such as Eve Bunting's *On Call Back Mountain,* they produce a wide range of responses about friendship, loss, and rebirth of the human spirit. It is interesting to observe these same prompts used across age levels with the same book as the developmental characteristic of response becomes obvious.

*Literature discussions.*     Oral response that builds from student-directed discussion groups (i.e., literature circles, grand conversations) provides developmentally appropriate response outlets for students in intermediate/middle-level classrooms. Based on the idea of building from the articulated thoughts and ideas of others, literature discussions provide a format for free comments limited only by the bounds of the literature being discussed. The emphasis on student-generated talk driven by minimal teacher facilitation provides a setting for authenticity and unique expression. Generally used with the reading of chapter books, literature discussions elicit deep thinking in response to books across genres like these Newbery-winning titles: *The Giver* (science fiction/fantasy), *Walk Two Moons* (realistic fiction), and *The Midwife's Apprentice* (historical fiction). Socially empowered response finds an audience within literature conversations.

## Written Response

The written mode of response encourages the reader to capture and record her or his personal transaction with literature. Whereas oral response is fleeting, written response secures a permanent record of thoughts, opinions, feelings, and reactions during the act of reading. As children leave their egocentric selves behind, they are often more inhibited in sharing innermost responses to literature. The written response often becomes a means for private expression of thoughts.

Typically recorded in a journal format, written responses can ultimately be shared in discussion groups, exchanged with a reading partner, reflected on personally, or shared privately with a teacher. They can become an impetus for extended writing or effect the creation of an original work. Although the written response can begin in the primary grades, it is often viewed as a higher level interaction with literature that reconstructs reading images and meaning into personalized thoughts on paper.

*Literature journals.*     A literature journal is best described as a repository of wanderings, wonderings, speculations, questions, and explorative thoughts recorded during the reading process (Hancock, 1993). It allows the reader to make discoveries, let the mind ramble, and create room for the evolving text. Several names and adaptations exist for the reading journal, but all encourage spontaneous, honest written response to the literature children read.

- **Literature response journal.**   This format allows for the free flow of thought throughout the entire reading process. Its unstructured format encourages the written recording of thoughts *as* they occur, rather than retrospectively following the reading event.

- **Dialogue journal.**   This format fosters continuous written dialogue between the reader and another respondent. Writing back and forth about a book being read creates a continuous conversation. The second respondent can be a peer, the classroom teacher, or another supervising adult (student teacher, paraprofessional, special education teacher). These responses read as letters between two readers.
- **Character journal.**   This format suggests a first-person interaction with the book by the reader assuming the guise of one of the book's characters. The "I" stance of the narrative creates strong involvement in the book and engages the reader with the persona of the character and the events.
- **Double entry draft.**   This format suggests the journal be divided in two columns. Readers record direct quotes, lists, or other pertinent information on the left side, and then record responses to these on the right side of each page.
- **Reading log.**   This format suggests a brief entry of the name of the book and author followed by a brief comment at the end of the book (picture book) or at the end of the day's reading (chapter book). More informal and less spontaneous, this writing is often kept in chart form as an ongoing process throughout the school year.

The freedom to write in most of these journals throughout the reading process preserves the spontaneous thoughts and interactions with the text. With practice and commitment to the response process, a full, rich range of written response can be revealed to most emotionally charged books. With teacher modeling of his or her own responses to a read-aloud on an overhead projector, children quickly acclimate themselves to the process. With strong teacher encouragement and frequent written feedback, children develop their own response styles and willingly internalize the written response process. Over time, the interplay between reading and written reflections slowly becomes a natural part of the reading process.

***Literature as a model for writing.***   Literature often serves as a springboard for extended writing activities that follow the format or genre structure of a book. Many researchers have pointed out the connections between reading literature and the writing process. Both Jane Hansen (1987) and Donald Graves (1983) pointed out the connections between the reading of quality literature and the production of quality writing. Golden (1984) demonstrated how readers draw on their concept of story during writing stories. A strategy for teaching story structure and its application to writing (Tompkins, 1994) includes the following suggestions:

- Focus on a single element of story structure or genre.
- Read literature emphasizing this element or genre.
- Discuss how the element was used in the genre read.
- Participate in prewriting activities that frame the element or genre (graphic organizers, retellings).
- Write stories incorporating the particular element or genre.

Sharing a *pourquoi* version of how a bear lost his tail may provide a model for students composing a parallel tale. Reading *Only Opal: The Diary of a Young Girl* provides an inspiration for keeping a diary of one's own. Jon Scieszka's *The True Story of the Three Little Pigs* has inspired countless point-of-view fairy-tale creations. Literature as a model for writing serves a meaningful purpose as children internalize genre, literary elements, and the writing craft and begin to utilize these components in their own writing.

These seven modes of response are not exclusive, distinct or isolated from one another. They tend to blend, overlap, and build on each other. Practitioners should never feel obliged to fit observations of children into one of these response modes. While the categorical organization of this chapter creates a framework for exploring the possibilities, reader response does not warrant exclusive inclusion in a single area. Categories overlap because response naturally defies certain categorization. Although the categories tend to be presented in a continuum from student-initiated response to teacher-initiated response-based activities, any mode can be spontaneous and can be generated by the reader rather than the literacy facilitator in a classroom setting.

# CLOSING THOUGHTS

The theoretical voice of Louise Rosenblatt speaks clearly to literature-based teachers. Rosenblatt's impact on both research and practice in the last decade is evidenced by the number of research studies and dissertations grounded in the transactional theory of reader response (Short, 1995). The impact of these studies evidences itself in the current content of university education courses, teacher inservices, and staff development seminars. Its impact is felt in the hearts of children as they build an endearing relationship with literature throughout the school day and across the school year. Its impact is seen in a teacher's decision to include trade books as a central core of the curriculum supported by a philosophy of natural learning. Literature-based classrooms form the ultimate tribute to the theoretical voice of Louise Rosenblatt that resounds clearly in elementary classrooms in which the individuality of the reader and the uniqueness of response are treasured commodities and desired outcomes of a democratic education (Pradl, 1996).

As Rosenblatt's theory enters the reality of the elementary/middle-level classroom, patterns of response to literature emerge. As teachers realize and explore the potential and the variety of modes of response to literature, they are better able to plan a balanced approach to response in the context of their literature-based curriculum. Response spans active participation, verbal acuity, the power of the written word, artistic creations, and the human need to share. Response addresses the varied learning styles of children and stirs creative minds and hearts. Response to literature moves children away from "correctness interpretation" and allows them the freedom to express the thoughts that linger in their hearts during and following a literature experience. Classrooms in which response to literature thrives are characterized by teachers valuing response as a factor in literacy growth (Martinez & Roser, 1991). When teachers provide opportunities for response, models of response, and receptiveness to response, children and literacy flourish.

This chapter has attempted to open your eyes to the possibilities of a response-based literature classroom. Subsequent chapters in this text further explore these natural modes of response to literature in greater depth. Valuing literature for literature's sake is central to a response-based teaching philosophy. Viewing literature as an avenue for response further allows for expression of a child's literary transaction with a book. As teachers attempt to bring variety, breadth, and depth to the natural response potential of children, an awareness of and understanding of several modes of response are essential for celebrating the response outcomes of a thriving literature-based classroom. Ultimately, the theory-into-practice link between Rosenblatt's transactional theory of reader response and the identified response modes of children evidences itself in the real classroom where engaged readers and quality books come together in a teaching/learning environment that supports quality literature and genuine response.

# REFERENCES

Applebee, A. N. (1978). *The child's concept of story: Ages two to seventeen.* Chicago, IL: University of Chicago Press.

Barone, D. (1990). The written responses of young children: Beyond comprehension to story understanding. *The New Advocate, 3,* 49–56.

Bleich, D. (1978). *Subjective criticism.* Baltimore: Johns Hopkins University Press.

Chase, N. D., & Hynd, C. R. (1987). Reader response: An alternative way to teach students to think about text. *Journal of Reading, 30,* 530–540.

Cox, C., & Many, J. E. (1992a). Reader stance towards a literary work: Applying the transactional theory to children's responses. *Reading Psychology, 13,* 37–72.

Cox, C., & Many, J. E. (1992b). Toward an understanding of the aesthetic response to literature. *Language Arts, 69,* 28–33.

Cullinan, B. E., Harwood, K. T., & Galda, L. (1983). The reader and the story: Comprehension and response. *Journal of Research and Development in Education, 16,* 29–37.

Egawa, K. (1990). Harnessing the power of language: First graders' literature engagement with Owl Moon. *Language Arts, 67,* 582–588.

Fry, D. (1985). *Children talk about books: Seeing themselves as readers.* Philadelphia, PA: Milton Keynes.

Galda, L. (1982). Assuming the spectator stance: An examination of the responses of three young readers. *Research in the Teaching of English, 16,* 1–20.

Golden, J. M. (1984). Children's concept of story in reading and writing. *The Reading Teacher, 37,* 578–584.

Graves, D. (1983). *Writing: Teachers and children at work.* Portsmouth, NH: Heinemann.

Hancock, M. R. (1991). Literature response journals: Insights beyond the printed page. *Language Arts, 69,* 36–42.

Hancock, M. R. (1993). Exploring the meaning-making process through the content of literature response journals. *Research in the Teaching of English, 27,* 335–368.

Hansen, J. (1987). *When writers read.* Portsmouth, NH: Heinemann.

Hepler, S. (1982). Patterns of response to literature: A one-year study of a fifth- and sixth-grade classroom (Doctoral dissertation, The Ohio State University, 1982). *Dissertation Abstracts International, 43,* 1419A. (University Microfilms No. 82-22100).

Hepler, S., & Hickman, J. (1982). "The book was okay. I love you"—Social aspects of response to literature. *Theory into Practice, 21,* 278–283.

Hickman, J. (1980). Children's responses to literature: What happens in the classroom. *Language Arts, 57,* 524–529.

Hickman, J. (1981). A new perspective on response to literature: Research in an elementary school setting. *Research in the Teaching of English, 15,* 343–354.

Hickman, J. (1983). Everything considered: Response to literature in an elementary school setting. *Journal of Research and Development in Education, 16,* 8–13.

Hickman, J. (1985). Looking at response to literature. In A. J. & M. T. Smith-Burke (Eds.), *Observing the language learner* (pp. 111–119). Newark, DE: International Reading Association and the National Council of Teachers of English.

Holland, N. N. (1968). *The dynamics of literary response.* New York: Norton.

Holland, N. N. (1975). *Five readers reading*. New Haven, CT: Yale University Press.

Hubbard, R. S., Winterbourne, N., & Ostrow, J. (1996). Visual responses to literature: Imagination through images. *The New Advocate, 9*, 309–323.

Hynds, S. (1989). Bring life to literature and literature to life: Social constructs and contexts of four adolescent readers. *Research in the Teaching of English, 23*, 30–61.

Iser, W. (1978). *The act of reading: A theory of aesthetic response*. Baltimore, MD: The Johns Hopkins University Press.

Kelly, P. R. (1990). Guiding young students' response to literature. *The Reading Teacher, 43*, 464–470.

Kiefer, B. (1983). The responses of children in a combination first/second grade classroom to picture books in a variety of artistic styles. *Journal of Research and Development in Education, 16*, 14–20.

Langer, J. A. (1990). The process of understanding: Reading for literary and informative purposes. *Research in the Teaching of English, 24*, 229–260.

Leal, D. (1993). The power of literary peer-group discussions: How children collaboratively negotiate meaning. *The Reading Teacher, 47*, 114–120.

Lundsteen, S. (1990). Learning to listen and learning to read. In S. Hynds & D. L. Rubin (Eds.), *Perspectives on talk and learning*. Urbana, IL: National Council of Teachers of English.

Madura, S. (1995). The line and texture of aesthetic response: Primary children study authors and illustrators. *The Reading Teacher, 49*, 110–118.

Many, J. E. (1991). The effects of stance and age level on children's literary responses. *Journal of Reading Behavior, 23*, 61–85.

Many, J. E., & Cox, C. (1992). *Reader stance and literary understanding: Exploring the theories, research, and practice*. Norwood, NJ: Ablex.

Martinez, M. G., & Roser, N. L. (1991). Children's responses to literature. In J. Flood, J. M. Jensen, D. Lapp, & J. R. Squire (Eds.), *Handbook of research on teaching the English language arts* (pp. 643–654). New York: Macmillan.

Monson, D. L., & Sebesta, S. (1991). Reading preferences. In J. Flook, J. M. Jensen, D. Lapp, & J. R. Squire (Eds.), *Handbook of research on teaching the English language arts* (pp. 664–673). New York: Macmillan.

Pantaleo, S. (1995). The influence of teacher practice on student response to literature. *Journal of Children's Literature, 21*, 38–47.

Pradl, G. M. (1996). Reading and democracy: The enduring influence of Louise Rosenblatt. *The New Advocate, 9*, 9–22.

Probst, R. E. (1984). *Adolescent literature: Response and analysis*. Columbus, OH: Charles E. Merrill.

Purves, A., & Rippere, V. (1968). *Elements of writing about a literary work: A study of response to literature* (Research Report No. 9). Urbana, IL: National Council of Teachers of English.

Richards, I. A. (1929). *Practical criticism: A study in literary judgment*. New York: Harcourt, Brace, and World.

Roller, C. M., & Beed, P. L. (1994). Sometimes the conversations were grand, and sometimes. . . . *Language Arts, 71*, 509–515.

Rosenblatt, L. M. (1938/1995). *Literature as exploration*. New York: Appleton-Century-Crofts. (5th ed., Modern Language Association)

Rosenblatt, L. M. (1978). *The reader, the text, the poem: The transactional theory of the literary work*. Carbondale, IL: Southern Illinois University Press.

Rosenblatt, L. M. (1994). The transactional theory of reading and writing. In R. B. Ruddell, M. R. Ruddell, & H. Singer (Eds.), *Theoretical models and processes of reading* (4th ed.) (pp. 1057–1092). Newark, DE: International Reading Association.

Schlager, N. (1978). Predicting children's choices in literature: A developmental approach. *Children's Literature in Education, 9*, 136–142.

Sebesta, S. L., Monson, D. L., & Senn, H. D. (1995). A hierarchy to assess reader response. *Journal of Reading, 38*, 444–450.

Short, K. G. (Ed. ) (1995). *Research & professional resources in children's literature: Piecing a patchwork quilt*. Newark, DE: International Reading Association.

Squire, J. R. (1964). *The responses of adolescents while reading four short stories*. Champaign, IL: National Council of Teachers of English.

Tompkins, G. E. (1994). *Teaching writing: Balancing process and product* (2nd ed.). Columbus, OH: Merrill/Macmillan.

Wollman-Bonilla, J. E., & Werchadlo, B. (1995). Literature response journals in a first-grade classroom. *Language Arts, 72*, 562–570.

Yocum, J. A. (1987). Children's responses to literature read aloud in the classroom. (Doctoral dissertation, The Ohio State University). *Dissertation Abstracts International, 48*, 2300A. (University Microfilms No. 87-26750)

# CHILDREN'S BOOKS CITED  [ P ] = K–2; [ I ] = 3–5; [ M ] = 6–8

Angelou, Maya (1993). *Life doesn't frighten me.* Paintings by Jean-Michel Basquiat. New York: Stewart, Tabori and Chang. [ I/M ]

Arnosky, Jim (1997). *Rabbits & raindrops.* New York: Putnam. [ P ]

Avi (1996). *Beyond the western sea. Book One: The escape from home.* New York: Orchard Books. [ I/M ]

Avi (1996). *Beyond the western sea. Book Two: Lord Kirkle's money.* New York: Orchard Books. [ I/M ]

Aylesworth, Jim (1998). *The gingerbread man.* Illus. by Barbara McClintock. New York: Scholastic. [ P ]

Barnwell, Ysaye M. (1998). *No mirrors in my Nana's house.* Illus. by Synthia Saint James. San Diego: Harcourt Brace. (CD included) [ P ]

Birdseye, Tom, & Birdseye, Debbie H. (1994). *She'll be comin' round the mountain.* Illus. by Andrew Glass. New York: Holiday House. [ P/I ]

Boulton, Judy (Adapter) (1994). *Only Opal: The diary of a young girl.* Illus. by Barbara Cooney. New York: Philomel Books. (From the diary of Opal Whiteley) [ I ]

Brett, Jan (Reteller) (1987). *Goldilocks and the three bears.* New York: Putnam. [ P ]

Brett, Jan (Reteller) (1989). *The mitten.* New York: Putnam. [ P ]

Bunting, Eve (1991). *Fly away home.* Illus. by Ron Himler. New York: Clarion. [ P/I ]

Bunting, Eve (1997). *On Call Back mountain.* Illus. by Barry Moser. New York: Blue Sky/Scholastic. [ P/I ]

Cannon, Janell (1997). *Verdi.* San Diego: Harcourt Brace. [ P ]

Carle, Eric (1997). *From head to toe.* New York: HarperCollins. [ P ]

Cauley, L. B. (1992 ). *Clap your hands.* New York: Putnam. [ P ]

Coerr, Eleanor (1993). *Sadako.* Illus. by Ed Young. New York: Putnam. [ P/I ]

Creech, Sharon (1994). *Walk two moons.* New York: HarperCollins. [ I/M ]

Cushman, Karen (1994). *Catherine, called Birdy.* New York: Clarion. [ M ]

Cushman, Karen (1995). *The midwife's apprentice.* New York: Clarion. [ M ]

Edwards, Pamela D. (1996). *Some smug slug.* Illus. by Henry Cole. New York: HarperCollins. [ P ]

Ehlert, Lois (1989). *Eating the alphabet.* Harcourt Brace. [ P ]

Ernst, Lisa Campbell (1995). *Little Red Riding Hood: A newfangled prairie tale.* New York: Simon & Schuster. [ P/I ]

Ginsburg, Mirra (1997). *Clay boy.* Illus. by Jos. A. Smith. Greenwillow. [ P ]

Henkes, K. (1990). *Julius, the Baby of the World.* Greenwillow. [ P ]

Henkes, K. (1991). *Chrysanthemum.* Greenwillow. [ P ]

Henkes, K. (1996). *Lily's purple plastic purse.* Greenwillow. [ P ]

Hesse, K. (1992). *Letters from Rifka.* New York: Holt. [ I/M ]

Hoberman, M. A. (1997). *The seven silly eaters.* Illus. by M. Frazee. San Diego: Browndeer Press/Harcourt Brace. [ P ]

Kroll, Virginia (1994). *Pink paper swans.* Illus. by Nancy Clouse. Wm. B. Eerdman's. [ P/I ]

Jorgensen, Gail (1997). *Gotcha!* Illus. by Kerry Argent. New York: Scholastic. [ P ]

Levitin, Sonia (1998). *Boom town.* Illus. by Cat Bowman Smith. New York: Orchard Books. [ P/I ]

Lewis, C. S. (1961). *The lion, the witch, and the wardrobe.* New York: Macmillan. [ I ]

Lowry, Lois (1994). *The giver.* Boston: Houghton Mifflin. [ M ]

MacDonald, Amy (1990). *Rachel Fister's blister.* Illus. by Marjorie Priceman. Boston: Houghton Mifflin. [ P/I ]

McCully, E. A. (1993). *Mirette on the high wire.* New York: Putnam. [ P ]

Miranda, A. (1997). *To market, to market.* Illus. by J. Stevens. San Diego: Harcourt Brace. [ P ]

Pandell, K., & Wolfe, A. (1996). *Animal action ABC.* Photographs by N. Sheehan. New York: Dutton. [ P ]

Paulsen, Gary (1987). *Hatchet.* New York: Bradbury. [ I/M ]

Paulsen, Gary (1992). *The haymeadow.* New York: Delacorte. [ I/M ]

Paulsen, Gary (1996). *Brian's winter.* New York: Delacorte. [ I/M ]

Platt, Richard (1994). *Stephen Beisty's cross-sections: Castles.* Illus. by Stephen Beisty. DK Publishing. [ I/M ]

Polacco, Patricia (1990 ). *Thundercake.* New York: Philomel Books. [ P ]

Prelutsky, Jack (1996). *A pizza the size of the sun.* Greenwillow. [ I ]

Priceman, Marjorie (1994). *How to make an apple pie and see the world.* New York: Knopf. [ P/I ]

Sanfield, Steve (1995). *Bit by bit.* Illus by Susan Garber. New York: Philomel Books. [ P ]

Scieszka, Jon (1989). *The true story of the three little pigs as told by A. Wolf.* Illus. by Lane Smith. New York: Viking/Penguin. [ I ]

Simon, Seymour (1989). *Storms.* New York: Morrow Junior Books. [ P/I ]

Stanley, Diane (1996). *Leonardo da Vinci.* New York: Morrow Junior Books. [ I/M ]

Stevens, Janet (1995). *Tops and bottoms.* San Diego: Harcourt Brace. [ P ]

Van Laan, Nancy (1990). *Possum come a-knockin'.* Illus. by George Booth. New York: Knopf. [ P ]

Wahl, Jan (1995). *Tailypo!* Illus. by Wil Clay. New York: Henry Holt. [ P ]

Westcott, Nadine (1990). *There's a hole in the bucket.* New York: Little, Brown. [ P ]

Yolen, Jane (1987). *Owl moon.* Illus by Jon Schoenherr. New York: Philomel Books. [ P ]

# PART II

# Celebrating Literature

The wonder and enjoyment of children's literature reside in the variety of ways in which books convey a story. While some stories emerge from the realm of make-believe, others ground themselves in the reality of everyday life. As some tales unfold through the art of the storyteller, others relate information in descriptive ways. While some stories share the lives of real people, other books build on the delight of words and rhyme. It is this variety that helps literature reach every reader with satisfaction. At the same time, it is this variety that creates a need for advocates of children's literature to organize literature using a common scheme as a basis for literary discussion.

To efficiently categorize and discuss the large number of children's books in print today, literary genres serve as a framework and an organizational scheme for classifying children's literature. Books that have a great deal in common with each other are placed in a literary genre according to similar traits. When books with these similar literary characteristics form a group, that group is called a literary genre (Jacobs & Tunnell, 1996).

Differentiation often begins with the two formats of a book: picture books or chapter books. Picture books (Chapter 3) are particularly distinguished because of their blend of art and text. They can contain stories from any genre. Literary genres are the organizational scheme for discussion in this part. They include Traditional Tales and Modern Fantasy (Chapter 4), Poetry (Chapter 5), Realistic and Historical Fiction (Chapter 6), and Biography and Informational Books (Chapter 7). In addition, "multicultural" literature, which flows across each genre, is discussed in Chapter 8.

In an attempt to celebrate the variety of children's literature, the next six chapters showcase picture books, the seven literary genres for children, and multicultural literature. The discussion for each genre includes a definition of the genre, lists characteristics of the genre, denotes categories of books within the genre, and discusses the value of the genre as part of a well-rounded literacy program. Reader response connections to each genre are summarized after each genre is presented. Readers are referred to extensive connections in Part III of this text.

The literary genre approach to presenting literature provides the most consistent organizational scheme used when studying or discussing children's literature (Pavonetti, 1997). While an issues approach or an inquiry approach to children's literature may be used, a general knowledge of literary genres supports practitioners who surround their students with a blend of high-quality books from the entire literary realm.

Jacobs, J. S., & Tunnell, M. O. (1996). *Children's literature, briefly.* Upper Saddle River, NJ: Merrill/Prentice Hall.

Pavonetti, L. (1997). Conversations among colleagues: A master class in teaching children's literature. *Journal of Children's Literature, 23,* 66–69.

## Chapter 3

# The Art of the Picture Book:
## *Blending Illustration and Text*

*P*atricia Polacco *creates another masterpiece in word and pictures in* The Bee Tree. *I enjoyed the many colorful, lively characters Polacco introduced who come along for the fun. You almost want to jump into the pages and follow Mary Ellen and Grampa. This would be an entertaining read-aloud when you are exploring insects. It also has a powerful ending that would be a great topic for a grand conversation. What a way to show kids that reading is an adventure into the unknown! Books like* The Bee Tree *remind me of my grandparents' farm in Missouri. The barns and the out-buildings could be the same ones. Patricia Polacco has won an active place in my classroom.*

Second-Grade Teacher Response to *The Bee Tree*
by Patricia Polacco

The picture book is a celebration of both text and art. The words that tell a story enhanced by artful illustrations blend into a magical reading and response experience. Kevin Henkes (1992), author/illustrator of *Chrysanthemum, Owen,* and *Lilly's Purple Plastic Purse,* celebrates the wonder of the picture book format for children's literature.

> The great thing about a successful picture book is you can't have great illustrations without a great text, and you can't have a great text without great illustrations. . . . The art form of the picture book is, in fact, all thirty-two pages—pictures and words—working together. (p. 39)

In this chapter, the term *picture book* is used as an umbrella term to denote the broad group of books containing illustrations, and, in most cases, words. Its broad terminology includes baby/board books, ABC books, engineered books, counting books, concept books, wordless books, picture storybooks, and transitional books (Lynch-Brown & Tomlinson, 1993). The term *picture storybook,* however, is a more specific term and is used in this text to refer to books that primarily convey stories through both the art of illustrating and the art of writing. Picture storybooks span several genres and appeal to readers of all ages. Most picture books that are published are picture storybooks so the blending of language and art is showcased during this chapter discussion. Distinguishing between the two terms becomes more significant as one becomes more acquainted with children's literature.

This chapter begins a celebration of children's literature by focusing on the popular picture book format. The picture book houses well-composed text and exceptional artwork across all literary genre. From George Shannon's *Tomorrow's Alphabet* (ABC) to Eric Kimmel's *Count Silvernose* (traditional tale), from Lynne Cherry's *Flute's Journey* (informational) to Barbara Esbensen's *Echoes for the Eye* (poetry), picture books thrive on the harmonizing of energetic text and imaginative art into this creative, cherished format. Picture books also address the art of visual literacy and its potential to assist with comprehension and aesthetic understanding (Kiefer, 1995).

The Caldecott Medal, named in honor of the nineteenth-century English illustrator Randolph Caldecott, is awarded each year to the artist of the most distinguished American picture book for children. Artists such as Mary Azarian, Paul Zelinsky, David Wisniewski, Emily Arnold McCully, and Peggy Rathmann have won this prestigious award for illustration. Appendix A contains a list of these winning illustrators and their books. Several honored award-winning books are mentioned throughout this chapter.

Besides highlighting quality picture books, this chapter includes discussions of the role of picture books in visual literacy; evaluative criteria for picture books; types of picture books available for reader enjoyment, delight, and response; the impression and importance of book design; art media, graphic techniques, and artistic style; and the power of illustration to blend with well-written text to tell a story. This chapter also serves as background for a study of the literary genres (Chapters 4 through 7) and multicultural literature (Chapter 8), which utilize the picture book as well as the chapter book formats to share both narrative and expository writing.

# THE PICTURE BOOK AND VISUAL LITERACY

Children today grow up in a visual world surrounded by a barrage of images on computer monitors, across Internet sites, on television and movie screens, and throughout their environment. The term *visual literacy* implies a level of discrimination that can sort through this constant deluge of visual images in an attempt to develop a personal sense of discretionary viewing and judgment. The illustrations in picture books naturally invite active participation in viewing. With the abundance of picture books available to children at home, school, bookstores, and libraries, it becomes increasingly important for children to develop a sense for judging quality and establishing personal taste in book illustration.

Many adults actually believe that children's book are "wasted" on children. Teacher comments on recent Caldecott award-winning illustrations including Paul Zelinsky's *Rapunzel* and David Wisniewski's *Golem* have been directed at their "lack of appeal" to children. Yet children tend to be more atune to detail and more aware of their perceptions than adults give them credit. Jacobs and Tunnell (1996) believe that as readers get older they tend to be "dulled by overload or by the real and imagined expectations our educational system have imposed on us which alter the way we view images" (p. 34). Children often learn to ignore their own personal reactions and the details in illustrations to fulfill narrowly focused views of learning. In becoming less aware, they become less sensitive to the differences in the art of the picture book and less discriminating in the process of developing personal tastes.

In *The Potential of Picture Books,* Barbara Kiefer (1995) describes visual literacy for children as the ability to "discriminate and interpret what they see. This process involves their attention, their recognition, and finally their understanding" (p. 8). Teachers, parents, and librarians play a crucial role in helping children develop the ability to "see" through picture book illustrations. By enriching discriminatory abilities and encouraging the development of personal taste in visual imagery in picture books, children can attain independence of expression and response. To accomplish this, however, teachers must learn more about children's book illustrations including style, medium, and design as well as more about the illustrators themselves. Enhancing visual literacy through picture books begins with a fresh view of illustrations through a child's eyes.

Picture books possess the potential for children to become discriminators of personal tastes in art. If all they view are cartoons, all they will appreciate are cartoon-like drawings. If, however, a knowledgeable, open-minded teacher, parent, or librarian attends to the choices, comments, and exuberance they exhibit toward a variety of illustrations, individual tastes can be cultivated. Teachers have long recognized the potential of picture books to develop reading and writing literacy. Now picture books stand poised to elicit the intellectual and emotional response of children to art. Picture books provide an exceptional means of cultivating visual literacy and artistic appreciation in an increasingly visual world. This chapter strives to share more about the art of the picture book with those who choose to work with children so their own visual literacy, as well as that of their students, can be extended through better informed picture book experiences.

# EVALUATING AND SELECTING PICTURE BOOKS

Picture books are a child's first invitation into the world of literature and the potential start of a lifelong adventure with reading. Quality time spent during the reading/listening event should be accompanied by the highest quality literature. Although children should be encouraged to choose their favorite books to be read and reread, adults must be responsible for selecting a pool of quality literature from which endearing favorites may grow. The following straightforward criteria adapted from John Stewig's *Looking at Picture Books* (1995) assist teachers, librarians, and parents in identifying the best of the world of the picture book so listeners and readers alike can engage in quality verbal and visual literary experiences.

Criteria for language in picture books:

- The author uses a variety of rich familiar and unfamiliar words to embrace the reader/listener's understanding of what they know and extend them toward what they have yet to learn.
- A variety of sentence structures introduces readers/listeners to sentence types as well as adding interest to the text.
- The author creatively uses literary devices to captivate the reader/listener. These may include repetitive words, phrases, or sentences that engage children in the text.
- The text invites reader response through participating, noticing, relating, or expressing feelings.

Criteria for art in picture books:

- The artist uses an original idea which allows the viewer to see something familiar in a new way or to introduce something not ever seen before.
- The art captivates the viewer because of style, medium, sequence, or placement on the page.
- The art enhances or extends the text, creating a greater understanding of the words through artistic images or additional details not mentioned in the text.
- The art invites viewer response through noticing, discussing, pointing, relating to text, discovering details, or expressing feelings.

In addition, picture books should be written about topics children find interesting. Adult enthusiasm can play an especially important role in introducing quality picture books to children. The ultimate evaluative criteria for a picture book is whether children will be engaged, entertained, and encouraged to continue on their lifelong reading adventure.

# TYPES OF PICTURE BOOKS

The picture book format includes many different types of books that appeal to the very young, to emergent readers, to older readers, and even to adults. Defining and discussing these books in sequence by age of reader to which they appeal emphasizes the breadth of the picture book format and the size of its audience and allows discovery of and distinguishing among the wide range of categories of picture books.

## Baby/Board Books

First books for babies receive increasing importance as continuing research points out connections between early reading to children and later academic success (Teale, 1986). These books are manufactured of thick cardboard, plastic, or cloth to withstand the wear and tear of eager hands. Many classic titles have taken on the board book format as the quality and popularity of these books have increased. Titles currently in board book format include Eric Carle's *The Very Busy Spider* and *Tomie de Paola's Mother Goose.* They serve as important lapsitting experiences as young hands begin to turn the pages, eager fingers point to bright colors, and a sense of story begins to take hold. Independent exploration with these books fulfills a need for a young child to discover the world of books. Response is typically in the form of physical book exploration tempered by spontaneous sounds of delight from the youngest bibliophiles. Figure 3.1 lists just a sampling of colorful, sturdy titles available for the very young.

## Mother Goose and Nursery Rhymes

The rhythm, rhyme, and predictability of Mother Goose and traditional nursery rhymes explain why these remain an appealing type of picture book for young children. Mother Goose books are often read over and over again as children begin to value and appreciate the sound

**FIGURE 3.1**   Books for young readers.

### Books for the Very Young

Hague, Michael (1993). *Teddy bear, teddy bear: A classic action rhyme.* New York: Morrow. (Board book)

Hoban, Tana (1993). *Black on white.* New York: Greenwillow. (Board book)

Hurd, Thatcher (1998). *Zoom city.* New York: HarperCollins. (Board book)

Martin, Bill Jr., & Archambault, John (1993). *Chicka Chicka ABC.* Illus. by Lois Ehlert. New York: Simon & Schuster. (Board book)

Miller, Margaret (1996). *At the seashore.* New York: Simon & Schuster. (Board book)

Oxenbury, Helen (1995). *I see.* Cambridge, MA: Candlewick Press. (Board book)

Newcome, Zita (1996). *Toddlerobics.* Cambridge, MA: Candlewick Press.

Rathmann, Peggy (1997). *Goodnight gorilla.* New York: Putnam. (Board book)

Wells, Rosemary (1997/1973). *Noisy Nora.* New York: Dial.

Wells, Rosemary (1998). *Max's breakfast.* New York: Dial. (Board book); see also *Max's bath, Max's bedtime, Max's birthday, Max's first word, Max's new suit, Max's ride,* and *Max's toys.*

Yorinks, Arthur (1996). *Frank and Joey eat lunch.* Illus. by Maurice Sendak. New York: HarperCollins. (Board book)

### Mother Goose and Nursery Rhymes

*Anholt, Catherine et. al. (1996). *The Candlewick book of first rhymes.* Cambridge, MA: Candlewick Press.

Cousins, Lucy (1996). *Jack and Jill and other nursery rhymes.* New York: Dutton. (Board book); see also *Humpty dumpty* (1996); *Wee Willie Winkie* (1997); and *Little Miss Muffet* (1997).

de Paola, Tomie (1985). *Tomie de Paola's Mother Goose.* New York: Putnam.

_____ (1993). *Mother Goose's nursery rhymes.* Everyman's Library Children's Classics series. New York: Random House. (Originally published as *The big book of nursery rhymes,* 1903)

Dyer, Jane (1996). *Animal crackers: A delectable collection of pictures, poems, and lullabies for the very young.* Boston: Little, Brown.

Lobel, Arnold (1997). *The Arnold Lobel book of Mother Goose.* New York: Knopf/Random House. (Former title: *Random House book of Mother Goose*)

Opie, Iona A. (1996). *My very first Mother Goose.* Illus. by Rosemary Wells. Cambridge, MA: Candlewick Press.

Rosenburg, Liz (1994). *Mama Goose: A new Mother Goose.* Illus. by Janet Street. New York: Philomel Books.

of language. These books serve as outstanding language models for children as they begin to experiment with language by attempting to repeat the well-loved rhymes. The illustrations in these books often have strong appeal to young children as characters like Old King Cole, Little Boy Blue, and Peter, Peter Pumpkin Eater come to life on the page. While new, colorful editions of Mother Goose rhymes continue to be published, such as *My Very First Mother Goose* (Opie, 1996) illustrated by Rosemary Wells, some of the classic editions bring the same exuberant response from children. Arnold Lobel's *Book of Mother Goose* (1997), for example, is a reissue of a popular 1986 title by Random House. Response is typically in the form of language repetition and physical delight (smiles, clapping, pointing) as children begin to recognize familiar characters and related language as valued friends. Figure 3.1 lists additional versions of these rhyming traditions.

## Engineered/Participation Books

Pop-up books, flap books, and toy books are included in the engineered or participation book category. Like board books, these books beg active involvement. The difference is that they are usually delicately produced and require special care. These are likely to appeal to grandparents as much as children, but often are intricate enough to discourage child engagement. *The 12 Days of Christmas* by Robert Sabuda incorporates artistic cutouts and pop-ups of doily-like white designs replicating the traditional gifts of the holiday. Although likely to be appreciated as read-alouds and responded to with "oohs" and "aahs," these books are special and often require a "hands off" order to younger children. While they serve their place by showing readers how things work and offer countless surprises along the way, librarians are reluctant to purchase them and teachers keep them on their personal bookshelves.

Books that beg to be shared with children and invite active involvement with the book itself fit the category of participation books. Participation books engage readers in tracing shapes with their fingers, sliding pages to uncover colorful images, or lifting flaps to reveal instant surprises. Titles that are meant for exploration by young children include Eric Carle's insect quartet (*The Very Hungry Caterpillar, The Very Quiet Cricket, The Very Busy Spider, The Very Lonely Firefly*) and Lois Ehlert's *Hands.* For older children, books like Thomas Bayley's *Sailing Ships: A Lift-the-Flap Discovery Book* and *Robert Crowther's Pop-Up Olympics* offer hours of enjoyment and lots of information. By becoming actively involved with books, an eagerness for books and an interest in reading begin to evolve. Response exhibits itself through active engagement and the related early language and social talk that results from the interactive nature of parent–child participation with these books.

## Alphabet Books

While initially associated with young children, today's alphabet books have appeal across all age levels. Their unique designs and simple, effective text combine to teach far more content than the ABCs. Widely used as books in thematic explorations, they cover a wide variety of topics and transmit an extensive amount of information. In addition to illustrations and a consistent organizational pattern, alphabet books generally have a uniform, short format. Those focused around a specific concept or theme can be characterized as informational in nature.

Pictures, format, content, and text form the structure of an alphabet book. The illustrations are the inherent feature of these books as artists create intriguing and interesting visual displays built on single letters. David Pelletier's *The Graphic Alphabet,* for example, promotes visual inquiry by using graphic design to illustrate the letterform while retaining the natural shape of the letter as well as representing the meaning of the word. To accomplish this, snow rests on the peaks of an "M" for mountain, a sideways "D" resembles a devil, and a brilliant red "r" echoes a rip across the page, all showcased on a stark black background. Imaginations are ignited in Max Grover's *The Accidental Zucchini* in which the reader hops in an "apple auto" for a journey down "cupcake canyon" to ride on a "macaroni merry-go-round."

Most alphabet books have a predictable organizational manner, are concise, and rarely exceed a 26-letter presentation. Anita Lobel's *Away from Home* shares boys' names and exotic places in alliterative fashion just as *Allison's Zinnea* shares girls' names paired with exotic flowers. In many cases, the content extends beyond the features of letter identification, letter–sound correspondence, and object identification traditionally associated with these books. In *ANTics!* by Catherine Hepworth, the emphasis is on language as "ant" becomes the basis of alphabetical ants depicting "*ant*ique," "devi*ant*," and "quar*ant*ine." The wide range of content complexity makes alphabet books usable with many age groups. Alphabet book text is typically written in poetic form, but narrative and expository text often appear in themed alphabet books.

Beyond their traditional use with emergent and beginning readers, alphabet books provide valuable information to readers of all ages. Chaney (1993) suggests alphabet books can provide students with:

1. An introduction to or an overview of a theme exploration (Kathy Darling's *Amazon ABC*)
2. A stimulus for further research (Anne Doubilet's *Under the Sea from A to Z*)
3. Oral and written language development (Bill Martin and John Archambault's *Chicka Chicka Boom Boom*)
4. Multicultural awareness (Virginia Stroud's *The Path of the Quiet Elk: A Native American Alphabet Book*).

While young children tend to respond to alphabet books through their predictable nature as in *Tomorrow's Alphabet* or through ties to phonemic awareness, response from older children is often in the form of inquiry piqued by oral comments on visual or textual representations. Figure 3.2 represents a cross-section of alphabet books for all ages and on all topics.

## Counting/Number Books

In their simplest form, counting books present material in a predictable, sequenced format that appeals to the young child. Numbers and/or number words are teamed with illustrations or photographs of correctly numbered objects. Diana Pomeroy's *One Potato: A Counting Book of Potato Prints* uses images of fruits and vegetables to illustrate numbers from 1 to 10 and from 10 to 100 by tens. The response to these books includes counting aloud, pointing to objects, and making number–print associations. Quality oral language results from the interactive nature of the counting book.

**FIGURE 3.2**    Alphabet books [ all P/I ].

Aylesworth, Jim (1992). *Old black fly.* Illus. by S. Gammel. New York: Holt.
Bender, Robert (1996). *The A to Z beastly jamboree.* New York: Lodestar Books.
Darling, Kathy (1996). *Amazon ABC.* New York: Lothrop, Lee & Shepard.
Doubilet, Anne (1991). *Under the sea from A to Z.* Photos by D. Doubilet. New York: Crown.
Ernst, Lisa Campbell (1996). *The letters are lost.* New York: Viking.
Grover, Max (1993). *The accidental zucchini: An unexpected alphabet.* San Diego: Harcourt Brace.
Hepworth, Catherine (1992). *ANTics!: An alphabet anthology.* New York: Putnam.
Jonas, Ann (1990). *Aardvarks, disembark!* New York: Greenwillow.
Lobel, Anita (1990). *Allison's zinnea.* New York: Greenwillow.
Lobel, Anita (1994). *Away from home.* New York: Greenwillow.
Martin, Bill Jr., & Archambault, John (1989). *Chicka chicka boom boom.* Illus. by Lois Ehlert. New York: Simon & Schuster.
McDonald, Flora (1997). *Flora McDonell's ABC.* Cambridge, MA: Candlewick Press.
Palotta, Jerry (1996). *The airplane alphabet book.* Watertown, MA: Charlesbridge.
Paul, Ann Whitford (1991). *Eight hands round: A patchwork alphabet.* Illus. by Jeannette Winter. New York: HarperCollins.
Pelletier, David (1996). *The graphic alphabet.* New York: Orchard Books.
Sandved, Kjeil B. (1996). *The butterfly alphabet.* New York: Scholastic.
Shannon, George (1996). *Tomorrow's alphabet.* Illus. by Donald Crews. New York: Greenwillow.
Slate, Joseph (1996). *Miss Bindergarten gets ready for kindergarten.* New York: Dutton.
Stroud, Virginia (1996). *The path of the quiet elk: A Native American alphabet book.* New York: Dial.
Stutson, Caroline (1996). *Prairie primer: A to Z.* Illus. by Susan Condie Lamb. New York: Dutton.
Viorst, Judith (1994). *The alphabet from Z to A (with much confusion on the way).* Illus. by Richard Hull. New York: Atheneum.
Wells, Ruth (1992). *A to Zen: A book of Japanese culture.* Illus. by Yoshi. Saxonville, MA: Picture Book Studio.

Although this type of picture book was traditionally associated with young children, it, too, like the alphabet book, has stretched its use to older children as well through expanded mathematical concepts. Amy Axelrod's *Pigs Will Be Pigs* based on money, *Pigs Go to Market* based on shopping and *Pigs in the Pantry* based on measurement move the counting book to older readers. *Roman Numerals I to MM* by Arthur Geisert brings Roman numerals to life by using a farm of pigs—first by introducing the symbols and then through practicing counting items in his detailed etchings.

An additional dimension to counting books includes picture storybooks that actually utilize numbers in a variety of ways to carry the plot. Jeanette Winter's *Josephina* portrays a Mexican artist who created her world (*un sol, dos angeles, tres casas*) through colorful clay images. Daniil Kharms's *First, Second* sequences its plot by ordinal number while prompting the reader to problem solve along with the whimsical characters. The ending actually encourages written response by suggesting a sequel of a new series of adventures by the imaginative reader.

As literature has expanded beyond counting across curricular boundaries to mathematics, more books of this type have been published. Figure 3.3 represents a sample of some of these beginning and early math concept titles.

**FIGURE 3.3**   Counting/number books [ all P/early I ].

Appelt, Kathi (1996). *Bat jamboree.* Illus. by Melissa Sweet. New York: Morrow.

Bang, Molly (1997/1983). *Diez, Nueve, Ocho.* Trans. by Clarita Kohen. New York: Greenwillow.

Bloom, Valerie (1996). *Fruits: A Caribbean counting poem.* Illus. by David Axtell. New York: Holt.

Brooks, Alan (1996). *Frogs jump: A counting book.* Illus. by Stephen Kellogg. New York: Scholastic.

Clark, Emma Chichester (1997). *Little Miss Muffet's count-along surprise.* New York: Doubleday.

Geisert, Arthur (1996). *Roman numerals I to MM.* Boston: Houghton Mifflin.

Greene, Rhonda Gowler (1997). *When a line bends . . . a shape begins.* Illus. by James Kaczman. Boston: Houghton Mifflin.

Grossman, Bill (1996). *My little sister ate one hare.* Illus. by Kevin Hawkes. New York: Crown.

Grover, Max (1995). *Amazing & incredible counting stories! A number of tall tales.* San Diego: Harcourt Brace/Browndeer Press.

Grover, Max (1996). *Circles and squares everywhere!* San Diego: Browndeer/Harcourt Brace.

Haskins, Jim, & Benson, Kathleen (1996). *Count your way through Ireland.* Illus. by Beth Wright. Minneapolis, MN: Carolrhoda. (*Count your way* series includes Africa, Arab world, Brazil, Canada, China, France, Germany, Greece, India, Israel, Italy, Japan, Korea, Mexico, and Russia.)

Hightower, Susan (1997). *Twelve snails to one lizard: A tale of mischief and measurement.* Illus. by Matt Novak. New York: Simon & Schuster.

Hoberman, Mary Ann (1997). *One of each.* Illus. by Marjorie Priceman. Boston: Little, Brown.

Kharms, Daniil (1996). *First, Second.* Trans. from the Russian by Richard Pevear. Illus. by Marc Rosenthal. New York: Farrar, Straus and Giroux.

Lavis, Steve (1996). *Cock-a-doodle-doo: A farmyard counting book.* New York: Lodestar.

Lyon, George Ella (1998). *Counting on the woods: A poem.* Photographs by Ann W. Olson. New York: DK Publishing.

Masurel, Claire (1997). *Ten dogs in the window.* Illus. by Pamela Paparone. New York: North-South Books.

Merriam, Eve (1993). *12 ways to get to 11.* Illus. by Bernie Karlin. New York: Simon & Schuster.

Moss, Lloyd (1995). *Zin! zin! zin!: A violin.* Illus. by Marjorie Priceman. New York: Simon & Schuster.

Nikola-Lisa, W. (1996). *One hole in the road.* Illus. by Dan Yaccarino. New York: Holt.

Noll, Sally (1997). *Surprise!* New York: Greenwillow.

O'Donnell, Elizabeth Lee (1997). *Winter visitors.* Illus. by Carol Schwartz. New York: Morrow.

Parker, Vic (1996). *Bearobics: A hip-hop counting story.* Illus. by Emily Bolan. New York: Viking.

Pinozes, Elinor J. (1996). *Arctic fives arrive.* Boston: Houghton Mifflin.

Pomeroy, Diana (1996). *One potato: A counting book of potato prints.* San Diego: Harcourt Brace.

Roth, Susan (1997). *My love for you.* New York: Dial.

Schlain, Miriam (1996). *More than one.* Illus. by Donald Crews. New York: Greenwillow.

Sierra, Judy (1997). *Counting crocodiles.* Illus. by Will Hillenbrand. San Diego: Gulliver/Harcourt Brace.

Stow, Jenny (1997). *Following the sun.* Minneapolis, MN: Carolrhoda Books.

Wakefield, Alice P. (1996). *Those calculating crows.* Illus. by Christy Hale. New York: Simon & Schuster.

Winter, Jeanette (1996). *Josephina.* San Diego: Harcourt Brace.

## Concept Books

As curiosity and wonder fill the eyes of young children and their unquenchable thirst for knowledge abounds, the inclusion of concept books in their reading repertoire can assist in creating a knowledge base of essential conceptual informational that can be used to expand their understanding of their surroundings. Concept books share shapes, colors, sizes, and objects with children in creative picture book formats. Illustrations initiate natural interaction for child/parent/teacher.

The author/photographer Tana Hoban is synonymous with bold, clear concept books that teach children about common aspects of their world. In *Just Look,* children peer through open circles on black pages to identify objects and animals through close-up and wide-range photographs. Her countless titles, including *Animal, Vegetable, or Mineral* and *Spirals, Curves, Fanshapes, and Lines,* engage children in early book encounters while building the parental bond through the lap reading experience. Shelley Rotner challenges children to take up-close looks at objects from three different viewpoints—*Close, Closer, Closest.* The concept of perspective and scale are modeled through vivid photography of a butterfly, a TV screen, a glove, and other familiar objects. The response to concept books results in a heightened interest and inquiry as exhibited by speculations and questions.

## Wordless Picture Books

Picture books without words allow the illustrations to tell the story on their own. The words to the story and the voice of the storyteller lie in the viewer's mind or are manufactured orally in the discussion with an adult or peer participant. Wordless picture books provide an opportunity for children to use picture clues to create the story. The opportunities for language development are rich and varied as children orally attempt to impose their developing sense of story on the illustrations.

Visual "readers" may eloquently project their feelings for Quentin Blake's *Clown* as he is discarded in a trash barrel with his other toy friends. The toy clown's journey through town takes him on a series of adventures as he tries to find a home. Cartoon-like drawings emotionally guide the reader through an action-filled plot without the use of a single word. Eric Rohmann's *Time Flies,* for older children, occurs in a natural history museum when dinosaurs seem to come to life as a bird enters their domain. In Lisa Maizlish's *The Ring,* photographs follow a boy's magical adventures as he finds a bright yellow ring in New York City. These books beg for spoken or unspoken words to accompany eloquent visual representations.

Responses to wordless picture books come in the form of oral stories to accompany the pictures. While young children's stories can be dictated to older students, older children might also write the text to share with their younger counterparts. Wordless books invite a language experience—oral or written—that reminds us that meaning resides within the illustrations in the intentional absence of the text. Jeannie Baker's *Window* and Istvan Banyai's *Re-zoom* simply invite text. Small in number, but high in creative oral and written responses, these books supply the illustration yet rely on the reader's imagination for the story.

## Picture Storybooks

The type of picture book that is generally associated with the term *picture book* is the picture storybook. The picture storybook shares a story with the reader through well-written text that is blended with effective illustrations. In contrast to a picture book, the continuity between the language and the illustrations takes on even more importance as pictures help tell the story showing action, character expressions, well-defined settings, and plot development. The stories within the covers of a picture storybook can belong to almost any literary genre including realistic fiction (Eve Bunting's *Smoky Nights*), historical fiction (Donald Hall's *Ox-Cart Man*), traditional tale (Ed Young's *Lon Po Po: A Red-Riding Hood Story from China*), modern fantasy (*Tuesday* by David Wiesner), biography (*Bill Peet: An Autobiography* by Bill Peet), and informational books (*Ashanti to Zulu: African Traditions* by Margaret Musgrove). Reader response to picture storybooks truly engages personal response modes as children react individually to the unfolding of spellbinding, humorous, or captivating stories. The majority of picture books that are published each year are picture storybooks; hence, the tendency to simply refer to them as picture books. The term *picture storybook* as used in this text carries a stronger connotation regarding the blending of story and illustration, which places special demands on both the author and the artist.

*My Great Aunt Arizona* by Gloria Houston is a picture storybook that shares the life, love, and hugs of a special teacher. The story is told through pictures that brightly portray a one-room school, Aunt Arizona's braids wound round her head, and her precious hugs. The words are well chosen and arranged repetitively at times for special effect. It is the unraveling of the story enhanced by visual characterization that make this a classic picture storybook. *Market!,* authored and illustrated by Ted Lewin, is another showcase for combining splendid words and vivid pictures of world markets. The opening invitation to journey to the great markets of the world is a masterfully written paragraph. Each two-page spread takes us to destinations that are enhanced by rich colored portraits of the people whose expressions tell the story of the international art of trading.

Picture storybooks provide a strong impetus for early response to literature through the use of prompts. Asking children how the story makes them feel, what it reminds them of from their own life, and what they notice about the story opens wide possibilities to response before, during, and after the book has been read aloud. Most picture storybooks are also the perfect length for the 5- to 10-minute read-aloud time designated by teachers. Allowing time for response to both the story and the illustrations makes for a richer read-aloud experience. Picture storybooks abound on the library and classroom shelves making many of them fine choices for independent reading by second- and third-grade students. Book buddies from upper grades long to share picture storybooks, especially of their own childhood favorites, with kindergartners and first graders. The perfect blend of illustrations and the language of story brings hours of enjoyment to the literacy classroom each day.

## Picture Books for Older Readers

Although the picture book format has been linked to young children and emergent readers, some picture book titles are intended for older readers and even adults. Because picture books have typically been housed in elementary (K–5) libraries or in the juvenile collections of public libraries, these special creations are often lost to the very audience for whom they were intended. The use of picture books in middle-school (grades 6–8) classrooms is no longer shunned, but encouraged. Picture books for older readers provide efficient read-alouds, powerful genre models, and exemplary models of narrative and expository writing. In addition, picture books for older readers send a continuous reminder of the joy of reading to students as favorite authors and illustrators from their past reappear in a comfortable, yet nonthreatening format with a captivating story written at their cognitive and developmental level. Chris Van Allsburg may be most famous for *The Polar Express,* but *The Sweetest Fig* reintroduces this author/illustrator to upper grade students with a continued sense of magic and fantasy. Books like Leontyne Price's *Aïda* and Diane Stanley and Peter Vennema's *Charles Dickens* read well even at the middle-school level. With a growing knowledge of children's literature, a teacher will readily recognize the content, reading level, and amount of text that tends to support the designation of picture books for older readers. Figure 3.4 designates those titles especially applicable to the interests and curricular focus of older students (grades 6–8).

## Transitional Picture/Chapter Books

Picture books particularly designed for independent reading are regarded as easy-to-read books. More text and fewer illustrations are common in this format. Because the text in many picture books is beyond the independent reading level of the reader, children need access to some books that build confidence in their own ability to read, yet retain the enjoyment of reading authentic literature. Limited vocabulary, simple plot, and a balance of words and pictures characterize easy-to-read books. Several books by Dr. Seuss which contain rhyming and repetitive elements fit this category. They fill a specific purpose in children's literature by ensuring success as emergent readers achieve the response of "I can read!" through the challenge and excitement of reading real books.

As reading competency increases, some children outgrow picture books and long to tackle full-length chapter books. This can be a big step and a formidable task for second- and third-grade students. The transitional picture/chapter book, however, typically has several short chapters, uses simplified vocabulary, and incorporates illustrations intermittently (at least every other page) to offer comprehension clues and entertainment to the child transitioning toward the chapter book format. Even the dimensional size approaches that of a chapter book. Several well-known children's authors have written transitional books that allow young, independent readers to transition from the world of picture books to the world of chapter books. Eve Bunting's *Some Frog!* consists of 10 chapters contained in a 48-page format with 12 full-page and 8 partial-page illustrations. Cynthia Rylant opts for a popular series of transitional books with *Henry and Mudge, Mr. Putter and Tabby,* and the new *Poppleton* series. Teachers praise these books as an important milestone on the journey toward lifelong reading. Besides being a transition between picture and chapter books, they also serve as ideal formats as readers transition from oral to written response explorations. Figure 3.5 (on p. 60) lists welcome additions to transitional picture book offerings as children strive to read earlier and find comfort and success with these titles.

**FIGURE 3.4**    Picture books for older readers [ all I/M ].

Cherry, Lynne. (1992). *A river ran wild.* San Diego: Harcourt Brace.
Craft, M. Charlotte (1996). *Cupid and Psyche.* Illus. by K. Y. Craft. New York: Morrow.
Fisher, Leonard Everett (1995). *Ghandi.* New York: Atheneum.
Helprin, Mark (1996). *A city in winter.* Illus. by C. Van Allsburg. New York: Viking.
Hooks, William H. (1990). *The ballad of Belle Dorcas.* Illus. by B. Pinkney. New York: Knopf.
LeGuin, Ursula (1992). *A ride on the red mare's back.* Illus. by J. Downing. New York: Orchard Books.
McKissack, Patricia, & McKissack, Frederick (1994). *Christmas in the big house, Christmas in the quarters.* Illus. by John Thompson. New York: Scholastic.
Paterson, Katherine (1992). *The king's equal.* New York: Harper.
Price, Leontyne (1990). *Aïda.* Illus. by Leo & Diane Dillon. San Diego: Harcourt Brace.
Ross, Stewart (1997). *Charlotte Bronte and Jane Eyre.* Illus. by R. Van Nutt. New York: Viking.
Say, Allen (1990). *El chino.* Boston: Houghton Mifflin.
Shakespeare, William (Retold by Ann Keay Beneduce) (1996). *The tempest.* Illus. by G. Spirin. New York: Philomel Books.
Sis, Peter (1996). *Starry messenger.* New York: Farrar, Straus and Giroux.
Stanley, Diane (1996). *Leonardo Da Vinci.* New York: Morrow. (Orbis Pictus Award, 1998)
Stanley, Diane, & Vennema, Peter (1993). *Bard of Avon: The story of William Shakespeare.* New York: Morrow.
Stanley, Diane, & Vennema, Peter (1993). *Charles Dickens: The man who had great expectations.* New York: Morrow.
Swift, Jonathon (Retold by Ann Keay Beneduce) (1993). *Gulliver's adventures in Lilliput.* Illus. by G. Spirin. New York: Putnam.
Van Allsburg, Chris (1983). *The wreck of the Zephyr.* Boston: Houghton Mifflin.
Van Allsburg, Chris (1986). *The stranger.* Boston: Houghton Mifflin.
Van Allsburg, Chris (1991). *The wretched stone.* Boston: Houghton Mifflin.
Van Allsburg, Chris (1993). *The sweetest fig.* Boston: Houghton Mifflin.
Wiesner, David (1991). *Tuesday.* New York: Clarion. (Newbery Medal, 1992)
Willard, Nancy (1991). *Pish, posh, said Hieronymous Bosch.* Illus. by Leo & Diane Dillon. San Diego: Harcourt.
Wisniewski, David (1997). *Golem.* New York: Clarion. (Newbery Medal, 1998)
Yolen, Jane (1996). *O Jerusalem.* Illus. by J. Thompson. New York: Blue Sky/Scholastic.

# ARTISTIC DESIGN IN PICTURE BOOKS

While the interplay of a picture book's text and illustrations achieves an optimal blend of literacy components, the design of a book extends visual literacy to another dimension. Book design reaches beyond the visual and verbal aspects of the picture book. A book's overall design is what intrigues children about a book in the first place. Design includes the book's size and shape, the book jacket, the endpapers, the front matter, the lettering, and the placement of art and text on the page. Design is one of the factors that attracts the child to a selection for independent reading as well. An attractive cover in compelling color with unique lettering invites students inside a book to explore both pictures and story. The blend of a picture book's text, illustrations, and elements of design results in a greater overall effect than any one of these components can achieve separately.

**FIGURE 3.5** Transitional picture/chapter books [ all P/early I ].

Alphin, E. M. (1996). *A bear for Miguel.* Illus. by J. Sandin. New York: HarperCollins.
Bauer, M. D. (1997). *Turtle dreams.* Illus. by D. D. Hearn. New York: Holiday House.
Brisson, P. (1997). *Hot fudge hero.* Illus. by D. C. Bluthenthal. New York: Holt (Redfeather book)
Brown, L. K. (1997). *Rex and Lilly schooltime.* Illus. by Marc Brown. Boston: Little, Brown.
Bunting, E. (1998). *Some frog!* Illus. by S. Medlock. San Diego: Harcourt Brace.
Calmenson, S., & Cole, J. (1997). *Rockin' reptiles.* Illus. by L. Munsinger. New York: Morrow.
Gerstein, M. (1998). *Stop those pants!* San Diego: Harcourt Brace.
Haas, J. (1996). *Clean house.* Illus. by Y. Abolafia. New York: Greenwillow.
Hoban, L. (1996). *Arthur's Back to School Day.* New York: HarperCollins.
Lawlor, L. (1997). *The biggest pest on Eighth Avenue.* Illus. by C. Fisher. New York: Holiday House.
Littlefield, H. (1996). *Fire at the Triangle Factory.* Illus. by M. O. Young. Minneapolis, MN: Carolrhoda
    Books.
McDonald, M. (1997). *Beezy.* Illus. by N. Poydar. New York: Orchard Books.
McDonald, M. (1998). *Beezy magic.* Illus. by N. Poydar. New York: Orchard Books.
Mills, C. (1997). *Gus and Grandpa.* Illus. by C. Stock. New York: Farrar, Straus and Giroux.
Mills, C. (1997). *Gus and Grandpa and the Christmas cookies.* Illus. by C. Stock. New York: Farrar,
    Straus and Giroux.
Mills, C. (1998). *Gus and Grandpa at the hospital.* New York: Farrar, Straus and Giroux.
Mills, C. (1998). *Gus and Grandpa ride the train.* New York: Farrar, Straus and Giroux.
Mills, C. (1999). *Gus and Grandpa and the two wheeled bike.* New York: Farrar, Straus and Giroux.
Porter, B. A. (1997). *Harry's pony.* Illus. by Y. Abolafia. New York: Greenwillow.
Rockwell, A. (1997). *Once upon a time this morning.* Illus. by S. Stevenson. New York: Greenwillow.
Rylant, C. (1997). *Henry & Mudge and the bedtime thumps.* New York: Greenwillow.
Rylant, C. (1998). *Henry & Mudge and the sneaky crackers.* New York: Greenwillow. (16th book)
Rylant, C. (1998). *Henry & Mudge and the starry night.* New York: Greenwillow. (17th book)
Rylant, C. (1997). *Mr. Putter and Tabby fly the plane.* Illus. by A. Howard. San Diego: Harcourt Brace.
Rylant, C. (1997). *Mr. Putter and Tabby row the boat.* Illus. by A. Howard. San Diego: Harcourt Brace.
Rylant, C. (1998). *Mr. Putter and Tabby toot the horn.* Illus. by A. Howard. San Diego: Harcourt Brace.
Rylant, C. (1997). *Poppleton: Book one.* Illus. by Mark Teague. New York: Blue Sky/Scholastic.
Rylant, C. (1998). *Poppleton everyday.* Illus. by Mark Teague. New York: Blue Sky/Scholastic.
Rylant, C. (1998). *Poppleton forever.* Illus. by Mark Teague. New York: Blue Sky/Scholastic.
Sanfield, S. (1996). *The great turtle drive.* Illus. by D. Zimmer. New York: Knopf.
Stevenson, J. (1996). *Yard sale.* New York: Greenwillow.
Stevenson, J. (1997). *Heat wave at Mud Flat.* New York: Greenwillow.
Stevenson, J. (1997). *The Mud Flat mystery.* New York: Greenwillow.
Stevenson, J. (1998). *Mud Flat April fool.* New York: Greenwillow.
Wetterer, M. K., & Wetterer, C. M. (1996). *The snow walker.* Illus. by M. O. Young. Minneapolis, MN:
    Carolrhoda.

## Book Size and Shape

Most picture books conveniently fit into an $8\frac{1}{2}$-inch by 11-inch format. These books tell compelling stories, feature award-winning presentations, and efficiently fit on library shelves. Occasionally, however, the text or illustration of a picture book lends itself to a special format. Awareness of these special instances and speculation about design decisions help children become higher level thinkers and problem solvers. Articulating reasons for special book formats is in itself a response to literature.

The postcard format of Barbara Willard's *The Magic Cornfield* requires a $9\frac{1}{2}$-inch by $7\frac{1}{2}$-inch size and shape for the contents. Getting lost in the Magic Cornfield on his way to Minneapolis requires Tottem to communicate with Cousin Bottom through postcards. The postcards fit effectively into this smaller, elongated book format, adding to writing authenticity in the midst of a fantasy setting. Fred Marcellino's illustrations for *The Tale of Little Babaji* (1996) update the text of Helen Bannerman's *The Tale of Little Black Sambo* (1899). Those who remember the original book format will recall its similar compact size, with the updated, unstereotyped new version set in India. The diminutive format still effectively captures the strength of four tigers as they melt into butter, yet manages to be large enough to hold a plate of "a Hundred and Sixty-nine" pancakes for Babaji.

Just as undersized formats can be useful, oversized formats can prove necessary if they hold special creations that require additional space. Janet Stevens's *Tops and Bottoms* requires a larger format so it can be read from "top to bottom" rather than the traditional left to right. Double-page spreads that take us down into the rabbit hole and those that combine lazy Bear on the porch with the energetic Hare family working the garden require the large format. Because the illustrator is also the author of this adapted tale, it is likely that the format was conceived from the book's inception. The bright, bold collage illustrations in Lois Ehlert's *Cuckoo/Cucu: A Mexican Folktale* warrant the choice of a large format ($10\frac{1}{2}$ inches by $12\frac{1}{2}$ inches) to hold the striking constructed shapes and designs inspired by Mexican crafts and folk art. In addition, each page must hold not only the English text of the Mayan tale of how the cuckoo lost her beautiful feathers, but also the Spanish translation. Vivid colored shapes fastened together with gold brads construct the cuckoo as the regal Mexican bird fills the oversized pages with strength and beauty.

## Book Jackets

A book jacket serves to protect a book and to provide information about its content, its author and/or illustrator, and its special features. Even more, the illustration on the front cover of the book jacket serves as an invitation to open the book and explore. The illustration on the back cover may serve as a reason to reflect, relive, or relate the book to one's own experiences. We actually teach a lesson in visual literacy when we ask children "What do you think this book is about?" prior to a read-aloud session. Children provide answers to that question by paying attention to initial cues on the book jacket that ignite engagement in literature. The book jacket does, in a sense, initiate the first response to a book.

Many book jackets contain wraparound art that provides a continuous poster-like scene from front to back. James Ransome's jacket for Angela Medearis's *Rum-A-Tum-Tum*

Wraparound book covers invite eager readers into a story before they even open the pages of a book. *From* Rum-A-Tum-Tum *by Angela Shelf Medearis. Illustrated by James E. Ransome. Copyright © 1997. Reprinted by permission of Holiday House.*

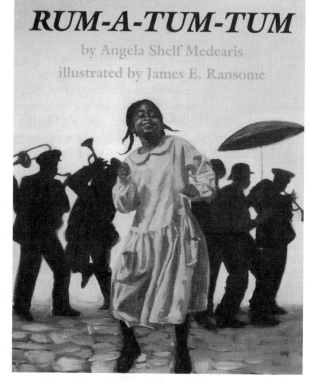

portrays a young girl in a vibrant blue dress dancing to the rhythm of a silhouetted New Orleans jazz band on the front cover. As the illustration continues to the back jacket, the panorama expands to a colorful marching band on the cobblestone streets of the French Quarter. Even before reading the text, the viewer joins in the tempo and rhythm of the music and appreciates the energetic culture of this Southern city.

Todd Doney's jacket illustration of Jonathan London's *Old Salt, Young Salt* highlights Aaron catching his first salmon from the sea. As the wraparound cover is opened to its full perspective, Aaron's father is shown helping net the prized catch. The total book jacket effect is to emphasize the father–son relationship that provides the story theme.

A book jacket may also have separate, but related, illustrations on the front and the back. Michael Garland's front illustration for Elizabeth Friedrich's *Leah's Pony* frames the joyful relationship between a girl and her treasured equine companion. The back cover, however, focuses on Leah, astride her pony, as Mr. B, the grocer, greets her on her trip to town. Between the jacket covers lies the heartwarming story of the Depression, its devastating effect on a farm family, the willingness of a girl to sacrifice, and the power of a penny auction to recapture a mutual friendship even during tough times. In this case, the front jacket captures the potential reader with warmth, while the back cover captures the caring spirit of the story.

Barbara Cooney's gentle artwork invites the viewer into the lumber camp life of a foster child in *Only Opal: The Diary of a Young Girl.* Framed by two tall firs and barren stumps, Opal views her home and her beloved forest surroundings. The back cover provides an inlay of Opal Whiteley in her pinafore on the forest path surrounded by her treasured wildflow-ers. The simple, detailed portrait summons the reader to reflect and revisit the story of Opal's oneness with nature and her struggle for love, self-worth, and a sense of belonging. These separate front and back artworks are, in their own way, very special because they house important story content between their contrasting picture frames.

## Endpapers

Endpapers serve a utilitarian function in that they attach the pages of a book to its casing. But they also provide an interesting transition from the exterior to the interior of a book. Initially, they may go unnoticed as the reader's momentum moves them toward the text. An astute teacher, however, can open children's eyes to these effective connecting links between book covers and text. Evidencing awareness, sharing discovery, and revealing connections to the text formulate responses to literature.

In their simplest forms, endpapers are colored, illustration-free paper. Even then, their colors are chosen to enhance the book jacket or to express a mood or feeling. May Lyn Ray's *Mud,* which captures the thawing of winter into spring, chooses a chocolate brown endcover for the book's opening. The dark, murky, muddy, oozing transition to spring is contrasted with vibrant, fresh green endpapers at the book's end to emphasize the rebirth of grass, trees, and life as the long-awaited season arrives. In *Fenwick's Suit,* David Small uses bright yellow endpapers crisscrossed with orange lines to foreshadow and recall the chaos that came into Fenwick's life when he wore a suit with this same colorful plaid pattern.

Many illustrators plan for endpapers that complement the story or the artwork that graces the book's interior. Diana Pomeroy's *Wildflower ABC* is an alphabet of potato prints. The endpapers are a shower of repeated patterns of golden poppies, purple asters, and wild roses, all created with the potato print motif that graces the book. Children can even revisit the text or use the informational glossary to identify these wildflowers. Karen Winnick's *Mr. Lincoln's Whiskers* showcases the letter from 11-year-old Grace Bedell to Abraham Lincoln in which she boldly suggested he grow whiskers to hide his thin face and appeal to the vot-ers. The endpapers appropriately replicate portions of the authentic return letter of Mr. Lincoln to Grace. A parchment background highlights the black-inked smudges and the dis-tinctive signature of A. Lincoln. These meaningful connections between story and endpa-pers make them worth noting, sharing, and responding to prior to or following a book reading experience. Once readers are made aware of their special connection to the book, they are certain to stop and note them independently as they begin their reading journey.

## Front Matter

In examining the visual qualities of a picture book, children become adept at discovering the importance of what comes before the text. The front matter includes the pages between the front endpapers and the first page of text. Besides supplying important copyright and publication information for adults, these pages often introduce prospective readers to the story's mood, character(s), setting, theme, or content. They may also provide important background regarding the origin of the story or insights into the illustrations.

***Title page.***    The title page introduces the reader to the book, showcases the full title, and distinguishes the author and/or illustrator and the publisher. The title page is commonly housed on a single page, but can extend across two pages as a double-page spread. Children can easily be made aware of its importance as a page to be examined prior to the reading of a story. Insights into the story can be gleaned by examining the illustrations on the title page, and the importance of differentiating author, title, and publisher can be confirmed.

A double-page spread by James Ransome invites the reader into the simple cabin and fenced-in yard of the slave quarters in Tony Johnston's *The Wagon.* While the bright sunlight and blooming sunflowers give the impression of impending joy, the dark cabin, absence of people, and shadowed fenceposts temper the mood. The open gate invites the reader to turn the page and become a part of this moment in history when the slaves realized that their dream of freedom had become a reality. Speculating on this illustration initiates predictive reader response prior to actual textual exposure.

***Dedication page.***    Dedications typically appear after the title page, or opposite or on the same page with the copyright and publishing information. While a dedication usually expresses appreciation to someone closely associated with the author or illustrator, it can also add a statement reflecting a message related to the text. For example, Patricia Polacco touchingly dedicates *The Trees of the Dancing Goats:* "In loving memory of my hero . . . my mother, Mary Gaw Barber, August 8, 1913–May 13, 1996." Gloria and Ted Rand, on the other hand, dedicate *Willy Takes a Walk* "For all search-and-rescue volunteers, who selflessly risk their own lives to aid others." While Willie's mouse wanderings in a junkyard appear humorous, the book shares an important message with would-be hikers.

Important related information can be found printed on or opposite the dedication page. Alan Schroeder's *Satchmo's Blues* contains a note pointing out that the book is a fictionalized account of Louis Armstrong's childhood. It also guides the reader to other printed sources for factual information. This page may also serve as a transition from the title page to the first page of text. Virginia Kroll's *Can You Dance, Dalila?* contains a two-page dedication spread by Nancy Carpenter that illustrates a footprint dancestep pattern that compels the reader to follow the steps. As children become more aware of the role of the dedication page, it is likely to be a page that is examined, not skipped, as a portion of the invitation to enter the world of a picture book.

## Borders

Some illustrators choose to use borders around their illustrations to artistically complement the main illustrations. Others incorporate borders to predict forthcoming happenings or to reveal an ongoing story taking place alongside the illustrations, but related to the text. The creative use of borders enhances artistic presentation, but can also extend meaning beyond the visual and verbal aspects of the book.

The simple, yet effective purple frames surrounding each page of William Steig's *The Toy Brother* serve to articulate each distinct illustration. A thin lined decorative frame surrounds David Small's illustrations in *The Library* by Sarah Stewart. A single narrow line separates the illustration from the text while another line, with corner decorations, frames the entire page. The eye appeal of simple frames such as these highlights the illustrations.

The masterful crafting of borders for import beyond the text is synonymous with the work of Jan Brett. Her classic retelling of *The Mitten* (1989) introduced the reader to the use of borders to review and predict events in the story. As Ms. Brett cleverly packed animals in the mitten one by one, she used mitten-shaped cutouts in the right and left borders of double-page spreads to review the previous mitten inhabitant and preview the impending occupant. She continues her border artwork in *Comet's Nine Lives* (1996) as frames made of shells, rope, and sealife encase each of a Nantucket cat's adventures. *The Hat* (1997) capitalizes on this border characteristic of Jan Brett's artistry. Sometimes the borders of a book go undetected, but knowledge of their inclusion makes the discerning eye aware of their role in book design.

## Lettering and Type

Type selection involves three critical decisions for the book designer or illustrator. The first choice of font selection is an important one because today more than 6,000 type fonts are available for printed text. The right choice of type to match a historical period, a story genre, or a mood or setting can add to successful presentation. The second choice includes size of type. Considerations of the age of the intended audience and of format size are primary factors in this decision. Finally, the choice of black type on a light background or white type on a dark background must be made. The combined effect of these three decisions provides an added dimension to the overall conceptualization of the picture book.

Color and size of type is an exaggerated and unique feature of Jon Scieszka's *The Stinky Cheese Man and Other Fairly Stupid Tales.* In the main fairy-tale retelling, the type begins with five characters per inch, reduces to nine characters per inch, and ends with type that is three characters per inch. The one-page retelling of "Jack's Story" ranges from 4 red characters per inch to an almost unreadable 28 black characters per inch as the story suggests continued repetition at the bottom of the page. Throughout the text, varying type reflects the humor of the tale—even the dedication is printed upside down.

In a poignant portrayal of the childhood of Booker T. Washington, Marie Bradby's text meshes with Chris Soentpiet's art in a meaningful way in *More Than Anything Else.* From sunup to sundown, the type is black set on the pure white background of the saltworks where Booker and his Papa arduously labor. Throughout most of the book, however, the type is rendered in yellow with dark backgrounds reflecting the light of the kerosene lanterns, candles, or fireplace on the faces and setting of the story. This technique is particularly effective in the book's final illustration in which Booker learns to write and read his name. These types of design decisions combine to make a picture book into a work of art.

## Use of Space

The location of text in relation to illustrations is another aspect of book design. Text can appear on the same side of the page or it can be alternated from right side to left side intermittently. Text can appear in the upper right and the lower left on each double-page spread or it can be alternated according to the illustrator's needs. In *Emma's Rug,* Allen Say chooses to effectively place the text on the left-hand page of his picture book while the right-hand page holds his masterful watercolor representations of an emerging young artist who ultimately realizes her creativity comes from within. Jean Craighead George's text blends into

Thomas Locker's landscape art and almost begs to be printed on the upper left of most pages in *To Climb a Waterfall*. The sky or treetops seem to aptly house the text for this well-crafted book. Occasionally, the text is moved to a rock or a stream, but the artwork itself seems to effortlessly provide a place for the text.

No single design element alone makes an outstanding picture book. It is the effective blending of all of these design elements with exquisite illustrations and powerful text that creates a cohesive whole. Then, and only then, does the picture book appeal to the eye and stir the imagination of the reader. Open any Caldecott award-winning title (see Appendix A) and note how several of these design techniques blend into an integrated whole—the picture book. As teachers and students open their eyes to an awareness of the intricacies of book design, they grow both in their appreciation of the artistic qualities of the picture book and in their ability to respond to the intricacies of book design.

# ARTISTIC STYLE IN PICTURE BOOKS

The style of an illustration is revealed by the way in which the artist uses the elements of art and the chosen media to create a visual image. Style results from a blend of color, line, and shape with the media choices an illustrator selects. Style is a result of all the decisions an illustrator makes in producing a final product, likened to placing a signature on a work of art. Illustrators typically become identified with a particular style, especially by children, although many choose to continue to explore, experiment, and extend their artwork during their emerging careers.

Six basic styles of art are recognized in children's book illustrations, just as they are in museum art. These include realism, surrealism, expressionism, impressionism, folk art, and cartoon art. With guidance and modeling, children can learn to recognize the characteristics of each of these styles and respond to illustrations by discussing the illustrator's style.

Realism or representational art incorporates a natural reproduction of people, nature, and objects as they actually appear in the real world. Allen Say's representations of his ancestors in *Grandfather's Journey* appear lifelike; their facial expressions and authentic forms bring reality to the viewer's eyes. In Patricia and Frederick McKissack's *Christmas in the Big House, Christmas in the Quarters,* John Thompson brings contrasting personalities to life from both sides of plantation life—slaves and masters—as they prepare for their holiday celebration. Ruth Sanderson's realism invades the oil paintings of *Snow White and Rose Red* as sisters outwit a crafty leprechaun. Photographic in their quality, realistic illustrations bring true-to-life qualities to characters, settings, and scenarios in literature.

Surrealism in children's illustrations skews realism in its attempts to represent the mingling of the unconscious with the dreamlike qualities of imagination. The haunting paintings of Rafal Olbinski in John Gruen's *Flowers & Fables* not only illuminate the text, but suggest further unfolding of tales to children. A spectacular world of whimsical paradoxes and playful contradictions "dreamed by" Audrey Wood and "imagined by" Don Wood lies between the covers of the digitally produced creation of *Bright and Early Thursday Evening*. Readers float between dreams and reality as as they attempt to unravel meaning in a landscape of backward clocks and animated skeletons. Children, perhaps more than adults, enjoy responding to and making sense of the fantastical portrayal of dreamlike states in surrealististic illustrations.

Expressionism uses bright colors and disproportionate figures to add strong emotions to a story.
*From CHATO'S KITCHEN by Gary Soto, illustrations by Susan Guevara. Copyright © 1995 by Susan Guevara, illustrations. Used by permission of G.P. Putnam's Sons, a division of Penguin Putnam Inc.*

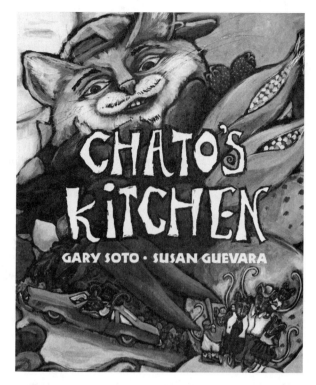

Expressionism makes use of bright colors and figures that are a bit disproportionate in giving form to strong inner feelings while presenting a modified or distorted reality. Faith Ringgold's characters in *Tar Beach* represent this style of art through characters and a rooftop setting. With an emphasis on inner feelings, the bright colors and unique angles and perspectives of Susan Guevara's illustrations in *Chato's Kitchen* also represent this stylistic mode. Recognized by children because of its vivid colors, exaggerated gestures, and extreme facial expressions, expressionism has become an increasingly popular mode of illustrator style.

Impressionism characteristically prioritizes light, movement, and color over definition of detail. Emily Arnold McCully captures the essence of this style in both her Caldecott award winner, *Mirette on the High Wire,* and in its sequel, *Starring Mirette and Bellini.* Either a light or dark background illuminates each illustration and dramatically allows rich watercolors to blend history, European culture, and a fine story. Michael Foreman's impressionistic renderings of the sea fill the pages of *Seal Surfer* and *The Little Ships* with pastel blues and greens as seasonal sunlight and moonlight reflect off the ocean's surface.

Folk art has a childlike characteristic in that it appears flat and lacks a sense of proportion. Claire Nivola's folk art in *Elisabeth* is well suited to a cross-generational story of a doll who makes her way through the years and across the ocean to her original owner. Jacob Lawrence has gained a national reputation for his sequences of narrative paintings dealing with important figures and issues in African-American history. His folk art style illustrations grace Walter Dean Myers's *Toussaint L'Ouverture: The Fight for Haiti's Freedom.* A more traditional style of folk art is found in the caricatures of Petra Mathers in Jacqueline

Briggs Martin's *Grandmother Bryant's Pocket* with diminutive characters interspersed throughout the book.

Cartoon art appeals to children so it is not surprising that some of children's favorite illustrators create in this style. Tomie de Paola is the master of cartoon art as evidenced in *Strega Nona: Her Story* and *Tom* as well as countless other creations. His memorable characters are easily recognized and loved by young children. Great respect was gained for the cartoon art style when the Caldecott award was bestowed to Peggy Rathmann for *Officer Buckle and Gloria*. The humor of the characters, the bright bold colors, and the movement she creates have made this a favorite with teachers and children alike. Kevin Henkes brings delightful mice to life in *Chrysanthemum, Owen,* and *Lilly's Purple Plastic Purse,* and Steven Kellogg has mesmerized children for decades with his own cartoon-like characters. Cartoon art has reached the informational genre as children delight in Bruce Degen's art in the *Magic School Bus* series. Popular with children, the bright colors and stark pen and ink outlines of this style focus reader/viewer attention and permanently etch these characters in children's hearts and minds.

As children are drawn to and recognize the art of favorite illustrators and the characteristics of styles of artistic expression, their interest and curiosity in children's book illustrations will deepen. A teacher does not have to be an art expert to respond aesthetically to the picture book (Kiefer, 1995). This quality artwork serves as an introduction to the real world of art as connections between the world of children's picture books and the broader world of art become apparent.

# ARTISTIC MEDIA IN PICTURE BOOKS

Examining the media illustrators use to create their works of art can help children understand and appreciate the pictures while encouraging them to respond by using these media in their own artistic explorations (Elleman, 1994). Information on media may be located on the copyright page or in the illustrator's biographical notes on the book jacket. If this information is not available, children can be encouraged to speculate by using clues from the techniques they have learned from previous illustrated books. Response to illustrations may include why an illustrator chose a particular medium and what effect is achieved through that medium. Children can compare this book with other titles by the same artist to see if the same medium was used.

Four common art media are repeatedly found in children's book illustrations. These include oil paints, watercolors, graphite pencils, and pastels/chalk. Mixed media refers to the blending of these and other types of media for a special, unique effect. Relating each medium to a distinguished artist will help to differentiate them as children become aware of their characteristic features.

Oil paints dominate the deep, rich illustrations of Thomas Locker in more than 20 picture books. Originally an adult landscape artist, Locker brought his painterly techniques to children's books, most recently those dealing with science. In *Water Dance,* inspiring oil illustrations accompany hundreds of facts about water as the reader journeys through the water cycle. In *Sky Tree: Seeing Science through Art* with Candice Christiansen, Locker paints 12 portraits of the same tree as it passes through the seasons of the year and explains how light affects each depiction. Because children are rarely exposed to oils, Locker's artwork, besides being enjoyed for its inherent quality, can also serve as an introduction to the art of the great masters.

Watercolor, a commonly used medium in picture books, has the power to portray a variety of moods from whimsical and lighthearted to serious and downcast. Jerry Pinkney performs magic with his use of watercolors to portray the racing tigers as "they melted into a pool of butter as golden as a dream come true" in *Sam and the Tigers* by Julian Lester. Watercolors add lip-smacking appeal to James Stevenson's *Sweet Corn*, making his illustrations taste just as good as his poems. Vivid tones and blended colors provide a celebration for viewers.

Graphite pencils define the shades of night as a father and son head to the mountains during *Night Driving* (Coy, 1996). Black, gray, and white cafes, gas pumps, and truck stops give striking realism to this nostalgic driving experience. Chris Van Allsburg's graphite drawings for *The Mysteries of Harris Burdick* and *Jumanji* often come to mind first when looking for connections to this medium.

Pastel drawings are made with compressed colored chalk that blends well and works best on rough paper. Pastels form the foundation of illustrations by Lisa Campbell Ernst whose *Potato: A Tale from the Great Depression* reflects the fine color and blending of this medium. Ernst also incorporates an ink outline and pencil cross-hatching to compliment the pastel drawings. Thomas B. Allen also uses pastels to color his charcoal-drawn illustrations. *Climbing Kansas Mountains* shows the rough tinted paper and blending of charcoal and pastels that have become the hallmark of Allen's many illustrated children's books.

More artists are introducing mixed media or new media to children's book illustrations. The reverse side of the title page often includes a small print reference to the type of media used to produce the illustrations. With each new publishing year, experimental media bring rich color, texture, and dimension to children's books.

The choice of graphite as an artistic medium effectively blends with the story of an overnight auto journey in *Night Driving*.
*From* Night Driving *by John Coy. Jacket illustration copyright © 1996 by Peter McCarty. Reprinted by permission of Henry Holt.*

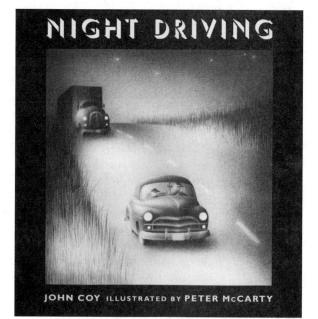

# GRAPHIC TECHNIQUES IN PICTURE BOOKS

Beyond selecting media with which to present their images, illustrators must choose creative techniques to transmit the visions carried in their minds. These techniques include woodcuts, scratchboards, engravings, collage, cut paper, and photography. Recognition of these art techniques is also important because they bring unique responses from children instilled by their own special characteristics.

Woodcuts give a strong and powerful impression and David Frampton's choice of this technique for *Whaling Days* (Carrick, 1993) is perfectly well suited to the subject. The big, bold images of the woodcuts blend the strength of the whale, the power of the ocean, and the determination of sailors to capture their catch. Bold black areas trimmed in gold and blue are simple choices to portray these compelling scenes. In this technique, an image is drawn on a woodblock, and the wood is cut away with special knives until only the lines of the drawing are standing. Ink is rolled on the lines and the wood is pressed onto paper to print the picture. The boldness and depth of black highlights this intricate technique. Mary Azarian, the 1999 Caldecott Medal recipient, skillfully uses crafted tinted woodcuts to capture the rural Vermont landscape and the rugged characters in *Snowflake Bentley*. (Martin, 1998)

Engravings are a related technique that adds a sense of permanence and strength to book illustrations. Barry Moser chose to use them for Patricia MacLachlan's *What You Know First* (1995). Both the author and illustrator chose photographs from their own family albums to serve as models for these intricate artworks. The engravings proved to be an effective choice for sharing nostalgic memories of childhood and home.

The scratchboard technique has become the specialty of Brian Pinkney. Scratchboard uses a white board covered with black ink into which a drawing is scratched with a sharp tool. Pinkney adds color with oil pastels or oil, wiping away any excess. This technique which was first demonstrated in William Hooks's *The Ballad of Belle Dorcas,* is readily apparent in Sans Souci's *Sukey & the Mermaid,* and most recently seen in Andrea Pinkney's *Bill Pickett: Rodeo-Ridin' Cowboy.* The use of light and shadow is particularly noteworthy as are the attention to detail both in animal representation and facial expressions. Children have been informally exploring this technique for years in school as they covered pieces of paper with black crayon and scratched out a drawing with a sharp object. Brian Pinkney has mastered the technique and made it his own.

Collage is an artistic composition made by gluing different materials onto a surface. The master of paper collage is Eric Carle, whose 25 years' worth of book illustrating reflect his ability to bring paper to life. He prepares his own colored tissue papers by using various brushes to splash or splatter, or by fingerpainting acrylic paint onto the tissue paper. The prepared paper is then cut or torn into shapes as needed and glued onto white illustration board. Carle's animals are particularly impressive as overlapped tissue paper giraffes, elephants, and roosters fill the page. Carle's insect quartet employs this technique with a caterpillar, a spider, a cricket, and a lightning bug. As this technique has become the hallmark of his work, his illustrations are perhaps the most recognizable by young children.

Cut paper layering is related to collage, but requires an even sharper eye for defining detail. David Wisniewski has been honored for this technique for *Golem,* the 1997 Caldecott Medal book. This artist uses colored paper for his cut illustrations, which are held together

*Golem* blends the dramatic flair of cut paper with the splendid retelling of an eloquent tale of Prague. *Jacket from GOLEM by David Wisniewski. Copyright © 1996 by David Wisniewski. Reprinted by permission of Clarion Books/ Houghton Mifflin Company. All rights reserved.*

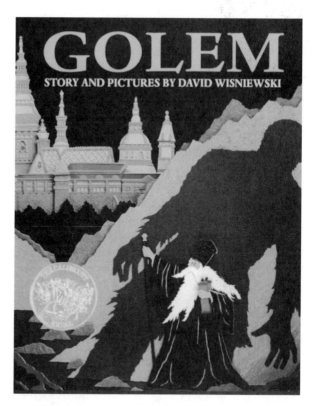

with double-stick photo mounts. To achieve depth between pieces of paper, he uses double-stick foam tape or places thicker matboard behind layers of paper. He uses a precise bladed knife and often uses between 800 and 1,000 blades to complete 16 illustrations in one book (Cummings, 1995). *Golem* represents the current apex of Wisniewski's picture book career. His cuttings of the city of Prague and the dominant monster-like Golem creatively fill the book's pages with varying perspectives and dramatic action. Double-page spreads provide a panoramic unfolding of events and the deep brown, black, red, and orange-toned papers aptly reflect the story elements. The cut of the paper is so acute that one can almost feel its sharpness. Golem blends the high drama of an eloquently retold story with the dramatic flair of the cut paper technique to form an award-winning picture book.

Photography is another technique used to create the foundation for text or as building blocks for additional media. Bruce McMillan's *Grandfather's Trolley* began with black-and-white photos. The prints were then given a brown tone before being tinted with oil colors. This technique was used to make color photographs during the turn of the century, so its use in *Grandfather's Trolley* makes it historically appropriate as well as pleasing to the eye.

Digitally illustrated books are beginning to appear on the market as this technology becomes available to book illustrators and publishing houses. Audrey Wood's *The Red Racer* was drawn entirely with a digital pen on a digital tablet by hand. Wood mixed colors on a digital palette and designed textured backgrounds as well. Uncertainty and disagreement have arisen over this technique's acceptance as authentic book illustration, yet children will be drawn to its vivid color, cartoon-like design, and the potential of software to contribute to their own book illustrating attempts.

Each illustrator brings special talents and choices to the art of the picture book. The variety of choices blended with unique artistic talents makes children's book illustrations an outstanding topic for response by both adults and the children with whom they share these works of art (Kiefer, 1989).

## CLOSING THOUGHTS

The world of picture books encompasses books for all ages and titles across all genres. The art of the picture book lies in the blend of its words and in its illustrations. Children, however, do not always recognize the beauty of the language of the text and the special types of illustrations without the guidance of a knowledgeable teacher. The more teachers learn about illustration, the more children will respond to the visual aspects of a book. The more teachers point out exceptional language, the more children will warm to the special word choices of an author. Early impressions of literature and reading begin with motivating readings and presentations of quality picture books. As children learn more about the blending of language and art, they develop their own artistic and literary tastes as they develop into readers.

Classroom time is precious and the books we choose to share as teachers can directly influence student motivation and attitude toward reading and literature. Because so many picture books are published each year, teachers need to selectively evaluate the ones they choose to use in their classrooms. An awareness of book design and format, a sense of quality writing, a knowledge of various art media, styles, and techniques, and a feel for the response potential of the book help in making informed decisions about which picture books to share with children. Over time, teachers should expose children to a variety of illustrators whose artistic styles combine with well-written text and blend into the extraordinary aesthetic experience that is the picture book.

## REFERENCES

Chaney, J. A. (1993). Alphabet books: Resources for learning. *The Reading Teacher, 47,* 96–104.

Cummings, P. (Ed.) (1995). *Talking with artists: Volume two.* New York: Simon & Schuster.

Elleman, B. (1994). Illustration as art. *Book Links, 3,* 28–31.

Henkes, K. (1992). The artist at work. *The Horn Book Magazine, 68,* 38–47.

Jacobs, J. S., & Tunnell, M. O. (1996). *Children's literature, briefly.* Upper Saddle River, NJ: Merrill/Prentice Hall.

Kiefer, B. Z. (1989). Picture books for all the ages. In J. Hickman & B. E. Cullinan (Eds.), *Children's literature in the classroom: Weaving Charlotte's web* (pp. 75–88). Needham Heights, MA: Christopher Gordon.

Kiefer, B. Z. (1995). *The potential of picture books: From visual literacy to aesthetic understanding.* Upper Saddle River, NJ: Merrill/Prentice Hall.

Kiefer, B. Z. (1995). Responding to literature as art in picture books. In N. L. Roser & M. G. Martinez (Eds.), *Book talk and beyond: Children and teachers respond to literature* (pp. 191–200). Newark, DE: International Reading Association.

Lynch-Brown, C., & Tomlinson, C. M. (1993). *Essentials of children's literature.* Boston: Allyn & Bacon.

Stewig, J. W. (1995). *Looking at picture books.* Fort Atkinson, WI: Highsmith Press.

Teale, W. H. (1986). Home background and young children's literacy development. In W. H. Teale & E. Sulzby (Eds.), *Emergent literacy: Writing and reading* (pp. 173–205). Norwood, NJ: Ablex.

# CHILDREN'S BOOKS CITED  [ P ] = K–2; [ I ] = 3–5; [ M ] = 6–8

Axelrod, Amy (1994). *Pigs will be pigs.* Illus. by Sharon McGinley-Nally. New York: Simon & Schuster. [ I ]

Axelrod, Amy (1997). *Pigs in the pantry.* Illus. by Sharon McGinley-Nally. New York: Simon & Schuster. [ I ]

Axelrod, Amy (1997). *Pigs go to market.* Illus. by Sharon McGinley-Nally. New York: Simon & Schuster. [ I ]

Baker, Jeannie (1991). *Windows.* New York: Greenwillow. [ P/I ]

Bannerman, Helen (1996). *The tale of Little Babaji.* Illus. by Fred Marcellino. New York: HarperCollins. [ P ]

Banyai, Istvan (1995). *Re-zoom.* New York: Viking. [ I ]

Bayley, Thomas (1998). *Sailing ships: A lift-the-flap discovery.* New York: Orchard Books. [ I ]

Blake, Quentin (1995). *Clown.* New York: Holt. [ P/I ]

Borden, Louise (1997). *The little ships: The heroic rescue at Dunkirk in World War II.* Illus. by Michael Foreman. New York: McElderry. [ I ]

Boulton, Judy (Adapter) (1994). *Only Opal: The diary of a young girl.* Illus. by Barbara Cooney. New York: Philomel Books. [ I ]

Bradby, Marie (1995). *More than anything else.* Illus. by Chris Soentpiet. New York: Orchard Books. [ P/I ]

Brett, Jan (1989). *The mitten.* New York: Putnam. [ P ]

Brett, Jan (1996). *Comet's nine lives.* New York: Putnam. [ P ]

Brett, Jan (1997). *The hat.* New York: Putnam. [ P ]

Bunting, Eve (1994). *Smoky nights.* Illus. by David Diaz. San Diego: Harcourt. [ P/I ]

Bunting, Eve (1998). *Some frog!* Illus. by S. Medlock. San Diego: Harcourt Brace. [ P/I ]

Carle, Eric (1968). *The very hungry caterpillar.* New York: Philomel Books. [ P ]

Carle, Eric (1984). *The very busy spider.* New York: Philomel Books. [ P ]

Carle, Eric (1990). *The very quiet cricket.* New York: Philomel Books.

Carle, Eric (1995). *The very lonely firefly.* New York: Philomel Books. [ P ]

Carrick, Carol (1993). *Whaling days.* Woodcuts by David Frampton. New York: Clarion. [ I/M ]

Cherry, Lynne (1997). *Flute's journey.* San Diego: Harcourt Brace. [ I ]

Coy, John (1996). *Night driving.* Illus. by Peter McCarty. New York: Holt. [ P/I ]

Crowther, Robert (1996). *Robert Crowther's pop-up Olympics: Amazing facts and record breakers.* Cambridge, MA: Candlewick Press. [ I ]

Darling, Kathy (1996). *Amazon ABC.* New York: Lothrop, Lee & Shepard. [ P/I ]

de Paola, Tomie (1985). *Tomie de Paola's Mother Goose.* New York: Putnam. [ P ]

de Paola, Tomie (1993). *Tom.* New York: Putnam. [ P ]

de Paola, Tomie (1996). *Strega Nona: Her story.* New York: Putnam. [ P ]

Doubilet, Anne (1991). *Under the sea from A to Z.* Photos by D. Doubilet. New York: Crown. [ P/I ]

Ehlert, Lois (1997). *Cuckoo/Cucu: A Mexican folktale.* San Diego: Harcourt Brace. [ P/I ]

Ehlert, Lois (1997). *Hands.* San Diego: Harcourt Brace. [ P ]

Esbensen, Barbara J. (1996). *Echoes for the eye: Poems to celebrate patterns in nature.* Illus. by Helen K. Davie. New York: HarperCollins. [ I ]

Foreman, Michael (1997). *Seal surfer.* San Diego: Harcourt Brace. [ I ]

Friedrich, Elizabeth (1996). *Leah's pony.* Illus. by Michael Garland. Honesdale, PA: Boyds Mill Press. [ I ]

Geisert, Arthur (1996). *Roman numerals I to MM.* Boston: Houghton Mifflin. [ I ]

George, Jean Craighead (1995). *To climb a waterfall.* Illus. by Thomas Locker. New York: Philomel Books. [ I ]

Grover, Max (1993). *The accidental zucchini: An unexpected alphabet.* San Diego: Harcourt Brace. [ P/I ]

Gruen, John (1996). *Flowers & fables.* Illus. by Rafal Olbinski. San Diego: Harcourt Brace. [ I/M ]

Hall, Donald (1979). *Ox-cart man.* Illus. by Barbara Cooney. New York: Viking. [ I ]

Henkes, Kevin (1991). *Chrysanthemum.* New York: Greenwillow. [ P ]

Henkes, Kevin (1993). *Owen.* New York: Greenwillow. [ P ]

Henkes, Kevin (1996). *Lilly's purple plastic purse.* New York: Greenwillow. [ P ]

Hepworth, Catherine (1992). *ANTics!: An alphabet anthology.* New York: Putnam. [ I ]

Hoban, Tana (1992). *Spirals, curves, fanshapes, and lines.* New York: Greenwillow. [ P ]

Hoban, Tana (1995). *Animal, vegetable, or mineral?* New York: Greenwillow. [ P ]

Hoban, Tana (1996). *Just look.* New York: Greenwillow. [ P ]

Hooks, William (1990). *The ballad of Belle Dorcas.* Illus. by Brian Pinkney. New York: Knopf. [ I/M ]

Houston, Gloria (1992). *My great aunt Arizona.* Illus. by Susan Lambe. New York: HarperCollins. [ I ]

Johnston, Tony (1996). *The wagon.* Illus. by James Ransome. New York: Tambourine. [ I ]

Kharms, Daniil (1996). *First, second.* Translated from the Russian by Richard Pevear. Illus. by Marc Rosenthal. New York: Farrar, Straus & Giroux. [ I ]

Kimmel, Eric (1996). *Count Silvernose.* New York: Holiday House. [ I ]

Kroll, Virginia (1996). *Can you dance, Dalila?* Illus. by Nancy Carpenter. New York: Simon & Schuster. [ P ]

Lester, Julian (1996). *Sam and the tigers.* Illus. by Jerry Pinkney. New York: Dial. [ P ]

Lewin, Ted (1996). *Market!* New York: Lothrop, Lee & Shepard. [ I ]

Lied, Kate (1997). *Potato: A tale from the great depression.* Illus. by Lisa Campbell Ernst. Washington, DC: National Geographic. [ P/I ]

Lobel, Anita (1990). *Allison's zinnea.* New York: Greenwillow. [ P/I ]

Lobel, Anita (1994). *Away from home.* New York: Greenwillow. [ P/I ]

Lobel, Arnold (Illus.) (1997). *Book of Mother Goose.* New York: Random House. [ P ]

Locker, Thomas (1997). *Water dance.* San Diego: Harcourt Brace. [ I ]

Locker, Thomas, with Candice Christiansen (1995). *Sky tree: Seeing science through art.* Illus. by Thomas Locker. New York: HarperCollins. [ I ]

London, Jonathan (1996). *Old salt, young salt.* Illus. by Todd Doney. New York: Lothrop, Lee & Shepard. [ P/I ]

MacLachlan, Patricia (1995). *What you know first.* Engravings by Barry Moser. New York: Joanna Cotler Books/HarperCollins. [ I ]

Maizlish, Lisa (1996). *The ring.* Photographs by L. Maizlish. New York: Greenwillow. [ P/I ]

Martin, Bill, Jr., & Archambault, John (1989). *Chicka chicka boom boom.* Illus. by Lois Ehlert. New York: Simon & Schuster. [ P ]

Martin, Jacqueline Briggs (1996). *Grandmother Bryant's pocket.* Illus. by Petra Mathers. Boston: Houghton Mifflin. [ I ]

Martin, Jacqueline Briggs (1998). *Snowflake Bentley.* Illus. by Mary Azarian. Boston: Houghton Mifflin. [ P/I ]

McCully, Emily Arnold (1992). *Mirette on the high wire.* New York: Putnam. [ P ]

McCully, Emily Arnold (1997). *Starring Mirette and Bellini.* New York: Putnam. [ P ]

McKissack, P. C., & McKissack, F. L. (1994). *Christmas in the big house, Christmas in the quarters.* Illus. by John Thompson. New York: Scholastic. [ I/M ]

McMillan, Bruce (1995). *Grandfather's trolley.* Photo-illustrated by Bruce McMillan. Cambridge, MA: Candlewick Press. [ I ]

Medearis, Angela (1997). *Rum-a-tum-tum.* Illus. by James Ransom. New York: Holiday House. [ P ]

Musgrove, Margaret (1976). *Ashanti to Zulu: African traditions.* Illus. by Leo & Diane Dillon. New York: Dial. [I]

Myers, Walter Dean (1996). *Toussaint L'Ouverture: The fight for Haiti's freedom.* Paintings by Jacob Lawrence. New York: Simon & Schuster. [ I/M ]

Nivola, Claire (1997). *Elisabeth.* New York: Farrar, Straus and Giroux. [ I ]

Opie, Iona A. (1996). *My very first Mother Goose.* Illus. by Rosemary Wells. Cambridge, MA: Candlewick Books. [ P ]

Peet, Bill (1989). *Bill Peet: An autobiography.* Boston: Houghton Mifflin. [ I ]

Pelletier, David (1996). *The graphic alphabet.* New York: Orchard Books. [ P/I ]

Pinkney, Andrea (1996). *Bill Pickett: Rodeo-ridin' cowboy.* Illus. by Brian Pinkney. New York: Four Winds Press. [ I ]

Polacco, Patricia (1996). *The trees of the dancing goats.* New York: Simon & Schuster. [ P/I ]

Polacco, Patricia (1993). *The bee tree.* New York: Putnam. [ P/I ]

Pomeroy, Diana (1997). *Wildflower ABC.* San Diego: Harcourt Brace. [ P ]

Pomeroy, Diana (1996). *One potato: A counting book of potato prints.* San Diego: Harcourt Brace.[ P ]

Price, Leontyne (1990). Aïda. Illus. by Leo and Diane Dillon. San Diego: Harcourt Brace. [ I/M ]

Rand, Gloria (1996). *Willy takes a walk.* Illus. by Ted Rand. San Diego: Harcourt Brace. [ P ]

Rathmann, Peggy (1995). *Officer Buckle and Gloria.* New York: Putnam. [ P ]

Ray, Mary Lyn (1996). *Mud.* Illus. by Lauren Stringer. San Diego: Harcourt Brace. [ P ]

Ringgold, Faith (1991). *Tar beach.* New York: Crown. [ P/I ]

Rohmann, Eric (1994). *Time flies.* New York: Crown. [ P/I ]

Rotner, Shelley (1997). *Close, closer, closest.* Photos by Richard Olivo. New York: Atheneum. [ P ]

Rylant, Cynthia (1998). *Henry & Mudge and the starry night.* (*Henry & Mudge* series). New York: Greenwillow. [ P/I ]

Rylant, Cynthia (1998). *Mr. Putter and Tabby toot the horn.* (*Mr. Putter and Tabby* series). San Diego: Harcourt Brace. [ P/I ]

Rylant, Cynthia (1998). *Poppleton everyday.* (*Poppleton* series). New York: Blue Sky/Scholastic. [ P/I ]

Sabuda, Robert (1996). *The 12 days of Christmas: A pop-up celebration.* Danbury, CT: Children's Press. [ P/I ]

Sanderson, Ruth (1997). *Snow White and Rose Red.* Boston: Little, Brown. [ P/I ]

San Souci, Robert (1992). *Sukey & the mermaid.* Illus. by Brian Pinkney. New York: Four Winds Press. [ I ]

Say, Allen (1993). *Grandfather's journey.* Boston: Houghton Mifflin. [ I ]

Say, Allen (1996). *Emma's rug.* Boston: Houghton Mifflin. [ P/I ]

Schroeder, Alan (1996). *Satchmo's blues.* Illus. by Floyd Cooper. New York: Doubleday. [ P/I ]

Scieszka, Jon (1992). *The stinky cheese man and other fairly stupid tales.* Illus. by Lane Smith. New York: Viking. [ P/I ]

Shannon, George (1993). *Climbing Kansas mountains.* Illus. by Thomas B. Allen. New York: Bradbury. [ P ]

Shannon, George (1996). *Tomorrow's alphabet.* Illus. by Donald Crews. New York: Greenwillow. [ P ]

Small, David (1996). *Fenwick's suit.* New York: Farrar, Straus and Giroux. [ I ]

Soto, Gary (1995). *Chato's kitchen.* Illus. by Susan Guevara. New York: Putnam. [ P ]

Stanley, Diane & Vennema, Peter (1993). *Charles Dickens: The man who had great expectations.* Illus. by Diane Stanley. New York: Morrow. [ I/M ]

Steig, William (1996). *The toy brother.* New York: HarperCollins. [ P ]

Stevens, Janet (1995). *Tops & bottoms.* San Diego: Harcourt Brace. [ P ]

Stevenson, James (1995). *Sweet corn: Poems.* New York: Greenwillow. [ I ]

Stewart, Sarah (1995). *The library.* Illus. by David Small. New York: Farrar, Straus and Giroux. [ P/I ]

Stroud, Virginia (1996). *The path of the quiet elk: A Native American alphabet book.* New York: Dial. [ I ]

Van Allsburg, Chris (1981). *Jumanji.* Boston: Houghton Mifflin. [ I ]

Van Allsburg, Chris (1984). *The mysteries of Harris Burdick.* Boston: Houghton Mifflin. [ I/M ]

Van Allsburg, Chris (1985). *The Polar Express.* Boston: Houghton Mifflin. [ P/I ]

Van Allsburg, Chris (1993). *The sweetest fig.* Boston: Houghton Mifflin. [ I/M ]

Wiesner, David (1991). *Tuesday.* New York: Clarion. [ I ]

Willard, Barbara (1997). *The magic cornfield.* San Diego: Harcourt Brace. [ I ]

Winnick, Karen (1996). *Mr. Lincoln's whiskers.* Honesdale, PA: Boyds Mills Press. [ I ]

Winter, Jeanette (1996). *Josephina.* San Diego: Harcourt Brace. [ P/I ]

Wisniewski, David (1996). *Golem.* New York: Clarion. [ I/M ]

Wood, Audrey (1996). *Bright and early Thursday evening: A tangled tale.* Illus. by Don Wood. San Diego: Harcourt Brace. [ P/I ]

Wood, Audrey (1996). *The red racer.* New York: Simon & Schuster. [ P ]

Young, Ed (1989). *Lon Po Po: A Red-Riding Hood story from China.* Trans. and illus. by Ed Young. New York: Philomel Books. [ P/I ]

Zelinsky, Paul O. (1997). *Rapunzel.* New York: Dutton. [ P/I ]

## Chapter 4

# Traditional Tales and Modern Fantasy:
## *The Domain of Imagination*

*W*OW! *What is happening? After Hannah opened the door, it was like she was in another world or gone back in time. How could this have happened? I bet she is scared. I must continue to read and find out what is happening!*

*Hannah is in another place at a different time. She is now looking out a door that is not the same door she opened earlier. Why were so many things familiar to Hannah—the phrase, the whistling tune sung by the bearded man, and why were they calling her Chaya? This is really strange.*

*Hannah [Chaya] was in another world. This situation seems all too real to be a dream. Is this a dream? Are Hannah's family playing a trick on her? Is she just passed out from the wine and dreaming all this? Chaya seems very scared and lonely. I feel sorry for her since she has just walked into a Polish village during World War II and she is Jewish.*

*Preservice Teacher Response to* The Devil's
Arithmetic *by Jane Yolen*

Traditional literature and fantasy dwell in the domain of imagination. Whether tales are told by word of mouth or written down for readers to savor, their origin lies in the imagination of those who originally created them. This chapter honors the inspiration of the storyteller whose tales were eventually recorded and the inventive genius of the creator of the fantastic who dreams the impossible, yet causes the reader to linger on the possible.

Traditional tales and fantasy transport the reader to worlds inhabited by talking animals, fairy princesses, and monumental heroes. They introduce the reader to memorable characters from the far corners of the world and issue invitations to embark on heroic quests. Acknowledging the otherworld of this imaginative domain results in a true appreciation of the creative genres of traditional literature and fantasy.

# TRADITIONAL LITERATURE

No one can be sure where and when stories originated. They were carried by the mesmerizing voices of storytellers as they moved from country to country. While interested listeners absorbed the details of each story, new retellers were likely to share their own versions with unique details to suit their own tastes, reflect their own cultures, and reach their own audiences. The oral tradition of communicating these tales from country to country lasted for centuries before the stories were finally recorded in print.

According to Jane Yolen (1981) in *Touch Magic: Fantasy, Faerie, and Folklore in the Literature of Childhood,* folk or traditional literature possesses two major functions. The most basic function is "to provide a landscape of allusion" (p. 15). Beginning with the first story a child hears, he or she builds a repertoire of stories filled with heroes and monsters, heroines and helpers, and even tricksters who manage to outwit even the wisest foes. As children hear more stories and tales, they become linked as their literary landscape is broadened and stretched with memorable characters who form the framework for further literary encounters. "Stories lean on stories" (p. 15) and a growing sense of familiarity is necessary as preparation for appreciating the literature children will encounter in their lifetimes as readers. The second function of folklore is "to provide a way of looking at another culture from the inside out" (p. 16). Superheroes and heroines of today spring from a need within our culture to replicate the glory and strength of characters of the past. Robin Hood, Anansi the spider, Sir Lancelot, and Sweet Betsey from Pike stem from the gods and goddesses of Greek, Roman, and Norse mythology. "Stories lean on stories, culture on cultures" (p. 16). Old stories and honored characters bridge the past and the present while providing the background needed for understanding ongoing encounters with literature.

The historical and cultural heritage of traditional tales is the birthright of children today. Yet traditional tales no longer seem to be an assumed rite of childhood. If children are denied access to the legacy of traditional stories, they will lack the essential literary insights and visions expressed through oral language for hundreds of years. This chapter celebrates the oral and written legacy of the genre of traditional tales and discusses titles that can be shared with children for their enjoyment and response.

Traditional literature includes those stories that originally passed to listeners through the oral tradition of storytelling. They are not attributed to individual authors, but are usually associated with the groups of people or cultures in which they originated. Ted Lewin's *The Storytellers* builds a sense of the oral tradition as words weave stories and stories take flight around the world. Although the oral tradition came first, the act of writing down a story actually performed its own magic on this genre as tales gained permanence through print. Traditional tales include folktales, fairy tales, fables, myths, and legends. This vast heritage of traditional tales finds written expression today in continued retellings that emphasize old values through their modern adaptations, especially in the picture book format. Traditional tales, in this text, also include the modern fairy tale because it echoes the resounding voice from the art of long ago storytelling.

## Characteristics of Traditional Tales

Traditional tales can be divided into different types, but they all possess some commonalities because they were shared orally for centuries.

> Like a kaleidoscope, a folktale is made up of large and small units—motifs—incidents that, like bits of colored glass, are picked up as the tale travels from story to story, from country to country, from culture to culture. Shake up the folktale kaleidoscope, and these motifs arrange themselves in an infinite variety of usable and attractive forms. (Yolen, 1981, p. 17)

The following characteristics of traditional tales reflect the storytelling tradition from which they were generated:

- *Simple story structure.* The beginning quickly identifies the setting and characters and introduces the problem. The middle builds the action through a series of conflicts moving toward a climax. The ending resolves the problem and brings closure to the story. Margaret Hodges' brief retelling of *The Hero of Bremen* tells the simple story of a humble shoemaker who proves himself a hero.
- *One-dimensional characters.* The characters in the stories usually possess a single dominant characteristic, typically good or evil, that makes them easy to identify (handsome prince, wicked stepmother). Jacob, in Eric Kimmel's version of *The Magic Dreidels,* portrays the forces of good, but his naive, impressionable nature makes him susceptible to those who are less than honest.
- *Indistinct settings.* Settings are inexplicit since the tales traveled from country to country. "Once upon a time. . . ." and "Long ago in a far away land. . . ." tend to reflect the secondary nature of setting to the story itself. Ruth Sanderson's *Rose Red & Snow White* is set "in a lonely cottage at the edge of the forest."
- *Succinct language.* Standard beginnings and endings encase simple, patterned motifs, typically in threes. Complicated descriptions are avoided. Repeated chants or refrains economize on total words. The opening line of Ed Young's *Donkey Trouble,* for example, reflects utter simplicity: "There was once a kind and simple man who lived in the desert with his kind and simple grandson" (n.p.).

- *Predictable themes.* Good triumphs over evil, hard work and effort breed success, and brains outwitting brawn encompass themes that are likely to prevail. *Comus,* based on an English fairy tale by John Milton and adapted by Margaret Hodges, tells of bewitchment by a wicked sorcerer, and the ultimate rescue by the heroine's brothers and the good spirits of the forest.
- *Happy endings.* ". . . and they lived happily ever after" keeps the young listener/reader satisfied and motivated to revisit this genre. *The Swan's Gift* retold by Brenda Seabrooke portrays an act of kindness as a swan, whose life is spared, puts food on the table and diamonds in the pocket of a poor farmer.

As these characteristics become familiar to children, they are likely to emerge as a natural part of their oral or written response to traditional tales.

## Types of Traditional Tales

To assist in classifying the wide realm of traditional tales, four groups are identified as a basis for discussion. As teachers introduce traditional literature to their students, they should include examples from each of these traditional literature subgenres. Building a strong foundation across this genre prepares readers for a lifetime of appreciation of literature.

*Folktales.*    Folktales originated from the lives and daily happenings and imaginations of the common folk. They form the most numerous type of traditional tale and one that has remained popular through the centuries. Although all traditional literature might be considered folktales, this category is used to describe several common types of folktales with their identifying characteristics:

- *Cumulative tales.* Based on built-on phrases, these tales encourage children to join in as new lines are added to a repeated refrain. The constant rhythm, simple plot, and humor tend to make this popular fare with the youngest children. Paul Galdone's *The Gingerbread Boy* (1984) invites participation as children quickly learn the repeated refrains. Perhaps the most famous example is *The House That Jack Built* (Stobbs, 1983).
- *Beast tales.* These tales of talking animals with human characteristics are likely to include a competition between animals. Cleverness and sharp wit typically triumph over size and physical prowess. *Pedro and the Monkey* (San Souci, 1996) tells the Puss-in-Boots variant of a farmer in the Philippines irritated by a monkey who stole his corn. After capturing him, the kind-hearted Pedro releases the monkey, and, in return, the monkey promises to arrange for Pedro to marry the daughter of a rich landowner. As the reader wonders how a monkey can accomplish that feat, the storyteller reveals how cleverness leads to fulfillment of a promise.
- *Pourquoi tales.* These tales give unscientific explanations of why things are the way they are in the natural world. The name comes from the French word pronounced "porquah" meaning "why." Lois Duncan's *The Magic of Spider Woman* reveals the reason why the Navajo blanket contains spirit trails which reflect the belief of keeping balance in our lives. Wandering Girl must overcome her passion to create the most beautiful blanket in all the world as Spider Woman shares a lesson with her.

- *Nonsense tales.* These tales focus on a simple-minded character whose lack of common sense leads him or her toward a series of silly mistakes. Also known as noodlehead or numbskull tales, the simpleton often travels through life surviving on luck rather than brains. *Onions and Garlic,* retold by Eric Kimmel, focuses on the youngest of three sons, Getzel, who is too kindhearted to make a good tradesman. When his father gives him a sack of onions to trade, Getzel travels from port to port to no avail. Unwittingly, he becomes shipwrecked and circumstances, rather than business sense, help him make his fortune.
- *Trickster tales.* Often a type of natural creature, the trickster outwits all other creatures in the story. Some tricksters are prankish or crafty, while others are wise and generous in their actions. Bodnar's *A Wagonload of Fish* features the clever fox as the trickster who gets the best of an old man and his greedy wife. Verna Aardema's *Anansi Does the Impossible* challenges Anansi the spider, the ultimate trickster, to enlist the help of his wife to buy back folktales from the sun. They must produce a live python, a real fairy, and 47 stinging hornets, a feat only a trickster can perform. Virginia Hamilton gathers an entire array of these cunning characters in *A Ring of Tricksters: Animal Tales from America, the West Indies, and Africa.*

Because traditional tales, including folktales, have their origin in the oral tradition, they were carried by word of mouth to the far corners of the world. Different versions of traditional tales span the globe and deserve recognition. Figure 4.1 shares only a sampling of recently published traditional tales from around the world. They span continents and cultures, but all have one commonality—they tell a good story. Whether read aloud or retold in the voice of the storyteller, these tales not only bring the traditional tale genre to children, they bring the world to readers as well.

***Fairy tales.*** Often identified as a type of magical folktale, the fairy tale contains dominant elements of magic and enchantment. Although often placed in the genre of modern fantasy, they are included here as a type of folktale because they are commonly told through storytelling. Recent interest in fairy-tale variants has renewed interest in this subgenre in elementary classrooms.

While shouldering an honored role in literary history, fairy tales maintain a unique place in child development. Bruno Bettleheim (1977) has long supported the role of fairy tales in satisfying emotional needs. In *The Uses of Enchantment,* he analyzes several tales in detail to relate how they enable children to cope with the reality of their emotions in their world. The fine line and personal connections between fairy tales and reality has been further explored by Favat (1977) who parallels components of fairy tales and the concepts of reality in 6- through 8-year-olds, a peak period of interest in these tales.

Fairy tales are typically the realm of elves, fairies, witches, wizards, magicians, and fairy godmothers. Magical objects touch their hands in the forms of wands, branches, or pixie dust. Transformations and spells of enchantment dominate their plots as princes turn into frogs and princesses fall into timeless sleep. These tales of magic, wonder, and the supernatural capture young children's attention as they are carried into a world of towering castles, talking mirrors, glass slippers, and magical beans. The imaginative and dreamlike qualities of fairy tales and the illusions made to them in everyday life identify them as an essential part of a child's literary background.

**FIGURE 4.1**   Folktales from around the world.

---

### Africa

Aardema, Verna (1996). *The lonely lioness and the ostrich chicks.* Illus. by Yumi Heo. New York: Knopf. (Masai tale) [ P ]

Berry, James (1996). *Don't leave an elephant to go and chase a bird.* Illus. by A. Grifalconi. New York: Simon & Schuster. (Ghana, Trickster tale) [ P/I ]

Davol, Marguerite (1996). *How snake got his hiss.* Illus. by M. McDonald. New York: Orchard Books. [ P ]

McDermott, Gerald (1992). *Zomo the rabbit: A trickster tale from West Africa.* San Diego: Harcourt Brace. [ P/I ]

### Australia/New Zealand

Bishop, Gavin (1996). *Maui and the sun: A Maori tale.* New York: North-South Books. (Trickster tale) [ P/I ]

### China

Chang, Margaret, & Chang, Raymond (1997). *The beggar's magic.* Illus. by D. Johnson. New York: McElderry Books. [ P/I ]

Demi (1990). *The empty pot.* New York: Holt. [ I ]

San Souci, Robert D. (1998). *Fa Mulan.* Illus. by Jean & Mou-Sien Tseng. New York: Hyperion. [ I ]

Tompert, Ann (1996). *The jade horse: The cricket and the peach stone.* Illus. by W. Trang. Honesdale, PA: Boyds Mills Press. [ P/I ]

Yep, Laurence (1997). *The Khan's daughter: A Mongolian folktale.* Illus. by J. & M. Tseng. New York: Scholastic. [ I ]

### Japan

Bodkin, Odds (1998). *The crane wife.* Illus. by G. Spirin. San Diego: Gulliver/Harcourt Brace. [ P/I ]

Johnston, Tony (1990). *The badger and the magic fan: A Japanese folktale.* Illus. by T. de Paola. New York: Putnam. [ P ]

Paterson, Katherine (1990). *The tale of the Mandarin ducks.* Illus. by L. & D. Dillon. New York: Lodestar. [ I ]

### India

Martin, Rafe (1998). *The brave little parrot.* Illus. by Susan Garber. New York: Putnam. [ P ]

Martin, Rafe (1985). *Foolish rabbit's big mistake.* Illus. by Ed Young. New York: Putnam. [ P ]

### Europe

Hodges, Margaret (1996). *Molly Limbo.* Illus. by E. Miles. New York: Atheneum. (Scotland) [ P/I ]

MacGill-Callahan, Sheila (1993). *The children of Lir.* Illus. by G. Spirin. New York: Dial. (Wales) [ P ]

Stewig, John W. (1991). *Stone soup.* Illus. by Margot Tomes. New York: Holiday House. (France) [ P ]

Sturges, Philemon, & Vojtech, Anna (1996). *Marushka and the month brothers.* Illus. by A. Vojtech. New York: North-South Books. (Czechoslovakia) [ P/I ]

**FIGURE 4.1**    Folktales from around the world. *(continued)*

## Russia

Johnson, Paul B. (1998). *A perfect pork stew.* New York: Orchard Books. (Baba Yaga tale) [ P ]
Kherdian, D. (1998). *The golden bracelet.* Illus. by N. Hogrogian. Toronto: Holiday House. [ I ]
Lottridge, Celia B. (1998). *Music for the Tsar of the sea.* Illus. by H. Chan. Toronto:
        Groundwood/Douglas & McIntyre. [ I ]
Polacco, Patricia (1993). *Babushka Baba Yaga.* New York: Philomel Books. [ P/I ]
San Souci, Robert D. (1998). *A weave of words.* Illus. by R. Colon. New York: Orchard Books.
        (Armenia) [ I ]

## Caribbean

Ada, Alma Flor (1993). *The rooster who went to his uncle's wedding.* Illus. by K. Kuchera. New York:
        Putnam. (Cuba) [ P ]
Hausman, Gerald (1998). *Doctor bird: Three lookin' up tales from Jamaica.* Illus. by A. Wolff. New
        York: Philomel Books. [ P/I ]
Jaffe, Nina (1996). *The golden flower: A Taino myth from Puerto Rico.* Illus. by E. Sanchez. New York:
        Simon & Schuster. [ P/I ]

## Mexico

Gollub, Matthew (1996). *Uncle snake.* Illus. by L. Martinez. New York: Tambourine/Morrow. (Porquoi)
        [ P/I ]
McDermott, Gerald (1997). *Musicians of the sun.* New York: Simon & Schuster. [ P/I ]

## Collective Cultures

Doherty, Berlie (1998). *Tales of wonder and magic.* Illus. by J. Wijngaard. Cambridge, MA:
        Candlewick Press. [ I/M ]
Walker, Paul R. (1997). *Little folk: Stories from around the world.* Illus. by J. Bernardin. San Diego:
        Harcourt Brace. [ I ]
See Chapter 8, Multicultural Literature, for examples of traditional tales of the African American,
Native American, Asian American, and Hispanic American cultures.

Retellings of popular fairy tales have created masterpieces of storytelling and illustration in recent years. Paul Zelinsky's (1997) Caldecott award-winning retelling of *Rapunzel* is a tribute to the importance of well-told tales in the literary lives of children. Drawing on elements from early French and Italian art, Zelinsky blends stunning oil paintings with a powerfully written version of this Grimm fairy tale. Zelinsky previously blended retelling and art successfully in *Rumpelstiltskin* (1986) and teamed with Rika Lesser for a retelling of *Hansel and Gretel* (1984). Trina Schart Hyman has also resurrected traditional fairy tales in inviting realistic formats through *Little Red Riding Hood* (1983), while Jan Brett eloquently portrayed *Beauty and the Beast* (1989) through her fine detailed drawings.

The imaginative and dreamlike qualities of fairy tales make them an essential part of a literary background.
*From* RAPUNZEL *by Paul O. Zelinsky. Copyright © 1997 by Paul O. Zelinsky. Used by permission of Dutton Children's Books, a division of Penguin Putnam Inc.*

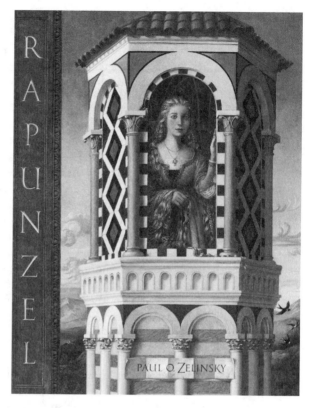

Several fairy tales have been expanded to full-length chapter book formats with great appeal to older readers. Robin McKinley's *Beauty: A Retelling of the Story of Beauty and the Beast* (1978) captures the essence of love. Just as in the original version, Beauty's growing admiration for the beast releases him from the spell and turns him into a handsome prince. Almost 20 years after the success of *Beauty,* the author has created *Rose Daughter* (1997), a captivating, fresh retelling of the same tale. Donna Napoli's *Zel* (1996) extends the Rapunzel story through the alternating voices of Rapunzel, her mother, and the prince while revealing the psychological motivations of the characters. On a lighter note, Gail Levine's *Ella Enchanted* (1997), a Newbery honor book, introduces Ella of Frell who struggles against a childhood curse that forces her to obey any order she receives. This refreshing version of Cinderella preserves its fairy-tale magic while adding ample humor in the guise of an intelligent, assertive heroine.

Fairy-tale variants are modern fairy tales that are slight alterations of original tales and provide a different perspective through character, details, setting, or ending. Jon Scieszka's groundbreaking point-of-view variant called *The True Story of the Three Little Pigs* is told from the perspective of A. Wolf. *The Frog Prince Continued . . .* provides the sequel to the marriage of the ex-frog prince to his princess and the ensuing problems in their less than perfect life. *The Tale of Little Red Riding Hood: A Newfangled Prairie Tale* changes the forest setting to the open prairie as an unsuspecting wolf encounters a liberated, feisty, tractor-driving grandma. New versions of traditional fairy tales abound as Charlotte Huck portrays *Princess Furball* as an independent, problem-solving Cinderella, and Renee proves to be a resourceful character of her own in the kind–unkind sister tale of *Toads and Diamonds.* Chapter 11 discusses in detail how these fairy tales can become a springboard for response-related writing activities.

***Fables.***     Fables tell a simple story that teaches a moral lesson or emphasizes a universal truth. Animal characters carry the action of these brief tales with the moral commonly stated at the tale's end. Aesop's fables are the best known collection of fables in the world with Arnold Lobel's award-winning *Fables* providing an outstanding format for younger children. Ed Young's *Seven Blind Mice* also provides a colorful means to introduce fables to students. *Androcles and the Lion,* retold by Dennis Nolan, conveys the timeless story of helping those in need and the value of friendship. Demi's *The Dragon's Tale and Other Animal Fables of the Chinese Zodiac* portrays universal truths through morals like "The more you know, the more you know there is to know." Paul Rosenthal's *Yo, Aesop! Get a Load of These Fables* and Jon Scieszka and Lane Smith's *Squids Will Be Squids: Fresh Morals, Beastly Tales,* on the other hand, provide a lighthearted, updated approach to these traditional bits of Aesop's wisdom. All maintain the essence of lessons to be learned and applied to life.

***Myths.***     Myths are stories that explain the origins of the world and its natural phenomena. Similar to pourquoi tales, myths feature Roman, Greek, or Norse gods and goddesses who control human fate from a heaven-like setting. Myths that are collected and ordered logically present a mythology of the entire universe. Because myths seem more abstract, they are generally popular with upper elementary students. Myths also encompass cultural creation tales as evidenced by Virginia Hamilton's *In the Beginning: Creation Stories from Around the World.* Creation tales depict the struggle to form the earth from darkness and chaos.

Anne Rockwell's *The One-Eyed Giant and Other Monsters from the Greek Myths* shares the ever popular myths of the Cyclops, Medusa, the Minotaur, and Sylla. *Favorite Norse Myths* retold by Mary Pope Osborne include "How Thor Got His Hammer" and "The Golden Apples." *The Illustrated Book of Myths: Tales and Legends of the World* retold by Neil Philip shares tales from around the globe with timeless universal stories that form our literary heritage. Many of these tales are accumulated in collections and are most appropriately shared with intermediate grade and middle-school students.

***Legends.***     Legends share the stories of extraordinary deeds accomplished by real or supposedly real heroes and heroines. Legends describe the daring feats of a person of lowly status whose good deeds or heroic quest is eventually rewarded with a high position. Heroes or heroines are often accompanied by a wise mentor who directs or guides them through unexpected challenges. Although their journey may be entered with trepidation, their self-determination and inner confidence allows these heroes and heroines to succeed. *Robin of*

*Sherwood* (Morpurgo, 1996), *Excaliber* (Talbott, 1996), *The Wanderings of Odysseus* (Sutcliff, 1995), and *Gawain and the Green Knight* (Shannon, 1994) are a few examples of legends that span time and settings.

Tall tales are legends in which seemingly common people with exaggerated character traits accomplish unbelievable tasks. American tall tale heroes parallel our country's historical expansion and include *Pecos Bill* (Kellogg, 1986) the Texas cowboy, and the tale of Paul Bunyan and his entire family told in *The Bunyans* (Wood, 1996). Margaret Hodges and Kim Root team to present Americana through *The True Tale of Johnny Appleseed*. Tall tale heroines have gained notice and might include *The Heroine of the Titanic: A Tale Both True and Otherwise of the Life of Molly Brown* (Blos, 1991) or *Sally Ann Thunder Ann Whirlwind Crockett* (Kellogg, 1995).

## Guidelines for Evaluating Traditional Tales

The following expectations for quality traditional literature assist in evaluating and selecting books from this wide-ranged literary genre.

- The story should be appropriate to the developmental age of the children who will read and enjoy it.
- The oral storytelling style of the original tale should be preserved in the book retelling as evidenced in an oral read-aloud.
- The integrity of the original culture of the tale should be retained through authentic names, cultural terminology, and cultural authenticity of language elements.
- The illustrated versions of traditional tales should be of high quality and provide assistance in interpreting story, plot, characters, and theme.

When these standards are applied to Walter Dean Myers's *How Mr. Monkey Saw the Whole World*, a beast tale, we see a traditional tale suited for an introduction to the folktale genre for young children. The writing begs to be delivered through an oral read-aloud in a storytelling voice. The illustrations by Synthia Saint James are bright, simple, and focus on story characters and events. The tale shares a special trick that Mr. Monkey has in mind for the ruthless, cold-hearted Mr. Buzzard. The tale exemplifies the enjoyment of the oral sharing of traditional tales with young children. Spontaneous responses include cheering, booing, and satisfaction with the outcome.

## Values of Traditional Tales

Traditional tales have been handed down through the oral tradition for centuries, yet they retain their ability to entertain their audience. During this time of growing cultural diversity, traditional tales serve important purposes in the lives of children.

- Traditional tales carry on the strong oral tradition of storytelling.
- Traditional tales provide an important introduction to simple story structure as repeated readings contribute to comfort and confidence through the predictable nature of the tales.
- Traditional tales provide a resource for classroom storytelling by teachers or retellings by children.

- Traditional tales provide an added dimension to a child's cultural literacy as she or he experiences tales from around the world.
- Traditional tales provide moral models for children as the struggle between good and evil is applied to incidents in their own lives.

## Reader Response to Traditional Tales

Reader response connections to traditional literature hold a wide range of possibilities because of the broadness of this literary genre. Traditional literature begs to be shared through retellings or storytelling with older children. The familiarity of plot and dialogue often assist in puppet presentations or dramatic improvisations. Children often respond to the moral themes of these tales as evidenced in both oral and written response. Fairy-tale variants, in particular, serve as springboards to ideas for writing one's own variant by changing a single aspect of the story—character, setting, ending. Tall tales and myths are also enthusiastically embraced as models for writing in these particular formats.

Mostly, however, children respond to good stories. Children love repeating the memorable lines of the characters in imitative voices. They readily share their favorite characters, how they would have approached a problem, or their opinions on the outcomes. Teachers should allow time before, during, and after reading for voices to surface. Traditional tales do not require prompting, just freedom to respond naturally and spontaneously.

Traditional tales provide a background of the oral heritage of literature that should become a part of a child's literary repertoire. An abundance of quality picture books originated from a variety of cultures and shared over a variety of times supplies the reader with extensive access to this literary genre. While initiation to this genre generally occurs in the home setting, teachers must be certain that children have opportunities to listen to, retell, and internalize these oral treasures in the school setting. The fairy tales, Greek myths, and tall tales we read as children are seldom forgotten. Often reread, powerfully retold, and always cherished, traditional literature holds a special place in a child's literary experience.

# MODERN FANTASY

Modern fantasy is characterized by a single element or set of complex elements that only exist in the imagination. The imaginary element provides the bridge that separates fantasy from realism. Fantasy suspends the reader's belief as he or she enters a new world or accepts a scientific impossibility in our own world. The conceptualization of fantasy reveals author ingenuity as imaginary settings, magical dimensions, and heroes and heroines possessing incredible powers compel the reader to transcend reality and willingly partake of a fanciful tale. Great fantasies can even reveal new insights into the world of reality.

In Jane Yolen's (1997) introduction to her recent collection of fanciful short stories, *Twelve Impossible Things Before Breakfast,* she shares her experience with fantasy writing.

> You fill the tale with creatures or people who never existed, or you take a spin on stories that are well-known and loved. And all the while you talk about the fantastic, you are actually writing about the real world and real emotions, the right-here and the right-now. It is a kind of literary displacement, a way of looking at what worries both writer and reader by glancing out of the corner of one's eye. (p. x)

Fantasy describes books in which magic causes impossible and wondrous events to occur. Fantasy tales can be set in our own everyday world or in a "secondary world" somewhat like our own. The existence of the magic cannot be explained, but certainly can be savored. The narrative storytelling of the fantasy genre is magical in its ability to enchant readers and draw them past the boundaries of the reality of their world and into the inexplicable magic of another. Fantasy, however, does not escape reality, but illuminates it by transporting readers to a world different from their own while demonstrating truths that persist in both worlds. Lynn (1995) describes fantasy as "imaginative, fanciful, visionary, strange, otherworldly, supernatural, mysterious, frightening, magical, inexplicable, wondrous, dreamlike, and, paradoxically, realistic" (p. xxv). A natural yearning for a sudden glimpse of something strange and different may lead the reader to a truer sense of reality.

Through the years, fantasy has played a vital role in popular children's literature. While E. B. White's *Charlotte's Web* transported the reader into the world of talking animals, Natalie Babbit's *Tuck Everlasting* caused deliberation on the consequences of eternal life. J. R. R. Tolkein's *The Hobbit* enthralled the reader with Bilbo Baggins and an introduction to the world of Middle Earth, while Lloyd Alexander transported participants to Taran and five incredible chronicles of the pigkeeper turned hero in *The Book of Three*. Some of the most memorable books from childhood are fantasies often read aloud by teacher or parents: *Alice's Adventures in Wonderland, The Wind in the Willows, James and the Giant Peach.* Once introduced to the realm of fantasy, children are likely to approach this genre with anticipation and excitement.

## Types of Fantasy

Important variations exist among the different types of fantasy that make subgenre classification both challenging and valuable. The breadth of the fantasy genre is intriguing as imagination enters the world of people, places, situations, and things. Because most fantasies are continuing quests or adventures, the trend in the fantasy genre has been to produce books as a trilogy, quartet, or series that follows a character through many adventures in a distinctive secondary imaginative world of magic. Figure 4.2 lists and elaborates on many fantasy series books, old and new, that will motivate children to become engaged in fantasy books.

While most of their titles are high fantasy, they also include animal fantasy and toy fantasy, two of the fantasy types discussed in this section. Because this is a genre often unfamiliar to or forgotten by unimaginative adults, it becomes even more important for them to build their own awareness of books in this genre.

*Animal fantasy.* Perhaps the most popular read-alouds from the fantasy genre, animal fantasies showcase animals who possess human qualities in addition to their natural characteristics. They are personified with human emotions, they reason through complex situations, and they communicate with other animals. Famous stars of rodent fantasies, for example, include Beverly Cleary's adventurous *Ralph S. Mouse,* E. B. White's diminutive *Stuart Little,* Robert O'Brien's Widowed *Mrs. Frisby,* courageous Miss Bianca in Margery Sharp's *The Rescuers,* and the melodramatic survivor in William Steig's *Abel's Island.* These endearing creatures possess humanitarian ideals and engage in challenging encounters in a

**FIGURE 4.2**    Fantasy series books.

---

### REDWALL SAGA by Brian Jacques. New York: Putnam. [ M ]

(1987). *Redwall.* Matthias Mouse defends Redwall Abbey from rats with plans to enslave mice.

(1988). *Mossflower.* (Prequel) Martin the Warrior battles wildcat Tsarmina for peace in the Woodlands.

(1990). *Mattimeo.* Matthias's son, enslaved by a Fox, is rescued by father while mother saves the Abbey.

(1992). *Mariel of Redwall.* The daughter of Joseph the bellmaker becomes a warrior in quest of Gabool.

(1993). *Salamandastron.* Martin's sword is stolen and the Castle is attacked by Ferahgo the Assassin.

Additional titles in this series include *Martin the Warrior* (1994), *The Bellmaker* (1995), *Outcast of Redwall* (1996), *The Long Patrol* (1997), *The Pearls of Lutra* (1997).

### THE CHRONICLES OF PRYDIAN by Lloyd Alexander. New York: Holt. [ I/M ]

(1964). *The Book of Three.* Taran, a young pigkeeper, and Gwydion, a warrior, battle the Horned King.

(1965). *The Black Cauldron.* Taran and Gwydion plan to destroy the black cauldron of the Lord of the Land of Death. (Newbery Honor book)

(1966). *The Castle of Llyr.* Taran and Gwydion rescue Princess Eilonwy, who has been kidnapped by the wicked steward.

(1967). *Taran Wanderer.* Taran, grown to a young man, journeys through Prydian seeking his identity.

(1968). *The High King.* The final struggle of the people of Prydian against the Lord of the Land of Death. (Newbery Medal, 1969)

### WESTMARK TRILOGY by Lloyd Alexander. New York: Dutton. [ I/M ]

(1981). *Westmark.* Theo and Mickle turn the tables on Cabbarus, the king's evil minister, when he tries to gain control of the throne.

(1982). *The Kestrel.* Theo becomes a blood-thirsty warrior defending his love, Queen Mickle of Westmark.

(1984). *The Beggar Queen.* Westmark is overthrown by ex-minister Cabbarus, forcing a resistance movement.

### THE DARK IS RISING SEQUENCE by Susan Cooper. New York: Macmillan/Atheneum. [ I/M ]

(1965). *Over Sea, Under Stone.* Simon, Jane, and Barney Drew set out to find King Arthur's grail.

(1973). *The Dark Is Rising.* Will Stanton travels into the past in search of six magic signs to hold back the forces of Darkness. (Newbery Honor book, 1974)

(1974). *Greenwich.* The sea creature holds the manuscript needed to interpret the inscription on the grail.

**FIGURE 4.2** Fantasy series books. *(continued)*

(1975). *The Grey King.* Will and Bran Davies search for the golden harp to waken King Arthur's knights. (Newbery Medal, 1976)

(1977). *Silver on the Tree.* Five children are summoned to Walse to search for the crystal sword while the Drews and King Arthur prepare for the ultimate battle against the Darkness.

**EARTHSEA QUARTET by Ursula LeGuin. New York: Parnassus/Atheneum. [ M ]**

(1968). *A Wizard of Earthsea.* Ged, studying wizardry, accidentally conjures up a terrifying creature that threatens the existence of the world of Earthsea.

(1971). *The Tombs of Atuan.* Ged invades the forbidden labyrinth of Atuan, forcing Tenar to make a choice. (Newbery Honor book, 1972)

(1972). *The Farthest Shore.* Ged and Prince Arren make a journey into the Shadow Kingdom of the dead.

(1990). *Tehanu: The Last Book of Earthsea.* Tenar heals both an abused child and Ged, who lost his magical powers in a struggle to save the world.

**THE CHRONICLES OF NARNIA by C. S. Lewis. New York: Macmillan. (Suggested reading order) [ I ]**

(1955). *The Magician's Nephew.* Digory and Polly borrow an uncle's magic rings and are transported to Narnia, just as Aslan is singing it into existence.

(1951). *The Lion, the Witch, and the Wardrobe.* Many years later, four children stumble through a magic wardrobe into Narnia where they struggle to break the White Witch's enchantment.

(1954). *The Horse and His Boy.* Shasta and Aravis and their talking horses flee into Narnia.

(1951). *Prince Caspian: The Return to Narnia.* The four children help Aslan restore Prince Caspian's throne.

(1952). *The Voyage of the Dawn Treader.* Sailing to World's End in search of seven missing noblemen.

(1953). *The Silver Chair.* Aslan sends Eustace and Jill on a quest to free Prince Rilian.

(1956). *The Last Battle.* Aslan calls all creatures who love Narnia to battle against the forces of evil.

**THE HARPER-HALL TRILOGY by Anne McCaffrey. New York: Macmillan. [ M ]**

(1976). *Dragonsong.* Menolly runs away and makes her home with a family of fire dragons.

(1977). *Dragonsinger.* Menolly struggles through Harper training while caring for her brood of fire dragons.

(1979). *Dragondrums.* Piemer, friend of Menolly, is trained as a drummer and sent on a mysterious journey.

**DAMAR SERIES by Robin McKinley. New York: Greenwillow Books. [ M ]**

(1982). *The Blue Sword.* Harry Crewe is kidnapped by Corlath, King of the Damarians, and realizes they possess the same mysterious powers. (Newbery Honor book, 1983)

(1984). *The Hero and the Crown.* (Prequel) Princess Aerin becomes a dragonslayer fulfilling her destiny. (Newbery Medal, 1985)

(1994). *A Knot in the Grain and Other Stories.* Four stories set in the world of Damar.

**FIGURE 4.2**   Fantasy series books. *(concluded)*

---

**HIS DARK MATERIALS TRILOGY by Philip Pullman. New York: Knopf. [ I/M ]**

(1996). *The Golden Compass.* Lyra Belacqua, accompanied by her daemon, Pantalaimon, sets out to prevent gruesome scientific experiments on children in the Far North.

(1997). *The Subtle Knife.* Lyra and her daemon help Will Parry in his search for his father and a magic knife.

(1999). *The Amber Spyglass.* Lyra and an intriguing cast of characters bring a startling resolution to their quest.

**LORD OF THE RINGS TRILOGY by J. R. R. Tolkein. Boston: Houghton Mifflin. [ I/M ]**

(1965). *The Fellowship of the Ring.* Frodo Baggins inherits a magic ring from Uncle Bilbo and begins a journey to protect it from the powers of evil. Set in Middle Earth.

(1965). *The Two Towers.* Frodo and Sam take the ring to the borders of the Dark Kingdom while the Company of the Ring battle the wizard Saruman and his goblin army.

(1965). *The Return of the King.* Frodo and Sam bring the ring to Mount Doom where it is destroyed to help the forces of good win over the Dark Lord.

**ENCHANTED FOREST CHRONICLES by Patricia C. Wrede. San Diego: Harcourt Brace. [ I ]**

(1991). *Dealing with Dragons.* Princess Cimorene, vowing to be eaten by a dragon rather than act the role of proper princess, volunteers to be captured by the powerful dragon Kazul.

(1991). *Searching for Dragons.* Cimorene and King Morwen set off on a flying carpet in search of Kazul.

(1993). *Calling on Dragons.* Queen Cimorene sets out to retrieve a stolen magic sword.

(1993). *Talking to Dragons.* Set 16 years later, Cimorene's son, Daystar, faces wizards and monsters as he tries to rescue his father.

**YOUNG MERLIN TRILOGY by Jane Yolen. San Diego: Harcourt Brace. [ I ]**

(1996). *Passager.* An 8-year-old is abandoned in the woods of England until a falconer captures and trains him.

(1996). *Hobby.* Young Merlin's adopted family dies in a fire, and he finds himself in a band of traveling performers. Renaming him Hobby, he is exploited for his talent for dreaming the future.

(1997). *Merlin.* Merlin falls into the hands of the wodewose only to have his dreaming mark him as an outcast—yet one who is predicted to be king.

---

quest for a better life for themselves or their owners. In its most effective form, animal fantasy permits the reader to view life through the eyes of an animal while gaining a clearer perspective on one's own values.

Most recently, *Poppy* epitomizes the strengths of the animal fantasy as Avi skillfully humanizes the deer mouse heroine who is forced to confront Mr. Ocax, a bully owl, who claims

Animal fantasy invites the reader to view reality through the eyes of a personified creature.
*From* Poppy *by Avi. Illustrated by Brian Floca. Illustration copyright © 1995 by Brian Floca. Reprinted by permission of the publisher, Orchard Books, New York.*

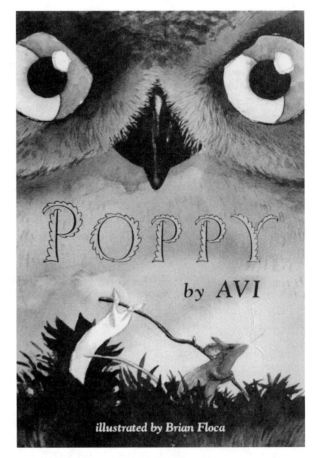

that he alone protects the mouse community from porcupines. Poppy reflects the best of both animal and human world as she embarks alone on a dangerous quest because her family is in danger of starving if they don't relocate to a home with a more plentiful food supply. Braving the forbidden woods, Poppy meets Ereth, the porcupine, who helps her understand the great horned owl's motives and fears. Eventually Poppy learns that porcupines never eat mice, battles Mr. Ocax, and enables her mouse family to move to the cornfields. The reader realizes that independence and courage win out over the oppressor, making a safer community for all. The popularity of this character has led to its sequel, *Poppy and Rye.* Poppy, mouse heroine, mourns the death of her fiancee, Ragweed, while discovering more flooding caused by dam building in her once serene woodland home. Poppy and Ragweed's younger brother, Rye, work side by side to battle the beavers. These quality read-alouds in primary classrooms serve as a strong introduction to the fantasy genre.

An extremely popular series of animal fantasy is the Redwall Saga series by Brian Jacques. In *Redwall* (1987) Matthias Mouse defends Redwall Abbey against marauding rats bent on enslaving the peaceful mice in residence there. Prequels and sequels (see Figure 4.2) engage other rodent heroes and heroines in bravely fought battles against animal foes. Other classic animal fantasies that deserve special recognition include Dick King-Smith's *Babe: The Gallant Pig*, Robert Lawson's *Rabbit Hill* and Robert O'Brien's Newbery award winner *Mrs. Frisby and the Rats of NIHM*. Traditionally, these titles have served as an invitation to the broader world of fantasy literature.

***Humorous fantasy.***     Talented authors introduce readers to humorous and exaggerated tales, including those with fast-paced, comedic plots, bizarre characters, and amusing incidents. Roald Dahl, a master of humorous fantasy, introduces the *BFG* (big friendly giant) who kidnaps Sophie and delivers her to Giant Country where "human beans" provide a steady diet for the inhabitants. In *Matilda,* Dahl introduces a brilliant first grader who triumphs over her parents and Miss Trunchbull, the school principal. Sid Fleischman's *By the Great Horn Spoon* and *Mr. Mysterious and Company* and several titles by Margaret Mahy and Daniel Pinkwater bring a smile to new fans of the funny side of fantasy. J. K. Rowling's enthralling *Harry Potter and the Sorcerer's Stone* promises to reignite reader interest in the fantasy genre.

***Magic adventure and toy fantasy.***     Fantasy can transport the reader to a world of strange happenings in which unearthly wonders surprise and delight. Imagine a world in which toys come to life, miniature people go about their daily lives, and strange occurrences confront the imagination. Memorable members of this extraordinary group of literary characters include Carolyn Bailey's *Miss Hickory,* a country doll with an applewood twig body and hickory nut head, Susan Cooper's ancient and mischievous Scottish spirit named *The Boggart,* Mary Norton's diminutive *Borrowers* and Sylvia Waugh's family of life-sized cloth and kapok rag dolls in *Mennyms Alone.*

A current popular series in this fantasy subgenre is the Magic Shop books by Bruce Coville. A magical ring (*The Monster's Ring*), a dragon's egg (*Jeremy Thatcher, Dragon Hatcher*), a talking amphibian (*Jennifer Murdley's Toad*), and a mysterious skull (*The Skull of Truth*) have lured many intermediate readers to the fantasy genre. Lynne Reid Banks's *The Indian in the Cupboard* follows the transformation of Patrick and Omri's toy cowboy and Indian into miniature people named Boone and Little Bear. Criticized for its stereotypical representation of Native American characters, the series continues through the French and Indian Wars (*The Return of the Indian*), the Old West (*The Secret of the Indian*), and tragic family history (*The Mystery of the Cupboard*). Nominated consistently for children's choice awards, these series provide yet another tempting invitation into the fantasy genre.

***Ghost fantasy.***     The world of the supernatural encompasses ghosts, mystery, and unexplainable happenings. A popular author of the supernatural world is Mary Downing Hahn whose books are consistently nominated and honored on children's choice lists. Her books take the reader to the borders of the supernatural in *The Doll in the Garden* and *A Time for Andrew.* Betty Ren Wright's *The Ghosts of Mercy Manor, The Ghost of Popcorn Hill,* and *A Ghost in the House* share similar popularity. Although ghost fantasy is popular reading, it is important to steer children toward quality selections. These mildly chilling stories do not include horror and often contain amusing rather than horrifying elements.

Other authors/titles of ghost fantasy include Eleanor Cameron's *The Court of the Stone Children* which finds the ghost of a 19th-century French girl whose father was executed for treason begging Nina Harmsworth to help prove his innocence. With a touch of ghostly humor, Sid Fleischman's *The Midnight Horse* introduces Touch and his ghostly friend, the Great Chuffalo, who work together to foil the dastardly deeds of Judge Henry Wigglesforth. Tales of ghosts and the supernatural fascinate readers of all ages. With scrutiny in selection, these titles can appeal to both intermediate and middle-level readers.

***Time travel fantasy.*** Time shift fantasy is based on characters who readily shift from a particular moment in the present to a point in someone else's past. Characters begin a story in their own safe world, yet find themselves instantly transported to another time having changed places with an individual from the period. The new place can be a parallel universe, existing at the same time, or a historical world, dispatching them to a situation from the past.

Primary-level readers can "get hooked" on time travel through Mary Pope Osborne's Magic Tree House series. Young readers are instantly transported to the Middle Ages, Egypt, the Ice Age, feudal Japan, Pompeii, or ancient China through brief, easy-to-read time travel fantasy. In Jon Scieszka's humorous Time Warp Trio, series (*The Good, the Bad & the Goofy; Knights of the Kitchen Table; The Not-So-Jolly Roger*) Joe, Fred, and Sam travel through time using a magic book given to Joe by his magician uncle. Easy-to-read humor makes these a popular choice as children grow into full-length chapter book time travel.

Dan Gutman's *Honus and Me: A Baseball Card Adventure* follows Joe Stoshack from a baseball card he finds in Miss Young's attic through time to the early 1900s to join baseball great Honus Wagner. Interspersed with authentic photographs and newspaper clippings, this time travel book draws a commendable fine line between fantasy and realism. Janet Lunn's *The Root Cellar* finds Rose opening a vine-covered root cellar door to enter the Civil War era, 100 years in the past. The strength and determination she requires during this trying time serve her well on her return to the present. Opening the door as a symbol of the Passover Seder steals Hannah away to a Polish village during the Holocaust of the 1940s in Jane Yolen's *The Devil's Arithmetic* (see opening journal reflection). Other noteworthy time travel fantasies include Peni Griffin's *Switching Well*, Pam Conrad's *Stonewords*, and Jan Slepian's *Back to Before*. Although time travel fantasy titles often cross the line toward the historical fiction genre, they do possess the identifying characteristic of travel across time with a return, enriched and informed, to the present.

***High fantasy.*** Heroic, dramatic quests are the hallmark of the popular high fantasy as readers are transported to secondary worlds with names like Narnia, Earthsea, or Prydain. These secondary worlds are close enough to reality to allow identification, yet far enough away to suspend reader belief. The main characters of high fantasy often possess lofty ideals and noble codes of honor that assist them on their searches and challenging missions. Their complex plots provide a formidable task for readers as heroes weave their way through intricate adventures against formidable foes. The never-ending battle between good and evil also forces the reader to confront philosophical truths along the adventurous journey.

The adventures of high fantasy often continue through several volumes (see Figure 4.2). The roots of high fantasy trace back to L. Frank Baum's 14 titles of The Wizard of Oz (1900) series (extended to 53 by additional authors), thus providing a century of high fantasy to children. Once a reader finds an adventure to follow, his or her imagination is fed through several sequential titles. The Narnia Chronicles of C. S. Lewis, for example, contain seven books while Lloyd Alexander's Prydain Chronicles number five. Once aware of high fantasy, readers easily look to new fantasy titles like Philip Pullman's *The Golden Compass* and *The Subtle Knife* and favorite authors like Anne McCaffrey or Robin McKinley (see Figure 4.2).

***Science fantasy.***    Set in a future world, science fantasy balances scientific fact and probabilities with fiction. Such books often raise questions about the future, causing readers to reflect on the direction of their values and their world. Historically, this subgenre has been graced with titles including Madeline L'Engle's *A Wrinkle in Time* and John Christopher's White Mountain quartet, often referred to as science fiction. With an increasing emphasis on story over scientific fact, the term *science fantasy* seems more appropriate for children's literature.

Science fantasy recently gained momentum and respect as a subgenre of fantasy with the publication of Lois Lowry's *The Giver,* winner of the 1994 Newbery Medal. Jonas lives in a seemingly idyllic, peaceful world as he awaits the Ceremony of the Twelve during which he will be assigned his life's work. His role as Receiver of the Memory designates him not only the keeper of events, but of feelings as well. Jonas comes to understand the fullness of human experience with its pain, joy, and color through the current Giver. Beginning to question the orderliness of his own existence and the price humanity has paid for a tranquil life, Jonas escapes with Gabriel, a foster child, and begins a journey that may result in his demise or return him to his lost humanity. While Jonas's people lacked choice, Lowry bestows this precious gift on her readers as she challenges them to ponder the future of their civilization. This richly rewarding fantasy has instilled new life in an often forgotten genre for children.

## Criteria for Quality Fantasy

While the number of books in the fantasy genre is smaller than other genres, guidelines for quality must still be applied in choosing the best fantasy to share with children. Standards include these:

- Fantasy convinces the reader of the possibility of the improbable. Readers must suspend belief and all that they know of reality and willingly enter the world of the impossible.
- Fantasy effectively establishes a unique setting that is original in both time and place. Authors of fantasy must create ingenious, creative worlds.
- Fantasy is compelling and well written with action and well-developed, plausible characters and language that reflects the extraordinary world in which it occurs.
- Fantasy continuously makes the fantastic element believable throughout the story. The element must remain central to the story and all details must remain consistent with the characteristics of the fantastic element.
- Fantasy creates belief in the unbelievable while maintaining a balance between imagination and what we perceive realism to be.

## Values of Fantasy

Fantasy fuels the imagination and begs readers to move beyond the real world into an imaginary world where anything is possible. Perhaps the greatest contribution of fantasy to literature lies in its ability to challenge and develop a child's imagination. Children are encouraged to pretend, to visualize, and to dream what might be. Too often today, imaginations are limited to the visual images children are bombarded with through television and movies. When the literary words create a vision of a new world and paint a portrait of a hero or heroine who captures the imagination, fantasy has achieved its primary goal.

Fantasy provides an escape from reality as readers are invited to take on the heroic characteristics of a person from a realm outside our own world. Identifying with the improbable not only entertains, but causes the reader to consider the deeper possibilities of an extraordinary world. Often the realities of life—abuse of power, life and death, justice under the law—are couched in fantasy and provide a reason to reflect on morality, values, mortality, community, society, and the larger world.

## Reader Response to Fantasy

An excellent connection and introduction to reader response to fantasy for younger students is picture books that border on fantastic worlds. Looking at the realm of the impossible makes read-alouds magical and calls for imaginative responses. Books like John Burningham's *Cloudland* and Audrey Wood's *The Flying Dragon Room* draw young eyes and ears into the world of fantastical places. Brian Jacques's *The Great Redwall Feast* is a picture book introduction to the abbey and creatures of Redwall and an inspiring invitation to future readers of the Redwall Saga series as reading ability and developmental maturity stretch.

Young children's responses will likely blur the probable and the possible, revealing their belief that such settings and possibilities do exist. They enjoy suspending belief and often respond as if the book is a real-world experience. While young children may respond to fantasy only as an adventure story, their ability to accept and revel in the presence of magic and impossibility may actually pave the way for continuing selection of books in this genre as they grow. Young children share an openness to accepting the fantastic more readily that they can then transfer to developing literary tastes.

With intermediate readers, response builds on the genre of fantasy as the innermost thoughts, reflections, and judgments find an audience with a teacher, peer, or literature conversation group. Young people can find adventure, humor, or nonsense in fantasy. They may also reflect beyond this level to a richer experience of sensing inner truths surrounding the entertaining tale. Begin with read-alouds of picture books like Colin Thompson's *How to Live Forever* or *The Tower to the Sun*. The text and illustrations tantalize the imagination and serve as a springboard for response. Middle-school readers will enjoy a read-aloud of Robin McKinley's romantic tale of *The Stone Fey*. This illustrated, brief fantasy serves as a special invitation to respond to the fantasy genre.

Journals work well with fantasy because time travel and heroic adventures in strange settings inspire participation in the text through writing. Artistic responses enable the reader to draw the secondary world of which they have momentarily been a part of and to envision the hero or heroine in his or her glory in a triumph over insurmountable challenges. Of all the genres, fantasy may be the most untapped resource for response and needs to be further considered and explored to truly uncover its potential.

# CLOSING THOUGHTS

Traditional tales and fantasy offer entertainment and escape while providing involvement, ideas and insights, and clarification of feelings and values. One of the special qualities of traditional tales and fantasy literature is that they invite the reader to share the hero or heroine's hopes, struggles, and triumphs and end on a note of hope for the future. Stories that illuminate, delight, and refresh are the type that create readers. Those who work with children need to make a special effort to share books from these genres with both young and older readers. Jane Yolen (1981), writer of numerous books of fantasy, fairies, and folklore invites participation in these genres.

> Knowing that, that magic has consequences, whether it is the magic of wonder, the magic of language, or the magic of challenging a waiting mind, then it is up to the artist, the writer, the storyteller [or the teacher] to reach out and touch that awesome magic. Touch magic—and pass it on. (p. 91)

# REFERENCES

Bettleheim, Bruno (1977). *The uses of enchantment: The meaning and importance of fairy tales.* New York: Vintage.

Favat, Andre (1977). *Child and tale: The origins of interest* (NCTE Research Report No. 19). Urbana, IL: National Council of Teachers of English.

Jacobs, J. S., & Tunnell, M. O. (1996). *Children's literature, briefly.* Upper Saddle River, NJ: Merrill/Prentice Hall.

Lynn, Ruth Nadelman (1995). *Fantasy literature for children and young adults: An annotated bibliography* (4th ed.). New Providence, NJ: R. R. Bowker.

Yolen, Jane (1981). *Touch magic: Fantasy, faerie and folklore in the literature of childhood.* New York: Philomel Books.

# CHILDREN'S BOOKS CITED: TRADITIONAL LITERATURE
## [ P ] = K–2; [ I ] = 3–5; [ M ] = 6–8

Aardema, Verna (1997). *Anansi does the impossible: An Ashanti tale.* Illus. by Lisa Desimini. New York: Atheneum. [ P/I ]

Blos, Joan (1991). *The heroine of the Titanic: A tale both true and otherwise of the life of Molly Brown.* Illus. by Tennessee Dixon. New York: Morrow. [ I ]

Bodnar, Judith Z. (1996). *A wagonload of fish.* Illus. by Alexi Natchev. New York: Lothrop, Lee & Shepard. [ P ]

Brett, Jan (Reteller). (1989). *Beauty and the beast.* New York: Clarion. [ P/I ]

Demi (1996). *The dragon's tale and other animal fables of the Chinese zodiac.* New York: Henry Holt. [ I ]

Duncan, Lois (1996). *The magic of spider woman.* Illus. by Shonto Begay. New York: Scholastic. [ I ]

Ernst, Lisa Campbell (1995). *The tale of Little Red Riding Hood: A newfangled prairie tale.* New York: Simon & Schuster. [ P/I ]

Galdone, Paul (1984). *The gingerbread boy.* Boston: Clarion. [ P ]

Hamilton, Virginia (1988). *In the beginning: Creation stories from around the world.* Illus. by Barry Moser. New York: Harcourt Brace. [ I/M ]

Hamilton, Virginia (1997). *A ring of tricksters: Animal tales from America, the West Indies, and Africa.*

Illus. by Barry Moser. New York: Blue Sky/Scholastic. [ I/M ]

Hodges, Margaret (1996). *Comus*. Illus. by Trina Schart Hyman. New York: Holiday House [ I/M ]

Hodges, Margaret (1993). *The hero of Bremen*. Illus. by Charles Mikolaycak. New York: Holiday House. [ P/I ]

Hodges, Margaret (1997). *The true tale of Johnny Appleseed*. Illus. by Kimberly B. Root. New York: Holiday House. [ I ]

Huck, Charlotte (1989). *Princess furball*. Illus. by Anita Lobel. New York: Greenwillow Books. [ P/I ]

Huck, Charlotte (Reteller) (1996). *Toads and diamonds*. Illus. by Anita Lobel. New York: Greenwillow Books. [ P/I ]

Hyman, Trina Schart (Reteller) (1983). *Little Red Riding Hood*. New York: Holiday House. [ P/I ]

Kellogg, Stephen (1986). *Pecos Bill*. New York: Morrow. [ P/I ]

Kellogg, Stephen (1995). *Sally Ann Thunder Ann Whirlwind Crockett*. New York: Morrow. [ P/I ]

Kimmel, Eric A. (Reteller) (1996). *Onions and garlic: An old tale*. Illus. by Katya Arnold. New York: Holiday House. [ P/I ]

Kimmel, Eric A. (Reteller) (1996). *The magic dreidels: A Hanukkah story*. Illus. by Katya Krenina. New York: Holiday House. [ P/I ]

King-Smith, Dick (1985). *Babe the gallant pig*. Illus. by Mary Rayner. New York: Crown. [ I ]

Lawson, Robert (1944). *Rabbit hill*. New York: Viking. [ I ]

Lesser, Rika (Reteller) (1984). *Hansel and Gretel*. Illus. by Paul O. Zelinsky. New York: Dodd/Mead. [ P/I ]

Levine, Gail C. (1997). *Ella enchanted*. New York: HarperCollins. [ I/M ]

Lewin, Ted (1998). *The storytellers*. New York: Lothrop, Lee & Shepard. [ P/I ]

Lobel, Arnold (1980). *Fables*. New York: Harper & Row. [ P ]

McKinley, Robin (1978). *Beauty: A retelling of the story of Beauty and the beast*. New York: Harper & Row. [ I/M ]

McKinley, Robin (1997). *Rose daughter*. New York: Greenwillow Books. [ I/M ]

Morpurgo, Michael (1996). *Robin of Sherwood*. Illus. by Michael Foreman. San Diego: Harcourt Brace. [ I/M ]

Myers, Walter Dean (1996). *How Mr. Monkey saw the whole world*. Illus. by Synthia Saint James. New York: Doubleday. [ P ]

Napoli, Donna J. (1996). *Zel*. New York: Dutton. [ M ]

Nolan, Dennis (1997). *Androcles and the lion*. San Diego: Harcourt Brace. [ P/I ]

O'Brien, Robert (1971). *Mrs. Frisby and the rats of NIHM*. New York: Atheneum. [ I/M ]

Osborne, Mary Pope (1996). *Favorite Norse myths*. Illus. by Troy Howell. New York: Scholastic. [ I/M ]

Philip, Neil (Reteller) (1995). *The illustrated book of myths: Tales and legends of the world*. Illus. by Nilesh Mistry. New York: Dorling Kindersley. [ I/M ]

Rockwell, Anne (1996). *The one-eyed giant and other monsters from the Greek myths*. New York: Greenwillow Books. [ I/M ]

Rosenthal, Paul (1998). *Yo, Aesop! Get a load of these fables*. Illus. by Marc Rosenthal. New York: Simon & Schuster.

Sanderson, Ruth (1997). *Rose Red & Snow White*. Boston: Little, Brown. [ I ]

San Souci, Robert D. (1996). *Pedro and the monkey*. Illus. by Michael Hays. New York: Morrow. [ P/I ]

Scieszka, Jon (1989). *The true story of the three little pigs as told to A. Wolf*. Illus. by Lane Smith. New York: Viking/Penguin. [ I ]

Scieszka, Jon (1991). *The frog prince continued*. Illus. by Steve Jackson. New York: Viking. [ I ]

Scieszka, Jon, & Smith, Lane (1998). *Squids will be squids: Fresh morals, beastly tales*. New York: Viking. [ I/M ]

Seabrooke, Brenda (1995). *The swan's gift*. Illus. by Wenhai Ma. Cambridge, MA: Candlewick Press. [ P ]

Shannon, Mark (1994). *Gawain and the green knight*. Illus. by David Shannon. New York: Putnam. [ I ]

Stobbs, William (1983). *The house that Jack built*. New York: Oxford University Press. [ P ]

Sutcliff, Rosemary (1995). *The wanderings of Odysseus: The story of the Odyssey*. Illus. by Alan Lee. New York: Delacorte. [ I/M ]

Talbott, Hudson (1996). *Excaliber: Tales of King Arthur*. New York: Morrow. [ I/M ]

Young, Ed (1992). *Seven blind mice*. New York: Philomel Books. [ P ]

Young, Ed (1995). *Donkey trouble*. New York: Atheneum. [ P ]

Wood, Audrey (1996). *The Bunyans*. New York: Blue Sky/Scholastic. [ P/I ]

Zelinsky, Paul O. (1997). *Rapunzel*. New York: Dutton. [ I/M ]

Zelinsky, Paul O. (1986). *Rumpelstiltskin*. New York: Dutton. [ P/I ]

# CHILDREN'S BOOKS CITED: MODERN FANTASY

Alexander, Lloyd (1964). *The book of three.* New York: Holt. (See additional titles in the Prydian Chronicles). [ I/M ]

Avi (1995). *Poppy.* Illus. by Brian Floca. New York: Orchard Books. [ I ]

Avi (1997). *Poppy and Rye.* Illus. by Brian Floca. New York: Avon. [ I ]

Babbitt, Natalie (1975). *Tuck everlasting.* New York: Farrar, Straus and Giroux. [ I ]

Bailey, Carolyn (1946/1962). *Miss Hickory.* Illus. by Ruth Gannett. New York: Viking. [ I ]

Banks, Lynne Reid (1981). *The Indian in the cupboard.* Illus. by Brock Cole. New York: Doubleday. [ I ]

Banks, Lynne Reid (1986). *The return of the Indian.* Illus. by William Geldard. New York: Doubleday. [ I ]

Banks, Lynne Reid (1989). *The secret of the Indian.* Illus. by Ted Lewin. New York: Doubleday.

Banks, Lynne Reid (1992). *The mystery of the cupboard.* Illus. by Tom Newsom. New York: Doubleday. [ I ]

Burningham, John (1996). *Cloudland.* New York: Crown. [ P ]

Cameron, Eleanor (1994). *The court of the stone children.* Magnolia, MA: Peter Smith. [ I ]

Carroll, Lewis (1865/1963). *Alice's adventures in wonderland and through the looking glass.* New York: Macmillan. [ I ]

Christopher, John (1967). *The white mountains.* New York: Macmillan. [ I ]

Cleary, Beverly (1982). *Ralph S. Mouse.* Illus. by Paul Zelinsky. New York: Morrow. [ P/I ]

Conrad, Pam (1990). *Stonewords.* NY: HarperCollins. [ I ]

Cooper, Susan (1993). *The boggart.* New York: McElderry Books. [ I ]

Coville, Bruce (1982). *The monster's ring.* San Diego: Harcourt Brace. [ I ]

Coville, Bruce (1991). *Jeremy Thatcher, dragon hatcher.* San Diego: Harcourt Brace. [ I ]

Coville, Bruce (1992). *Jennifer Murdley's toad.* San Diego: Harcourt Brace. [ I ]

Coville, Bruce (1997). *The skull of truth.* San Diego: Harcourt Brace. [ I ]

Dahl, Roald (1961). *James and the giant peach.* Illus. by Nancy E. Burkert. New York: Knopf. [ P/I ]

Dahl, Roald (1982). *BFG.* Illus. by Quentin Blake. New York: Farrar, Straus & Giroux. [ P/I ]

Dahl, Roald (1988). *Matilda.* Illus. by Quentin Blake. New York: Viking. [ P/I ]

Fleischman, Sid (1963). *By the great horn spoon.* Illus. by Eric Von Schmidt. Boston: Little Brown. [ P/I ]

Fleischman, Sid (1990). *The midnight horse.* Illus. by Peter Sis. New York: Greenwillow. [ I ]

Fleischman, Sid (1997). *Mr. Mysterious and company.* Illus. by Eric Von Schmidt. New York: Greenwillow. [ P/I ]

Grahame, Kenneth (1908/1940). *The wind in the willows.* Illus. by E. H. Shepard. New York: Scribner's. [ P/I ]

Griffin, Peni (1993). *Switching well.* New York: McElderry. [ I ]

Gutman, Dan (1997). *Honus and me.* New York: Avon.

Hahn, Mary Downing (1989). *The doll in the garden: A ghost story.* Boston: Houghton Mifflin. [ I ]

Hahn, Mary Downing (1994). *A time for Andrew: A ghost story.* Boston: Clarion. [ I ]

Jacques, Brian (1987). *Redwall.* (Redwall Saga series). New York: Putnam. [ I/M ]

Jacques, Brian (1995). *The bellmaker.* Philomel Books. (See additional titles in the Redwall Saga series.) [ I/M ]

Jacques, Brian (1996). *The great Redwall feast.* Illus. by Christopher Denise. New York: Philomel Books. [ P/I ]

L'Engle, Madeline (1962). *A wrinkle in time.* New York: Farrar, Straus and Giroux. [ I ]

Lewis, C. S. (1961). *The lion, the witch, and the wardrobe.* Illus. by Pauline Baynes. New York: Macmillan. (See additional titles in The Narnia Chronicles.) [ I ]

Lowry, Lois (1993). *The giver.* Boston: Houghton Mifflin. [ I/M ]

Lunn, Janet (1983). *The root cellar.* New York: Scribner's. [ I/M ]

McKinley, Robin (1998). *The stone fey.* Illus. by John Clapp. San Diego: Harcourt Brace. [ M ]

Norton, Mary (1953). *The borrowers.* Illus. by Beth and Joe Krush. New York: Harcourt Brace. [ I ]

O'Brien, Robert C. (1971). *Mrs. Frisby and the rats of NIHM.* New York: Atheneum. [ I ]

Pullman, Philip (1996). *The golden compass.* New York: Knopf. [ I/M ]

Pullman, Philip (1997). *The subtle knife.* New York: Random House. [ I/M ]

Rowling, J. K. (1998). *Harry Potter and the Sorcerer's Stone.* New York: Scholastic. [ I ]

Scieszka, Jon (1991). *Knights of the kitchen table* (Time Warp Trio series). Illus. by Lane Smith. New York: Viking. [ I ]

Scieszka, Jon (1991). *The not-so Jolly Roger* (Time Warp Trio series). Illus. by Lane Smith. New York: Viking. [ I ]

Scieszka, Jon (1992). *The good, the bad, & the goofy* (Time Warp Trio series). Illus. by Lane Smith. New York: Viking. [ I ]

Sharp, Margery (1959). *The rescuers.* Illus. by Garth Williams. Boston: Little, Brown. [ P/I ]

Slepian, Jan (1994). *Back to before:* New York: Putnam. [ I ]

Steig, William (1976). *Abel's island.* New York: Farrar, Straus and Giroux. [ I ]

Thompson, Colin (1995). *How to live forever.* New York: Knopf. [ I ]

Thompson, Colin (1996). *The tower to the sun.* New York: Knopf. [ I ]

Tolkein, J. R. R. (1938). *The hobbit.* Boston: Houghton Mifflin. [ I/M ]

Waugh, Sylvia (1996). *Mennyms alone.* New York: Greenwillow Books. [ I ]

White, E. B. (1952). *Charlotte's web.* Illus. by Garth Williams. New York: Harper & Row. [ P/I ]

White, E. B. (1945). *Stuart Little.* Illus. by Garth Williams. New York: Harper & Row. [ P/I ]

Wood, Audrey (1996). *The flying dragon room.* Illus. by Mark Teague. New York: Blue Sky/Scholastic. [ P/I ]

Wright, Betty Ren (1991). *A ghost in the house.* New York: Scholastic. [ I ]

Wright, Betty Ren (1993). *The ghost of Popcorn Hill.* New York: Holiday House. [ I ]

Wright, Betty Ren (1993). *The ghosts of Mercy Manor.* New York: Scholastic. [ I ]

Yolen, Jane (1990). *The devil's arithmetic.* New York: Viking/Penguin. [ I/M ]

Yolen, Jane (1997). *Twelve impossible things before breakfast.* San Diego: Harcourt Brace. [ I/M ]

## Chapter 5

# Poetry
## *The Power and Pleasure of Language*

*Poetry full of rich, playful language is what you encounter as you read the poems found in this collection. The unusual linoleum cuts used for the illustrations convey the strength yet vulnerability of the nature described in the poems. The language is dynamic! Listen to the following examples: "Brown sugar nights" and "Sweet spoonfuls of July" come from "Honeycomb Days." From "Puppy" we hear "Summer is a long yellow gown" and "Buttoned to a blue-necked sky." Poetry seems to be a natural for teaching word choice and voice in writing.*

*I never make the time to sit and enjoy the kinds of literature I like. Sharing literature with my children and students is second nature, but to pick up a poetry book for my own enjoyment . . . I had almost forgotten how. You almost feel guilty doing it because it feels so good to read it and soak it up.*

Second-Grade Teacher Response to *Earth Verses and Water Rhymes* by J. Patrick Lewis

Like the onion, poetry is a constant discovery. Peel the onion, layer after layer, until its very heart is reached; every cell contains myriad worlds. Place the onion in the ground, and with care, new onions will grow. Cut the onion, tears can come to the eyes.

> Poetry is the onion of readers. It can cause tears, be peeled layer by layer, or be replanted to grow into new ideas. And it adds taste, zest, and a sharp but sweet quality that enriches our lives.*

Ruth Gordon's (1993) reader's note to her poetry anthology, *Peeling the Onion*, captures the essence of the genre of poetry. Its multilayered meanings, its regeneration in the imagination of children, its nurturing effect on the reader, and its solid emotional core form the genre that is poetry.

Poetry is an invitation to celebrate language and emotions. Poetry delights our funny bones, touches our hearts, titillates our senses, and heightens our awareness. Poetry with its focus on reflection and emotion is "necessary nourishment for the soul" (Bownas, McClure, & Oxley, 1998, p. 48). Extending and intensifying everyday experiences, poetry enhances and enriches our appreciation for the power of words to capture the essence of objects, thoughts, and feelings. Poetry should be a valued part of a child's everyday life, both in and out of school (Harms & Lettow, 1991).

Poetry naturally invites a response from children. The effective language selectively chosen for sound and meaning, the structured patterning of words, and the flow of those words from our lips make active response a natural tendency rather than an option. Poetry demands response from our total being as it engages our intellect, emotions, senses, and imaginations. Poetry has the power to open doors so children can expand their view of the world while celebrating even the commonplace as a fresh experience.

## THE ELEMENTS OF POETRY

Poetry is more than an emotional experience. The essence of poetry lies in its selective language. Eve Merriam, honored children's poet, shared:

> I've sometimes spent weeks looking for precisely the right word. It's like having a tiny marble in your pocket, you can just feel it. Sometimes you find a word and say, "No, I don't think this is it. . . ." Then you discard it, and take another and another until you get it right. I do think poetry is great fun. That's what I'd like to stress more than anything else: the joy of the sounds of language.*

The elements of poetry are essentially language related. There is no emphasis on plot or character, neither setting nor point of view. There is, however, language—in all its glory and with all its propensity to capture objects, emotions, and thoughts. The elements of poetry include rhythm, rhyme and sound, imagery, figurative language, and shape and spacing. When children unpeel the onion skin of poetry, they are exposing and feasting on the language that surrounds the poetic experience.

Children should be made aware of, but not required to analyze, the elements of poetry. These language elements are shared to heighten adult awareness of the wonders of this genre and to assist them in selecting the best to share with children. A knowledge of the language impact on poetry impacts one's attitude toward poetry, the way it is read, and the manner in which it is shared. For poetry to become a steady diet across the curriculum and throughout the school day, teachers must feel a sense of wonder in its language roots.

## Rhythm

Rhythm can be described as the flow of language that creates a sense of movement in the listener. Poetic rhythm can best be detected through a read-aloud in which the reader's voice captures the hand clapping or foot stomping pattern of words. Children respond naturally to rhythm as poems possess a music of their own that invite response. Many traditional poems by timeless poets share this poetic trait. Listen to the simple, traditional, but present rhyme of Walter de la Mare's "Silver."

> Slowly, silently, now the moon
> Walks the night in her silver shoon;
> This way, and that, she peers, and sees
> Silver fruit upon silver trees;
> One by one the casements catch
> Her beams beneath the silvery thatch;
> Couched in his kennel, like a log,
> With paws of silver sleeps the dog;
> From their shadowy cote the white breasts peep
> Of doves in a silver-feathered sleep;
> A harvest mouse goes scampering by,
> With silvery claws, and silver eye;
> And moveless fish in the water gleam,
> By silver reeds in a silver stream.*

## Rhyme

Just as children respond to rhythm, so, too, do they respond to the rhyme created by the words. Rhyme is the "sing-songedness" of the chosen words painstakingly selected by the poet. As children are engaged in first experiences with poetry, it is the rhyme of the poems that can build a positive response to the genre. The well-loved rhyme and rhythm of Mother Goose, like those shared in Iona Opie's *My Very First Mother Goose* or Jane Dyer's *Animal Crackers*, are actually a strong introduction to this poetic element. Rebecca Kai Dotlich's title poem from *Lemonade Sun and Other Summer Poems* contains the simple rhyme young children love to hear, repeat, and internalize.

**LEMONADE SUN**

Popsicle stains.
Fudgesicle fun.
Strawberry sizzle—
lemonade sun.[†]

Rhyme is related to the sound of words and certain literary devices are well suited to creating the sounds that result in rhyme. Alliteration, the repetition of initial consonant sounds, can be effective in creating rhyme. For example, Lew Sarett's "Four Little Foxes" begins: "Speak gently, Spring, and make no sudden sound. . . ." Similarly, assonance is the repetition of vowel sounds which typically results in internal, rather than external, rhyme. David McCord's "The Pickety Fence" uses wonderful, imaginative word choices like *pickety, clickety, lickety,* and *rickety* to repeat the same sound and establish internal rhyme that appeals to the ear and eye.

## Imagery

Language can create sensory experiences for children as it arouses their senses of sight, touch, taste, smell, and sound. Descriptions of a lofty buffalo, a scaly snake, blackberry jam, an evergreen forest, or a chirping cricket can stimulate the sensory images children create in their minds. Words vividly paint pictures for children—pictures that open the door to discovery of everyday things in the complex world. Ralph Fletcher's collection titled *Ordinary Things: Poems from a Walk in Early Spring* bursts with imagery. Picture this . . .

**DAFFODILS**

they put on a little show
simply by being so yellow
their stems darkly green
against the faded brown barn.[*]

## Figurative Language

Because words are vital to creating images in a poem, poets often rely on literary devices to assist them in economizing on words, yet creating sensory images that appeal to children. Poets may compare two like objects so the connection of one to the other adds meaning for the reader. When writers use the words *like* or *as* to make a comparison, the literary device is called a simile. In a metaphor, the poet refers to another object as if it were the object or idea. For example, Tony Johnson portrays winter as a cat in *Once in the Country:*

[†]"From *Lemonade Sun and Other Summer Poems* (p. 6) by Rebecca Kai Dotlich. Copyright © 1998. Published by Boyds Mills Press, Inc. Reprinted by permission.

[*]Reprinted with the permission of Atheneum Books for Young Readers, an imprint of Simon & Schuster Children's Publishing Division from *Ordinary Things* (p. 44) by Ralph Fletcher. Text copyright © 1997 Ralph Fletcher.

**WHITE CAT WINTER**

White cat Winter
prowls
the farm,
tiptoes
soft
through withered corn,
creeps
along low walls
of stone,
falls asleep
beside
the barn.*

It is not so important for children to distinguish between these two forms of figurative language. Their importance lies in teacher recognition of figurative language so children may be drawn to and respond to these types of comparisons.

Personification casts inanimate objects and animals in a human light. Children typically recognize this literary device because they personify some of their own possessions during play. In "December" James Stevenson personifies this winter month:

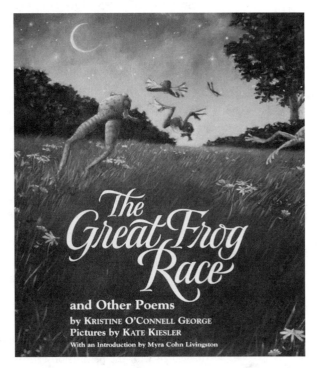

*Jacket cover from THE GREAT FROG RACE AND OTHER POEMS by Kristine O'Connell George. Jacket illustration copyright © 1997 by Kate Kiesler. Reprinted by permission of Clarion Books/Houghton Mifflin Company. All rights reserved.*

*"White Cat Winter" from *Once in the Country* (p. 26) by Tony Johnson. Copyright © 1996 by Tony Johnson. Used by permission of G. P. Putnam's Sons, a division of Penguin Putnam, Inc.

Across the front of the pale gray woods
Deep red sumac sway on stilts.
Clusters of half-notes.
Scribble a crimson score.[†]

## Shape and Spacing

The arrangement of words on the page is one of the simple, yet important distinguishing features between poetry and prose in the eyes of children. Stanzas, indentations, variations in line length, centering, margins, and shape are all features children notice when they begin to read poetry independently. These elements also influence children as writing models when they begin to compose their own poems. Examine the placement of words in "Egg" by Kristine O'Connell George from her collection titled *The Great Frog Race and Other Poems*.

There are
No tags, no tabs
Or wrapping paper,
Nor flaps, nor string,
Sticky tape or ribbon.
Never hidden up high
On a cupboard shelf.
Egg is a package
That can open
Itself.[*]

Rhythm, rhyme, language, and shape all combine to create the total response to a poem. While children may react to isolated elements, it is the response to the whole that creates emotion in the reader. Adults should never make poetic elements the objective of sharing poetry. Children should have an opportunity to hear a poem, to respond to a poem, and to relate a poem to familiar poems, but never to analyze a poem. Teachers, however, need to be aware of these poetic elements so they may select only the best poems to share with children.

# FORMS OF POETRY

Just as with other literary genres, poetry can be classified to better discuss the variation in the poetic genre. Forms of poetry are useful to adults to ensure they select poems that expose children to all variations in form. Although terminology may be shared with children, it is not necessary for them to recognize form. Enjoyment of poetry, in any form, should be our outcome in sharing this genre with children.

## Narrative Poems

Popular with children, narrative poems tell a story. In reading classic poems like *The Night Before Christmas* or *Paul Revere's Ride,* the poetic elements merge with story to create reading pleasure. The favorite narratives of children today come from the poetic minds of Shel Silverstein and Jack Prelutsky. The characters they create and the situations they share bring a smile to every listener. Shel Silverstein shares the following tale of the dilemma of pirate's treasure in his newest collection titled *Falling Up:*

**MORGAN'S CURSE**

Followin' the trail on the old treasure map,
I came to the spot that said "Dig right here."
And four feet down my spade struck wood
Just where the map said a chest would appear.
But carved in the side were written these words:
"A curse upon he who disturbs this gold."
Signed, Morgan the Pirate, Scourge of the Seas.
I read these words and my blood ran cold.
So here I sit upon untold wealth
Tryin' to figure which is worse:
How much do I need this gold?
And how much do I need this curse?*

Children are likely to respond to this narrative by continuing the saga and expounding on the consequences of a wise or fateful decision.

## Lyrical Poetry

Lyrical poetry is descriptive poetry that imbibes an object, scene, or feeling through language that reflects a songlike quality. Lyric poems don't read, they *sing* their way into our minds and hearts. In a traditional sense, several of Robert Louis Stevenson's poems from *A Child's Garden of Verses* create a melodic quality that keeps them in our minds. A newer collection of night poems for children, *The Sky Is Not So Far Away* by Margaret Hillert, captures that songlike quality at bedtime, particularly in "Night Sky."

The sky is not so far away.
It reaches to the ground.
I'm standing right inside of it.
It doesn't make a sound.
And once I almost held a star,
A small and shining light
That turned into a firefly
And flickered out of sight.*

*"Morgan's Curse" from *Falling Up: Poems and Drawings by Shel Silverstein* (p. 22) by Shel Silverstein. Copyright © 1996 by Shel Silverstein. Reprinted by permission of HarperCollins Publishers.

*Text copyright © 1996 by Margaret Hillert from *The Sky Is Not So Far Away* by Margaret Hillert. Published by Boyds Mills Press, Inc. Reprinted by permission.

## Limericks

Particularly popular with children, this nonsense verse is a formula poem. The five-line poem (first lines rhymes with second line, third and fourth line rhyme, fifth line rhymes with first and second lines) is a humorous statement that creates a character, a setting, an ironic twist. Although Ogden Nash is considered the grandmaster of this poetic form, Arnold Lobel took it on more recently in *The Book of Pigericks,* limericks about pigs across the United States. X. J. Kennedy's *Brats* humorously uses the limerick form to tell tales of famous brats that surround our lives. In *Uncle Switch,* a collection of limericks built on the antics of a single character, Kennedy again tickles the reader's funnybone.

> Uncle Switch, at the beach for a swim,
> Never jumps in. Instead, it's his whim
> On his blankets to lie
> Till the tide rises high—
> He insists that the sea come to *him.*[†]

Children do enjoy responding to limericks by writing them. Since they are nonsense, almost any topic works and the rhyme scheme is straightforward and achievable for intermediate grade students.

## Free Verse

Gaining increasing popularity and deserved respect as a poetic form, free verse has no discernible pattern. Free verse flows freely on the printed page and does not contain the rhyme which children typically associate with poetry. Children who listen to free verse read aloud will be released from the rhymed poem stereotype. Void of external rhyme, free verse does contain an internal rhythm that makes it read well aloud. Sample the sound of "Spirals" from Barbara Esbensen's *Echoes for the Eye.*

> Every spring
> lifting out of the damp earth,
> ferns
> like coiled green wires
> push up through leafmold
> into the new sun
> Spiral shapes wound tight
> curled underground
> all winter
> unwind
> like green
> mainsprings inside the earth's
> dark clock*

[†]Reprinted with the permission of Margaret K. McElderry Books, an imprint of Simon & Schuster Children's Publishing Division from *Uncle Switch: Loony Limericks* by X.J. Kennedy. Text copyright © 1997 X.J. Kennedy.

*Text copyright © 1996 *Echoes for the Eye* by Barbara Juster Esbensen. Illustrations copyright © 1996 by Helen K. Davie. Used by permission of HarperCollins Publishers.

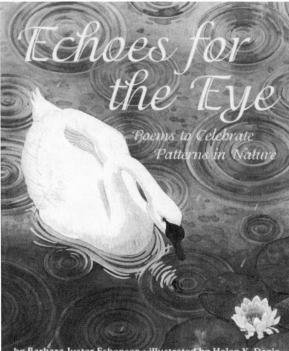

## Haiku

A deceptively simple form of poetry, haiku originated in Japan in the 13th century. In its purest sense, haiku contains 17 syllables in three lines (5 syllables/7 syllables/5 syllables) focusing on a season or a symbol of a season. Many haiku writers today write about almost any topic from the natural world and do not necessarily adhere to the original syllable formula. In spite of their simple form, haiku share complex ideas for deeper reflection. J. Patrick Lewis (1995) in an introduction to his original haiku collection, *Black Swan White Crow*, believes, "The best haiku make you think and wonder for a lot longer than it takes to say them" (n.p.). Because haiku elicit reflection, they provide effective poetry to share for reader response connections. Haiku is an abstract form of poetry that should be reserved for intermediate/middle-level students. Asking children to write haiku distorts the complexity and natural spirit that forms the heart of this ancient poetic form. Enjoy the flow, simplicity, and natural connection of haiku from Lewis's collection. Reflection and response flows naturally from the listener.

> The meadow reddens—
> my old black lab fills
> the sky with quail

The spider yo-yos
down August to a hemlock
petalworth of shade*

Chris Manson's woodcut prints provide essential visual balance for each haiku—suggestive, eye-pleasing, and quietly satisfying.

## Concrete Poetry

Sometimes the message of a poem is not only delivered through its words, but through the visual presentation of the words on the page. Concrete poetry is poetry that carries a portion of its meaning through its shape. Once children are visually introduced to this kind of poetry, they want to write their own. Initial emphasis on meaning must supercede the drawing or the poetic flavor will be lost. Jack Prelutsky shares several concrete poems in *A Pizza the Size of the Sun*.

*An example of concrete poetry. "I Was Walking in a Circle" from* A Pizza the Size of the Sun *by Jack Prelutsky. Copyright © 1994/1996. Reprinted by permission of Greenwillow Books, a division of William Morrow & Company.*

**I Was Walking in a Circle**

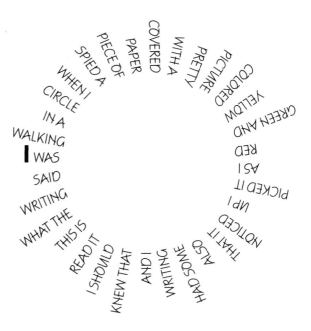

*Reprinted with the permission of Atheneum Books for Young Readers, an imprint of Simon & Schuster Children's Publishing Division from *Black Swan White Crow* by J. Patrick Lewis. Text copyright © 1995 J. Patrick Lewis.

Teachers should share all types of poetry with their students, exposing them to the breadth and depth of this genre. The library typically abounds with poetry books and anthologies, making poetry books accessible for classroom independent reading, poet displays, or integration with themed units. Teachers need to document or record the types of poetry they select, keeping an eye on balance and variety as they share this inspiring genre with children.

# TYPES OF POETRY COLLECTIONS

Besides categorizing poetry by its form, poetry can also be discussed in general terms by focusing on its organization or content. This classification ranges from comprehensive collections to specialized collections by a single author. The increased publication of poetry books for children necessitates an additional means to view the breadth and depth of this genre.

## Comprehensive Anthologies

Anthologies are collections of children's poems that contain a large number of poems from many well-known poets. Anthologists select poems, gain permission to reprint them, and arrange them in a meaningful format. Most teachers like to keep a poetry anthology on their desk so they can locate a poem on a topic during a teachable moment. Two of the most useful in print are *Sing a Song of Popcorn,* edited by Beatrice Schenk de Regniers, and *The Random House Book of Poetry for Children,* edited by Jack Prelutsky. One of the most recent anthologies, although not quite as comprehensive in nature, is *A Jar of Tiny Stars: Poems by NCTE Award-Winning Poets,* which offers a collection of poems selected by children from the offerings of David McCord, Aileen Fisher, Karla Kushkin, Myra Cohn Livingston, Eve Merriam, John Ciardi, Lilian Moore, Arnold Adoff, Valerie Worth, and Barbara Esbensen. These poets were judged to be the very best in their genre and honored for a distinguished body of poetic work over time.

## Specialized Collections

A trend in poetry publication has been to produce shorter collections of poems on a specific topic. Either authored by a single poet or collected from the works of several poets, the narrower scope and reduced number of poems truly suit the style of thematic, interdisciplinary instruction teachers are sharing in classrooms. Lee Bennett Hopkins carries a reputation as a respected anthologist whose selections in *School Supplies* and *April Bubbles Chocolate: An ABC of Poetry* catch the interest of young poetry lovers. Doug Florian's themed titles fit the model of specialized collections by a single author. *Insectlopedia* presents a swarm of insect poems, while *In the Swim* blends poetry naturally into themes on creatures of the sea. Jane Yolen's *Sky Scrape/City Scape: Poems of City Life* and Kathy

Henderson's *A Year in the City* provide varying perspectives on urban life. In contrast stands Tony Johnson's *Once in the Country: Poems of a Farm.*

Many strong themed collections authored by a single poet belong to Myra Cohn Livingston. One of her last collections, *Festivals,* contains original poems for celebrations of Chinese New Year, Mardi Gras, Ramadan, The Day of the Dead, and Kwanzaa. Enhanced by color drawings of Leonard Everett Fisher, this collection will readily find its way into seasonal, cultural, and varied theme explorations. Through years of writing, her poems have emotionally touched generations of poetry lovers. Other themed collections like *Grassroots: Poems by Carl Sandberg* highlight the work of a single author and are further enhanced by the reflective illustrations of artists like Wendell Minor. These collections carry poetry into thematic explorations across the curriculum.

## Poem Picture Books

A special showcase for a single poem is a picture book format in which the text of the poem is blended with striking illustrations for both a visual as well as an oral reading experience (Glazer & Lamme, 1990). The poem picture book has become more popular since its inception with traditional poems like Edward Lear's *The Owl and the Pussycat* romantically presented in a Caribbean setting while intricate details in Jan Brett's illustrations extend the poem. Diane Siebert's *Heartland* has language that flows across the page like the wind across this huge expanse of our country. Eve Bunting's *Sunflower House* is a picture storybook written in rhymed couplets that captures the imaginative world of children's play as seasonal sunflowers come and go. A special blend of language and illustration is Bill Martin and John Archambault's *Listen to the Rain* and Harry Behn's *Trees.* Response can take the form of drawing illustrations inspired by the words of these language experiences. Jean Marzollo's *Home Sweet Home* blends simple, rhymed text with Ashley Wolff's vibrant paintings. Children eagerly join in with the poetic text prompted by cues from the lushly detailed illustrations creating a strong introduction to the sounds and visions of poetry.

# SORTING POETRY BY CONTENT

## Humorous Verse

The poetry collections with the highest circulation rate are works of humorous verse. The placement of the poem surrounded by the space on the page often invites even reluctant readers to browse and sample the varied fare of children's humorous poets. Shel Silverstein (*A Light in the Attic*) and Jack Prelutsky (*A Pizza the Size of the Sun*) never fail to bring a smile to children's faces even at the mention of their names. Both *A Thousand Cousins: Poems of Family Life* and Ogden Nash's *Custard the Dragon and the Wicked Knight* entertain children eager for fun with words and rhyme.

## Nature Poetry

Children's natural curiosity can open their eyes to well-selected poems whose words paint the wonders of nature. Whether integrating these with a science unit or merely sharing them as good poetry, nature poems restore our sense of wonder. Constance Levy's *A Tree Place and Other Poems* and *When Whales Exhale and Other Poems* share the wonder and simplicity of the rarities and everyday pleasures of nature. In "Tail Flukes," Levy discovers beauty in a whale's tail.

> The humpback whale will charm you
> with the ballet of its dive
> shaping itself
> like the downstroke
> of a wave,
> its tail flukes,
> great butterfly wings,
> spread wide.*

## Versatility in Poems

Some poets write poems about a wide variety of experiences and topics. While difficult to classify, these poets should be honored for the versatility they bring to the poetic genre. Eve Merriam's *Blackberry Ink,* David McCord's *One at a Time,* Nancy Larrick's *Mice are Nice,* Alice Schertle's *Keepers,* Deborah Chandra's *Rich Lizard and Other Poems,* and Barbara Esbensen's *Dance with Me* share poetic talent that demands appreciation. They write poems about daily experiences, nature, animals, and feelings while spanning many poetic forms.

# SELECTING QUALITY POETRY

The value of poetry is measured by the overall emotional impact and the creative use of language of the poems. One of the best ways of evaluating poetry is to read it aloud. If the words flow and create excitement within you, if the poem appeals to your senses, if the poem makes you stop and reflect long after it is over, if a phrase or word keeps reoccurring in your mind, then perhaps you have found a special poem.

Joan Glazer (1997) cites five basic criteria that distinguish great poems from good poems. These criteria reflect standards to apply when assessing a poem:

1. A fresh or original view of the subject is presented.
2. Insight or emotion is shown or felt.
3. Poetic devices are used effectively.

*Reprinted with the permission of Margaret K. McElderry Books, an imprint of Simon & Schuster Children's Publishing Division from *When Whales Exhale and Other Poems* (p. 11) by Constance Levy. Text copyright © 1996 Constance Kling Levy.

4. Language is used effectively.
5. The voice or persona within the poem appears to be sincere. (p. 278)

Children come to school with a natural appreciation for the rhyme, rhythm, and sounds of language. Teachers need to capitalize on that tendency by selecting poems that appeal to those natural preferences. As children develop as listeners and readers, teachers need to deepen their poetic appreciation with a variety of poetic forms and surround them with the best of the genre.

One of the areas with which to begin the decision-making process in poetry selection is to consider the poetry reading preferences of children. Studies of primary (grades 1–3) students' preferences (Fisher & Natarella, 1982), of intermediate (grades 4–6) students' preferences (Terry, 1974), and middle-level (grades 7–9) preferences (Kutiper, 1985) confirmed the findings of Terry's (1972) original study, some of which are shared here:

1. The narrative form of poetry was popular with readers of all ages, while free verse and haiku were the most disliked forms.
2. Students preferred poems that contain rhyme, rhythm, and sound.
3. Children most enjoyed poetry that contained humor, familiar experiences, and animals.
4. Younger students preferred contemporary poems.
5. Students disliked poems that contained visual imagery or figurative language. (Kutiper & Wilson, 1993, p. 29)

A library circulation study of poetry books reinforced these findings as humorous titles by Silverstein (*A Light in the Attic, Where the Sidewalk Ends*), Prelutsky (*The New Kid on the Block, Something Big Has Been Here*), and Viorst (*If I Were in Charge of the World and Other Worries*) revealed the highest school circulation figures (Kutiper & Wilson, 1993). The rhyme, rhythm, humor, and narrative form of these student-selected poems align with children's designated preferences.

The findings of these studies do not imply that teachers should prioritize children's likes over dislikes in sharing poetry. The implication for teachers is to initiate poetry exposure with student preferences and gradually bridge those experiences toward those poetic forms which they typically avoid. If we limit children's exposure to poetry to a few popular poets, the rich possibilities of this genre will be left unexplored and unappreciated. Teachers may include poetry in interdisciplinary studies, provide classroom poetry collections, and read aloud poetry on a regular basis. The greater the diversity of poems, the more opportunities for response to and appreciation for this genre to develop.

While this chapter includes many quality poetry collections and poets within its pages, the list given in Figure 5.1 adds even greater depth to a poetry repertoire. Both classic poets who have gained recognition through the years and contemporary poets whose books have special appeal for today's children are included in this list.

# READER RESPONSE TO POETRY

Response to poetry with young children takes the form of oral response as children repeat words, phrases, and rhymes that capture their language sensations (Bownas et al., 1998). Choral reading experiences bring appreciation to the sounds of poetry as large and small groups use voice to project the poetic emotions beyond the printed page.

**FIGURE 5.1** Additional poetry to share with children of all ages.

---

## Classic Poetry

Bodecker, N. M. (1974). *Let's marry said the cherry and other nonsense poems.* New York: Atheneum. [ P/I ]

Ciardi, John (1962). *You read to me, I'll read to you.* Illus. by Edward Gorey. Philadelphia: Lippincott. [ P/I ]

Cole, William (Ed.) (1966). *Oh, what nonsense!* Illus. by Tomi Ungerer. New York: Viking. [ P/I ]

Fleischmann, Paul (1988). *Joyful noise: Poems for two voices.* Illus. by Eric Beddows. New York: Harper. [ I/M ]

Greenfield, Eloise (1978). *Honey, I love, and other love poems.* Illus. by Diane & Leo Dillon. New York: Crowell. [ P/I ]

Kennedy, X. J., & Kennedy, Dorothy J. (Compilers) (1982). *Knock at a star: A child's introduction to poetry.* Illus. by K. A. Weinhaus. Boston: Little, Brown. [ P/I ]

Kuskin, Karla (1972). *Any me I want to be.* New York: Harper & Row. [ P ]

Larrick, Nancy (1985/1968). *Piping down the valleys wild.* Illus. by Ellen Raskin. New York: Delacorte. [ P/I ]

Livingston, Myra Cohn (1982). *A circle of seasons.* Illus. by Leonard Everett Fisher. New York: Holiday House. [ P/I ]

Merriam, Eve (1964). *It doesn't always have to rhyme.* Illus. by Malcolm Spooner. New York: Atheneum. [ P/I ]

O'Neill, Mary (1989/1961). *Hailstones and halibut bones.* Illus. by Leonard Weisgard. New York: Doubleday. [ P/I ]

Prelutsky, Jack (1984). *The new kid on the block.* Illus. by James Stevenson. New York: Greenwillow Books. [ P/I ]

Silverstein, Shel (1974). *Where the sidewalk ends.* New York: Harper & Row. [ P/I ]

Untermeyer, Louis (Ed.) (1985). *Rainbow in the sky.* Illus. by Reginald Birch. San Diego: Harcourt Brace.

Viorst, Judith (1982). *If I were in charge of the world and other worries: Poems for children and their parents.* Illus. by Lynne Cherry. New York: Atheneum. [ I ]

Willard, Nancy (1981). *A visit to William Blake's Inn: Poems for innocent and experienced travellers.* Illus. by Alice & Martin Provensen. San Diego: Harcourt Brace. [ P/I ]

Worth, Valerie (1972). *Small poems.* Illus. by Natalie Babbitt. New York: Farrar, Straus & Giroux. [ P/I ]

## Contemporary Poetry

Adoff, Arnold (1991). *In for winter, out for spring.* Illus. by Jerry Pinkney. San Diego: Harcourt Brace. [ P/I ]

Carlson, Lori M. (Ed. ) (1994). *Cool salsa: Growing up Latino in the United States.* New York: Holt. [ M ]

Cassedy, Sylvia (1993). *Zoomrimes: Poems about things that go.* Illus. by Michele Chessare. New York: HarperCollins. [ P ]

Chandra, Deborah (1993). *Rich lizards and other poems.* Illus. by Leslie Bowman. New York: Farrar, Straus and Giroux. [ I ]

Esbensen, Barbara J. (1995). *Who shrank my grandmother's house?* Illus. by Eric Beddows. New York: HarperCollins [ P/I ]

**FIGURE 5.1**    Additional poetry to share with children of all ages. *(continued)*

Hopkins, Lee Bennett (1990). *Good books, good times!* Illus. by Harry Stevenson. New York: Harper-
   Collins. [ P/I ]
Janeczko, Paul B. (1998). *That sweet diamond: Baseball poems.* Illus. by Carole Katchen. New York:
   Atheneum. [ I/M ]
Moore, Lilian (1997). *Poems have roots.* Illus. by Tad Hills. New York: Atheneum. [ I/M ]
Mora, Pat (1998). *The big sky.* Illus. by Steve Jenkins. New York: Scholastic. [ I ]
Nye, Naomi Shihab (Ed.) (1992). *This same sky: A collection of poems from around the world.* New
   York: Four Winds. [ M ]
Prelutsky, Jack (1993). *The dragons are singing tonight.* Illus. by Peter Sis. New York: Greenwillow
   Books. [ P/I ]
Schertle, Alice (1995). *Advice for a frog.* Illus. by Norman Green. New York: Lothrop, Lee &
   Shepard. [ P/I ]
Stevenson, James (1998). *Popcorn.* New York: Greenwillow Books. [ I ]
Yolen, Jane (1998). *Snow, snow: Winter poems for children.* Photographs by Jason Stemple.
   Honesdale, PA: Boyds Mills Press. [ P ]
See additional multicultural poetry listed in Chapter 8, Multicultural Literature.

Children can also respond to poetry, especially poem picture books, through art.
Drawing what you see when you listen to a lyrical poem or sketching an interpretion of a
haiku usually reflects differences in how words and images are perceived. Groups or individuals can create an anthology of favorite poems by selecting and documenting the work
of popular poets during theme explorations. Selecting poems that relate to the sea during
an ocean theme, for example, brings together a vast array of quality poetry.

The written response to a poem through personal interpretation, literary analysis,
or self-created poetry is not encouraged until children have learned to love poetry. In
most cases, the reader must be immersed and drenched in poetry long before the written assignment of a poem occurs. Poetry must speak enjoyment to the reader before it
can become the writing model. Although poetry and writing can be addressed as response (see Chapter 11), it is far more important to savor its word choice, its texture, its
emotions, and its ability to inspire reflection during the early stages of appreciation.
When appreciation takes hold, the time may be ripe for the written response through
self-created poetry.

Meanwhile, teachers can support responses to poetry on a daily basis through an interactive poetry session in the classroom. Rather than turning these experiences into lessons,
they should occur spontaneously as the rich experience of poetry unfolds.

- Read aloud and savor poetry on a regular basis.
- Linger over the language of poetry to appreciate wordcrafting.
- Invite children to participate in poetry by joining in on repeated phrases or responding
  to rhythm or rhyme through movement.
- Read aloud a few poems from a collection inviting children to venture through the rest
  of the collection on their own.

- Encourage children to select favorite poems and share orally during poetry sharing sessions.
- Build a repertoire of poems so children can compare, discuss, respond, relate, recall, and develop personal tastes in poetry.
- Share poet studies to build familiarity with quality writers in this genre.
- Provide opportunities for choral reading of poetry for individual, partner, book buddy, small group, or whole class performances.
- Add the aesthetic dimension of poetry across the curriculum.
- Build appreciation for languages and dialects of other cultures through multicultural poetry.
- Appreciate the universality of poetry to address common objects, emotions, and themes through the power of language.

One of the most respected children's poets, Eve Merriam, makes a suggestion on relishing the joy of poetry in selected lines of "How to Eat a Poem."

> Pick it up with your fingers and lick the juice
> that may run down your chin.
> It is ready and ripe now, whenever you are.*

Savor the flavor and message of poetry as you select and share the wealth of this genre with children of all ages.

# CLOSING THOUGHTS

This chapter celebrates the genre of poetry through which well-chosen words invite readers to ponder, observe, smile, reflect, or laugh. Young children "take to poetry as naturally as breathing, and . . . [poetry] is as essential to their well-being as air that is clean" (Schliesman, 1998, p. 35). Older children attach to poetry as both readers and listeners. A wealth of recent innovative poetry in single poet collections and anthologies celebrates opportunities to engage readers beyond their early years toward poetic experiences for a lifetime. Regardless of the age of the child, it is important to remember that meanings in poems lie in the individual hearts and minds of the reader. Myra Cohn Livingston (1990), children's poet/author/anthologist, articulately supports the uniqueness of poetic response,

> There is no poem that can live, come alive, without a reader. The reader, the listener, breathes into each work of art his own experience, his own sensitivity, and re-creates it in meaningful terms. (p. 207)

Response to poetry makes way for the diverse emotions, delights, challenges, and understandings it stirs within the individual child. Response to poetry creates lifelong lovers of language, words, and the poetic genre.

*In Cullinan, Bernice E. (Ed.) (1996). *A jar of tiny stars* (p. 34). Honesdale, PA: Wordsong/Boyds Mills Press.

# REFERENCES

Bownas, J., McClure, A. A., & Oxley, P. (1998). Talking about books: Bringing the rhythm of poetry into the classroom. *Language Arts, 75,* 48–55.

Fisher, C. J., & Natarella, M. A. (1982). Young children's preferences in poetry: A national survey of first, second, and third graders. *Research in the Teaching of English, 16,* 339–354.

Glazer, J. I. (1997). *Introduction to children's literature* (2nd ed.). Upper Saddle River, NJ: Merrill/Prentice Hall.

Glazer, J. I., & Lamme, L. L. (1990). Poem picture books and their uses in the classroom. *The Reading Teacher, 44,* 102–109.

Harms, J. M., & Lettow, L. J. (1991). Recent poetry for children. *The Reading Teacher, 45,* 174–279.

Kutiper, K. (1985). A survey of the adolescent poetry preferences of seventh, eighth, and ninth graders. Unpublished doctoral dissertation, University of Houston, Houston, TX.

Kutiper, K., & Wilson, P. (1993). Updating poetry preferences: A look at the poetry children really like. *The Reading Teacher, 47,* 28–35.

Livingston, M. C. (1990). *Climb into the bell tower: Essays on poetry.* New York: Harper & Row.

Schliesman, M. (1998). Poetry for every child. *Book Links, 7,* 35–39.

Terry, A. (1972). A national study of children's poetry preferences in the fourth, fifth, and sixth grades. Unpublished doctoral dissertation, Ohio State University, Columbus.

Terry, A. (1974). *Children's poetry preferences: A national survey of upper elementary grades* (NCTE Report No. 16). Urbana, IL: National Council of Teachers of English.

# CHILDREN'S BOOKS CITED
# [ P ] = K–2; [ I ] = 3–5; [ M ] = 6–8

Behn, Harry (1947/1992). *Trees.* Illus. by James Endicott. New York: Henry Holt. [ P/I ]

Bunting, Eve (1996). *Sunflower house.* Illus. by Kathryn Hewitt. San Diego: Harcourt Brace. [ P ]

Chandra, Deborah (1993). *Rich lizard and other poems.* Illus. by Leslie Bowman. New York: Farrar, Straus and Giroux. [ I ]

Cullinan, Bernice E. (Ed.) (1996). *A jar of tiny stars: Poems by NCTE award-winning poets.* Honesdale, PA: Wordsong/Boyds Mills Press & National Council of Teachers of English. [ P/I ]

de Regniers, Beatrice Schenk (Ed.) (1988). *Sing a song of popcorn.* Illus. by nine Caldecott Medal artists. New York: Scholastic. [ P/I ]

Dotlich, Rebecca Kai (1998). *Lemonade sun and other summer poems.* Illus. by Jan Spivey Gilchrist. Honesdale, PA: Wordsong/Boyds Mills Press. [ P/I ]

Dyer, Jane (1996). *Animal crackers: A delectable collection of pictures, poems, and lullabies for the very young.* Boston: Little, Brown. [ P ]

Esbensen, Barbara Juster (1995). *Dance with me.* Illus. by Megan Lloyd. New York: HarperCollins. [ P/I ]

Esbensen, Barbara Juster (1996). *Echoes for the eye: Poems to celebrate patterns in nature.* Illus. by Helen K. Davie. New York: HarperCollins. [ I ]

Fletcher, Ralph (1997). *Ordinary things: Poems from a walk in early spring.* Illus. by Walter Lyon Krudop. New York: Atheneum. [ I ]

Florian, Douglas (1997). *In the swim.* San Diego: Harcourt Brace. [ I/M ]

Florian, Douglas (1998). *Insectlopedia.* San Diego: Harcourt Brace. [ I/M ]

George, Kristine O'Connell (1997). *The great frog race and other poems.* Illus. by Kate Kiesler. Boston: Clarion. [ I/M ]

Gordon, Ruth (Selector) (1993). *Peeling the onion: An anthology of poems.* New York: Charlotte Solotow Book/HarperCollins. [ M ]

Harrison, David L. (1996). *A thousand cousins: Poems of family life.* Illus. by Betsy Lewin. Honesdale, PA: Wordsong/Boyds Mills Press. [ P/I ]

Henderson, Kathy (1996). *A year in the city.* Illus. by Paul Howard. Cambridge, MA: Candlewick Press. [ P/I ]

Hillert, Margaret (1996). *The sky is not so far away: Night poems for children.* Illus. by Thomas Werner. Honesdale, PA: Wordsong/Boyds Mills Press. [ P ]

Hopkins, Lee Bennett (Selector) (1994). *April bubbles chocolate: An ABC of poetry.* Illus. by Barry Root. New York: Simon & Schuster. [ P/I ]

Hopkins, Lee Bennett (Selecter) (1996). *School supplies: A book of poems.* Illus. by Renee Flower. New York: Simon & Schuster. [ I ]

Johnson, Tony (1996). *Once in the country: Poems of a farm.* Illus. by Thomas B. Allen. New York: Putnam. [ P/I ]

Kennedy, X. J. (1986). *Brats.* Illus. by James Watts. New York: Atheneum. [ I ]

Kennedy, X. J. (1997). *Uncle Switch: Loony limericks.* Illus. by John O'Brien. New York: McElderry Books. [ I ]

Larrick, Nancy (1990). *Mice are nice.* Illus. by Ed Young. New York: Philomel Books. [ P/I ]

Larrick, Nancy (1992). *The night of the whippoorwill.* Illus. by David Ray. New York: Philomel Books. [ P/I ]

Lear, Edward (1991). *The owl and the pussycat.* Illus. by Jan Brett. New York: Putnam. [ P/I ]

Levy, Constance (1994). *A tree place and other poems.* Illus. by R. Sabuda. New York: McElderry Books. [ I/M ]

Levy, Constance (1996). *When whales exhale and other poems.* Illus. by Judy LaBrasca. New York: McElderry Books. [ I/M ]

Lewis, J. Patrick (1991). *Earth verses and water rhymes.* Illus. by Robert Sabuda. New York: Atheneum. [ I ]

Lewis, J. Patrick (1995). *Black swan white crow.* Woodcuts by Chris Manson. New York: Atheneum. [ I ]

Livingston, Myra Cohn (1996). *Festivals.* Illus. by Leonard Everett Fisher. New York: Holiday House. [ P/I ]

Lobel, Arnold (1983). *The book of pigericks.* New York: Harper & Row. [ P/I ]

Longfellow, Henry Wadsworth (1990). *Paul Revere's ride.* Illus. by Ted Rand. New York: Dutton. [ I/M ]

Martin, Bill Jr., & Archambault, John (1988). *Listen to the rain.* Illus. by James Endicott. New York: Henry Holt. [ P/I ]

Marzollo, Jean (1997). *Home sweet home.* Illus. by Ashley Wolff. New York: HarperCollins. [ P ]

McCord, David (1977). *One at a time.* Illus. by Henry B. Kane. Boston: Little, Brown. [ P ]

Merriam, Eve (1985). *Blackberry ink.* Illus. by Hans Wilhelm. New York: Morrow. [ P ]

Moore, Clement C. (1980). *The night before Christmas.* Illus. by Tomie de Paola. New York: Holiday House. [ P ]

Nash, Ogden (1961/1996). *Custard the dragon and the wicked knight.* Illus. by Lynn Munsinger. Boston: Little, Brown. [ P/I ]

Opie, Iona (Ed.) (1996). *My very first Mother Goose.* Illus. by Rosemary Wells. Cambridge, MA: Candlewick Press. [ P ]

Prelutsky, Jack (Ed.) (1983). *The Random House book of poetry for children.* Illus. by Arnold Lobel. New York: Random House. [ I/P ]

Prelutsky, Jack (1984). *The new kid on the block.* Illus. by James Stevenson. New York: Greenwillow Books. [ I ]

Prelutsky, Jack (1990). *Something big has been here.* Illus. by James Stevenson. New York: Greenwillow Books. [ I ]

Prelutsky, Jack (1996). *A pizza the size of the sun.* Illus. by James Stevenson. New York: Greenwillow Books. [ I ]

Sandberg, Carl (1998). *Grassroots.* Illus. by Wendell Minor. San Diego: Browndeer Press/Harcourt Brace. [ I/M ]

Schertle, Alice (1996). *Keepers.* Illus. by Ted Rand. New York: Lothrop, Lee & Shepard. [ I ]

Siebert, Diane (1989). *Heartland.* Illus. by Wendell Minor. New York: Crowell. [ I/M ]

Silverstein, Shel (1974). *Where the sidewalk ends.* New York: Harper & Row. [ I ]

Silverstein, Shel (1981). *A light in the attic.* New York: Harper & Row. [ I ]

Silverstein, Shel (1996). *Falling up.* New York: HarperCollins. [ I ]

Stevenson, James (1995). *Sweet corn.* New York: Greenwillow Books. [ I ]

Stevenson, Robert Louis (1885/1947). *A child's garden of verses.* Illus. by Tasha Tudor. New York: Oxford University Press. [ P/I ]

Viorst, Judith (1982). *If I were in charge of the world and other worries.* Illus. by Lynne Cherry. New York: Atheneum. [ I/M ]

Yolen, Jane (Selecter) (1996). *Sky scrape/city scape: Poems of City Life.* Illus. by Ken Condon. Honesdale, PA: Wordsong/Boyds Mills Press. [ P/I ].

## Chapter 6

# Realistic and Historical Fiction
## *The Boundary of Reality*

*W*hat a huge responsibility rested on Rifka's shoulders to divert the soldiers from their work
of inspecting the boxcars! What chances families will take to gain freedom! This is something we
take for granted—our freedom. And Rifka's comment, "How could Papa ever think I had such
courage?" How heartwrenching for a parent to have to use their 12-year-old child because of the
physical characteristics which can pass for a Russian peasant. . . .

Rifka's life with so many adult responsibilities and expectations is not unlike what some children go through today in families and relationships when we would like children to be able to be
carefree and play. What persecution and the desire for freedom pushes you to do! Uncle Avrum
said Papa could not let the fate of the entire family rest on the shoulders of a child. I readily agree.

Fourth-Grade Teacher Response to
*Letters from Rifka* by Karen Hesse

Realistic stories about people like themselves set in both contemporary or historical times
appeal to children as readers. The ability to identify with a character challenged by contemporary problems or surrounded by historical events engages the reader in literature. Fiction
provides a realistic view of people and issues while keeping the reader at a safe distance from
their actual occurrence. Realistic fiction set in contemporary times addresses the commonalities of family, friendship, humor, and growing up. On a more serious side, realistic fiction

addresses hardships, cruelties, and problems that face society and touch children's lives. Historical fiction, on the other hand, transports the reader to historical contexts in which heroism and courage become real attributes of character. Universal problems set in historical times and circumstances cause readers to make connections to their own lives today.

This chapter on the fictional genres of realistic and historical fiction covers literature that contains truth, but keeps the reader distanced from the harsh realities that life poses in both contemporary and historical times. The book becomes an opportunity to experience life, either yesterday or today, and learn that we are not alone. Characters in realistic and historical fiction face challenges and frustrations, succeed and fail just like the reader. Perhaps the genres with most appeal to independent readers, realistic fiction and historical fiction play an important role in engaging and developing lifelong readers.

# CONTEMPORARY REALISTIC FICTION

The genre of realistic fiction contains stories that reflect contemporary life, take place in familiar settings, and present common situations with which the reader can identify. Grounded in the common perception of what life is really like, realistic fiction strives for a balance between reality (realism) and make-believe (fiction). Quality realistic fiction is so true to life, however, that children read these novels as if they are indeed real.

The protagonists in realistic fiction face real-life problems (abuse, divorce, illness, disability, drugs, death), confront them, and mature from the life experience. Readers can gain insights into challenging situations they are facing or may face while learning about handling the problem with determination, forethought, and control. Because realistic fiction is a reflection of our society, the types of problems faced by the main characters change with time. Whereas the heroes and heroines of the 1970s may have faced divorce, foster homes, and death, today's characters face those challenges as well as abuse, drug problems, AIDS, and their own sexuality. Because societal changes warrant changes in realistic fiction, at any given time some number of books in this genre will be considered controversial and possibly even subject to censorship, particularly in a school setting. The issues of selection and censorship are discussed later in this chapter.

Realistic fiction is the most popular genre of children's literature with readers. When children walk into the library/media center and ask for a mystery, an adventure, a humorous story, or a sports story, they are actually requesting realistic fiction. Its popularity lies in the reality and believability of characters, situation, and settings. Children often read these books as if they are real and their responses reflect their involvement with the story. When children can slip into a character's life because it parallels their own or that of their peers, they are more inclined to read a book.

A recent study (Hancock, 1996) analyzed state children's choice book awards based on the votes of the children who either read nominated books independently or had nominated books read to them. The most popular children's choice books between 1985 and 1995 were all realistic fiction and included *Shiloh* (20 state awards), *There's a Boy in the Girl's Bathroom* (17 state awards), *Maniac Magee* (14 state awards), and *Hatchet* (12 state awards). The most popular children's choice authors included respected writers of realistic fiction including Mary Downing Hahn (26 state awards for 6 titles), Phyllis Reynolds Naylor (24 state awards/4 titles), Louis Sachar (21 awards/2 titles), Lois Lowry (18 awards/7 titles), and Jerry Spinelli (17 state awards/3 titles). In fact, almost half (48%) of all state children's choice awards between 1985 and 1995 were received by works of contemporary realistic fiction. These findings provide further support for the popularity of this genre, particularly with children who are independent readers of chapter books.

## Types of Realistic Fiction

Because realistic fiction covers such a broad range of contemporary life situations, this genre is commonly divided into narrower categories for discussion. Three major categories posed by Huck, Hepler, Hickman, & Kiefer (1997) with major subthemes comprehensively reflect all contemporary realistic fiction.

The first category, "Becoming One's Own Person," covers the transition from being a child and growing into an adult. The nurturing warmth of the traditional family, challenging relationships within the family, the role of extended families, and living through families in transition provide realistic themes about the role of family in growing up. Patricia MacLachlan's *Journey,* Cynthia Voigt's Tillerman family series including *Homecoming* and *Dicey's Song,* and Sharon Creech's *Walk Two Moons* address the role of families in our lives. Realistic fiction also includes stories of living with others including the struggle for peer acceptance and the importance of friendship. Readers of Katherine Paterson's *Bridge to Terabithia* and Jerry Spinelli's *Maniac Magee* witness the struggle for acceptance and the bond of strong relationships. Titles in this category hold the reader's interest, connect to the reader's life, and touch the reader's heart with their sincerity and authenticity.

The second category of "Coping With Problems of the Human Condition" includes the challenges of physical disabilities and mental disabilities, growing old, and death and dying. *The Man Who Loved Clowns* and *When Pigs Fly* by June Rae Wood put the reader in honest, empathetic touch with Down syndrome characters. Janet Hickman's *Jericho* emphasizes the gulf that separates two generations, while Dick King-Smith's *Stray* poignantly brings family and love to 75-year-old Henny who runs away from her old age home. Cynthia Rylant's *Missing May,* Sharon Creech's *Chasing Redbird,* and Barbara Park's *Mick Harte Was Here* address coping with the aftermath of the death of a loved one. Figure 6.1 lists criteria for selecting books on these issues and shares other examples of quality literature that address these important realities of life.

The final category focuses on "Living in a Diverse World" and addresses racial and ethnic diversity, stories about minorities, and stories set in the context of world cultures. Beverly Naidoo's *Journey to Jo'burg* shares the realities of apartheid, while Walter Dean Myers's books present a less grim look at urban life in America. Suzanne Fisher Staples's *Dangerous Skies* confronts the issues of racism and hypocrisy and fills the reader with rage and pain. Her previous Newbery Honor book, *Shabanu: Daughter of the Wind,* takes the reader to the desert culture of Pakistan and its expectations within our modern world. This category is elaborated on in Chapter 8 on multicultural children's literature.

These three categories are especially, but not exclusively, applicable to older readers in the upper elementary and middle schools through realistic fiction chapter books. While these subgenre form a comprehensive scheme with which professionals can organize children's realistic fiction, younger children are more apt to relate to the realistic fiction genre

**FIGURE 6.1**    Realistic fiction: coping with problems of the human condition.

---

**Criteria for Selecting Books Incorporating Disabilities or Chronic Illness**

- Promotes empathy, not pity and depicts acceptance, not ridicule.
- Emphasizes success rather than, or in addition to, failure.
- Promotes positive images of persons with disabilities.
- Assists children's growth in understanding of the disability while modeling respect.
- Promotes an attitude of "one of us" rather than "one of them."
- Utilizes language that stresses person first, disability second (i.e., Mark who is deaf).
- Depicts person with disability in real settings, activities, or occupations.

Adapted from Blaska, J. K. (1996). *Using children's literature to learn about disabilities and illness.* Moorhead, MN: Practical Press.

**Physical Disabilities**

Foreman, Michael (1996). *Seal surfer.* San Diego: Harcourt Brace. (Picture book) [ P ]
Although on crutches, a boy goes to the beach with his grandfather where he develops a continuing special bond with a seal.
Konigsburg, E. L. (1996). *The view from Saturday.* New York: Atheneum. [ I/M ]
A sixth-grade teacher, a paraplegic, helps four students develop a special bond as they compete in an Academic Bowl competition.
Paulsen, Gary (1991). *The monument.* New York: Delacorte. [ M ]
Rocky is self-conscious of the braces on her leg until a remarkable artist who comes to her small town to design a monument changes her life.
Platt, Chris (1998). *Willow king.* New York: Random House. [ I/M ]
Katie, a physically challenged 13-year-old, saves a crippled foal and nurses him back to health and eventual championships.

**Mental Disabilities**

Conly, Jane L. (1993). *Crazy lady!* New York: HarperCollins. [ M ]
As he comes to terms with his mother's death, Vernon finds comfort with the neighborhood outcasts, an alcoholic woman and her son, a child with mental retardation.
Fleming, Virginia (1993). *Be good to Eddie Lee.* Illus. by Floyd Cooper. New York: Philomel Books. (Picture book) [ P/I ]
Christy considers Eddie, a Down syndrome child, a real pest. But when he follows her into the woods, he shares special discoveries with her to indeed show he is a special person.
Fox, Paula (1997). *Radiance descending.* [ I ] New York: D.K. Inc. Note: Dorling Kindersley changed their name to D.K. Ink.
Paul scarcely is able to accept his 7-year-old brother, who has Down syndrome. With the love of his grandfather and neighbors, Paul is able to recognize the qualities that make Jacob a special person.
Philbrick, Rodman (1993). *Freak the mighty.* New York: Blue sky/Scholastic. [ M ]
Max, who has a learning disability, and his brilliant friend Freak, born with a birth defect, combine forces to make a powerful team.

**FIGURE 6.1**    Realistic fiction: coping with problems of the human condition. (*continued*)

Stone, Kimberly W. (1998). *My Louisiana sky.* New York: Henry Holt. [ I/M ]
After her grandmother's death, 12-year-old Tiger Ann Parker struggles to accept her parents, who
   have mental disabilities. She soon realizes their love and personal capabilities contribute to her
   sense of family and home.
Wood, June Rae (1992). *The man who loved clowns.* New York: Putnam. [ I/M ]
Delrita loves her Uncle Punky, but sometimes feels ashamed of his behavior because he has Down
   syndrome. Her developing understanding of love and loss creates two memorable characters.

**Chronic Illness/AIDS**

Nelson, Theresa (1994). *Earthshine.* New York: Orchard Books. [ M ]
Slim's father has AIDS and she learns to deal with the anger and guilt that diminish her own spirit. A
   support group and Isaiah, whose mother has AIDS, help Slim to cope as her father moves closer
   to death.
Porte, Barbara A. (1994). *Something terrible happened.* New York: Orchard Books. [ I/M ]
When Gillian's mother dies of AIDS, she returns to her deceased father's family in Tennessee to deal
   with death. Her biracial ancestry brings her a new understanding of herself as a stable family
   helps her cope.

through a simplified scheme that addresses children's choices and favorites. While it is important to be knowledgeable about the higher level categorization scheme, teachers may find intermediate elementary students more highly motivated by the simple terminology of the following popular categories:

***Family stories.***    Most children share the common life experience of having a family. Although the configuration of that family differs, it supports, loves, and nurtures the child in a way that makes a difference in his or her life. Beverly Cleary's timeless Ramona series and Lois Lowry's Anastasia books humorously invite us into the Quimby and Krupnik families for a taste of sibling life. Children thrive on stories that share the joys, challenges, and sadnesses of growing up as a member of the unit they call family.

***School stories.***    Stories that take place in school bring a universal setting to young readers. Here the cast of characters includes a special teacher, classmates, the class bully, the custodian, the principal, and the projects and celebrations that fill the school year. *Frindle* is an invented name for a ball point pen that takes a school and a nation by storm. Elvira Woodruff's *Dear Napoleon, I Know You're Dead, But. . .* fulfills a class assignment of writing letters to famous people and, somehow, getting answers. The close connections to children's own lives make these titles not only popular read-alouds, but books children choose on their own again and again.

***Animal stories.***    Few readers can encounter an animal story without wiping away a tear as our affinity with animals puts response at an emotional high. While sharing love and receiving loyalty in return provide a major theme of these books, it is typically the character who grows because of his or her encounter with an animal friend. Phyllis Reynolds Naylor's Shiloh trilogy, John Gardiner's *Stone Fox,* and Wilson Rawls's *Where the Red Fern Grows* are timeless stories that reach the response core of the reader. Karen Hesse's *Sable* and Betsy Hearne's *Eliza's Dog* are newer titles that add to this beloved subgenre.

***Adventure/survival stories.***   Survival stories hold powerful appeal to students in the middle grades. Without adult assistance, characters encounter situations that require quick thinking, problem solving, and inner strength. Reflecting on their ordeals, they realize that they have grown, not only in physical prowess, but in confidence and independence. Gary Paulsen's survival quartet (*Hatchet, The River, The Haymeadow,* and *Brian's Winter*) fosters response discussion on qualities and kinds of survival. Kirkpatrick Hill's *Winter Camp,* Will Hobbs's *Far North,* and Ben Mikaelsen's *Rescue Josh McGuire* reflect the strong reader attraction to the adventure story.

***Humorous stories.***   Humorous realistic fiction finds characters involved in amusing predicaments that are solved in clever ways. Books like Lois Lowry's *See You Around, Sam* and Paula Danzinger's Amber Brown series serve to introduce younger readers to the realistic fiction genre. Especially appealing to transitional readers, each chapter often stands alone as an episode in the life of the character.

***Serious stories.***   Stories that focus on societal issues fit this category. Betsy Byars's *Cracker Jackson,* for example, addresses the issue of domestic abuse while Ruth White's *Belle Prater's Boy* seeks the answers to a mother's disappearance. These are the stories of which aesthetic response can become the focus as they attempt to identify the reader with flesh-and-blood characters within the context of real-life issues.

***Mysteries.***   During some stage of a young reader's life, mystery has a role in motivating reading. While generations of readers were raised on Nancy Drew and the Hardy Boys as supersleuths, today's readers have greater variety and quality. The titles in Phyllis Reynolds Naylor's Bessledorf mystery series such as *The Bomb in the Bessledorf Bus Depot* possess the intriguing, fast action plots that hook readers. Perhaps this subgenre exists to introduce young readers to realistic fiction and, after a time, send them off to further explore the genre.

The genre of contemporary realistic fiction is indeed diverse in that it shares situations that are real and characters who must respond with maturity to deal with the real world of growing up. This most popular genre among school-age readers is a thriving one and naturally invites reader response.

# CONSIDERING LITERARY ELEMENTS IN REALISTIC FICTION

Works of children's realistic fiction must adhere to the high standards of the use of literary elements applicable to all quality fiction. Literary elements appropriate for discussion and evaluation in children's literature include plot, character, setting, theme, and point of view. While all literature justifies mention of these elements, it is in the narrative form of

Quality authors share their writing craft by skillfully incorporating literary elements in realistic function.

*From* Wringer *by Jerry Spinelli. Jacket illustration copyright © 1997 by Cliff Nielson. Used by permission of HarperCollins Publishers.*

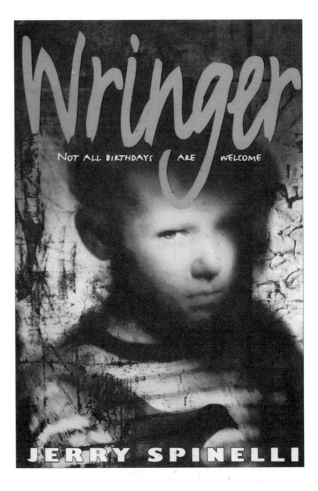

contemporary realistic fiction where these elements may best be modeled. Examining the complexity of story structure begins with the recognition of these five literary elements in the context of authentic literature. The beginnings of children's writing are grounded in the use of these elements throughout quality literature. In the following discussion, a recent example of realistic fiction, Jerry Spinelli's *Wringer,* will be used to exemplify each element.

***Plot.*** Plot is the sequence of events that occur to characters in situations in the beginning, middle, and end of a story. Conflict is the tension within the plot between a character and nature, a character and society, between characters, or even *within* the character. The unfolding conflict and ultimate resolution are what keep readers reading. Plot development occurs when the problem and conflict are introduced, continues as roadblocks are placed in the face of the character, reaches a high point when the problem is about to be solved, and concludes with the solution of the problem and removal of roadblocks at the end of the story (Tompkins, 1994).

For example, the beginning of *Wringer* transports the reader to the ninth birthday celebration of Palmer LaRue who is already experiencing peer pressure and agonizing over his impending tenth birthday. Turning 10 involves becoming a "wringer"—a boy who wrings the necks of pigeons at the town's annual Pigeon Day shoot. As the plot unfolds, Palmer (alias Snots) instinctively knows he will not be able to follow the desires of the "gang" and his father. Continuous events keep getting in the way of his ability to speak out for what he believes. Matters are brought to a climax when Palmer befriends a pigeon and must hide its presence from his peers. The plot resolution occurs when Palmer defies tradition, saves the life of the pigeon Nipper, and remains true to his ethical self.

***Setting.***      Although setting is often described as where the story takes place, setting can also include dimensions of location, weather, time, or time period (Tompkins, 1994). Some stories have backdrop settings, barely sketched, while others have specific, well-described locations. In realistic fiction, the time frame of the story focuses on a contemporary setting over a relatively short time span.

The setting for Spinelli's *Wringer* is a town called Waymer known for its 63rd annual Pigeon Day sharpshooter competition. Although the story begins a year prior to this event, the story revolves around the proximity of Palmer LaRue's tenth birthday as the day he becomes a "wringer." Details of the setting evolve from a newspaper clipping at the book's opening that alludes to a small, rural community of 4,000 people.

***Character.***      Characters in realistic fiction are those involved in the story. The main characters are fully developed, while supporting characters are minimally portrayed. Authors develop characters through appearance, action, dialogue, and monologue (Tompkins, 1994). Award-winning realistic fiction is often remembered because of unforgettable characters and personal growth.

Palmer LaRue is portrayed as a typical 9-10-year-old boy. Prone to peer pressure, but striving to define and live by his own set of standards, Palmer's actions gradually lead away from the "gang" toward supporting his own values. His speech with his peers (Beans, Mutto, Henry) expresses a playful camaraderie and need to belong, while his words to next-door-neighbor, Dorothy (Fishface), reveal a sensitive, caring individual. Palmer's innermost thoughts or monologue reveals his personal struggle to overcome peer pressure and societal expectations and to resolve his sense of doing what's right. Jerry Spinelli skillfully includes minor characters of opposing viewpoints, including a pigeon, to allow Palmer to struggle with those feelings and resolve his ethical issues.

***Theme.***      Theme is the underlying meaning or message of a story that encompasses truths about human nature and/or society. Usually dealing with the character's emotions or values, themes are either openly stated or implied in a character's actions. Friendship, courage, responsibility, truth, and justice are common themes used in children's literature (Tompkins, 1994).

The theme for *Wringer* focuses on the moral issue of killing an animal. Palmer cannot accept society's thrill over the shooting and death of pigeons. His decisive action includes recklessly dashing onto the shooting field on Pigeon Day to rescue his beloved Nipper. "Cradling his pigeon in both hands, Palmer walked from the field " (p. 228). Palmer's decision is the story's theme. The value of life becomes a priority over peer acceptance, while self-knowledge triumphs over the general view of society. Although not directly stated by the author, the theme can easily be discerned by the discriminating reader.

*Viewpoint.* The focus of the narrator determines the believability of the plot and the reader's understanding of the story. In children's literature read by intermediate and middle-level readers, the first-person point of view and the omniscient view are most commonly used. A story told through the eyes of the main character using the narrative "I" is first person. The narrator is both an eyewitness and a story participant. The omniscient viewpoint, on the other hand, sees and knows all. The author informs the reader of a character's thoughts and feelings.

In *Wringer,* the author knows every action, feeling, and thought of Palmer and shares them with the reader through a third-person perspective. Although the reader knows that Palmer is struggling with his impending decision, the reader is not quite certain until Palmer acts on his emotions. Yet it is the author who ultimately informs the reader of his final stand.

These five literary elements—plot, character, setting, theme, and viewpoint—are well defined and modeled in quality realistic fiction. These elements become the basis of the criteria for evaluating quality realistic fiction for children and positively influence readers as writers of fiction.

## Realistic Fiction Series Books

Because of this genre's appeal to young readers, realistic fiction often appears in the form of series books. Series books are formula fiction written with predictable plots, standard characters, and simplified writing style. Their predictable formulas may stretch a plot over several titles, describe different characters in similar situations, or carry the same character through different situations. These books with simple variations provide comfort in "their confirmation of previous expectations" (Nodelman, 1992) and the security of knowing that the story goes on even as the final page is turned.

Although literary experts typically view series books as a "lesser" type of literature, generations of young readers have thrived on a comforting familiarity within these titles. Grandparents may have grown up on a steady diet of the Bobbsey Twins or Tom Swift series, while many of today's parents enjoyed a steady diet of Nancy Drew and Hardy Boy mysteries. Many of today's college students might eagerly admit their attachment to Encyclopedia Brown (Donald Sobol), the Sweet Valley Twins (Francine Pascal), or the Baby-Sitters Club (Ann Martin) series. Many ardent adult readers attribute their zest for reading to their emerging adolescence when series books presented predictable characters and absorbing plots that built confidence in oneself both as a reader and as a person. Nodelman (1992) speculates that learning basic story patterns as the foundation of all fiction builds a schema for the divergent patterns in the quality literature that lies beyond the series book.

Fortunately, several recognized children's authors have taken on the task of writing books in a series. Bruce Brooks, twice recipient of a Newbery Honor award, currently authors the Wolfbay Wings series. A squirt ice hockey team led by rookie Dixon Woods (*Woodsie,* #1) attempts to lead the team to a league championship. New characters in each book continue to show skating and personal prowess for the sake of the team. Betsy Byars,

Newbery award medalist, introduces the Herculeah Jones mystery series, in which a budding spy helps his private investigator mother solve a series of intriguing cases. Newbery medalist Phyllis Reynolds Naylor presents Alice McKinley (*Alice-in-Between, Alice in Lace*) as she takes on the task of growing up female in an all-male household. Chris Lynch, author of highly acclaimed young adult books, brings humor to the eternal battle of the sexes in the He-Man Women Haters Club series. Titles like *Johnny Chesthair* and *Scratch and the Sniffs* have particular appeal to even reluctant middle-grade readers. The gravitation of quality authors into the realm of series book has recently brought a more positive view to this aspect of the realistic fiction genre.

Figure 6.2 presents a listing of both contemporary and classic series realistic fiction books that are likely to find their way into the self-selected readings of intermediate and middle-school students. School librarians, classroom teachers, and parents should be aware of their appeal and their ability to "hook" readers on reading. As mentioned in Chapter 2, readers' choices are genuine responses to literature. While these books awaken readers to the enjoyment of reading, the continuing selection of titles in a series is indeed a valid form of reader response.

**FIGURE 6.2**   Realistic fiction series books.

### Brooks, Bruce

The Wolfbay Wings series, New York: HarperCollins. [ I/M ]
   (1997). *Woodsie.*
   (1997). *Zip.*
   (1997). *Cody.*
   (1998). *Boot.*
   (1998). *Prince.*
   (1998). *Shark.*
   (1998). *Billy.*

### Byars, Betsy

Herculeah Jones mystery series, New York: Viking. [ I ]
   (1994). *The dark stairs.*
   (1995). *Tarot says beware.*
   (1996). *Dead letter.*
   (1997). *Death's door.*
   (1998). *Disappearing acts.*

### Cameron, Ann

Julian and Henry series, New York: Knopf. [ I ]
   (1995). *The stories Huey tells.*
   (1997). *More stories Huey tells.*
   (1981). *Stories Julian tells.*
   (1986). *More stories Julian tells.*

**FIGURE 6.2** Realistic fiction series books. *(continued)*

---

### Danziger, Paula

The Amber Brown series, New York: Putnam. [ I ]
  (1994). *Amber Brown is not a crayon.*
  (1995). *Amber Brown goes fourth.*
  (1995). *You can't eat chicken pox.*
  (1996). *Amber Brown wants extra credit.*
  (1996). *Forever Amber Brown.*
  (1997). *Amber Brown sees red.*
  (1998). *Amber Brown is feeling blue.*

### Howe, James

Sebastian Barth series, New York: Atheneum. [ I ]
  (1986). *Eat your poison, dear.*
  (1990). *Dew drop dead.*
  (1995). *What Eric knew.*
  (1995). *Stage fright.*

### Hurwitz, Joanna, New York: Morrow. [ I ]

  (1987). *Class clown.*
  (1988). *School spirit.*
  (1991). *School's out.*
  (1988). *Teacher's pet.*
  (1990). *Class president.*
  (1997). *Spring break.*
  (1985). *The hot and cold summer.*
  (1988). *The cold and hot winter.*
  (1993). *The up and down spring.*
  (1996). *The down and up fall.*

### Lowry, Lois

Anastasia Krupnik series, Boston: Houghton Mifflin. [ I ]
  (1979). *Anastasia Krupnek* and numerous other titles including
  (1986). *Anastasia has the answers.*
  (1987). *Anastasia's chosen career.*
  (1991). *Anastasia at this address.*
  (1992). *Attaboy, Sam!* (Anastasia's brother)
  (1995). *Anastasia, absolutely.*
  (1996). *See you around, Sam.* (Anastasia's brother)

### Lynch, Chris

The He-Man Woman Haters Club series, New York: HarperCollins. [ M ]
  (1997). *Johnny Chesthair.*
  (1997). *Babes in the woods.*

**FIGURE 6.2**   Realistic fiction series books. *(continued)*

---

(1997). *Scratch and the Sniffs.*
(1997). *Ladies' choice.*
(1998). *The wolf gang.*

### Mills, Claudia

Dinah Seabrook series [ I ]
(1990). *Dynamite Dinah.* New York: Macmillan.
(1992). *Dinah for president.* New York: Simon & Schuster.
(1993). *Dinah in love.* New York: Simon & Schuster.
(1995). *Dinah forever.* New York: Farrar, Straus & Giroux.

### Naylor, Phyllis Reynolds

Alice McKinley series, New York: Atheneum. [ I ]
(1985). *Agony of Alice* and numerous other titles including
(1994). *Alice in-between.*
(1994). *All but Alice.*
(1995). *Alice the brave.*
(1996). *Alice in lace.*
(1997). *Outrageously Alice.*
(1998). *Achingly Alice.*

### Bessledorf Mysteries series, New York: Atheneum [ I ]

(1990). *Bernie and the Bessledorf ghost.*
(1991). *The mad gasser of Bessledorf Street.*
(1992). *The bodies in the Bessledorf Hotel.*
(1993). *The face in the Bessledorf funeral parlor.*
(1996). *The bomb in the Bessledorf bus depot.*
(1998). *The treasure of Bessledorf hill.*

### Hartford Boys/Malloy Girls series, New York: Delacorte. [ I ]

(1993). *The boys start the war.*
(1993). *The girls get even.*
(1994). *The boys against the girls.*
(1998). *The girls' revenge.*

### Peck, Robert Newton

Soup series [ P/I ]
(1974). *Soup* and numerous titles in the 1970s, 1980s, and 1990s including
(1990). *Soup's hoop.* New York: Delacorte.
(1992). *Soup in love.* New York: Delacorte.
(1994). *Soup ahoy.* New York: Knopf.
(1995). *Soup 1776.* New York: Knopf.

# Criteria for Evaluating Quality Realistic Fiction

Because realistic fiction is such a popular genre, it does require careful scrutiny for inclusion in the classroom or library/media center. Because realistic fiction reflects the social conditions of our times, the issues addressed and the situations rendered may create controversy in a school setting. Criteria to locate quality titles in this genre include the following:

- Realistic fiction must, first and foremost, share a good story that engages the reader so much that they actually care about the outcome of the book.
- Realistic fiction must embrace realistic characters, situations, and settings that reflect life in a believable way.
- Character development forms an integral part of the story. The characters must grow and learn about themselves during the course of the book.
- The plot must be fresh and carry the reader into a challenging situation that requires problem solving or reflections on moral or value issues.
- Realistic fiction must maintain an optimistic view of our lives in spite of the problems that surround the story. The reader must be left with the message that people do have control over their lives and problems can be overcome, dealt with, and solved.
- Realistic fiction should reflect a balance of the different subgenre types and incorporate both males and females as protagonists who face problems with determination and courage, regardless of the eventual outcome.

# Values of Realistic Fiction

Although it seems somewhat redundant to enumerate the strengths of this genre, the following list emphasizes why this genre plays such an important role in both reading for pleasure and personal/social development of the reader.

- Realistic fiction invites the reader to gain insights into themselves and their peers in the context of realistic relationships and problems that form the core of our lives.
- Realistic fiction fosters reader engagement and understanding because situations and events are familiar to the reader. This factor actually contributes to the popularity of this genre.
- Realistic fiction presents a model of confronting life experiences in which the reader serves as a spectator as characters cope with contemporary issues.
- Realistic fiction provides readers with a safe distance between unknown areas while building reader awareness of their existence. Rather than sheltering, realistic fiction invites readers to observe and empathize with the problems of others that may never touch their own lives.
- Realistic fiction depicts life in other cultures set in geographic regions around the world allowing for a broader perspective on viewing the world.

# Reader Response Connections

Realistic fiction provides sound support for reader response through literature response journals, character journals, and literature conversations. Some of the richest personal responses are elicited from realistic fiction. Responses to living through the experiences of others reflect an empathy and preparedness for confronting problems in one's own life. The real world of growing up is a challenge, but realistic fiction books provide a connection to that world so readers experience the fact that they are not alone with the problems they face.

The written response is perhaps the strongest mode gleaned from interactions with realistic fiction (see Chapter 10). Because of the private nature of written reader response, the reader is more confident sharing connections with his or her own life as literature and reality bridge a challenging time in a young person's life. Realistic fiction holds the key to better understanding oneself and others as the realities of contemporary life confront us.

# HISTORICAL FICTION

*The Ballad of Lucy Whipple* by Karen Cushman exemplifies the true-to-life characters, historical realism, and authentic background that make historical fiction a popular literary genre. Unwillingly uprooted from her Massachusetts home, 12-year-old California Morning Whipple (self-named Lucy) becomes an involuntary citizen of Lucky Diggins. A lifelong dream of her deceased father causes her adventurous mother and siblings to journey by ship to California in 1849. Instead of gold, Lucy finds only tattered tents, no lending library, and rough and boisterous miners. Emotional letters back home reflect Lucy's rebellious, outspoken nature as well as her genuine misery and misgivings. While Lucy is slow to admit that the unsettled nature of the western wilderness is the perfect match for her imagination, her love of reading eventually provides a reason to call California home.

Historical fiction is realistic fiction set in the historical past. While the story is imaginary, characters and events introduced could really have occurred in this historical context. Based on historical facts, the story is skillfully blended with historical settings, historical figures, and historical events. Not only does historical fiction convey a sense of historical period, but it shares a rousing story that actually could have taken place.

Widely used in literature-based classrooms, historical fiction has become an effective link between social studies and literacy instruction (Farris & Cooper, 1997; James & Zarillo, 1989; Johnson & Ebert, 1992; Tunnell & Ammon, 1993). The parallel study of historical facts beside a dazzling story set during the same period provides a motivating means of breathing life into the curriculum. Karen Cushman's *The Midwife's Apprentice,* for example, integrated with a middle-level study of the Middle Ages, brings the attitudes, social customs, and physical surroundings of the period to life. In addition, a sound story of self-respect and self-worth evolves. The quality of historical fiction, evidenced by its repeated connections between history and the realities of life, makes this genre a welcome choice by both students and their teachers. Through both historical fiction picture books and chapter books, this genre provides a meaningful link to interdisciplinary instruction.

## Types of Historical Fiction

Even though all historical fiction tells an energizing story set in a historical time period, variations do exist between types of historical fiction books.

***Historically researched with imaginary characters.*** Most historical fiction is of this type. Set in an authentic period, the invented main character lives amid authentic events, settings, and issues. Katherine Paterson's *Lyddie* remains a memorable literary character as circumstances take her from Vermont to the factory mills of Lowell, Massachusetts. The long, hard hours of factory workers during America's Industrial Revolution are showcased through the eyes of believable characters. Author notes acknowledge research sources that authentically support the writing of this strong example of historical fiction.

***Historical period piece.*** The historical context is the focus as the social conventions, customs, morals, and values of the historical period are showcased around a character. The early years of westward expansion set the stage for Mary Jane Auch's *Journey to Nowhere* set in 1815 on a difficult trek from Hartland, Connecticut, to Genesee County, New York. Inspired by knowledge of the hardships of early settlement, the author begins her planned trilogy as Mem Nye and her family set off in a covered wagon facing innumerable hardships in their struggle to establish a permanent home. Exact location, time period, events, and an author's note attest to the historical authenticity of this title as the reader is immersed in a historically accurate way of life during eastern settlement.

***Time travel.*** Contemporary characters are transported to the past as time travel sets them in another historical context. The character lives through actual events and returns to the present with a deeper understanding of history. Elvira Woodruff's *The Orphan of Ellis Island* transports Dominic Cantori from a class visit to Ellis Island back to Italy in 1908 as he unlocks the doors to his past. After the author visited the museum at Ellis Island, she sensed the importance of family in history and used this time travel adventure to reinforce her message. Often classified as a type of fantasy (see Chapter 5), the heavy historical emphasis of some titles comfortably places these books in the historical fiction genre as well.

***Personal chronicle.*** The author actually experienced a historical period and writes about his or her own life through authentic memories or documented journal entries. The reader relives moments from the author's life, usually as a child, and learns about growing up and living in a particular historical period. Laura Ingalls Wilder's Little House series takes the reader to a bygone time, yet documents the simple pleasures and joys of growing up on the prairie.

## Judging Quality Historical Fiction

First presented in 1984, the Scott O'Dell Award (see Appendix A) is given to the author of a distinguished work of historical fiction written for children or adolescent readers. The award was originated by Scott O'Dell, author of quality historical fiction including *Island of the Blue Dolphins*, *Sing Down the Moon*, and *Sarah Bishop*. Winners of this award constitute a sound starting point for selecting the best of the genre. Recent winners provide many of the examples throughout this chapter.

While historical fiction must first and foremost deliver a good story, several specific criteria should be considered in judging the best of this genre. Parallel examples from Karen

Historical fiction must be authentically presented, historically accurate, and weave historical detail into a good story.
*Cover from* CATHERINE, CALLED BIRDY *by Karen Cushman. Jacket illustration copyright © 1994 by Trina Schart Hyman. Reprinted by permission of Clarion Books/Houghton Mifflin Company. All rights reserved.*

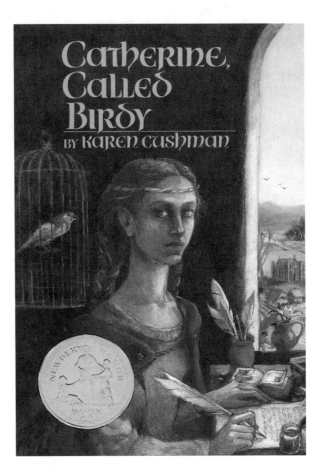

Cushman's *Catherine, Called Birdy,* 1994 Newbery Honor book, connect to each criteria to better reflect the quality of this genre of literature.

***History should be authentically presented.***     No attempt should be made to shelter the reader from the realities of the time period. The barbaric eating and drinking habits of medieval times shared in *Catherine, Called Birdy* may be considered vulgar, but they do replicate the feudal system hierarchy and the authentic life surrounding it. Likewise, the language of the period, while harsh, reflects the language of the times.

***Historical accuracy must be a priority.***     Historical fiction is grounded in historical fact and authenticity must be preserved. While fictitious characters and contrived conversations abound, the context must truly reflect the times. Catherine, for example, snatches a glimpse of King Edward I in a death procession of the Queen, Eleanor of Castile, a verified historical event for 1290. Catherine is appalled by the dancing bear at the fair. Partially fictionalized, fairs and animal entertainment were, however, popular during the Middle Ages and the event holds true to the happenings of the times.

***The story must recreate the times through setting, daily life, and customs.*** The reader should be able to visualize the physical surroundings, imagine the clothing, taste the meals, and note the traditions of the times. *Catherine, Called Birdy* transports the reader to both the fervor of the raucous banquet hall and the reality of the cold privy in medieval times. Readers may be appalled by the thought of eel pie, but this was indeed a food of the times. The thought of Catherine at 14 marrying a man of 50 may seem disturbing to the adolescent reader, but negotiated marriages were the rule of the time reflecting the social hierarchy, family expectations, and accepted customs of the Middle Ages.

***The story reveals history through a character of similar age to the reader.*** By becoming involved with the protagonist, male or female, the reader generally assimilates history while empathizing with a character. The character's actions, beliefs, and values must be aligned with the time period. The language of the character should be appropriate to the period, including figures of speech that reflect the times. While dialogue must convey a feeling of the period, it must accomplish this without overwheming the reader. Fourteen-year-old Birdy's diary reflects the bold language of the period and her entrapment by the stereotypes of her times. Her quest to find a word that expresses her sentiments, "Corpus bones," puts an even further emphasis on language.

***The writing style should unobtrusively weave historical detail into a good story.*** The reader should be immersed in history without actually realizing that's what is happening. Birdy's diary format highlighted by the saint's day notes provides a historical sequencing and attests to religion's impact on the times, while each entry reflects the evolving growth, resignation, and realization as Birdy becomes a young woman. The challenge of achieving this literary blend is a demanding one and attained by several talented writers who specialize in this genre.

## Literary Elements in Historical Fiction

Just as this chapter looked at the five literary elements in the context of realistic fiction, so will it view them in the context of historical fiction. An exemplary choice for discussing these elements is Karen Hesse's *Out of the Dust,* the Newbery Medal winner for 1998. The Newbery Medal is awarded annually to the author of the most distinguished contribution to American literature for children. This recent winner exemplifies the effective use of literary elements in writing historical fiction. Although presented in a nontraditional historical format as a novel in free verse, this book captures the spirit of the Depression and the devastated lives of the victims of drought, dust, and poverty.

The **setting** of *Out of the Dust* is Cimarron County, Oklahoma, during the dust bowl years of the Great Depression. The book is divided into five sections covering the period from Winter 1934 to Summer 1935. Each entry is labeled with the exact month and year making the historical chronology of the weather and economic conditions even more real. The **plot** involves 14-year-old Billie Jo who is faced with the guilt of accidentally being responsible for the tragic death of her mother and unborn brother. A fire causes fatal burns as well for Billie Jo whose hands are disfigured in the flames. The family's loss and their struggle to deal with inward emotions and the never-ending dust and poverty of the Dust Bowl years form the storyline of this historical account of fragile lives in difficult times.

The main **character,** Billie Jo, possesses a passion for playing the piano and loving and respecting her family. The tragic loss of this family compounded by the ghastly ecological conditions cause her to feel isolated, alone, and disconnected from the place she has called home. Yet her attempt to leave her feelings and guilt behind are thwarted as she feels the pull of family, roots, and home. Billie Jo is able to dig deep within to begin anew like so many victims of the terrible Dust Bowl that devasted the Great Plains during the 1930s. The historical account is revealed through her first-person **viewpoint** as the strong voice of "I" shares emotions and unfolding events. The **theme** of this painful account of personal and geographic tragedy is the persistence of the human spirit in desperate times. Not only does the reader learn of the history and vivid conditions of the Oklahoma Dust Bowl, but also the reality of the human will to survive in spite of personal and environmental conditions.

The five literary elements are well represented by Karen Hesse's quality writing and further support the importance of observing, noting, and discussing the role of literary elements in creating quality fictional works. Any Newbery award historical fiction title or any Scott O'Dell award books (see Appendix A) could be evaluated through a similar literary element lens.

## Trends in Historical Fiction

The chapter book has provided the mainstay of the historical fiction genre for decades. Walter Edmonds's *The Matchlock Gun,* Marguerite de Angeli's *Door in the Wall,* Carolyn Reeder's *Shades of Gray,* and Graham Salisbury's *Under the Blood Red Sun* exemplify award-winning titles in chapter book form across 50 years. The 1990s, however, witnessed some invigorating format additions to the historical fiction genre that appeal to a wider range of readers. Most notable are the historical fiction picture book and historical fiction titles in a series.

The picture book is not entirely new to historical fiction, but many more books are being published today that carry illustrated versions of fictionalized historical events. Based on historical facts, Michael Tunnell's *Mailing May* portrays travel in the West of 1914, while Elizabeth Friedrich's *Leah's Pony* captures a family's hard times during the Depression of the 1930s. Candace Fleming's *The Hatmaker's Sign: A Story by Benjamin Franklin* and Karen Winnick's *Mr. Lincoln's Whiskers* both share fictionalized accounts of real moments in history. Vivid portrayals of slavery in Veronica Chamber's *Amistad Rising: A Story of Freedom* and Ken Mochizuki's *Baseball Saved Us* share the stories of heroic efforts in authentic contexts in American history.

The picture book format provides a way to introduce the historical fiction genre to younger children. But it also provides an appealing, time-effective means of introducing history to intermediate/middle-level students of history. Connecting humanity to historical times is a strength of the focus of the picture book topic and format for disseminating the personal side of history.

The second trend in historical fiction is the advent of the historical fiction series book. Although series books have been popular in realistic fiction, only recently has historical fiction taken on the series appeal. A quality example of a historical fiction series is the Dear America series, which utilizes journal entries to deliver historically accurate information about the growth of our country through the words of children. The appeal of journal reading, the American history connections to the elementary social studies curriculum, and the continuing saga of young female characters during various historical periods blend to appeal to intermediate-level readers. The series began with early titles such as *A Journey to the New World: The Diary of Remember Patience Whipple*, *The Winter of Red Snow: The Revolutionary War Diary of Abigail Jane Stewart*, and *When Will This Cruel War Be Over? The Civil War Diary of Emma Simpson*.

The Dear America series has extended to include stories of slavery, westward expansion, and immigration and has grown in quality with authors such as Kathryn Lasky, Patricia McKissack, and Jim Murphy. *I Thought My Soul Would Rise and Fly: The Diary of Patsy, a Freed Girl* won a Coretta Scott King honor book award. Each title is authenticated with historical notes, author notes, archival photographs, maps, recipes, sheet music, and other indications of life during the historical period. With increased popularity, the series has branched out with the My Name Is America series, which focuses on male characters including *The Journal of William Thomas Emerson: A Revolutionary War Patriot* and *The Journal of James Edmond Pease: A Civil War Union Soldier*. The series appeal with titles tied to American history has led to their use in classrooms and they are popular items on library shelves.

## Values of Historical Fiction

Beyond the value of enjoying a well-written story, historical fiction offers several benefits to the reader.

- Historical fiction represents historical facts through the everyday life of young people living during a particular historical period. Historical facts shared through realistic characters and settings bring history to life for readers (Cianciolo, 1981). *The Apprenticeship of Lucas Whitaker* focuses on consumption during the mid-1800s as this scourge leaves Lucas an orphan. As an apprentice to Doc Beecher, Lucas exposes beliefs and attitudes of the day regarding health and witchcraft as he even digs up coffins to ward off the affliction. The extraordinary advances in medical knowledge through the last century stand in stark contrast to the beliefs of this period.
- Historical fiction provides personal interaction with and understanding of the people, places, and events related to a particular historical period. Katherine Paterson's *Jip: His Story* evokes the attitudes and social conditions of the 1850s. The plot revolves around Jip, a gypsy who as an infant fell from a wagon 8 years before the story opens. He becomes a resident of the town poor farm and seems doomed to permanent servitude. Jip befriends an elderly man, who is prone to fits of violence and confined to a wooden cage. His growing awareness of the wretched conditions and the concern of a new teacher lead to a startling revelation about Jip's origins. Carefully planned by a master of this genre, this book shares a historical period through outstanding writing.
- Historical fiction provides enjoyment in reading a literary genre steeped in historical accuracy, yet focused on strong characters whose lives are set in a historical context. Avi's two-volume *Beyond the Western Sea* (*Book One: The Escape from Home*; *Book Two: Lord Kirkle's Money*) tells a fast-paced story based on the escape of Irish emigrants

from the Great Famine. A wealth of characters, short chapters, and the talent of Avi as a writer combine to keep the reader involved from start to finish. A superb read-aloud that represents historical fiction at its best, this remarkable saga shares the pleasure and fulfillment of this genre, which can lead to lifelong reading experiences.

## Reader Response to Historical Fiction

Reader response to historical fiction, typically in the form of chapter books for intermediate/middle-level readers, is through literature conversations and response journals, but especially through character journals, which invite the reader to become a part of history through character identification (see Chapter 10). Choosing either Edward or Simon from Carolyn Reeder's Civil War novel, *Across the Lines,* helps create empathy for people and the situations surrounding this period in American history. Historical fiction begs dramatic reenactments of scenes and dialogue from the text or adaptation to a readers' theater script (see Chapter 12). Honored works of historical fiction, such as Elizabeth Speare's *The Witch of Blackbird Pond,* the Colliers' *My Brother Sam is Dead,* Avi's *The True Confessions of Charlotte Doyle,* Patricia Beatty's *Charley Skedaddle,* Patricia MacLachlan's *Sarah, Plain and Tall,* Scott O'Dell's *Island of the Blue Dolphins,* and Lois Lowry's *Number the Stars,* provide a chronological look at history that invites written response through reader immersion in another time and another place.

Some of the most honored children's books grace the historical fiction genre. While seemingly reserved for older readers, many excellent picture books also stand as an introduction to this genre for both younger and older readers. Patricia Polacco's *Pink and Say* shares a poignant friendship cast in the divisiveness of the Civil War. Elisa Bartone's *Peppe the Lamplighter* captures the dream of immigrants while Gloria Houston's *But No Candy* opens our hearts as World War II touches young lives. These titles invite younger readers into this genre and open literature connections to history in early elementary classrooms.

Well-written historical fiction can help children find their place in the vast framework of history. Quality historical fiction breathes life into history and the curriculum and connects across time with personal feelings and experiences. As children savor historical fiction, they realize that today's events rapidly become a part of tomorrow's history.

# ISSUES OF SELECTION AND CENSORSHIP

The genres of realistic and historical fiction cannot be mentioned without addressing the responsibility of selection of literature from those genres for individual reading or classroom use. Selection, however, assumes the companion issue of censorship.

> Once upon a time and far away children's books were perceived as simple things, concerned with naughty little rabbits, perplexed toy bears, and fairy princesses. Today they're often viewed as a pernicious enemy with the ability to corrupt impressionable minds and destroy our country. Those who hold this opinion seek then to remove these terrible influences from classrooms and libraries. (McClure, 1995, p. 3)

When teachers and librarians/media center directors believe that children must be exposed to meaningful literature for reading to come alive, they also believe that they must read what is personal and important to them. For many children, those issues include those they confront on a daily basis both in and out of school—divorce, death, disability, substance abuse, physical abuse, cultural differences, nontraditional families, and prejudice. Exposure to books on these topics may lead children to become better readers and better able to cope with issues in their own lives (Rasinski & Gillespie, 1992). Yet in well-intentioned efforts to develop sensitivity, respect, and tolerance within the traumatic contexts of children's lives, teachers and librarians may be opening their literary choices to criticism from the community beyond the school. In an honest attempt to show children "they are not alone," the issue of censorship becomes an issue for consideration as part of the literature environment in a response-based reading program.

In her introduction to *Battling Dragons,* a collection of authors' voices on issues dealing with censorship, Susan Lehr (1995) points to the growing number of authors writing about the diverse and somewhat frightening experiences of children today and in the past. Episodes from *The Clay Marble* (Ho, 1991), *Fly Away Home* (Bunting, 1991), or *Monkey Island* (Fox, 1991) represent but a few examples of the violence and neglect that real children experience as recaptured in children's literature. "The books provide real and often disturbing views of life, challenging readers to think about issues from which some would rather shelter children" (p. xiii). Whether censors are politically motivated or moved by a sense of morality, they attempt to monitor and control the books children read rather than having reading selection be a matter of personal choice. The commonality among censors (parents, teachers, librarians, community members) is their desire to protect children from influences they perceive as evil or harmful.

Julie Wollman-Bonilla's (1998) recent study of preservice and inservice teachers' criteria for rejecting works of children's literature from their classrooms are enlightening and, unfortunately, indicative of a conservative attitude observed in the professional teaching community. ". . . [t]eachers commonly objected to texts that reflect gender, ethnic, race, or class perspectives or experiences that differed from their own." (p. 289). These are the three rationale behind text inappropriateness and examples cited in this study:

1. The belief that a text is inappropriate for children because it might frighten or corrupt them by introducing them to things they don't or shouldn't know about. [Examples cited: *Fly Away Home* (Bunting, 1991)—homelessness; *Bridge to Terabithia* (Paterson, 1977)—death; *Smoky Night* (Bunting, 1994)—riots; *Roll of Thunder, Hear My Cry* (Taylor, 1976)—discrimination.]
2. The belief that a text is inappropriate for children because it fails to represent dominant social values or myths. [Examples cited: *Amazing Grace* (Hoffman, 1991)—nontraditional families and improper English; *Tar Beach* (Ringgold, 1991)—struggle for financial security and challenges work ethic as a key to happiness.]
3. The belief that a text is inappropriate for children because it identifies racism or sexism as a social problem. [Examples cited: *Nettie's Trip South* (Turner, 1987)—blacks considered three fifths of a person in the Constitution; *William's Doll* (Zolotow, 1972)—challenges traditional gender roles.]

Wollman-Bonilla (1998) further suggests teachers are quite conscious of their criteria for text rejection, yet challenges their thinking on each criterion. Rejecting texts because they might frighten or corrupt actually separates schools and society rather than using schools as a place in which children are taught to act responsibly and exhibit openmindedness in a diverse world. Using books as a means to uphold mainstream norms does not teach reading as a critical thinking process or recognize that readers construct meaning from their personal backgrounds and experiences. Finally, believing that if they avoid a discussion of racism and sexism, it will go away typically reveals the status quo embedded within these real issues. With a desire to do what is "best" for children, the question still remains: "Who decides what is best for children?" (p. 292).

In the school setting, professional guidelines should serve both teachers and librarians in making selections for the classroom or the media center. "Selection" takes a more positive view of literature choices (than censorship) by *including* specific materials, *intending* to advise and educate, and *increasing* access to ideas and information. Collecting reviews from respected professional sources (see Appendix B), applying guidelines for literary quality (see Chapters 3–8), and following policy statements to back up choices generally ensures quality literary choices for children.

Selecting quality realistic and historical fiction (and all genres, for that matter) demands that those who decide what is "best" for children recognize their own biases and offset them by providing a balanced program that assists students in becoming both effective readers and lovers of literature. Providing time for discussion and response following the reading of all books may be the most appropriate means of ensuring this needed balance. Building a strong classroom and library/media center collection that represents diversity of thought and peoples through realistic and historical fiction (as well as other genres) should be a priority.

# CLOSING THOUGHTS

The genres of realistic and historical fiction hold strong appeal for independent readers in the intermediate/middle-level grades. The appeal often lies in the reality of the characters and the challenging problems in their lives. Whether the setting is contemporary or historical, a fictional character and an involved reader form a strong bond. That bond is often evidenced in oral or written response connections to these powerful genres. Identifying with a character of a similar age seems to draw readers to books. Whether set in a historical context or in hometown/urban contemporary America, these characters face problems, encounter obstacles, and falter in their attempts to grow up. Yet they maintain an admirable persistence, a growing maturity, and a problem-solving capability that provides a role model to the reader.

Teachers need to revere these genres because realistic and historical fiction can change readers in classrooms into lifelong readers. Reading popular authors aloud brings these genres to life at a critical time as children determine their literacy futures. The incredible blend between social studies and historical fiction makes their inclusion viable in interdisciplinary connections. The meaningful relationship between a contemporary character and a reader of realistic fiction makes this genre mandatory as children strive to grow up. The inclusion of realistic fiction and historical fiction ensures an opportunity for growth as a consumer of literature and as a maturing individual.

# REFERENCES

Blaska, J. K. (1996). *Using children's literature to learn about disabilities and illness.* Moorhead, MN: Practical Press.

Cianciolo, P. (1981). Yesterday comes alive for readers of historical fiction. *Language Arts, 59,* 452–462.

Farris, P. J., & Cooper, S. M. (Eds.) (1997). *Elementary and middle school social studies: A whole language approach* (2nd ed.). Madison, WI: Brown & Benchmark.

Hancock, M. R. (1996). *State children's choice book awards: Instructional insights through children's literary preferences.* Paper presented at the 41st Annual Convention of the International Reading Association, New Orleans, LA.

Huck, C., Hepler, S., Hickman, J., & Kiefer, B. Z. (1997). *Children's literature in the elementary school* (6th ed.) Madison, WI: Brown & Benchmark.

James, M., & Zarillo, J. (1989). Teaching history with children's literature: A concept-based interdisciplinary approach. *Social Studies, 80,* 153–158.

Johnson, N. M., & Ebert, M. J. (1992). Time travel is possible: Historical fiction and biography— Passport to the past. *The Reading Teacher, 45,* 488–495.

Lehr, S. (Ed.) (1995). *Battling dragons: Issues and controversies in children's literature.* Portsmouth, NH: Heinemann.

McClure, A. (1995). Censorship of children's books. In S. Lehr (Ed.), *Battling dragons: Issues and controversies in children's literature* (pp. 3–25). Portsmouth, NH: Heinemann.

Nodelman, P. (1992). *The pleasures of children's literature.* New York: Longman.

Rasinski, T. V., & Gillespie, C. S. (1992). *Sensitive issues: An annotated guide to children's literature K–6.* Phoenix, AZ: Oryx Press.

Tompkins, G. (1994). *Teaching writing.* Upper Saddle River, NJ: Merrill/Prentice-Hall.

Tunnell, M. O., & Ammon, R. (1993). *The story of ourselves: Teaching history through children's literature.* Portsmouth, NH: Heinemann.

Wollman-Bonilla, J. E. (1998). Outrageous viewpoints: Teachers' criteria for rejecting works of children's literature. *Language Arts, 75,* 287–295.

# CHILDREN'S BOOKS CITED: REALISTIC FICTION

Brooks, Bruce (1997). *Woodsie.* (The Wolfbay Wings series). New York: HarperCollins. [ I/M ]

Bunting, Eve (1991). *Fly away home.* Illus. by Ronald Himler. Boston: Clarion/Houghton Mifflin. [ P/I ]

Bunting, Eve (1994). *Smoky night.* Illus. by David Diaz. San Diego: Harcourt Brace. [ P/I ]

Byars, Betsy (1985). *Cracker Jackson.* New York: Viking. [ I/M ]

Cleary, Beverly (1968). *Ramona the pest.* Illus. by Lois Darling. New York: Morrow. [ P/I ]

Clements, Andrew (1996). *Frindle.* Illus. by Brian Selxnick. New York: Simon & Schuster. [ I ]

Creech, Sharon (1994). *Walk two moons.* New York: HarperCollins. [ I/M ]

Creech, Sharon (1997). *Chasing redbird.* New York: Joanna Cottler/HarperCollins. [ I/M ]

Danzinger, Paula (1997). *Amber Brown sees red.* New York: Putnam. [ I ]

Fox, Paula (1991). *Monkey island.* New York: Orchard. [ I ]

Gardiner, John (1980). *Stone fox.* Illus. by Marcia Sewall. New York: Crowell. [ P/I ]

Hearne, Betsy (1996). *Eliza's dog.* New York: McElderry Books. [ I ]

Hesse, Karen (1994). *Sable.* Illus. by Marcia Sewall. New York: Holt. [ P/I ]

Hickman, Janet (1994). *Jericho.* New York: Greenwillow Books. [ I ]

Hill, Kirkpatrick (1993). *Winter camp.* New York: McElderry Books. [ I ]

Ho, Minfong (1991). *The clay marble.* New York: Farrar, Straus & Giroux. [ I/M ]

Hoffman, Mary (1991). *Amazing Grace.* Illus. by Caroline Binch. New York: Dial. [ P/I ]

Hobbs, Will (1996). *Far North.* New York: Morrow. [ M ]

King-Smith, Dick (1996). *Stray.* Illus. by Wayne Parmenter. New York: Crown. [ I ]

Lowry, Lois (1979). *Anastasia Krupnik.* (Anastasia series) Boston: Houghton Mifflin. [ I ]

Lowry, Lois (1996). *See you around, Sam!* Boston: Houghton Mifflin. [ I ]

Lynch, Chris (1997). *Johnny Chesthair.* New York: HarperCollins. [ M ]

Lynch, Chris (1997). *Scratch and the sniffs.* New York: HarperCollins. [ M ]

MacLachlan, Patricia (1991). *Journey.* New York: Delacorte. [ I/M ]

Mikaelsen, Ben (1991). *Rescue Josh McGuire.* New York: Hyperion. [ I ]

Naidoo, Beverly (1986). *Journey to Jo'burg.* Philadelphia: Lippincott. [ I/M ]

Naylor, Phyllis Reynolds (1991). *Shiloh.* New York: Atheneum. [ I ]

Naylor, Phyllis Reynolds (1994). *Alice in-between.* New York: Atheneum. [ I ]

Naylor, Phyllis Reynolds (1996). *Alice in lace.* New York: Atheneum. [ I ]

Naylor, Phyllis Reynolds (1996). *The bomb in the Bessledorf bus depot.* New York: Atheneum. [ I ]

Naylor, Phyllis Reynolds (1996). *Shiloh season.* New York: Atheneum. [ I ]

Naylor, Phyllis Reynolds (1997). *Saving Shiloh.* New York: Atheneum. [ I ]

Park, Barbara (1995). *Mick Harte was here.* New York: Apple Soup. [ I ]

Paterson, Katherine (1977). *Bridge to Terabithia.* New York: Crowell. [ I/M ]

Paulsen, Gary (1987). *Hatchet.* New York: Bradbury. [ I/M ]

Paulsen, Gary (1991). *The river.* New York: Delacorte. [ I/M ]

Paulsen, Gary (1992). *The haymeadow.* New York: Delacorte. [ I/M ]

Paulsen, Gary (1996). *Brian's winter.* New York: Delacorte. [ I/M ]

Rawls, Wilson (1961). *Where the red fern grows.* New York: Doubleday. [ I/M ]

Ringgold, Faith (1991). *Tar beach.* New York: Crown. [ P/I ]

Rylant, Cynthia (1992). *Missing May.* New York: Orchard Books. [ I/M ]

Sachar, Louis (1987). *There's a boy in the girl's bathroom.* New York: Knopf. [ I ]

Spinelli, Jerry (1990). *Maniac Magee.* New York: HarperCollins. [ I ]

Spinelli, Jerry (1997). *Wringer.* New York: HarperCollins. [ I ]

Staples, Suzanne Fisher (1989). *Shabanu: Daughter of the wind.* New York: Knopf. [ M ]

Staples, Suzanne Fisher (1996). *Dangerous skies.* New York: Farrar, Straus and Giroux. [ M ]

Voigt, Cynthia (1981). *Homecoming.* New York: Atheneum. [ M ]

Voigt, Cynthia (1983). *Dicey's song.* New York: Atheneum. [ M ]

White, Ruth (1996). *Belle Prater's boy.* New York: Farrar, Straus and Giroux. [ I/M ]

Woodruff, Elvira (1992). *Dear Napoleon, I know you're dead, but . . . .* New York: Holiday House. [ I ]

Woods, June Rae (1993). *The man who loved clowns.* New York: Putnam. [ I/M ]

Woods, June Rae (1994). *When pigs fly.* New York: Putnam. [ I/M ]

Zolotow, Charlotte (1972). *William's doll.* Illus. by William Pene Du Bois. New York: HarperCollins. [ P ]

# CHILDREN'S BOOKS CITED: HISTORICAL FICTION
## [ P ] = K–2; [ I ] = 3–5; [ M ] = 6–8

Auch, Mary Jane (1997). *Journey to nowhere.* New York: Holt. [ I ]

Avi (1990). *The true confessions of Charlotte Doyle.* New York: Orchard Books. [ M ]

Avi (1996). *Beyond the western sea. Book One: The escape from home.* New York: Orchard Books. [ I/M ]

Avi (1996). *Beyond the western sea. Book Two: Lord Kirkle's money.* New York: Orchard Books. [ I/M ]

Bartone, Elisa (1993). *Peppe the lamplighter*. Illus. by Ted Lewin. New York: Lothrop, Lee & Shepard. [ P ]

Beatty, Patricia (1987). *Charley Skedaddle*. New York: Morrow. [ I ]

Chambers, Veronica (1998). *Amistad rising: A story of freedom*. Illus. by Paul Lee. San Diego: Harcourt Brace. [ I/M ]

Collier, James Lincoln, & Collier, Christopher (1974). *My brother Sam Is dead*. Four Winds. [ I/M ]

Cushman, Karen (1994). *Catherine, called Birdy*. Boston: Clarion. [ M ]

Cushman, Karen (1995). *The midwife's apprentice*. Boston: Clarion. [ M ]

Cushman, Karen (1996). *The ballad of Lucy Whipple*. Boston: Clarion. [ I/M ]

de Angeli, Marguerite (1949). *Door in the wall*. New York: Doubleday. [ I ]

DeFelice, Cynthia (1996). *The apprenticeship of Lucas Whitaker*. New York: Farrar, Straus and Giroux. [ I/M ]

Denenberg, Barry (1996). *When will this cruel war be over? The Civil War diary of Emma Simpson* (Dear America series). New York: Scholastic. [ I ]

Denenberg, Barry (1998). *The journal of William Thomas Emerson: A Revolutionary War patriot* (My Name Is America series). New York: Scholastic. [ I ]

Edmonds, Walter (1941). *The matchlock gun*. Illus. by Paul Lantz. New York: Dodd. [ I ]

Fleming, Candace (1998). *The hatmaker's sign: A story by Benjamin Franklin*. Illus. by Robert Andrew Parker. New York: Orchard Books. [ P/I ]

Friedrich, Elizabeth (1996). *Leah's pony*. Illus. by Michael Garland. Honesdale, PA: Boyds Mills Press. [ P/I ]

Gregory, Kristina (1996). *The winter of red snow: The Revolutionary War diary of Abigail Jane Stewart* (Dear America series). New York: Scholastic. [ I ]

Hansen, Joyce (1997). *I thought my soul would rise and fly: The diary of Patsy, a freed girl* (Dear America series). New York: Scholastic. [ I ]

Hesse, Karen (1997). *Out of the dust*. New York: Scholastic. [ I/M ]

Houston, Gloria (1992). *But no candy*. Illus. by Lloyd Bloom. New York: Philomel Books. [ I ]

Lasky, Kathryn (1996). *A journey to the New World: The diary of Patience Whipple* (Dear America series). New York: Scholastic. [ I ]

Lowry, Lois (1989). *Number the stars*. Boston: Houghton Mifflin. [ I ]

MacLachlan, Patricia (1985). *Sarah, plain and tall*. New York: Harper & Row. [ P/I ]

Mochizuki, Ken (1993). *Baseball saved us*. Illus. by Dom Lee. New York: Lee & Low. [ I/M ]

Murphy, Jim (1998). *The journal of James Edmond Pease: A Civil War Union soldier* (My Name Is America series). New York: Scholastic. [ I ]

O'Dell, Scott (1960). *Island of the blue dolphins*. Boston: Houghton Mifflin. [ I/M ]

O'Dell, Scott (1970). *Sing down the moon*. Boston: Houghton Mifflin. [ I/M ]

O'Dell, Scott (1980). *Sarah Bishop*. Boston: Houghton Mifflin. [ I/M ]

Paterson, Katherine (1991). *Lyddie*. New York: Dutton. [ M ]

Paterson, Katherine (1996). *Jip: His story*. New York: Lodestar. [ M ]

Polacco, Patricia (1994). *Pink and Say*. New York: Philomel. [ I ]

Reeder, Carolyn (1989). *Shades of gray*. New York: Macmillan. [ I/M ]

Reeder, Carolyn (1997). *Across the lines*. New York: Atheneum. [ I/M ]

Salisbury, Graham (1994). *Under the blood red sun*. New York: Delacorte. [ I/M ]

Speare, Elizabeth (1958). *The witch of blackbird pond*. Boston: Houghton Mifflin. [ M ]

Taylor, Mildred (1976). *Roll of thunder, hear my cry*. Illus. by Jerry Pinkney. New York: Dial. [ I ]

Tunnell, Michael O. (1997). *Mailing May*. Illus. by Ted Rand. New York: Tambourine/Greenwillow Books. [ P/I ]

Turner, Ann (1987). *Nettie's trip South*. Illus. by Ronald Himler. New York: Macmillan. [ P/I ]

Wilder, Laura Ingalls (1932/1953), *Little house in the big woods*. Illus. by Garth Williams. (Little House series) New York: Harper & Row. [ P/I ]

Winnick, Karen B. (1996). *Mr. Lincoln's whiskers*. Illus. by the author. Honesdale, PA: Boyds Mills Press. [ P/I ]

Woodruff, Elvira (1997). *The orphan of Ellis Island: A time travel adventure*. New York: Scholastic. [ I ]

## Chapter 7

# Biography and Informational Books

## *The Realm of Nonfiction*

*I don't remember informational books being this alive, this colorful, or this energetic when I was a child. When I first picked this book up, I thought "Boring!" and "Ho, hum, just another book about the ocean." Somehow I have the idea that nonfiction is dry and lifeless. I don't know why, but I noticed the visual aspects of this book first—starfish above chapter titles, mesmerizing photographs, captions in large print, sidebar information, lists of facts. These captured my attention even before I read it! Chapter titles like "Spineless Superstars" and "Far-Out Fish" would really appeal to my reluctant readers. The three sizes of text would really address the many different reading levels in my classroom. The photographs make you want to read the text to find out more.*

*I've learned all about wonders below the sea from this book. I used to send my students to the encyclopedia to get information. I will have to begin sending them to the nonfiction shelves if other books are like this one. If a teacher from a landlocked state can become interested in the ocean from a children's book, imagine the impact this book and other nonfiction could have on my students.*

Sixth-grade teacher response to
*Safari Beneath the Sea* by Diane Swanson

Nonfiction literature for children is flourishing. Not only has nonfiction become more plentiful in numbers published, but it has attained a high quality of literary distinction with well-written text and superb illustrations or photographs that blend into an adventure in informational reading. Nonfiction literature consists of the genres of biography (including autobiography, memoirs, fictionalized biography) and informational books (including both informational picture books and informational chapter books). In many classrooms, the well-written and designed nonfiction books available today have taken priority over traditional textbooks as informational resources (Bamford & Kristo, 1998). Nonfiction comfortably builds on the natural curiosity of the learner to inquire, know, and investigate. The informational age of the 1990s and the impending millennium continue to deliver an explosion of data. That information is most effectively delivered to children through quality children's nonfiction literature.

# BIOGRAPHY

A biography shares the life of an authentic person from the past or present, celebrates his or her challenges and accomplishments, and inspires the reader with dedication and determination to lead one's own successful life. Biographies are written about people who have had a positive impact on society leaving the reader with an optimistic view of his or her potential as a contributor to our society (Zarnowski, 1990).

According to Levstik (1993), elementary students link themselves closely to biographical characters. Biographies enable readers to experience real life by vicariously tapping the experiences of achievers while often providing a historical context for understanding such people's lives. Biography has had a natural appeal to readers and an effective link to all the disciplines through the years. While the serial biographies of the past provided rather dry, formula factual information about famous people, today's biographies present flesh-and-blood individuals, with both strengths and weaknesses, in an entertaining manner. The past decade has given rise to the picture book biography as a means for the primary and intermediate reader (K–5) to engage with this genre. Titles such as Barbara Younger's *Purple Mountains Majesty: The Story of Katherine Lee Bates and "America the Beautiful"* and Josephine Poole's *Joan of Arc* become outstanding read-alouds for sharing the biography genre across the curriculum. In addition, authors such as Jean Fritz, Leonard Everett Fisher, Russell Freedman, and Diane Stanley have carried this genre to new heights as they honestly introduce students to the multidimensional, human characteristics of famous people in both their public and private lives.

## Types of Biography

Biographies can be discussed across four dimensions: (1) the degree of authenticity presented in the text, (2) the amount of coverage of the subject's life, (3) the treatment of a single or multiple subject(s) and (4) the perspective from which a biography is told. Awareness of these organizational categories of biography assist in determining the multilayered facets and possibilities of this genre across the entire curriculum.

***Degree of authenticity.***    The degree of authenticity relates to the amount of historical accuracy, documentation, and research that is brought to the biographical presentation. Although most biographies are grounded in some degree of authenticity, it is the depth of that authenticity that differentiates biographies from one another.

***Factual portrait.***    The most authentic type of biography, the factual portrayal supports all factual information through direct documentation of letters, diaries, interviews, and eyewitness accounts. Reliable resource bibliographies and acknowledgments to museums and historical societies often verify that intensive research has taken place. Authentic photographs, verifiable quotations, facsimiles of writing, and original maps can also substantiate the information on the subject.

*Lincoln: A Photobiography* by Russell Freedman provides the highest quality example of a factual portrait. Not only did this title win a Newbery Medal, it also opened the genre to new attention and exploration by authors and publishers. The book is filled with photographs, letters, diary entries, campaign posters, and other authentic documentation of research into Lincoln's life. An extensive bibliography further documents the author's research, showing that the utmost attention was paid to authentic reporting of factual information through well-written text.

Jean Fritz epitomizes the best of factual portraits. Her early books on figures of American history such as *And Then What Happened, Paul Revere?* combine humor and dialogue based on a rich foundation of documented factual information. Her later biographies like *Bully for You, Teddy Roosevelt* and *The Great Little Madison* follow the factual portrait within a chapter book format. Endnotes by the author always verify sources of information and the technical research that supports the comfortable delivery of facts about the lives of great Americans.

***Fictional portrait.***    Although tied to historical fact, the fictional portrayal reflects the author's creative addition of scenes, dialogue, or thoughts for which there is no documented basis. Based on careful research, the author paints factually grounded scenes through contrived conversation between or among characters. Clever authors skillfully weave fictionalized dialogue around existing facts in a reasonable and believable manner. The degree of fictionalization varies greatly from minor alterations to major changes to accommodate story delivery. Ann Rinaldi's *Hang a Thousand Trees with Ribbons: The Story of Phyllis Wheatley* is structured around pertinent facts about the subject's prowess as a black poet, but the actual words and thoughts of the character and dialogue between characters are invented by the author. Lynn Joseph's *Fly, Bessie, Fly* tells the story of black aviator Bessie Coleman with adequate facts, but is also filled with re-created dialogue that makes the story flow for younger readers.

***Biographical fiction.***    Some biographies appear to be more fiction than fact, and are termed biographical fiction. *Satchmo's Blues* by Alan Schroeder is a picture book that shares the life of Louis Armstrong, the amazing trumpet player from New Orleans. An author's note actually describes the book as "a fictional re-creation" and refers the reader to two biographies for factual information. At first sight, this book shouts biography, but a closer look reveals an excellent example of biographical fiction.

***Amount of coverage.*** The amount of coverage within the subjects' lives carries a wide range of possibilities while filling a wide range of needs for the reader.

### *Comprehensive biography.* 
This type covers the entire life of a subject from birth to death. Comprehensive biographies enable readers to see how the complexities of childhood, academic background, or life experiences can intricately shape the personality of an adult. Typically a chronological journey, the comprehensive account appeals to readers who want or need every fact and detail about a subject from the past. David Adler's picture book biography, *Lou Gehrig: The Luckiest Man,* takes the reader from 1903, the year of the baseball great's birth, through his grade school years, through his glory as a New York Yankee, and concludes on the day of his death on June 2, 1941.

### *Partial biography.* 
Covering only a part of a subject's life, this format is typically selected in biographies for young children that often cover the childhood of their subject. Barbara Cooney's *Eleanor* tells of the childhood and the growing up years of Eleanor Roosevelt. While an endnote tells of Eleanor Roosevelt's later confidence, independence, and contributions to her country, the illustrated biography focuses on a sad childhood. Kathryn Lasky's *A Brilliant Streak: The Making of Mark Twain* focuses on this young boyish adventurer before Samuel Clemens became the writer we know as Mark Twain. Partial biographies also tend to be accounts of living persons whose active lives and varied accomplishments are still evolving.

***Single-subject/collective biography.*** Persons' lives can be shared as single-subject biographies or grouped in a collection of several similar subjects with some common strand in their lives.

### *Single-subject biography.* 
In this case, the personality of the selected subject is typically well known, highly respected, and has earned a place in history for his or her accomplishments. The subjects can be scientists, sports figures, explorers, artists, authors, politicians, or simply ordinary people who overcome great adversity. Most biographies in both picture books and chapter book formats today rely on single-subject coverage. Both Leonard Everett Fisher through his stark black-and-white illustrations in *Gandhi* and John B. Severance through photographs and well-developed text in a chapter book titled *Gandhi: Great Soul* focus on the life of Mohandas Gandhi and his lifetime dedication to free the people of India from British rule.

### *Collective biography.* 
The life stories of several people in one book are connected by a common strand that runs through the subjects' lives. The subjects may be part of the same profession as in Pat Cummings's *Talking with Artists* or Kathleen Krull's *Lives of the Athletes: Thrills, Spills (and What the Neighbors Thought).* Not nearly as popular or

plentiful as the single-subject biography, they serve the purpose of bringing human similarities together for potential comparison and contrast.

***Biography series.***   Many children's authors have become specialists in writing in the biographical genre and have applied their research skills to the lives of several individuals. More than formula writing, the newer series biography may carry a common theme that flows throughout the series. Rizzoli has published a series of Weekend with the Artist books including *Weekend with Van Gogh* that integrates biography and art. Kathleen Krull's illustrated collective biography series includes *Lives of the Presidents: Fame, Shame (and What the Neighbors Thought),* as well as books on artists, musicians, and writers. Although biographical series have typically been frowned on as formula writing, today's series reflect a higher quality of writing and greater selectivity of subjects to share with children. For example, David Adler's picture book series on famous Americans includes *A Picture Book of John F. Kennedy* and *A Picture Book of Rosa Parks.*

***Biographical perspectives.***   Biographies can also differ in the perspective from which the stories of people's lives are told.

***Autobiography.***   Told, and usually written by the subject of the book, an autobiography is a first-person account of a subject's life. It is likely to be near factual in delivery as a person reflects on the true details of the joys and sorrows of one's own life. Autobiographies tend to be highly personalized, leaving the reader with an emotional perspective on events in the subject's life. Peg Kehret, popular adolescent author, emotionally shares her childhood years and the experience of being a victim of polio in *Small Steps: The Year I Got Polio.* A series of autobiographies by popular children's authors and illustrators by Richard C. Owens Publishers shares the voice of subjects familiar to children in a direct, first-person voice. These include *Under My Nose* by Lois Ehlert and *Firetalking* by Patricia Polacco. *On the Bus with Joanna Cole* and *In Flight with David McPhail* are part of another author series by Heinemann. These autobiographies focus not only on the lives of the subjects, but on the personal views of the subjects on the art of writing as well. The first-person voice of the writer provides a powerful testimony of a person's life to a young reader.

***Memoir.***   Related to autobiography is a memoir, a record of events based on the writer's own observations. In children's books, this is often a retrospective account that focuses on a memorable or tragic event in the author's life. *Red Scarf Girl: A Memoir of the Cultural Revolution* by Ji-Li Jiang shares 12-year-old Ji-li's view of the terrifying impact of Chairman Mao's New China on herself, friends, neighbors, and family. Livia Bitton-Jackson's *I Have Lived a Thousand Years: Growing Up in the Holocaust* presents the memoir of 13-year-old Elli Friedman who descends into the hell of Auschwitz in March 1944. Elli (actually the author) recounts what it was like to be an inmate and how she managed to survive impending extermination. In more contemporary times, *Zlata's Diary: A Child's Life in Sarajevo* shares entries written of Zlata Filipovic's experiences during the bombings of the 1990s. These accounts, told with innocence and grace, all share courageous stories of young women trapped in unfolding political trauma. Often written as a chronology or diary, the memoir is characterized by the strong, emotional first-person voice of one who relives the memory through writing.

### *Narrated biography.*

The most common type of biography is that told by an author through a third-person voice. The voice is one of authority and is aided by research and documentation that makes the delivery of information believable. This is also the likely writing style of a child when asked to share biographical information on a subject.

Russell Freedman's *Out of Darkness: The Story of Louis Braille* reflects the narrated style of writing in children's biography. The narrated style overrides the traditional bland, expository mode while delivering facts to children through motivating text supported by the strong voice of the author. Listen while reading a select portion of the first page of this quality title:

> The dormitory was dark and still. Only one boy was still awake. He sat on the edge of his bed at a far corner of the room, holding a writing board and a sheet of thick paper on his lap. Working slowly, deliberately, he punched tiny holes across the page with the sharp point of a stylus. (p 1)

### *Outsider biography.*

Often a biography can be told by an individual distanced from the subject. The third-person voice can present a detached view of a famous figure. For example, *When Willard Met Babe Ruth* tells the story of the great baseball player as his life touched one family. Told by a small boy, Willard Babson, the biography spans Babe Ruth's baseball career, but the emphasis is on how this player and the sport of baseball bound generations of this family together. Another example is Louise Borden's *Good-bye, Charles Lindbergh,* which focuses on an accidental, but true encounter between a boy and the revered aviator. This unique style is quite uncommon, but presents an interesting slant on a major figure in the context of the real world, rather than isolated from it.

Examining a recent biography to see how the characteristics just discussed apply to quality titles assists us in understanding the quality and depth of this genre. *Wilma Unlimited: How Wilma Rudolph Became the World's Fastest Woman,* skillfully written by Kathleen Krull, is a single-subject, fictionalized biography of a great woman athlete. Based almost entirely on fact, the reader follows Wilma from her childhood bout with polio to her dramatic persistence in running in the Olympics. The author incorporates only a few contrived situations and statements that cannot be historically documented. For the most part, however, the facts speak clearly through dates and actual events. This book is an example of a partial, slice-of-life biography covering the childhood, battle with polio, and triple Olympic medal-winning performance of Wilma Rudolph. The book is intended to highlight her greatest victories, with only an author's note following the story that reveals her later life and death. This is an outstanding picture book biography illustrated with the bright, bold paintings of David Diaz that capture Wilma's determination to overcome a physical obstacle and triumph in her life. Picture book biographies like this one have become increasingly popular with younger children and allow children to be introduced to biography as a genre during the primary grades.

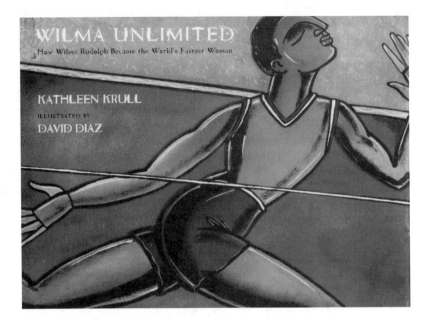

Characteristics of biography are skillfully blended around courageous lives.
*From* Wilma Unlimited: How Wilma Rudolph Became the World's Fastest Woman *by Kathleen Krull. Jacket illustration copyright © 1996 by David Diaz. Reproduced by permission of Harcourt Brace & Company.*

## Criteria for Evaluating Biography

Because biographies involve real people and their lives, the importance of factual accountability is a major focus of the criteria for quality in this genre.

***Accuracy of fact and detail.***    The top priority in assessing biography must be the historical accuracy of the text and the integrity of the author's presentation. Authors must admit gaps in their research so readers themselves can judge the accuracy of the portrayal. All sides of a subject should be shared, including weaknesses and character faults. A shaded view of a less than human character reflects on the honesty and credibility of the author. Although the age of the audience must be considered, the biography needs to focus on accuracy without risking an overglorified portrayal of a subject. The biography should be scanned for author references and acknowledgments to museums, libraries, and individuals who shared expertise on the subject.

*John Burroughs: The Sage of Slabsides* by Ginger Wadsworth exemplifies accuracy of fact and detail. An author of nature essays, Burroughs read, wrote, and entertained at his cabin in the Catskills of New York. His friendships with Walt Whitman, Henry Ford, John Muir, and Theodore Roosevelt make him an intriguing subject for a biography. Author acknowledgments reflect appreciation to museums, associations, libraries, universities, and relatives for their assistance in collecting factual details, essays, and photographs of this naturalist's life. Included is a list of books by Burroughs, a selected bibliography documenting author sources, and a related list of books for young readers. This title exemplifies the best of the genre and the recent trend toward high-quality biography.

***Quality writing.***    The biography genre has soared beyond the formula writing of the Landmark biographies of the 1950s and 1960s. Although children may be interested in a biography subject, they need good writing to gently motivate them through the flow of information. Biographies that overwhelmingly consist of expository text often scare off prospective readers, whereas those that skillfully present biography as story seem to hold their attention.

Robert Burleigh's *Black Whiteness: Admiral Byrd Alone in the Antarctic* exemplifies the quality of writing that captures the wonder, the terror, and the will of one man to stay alive under brutal frigid conditions. Burleigh intersperses his own poetic prose with plausible journal excerpts from Byrd's diary.

> Cold, terrible cold:
> At −50°F a flashlight dies in his hand;
> at −55°F kerosene freezes;
> at −60°F rubber turns brittle and snaps,
> juice bottles shatter,
> canned food from the tunnel becomes hard as rock.
> Outside, he hears his breath freeze as it floats away,
> making a sound like firecrackers.
> Sometimes the frozen breath hangs above his head like a small cloud;
> if he breathes too deeply, his lungs burn with invisible fire.*

This quality of writing is becoming more common in biographical portrayals and is certain to inspire children to sample this genre during self-selection and independent reading.

***Contextual immersion.***    Besides presenting factual information on a subject, the author must surround the reader in the social context of the times. The mention of prominent figures of the times, descriptions of clothing, and timely news events immerse the reader in the social context of the subject's life, thus building a greater sense of understanding and a broader historical perspective. Diane Stanley's biography *Leonardo da Vinci,* immerse the reader in the historical period of the Renaissance both through her writing and through her exacting illustrations which showcase the dress, architecture, and Italy of this period of rebirth in Europe.

In light of these three criteria, *Anastasia's Album* by Hugh Brewster exemplifies authenticity, from its inclusion of family photographs to its endpapers, which replicate the personal scrapbook of Princess Anastasia, the daughter of Tsar Nicholas II of Russia. Authenticity is documented through a list of primary works and sources, picture credits, and acknowledgments to museum officials in Russia. Quality writing tells the story of the youngest daughter of the tsar highlighted by quotes from memoirs and letters. Immersion in the Russian revolution as a cultural experience is confirmed by the chronological events

*From *Black Whiteness: Admiral Byrd Alone in the Antarctic* (p. 8). Text copyright © 1998 by Robert Burleigh. Reprinted by permission of Atheneum Books for Young Readers.

that led to the downfall of imperial Russia. A masterpiece in format and an authentic reflection on the life of the last ruling family of Russia, this title sets the standards for high-quality biographies.

## Values of Biography

The value of biography begins with the presentation of models of people whose hard work and determination help them overcome obstacles and achieve high goals. Many biographical subjects are ordinary people who accomplish extraordinary deeds, compelling children to build from their own strengths and set high goals for themselves. *Free to Dream: The Making of a Poet, Langston Hughes* portrays a passed around child in white Kansas towns who achieved success as the greatest Harlem poet.

Biography models a process of collecting and presenting research on a person. By reading this genre and studying its authors, children become aware of how investigation of multiple resources and transmission of facts through quality writing bring a subject to life for the reader. Andrea Pinkney's *Bill Pickett: Rodeo-Ridin' Cowboy* supplies acknowledgments of multiple resources, additional factual information at the book's conclusion, and a strong bibliography for further research.

Biography provides a curricular connection across disciplines. Biographies of figures from science, history, mathematics, the humanities, and the arts enrich the study of these content areas. Peter Sis's *Starry Messenger: Galileo Galilei,* for example, depicts the life of the famous scientist, mathematician, astronomer, philosopher, and physicist, making a natural link to mathematics and science curricula. Almost all theme explorations should include a biography of a related person such as *Capturing Nature,* an edited autobiography of John James Audubon for studying birds, or *Nobody Owns the Sky: The Story of "Brave Bessie" Coleman* for integrating into a unit on flight.

Biography extends beyond famous Americans to those renowned around the world and increases student awareness of the traits that characterize global leaders, past and present. Students are immersed in different times and different cultures, opening a window on the world of humankind. Aliki's *The King's Day: Louis XIV of France* represents the history of France, whereas Diane Stanley's *Peter the Great* immerses the reader in Russia's rich history.

## Reader Response to Biography

Biography presents a wide variety of reader response options for children. Reading several biographies on a single subject can lead to comparison and contrast of a subject's strengths and weaknesses. Such scrutiny may even reveal conflicting information on a subject. Biography can model research as children try their own use of documentation as they compose an autobiography (Zarnowski, 1990) or fictionalized biography (Zarnowski, 1988). Response to biography can take the form of further reading because bibliographies lead children to other sources on a subject. Biography is easily coordinated with other content areas and themes. Students even enjoy dressing as the biography subject and sharing their lives in the first-person voice. Chapter 13 suggests several other options as response to biography.

Many possibilities exist as children are exposed to the biography genre. This genre grew tremendously in quality and quantity the during the 1990s and warrants inclusion for independent reading, read-alouds, research, and reading enjoyment. Perhaps picture book biographies have provided the greatest momentum to the growth of biography as younger readers engage themselves in a genre that has traditionally been focused on older readers. Biography shares quality writing and models of determined, hardworking people that can inspire children to set high goals and achieve success in life.

# INFORMATIONAL BOOKS

The quantity and quality of informational books soared in the 1990s in response to the huge information explosion, the increased use of factual books across academic curricula, and the high quality and dynamic presentation of knowledge by publishers. Although informational books have traditionally been used exclusively for research, the proliferation of books in this genre has led to an expanded scope in the classroom that includes reader enjoyment, curricular integration, and personal inquiry.

Informational books are factual presentations of documented knowledge. Their purpose is to instill information and inquiry in the reader. Informational books cover a wide range of topics in all disciplines including the sciences, social sciences, and the humanities. Although most informational books are written in expository text to transmit information, many informational books have gained prominence by using a narrative approach to delivering information.

Traditionally, informational books had little or no appeal to teachers beyond their expected use for report writing. Rarely have informational books been used for pleasure reading or selected as a source for a class read-aloud. Almost all books chosen to model reading to children have been fiction with a strong narrative voice and an imaginative story. Children's visits to the informational section of the library are infrequent and often unrewarding because they associate this genre with teacher-assigned research rather than personal inquiry. Few children have been shown that informational reading and browsing can be personally fulfilling. Informational books carry the reputation of being boring. Traditionally filled with facts and simple illustrations, children viewed them only as an extension of their textbooks.

In the past few years, however, informational books have gained new respect, well-deserved literary honors, and a growing reputation for quality. Reputable authors and illustrators, motivating formats, colorful presentations, and interesting means of disseminating facts have improved the nonfiction genre.

## Types of Informational Books

The following categories of informational books are based on the formats the books use to transmit knowledge to the reader. Outstanding titles exist in all of these formats and they provide information to children of varying age and reading ability levels.

***Informational chapter books.***    This format features mostly text organized in chapters or sections. While graphics and illustrations supplement the words, primary information is delivered through the text. Although Milton Meltzer's *Weapons and Warfare* contains simple pencil sketches, it is the text that carries a chronological account of the development of the weapons of war and the impact they have had on society. Divided into 59 sections, the book invites browsing as well as cover-to-cover reading.

***Informational picture books.***    These present factual information in a picture book format. The text and illustrations both play a vital role in contributing to the understanding of the topic. Before the reader's eyes unfolds a visual world of color and a textual world of intriguing information. Brenda Guiberson's *Into the Sea* combines compelling text with exquisite illustrations that reveal the life cycle of the sea turtle from hatching and entry into the ocean to the instinctive return to the shore where she was hatched to lay her own eggs.

***Photographic essays.***    Presentation of information is both through the text and the breathtaking photographs that accompany it. Unlike the picture book, the visual presentation is authentic, either historic, panoramic, or microscopic, with the book offering both visual and textual appeal. *A Drop of Water* shares spectacular photographs of water through stop action and magnification photography. Readers can examine a drop of water through all its states as it falls from the faucet, splashes on a hard surface, crystalizes into a snowflake, and forms clouds. An insert about the expertise of the author/photographer reinforces the professionalism of Walter Wick's text and visual display

***Informational books with a narrative blend.***    Several new books present a blend of fact and fiction with information typically presented in a narrative style. Intended to both inform and entertain, these books lure the avid reader into the informational realm as well as captivate the reluctant reader by surrounding intriguing facts with a motivating text. *Flute's Journey* by Lynne Cherry personifies a wood thrush into a story character and documents its migrational flight to and from South America. Reading like a fictional story, the text carries actual facts about the wonders of this yearly journey.

## Trends in Informational Books

Freeman and Person (1992) point out several trends in informational books during the 1990s beyond the increased quality and quantity already mentioned. Their book *Using Nonfiction Trade Books in the Elementary Classroom: From Ants to Zeppelins* has provided impetus in the creative inclusion of informational books across the curriculum.

***Evidence of research documentation.***    Increasingly, informational books have highlighted the authenticity of the knowledge being disseminated to children. Book jackets share biographical information reflecting the expert credentials of authors, illustrators, and photographers. Extended list of references to document the authenticity of the text are included as well as bibliographies of related children's books for more extensive research. Glossaries, time lines, and maps further extend the research efforts brought to the book. A brief view of *Safari Beneath the Sea: The Wonder of the North Pacific Coast,* the 1995 Orbis

Pictus Award book for Outstanding Nonfiction for Children, will make the reader aware of the quality and quantity of research that made this book possible. Informational books actually serve as a model format of high-quality, documented research for children.

***The growing importance of illustration.***   If children's attention is to be captured, information must reach beyond the text. Indeed it is often the colorful illustrations or photographs that motivate a child to delve into the text for additional information. One need only look at *Dolphin Man: Exploring the World of Dolphins* by Laurence Pringle to realize how children can be captivated and invited into the text by the appeal of visual photographic presentation. The same seems true for the colorful drawings of Gail Gibbons which invite children into the life and work of *The Honeymakers*.

***Unconventional formats and approaches.***   Boring formats have been cast aside in favor of pop-up books, cartoon style art, and cross-section drawings. The ability of the format itself to disseminate information has had a tremendous impact on the popularity of informational books. Adults are even more likely to purchase informational books because of their clever appeal. *Robert Crowther's Pop-Up Olympics* and *Stephen Beisty's Incredible Cross-Sections: Man of War* share information without children realizing that it is information and not entertainment. *Robert Snedden's Yuck!: A Big Book of Little Horrors* provides colorful microscopic views of everyday things from dust to food. Pull-out pages and huge print further enhance the presentation format of this awe-inspiring book of micromarvels.

***Informational books for the very young.***   With increased emphasis on early literacy, publishers have simplified advanced topics so they can be shared with younger children. The Eye-openers series and Junior Eyewitness books limit information but provide motivating presentation to capture children's natural interest at a young age.

***Specialized topics.***   The narrower lens of specific informational books has created a specialized focus on rather obscure, but interesting topics. Many books abound on wildflowers, but there is also a book on the life cycle of a *single* wildflower titled *Jack-in-the-Pulpit*. Broad books on great disasters, for example, have now been narrowed to individual titles like Robert Ballard's *Exploring the Titanic* and Jim Murphy's *The Great Fire*. The specialized topic book often creates a sense of inquiry that allows children to broaden their level of interest to a wider domain.

***Recognition and awards.***   The creation of the Orbis Pictus Award for Outstanding Nonfiction for Children by the National Council of Teachers of English marked a milestone in the respect given to informational books. Established to promote and recognize excellence in the writing of nonfiction for children, this award has brought the informational genre to national attention for teachers. The 1998 Orbis Pictus Award Book was presented to Laurence Pringle's *An Extraordinary Life: The Story of a Monarch Butterfly,* an optimal blend of narrative/informational text and stunning oil paintings by Bob Marstall.

Children possess a natural curiosity to ask questions and seek answers and the inquiry process has been revitalized through the new appealing books in this genre. As informational trade books take on an increasingly important role in literature-based classrooms, the quality and quantity of knowledge they provide children through inviting formats is making a critical impact on both literacy and interdisciplinary instruction.

## Criteria for Evaluating Informational Books

As informational books have gained new respect and an expanded role in the classroom curriculum beyond report writing, this genre has become more intensely scrutinized. The quality of the books being published has actually raised the standards for their selection. Five challenging criteria set the benchmark that informational books must reach to gain high regard in the information book genre.

***Accuracy and authenticity.***    The standards of correct and documented information begin with the author. Verifying the credentials of the transmission of knowledge does much to ensure the reader that only up-to-date information from an expert in the field is being shared. An example is Seymour Simon whose countless books on the universe including *Our Solar System* emphasize his expertise as a scientist and award recipient. Expert qualifications, reputation, and previous experiences equate with accuracy of information. Acknowledgments are often bestowed on experts in the field, museum, or professional collections further documenting validity of information.

Accuracy of facts is one of the criteria set by the National Science Teacher Association (*Outstanding Science Trade Books for Children*) and the National Council for the Social Studies (*Notable Children's Trade Books*) (see Appendix A for listings) in their yearly selection standards. Information needs to be as up to date as possible at the time of publication because knowledge changes so rapidly. Another related criterion includes the inclusiveness of information. All significant facts must be included and no relevant information should be omitted. Additional criteria related to accuracy and authenticity include stereotypes. In gender issues, women should be readily portrayed as scientists and truck drivers while men should be shown as nurses and beauticians. Ethnic portrayal is also important because scientists, politicians, and inventors span the multicultural mix of our society. Authors should also distinguish between fact and theory with the use of terms like "as far as we know . . ." or "we believe . . ." for sharing unverified statements. This lengthy list of considerations reflects the high standards and importance of accurate, up-to-date, documented information in transmitting knowledge to children.

***Content and perspective.***    The intended audience should be targeted for the presentation of information. Topic matched to a particular grade, age, and interest level is an important consideration in finding the most appropriate informational books. The book should have adequate coverage with just the right amount of information without overwhelming the reader. The book should reflect a spirit of inquiry and a modeling of the scientific method so children can experience the process of inquiry, the excitement of discovery, the value of observation, and the challenge of prediction. The perspective of the book should vary, and the facts can be told in expository, narrative, or poetic format. In *Stephen Kramer's Eye of the Storm*, for example, readers are provided with an eyewitness account of tracking tornadoes, hurricanes, and thunderstorms as they accompany storm chaser and photographer Warren Faidley in search of the beauty and danger of weather.

***Language style.***   Informational writing must be clear and direct if facts are to be accurately understood. The level of reading difficulty must be considered and new terms must be defined in context. Reader involvement is a critical factor in delivery style. Where direct expository text is traditional, children are likely to be more engaged by the use of the second-person "you" as Karen Wallace uses it in *Imagine You Are a Crocodile.* Authors might ask direct questions that lead children to speculate, gather information, and guide them toward an answer. Writing in the present tense makes information more accessible and believable as well. The use of vivid language is just as crucial to informational writing as for narrative writing. The writing should read aloud well, involve the child, and share information in a meaningful way.

***Organization.***   The structure, or clear order of information, must reflect a meaningful arrangement. This criterion is made evident by chapter titles, headings, and subheadings as indicated in the table of contents, and can also be assessed by reference aids appended to the book. The index, glossaries, bibliography, and appendixes should reflect important terminology, topics, and related material as a part of the book. These supplements form vital connections to and a framework for further inquiry. *Hawk Highway in the Sky* by Caroline Arnold joins the Hawk Watch International team as they gather information on raptor migration. The book opens with a page of acknowledgments listing address, phone, and Web page information on Hawk Watch. At the end of the book, a list of day-flying raptors, a location map for watching raptors, and an alphabetical index provide additional information to motivated learners.

***Visual selections and format.***   Whether pencil sketches, intricate pen-and-ink drawings, or photographs support the text, visual representations serve to clarify and extend textual information. The suitability of the media for the topic should be considered. For example, Leonard Everett Fisher's stark, bold vision of *The Great Wall of China* in blacks, grays, and whites does not detract from, but instead enhances, the topic. The same is true for Dorothy Henshaw Patent's *Back to the Wild,* which uses incredible color photographs to capture the struggle to save and reintroduce endangered animals into nature. William Munoz's photographs have captions that relate to the text, but provide an additional fact or perspective to the book's content. As with all books, the format should be attractive with meaningful placement of text and pictures, ornamented headings to invite interest, varying type sizes for differing levels of information, and adequate margins to avoid information overload.

## Value of Informational Books

Informational books add a new perspective to the reading realm of children. Their role is an important one as children emerge into reading and research.

- Informational books invite children into the world of nonfiction reading for both learning and enjoyment.
- Informational books cover a wealth of topics, so readers can readily locate a title on a subject of immediate interest.

- Informational books become a valuable resource for content area or interdisciplinary instruction providing different information and perspectives on a topic.
- Informational books can stimulate a child's interest on an unfamiliar topic, thus opening a world of inquiry and beginning a quest of generating questions and pursuing answers.
- Informational books provide a model for conducting research by showing how an expert gathers, evaluates, organizes, and shares information with an audience.

Figure 7.1 reviews a number of outstanding authors of both biography and informational books for children. In addition to the nonfiction titles mentioned throughout the chapter, this bibliography extends their writing accomplishments to better represent the quantity and quality of outstanding authors of nonfiction for children.

**FIGURE 7.1**   Noteworthy Nonfiction Authors

---

**David Adler (First biography series)**

(1992). *A picture book of Harriet Tubman.* Illus. by Samuel Byrd. New York: Holiday House. [ P/I ]
(1991). *A picture book of Eleanor Roosevelt.* New York: Holiday House. [ P/I ]

**Aliki**

(1993). *My visit to the aquarium.* New York: HarperCollins. [ P ]
(1989). *The king's day: Louis XIV of France.* New York: Crowell. [ P/I ]

**George Ancona**

(1998). *Fiesta fireworks.* New York: Lothrop, Lee & Shepard. [ P/I ]
(1998). *Barrio: Jose's neighborhood.* San Diego: Harcourt Brace. [ P/I ]
(1994). *The piñata maker/El pinatero.* San Diego: Harcourt Brace. [ P ]

**Caroline Arnold**

(1997). *Stone age farmers beside the sea: Scotland's prehistoric village of Skara Brae.* Boston: Clarion. [ I/M ]
(1994). *Killer whale.* Photographs by Richard Hewett. New York: Morrow. [ I/M ]
(1993). *On the brink of extinction: The California condor.* San Diego: Harcourt Brace. [ I/M ]

**Jim Arnosky**

(1997). *Nearer nature.* New York: Lothrop, Lee & Shepard. [ I/M ]
(1996). *Crinkleroot's guide to knowing butterflies and moths.* New York: Simon & Schuster. [ P ]

**Brent Ashabranner**

(1997). *To seek a better world: The Haitian minority in America.* New York: Cobblehill/Dutton. [ M ]
(1996). *A strange and distant shore: Indians of the Great Plains in exile.* New York: Cobblehill/Dutton. [ M ]

**FIGURE 7.1**    Noteworthy Nonfiction Authors *(continued)*

## Rhoda Blumberg

(1996). *Full speed ahead: The race to build a transcontinental railroad.* Washington, D.C.: National Geographic. [ I/M ]

(1989). *The great American gold rush.* New York: Bradbury. [ I/M ]

## Jim Brandenburg

(1996). *Scruffy: A wolf finds his place in the pack.* Edited by J. B. Guernsey. New York: Walker. [ P/I ]

(1995). *An American safari: Adventures on the North American prairie.* New York: Walker. [ I ]

(1993). *To the top of the world: Adventures with Arctic wolves.* New York: Walker. [ I/M ]

## Joanna Cole (Magic School Bus series)

(1996). *The magic school bus inside a beehive.* Illus. by Bruce Degen. New York: Scholastic. [ P/I ]

(1995). *The magic school bus inside a hurricane.* Illus. by Bruce Degen. New York: Scholastic. [ P/I ]

## Molly Cone

(1996). *Squishy, misty, damp & muddy: The in-between world of wetlands.* San Francisco: Sierra Club. [ I/M ]

(1992). *Come Back, Salmon: How a group of dedicated kids adopted Pigeon Creek and brought it back to life.* Photographs by S. Wheelwright. San Francisco: Sierra Club. [ I ]

## Leonard Everett Fisher

(1995). *Ghandi.* New York: Atheneum.

(1994). *Marie Curie.* New York: Macmillan.

## Russell Freedman

(1996). *The life and death of Crazy Horse.* Drawings by Amos Bad Heart Bull. New York: Holiday House. [ M ]

(1993). *Eleanor Roosevelt: A life of discovery.* Boston: Clarion. [ M ]

(1987). *Lincoln: A photobiography.* Boston: Clarion. [ I/M ]

## Jean Fritz

(1991). *Bully for you, Teddy Roosevelt.* New York: Putnam. [ I/M ]

(1989). *The great little Madison.* New York: Putnam. [ I/M ]

(1973). *And then what happened, Paul Revere?* Illus. by Margot Tomes. New York: Coward/McCann. [ P/I ]

## Gail Gibbons

(1998). *Soaring with the wind: The bald eagle.* New York: Morrow. [ P/I ]

(1997). *The honeymakers.* New York: Morrow. [ P/I ]

(1994). *Nature's green umbrella: Tropical rain forests.* New York: Morrow. [ P/I ]

**FIGURE 7.1**   Noteworthy Nonfiction Authors *(continued)*

## James Cross Giblin

(1995). *When plague strikes: The Black Death, smallpox, AIDS.* Woodcuts by David Frampton. New York: HarperCollins. [ I/M ]

(1994). *Thomas Jefferson: A picture book biography.* Illus. by Michael Dooling. New York: Scholastic. [ P/I ]

## Diane Hoyt-Goldsmith

(1995). *Apache rodeo.* Photographs by Lawrence Migdale. New York: Holiday House. [ I ]

(1993). *Cherokee summer.* Photographs by Lawrence Migdale. New York: Holiday House. [ I ]

## Kathryn Lasky

(1998). *Shadows in the dawn: The lemurs of Madagascar.* Photographs by Christopher G. Knight. San Diego: Gulliver Green/Harcourt Brace. [ I ]

(1997). *The most beautiful roof in the world: Exploring the rainforest canopy.* Photographs by Christopher G. Knight. San Diego: Harcourt Brace. [ I ]

(1994). *The librarian who measured the earth.* Illus. by Kevin Hawkes. Boston: Little, Brown. [ I ]

## Patricia Lauber

(1996). *Flood: Wrestling with the Mississippi.* Washington, D.C.: National Geographic. [ I/M ]

(1996). *Hurricanes: Earth's mightiest storms.* New York: Scholastic. [ I/M ]

## David Macauley

(1997). *Rome Antics.* Boston: Houghton Mifflin.

(1998). *The way things work.* Boston: Houghton Mifflin. [ I/M ]

(1973). *Cathedral: The story of its own construction.* Boston: Houghton Mifflin. [ I/M ]

## Milton Meltzer

(1993). *Lincoln: In his own words.* Illus. by Stephen Alcorn. San Diego: Harcourt Brace. [ I/M ]

(1992). *The amazing potato.* New York: HarperCollins. [ I/M ]

## Jim Murphy

(1996). *A young patriot: The American Revolution as experienced by one boy.* Boston: Clarion. [ I/M ]

(1995). *The great fire.* New York: Scholastic. [ I/M ]

(1993). *Across America on an emigrant train.* Boston: Clarion. [ I/M ]

## Dorothy Henshaw Patent

(1997). *Back to the wild.* Illus. by William Munoz. San Diego: Harcourt Brace. [ I/M ]

(1996). *Prairies.* Photographs by William Munoz. New York: Holiday House. [ I/M ]

160

**FIGURE 7.1**  Noteworthy Nonfiction Authors *(concluded)*

**Laurence Pringle**

(1997). *Extraordinary life: The story of a monarch butterfly.* Illus. by Bob Marstall. New York: Orchard Books. [ I/M ]

(1995). *Dolphin man: Exploring the world of dolphins.* Photographs by Randall S. Wells and Dolphin Biology Research Institute. New York: Atheneum. [ I/M ]

(1995). *Fire in the forest: A cycle of growth and renewal.* Paintings by Bob Marstall. New York: Atheneum. [ I/M ]

**Seymour Simon**

(1998). *Muscles.* New York: Morrow [ P/I ]. Human body series.

(1998). *The universe.* New York: Morrow [ P/I ]. Solar system/space series

(1997). *Ride the wind: Airbourne journeys of animals and plants.* Illus. by Elsa Warnick. San Diego: Browndeer Press/Harcourt Brace. [ P/I ] Mystery of Animal Migration series

(1997). *Lightning.* New York: Morrow. [ P/I ] Weather element series.

(1995). *Sharks.* New York: HarperCollins. [ P/I ] Animal series.

**Diane Stanley**

(1996). *Leonardo da Vinci.* New York: Morrow. [ I/M ]

(1993). *Charles Dickens: The man who had great expectations.* With Peter Vennema. New York: Morrow. [ I/M ]

(1992). *Bard of Avon: The story of William Shakespeare.* With Peter Vennema. New York: Morrow. [ I/M ]

(1990). *Good Queen Bess: The story of Elizabeth I of England.* With Peter Vennema. New York: Four Winds. [ I/M ]

**Jerry Stanley**

(1997). *Digger: The tragic fate of the California Indians from the missions to the Gold Rush.* New York: Crown. [ M ]

(1994). *I am an American: A true story of Japanese internment.* New York: Crown. [ I/M ]

(1992). *Children of the Dustbowl: The true story of the school at Weedpatch Camp.* New York: Random. [ I/M ]

**Diane Swanson**

(1996). *Buffalo sunrise: The story of a North American giant.* San Francisco: Sierra Club. [ I ]

(1994). *Safari beneath the sea: The wonder world of the north Pacific coast.* Photographs by the Royal British Columbia Museum. San Francisco: Sierra Club. [ P/I/M ]

**Kate Waters**

(1996). *On the Mayflower: Voyage of the ship's apprentice and a passenger girl.* Photographs by Russ Kendall. New York: Scholastic. [ P/I ]

(1993). *Samuel Eaton's day: A day in the life of a Pilgrim boy.* Photographs by Russ Kendall. New York: Scholastic. [ P/I ]

(1989). *Sarah Morton's day: A day in the life of a Pilgrim girl.* Photographs by Russ Kendall. New York: Scholastic. [ P/I ]

## Reader Response to Informational Books

Informational books set the stage for both oral and written response in the forms of readers' theater, written aesthetic response, diary entries, and book selection. Response can even be measured by additional research stimulated by the introduction of an inspiring informational book. The formats of informational books provide models for delivering student research as well. Chapter 13 contains an entire range of prompts and response-based activities focused on informational books.

There is an informational book to arouse and feed each child's area of interest. Whether satisfying an insatiable appetite for dinosaurs, fulfilling a dream to explore the outer limits of the universe, or experiencing the quest to discover new countries and cultures, informational books fulfill personal needs. Because these books account for more than half of library acquisitions and circulation, their importance with children is magnified. Teachers have placed a lopsided emphasis on fiction in the classroom. Perhaps with the inclusion of informational books, teachers can reach that child who does not readily respond to fiction. Informational books have the power to teach, to inspire, to answer, to stretch, to challenge, and to fulfill. Their current popularity attests to their importance in children's natural inquiry and their need to stretch beyond their own borders. A superlative resource for literature-based teachers, informational books have found a permanent home across the elementary/middle-level curriculum.

# CLOSING THOUGHTS

Today's biography and informational books reach far beyond the traditional research demands of the classroom. Through read-alouds, choices for independent reading, and as a natural springboard to content area study, children's nonfiction has risen to new heights. The quality and quantity of information delivered through these nonfiction genres makes nonfiction a viable choice for inclusion across the curriculum as well as for reading enjoyment.

As lifelong readers, many literate adults favor nonfiction titles for leisure reading. A renewed emphasis on expository reading has reinvigorated the nonfiction genres. The expository nature of biography and nonfiction demands introduction at an even earlier stage of reading development. The abundance of quality authors and quality works of nonfiction blended with the expertise and enthusiasm of a teacher can move the inclusion of nonfiction across grade levels, and curricular areas can encompass both research and reading to be viewed through both efferent and aesthetic lenses.

# REFERENCES

Bamford, R. A., & Kristo, J. V. (Eds.) (1998). *Making facts come alive: Choosing quality nonfiction literature K–8*. Norwood, MA: Christopher-Gordon.

Freeman, E. B., & Person, D. G. (Eds.) (1992). *Using nonfiction trade books in the elementary classroom: From ants to zeppelins*. Urbana, IL: National Council of Teachers of English.

Levstik, L. S. (1993). "I wanted to be there": The impact of narrative on children's thinking. In M. O. Tunnell & R. Ammon, (Eds.), *The story of ourselves: Teaching history through children's literature.* Portsmouth, NH: Heinemann.

Zarnowski, M. (1988). Learning about fictionalized biography: A reading and writing approach. *The Reading Teacher, 42,* 136–142.

Zarnowski, M. (1990). *Learning about biographies: A reading-and-writing approach for children.* Urbana, IL: National Council of Teachers of English.

# CHILDREN'S BOOKS CITED: BIOGRAPHY
## [P] = K–2; [I] = 3–5; [M] = 6–8

Adler, David (1990). *A picture book of John F. Kennedy.* Illus. by John and Alexandra Wallner. New York: Holiday House. [ P ]

Adler, David (1993). *A picture book of Rosa Parks.* Illus. by Robert Casilla. New York: Holiday House. [ P ]

Adler, David (1997). *Lou Gehrig: The luckiest man.* Illus. by Terry Widener. San Diego: Gulliver Books/Harcourt Brace. [ P/I ]

Aliki (1989). *The king's day: Louis XIV of France.* New York: Crowell. [ P/I ]

Bitton-Jackson, Livia (1997). *I have lived a thousand years: Growing up in the Holocaust.* New York: Simon & Schuster. [ M ]

Borden, Louise (1998). *Good-bye, Charles Lindbergh.* Illus. by Thomas B. Allen. New York: McElderry Books. [ P/I ]

Brewster, Hugh (1996). *Anastasia's album.* New York: Madison Press/Hyperion. [ I/M ]

Burleigh, Robert (1998). *Black whiteness: Admiral Byrd alone in the Antarctic.* Illus. by Walter Lyon Krudop. New York: Atheneum. [ I/M ]

Cole, Joanna, & Saul, Wendy (1996). *On the bus with Joanna Cole: A creative autobiography.* Portsmouth, NH: Heinemann. [ I ]

Cooney, Barbara (1996). *Eleanor.* New York: Viking. [ P/I ]

Cummings, Pat (Ed.) (1992). *Talking with artists.* New York: Bradbury. [ I/M ]

Cummings, Pat (Ed.) (1995). *Talking with artists: Volume two.* New York: Simon & Schuster. [ I/M ]

Ehlert, Lois (1996). *Under my nose.* (Meet the Author series) Photographs by Carlo Ontal. Katonah, NY: Richard C. Owen Publishers. [ P/I ]

Filipovic, Zlata (1994). *Zlata's diary: A child's life in Sarajevo.* New York: Viking. [ I/M ]

Fisher, Leonard Everett (1995). *Gandhi.* New York: Atheneum. [ I ]

Freedman, Russell (1987). *Lincoln: A photobiography.* Boston: Clarion. [ I/M ]

Freedman, Russell (1997). *Out of darkness: The story of Louis Braille.* Illus. by Kate Kiesler. Boston: Clarion. [ I ]

Fritz, Jean (1973). *And then what happened, Paul Revere?* Illus. by Margot Tomes. New York: Coward. [ I ]

Fritz, Jean (1989). *The great little Madison.* New York: Putnam. [ I/M ]

Fritz, Jean (1991). *Bully for you, Teddy Roosevelt.* Illus. by Mike Wimmer. New York: Putnam. [ I/M ]

Hall, Donald (1996). *When Willard met Babe Ruth.* Illus. by Barry Moser. San Diego: Browndeer Press/Harcourt Brace. [ P/I ]

Jiang, Ji-Li (1997). *Red scarf girl: A memoir of the Cultural Revolution.* New York: HarperCollins. [ I/M ]

Joseph, Lynn (1998). *Fly, Bessie, fly.* Illus. by Yvonne Buchanan. New York: Simon & Schuster. [ I ]

Kehret, Peg (1996). *Small steps: The year I got polio.* Morton Grove, IL: Albert Whitman. [ I/M ]

Krull, Kathleen (1996). *Wilma unlimited: How Wilma Rudolph became the world's fastest woman.* Illus. by David Diaz. San Diego: Harcourt Brace. [ P/I ]

Krull, Kathleen (1997). *Lives of the athletes: Thrills, spills (and what the neighbors thought).* Illus. by Kathryn Hewitt. San Diego: Harcourt Brace. [ I/M ]

Krull, Kathleen (1998). *Lives of the presidents: Fame, shame (and what the neighbors thought).* Illus. by Kathryn Hewitt. San Diego: Harcourt Brace. [ I/M ]

Lasky, Kathryn (1998). *A brilliant streak: The making of Mark Twain.* Illus. by Barry Moser. San Diego: Harcourt Brace. [ M ]

Lindbergh, Reeve (1996). *Nobody owns the sky: The story of "brave Bessie" Coleman.* Illus. by Pamela Paparone. Cambridge, MA: Candlewick Press. [ P/I ]

McPhail, David (1996). *In flight with David McPhail: A creative autobiography.* Portsmouth, NH: Heinemann. [ P/I ]

Osofsky, Audrey (1996). *Free to dream. The making of a poet, Langston Hughes.* New York: Lothrop, Lee & Shepard. [ I/M ]

Pinkney, Andrea D. (1996). *Bill Pickett: Rodeo-ridin' cowboy.* Illus. by Brian Pinkney. San Diego: Gulliver Books/Harcourt Brace. [ P/I ]

Polacco, Patricia (1994). *Firetalking.* (Meet the Author series) Katonah, NY: Richard C. Owens Publishers. [ P/I ]

Poole, Josephine (1998). *Joan of Arc.* Illus. by Angela Barrett. New York: Knopf. [ I/M ]

Rinaldi, Ann (1996). *Hang a thousand trees with ribbons: The story of Phillis Wheatley.* San Diego: Harcourt Brace. [ M ]

Roop, Peter, and Roop, Connie (Eds.) (1993). *Capturing nature: The writings and art of John James Audubon.* New York: Walker. [ I/M ]

Schroeder, Alan (1996). *Satchmo's blues.* Illus. by Floyd Cooper. New York: Doubleday. (Fictionalized biography) [ P/I ]

Severance, John B. (1997). *Gandhi: Great soul.* Boston: Clarion. [ I/M ]

Sis, Peter (1996). *Starry messenger: Galileo Galilei.* New York: Farrar, Straus and Giroux. [ P/M/I ]

Skira-Vertura, Rosabianca (1994). *Weekend with Van Gogh.* New York: Rizzoli International.

Stanley, Diane (1986). *Peter the Great.* New York: Four Winds. [ I ]

Stanley, Diane (1996). *Leonardo da Vinci.* New York: Morrow. [ I/M ]

Wadsworth, Ginger (1997). *John Burroughs: The sage of Slabsides.* Boston: Clarion. [ I/M ]

Younger, Barbara (1998). *Purple mountains majesty: The story of Katharine Lee Bates and "America the Beautiful."* Illus. by Stacey Schuett. New York: Dutton. [ I ]

# CHILDREN'S BOOKS CITED: INFORMATIONAL BOOKS

Arnold, Caroline (1997). *Hawk highway in the sky: Watching raptor migration.* Photographs by Robert Kruidenier. San Diego: Gulliver Green/Harcourt Brace. [ I ]

Ballard, Robert (1988). *Exploring the Titanic.* New York: Scholastic. [ I/M ]

Cherry, Lynne (1997). *Flute's journey.* San Diego: Gulliver Green/Harcourt Brace. [ I ]

Crowther, Robert (1996). *Pop-up Olympics: Amazing facts and record breakers.* Cambridge, MA: Candlewick Press. [ I ]

Fisher, Leonard Everett (1986). *The great wall of China.* New York: Simon & Schuster. [ I ]

Gibbons, Gail (1996). *The honeymakers.* New York: Morrow. [ P/I ]

Guiberson, Brenda (1996). *Into the sea.* Illus. by Alix Berenzy. New York: Henry Holt. [ I ]

Kramer, Stephen (1997). *Eye of the storm: Chasing storms with Warren Faidley.* Photographs by Warren Faidley. New York: Putnam. [ I ]

Meltzer, Milton (1996). *Weapons and warfare: From the stone age to the space age.* Illus. by Sergio Martinez. New York: HarperCollins. [ I/M ]

Murphy, Jim (1995). *The great fire.* New York: Scholastic. [ I/M ]

National Science Teacher Association (NSTA) and the Children's Book Council (CBC). (Annual). Outstanding Science Trade Books for Children. *Science and Children,* March issue.

National Council for the Social Studies (NCSS) and the Children's Book Council (CBC). (Annual). Notable Children's Trade Books in the Field of Social Studies. *Social Education,* April/May issue.

Patent, Dorothy Henshaw (1997). *Back to the wild.* Photographs by William Munoz. San Diego: Gulliver Green/Harcourt Brace. [ I ]

Platt, Richard (1992). *Stephen Beisty's incredible cross-sections: Man of war.* Illus. by Stephen Beisty. New York: Knopf. [ I ]

Pringle, Laurence (1995). *Dolphin man: Exploring the world of dolphins.* Photographs by Randall S. Wells and the Dolphin Biology Research Institute. New York: Atheneum. [ I ]

Pringle, Laurence (1997). *An Extraordinary life: The story of a monarch butterfly.* Illus. by Bob Marstall. New York: Orchard Books.

Simon, Seymour (1992). *Our solar system.* New York: Morrow. [ P/I ]

Snedden, Robert (1996). *Yuck!: A big book of little horrors.* New York: Simon & Schuster. [ I ]

Swanson, Diane (1995). *Safari beneath the sea: The wonder of the north Pacific coast.* San Francisco: Sierra Club Books. [ P/I ]

Wallace, Karen (1997). *Imagine you are a crocodile.* Illus. by Mike Bostock. New York: Henry Holt. [ P/I ]

Wexler, Jerome (1993). *Jack-in-the-pulpit.* New York: Dutton. [ I ]

Wick, Walter (1997). *A drop of water: A book of science and wonder.* New York: Scholastic. [ I ]

## Chapter 8

# Multicultural Literature
### *Sharing a Global Perspective*

*We hear someone yelling outside our tent. It is the Afghan. Wardak. He scares me. I don't like the way he looks. Dadi goes out to talk with him. I watch from behind the tent flap. Dadi is a brave man and does not let this man push him around. I can't hear what they are saying, but I follow every gesture they make. Finally Wardak pulls out a bundle of money and I see Dadi reach for it. I know what he has done. How could he! This is not possible. How could he sell Guluband? I run out of the tent toward Wardak screaming for him to stop. Dadi stops me and I kick and fight. I feel as furious as the storm raging around us. I wince, but all I can think about is Guluband, my favorite, my best camel, my friend. I watch as he is led away knowing I can do nothing. I am defeated. Dadi takes me back to the tent, but I am numb. I don't want to talk or look at Dadi. How could he do this! It is so unfair. My heart aches.*

K–12 Librarian Character Journal Response to
*Shabanu: Daughter of the Wind* by
Suzanne Fisher Staples

Multicultural literature transports the reader to many lands and surveys many cultures as it attempts to share differences among peoples of the world. Yet in its showcase of diversity, it encourages the recognition of commonalities among cultures. Although cultural contexts change, people retain their sameness, revealing similarities in emotions, commitments, dreams, and expectations.

The text of Mem Fox's (1997) *Whoever You Are* joyfully celebrates the emotional bonds that unite all humanity. *Joys are the same, and love is the same. Pain is the same, and blood is the same. Smiles are the same, and hearts are just the same . . .* * Multicultural children's literature opens the world of all peoples to children by inviting young readers to gain understandings about heritages, beliefs, and values that are, as they may soon discover, not so different from their own. Literature of a parallel culture—African American, Asian Pacific American, Mexican American, Native American—opens the culture's heart to the reading audience, showing the culture's joy and grief, love and hatred, hope and despair, expectations and frustrations, and the effects of living in a society where differences are not always readily accepted (Cai & Bishop, 1994). Language provides the connection between the common cultures of humanity as it serves as the means to transmit history and ideals through quality literature.

Multicultural literature serves a dual purpose in the lives of children. When a child sees him- or herself—one's own color, one's own heritage, one's own traditions—in a text, he or she feels pride, acceptance, and belonging. During a poetry unit, for example, an African American fourth-grade girl spent her recess in the media center when she discovered Eloise Greenfield was a poet of her culture. She proudly displayed *Honey, I Love* (1978) as her peers returned from the playground and kept the book close at hand for the entire week. The other purpose of multicultural literature involves mainstream or "ethnically encapsulated" (Banks, 1988) children. These are readers who often remain isolated in their own world and lack exposure to other colors and cultures. These are the young readers who open their eyes to Donald Crews' *Bigmama's* and Patricia McKissack's *Ma Dear's Aprons* and readily identify with their own family members. These are the readers who open their hearts to Dee Willis, an African American, who must adjust to an all-white suburb when her family moves in Andrea Davis Pinkney's *Hold Fast to Dreams*. Exposure to multicultural literature provides both a mirror into one's own world and a door into the culture and lives of others.

In this text multicultural literature is not considered a genre of literature, but a mirror that reflects the story of humankind *across all genres*. Although multicultural titles have been included throughout the genre chapters of this text, this chapter provides an opportunity to showcase authors, titles, and response connections that share a special purpose in touching the hearts, minds, and souls of readers while broadening their knowledge and experiences about people.

# ISSUES SURROUNDING MULTICULTURAL LITERATURE

Five issues surround multicultural literature and provide an ongoing agenda for discussion on the topic. These issues become the framework for this opening section of the chapter. First, the inclusiveness of various *definitions* of multicultural literature will be clarified.

Second, the issue of *authenticity*, the "insider" versus the "outsider" author perspective, will be examined. Third, *selection criteria* that encompass or exclude certain titles must be considered. Fourth, the *curricular relevance* of multicultural literature requires a supportive discussion. Finally, the past, current, and future *availability* of multicultural literature that meets the criteria for authenticity, cultural and historical accuracy, and aesthetic pleasure must be assessed. The following discussion should broaden the reader's knowledge of these important perspectives on children's literature and provide information to enhance judgment when selecting and naturally including multicultural literature across the curriculum.

## Definitions of Multicultural/Multiethnic Literature

Junko Yokota (1993) defined multicultural children's literature as "literature that represents any distinct cultural group through accurate portrayal and rich detail" (p. 157). Her definition allows inclusion of not only people of color, but other distinct cultural/religious groups as well as European cultural groups. This definition would not only include Walter Dean Myers' *Harlem,* but also provide for sharing Patricia Polacco's tales of her grandmother's Ukranian heritage in *Rechenka's Eggs.*

Violet Harris (1992) focused her definition of multicultural literature in *Teaching Multicultural Literature in Grades K–8* on any group that has marginal status and lacks complete access to mainstream institutions. This label includes people of color (African, Asian, Hispanic, Native American), religious minorities (Amish, Jewish), regional cultures (Appalachian, Cajun), people with disabilities (physical, mental), the aged, and, to some extent, women and girls. Using this definition, titles ranging from *Abuela* (Dorris, 1991) to Cynthia Rylant's *Appalachia: The Voices of Sleeping Birds* would be included.

In her most recent edition of *Using Multiethnic Literature in the K–8 Classroom,* Harris (1997) narrows her definition and focus by referring to literature exclusively about people of color—African, Asian, Hispanic, Native American—as "multiethnic literature." This chapter includes mostly "multiethnic literature," but also some "multicultural" titles that share specific cultures from around the globe. In addition, many of the titles mentioned span more than one culture and present a multiple perspective on people around the world.

## Authenticity

For years, scholars have debated the authenticity of multicultural literature written by authors inside and outside the culture. Although most agree that an author need not be of the culture about which he or she is writing, the fact remains that the farther one is removed from a heritage, the more difficult authenticity is to attain. To achieve authenticity, the author must either be of the culture or take on the perspective of other people living in the culture. Unfortunately, few people have the opportunity to live within a culture and note its distinctive nuances. Paul Goble is one of the few authors given genuine recognition for an "outsider" perspective on the Plains Indians (i.e., *The Return of the Buffaloes*) after actually living with Native Americans for more than a decade. Suzanne Fisher Staples spent years as a journalist in Pakistan before writing *Shabanu: Daughter of the Wind.* Authors must fill in their own cultural gaps before presuming to bridge cultural gaps for readers.

Cai and Bishop (1994) address the authenticity issue by discussing a hierarchy of multicultural literature based on the inside–outside perspective. *World literature* includes folktales and fiction from non-Western countries or other underrepresented groups outside the United States. This category includes adaptations by both American writers as well as literature directly from root cultures. For example, Geraldine McCaughrean's *The Golden Hoard* includes myths from China and Persia and legends from Wales to Australia. Mary Pope Osborne's *One World, Many Religions* shares the way people worship across the seven religions of the world. *Cross-cultural literature* focuses on the unique experiences of a cultural group or books written by an author outside the culture. The intention of these titles is to foster acceptance of cultural diversity or to encourage constructive intercultural relationships. Tony Johnson shares the mixed emotions of the moment of emancipation in *The Wagon*. Although outside the African American culture, Johnston's words capture the slaves' longings for freedom tempered by their sadness at the loss of President Lincoln, the Great Emancipator. Finally, *parallel culture literature* is written by authors from a cultural group who represent the experience and images developed as a result of being acculturated and socialized within the culture itself. A focused example is Walter Dean Myers's *Harlem* which poetically portrays the sounds, sights, and memories of this section of New York in which he was raised. Christopher Myers's collage art resonates strong emotions and adds another dimension to the understanding of this African American urban culture. While the "inside" perspective is still viewed by most multicultural specialists as the most "authentic," the acceptance of different levels of involvement within a culture broadens the number of books that attain varying degrees of authenticity.

Authenticity reflects accuracy of portrayal. This remains a topic for debate especially among those who apply authenticity as the main criteria in determining the quality of a title of multicultural literature. Although this discussion is likely to continue, an awareness of the variable tiers of authenticity may bring some degree of acceptance to a wider span of quality books from authors both inside and outside, yet well informed about the culture.

## Selection Criteria

Many teachers and librarians lack confidence in their ability to make informed decisions about multicultural titles, believing they do not have the cultural knowledge to select literature that does not foster stereotypes of a particular group. Whereas wide reading over time about a particular cultural group will assist in developing cultural sensitivities, they often request assistance in making difficult choices.

A reputable identification of quality multicultural literature comes from book award winners that have been carefully scrutinized by children's literature experts. The Coretta Scott King Award honors outstanding African American authors and illustrators of books for children and young adults. (See Appendix A for a complete listing of winning books). Former winning authors include Virginia Hamilton, Walter Dean Myers, and Frederick and Patricia McKissack. Coretta Scott King Award-winning illustrators include Tom Feelings for *Soul Looks Back in Wonder* (1993) and *The Middle Passage* (1995) and Jerry Pinkney for *Minty: A Story of Young Harriet Tubman* (Schroeder, 1996).

The Pura Belpé Award (see Appendix A) honors Latino writers and illustrators whose work best portrays, affirms, and celebrates the Latino cultural experience in the work of literature for youth. A relatively new award, winners include Stephanie Garcia for illustrations in *Snapshots from the Wedding* (Soto, 1997) and Victor Martinez for *Parrot in the Oven: Mi Vida* (1997).

The Notable Books for a Global Society provides an annual list of outstanding trade books for enhancing student understanding of people and cultures throughout the world (see Appendix A). The notable multicultural books selected must meet one or more of the following criteria:

1. Portray cultural accuracy and authenticity of characters in terms of:
   a. physical characteristics
   b. intellectual abilities and problem-solving capabilities
   c. leadership and cooperative dimensions
   d. social and economic status.
2. Be rich in cultural details.
3. Honor and celebrate diversity as well as common bonds in humanity.
4. Provide in-depth treatment of cultural issues.
5. Include characters with a cultural group or between two or more cultural groups who interact substantively and authentically.
6. Include members of a "minority" group for a purpose other than filling a "quota."
7. Invite reflection, critical analysis, and response.
8. Demonstrate unique language or style.
9. Meet generally accepted criteria of quality for the genre in which they are written.
10. Have an appealing format and be of endearing quality.

Recent recipients of this honor include Joseph Bruchac's *Between Earth and Sky: Legends of Native American Sacred Places,* Ann Rinaldi's *Hang a Thousand Trees with Ribbons: The Story of Phillis Wheatley,* Rafe Martin's *Mysterious Tales of Japan,* and Carmen Garza's *In My Family/En Mi Familia.*

Both children's literature and multicultural literacy experts offer general guidelines for evaluating and selecting multicultural literature that meet high standards (Diamond & Moore, 1995; Finazzo, 1997; Glazer, 1997; Huck, Hepler, Hickman, & Kiefer, 1997; Jacobs & Tunnell, 1996). All multicultural literature must first and foremost fulfill the same standards for literary traits that are used to scrutinize all types of quality children's literature. In addition, the following criteria blend into a structured template for scrutinizing quality multicultural literature across genres.

Characters:  Characters should authentically reflect the distinct cultural experience of a specific cultural group.

Names of characters should be culturally authentic and their personalities should reflect believable attributes.

Characterization should be true to life and balanced, representing both positive and negative behaviors and traits.

Perpetuation of cultural stereotypes must be avoided.

Gender roles within the culture should be portrayed authentically, reflecting the changing roles and status of women and men in cultures.

| | |
|---|---|
| Settings: | Settings should be representative of and consistent with a historical or contemporary time, place, or situation of a particular culture. |
| | Factual information describing a historical setting must be accurate in detail. |
| | Contemporary settings must align with current situations of a cultural group. |
| Themes: | Themes should be consistent with the values, beliefs, customs, traditions, and conflicts of the specific cultural group. |
| | Social issues and conflicts related to cultural groups should be treated honestly, accurately, and openly. |
| Language: | Language should reflect the distinctive vocabulary, style, and patterns of speech of the cultural group. |
| | Dialect should be natural and blend with plot and characterization while not being perceived as substandard language. |
| | Language should represent sensitivity to a people; derogatory terms should be excluded unless essential to a conflict or used in historical context. |
| Illustrations: | Physical characteristics of people of a diverse culture should replicate natural appearance and avoid stereotypes. |
| | Illustrations should reflect accurate cultural setting. |
| | Characters should be portrayed as unique individuals within a culture. |
| | Illustrations should complement and enhance imagery of the story. |

The application of these criteria ensures that children of all cultures who see themselves in a book will experience self-worth from the illustrations they view, the words they read, and the characters with whom they identify. A book should fill the reader of another culture with a positive view and clearer understanding of the represented culture. All readers should depart the multicultural reading experience with a more accurate understanding of both themselves and others.

## Multicultural Literature's Role in the Response Curriculum

Banks (1989) described a hierarchy of four curricular models for integrating multicultural/multiethnic content into the curriculum. These models have been explored in relation to literature connections by Rasinski and Padak (1990) and Bieger (1996). They provide a meaningful framework through which to address possible response-based connections between the reader and multicultural literature. Teachers must view these as models that can be addressed within the existing curriculum, rather than perceiving them as an addendum to the already weighty burden of content specific curriculum. This discussion serves to link these curricular models with current literature and response-based activities.

The lowest level of the multicultural hierarchy is the *contributions approach* in which readers read about and discuss ethnic holidays, heroes, and customs. The teacher may read *I Have a Dream* (King, 1997) to commemorate the birthday of Dr. Martin Luther King or share *Frederick Douglass: The Last Days of Slavery* (Miller, 1995) during Black History month. Unfortunately, this is the multicultural level at which most classrooms currently function, yet it serves as a springboard for higher level connections through response. Because biographies so readily fit the contributions approach, biopoems and prompts that address character traits are highly appropriate response connections. Suggesting that students design a bulletin board based on literature titles or research facts on a hero or holiday also extends response.

The second level is the *ethnic additive approach* in which content and themes that reflect other cultures are added to the existing curriculum, maintaining its purpose and structure. Multicultural literature is added to curriculum, but not necessarily viewed from a cultural perspective. For example, a kindergarten teacher may read *Kente Colors* (Chocolate, 1996) because recognizing colors in a learning outcome. The teacher emphasizes the colors described rather than discussing the culturally distinctive kente cloth. Folktales also abound at this level as they carry the reader to a variety of cultures that share similar stories. A prime example is the multicultural versions of Cinderella ranging from *Mufaro's Beautiful Daughters* (Steptoe, 1987), which carries the reader to Zimbabwe, or *Yeh-Shen* (Louie, 1982), which is embedded in Chinese lore. In this scenario, comparison/contrast serves as a higher level interpretive response.

The third level, the *transformation approach,* actually changes the structure of the curriculum to enable readers to view problems and themes from the perspective of different ethnic and cultural groups. An appropriate example is a study of Lewis and Clark, the Louisiana Purchase, and the expedition West during the early 1800s. An important part of American history, it has been viewed through the unlikely eyes of York, a black slave who accompanied them on the journey. *My Name Is York* (Van Steenwyk, 1997) reveals the perspective of Captain Clark's slave who dared to dream of freedom as he gazed at the vastness of the wilderness yet unexplored. Carolyn Reeder's *Across the Lines* reveals the contrasting human sides of the Civil War as Edward, a plantation owner's son, and Simon, his black companion and servant, share their close friendship, different choices, and the demands of the new freedom from alternating points of view. Insights gained through a fresh historical perspective may be gathered in a character journal or a literature response journal. Viewing historical events from an alternative point of view makes this approach to multicultural inclusion invigorating for both teacher and students.

The highest level of Banks' hierarchy is the *social action approach.* Readers are challenged to identify social problems, make decisions, and take action to resolve problems. Identification through literature, critical response analysis, and a plan of action related to cultural differences provides an outstanding outlet for response to literature. The cognitive aspects of reader response (prediction, speculation, problem solving, decision making) become paramount as societal issues are the focus of discussion and personal thought. For example, the issue of racial discrimination can be introduced through Evelyn Coleman's *White Socks Only.* This picture book highlights places children could not go or things they could not do because of color. Response takes the form of discussing ways in which discrimination still exists and what can be done to alleviate discrimination in our schools, our communities, and our nation.

These four levels of multicultural involvement through literature set high standards and a hierarchical ladder of participation for teachers and students. Teachers often lack confidence to move beyond the first level, because their lack of comfort with multicultural literature creates uncertainty in how they can increase its effective use in their class-rooms. Banks's categories, supported by a growing knowledge of multicultural titles, provide the sense of direction they need for gradual, but committed growth to multi-cultural education.

## Availability of Quality Multicultural Literature

As children of culturally and linguistically diverse backgrounds continue to be a growing portion of our country's population, the need and desire for publication of multicultural children's literature remains strong. Children's literature has not always represented children of diverse backgrounds in positive ways, so continued emphasis in this area is crucial. Strong literature-based programs in our schools demand that children of color have access to literature that is relevant to their own lives and which portrays all children, not merely those of the dominant culture. Our growing consciousness of our global society requires that all children be exposed to a multicultural perspective, and multicultural literature provides a means for accomplishing this end.

In the first edition of *Kaleidoscope: A Multicultural Booklist for Grades K–8,* Rudine Sims Bishop (1994) reported that almost 18,000 books for children were published during 1990 through 1992, yet only about 600 titles (3% to 4%) were books relating to people of color. The second edition of *Kaleidoscope* (Barrera, Thompson, & Dressman, 1997) recognizes about 900 books (5% to 6%) of the 18,000 published during 1993 through 1995 as multi-cultural literature. The slight increase is still quite limited compared to the proportion of people of color in the United States and children of color in our nation's schools. Many of these titles only minimally address cultural issues. The editors contend, ". . . the transfor-mation of children's literature into a mirror that reflects the diversity of America's children, and the application of that literature toward the advancement of our multicultural society, has hardly begun" (p. xii). Tokenism, indifference, and rejection must be overcome in pub-lishing as well as in the attitude of professional educators if multicultural literature is to be-come an essential component of our school curriculum.

# RESPONSE TO MULTICULTURAL LITERATURE

Response to literature that reflects a global society provides essential opportunities for read-ers to interact with texts by expressing opinions and reactions to similarities and differences in cultures other than their own. All response activities discussed throughout this entire text are also applicable to multicultural titles. This section of this chapter, however, travels through each genre, citing response connections specific to the genre while providing spe-cific response activities for quality multicultural titles. A genre approach provides an effec-tive means to present the linking of reader response and multicultural literature.

Each of the following sections suggests types of response connections to multicultural literature in each genre and is supplemented by a list of quality multicultural titles from the genre. The titles represent literature of "people of color" (multiethnic literature) as well as a few titles representing multiple cultures. Each bibliographic entry lists the represented

Children readily connect a sense of family and tradition across cultures. *From SNAPSHOTS FROM THE WEDDING by Gary Soto, illustrated by Stephanie Garcia. Copyright © 1997 by Stephanie Garcia. Used by permission of G. P. Putnam's Sons, a division of Penguin Putnam Inc.*

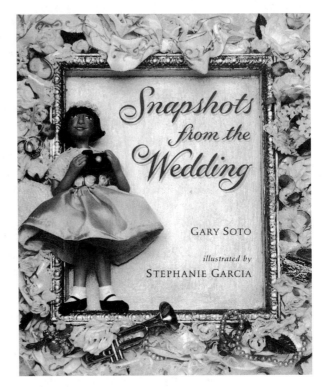

culture and the suggested grade level (P = grades K–2; I = grades 3–5; M = grades 6–8) for response connections. While the lists may seem numerically out of balance in favor of African American literature, the listings closely reflect the proportion of titles currently published for varied cultures.

## Response to Picture Storybooks

Reader response to multicultural literature may begin with the simple length—but meaningful content—of a multicultural picture storybook. Many of these titles reflect a character of a specific culture, but share a universal message. Response begins with a memorable read-aloud followed by response prompts designed to impart a personal response to the book (see Chapter 10). A Hispanic American selection such as Gary Soto's *Snapshots from the Wedding* might result in a read-aloud and response that indicates connections between Maya's life and the reader's own family wedding traditions. The story reflects a strong sense of family and its message is applicable across cultures.

A culturally specific read-aloud of Allen Say *Grandfather's Journey* results in aesthetic connections reflecting the struggle between the anticipation of a new home in a strange land and constant yearning for one's homeland and cultural heritage. Many children in today's classroom will readily identify with the meaning and message of titles like these. Children may respond to Tamar's *The Garden of Happiness* by noting how people of all cultures cooperate to produce an aesthetic garden in an urban neighborhood. Avoiding didacticism, these titles invariably pull children of all cultures together through common human expe-

**FIGURE 8.1**    Multicultural picture storybooks

Belton, Sandra (1994). *May'naise sandwiches & sunshine tea.* Illus. by Gail Gordon Carter. New York: Four Winds Press. AFRICAN AMERICAN. [ P ]

Bunting, Eve (1994). *A day's work.* Illus. by Ronald Himler. New York: Clarion Books. HISPANIC AMERICAN. [ P/I ]

Coleman, Evelyn (1998). *To be a drum.* Illus. by Aminah Robinson. Morton Grove, IL: Albert Whitman. AFRICAN AMERICAN. [ P/I ]

Ho, Minfong (1996). *Hush: A Thai lullaby.* Illus. by Holly Meade. New York: Orchard. ASIAN. [ P ]

Lauture, Denize (1996). *Running the road to ABC.* Illus. by Reynold Ruffin. New York: Simon & Schuster. HAITIAN. [ P ]

McKissack, Patricia C. (1997). *Ma Dear's aprons.* Illus. by Floyd Cooper. New York: Atheneum. AFRICAN AMERICAN. [ P/I ]

Medearis, Angela Shelf (1997). *Rum-a-tum-tum.* Illus. by James Ransome. New York: Holiday House. AFRICAN AMERICAN. [ P/I ]

Mitchell, Margaree King (1993). *Uncle Jed's barbershop.* Illus. by James Ransome. New York: Simon & Schuster. AFRICAN AMERICAN. [ P/I ]

Pinkney, Gloria Jean (1994). *The Sunday outing.* Illus. by Jerry Pinkney. New York: Dial Books. AFRICAN AMERICAN. [ P/I ]

Say, Allen (1993). *Grandfather's journey.* Boston: Houghton Mifflin. JAPANESE AMERICAN. [ P/I ]

Schertle, Alice (1995). *Down the road.* Illus. by E. B. Lewis. San Diego: Browndeer Press/Harcourt Brace. AFRICAN AMERICAN. [ P/I ]

Soto, Gary (1993). *Too many tamales.* Illus. by Ed Martinez. New York: Putnam. HISPANIC AMERICAN. [ P/I ]

Soto, Gary (1995). *Chato's kitchen.* Illus. by Sasan Guevara. New York: Putnam. HISPANIC AMERICAN. [ P/I ]

Soto, Gary (1997). *Snapshots from the wedding.* Illus. by Stephanie Garcia. New York: Putnam. HISPANIC AMERICAN. [ P/I ]

Tamar, Erika (1996). *The garden of happiness.* Illus. by Barbara Lambase. San Diego: Harcourt Brace. MULTICULTURAL. [ P/I ]

riences. Experiential prompts provide the most effective responses to these stories of true-to-life people of all the colors of the human race. The picture storybooks listed in Figure 8.1 are brief read-alouds, but have a powerful impact as children of all cultures reflect and connect to their own lives.

## Response to Traditional Literature

The genre that has the power to transport the reader around the entire globe through simple story is traditional literature—myths, legends, and folktales. Whether reading common tales across cultures or following a global journey across continents and cultures, traditional tales provide a valuable source for response to their multicultural nature. Three response goals are paramount in sharing multicultural traditional tales:

1. Identifying visual and verbal cues to the specific culture
2. Identifying intertextual connections and commonalities between and among tales of varying cultures
3. Creating a pleasurable, interesting experience with the literature of another culture.

Most traditional tales are published in the picture book format, inviting readers to respond to cultural specifics through both text and illustrations. Children's response might initially focus on the unique apparent differences of a culture—clothing, language, names, homes. With appropriate prompts and teacher planning, children can grow toward a recognition of cultural commonalities—role of family, valued human traits, cleverness and wit, the triumph of good over evil. A sound background of traditional literature deemed important in one's own culture is essential for these higher level connections to occur between and among cultures.

Because traditional tales have roots in the oral tradition, response to these tales results from oral retellings, storytelling, or dramatic reenactments. Memorable characters, specific themes, and repetitive actions provide structure for oral response. Lucia Gonzales's *Senor Cat's Romance,* a story in rhyme from Spain, begs response through choral reading. The blend of rhyme, monologue, and sound effects combines for an enjoyable oral response. Joseph Bierhorst's *The Dancing Fox: Arctic Folktales,* a collection of 18 brief Inuit tales, invites retelling by intermediate-level students. The oral nature of traditional literature across all cultures provides a meaningful focus for response. The titles listed in Figure 8.2 celebrate the oral tradition and invite oral response.

**FIGURE 8.2**    Multicultural traditional tales

---

Bierhorst, John (Reteller) (1993). *The woman who fell from the sky: The Iroquois story of creation.* Illus. by Robert Andrew Parker. New York: Morrow. IROQUOIS LEGEND (Picture book). [ P/I/M ]

Bierhorst, John (Ed.) (1997). *The dancing fox: Arctic folktales.* Illus. by Mary K. Okheena. New York: Morrow. INUIT. [ I/M ]

Bruchac, Joseph (Reteller) (1993). *The first strawberries: A Cherokee story.* Illus. by Anna Vojtech. New York: Dial. CHEROKEE LEGEND (Picture Book). [ P/I ]

Gonzales, Lucia M. (1997). *Senor Cat's romance and other favorite stories from Latin America.* Illus. by Lulu Delacre. New York: Scholastic. HISPANIC (Picture book). [ P/I ]

Hamilton, Virginia (Reteller) (1995). *Her stories: African American folktales, fairy tales, and true tales.* Illus. by Leo & Diane Dillon. NY: Blue Sky/Scholastic. AFRICAN AMERICAN. [ I/M ]

Hamilton, Virginia (Reteller) (1996). *When birds could talk & bats could sing.* Illus. by Barry Moser. New York: Blue Sky/Scholastic. AFRICAN AMERICAN, SOUTHERN US, FOLKTALES. (Picture book). [ P/I ]

Hamilton, Virginia. (Reteller) (1997). *A ring of tricksters: Animal tales from America, the West Indies, and Africa.* Illus. by Barry Moser. New York: Blue Sky/Scholastic. AFRICAN AMERICAN. [ P/I ]

Lester, Julius (1994). *John Henry.* Illus. by Jerry Pinkney. New York: Dial. AFRICAN AMERICAN FOLKTALE (Picture book). [ P/I ]

McDermott, Gerald (1993). *Raven: A trickster tale from the Pacific Northwest.* San Diego: Harcourt Brace. NATIVE AMERICAN LEGEND (Picture book). [ P/I ]

San Souci, Robert D. (1993). *Cut from the same cloth: American women of myth, legend, and tall tale.* Illus. by Brian Pinkney. New York: Philomel Books. MULTICULTURAL. [ I/M ]

San Souci, Robert D. (1995). *The faithful friend.* Illus. by Brian Pinkney. New York: Simon & Schuster. CARIBBEAN FOLKTALE (Picture book). [ P/I ]

Yep, Laurence (Reteller) (1993). *The shell woman and the king.* Illus. by Yang Ming-Yi. New York: Dial. CHINESE FOLKTALE. [ P/I ]

Young, Ed (1995). *Night visitors.* New York: Philomel Books. CHINESE FOLKTALE (Picture book). [ P/I ]

A common classroom response activity is to compare/contrast variants of traditional tales from various cultures. The 500 variants of Cinderella, for example, differ in name, characters, objects, and settings, but the literary element of theme remains constant and binds various cultures around the world together. An in-depth study and comparative response to Cinderella variants enhance understandings, appreciations, and respect for various cultural groups (Yang, Siu-Runyan, Vilscek, 1997). Comparisons among settings, characters' appearances, cultural values, as well as themes provide opportunities for personal response through cultural charts, story maps, or oral discussion. The titles listed in Figure 8.3 are intended for both primary and intermediate levels and provide only a cross-section of the cultures that embrace the Cinderella tale.

Finally, multicultural traditional tales should be enjoyed aesthetically for the wonderful stories they tell. These are often the stories that stay with the reader long after the read-aloud and the response. The staying power of *Mangaboom* (Pomerantz, 1997), for example, is in the larger-than-life character who speaks both English and Spanish, and in Anita Lobel's exquisite illustrations, which present a charming, female, bilingual giant to its di-

**FIGURE 8.3**   Multicultural versions of the Cinderella tale

Bernhard, Emery (1994). *The girl who wanted to hunt: A Siberian tale.* Illus. by Durga Bernhard. New York: Holiday House.
Brown, Marcia (1971). *Cinderella or the little glass slipper.* New York: Charles Scribner's Sons. (France)
Climo, Shirley (1989). *The Egyptian Cinderella.* Illus. by Ruth Heller. New York: HarperCollins.
Climo, Shirley (1993). *The Korean Cinderella.* Illus. by Ruth Heller. New York: HarperCollins.
Hamilton, Virginia (1995). Catskinella. In *Her stories: African American folktales, fairy tales, and true tales* (pp. 23–27). Illus. by Leo and Diane Dillon. New York: Blue Sky/Scholastic.
Han, Oki S. (1996). *Kongi and Potgi: A Cinderella story from Korea.* Illus. by Stephanie Plunkett. New York: Dial.
Hooks, William H. (1987). *Moss gown.* Illus. by Donald Carrick. Boston: Clarion. (N. Carolina)
Huck, Charlotte (1989). *Princess Furball.* Illus. by Anita Lobel. New York: Greenwillow. (Germany)
Jacobs, Joseph (1989). *Tattercoats.* Illus. by Margot Tomes. New York: Putnam. (England)
Louie, Ai-Ling (1982). *Yeh-shen: A Cinderella story from China.* Illus. by Ed Young. New York: Philomel Books.
Martin, Rafe (1992). *The rough-face girl.* Illus. by David Shannon. New York: Putnam. (Algonquin/Native American)
Pollock, Penny (1996). *The turkey girl.* Illus. by Ed Young. Boston: Little, Brown. (Zuni/Native American)
San Souci, Robert D. (1989). *The talking eggs.* Illus. by Jerry Pinkney. New York: Dial. (Louisiana)
San Souci, Robert D. (1994). *Sootface: An Ojibwa Cinderella story.* Illus. by Daniel San Souci. New York: Bantam Doubleday Dell. (Native American)
Schroeder, Alan. (1997). *Smoky Mountain Rose: An Appalachian Cinderella.* Illus. by Brad Sneed. New York: Dial.
Steptoe, John (1987). *Mufaro's beautiful daughter: An African tale.* New York: Lothrop, Lee & Shepard.
Wilson, Barbara Ker (1993). *Wishbones: A folk tale from China.* Illus. by Meilo So. New York: Bradbury.
Winthrop, Elizabeth (1991). *Vasilissa the beautiful: A Russian folktale.* Illus. by Alexander Koshkin. New York: HarperCollins.

verse readers. Encourage readers to make their own aesthetic connections with these stories as their themes transcend culture.

## Response to Poetry

Multicultural poetry strikes the same emotional chord within us that all poetry does. Its rhyme and rhythm, its flowing lines appeal to our inner senses. The experiences it shares allow for immediate connections to our own. The carefully selected word choices make us appreciate the power of language. Multicultural poetry, however, inspires all of these authentic responses within the context of a specific culture. Having poems read aloud by a member of a culture makes for a special response experience. The emphatic articulation, appropriate pauses, and authentic dialect of an African American or Hispanic American voice brings special life and light to the poetry presentation.

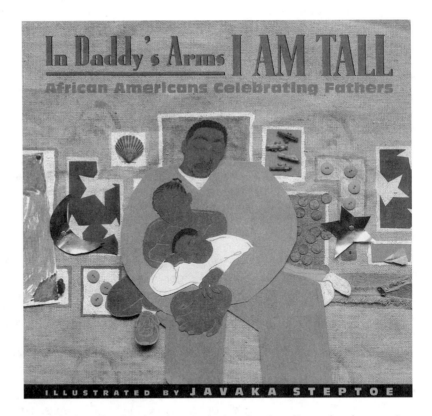

The rhyme and rhythm of multicultural poetry invites choral reading and oral connections to the reader's own life.
*From* In Daddy's Arms I Am Tall: African Americans Celebrating Fathers. *Illustration by Javaka Steptoe. Copyright © 1997 by Javaka Steptoe. Reprinted by permission of Lee & Low Books.*

Children's responses to multicultural poetry begin with the oral connection. Javaka Steptoe selected and illustrated *In Daddy's Arms I Am Tall: African Americans Celebrating Fathers* (Coretta Scott King Illustrator Award 1998). Inventive mixed media illustrations accompany a series of poems by African American poets celebrating fatherhood. Children will readily respond to the illustrations and well-chosen poems that pay tribute to the role black fathers have for sons, daughters, and grandchildren. Stories of their own fathers as personal heroes will abound as children respond to the prompt "Who does this remind you of in your own life?" Steptoe's selection of poems sensitively portrays all kinds of fathers, so no child will feel excluded from the discussion.

Primary readers especially want to become a part of the poem through choral reading. Providing a cultural read-aloud model followed by direct participation may itself provide a cultural response as children attempt to match rhythm, tempo, and the authentic language of the poem. For example, Pat Mora's *Confetti* contains a simple poem titled "Dancing Paper" that encourage the words *pinata, papel picado, marimba,* and *cascarones* to flow from the lips of the reader. The words offer an invitation to learn more about the culture and that research itself becomes a response.

Response to multicultural poetry can also be extended through an artistic response. As children examine the intriguing mixed-media constructions in Brian Swann's *Touching the Distance: Native American Riddle-Poems,* they can share the solutions to the riddles through their own art. Emotions can be captured through artwork in response to Maya Angelou's *Life Doesn't Frighten Me.* While oral discussion on the meaning or messages of poems can bring about cultural understandings, the beauty and distinction of a multicultural poem lies in its use of language to capture the values, priorities, and visions of a culture (see Figure 8.4). An appreciation of and response to the special language of poetry would be a desired response at any age level.

## Response to Realistic Fiction

The straightforward appeal of character's personalities and authentic actions in multicultural realistic fiction invite personal connections and reader response. Primarily chapter books, these multicultural titles lend themselves naturally to literature response journals (see Chapter 10) for the intermediate/middle-level reader. They invite spontaneous, ongoing response as the story unfolds and the character develops.

Minimal research has been conducted comparing responses of mainstream readers and readers of a specific culture to multicultural literature. Realistic fiction, however, provides an avenue for response by readers from both within and from those outside the culture. Sharing these perspectives in literature conversations or in peer sharing sessions might open readers' minds to varying perspectives on a cultural incident or set of values. Because of their contemporary settings and characters close to the age of readers, the appeal of this genre, especially to the grade 5–8 student, is apparent. The realistic fiction titles listed in Figure 8.5 contain the level of emotion and conflict that inspire heartfelt response.

**FIGURE 8.4**   Multicultural poetry

---

Angelou, Maya (1993). *Life doesn't frighten me.* Illus. by Jean-Michel Basquiat. New York: Stewart, Tabori and Chang. MULTICULTURAL (Picture book). [ I/M ]

Begay, Shonto (1995). *Navajo: Visions and voices across the mesa.* New York: Scholastic. NAVAJO (Picture book). [ M ]

Bryan, Ashley (1997). *Ashley Bryan's ABC of African American poetry.* New York: Atheneum. AFRICAN AMERICAN. [ P/I ]

Carlson, Lori M. (1994). *Cool salsa: Bilingual poems on growing up Latino in the United States.* New York: Holt. LATINO. [ I/M ]

Feelings, Tom (1993). *Soul looks back in wonder.* New York: Dial. AFRICAN AMERICAN (Picture book). [ P/I ]

Greenfield, Eloise (1995). *Honey, I love.* Illus. by Jan Spivey Gilchrist. New York: HarperCollins. AFRICAN AMERICAN (Picture book). [ P/I ]

Grimes, Nikki (1994). *Meet Danitra Brown.* Illus. by Floyd Cooper. New York: Lothrop, Lee & Shepard. AFRICAN AMERICAN. [ P/I ]

Gunning, Monica (1993). *Not a copper penny in me house.* Illus. by Frane Lessac. Honesdale, PA: Boyds Mills Press. CARIBBEAN. [ P/I ]

Gunning, Monica (1998). *Under the breadfruit tree: Island poems.* Illus. by Fabricio Vanden Broeck. Honesdale, PA: Wordsong/Boyds Mills Press. CARIBBEAN. [ I ]

Hamanaka, Sheila (1994). *All the colors of the earth.* New York: Morrow Junior Books. MULTICULTURAL (Picture book). [ P/I ]

Ho, Minfong (1996). *Maples in the mist: Children's poems from the Tang Dynasty.* Illus. by Jean & Mou-sien Tseng. New York: Lothrop, Lee & Shepard. CHINESE. [ P/I ]

Johnson, James Weldon (1995). *Lift every voice and sing.* Illus. by Jan Spivey Gilchrist. New York: Scholastic. AFRICAN AMERICAN (Picture book). [ P/I/M ]

Mora, Pat (1994). *The desert is my mother/El desierto es mi madre.* Illus. by Daniel Lechon. Houston, TX: Piñata Books. HISPANIC AMERICAN (Picture book). [ I ]

Mora, Pat (1996). *Confetti: Poems for children.* Illus. by Enrique O. Sanchez. New York: Lee & Low Books. HISPANIC AMERICAN (Picture book). [ P/I ]

Myers, Walter Dean (1997). *Harlem.* Illus. by Christopher Myers. New York: Scholastic. AFRICAN AMERICAN. [ I/M ]

Nye, Naomi Shihab (Ed.) (1995). *The tree is older than you are: A bilingual gathering of poems and stories from Mexico with paintings by Mexican artists.* New York: Simon & Schuster. MEXICAN (Includes stories). [ I/M ]

Steptoe, Javaka (1997). *In Daddy's arms I am tall: African Americans celebrating fathers.* New York: Lee & Low Books. AFRICAN AMERICAN. [ P/I ]

Thomas, Joyce Carol (1993). *Brown honey in broomwheat tea.* Illus. by Floyd Cooper. New York: HarperCollins. AFRICAN AMERICAN (Picture book). [ P/I ]

Wong, Janet S. (1994). *Goodluck gold and other poems.* New York: McElderry Books. ASIAN AMERICAN. [ I/M ]

Wong, Janet S. (1996). *A suitcase of seaweed and other poems.* New York: McElderry Books. ASIAN AMERICAN. [ I/M ]

**FIGURE 8.5** Multicultural realistic fiction

Cofer, Judith Ortiz (1995). *An island like you: Stories of the barrio.* New York: Orchard Books. PUERTO RICAN (Short stories). [ M ]
Dorris, Michael (1997). *The window.* New York: Hyperion. AFRICAN/NATIVE AMERICAN. [ M ]
Draper, Sharon M. (1997). *Forged by fire.* New York: Atheneum. AFRICAN AMERICAN. [ M ]
Fenner, Carol (1995). *Yolonda's genius.* New York: McElderry Books. AFRICAN AMERICAN. [ I ]
Fleischman, Paul (1997). *Seedfolks.* New York: Joanna Cotler Books/HarperCollins. MULTICULTURAL. [ M ]
Johnson, Angela (1993). *Toning the sweep.* New York: Orchard Books. AFRICAN AMERICAN. [ M ]
Nye, Naomi Shihab (1997). *Habibi.* New York: Simon & Schuster. MIDDLE EAST. [ M ]
Staples, Suzanne Fisher (1990). *Shabanu: Daughter of the wind.* New York: Knopf. PAKISTAN. [ I ]
Staples, Suzanne Fisher (1996). *Dangerous skies.* New York: Farrar, Straus and Giroux. AFRICAN AMERICAN. [ I/M ]
Woodson, Jacqueline (1994). *I hadn't meant to tell you this.* New York: Blue Sky/Scholastic. AFRICAN AMERICAN. [ M ]
Woodson, Jacqueline (1995). *From the notebooks of Melanin Sun.* New York: Blue Sky/Scholastic. AFRICAN AMERICAN. [ M ]
Yep, Laurence (1996). *Ribbons.* New York: Putnam. CHINESE AMERICAN. [ I/M ]

## Response to Historical Fiction

Historical fiction provides an excellent backdrop through which one can experience the life of a character in another historical time and place. A character journal (see Chapter 10) supplies an effective means for taking on the guise of a character and experiencing life from a historical perspective. Multicultural literature provides an additional layer to this simulated experience. The reader not only takes on the persona of the character, but also attempts to acquire the perspective of a cultural character feeling the devastation of war, the ache of discrimination, or the scar of prejudice. The character journal in no way equates the experience of the reader with that of the cultural character. It does, however, attempt to bring a varied perspective to the reader that might otherwise be missed or dismissed during reading. In Mildred Taylor's *Mississippi Bridge*, 10-year-old Jeremy Sims witnesses a bus driver ordering blacks off a bus to make room for whites, only to see it then skid off the bridge drowning its passengers. The written response to a culturally defined historical novel enhances the perspective with which historical events and characters may be viewed by the outside culture. A dramatic reenactment or readers' theater script of several of the emotional scences in the titles listed in Figure 8.6 creates emotional responses to both historical events and human attitudes as well as to literature.

## Response to Biography/Autobiography

The lives of people of color outside the mainstream culture stand as an inspiration to readers from both within and outside a cultural group. People of all cultures show ambition to

**FIGURE 8.6** Multicultural historical fiction

Balgassi, Haemi (1996). *Peacebound trains.* Illus. by Chris K. Soentpiet. Boston: Clarion. KOREAN AMERICAN (Korean War 1950–53). [ I/M ]

Breckler, Rosemary (1996). *Sweet dried apples: A Vietnamese wartime childhood.* Illus. by Deborah Kogan Ray. Boston: Houghton Mifflin. VIETNAM (Vietnam War). [ P/I ]

Coerr, Eleanor (1993). *Sadako.* Illus. by Ed Young. New York: Putnam. JAPANESE AMERICAN (World War II, Hiroshima). [ I ]

Curtis, Christopher Paul (1995). *The Watsons go to Birmingham—1963.* New York: Delacorte Press. AFRICAN AMERICAN (Civil rights movement). [ I/M ]

Dorris, Michael (1994). *Guests.* New York: Hyperion. NATIVE AMERICAN (Discovery of America). [ I ]

Johnson, Tony (1996). *The wagon.* Paintings by James Ransome. Tambourine/Morrow. AFRICAN AMERICAN (Emancipation). [ P/I ]

Mochizuki, Ken (1993). *Baseball saved us.* Illus. by Dom Lee. New York: Scholastic. JAPANESE AMERICAN (World War II). [ P/I ]

Polacco, Patricia (1994). *Pink and Say.* New York: Philomel Books. AFRICAN AMERICAN (Civil War). [ I/M ]

Salisbury, Graham (1994). *Under the blood-red sun.* New York: Delacorte. JAPANESE AMERICAN (World War II). [ I/M ]

Taylor, Mildred D. (1990). *Mississippi bridge.* New York: Dial. AFRICAN AMERICAN. [ I ]

Taylor, Mildred D. (1995). *The well: David's story.* New York: Dial. AFRICAN AMERICAN. [ I ]

personally succeed, determination to contribute to a better world, skills to lead armies to victory, and the desire to uncover the secrets of science. The valued personal qualities of the human race are exemplified through people of all cultures. Exposure to biography across cultures is vital for all children. For years, a steady diet of mainstream heroes took precedence over a cultural mix of heroes and heroines. A concerted effort must be made to include multicultural biographies throughout the entire curriculum, avoiding tokenism by showcasing them throughout the entire school year. Consider the fairness and importance to each child, whatever his or her color, of seeing him- or herself as part of the true account of a famous person of his or her race, ethnic group, color, or culture.

Response to biographical accounts of multicultural lives should focus both on personal traits and cultural contributions of the subject (see Figure 8.7). A biopoem composition following the reading of a Rosa Parks, Nelson Mandela, Sitting Bull, or Langston Hughes biography reflects personal, historical, and cultural contributions (see Chapter 13). More importantly, it reflects the personal strengths that all people require to make a difference in our world. The commonalities of the human spirit are paramount to cultural differences and are reflected through biographical response.

**FIGURE 8.7**   Multicultural biography

Adler, David A. (1993). *A picture book of Rosa Parks.* Illus. by Robert Casilla. New York: Holiday House. AFRICAN AMERICAN (Picture book). [ P ]

Bradby, Marie (1995). *More than anything else.* Illus. by Chris Soentpiet. New York: Orchard Books. AFRICAN AMERICAN (Booker T. Washington, picture book). [ P ]

Bruchac, Joseph (1994). *A boy called slow: The true story of Sitting Bull.* Illus. by Rocco Baviera. New York: Philomel Books. LAKOTA SIOUX (Picture book). [ I ]

Cooper, Floyd (1994). *Coming home: From the life of Langston Hughes.* New York: Philomel Books. AFRICAN AMERICAN (Picture book). [ P/I ]

Cooper, Floyd (1996). *Mandela: From the life of the South African statesman.* New York: Philomel Books. AFRICAN (Picture book). [ I/M ]

Freedman, Russell (1996). *The life and death of Crazy Horse.* Illus. by Amos Bad Heart. New York: Holiday House. NATIVE AMERICAN. [ I/M ]

Krull, Kathleen (1996). *Wilma unlimited: How Wilma Rudolph became the world's fastest woman.* Illus. by David Diaz. San Diego: Harcourt Brace. AFRICAN AMERICAN. [ P/I ]

Lyons, Mary E. (1993). *Starting home: The story of Horace Pippin, painter.* New York: Charles Scribner's Sons. AFRICAN AMERICAN (African American Artists and Artisans series). [ I ]

McKissack, Patricia, & McKissack, Frederick (1994). *African-American inventors.* Brookfield, CT: Millbrook Press. AFRICAN AMERICAN. [ I/M ]

Meltzer, Milton (Ed.) (1995). *Frederick Douglass: In his own words.* Illus. by Stephen Alcorn. San Diego: Harcourt Brace. AFRICAN AMERICAN. [ I ]

Miller, William (1997). *Richard Wright and the library card.* Illus. by Gregory Christie. New York: Lee & Low Books. AFRICAN AMERICAN. [ P/I ]

Osofsky, Audrey (1996). *Free to dream. The making of a poet, Langston Hughes.* New York: Lothrop, Lee & Shepard. AFRICAN AMERICAN. [ I/M ]

## Response to Informational Books

Nonfiction titles that extend knowledge about cultural groups provide a factual addition to information on a culture. Historical understandings and aesthetic interactions are enriched through the informational perspective on a topic. Response to informational books moves beyond efferent knowledge toward aesthetic connections to people of color and cultural experiences. Patricia and Frederick McKissack's *Christmas in the Big House, Christmas in the Quarters* not only provides factual information on plantation life prior to the emancipation of slaves, but aesthetically touches the reader's heart as both sides of society possess common needs, traditions, celebrations, and hope for the future. Reading informational texts efferently builds factual background, while reader response to informational text builds aesthetic empathy and greater understanding of the human element that links all colors and cultures (see Figure 8.8).

**FIGURE 8.8**    Multicultural nonfiction

Ancona, George (1993). *Powwow.* Photographs by George Ancona. San Diego: Harcourt Brace. NATIVE AMERICAN. [ P/I ]

Ancona, George (1997). *Mayeros: A Yucatec Maya family.* Photographs by George Ancona. New York: Lothrop, Lee & Shepard. MAYAN. [ I/M ]

Ashabranner, Brent (1996). *Our beckoning borders: Illegal immigration in America.* Photographs by Paul Conklin. New York: Cobblehill/Dutton. HISPANIC AMERICAN. [ I/M ]

Barboza, Steven (1994). *Door of no return: The legend of Goree Island.* New York: Cobblehill/Dutton. AFRICAN AMERICAN. [ I/M ]

Hamilton, Virginia (1993). *Many thousand gone: African Americans from slavery to freedom.* Illus. by Leo & Diane Dillon. New York: Knopf. AFRICAN AMERICAN. [ I/M ]

Hoyt-Goldsmith, Diane (1994). *Day of the dead: A Mexican-American celebration.* Photographs by Lawrence Migdale. New York: Holiday House. HISPANIC AMERICAN. [ I ]

Lewin, Ted (1996). *Market!* New York: Lothrop, Lee & Shepard. MULTICULTURAL (Picture book). [ P/I ]

McKissack, Patricia C., & McKissack Frederick L. (1994). *Christmas in the big house, Christmas in the quarters.* Illus. by John Thompson. New York: Scholastic. AFRICAN AMERICAN. [ I/M ]

Onyefulu, Ifeoma (1996). *Ogbo: Sharing life in an African village.* San Diego: Gulliver Books/Harcourt Brace. AFRICAN. [ I ]

Schlissel, Lillian (1995). *Black frontiers: A history of African American heroes in the old West.* New York: Simon & Schuster. AFRICAN AMERICAN. [ I/M ]

Sneve, Virginia Driving Hawk (1995). *The Nez Perce.* Illus. by Ronald Himler. New York: Holiday House. NATIVE AMERICAN (First American series). [ P/I ]

Stanley, Jerry (1994). *I am an American: A true story of Japanese internment.* New York: Crown. JAPANESE AMERICAN. [ I/M ]

# CLOSING THOUGHTS

Multicultural literature celebrates the diversity of the people who represent our communities, our country, and our world. Its inclusion in the curriculum needs to be natural, sincere, and elevated to its proper level of importance. Although multicultural children's literature focuses on literature by and about people who are underrepresented in the school curriculum, we still have a long way to go in believing that multicultural literature should be about all people. In our own honest response to choosing multicultural literature, we must look for authenticity in character, setting, language, clothing, and action. Stereotypes remain pervasive and the number of books produced about people of color still remains comparatively small.

The link between multicultural literature and aesthetic response might contribute to the building of understandings beyond one's personal realm of experience. As readers, we can move beyond being expressions of our own culture. Readers can transcend culture and they may begin to understand others and their feelings toward others more clearly. Exposure to multicultural literature enriched by the challenge of honest response challenges children to share their feelings, including fears and misunderstandings. Response causes the reader to view the human side of all cultures, to think more clearly, and to handle our feelings toward others. Multicultural literature provides a means for opening more honest discussions about the oneness of humanity and the equality of all people.

# REFERENCES

Banks, J. A. (1988). *Multicultural education: Issues and perspectives.* Boston: Allyn and Bacon.

Banks, J. A. (1989). Multicultural education: Characteristics and goals. In J. A. Banks & C. A. M. Banks (Eds.), *Multicultural education: Issues and perspectives* (pp. 2–26). Needham Heights, NJ: Allyn and Bacon.

Barrera, R. B., Thompson, V. D., & Dressman, M. (Eds.) (1997). *Kaleidoscope: A multicultural booklist for grades K–8* (2nd ed.). Urbana, IL: National Council of Teachers of English.

Bieger, E. M. (1996). Promoting multicultural education through a literature-based approach. *The Reading Teacher, 49,* 308–312.

Bishop, Rudine Sims (Ed.) (1994). *Kaleidoscope: A multicultural booklist for grades K–8.* Urbana, IL: National Council of Teachers of English.

Cai, M., & Bishop, R. (1994). Multicultural literature for children: Towards a clarification of the concept. In A. Dyson & C. Genishi (Eds.), *The need for story: Cultural diversity in classroom and community* (pp. 57–71). Urbana, IL: National Council of Teachers of English.

Diamond, B. J., & Moore, M. A. (1995). *Multicultural literacy: Mirroring the reality of the classroom.* White Plains, NY: Longman.

Finazzo, D. A. (1997). *All for the children: Multicultural essentials of literature.* Albany, NY: Delmar.

Glazer, J. I. (1997). *Introduction to children's literature* (2nd ed.). Upper Saddle River, NJ: Merrill/Prentice Hall.

Harris, V. (Ed.) (1992). *Teaching multicultural literature in grades K–8.* Norwood, MA: Christopher-Gordon.

Harris, V. (Ed.) (1997). *Using multiethnic literature in the K–8 classroom.* Norwood, MA: Christopher-Gordon.

Huck, C. S., Hepler, S., Hickman, J., & Kiefer, B. Z. (1997). *Children's literature in the elementary school.* Madison, WI: Brown & Benchmark.

Jacobs, J. S., & Tunnell, M. O. (1996). *Children's literature, briefly.* Englewood Cliffs, NJ: Merrill/Prentice Hall.

Rasinski, T. V., & Padak, N. (1990). Multicultural learning through children's literature. *Language Arts, 67,* 576–580.

Yang, S., Siu-Runyan, Y., & Vilscek, E. (1997). Stories of Cinderella from around the world. *The Dragon Lode, 15,* 9–15.

Yokota, J. (1993). Issues in selecting multicultural children's literature. *Language Arts, 70,* 156–167.

# CHILDREN'S BOOKS CITED [ P ] = K–2; [ I ] = 3–5; [ M ] = 6–8

Angelou, Maya (1993). *Life doesn't frighten me.* Illus. by Jean-Michel Basquiat. New York: Stewart, Tabori, and Chang. [ I/M ]

Bierhorst, Joseph (Ed.) (1997). *Dancing fox: Arctic folktales.* Illus. by Mary Okheena. New York: Morrow. [ I/M ]

Bruchac, Joseph (1996). *Between earth and sky: Legends of Native Americans sacred places.* Illus. by Thomas Locker. San Diego: Harcourt Brace. [ I/M ]

Chocolate, Debbi (1996). *Kente colors.* Illus. by John Ward. New York: Walker. [ P ]

Coleman, Evelyn (1996). *White socks only.* Illus. by Tyrone Geter. Morton Grove, IL: Albert Whitman. [ P/I ]

Crews, Donald (1991). *Bigmama's.* New York: Greenwillow. [ P ]

Dorris, Arthur (1991). *Abuela.* Illus. by Elisa Kleven. New York: Dutton. [ P ]

Feelings, Tom (1993). *Soul looks back in wonder.* New York: Dial. [ I ]

Feelings, Tom (1995). *The middle passage: White ships/black cargo.* New York: Dial. [ M ]

Fox, Mem (1997). *Whoever you are.* Illus. by Leslie Staub. San Diego: Harcourt Brace. [ P ]

Garza, Carmen Lomas (1996). *In my family/En mi familia.* Emeryville, CA: Children's Book Press. [ P ]

Goble, Paul (1996). *The return of the buffaloes.* Washington, DC: National Geographic Society. [ I ]

Gonzales, Lucia M. (Reteller) (1997). *Senor Cat's romance.* Illus. by Lulu Delacre. New York: Scholastic. [ P/I ]

Greenfield, Eloise (1978). *Honey, I love: And other poems.* Illus. by Leo & Diane Dillon. New York: Harper & Row. [ P/I ]

Johnson, Tony (1996). *The wagon.* Illus. by James Ransome. New York: Tambourine/Morrow. [ I ]

King, Dr. Martin Luther, Jr. (1997). *I have a dream.* Illus. by Coretta Scott King Award and Honor Book artists. New York: Scholastic. [ I ]

Louie, Ai-Ling (1982). *Yeh-Shen: A Cinderella story from China.* Illus. by Ed Young. New York: Philomel Books. [ I ]

Martin, Rafe (Reteller) (1996). *Mysterious tales of Japan.* Illus. by Tatsuro Kiuchi. New York: Putnam. [ I/M ]

Martinez, Victor (1996). *Parrot in the oven; Mi Vida.* New York: HarperCollins. [ M ]

McCaughrean, Geraldine (1995). *The golden hoard: Myths and legends of the world.* Illus. by Bee Willey. New York: McElderry Books. [ I/M ]

McKissack, Patricia C., & McKissack, Frederick (1994). *Christmas in the big house, Christmas in the quarters.* Illus. by John Thompson. New York: Scholastic.

McKissack, Patricia C. (1997). *Ma Dear's aprons.* Illus. by Floyd Cooper. New York: Atheneum. [ P ]

Miller, William (1995). *Frederick Douglass: The last days of slavery.* Illus. by Cedric Lucas. New York: Lee & Low Books. [ I ]

Mora, Pat (1996). *Confetti: Poems for children.* Illus. by Enrique O. Sanchez. New York: Lee & Low Books. [ P/I ]

Myers, Walter Dean (1997). *Harlem.* Illus. by Christopher Myers. New York: Scholastic. [ I/M ]

Osborne, Mary Pope (1996). *One world, many religions: The way we worship.* Illus. with photographs. New York: Knopf. [ I/M ]

Pinkney, Andrea Davis (1995). *Hold fast to dreams.* New York: Morrow. [ I ]

Polacco, Patricia (1988). *Rechenka's eggs.* New York: Putnam. [ P ]

Pomerantz, Charlotte (1997). *Mangaboom.* Illus. by Anita Lobel. New York: Greenwillow. [ P/I ]

Reeder, Carolyn (1997). *Across the lines.* New York: Atheneum. [ I/M ]

Rinaldi, Ann (1996). *Hang a thousand trees with ribbons: The story of Phillis Wheatley.* San Diego: Harcourt Brace. [ M ]

Rylant, Cynthia (1991). *Appalachia: The voices of sleeping birds.* Illus. by Barry Moser. San Diego: Harcourt Brace. [ I ]

Say, Allen (1993). *Grandfather's journey.* Boston: Houghton Mifflin. [ P/I ]

Schroeder, Alan (1996). *Minty: A story of young Harriet Tubman.* Illus. by Jerry Pinkney. New York: Dial. [ I ]

Soto, Gary (1997). *Snapshots from the wedding.* Illus. by Stephanie Garcia. New York: Putnam. [ P/I ]

Staples, Suzanne Fisher (1989). *Shabanu: Daughter of the wind.* New York: Knopf. [ M ]

Steptoe, Javaka (Selector) (1997). *In daddy's arms I am tall: African Americans celebrating fathers.* Illus. by Javaka Steptoe, New York: Lee & Low Books. [ P/I/M ]

Steptoe, John (1987). *Mufaro's beautiful daughters: An African tale.* New York: Lothrop, Lee & Shepard. [ P/I ]

Swann, Brian (1998). *Touching the distance: Native American riddle-poems.* Illus. by Maria Rendon. San Diego: Browndeer Press/Harcourt Brace. [ P/I ]

Tamar, Erika (1996). *Garden of Happiness.* Illus. by Barbara Lambase. San Diego: Harcourt Brace. [ P/I ]

Taylor, Mildred (1990). *Mississippi bridge.* New York: Dial. [ I ]

Van Steenwyk, Elizabeth (1997). *My name is York.* Illus. by Bill Farnsworth. Flagstaff, AZ: Rising Moon/Northland Publications. [ I ]

# Celebrating Response Connections

$B$uilding upon the sound knowledge of literary genres acquired in the previous section of this text, Part III of *A Celebration of Literature and Response* showcases the reader's personal response engagement with literature. No children's literature title truly exists without the response of the reader—the lump in the throat, the grin of delight, the tear in the eye, the spontaneity of applause. The desire to connect personal lives to literary experiences forms the framework of reader response. While these connections have been somewhat minimalized in teaching settings, Louise Rosenblatt (1978) reawakened teachers to the import of the reader in the literature-response engagement. The interaction between the literature and the reader creates the unique response that text seeks to elicit through meaningful modes of expression. Part III of this text, therefore, attends to the critical role of the reader of children's literature and the value of personal response through direct engagement and connection with the text.

Chapter 9 presents a developmental approach to the oral response to literature. From first responses to storybook reading in the home environment to interactive storybook reading in the primary classroom, children learn to voice their honest emotions and enthusiasm for literature through talk. As oral expression and literary experiences grow, informal literature discussions including retellings and storytelling ensue. Eventually, structured guidelines and assigned roles for literature conversations formalize and encourage an open forum for oral response in classroom settings.

Chapter 10 suggests an approach that developmentally transitions the reader from oral to written response. As readers gain adeptness with writing as a mode of personal expression, both prompted and unstructured literature response journals become an important vehicle for response. Building on the uniqueness of written response, Chapter 11 honors the model and role of literature in a young writer's apprenticeship. Even inexperienced writers utilize patterned or predictable books, fairy tale variants, and various writing connections as springboards to their own early writing experiences. For maturing young authors, literature serves as a model of the ideas, organization, voice, word choice, sentence fluency, and conventions that gradually emerge in their own creative written ventures.

While oral and written responses seem to dominate response to literature in classrooms, the expressive arts share an additional option for creative response in Chapter 12. Drama, art, and music provide opportunities to revisit and reengage with the text through movement, readers' theater, and puppetry or through varied art medium/techniques and musical performance/selection.

Finally, Chapter 13 emphasizes the challenge and possibility of blending efferent and aesthetic response to nonfiction literature. Traditionally reserved for seeking efferent information, nonfiction has the potential to elicit aesthetic response to read alouds, biographical formats, photographic essays, and informational picture books. This unheralded context for response invites readers to fling their arms wide to incorporate response to the nonfiction genre. The unexplored potential of response to nonfiction provides a unique challenge to both teachers and readers.

Janet Hickman (1995) supports the "not by chance" planning and nurturing of children's responses to literature by "teachers who consistently provide multiple avenues to reading and responding." The breadth of response options in Part III provides a diverse menu from which the reader or the teacher may choose the response engagement that best captures the special transaction with a unique title from the vast store of children's literature.

Hickman, Janet (1995). Not by chance: Creating classrooms that invite responses to literature. In Roser, N. L., & Martinez, M. G. (Eds.), *Book talk and beyond: Children and teachers respond to literature* (pp 3–9). Newark, DE: International Reading Association.

Rosenblatt, L. M. (1978). *The reader, the text, the poem: The transactional theory of a literary work.* Carbondale, IL: Southern Illinois University Press.

## Chapter 9

# Talking About Books

## *From Oral Response to Literature Conversations*

C:     *My heart is breaking for Phoebe. All that guilt that she feels is overwhelming for a child.*

M:    *I think about the father. When he unloads on Phoebe, it leaves a lump in my throat. Being a parent and losing a child has to be the worst thing that can ever happen to you.*

K:    *This accident was absolutely avoidable. Why do we have helmets? The parents are responsible and should feel terrible. Why don't parents watch their children or pick them up after school?*

C:     *When I was in grade school, a boy in our class was hit by a car when he was riding his bike. He only broke his leg, but all of us began to pay better attention to safety. I'm sure the author wrote this book at a third-grade level so all kids would wake up to the importance of safety. Did you notice the note at the back?*

M:    *I wonder what I'd do if I were Mick Harte's teacher. Or Phoebe's teacher. What do you say to the kids in your class? What do you say to Phoebe to ease the pain? We sure don't get those answers in education courses.*

L:     *I have a little brother about Mick Harte's age. I just want to go home and hug him and tell him to take care of himself. I cried when I read this book. He is so much like Mick.*

K:    *Don't get so emotional. This is only a book.*

L:      *It seems so real to me. This could be any child, anywhere. Don't be so insensitive. This story is so real it could happen in any of our families or to any of our students.*

Literature Conversation of
Four Preservice Teachers About
*Mick Harte Was Here* by Barbara Park

The most natural response to literature, either read aloud or independently savored, is to talk about it. Primary children can't wait to share their spontaneous reactions, their personal connections, or their likes or dislikes following the reading of a book. Intermediate/middle-level readers look forward to verbal interactions with a teacher and peers—an opportunity to voice their opinions while gaining new perspectives from other readers. These natural responses capture the individualized response to literature through the oral medium. Oral responses can be shared between two individuals, within a small group, or among an entire class. Oral response is spontaneous and builds strong oral communication skills, while allowing for the risk taking and uniqueness encouraged by reader response.

This chapter presents a developmental perspective on oral response to literature. Beginning with early childhood, literature encounters include repetition, language exploration, and interactive participation. Retellings and simple storytelling provide additional oral avenues for developing a sense of story and practicing oral language skills as response to literature. Gradually, open-ended prompts provide primary children with a flexible framework to extend their oral response. By the intermediate level, readers enjoy the freedom of literature conversations in which they are encouraged to share thoughts, opinions, feelings, and reactions with peers through oral discussion. This chapter's emphasis on the development of oral response showcases the importance of the verbal response mode in building a strong basis for sharing understandings and interactions with literature.

## MEMORABLE LITERATURE ENCOUNTERS: EARLY CHILDHOOD (PREK–K)

Memorable early experiences with literature inspire young children toward lifelong reading. Rather than assigning a passive role to the listener, astute teachers choose literature that encourages active engagement. Active involvement in the early reading process can genuinely motivate an emergent learner toward becoming an independent reader. Making reading memorable through participation in literature moves reading and the reader toward a positive lifelong experience. Active involvement through literature begins with insightful oral response to quality read-alouds. The teacher read-aloud provides a gentle group setting for sharing the story and eliciting response. In its earliest stage, oral response to literature may focus on the language of literature. Young children warm to repeated phrases, the rhyme and rhythm of words, and the enjoyment that oral language brings.

## Listen to the Language of Literature

The language of children's literature provides an essential resource for the acquisition, development, and enrichment of oral language in young children. Savoring the language of literature and reveling in rhyming texts are productive ways in which literature contributes to early language enrichment. These are the books whose alliterative titles flow off the tongue and are pure fun to repeat—*Some Smug Slug* (Edwards, 1996), *Dinorella* (Edwards, 1997), and *Barnyard Banter* (Fleming, 1994). These are the titles whose texts are written in playful language and provide word choices that invite exploration—*Alpha, Beta, Chowder* (Steig, 1992), and *Mr. Fine, Porcupine* (Joly, 1997). These are the poetic picture storybooks that revel in simple rhyme and demand repetition—*A House by the Sea* (Ryder, 1994), and *What Can You Do with a Shoe?* (deRegniers, 1955/1997). These are the concept books that introduce the alphabet, numbers, and the basic concepts that form a foundation for further learning—*Bearobics* (Parker, 1997), and *There Was an Old Lady Who Swallowed a Fly* (Taback, 1997). These are the multicultural titles that share the beauty of a second language—*Los pollitos dicen/The baby chicks sing* (Hall & Syverson-Stork, 1994), and *Cuckoo/Cucu* (Ehlert, 1997). These language-focused titles beg children to experiment with language—to listen, to engage, to create. All of the following books and response-related activities provide the necessary precursors that build emergent readers and early oral response.

***Listen to the language that invites play.*** The natural response of young children as they listen to alliterative language is to repeat it over and over and over again. As a kindergarten teacher read aloud Bill Martin and John Archambault's *Chicka Chicka Boom Boom,* the children started chanting the phrase. Not only was it fun to say, it had lasting power as well. As they retreated to the playground for recess, many of them skipped as they chanted the memorable phrase and shrieks of "chicka chicka boom boom" echoed from the swing set for the next week. Children naturally love language, and language-based participation invites language practice and exploration. Thus begins oral response to literature.

A similar response proved true for another group of kindergarteners whose teacher was reading *Rata-Pata-Scata-Fata: A Caribbean Story* (Gershator, 1994). The phrase "rata-pata-scata-fata" proved magical for both Junjun who used it to get his chores done and for the students who used it throughout the day in hopes of applying its special power to their academic tasks. Later in the day, the warm story of *The Little Black Truck* (Gray, 1994) quickly engaged the same children in the sounds of "perka, perka/pop, pop," "sluggedy slug," and "hummedy hum." The desire to play with the language of literature captures the enjoyment of the wonder of words and encourages spontaneous response to language itself.

***Listen to the language of rhyme.*** Picture storybooks written in rhyme contain the language of literature that appeals to young children and encourages early oral response. The natural response to rhyme is to identify it, chant it, and even create it. Imagine an energetic multiage primary classroom magically converted to a barnyard during a reading of Denise Fleming's *Barnyard Banter.* Listen to the rhyming text:

*Donkeys in the paddock, hee, haw, haw*
*Crows in the cornfield, caw, caw, caw*

> *Crickets in the stone wall, chirp, chirp, chirp!*
> *Frogs in the farm pond, burp, burp, burp.*

Superimposed as a guessing game is the repeated phrase "*But where's goose?,*" which is eagerly screamed on cue by participants who also willingly join in the honking at the end of the story. Active involvement creates a foundation for emergent oral response to literature.

In *Tangle Talk,* author Nikola-Lisa creates a topsy-turvy world in which a city is called May, a month is named Boston, flowers sing, birds bloom, babies fly, and hilarious rhyming incongruities abound. Imagine the repetitive, predictable responses to these ingenious lines:

> *A mouse flew by my window.*
> *Butterflies nibbled cheese.*
> *My canary swam in circles*
> *While the goldfish chirped in the breeze.*

Rhyme brings predictability to language while children enjoy repeating and giggling as they share their smiling responses.

## The Role of the Big Book in Early Oral Response

For more than a decade, both teachers and researchers have advocated the inclusion of the big book format in children's early engagement with literature (Combs, 1987; Slaughter, 1983; Trachtenburg & Ferruggia, 1989). A big book is an enlarged version of an authentic piece of children's literature that makes both illustrations and text highly visible to the child during a read-aloud event. Often referred to as a "shared reading experience" (Holdaway, 1982), the big book reading event replicates the lap reading time many children have sadly never experienced at home. The warmth and closeness to a picture book in a read-aloud setting encourages children to note the connection between the teacher's voice and the printed word as he or she points to the text during this experience (Strickland, 1988). Gradual "reading" participation becomes both an early type of oral response to literature and a milestone in emergent literacy.

Many popular titles of children's books with predictable text that invite reading participation are available in big book formats. For the novice teacher, a word of caution is necessary. All big books, unfortunately, are not authentic literature. The popularity of the big book format has encouraged publishers to create predictable texts released in big book format. In full support of authentic literature-based instruction, always check the library to locate the hardback trade book version of the big book. If the text and illustrations are the same, you have likely located an authentic big book from real literature. The authenticity factor gains importance as children excitedly discover the "real book" version in the library for later independent reading.

Big book engagement leads to early oral response. Whether children are simply joining in on repetitive phrases or actually making sound/symbol relationships on the road to becoming a reader, the big book format invites response. It continues to play a meaningful role both in the development of the emergent reader and in the foundational aspects of early reader response.

# ORAL RESPONSE PROMPTS: PRIMARY GRADE RESPONSE (K–2)

Although young children's spontaneous thoughts and oral reactions to read-aloud books constitute a highly valued response to literature, teachers can introduce a more structured, yet open-ended approach to encourage thought and expand response offerings. The use of open-ended reader response prompts following a read-aloud event invites readers to focus, feel, connect, and relate literature. Some response purists voice opposition to the notion of teacher-initiated prompts as distorting the natural response process. Yet experience with children in classroom-based research illustrates the power of the prompt in challenging children to stretch their thinking without distorting their natural response to a book.

A reader response prompt can be defined as an open-ended question designed to encourage the reader/listener to respond at the end of a read-aloud event. Unlike a traditional closed-end comprehension question, a reader response prompt has no predetermined right or wrong answer. The response lies within each child and each response is expected to be unique. David Bleich (1978) improvised three prompts, which provide the basis for responding orally to any piece of literature at any level:

- What did you notice in the story?
- How did the story make you feel?
- What does the story remind you of from your own life?

While these at first appear quite simple, they actually open vistas of response to children that otherwise might be left unexplored. Kelly (1990) utilized these prompts with third graders over an entire school year and documented remarkable growth in quality, quantity, and depth of oral response. At first, children responded to these three prompts following teacher read-alouds. Later on, these prompts guided discussion for independent reading. Initially, many respondents seem confused by the prompts since they are quite different from the narrowly focused comprehension questions to which they may have become accustomed. With some teacher modeling and with experience over time, these prompts become internalized. Teachers no longer need to state the prompts—they automatically become the framework for oral response.

As children grow in response to the three basic prompts, teachers may choose to pose other open-ended prompts to their students. These continue to invite individual response and encourage independent thought. Additional response prompts may include:

- What special meaning or message does the story have for you?
- What did you like or dislike about the story?
- What was the most important part of the story?
- What would it feel like to be (*name a character*)?
- Who have you known that was like (*name a character*)?
- What have you experienced that was like what (*name a character*) experienced?
- What do you think will happen to (*name a character*) in the future?
- What else do you have to say about what we've just read?

While these prompts lead young children toward more extensive oral response sharing, these prompts should *not* become a standard routine following each read-aloud. A knowledgeable teacher familiar with each book title will realize that a few specific prompts lend themselves to a particular title, while others might elicit thoughts more effectively from another book. A steady diet of the same prompts can become just as inhibiting as closed-end comprehension questions at the end of a basal reader story. Choose prompts wisely, ascertain their connectedness to the literature, and present the prompts effectively and in a nonthreatening format.

Teachers can enhance oral response by providing a consistent environment in which book talk is valued. Not only must children be given ample time to talk during formal oral sharing, but they must be provided time for informal responses as well. When they arrive in the morning, when they get ready to go home, and the many times between are all appropriate times to talk about books. Response is not built through a drill-and-practice routine, but through a natural environment of acceptance of unique thoughts and responses to the literature that is read to them or that they read independently.

# INTERACTIVE STORYBOOK READING: PRIMARY GRADE RESPONSE (K–2)

Teachers differ in their read-aloud styles and in the amount of dialogue in which they engage children during and after reading (Martinez & Teale, 1993). All children, but especially those who enter school with limited storybook reading experience, benefit from interactive read-alouds (Klesius & Griffith, 1996). Intended to build language and literacy understanding with young children, interactive read-alouds also encourage oral responses to literature. As teachers read stories interactively, they encourage children to interact orally with the text, their peers, and the teacher during, rather than following, the read-aloud. During interactive reading, teachers pose questions that lead readers to make sense of the text while eliciting aesthetic, personal response (Barrentine, 1996). This process facilitates a child's growing ability to orally respond to story.

The process of using ongoing conversation during a read-aloud without distracting from the story is more challenging than it may appear. Barrentine (1996) suggests selecting "a high-interest picture book with rich language, absorbing plots, lively characters and multiple layers of meaning" (p. 41). The following steps for planning an interactive read aloud to encourage student response are also included:

1. Read the book several times to yourself.
2. Think about the reading goals you have for your students and identify the process and strategy information at work in the story.
3. Identify where students' predictions about the developing story should be sought and shared.
4. Anticipate where you may need to build students' background knowledge.

5. Think through how you will phrase your questions and predicting invitations, and anticipate student responses.
6. After you have planned the read-aloud event, be prepared to relinquish your plans.
7. After reading, devise opportunities for students to explore stories in personal and exciting ways (Barrentine, 1996, pp. 41–42).

Phyllis Root's *One Duck Stuck*, well suited for a light interactive read-aloud, is a story in rhyme, a counting book, and an adventure to a swamp. The bright, spirited illustrations by Jane Chapman assist in inviting children into the story. The predictability of the story and the repetition of phrases guide the interactive framework of the read-aloud. The story begins: "Down by the marsh,/ by the sleepy,/ slimy march,/one duck/gets stuck in the muck/down by the/deep green marsh." The pattern set by the text quickly allows children to note the number of various types of animals (1–10), the repeated phrase (No luck,/ the duck stays stuck,/ deep in the muck,/ down by the/ _____ , _____ marsh). Teacher prompts can help the children predict the next number of swamp creature (grades K–1) or the next kind of animals/insects (grades 1–2) by drawing on knowledge of swamp critters or the sound that the creatures will make. Children can join in on well-chosen alliterative language for each critter (splish, splish—fish; clomp, clomp—moose) and on a repeated phrase ("Help! Help! Who can help?") that marks the turning of each page. Small groups can take the time to count the swamp inhabitants featured on each page. Words describing the marsh (squishy, pricky, croaky, soggy, mossy) can be discussed for vocabulary building. Predicting

Books with predictable text and repetitive language foster interactive storybook reading.
*From* One Duck Stuck *by Phyllis Root. Jacket illustration copyright ©1998 by Jane Chapman. Reprinted by permission of Candlewick Press.*

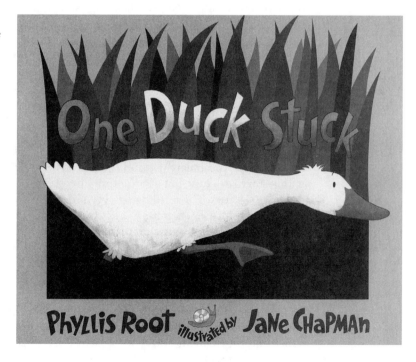

the final ending means listening to the text and observing the colorful illustrations through-out the read-aloud.

Not every read-aloud justifies an interactive approach, but the interactive read-aloud does consistently engage students with literature and encourage response throughout a read-aloud, rather than limiting response to a retrospective nature.

# RETELLING: BEYOND COMPREHENSION TO ORAL RESPONSE

For years, reading followed by retelling has been used as an oral response mechanism for as-sessing comprehension or as an instructional tool to facilitate readers' understanding of the reading process (Morrow, 1986). More recently, retelling has been viewed as a device to col-lect reader response to literature through oral language. Retellings are a powerful departure from recall questions, and, with teacher encouragement, reflect personal meaning making. Retellings can personalize a story by drawing on sense of story, personal experience, and feelings and reactions to a story. While retelling may be aided by visual representations in younger children, they still share the individual voice and style of the reader and draw from the personal interaction with text.

Morrow (1986) found that repeated retellings have a positive effect on the future oral dictation of original stories as children improve their story sense and knowledge of story el-ements. Retellings provide the opportunity to express understanding in a nonthreatening way. While traditional comprehension questions may set children up for failure, retelling challenges the child to state everything they remember in their own words without the threat of being wrong. Encouragement and praise is given for details, story elements, and personal reactions that are included. Over time, personal improvement through retellings becomes evident and growth in meaning making and oral articulation are the ultimate outcomes.

Stories with strong story structure and literary elements are considered optimal for retellings. These may include fairy tales, which typically have a definite setting, well-defined heroes/heroines/villains, and a sequenced plot, often containing three actions in a series. Schurle-Dillon (1996) reports a case study of Daisy that reflects individual response through retellings of various versions of Cinderella. Daisy's retellings of introductions, set-tings, episodes, vocabulary use, and endings not only reflected growing ability in orally pre-senting story structure, but also captured her unique oral responses and response style to the books she read. The retelling strategy not only improves comprehension skills, but of-fers another outlet for response to literature.

Several titles lend themselves to retelling because of both story structure and repetition. *Bearsie Bear and the Surprise Sleepover Party* (Waber, 1997) contains the perfect elements for successful retelling. Characters' names like Cowsie Cow and Moosie Moose are easily re-membered. Repetitive scenes of knocks on the door and requests to stay overnight form a pattern for the reteller. Repetitive dialogue (i.e., "Good night!" "Piggie Pig may sleep over.") also provides confidence for new story retellers. Remembering that Porkie Porcupine ini-tially has a different fate than the other animals reveals comprehension. The oral inflections of dialogue, the changing voices of characters, and the revealed reaction to the story ending provide meaningful outlets for oral response through a retelling.

Teachers should be aware of the following elements in considering level of performance of retellings or in modeling their own retelling.

| | |
|---|---|
| Setting | Begins story with an introduction. Includes time and place of story. |
| Characters | Names main character. Names some secondary characters. |
| Problem | States the main problem in the story. |
| Episodes | Recalls episodes in the story. Sequences episodes properly. |
| Solution | Identifies the solution to the problem. Provides story ending. |

The use of retellings to improve the quality and the understanding of story elements is convincing, especially when monitored over time.

# STORYTELLING AS RESPONSE: RETAINING ORAL TRADITIONS

While being loosely linked to retellings, the art of storytelling is built on personal response to literature. Storytelling differs from retelling because of its creative nature. Not only is a story being told, but the drama and language behind the story add an important dimension to the personal response. This oral response mode seems particularly well suited to intermediate-level students who might share their oral talent with primary-level students in their school setting.

*Tailypo,* retold by Jan Wahl, is a scary tale set in the bayou country of Louisiana. The storytelling strength of the story lies in the characters (old man, monster, and dogs), in the setting (cabin in the marshy woods), and in the repeated words ("Tailypo, Tailypo, all I want is my tailypo."). This story was told by a sixth grader to second graders and their response included gasps, giggles, oohs and aahs, and genuine fear. Like retelling, storytelling retains most of the language and story structure of the original text. Portions may be deleted, but characteristic vocabulary, introduction, description of setting, and repetitive phrases are retained in their original form. Storytelling includes performance response as the storyteller often sets the mood through lighting, engages interest through props, and captures the audience through vocal intonations. While storytelling preparation can be time consuming, its presentation as an individual oral response to literature not only showcases an individual mode of response, but allows younger listeners to appreciate the classic oral tradition of literature.

Books that might be used for storytelling as oral response typically belong to the genre of traditional tales because of their oral tradition. *Anansi Does the Impossible: An Ashanti Tale* (Aardema, 1997) revisits the beloved trickster spider as he and his wife outsmart the Sky God and win back the folktales of their people. A storytelling prior to a fourth-grade class's unit on folktales would be a motivating opening to an exciting genre study. Similarly, storytelling Steven Kellogg's contemporary version of *The Three Little Pigs* (Percy, Pete, and

Prudence) will prove successful for an older student who shares it with a group of first graders who have just read the original version. Giggles are ensured as Tempesto the wolf bellows, "Open up, Pork Chop! Or I'll huff and I'll puff and I'll flatten this dump!"

A multicultural storytelling might include *Mama Provi and the Pot of Rice* (Rosa-Casanova, 1997) as a simple pot of *arroz xon pollo* (chicken and rice) becomes a feast as it makes its way up eight floors of an ethnic apartment building. The sequence of events and the various ingredients add to a structural framework for storytelling. A serious storytelling of *When Jessie Came Across the Sea* (Hest, 1997) might prove a strong introduction to a unit on immigration to America. Many picture books share stories in a sequential framework, include strong dialogue, and contain excellent descriptions that can be savored and expressed in the storytelling mode of response.

# LITERATURE CONVERSATIONS: TALKING ABOUT BOOKS

As children enter both early and advanced stages of independent reading, teachers strive to provide more experiences of reading wonderful books and talking about them with others. Small groups of students with similar interests read and discuss picture books, short chapter books, and full-length chapter books, using a higher level of thinking to discuss and respond to what they have read. Originally called literature circles (Harste, Short, & Burke, 1988) and later referred to as grand conversations (Peterson & Eeds, 1990), these small discussion groups explore "rough draft understandings" (Short & Pierce, 1990) of literature with other readers.

Literature conversation groups are based on the belief that reading is a transactional process as students bring meaning to and take meaning from the text. Built on aesthetic response to literature, students engage in collaborative listening, thinking, and understanding as dialogue leads participants to new perspectives on a book. They generally are composed of only four to six students who ideally, over time, build a dining room table style of conversation to response sessions (Atwell, 1987). A sense of community and an acceptance of risk taking are necessary components that lead to the success of literature conversations. Because there are no correct responses in a conversation, the session must be viewed as dialogue among readers rather than the fulfillment of a teacher-generated agenda. Honesty and personal impressions are valued, honored, and used as a springboard for ongoing discussion.

Owens (1995) suggests a sound rationale for utilizing literature conversations as a support framework for sharing and celebrating response. She justifies the inclusion of literature conversations as oral response because they:

- Promote a love for literature and build positive attitudes toward reading.
- Reflect a constructivist, child-centered model of literacy.
- Encourage extensive and intensive reading.
- Invite natural discussions that lead to student inquiry and critical thinking.
- Support diverse response to texts.
- Foster interaction and collaboration.
- Provide choice and encourage responsibility.

- Expose children to literature from multiple perspectives.
- Nurture reflection and self-evaluation (p. 3).

Recent reports of the inclusion of literature conversations in a response-based reading program point to progress in literacy, literary, and social outcomes (Eeds & Wells, 1989; Goldenberg, 1992/93; Hepler, 1991; Lehman & Scharer, 1996; Strickland, Dillon, Funkhouser, Glick, & Rogers, 1989). These classroom-based studies highlight the potential of literature conversations to improve the ability to communicate personal thoughts about literature, become a critical listener and speaker, and keep an open mind to new perspectives on a literary text.

# LITERATURE CONVERSATIONS WITH YOUNG CHILDREN (1–2)

Many teachers of young children assume that literature conversations are only for intermediate- and middle-level readers. Although adjustments must be made for developmental levels and reading capabilities in the lower primary grades, the tasks of exploring meaning and engaging in conversations about literature are still paramount. Although a facilitator (parent, intern, upper grade student) is necessary with young children, the teacher steps back and allows personal thoughts to provide the script of the conversation.

The first adaptation of the primary-level literature conversation begins with book selection. Because most first- and second-grade students are unable to read substantiative picture books on their own, the literature conversation typically begins with a teacher read-aloud. The book should be read at least two times so children are better prepared to absorb its content and establish their personalized response. With repeated readings, many of the children are able to read the book independently by the day of the scheduled literature conversation. Children should be asked to draw their response to the book and to bookmark a favorite part in preparation for the small group discussion.

The importance of rereading or revisiting old favorites for literature conversations with young children cannot be stressed enough. Understandings are difficult to articulate on a first reading and multiple readings improve the quality of discussions. A "whole class" literature conversation serves as a model and conceptual foundation before moving to small groups. With short attention spans and a strong desire to talk, four children seems the optimal size.

Young children may begin literature conversations by talking about favorite parts of the book and relating the story to experiences from their own lives. From there they move on to elaborations of their own drawings in response to the story. A teacher, student intern, or adult facilitator is necessary with young conversationalists to assist in focusing on specific issues and building the framework of the decision.

With significant modeling and the selection of appropriate titles to discuss, young children can succeed in talking about literature in a small group format. Literature-based teachers report the success of literature conversations in their primary classrooms (Roller & Beed, 1994; Schlick Noe, 1995) and strongly encourage their peers to venture into this oral response realm with younger children.

Not all picture books, not even those that are our own favorites, will sustain literature conversations. The following list considers criteria of

- A well-crafted story with meaningful theme
- Sufficient depth to provide discussion
- The inclusion of memorable language
- Diverse characters in real world situations.

Figure 9.1 contains the thought-provoking titles necessary to stimulate natural response in a literature conversation with young readers.

# GRAND CONVERSATIONS: INTERMEDIATE AND MIDDLE LEVELS (3–8)

As independence in reading grows, so too grows the quality of talk linked to literature conversations. Cognitive development and social growth provide additional support to the small group conversation. Whereas young children require more guidance, many older students are capable of and eager to independently facilitate a literature conversation.

With proper modeling and experience, literature conversations often include the following oral engagements and response. They typically proceed in the designated order with common lulls between each stage of conversational development.

- Impressions and personal responses to the book (favorite parts, initial enjoyment of the book)
- Connections to personal experiences and other book titles (text-to-life and text-to-text connections)
- Specific conversational focus (critical dialogue, careful consideration of others' thoughts, focus on specific aspect of the book)
- Expansion and textual support of personal responses and building off of participant comments
- Determination of focus for next meeting (a starting point for the next day's conversation).

In many cases, however, teachers quickly discover that turning students loose to talk about books requires more structure and organization. To keep older students on the task of reader response, roles may be assigned that focus on sharing response without limiting or inhibiting the freedom it demands. Daniels (1994) describes six possible roles that students can assume within a grand conversation group.

- The *discussion director,* who makes certain the group has brought along questions for the discussion and helps keep the group focused on the purpose of the discussion
- The *literary luminary,* who locates sections of the book that read aloud well or provide deeper insight into the discussion
- The *connector,* who specifically looks for connections between the book and the real-world experiences of the readers
- The *illustrator,* who creates any type of visual or graphic representation to describe what has been read

**FIGURE 9.1**  Books for literature conversations

## Grades 1–2

Aliki (1998). *Marianthe's story: Spoken memories, painted words.* New York: Greenwillow.
Bunting, Eve (1991). *Fly away home.* Illus. by R. Himler. Boston: Clarion.
Henkes, Kevin (1992). *Chrysanthemum.* New York: Greenwillow.
Isaacs, Anne. (1994). *Swamp angel.* Illus. by Paul Zelinsky. New York: Dutton.
Johnson, Angela (1992). *The leaving morning.* Illus. by D. Soman. New York: Orchard Books.
MacLachlan, Patricia (1994). *All the places to love.* Illus. by M. Wimmer. New York: HarperCollins.
McCully, Emily Arnold (1992). *Mirette on the high wire.* New York: Putnam.
Polacco, Patricia (1992). *Chicken Sunday.* New York: Philomel Books.
Polacco, Patricia (1994). *My rotten redheaded older brother.* New York: Simon & Schuster.
Yolen, Jane (1994). *Granddad Bill's song.* Illus. by M. B. Mathis. New York: Philomel Books.

## Grades 3–5

Bauer, Marion Dane (1994). *A question of trust.* Boston: Houghton Mifflin.
Conly, Jane (1993). *Crazy lady!* New York: HarperCollins.
Cooper, Susan (1993). *The boggart.* New York: Macmillan.
deFelice, Cynthia (1991). *Weasel.* New York: Avon.
Fenner, Carol (1991). *Randall's wall.* New York: Macmillan.
Filipovic, Zlata (1994). *Zlata's diary.* New York: Viking.
Fox, Paula (1991). *Monkey island.* New York: Greenwillow.
Hahn, Mary Downing (1991). *Stepping on the cracks.* New York: Avon.
Hesse, Karen (1998). *Just Juice.* New York: Scholastic.
Kinsey-Warner, Natalie (1989). *The Canada geese quilt.* New York: Dell.
Lord, Bette Bao (1984). *In the year of the boar and Jackie Robinson.* New York: Harper & Row.
Mikaelsen, Ben (1991). *Rescue Josh McGuire.* New York: Hyperion.
Naylor, Phyllis Reynolds (1994). *The fear place.* New York: Atheneum.
Paterson, Katherine (1994). *Flip-flop girl.* New York: Lodestar.
Smith, Doris Buchanan (1973). *A taste of blackberries.* New York: Crowell.
Smith, Robert Kimmel (1984). *The war with Grandpa.* New York: Delacorte.
Tate, Eleanora E. (1990). *Thank you, Dr. Martin Luther King, Jr!* New York: Bantam.
Taylor, Mildred (1990). *Mississippi bridge.* New York: Bantam.
Walter, Mildred Pitt (1986). *Justin and the best biscuits in the world.* New York: Lothrop, Lee & Shepard.

## Grades 6–8

Avi (1991). *Nothing but the truth.* New York: Avon.
Avi (1996). *Beyond the western sea: The escape from home & Beyond the western sea: Lord Kirkle's money.* New York: Orchard Books. (two-volume set)
Blackwood, Gary (1998). *The Shakespeare stealer.* New York: Dutton.
Freedman, Russell (1990). *Franklin Delano Roosevelt.* New York: Scholastic.
Freedman, Russell (1993). *Eleanor Roosevelt: A life of discovery.* Boston: Clarion.
George, Jean C. (1994). *Julie.* New York: HarperCollins.
Lowry, Lois (1993). *The giver.* Boston: Houghton Mifflin.
MacLachlan, Patricia (1991). *Journey.* New York: Dell.
Myers, Walter Dean (1996). *Slam!* New York: Scholastic.
Paterson, Katherine (1980). *Jacob have I loved.* New York: HarperCollins.
Sachar, Louis (1998). *Holes.* New York: Farrar, Straus and Giroux.
Staples, Suzanne Fisher (1989). *Shabanu: Daughter of the wind.* New York: Knopf.
Staples, Suzanne Fisher (1993). *Haveli.* New York: Knopf.

- The *vocabulary enricher,* who looks for important word choices that enrich the writing or deepen the understanding of the reader
- The *summarizer,* who wraps up the reading for the day by assimilating the discussion and making a final statement as the group comes to closure.

These roles may also be viewed as directed responses to literature since each student focuses on a specific aspect of the literature experience. While the group contains the same students over a period of time, the roles rotate to share responsibilities, create response possibilities, and maintain interest.

Another means of keeping students on task is to provide guidelines for conversational response (see Figure 9.2). Prepared by the teacher for a specific title, the guidelines serve to facilitate oral response *only* when other personal responses has been exhausted. Experienced

**FIGURE 9.2**    *The true confessions of Charlotte Doyle* (Avi, 1991 Newbery Honor book) literature conversations guidelines

---

- Discuss these characters for their strengths, weaknesses, triumphs, and downfalls.

| Charlotte | Zachariah | Charlotte's father |
| Capt. Jaggery | Mr. Hollybrass | Keetch |

- If this book were to be made into a movie, who do you envision playing these roles?
- Discuss the story setting/period in terms of the following aspect of mid-nineteenth century sealife:

| the role of women | piracy on the high seas | a sailor's life |

- Locate and respond to your favorite passage.
- How did you feel when you realized that Charlotte would defy her parents and go back to the sea?
- What meaning or message about "being true to yourself" do you gain from the book?
- What will happen to Charlotte as the book ends?
- What did you like/dislike about the book? How would you change it?

How did you react to:
Charlotte's adjustment to seasickness and her quarters
Charlotte's early impressions of Capt. Jaggery
The mutiny
Charlotte's climbing of the ropes
The trial
The end of Capt. Jaggery
Charlotte's father's control of his daughter

Read a response from your journal in which you:
- Use a quote from the book
- Talk to a character
- Judge a character
- Give advice to a character
- Indicate questions or confusion
- Make a text-to-text connection
- Make a text-to-life connection
- Laughed out loud
- Felt tears roll from your eyes

groups may never need these springboards for response, but novice conversationalists are likely to depend heavily on them to sustain talk for 20 to 30 minutes.

Documented success with literature conversations in the intermediate/middle-level setting has been reported by Keegan and Shrake (1991) and Nystrand, Gamoran, and Heck (1993). The greatest challenge is often the changing role of the teacher, who must relinquish rights to directing a discussion. Eeds and Peterson (1991) refer to the new role of "teacher as curator" (p. 118) who must now collect response, nurture it, and delight in the independent thoughts of readers. O'Flahavan (1994/95) describes the new role of the teacher as "scaffolding" during the discussion and "coaching" before and after the conversation. Teachers strive to balance between retaining some control of the social and interpretive dimensions of response and relinquishing total control to students. Too much teacher participation subverts authenticity of response, particularly with older students. Teachers, therefore, must learn to listen instead of talk, while still providing verbal support and direction when students demonstrate that they need it.

Not all books intended for intermediate/middle-level readers will sustain literature conversations. The previous list of titles (Fig. 9.1) draws from criteria suggested by Dianne Monson (1995). She imparts three questions to scrutinize appropriate literature:

1. Does the book succeed in arousing my emotions and will it arouse children's emotions?
2. Is the book well-written?
3. Is the book meaningful? (p. 113)

The titles in Figure 9.1 fit these criteria and share books that will stimulate and impart critical thinking and authentic response.

# CLOSING THOUGHTS

The developmental trail of oral response to literature begins with children's early read-aloud events to which they respond to language, repetition, and the joy of memorable literature experiences. As they begin school, oral response to literature gains a more structured, intentional nature as teachers insert prompts both during and after stories to create interactive storybook reading and retrospective reflections on books. Retellings and storytellings provide structured frameworks for emerging oral response. Literature conversations provide a group format for sharing response. While young children require some modeling and guidance, older students revel in the freedom of open conversations on literature. Through designated roles, the use of guidelines, or teacher scaffolding in a natural sharing configuration, readers learn to become listeners and build meaning through valued shared perspectives on literature.

The advantages of oral response to literature include its spontaneity, its developmental nature, and its time efficiency. While focusing on communication skills, oral response also demands listening to the responses of others to enhance one's own interactions with the text. Oral response should *not* be limited to young children based on their lack of reading proficiency or developmental difficulty with written response modes. Oral response needs to be encouraged throughout the K–8 classroom as foundations are built through read-alouds, frameworks are established through prompts, and social interactions about books are nurtured through literature conversations. The major mode of reader response for adult readers consists of informal conversation through engagements with other readers. Thus, the oral response encourages and preserves the authenticity of response by its very nature and progresses developmentally from simple responses to read-alouds toward mature conversations about literature.

# REFERENCES

Atwell, N. (1987). *In the middle: Writing, reading, and learning with adolescents*. Portsmouth, NH: Heinemann.

Barrentine, S. J. (1996). Engaging with reading through interactive read alouds. *The Reading Teacher, 50*, 36–43.

Bleich, D. (1978). *Subjective criticism*. Baltimore, MD: The Johns Hopkins University Press.

Combs, M. (1987). Modeling the reading process with enlarged text. *The Reading Teacher, 40*, 422–426.

Daniels, H. (1994). *Literature circles: Voice and choice in a student-centered classroom*. York, ME: Stenhouse.

Eeds, M., & Peterson, R. (1991). Teacher as curator: Learning to talk about literature. *The Reading Teacher, 45*, 118–126.

Eeds, M., & Wells, D. (1989). Grand conversations: An exploration of meaning construction in literature study groups. *Research in the Teaching of English, 23*, 4–29.

Goldenberg, C. (1992/93). Instructional conversations: Promoting comprehension through discussion. *The Reading Teacher, 46*, 316–326.

Harste, J., Short, K., & Burke, C. (1988). *Creating classrooms for authors: The reading–writing connection*. Portsmouth, NH: Heinemann.

Hepler, S. (1991). Talking our way to literacy in the classroom community. *The New Advocate, 4*, 179–191.

Holdaway, D. (1982). Shared book experience: Teaching reading using favorite books. *Theory into Practice*, Autumn, 293–300.

Keegan, S. & Shrake, K. (1991). Literature study groups: An alternative to ability grouping. *The Reading Teacher, 44*, 542–547.

Kelly, P. R. (1990). Guiding young students' response to literature. *The Reading Teacher, 43*, 464–470.

Klesius, J., & Griffith, P. (1996). Interactive storybook reading for at-risk learners. *The Reading Teacher, 49*, 552–560.

Lehman, B. A., & Scharer, P. (1996). Reading alone, talking together: The role of discussion in developing literary awareness. *The Reading Teacher, 50*, 26–35.

Martinez, M. G., & Teale, W. H. (1993). Teacher storybook reading style: A comparison of six teachers. *Research in the Teaching of English, 27*, 175–199.

Monson, D. (1995). Choosing books for literature circles. In B. Campbell Hill, N. Johnson, & K.L. Schlick Noe, *Literature Circles and Response* (pp. 113-130). Norwood, MA: Christopher Gordon.

Morrow, L. M. (1986). Effects of structural guidance in story retelling on children's dictation of original stories. *Journal of Reading Behavior, 2*, 135–151.

Nystrand, M., Gamoran, A., & Heck, M. J. (1993). Using small groups for response to and thinking about literature. *English Journal, 82*, 14–22.

O'Flahavan, J. F. (1994/95). Teacher role options in peer discussion about literature. *The Reading Teacher, 48*, 354–356.

Owens, S. (1995). Treasures in the attic: Building the foundation for literature circles. In B. Campbell Hill, N. J. Johnson, & K. L. Schlick Noe (Eds.), *Literature circles and response* (pp. 1–12). Norwood, MA: Christopher-Gordon.

Peterson, R., & Eeds, M. (1990). *Grand conversations: Literature groups in action*. New York: Scholastic.

Roller, C. M., & Beed, P. L. (1994). Sometimes the conversations were grand, and sometimes. . . . *Language Arts, 71*, 509–515.

Schlick Noe, K. L. (1995). Nurturing response with emergent readers. In B. Campbell Hill, N. J. Johnson, & K. L. Schlick Noe (Eds.), *Literature circles and response* (pp. 41–54). Norwood, MA: Christopher-Gordon.

Schurle-Dillon, K. (1996). Retelling: A strategy for enhancing story structure through Cinderella tales. *Kansas Journal of Reading, 12*, 27–34.

Short, K., Harste, J., & Burke, C. (1996). *Creating classroom for authors and inquirers* (2nd ed.). Portsmouth, NH: Heinemann.

Short, K., & Pierce, K. M. (Eds.) (1990). *Talking about books: Creating literate communities.* Portsmouth, NH: Heinemann.

Slaughter, J. P. (1983). Big books for little kids: Another fad or a new approach for teaching beginning reading? *The Reading Teacher, 36,* 758–762.

Strickland, D. S. (1988). Some tips for using big books. *The Reading Teacher, 41,* 966–968.

Strickland, D. S., Dillon, R., Funkhouser, L., Glick, M., & Rogers, C. (1989). Research currents: Classroom dialog during literature response groups. *Language Arts, 66,* 192–200.

Trachtenburg, R., & Ferruggia, A. (1989). Big books from little voices: Reaching high risk beginning readers. *The Reading Teacher, 42,* 284–289.

# CHILDREN'S BOOKS CITED [ P ] = K–2; [ I ] = 3–5; [ M ] = 6–8

Aardema, Verna (1997). *Anansi does the impossible: An Ashanti tale.* Illus. by Lisa Desimini. New York: Atheneum. [ I ]

Avi (1990). The true confessions of Charlotte Doyle. New York: Orchard. [ M ].

deRegniers, Beatrice Schenk (1955/1997). *What can you do with a shoe?* Illus. by Maurice Sendak. New York: McElderry Books. [ P ]

Edwards, Pamela Duncan (1996). *Some smug slug.* Illus. by Henry Cole. New York: HarperCollins. [ P ]

Edwards, Pamela Duncan (1997). *Dinorella: A prehistoric fairy tale.* Illus. by Henry Cole. New York: Hyperion. [ P ]

Ehlert, Lois (1997). *Cuckoo/Cucu.* San Diego: Harcourt Brace. [ P/I ]

Fleming, Denise (1994). *Barnyard banter.* New York: Henry Holt. [ P ]

Gershator, Phillis (1994). *Rata-pata-scata-fata: A Caribbean story.* Illus. by Holly Meade. Boston: Little, Brown. [ P ]

Gray, Libba Moore (1994). *The little black truck.* Illus. by Elizabeth Sayles. New York: Simon & Schuster. [ P ]

Hall, Nancy A., & Syverson-Stork, Jill (1994). *Los pollitos dicen/The baby chicks sing: Traditional games, nursery rhymes, and songs from Spanish-speaking countries.* Illus. by Kay Chorao. Boston: Little, Brown. [ P ]

Hest, Amy (1997). *When Jessie came across the sea.* Illus. by P. J. Lynch. Cambridge, MA: Candlewick Press. [ I ]

Joly, Fanny (1997). *Mr. Fine, porcupine.* Illus. by Remi Saillard. San Francisco: Chronicle Books. [ P ]

Kellogg, Steven (Reteller) (1997). *The three little pigs.* New York: Morrow. [ P ]

Martin Jr., Bill, & Archambault, John (1989). *Chicka chicka boom boom.* Illus. by Lois Ehlert. New York: Simon & Schuster. [ P ]

Nikola-Lisa, W. (1997). *Tangle talk.* Illus. by Jessica Clerk. New York: Dutton. [ P ]

Park, Barbara (1995). *Mick Harte was here.* New York: Knopf. [ I ]

Parker, Vic (1997). *Bearobics.* Illus. by Emily Bolam. New York: Viking. [ P ]

Root, Phyllis (1998). *One duck stuck.* Illus. by Jane Chapman. Cambridge, MA: Candlewick Press. [ P ]

Rosa-Casanova, Sylvia (1997). *Mama Provi and the pot of rice.* Illus. by Robert Roth. New York: Atheneum. [ I ]

Ryder, Joanne (1994). *A house by the sea.* Illus. by Melissa Sweet. New York: Morrow. [ P ]

Steig, Jeanne (1992). *Alpha, beta, chowder.* Illus. by William Steig. New York: HarperCollins. [ P/I ]

Taback, Simms (1997). *There was an old lady who swallowed a fly.* New York: Viking. [ P/I ]

Waber, Bernard (1997). *Bearsie Bear and the surprise sleepover party.* Boston: Houghton Mifflin. [ P ]

Wahl, Jan (1991). *Tailypo.* Illus. by Wil Clay. New York: Henry Holt. [ P/I ]

# Literature Response Journals
*Written Reflections During Reading*

*C*hapter 10. *The most wonderful thing happened today. Nothing in the factory mind you. Oh no! It came after work, really when I was too tired to really appreciate it. Betsy read part of her novel to me. It's the most wonderful story about a little boy named Oliver. The poor little thing has had an awful thing happen to him. He's to be hung for wanting more to eat. Can you imagine such a thing? How cruel the poorhouse overseer seems. He's like the mistress at the tavern—bossy, greedy, unfair. Betsy has promised to read more of the book to me. Hopefully, with Diana's help, I'll be able to read the book by myself someday. Wouldn't Charlie be proud of me! His own sister, a rich factory girl who can read!*

*Chapter 11. I don't need Diana's help! I can teach myself to read! I have purchased my own copy of* Oliver Twist *at the shop in town. It was dreadfully expensive, two dollars, but it is the most beautiful thing I have ever seen. The cover is leather and has the title stamped in gold letters on the spine, and it's mine! I've decided to copy pages on paper and hang them up on the frame of my loom. It's just like the other girls have done with the magazine pages and poetry on the windowsill. I'll be able to study my words while watching the looms I'm tending. I may even get good enough to read the book to Betsy when she returns from her holiday! Wouldn't that be fun! Betsy would be so surprised!*

Fourth-Grade Teacher Character
Journal Response to *Lyddie*
by Katherine Paterson

As a book is read, fleeting thoughts, reactions, opinions, connections, and predictions flash through the mind of the reader. Once the journey is completed, most of those fleeting ideas cannot be rekindled in their genuine, spontaneous form. In fact, the vital remnants of the reading process are actually lost when response is reserved until after the reading event is completed. A child's responses to Paula Fox's *One-Eyed Cat* are more context specific and emotionally richer when recorded throughout the text rather than only at the book's conclusion (Hancock, 1992). Compare these responses written during and following the reading of this introspective story of a boy disobediently shooting his gun in the dark of night and hiding the truth from his parents.

> Ned your lying again your living a life of lies are you proud? Are you happy? Look at what your doing living a big lie. You can't see me, you can't be me, but I can see you and I can be you and I am so sick living in your lying world.

> (Sixth-grade response on p. 102 of *One-Eyed Cat*)

> The book wasn't all that boring. It had a happy ending and a psychological theme. I'm surprised he told his mom but it would be hard to keep it a secret that long. I can understand why this is a Newbery honor book.

> (Sixth-grade response on the final page of *One-Eyed Cat*)

While the first entry reflects reader involvement and actually speaks to the character, the second entry, written by the same reader, reflects only a bland retrospective overview of the text.

Because the reading process is an ongoing accumulation of plot information, character insights, and personal connections, it is crucial to capture those thoughts throughout the reading journey, rather than waiting until the journey is complete. Written response to literature is the vehicle for accomplishing this task. The written response creates a permanent record of the reader's thoughts before, during, and following reading. The written record can be drawn on for later discussion, revisiting the book, or as a seed for more extensive writing. The written response deserves particular attention in celebrating the value of response in exposing the individuality of the reader.

The purpose of this chapter is to explore the possibilities of written response across age/grade levels and to encourage literature-based professionals to consistently inspire their students to realize the full potential of this response option. Because response is developmental in nature, a gradual approach to transitioning to the written response is suggested. Categories for both primary and intermediate/middle-level responses are suggested as options and a means of exploring an expanding response potential. Complete guidelines for utilizing literature response journals and introspective character journals also highlight this chapter. Written response establishes the permanence of the reader's passing ideas, enabling him or her to revisit and build from them through continual growth in the understanding of and appreciation for literature.

# TRANSITIONING FROM ORAL TO WRITTEN RESPONSE

The written response to literature captures the fleeting thoughts of readers in print, creating a permanent record of the ongoing responses of a reader to literature. Developmentally, written response builds on all of the other response modes and finds itself near the peak of the developmental hierarchy of response. While young children's oral abilities allow them to verbalize response, older students in intermediate and middle grades acquire increasing ability to transfer their spontaneous thoughts and reflections from their heads and hearts to a journal format. This transition from oral to written response can be guided by including structured reading, the use of prompts, and teacher modeling before complete freedom in written response is granted. Some students will make this transition smoothly and effectively, but many will require that interim steps be taken on the road to independent written response.

***Transitioning through picture books.***    While the oral response to literature is valued and encouraged, the teacher must provide ways to help students transfer their rich oral responses to written form. The beginning of written response in a journal might be initiated with daily read-alouds of picture books (see Figure 10.1) followed by an open-ended prompt or choice of prompts for journal writing (see discussion of oral prompts in Chapter 9). Initially, allow students to discuss their responses orally, a familiar routine for most. Then request that students capture those very thoughts from their minds and hearts on paper. Allow 5 to 8 minutes to write a personal response. Over time, growth will be seen in honesty and depth of response. In fact, students are likely to begin requesting even more time for writing.

***Transitioning through chapter books.***    Teachers may next want to read aloud short chapter books (see Figure 10.1) to their students each day and follow the read-aloud with response prompts designed exclusively for the read-aloud title. Initially, they may again respond orally and then transfer their oral response to the written form in a journal. Written responses may be read orally the next day before the read-aloud or kept private at the discretion of the student. Teachers may even seek permission to make a few response entries into overhead transparencies to serve as the written model of internal thoughts.

Another transitioning model involves teacher composition of a response on an overhead or computer with a projection screen. Immediately following the read-aloud chapter, the teacher can model his or her thoughts by spontaneously composing a journal entry. Attention should be given to flow of reaction with minor concern for conventions. By listening and watching, students hear and witness the response process in action and realize that words can fluently move from their heads to their paper.

Once the students have made the transition from oral to written response, the teacher can facilitate and expand the breadth and depth of the quality of response through varied response prompts. While some reader response advocates disagree with the use of prompts to extend response, others have experienced the growth that occurs when prompts encourage various levels of interaction in readers.

# TEACHER-CONSTRUCTED PROMPTS

There are distinctive response prompts that can be utilized to encourage diverse response at four levels of reader interaction with literature: experiential prompts, aesthetic prompts, cognitive prompts, and interpretive prompts. Either a teacher reads the story aloud, chap-

**FIGURE 10.1**    The transition from oral to written response

---

### Picture Books

Blake, Robert J. (1994). *Dog.* New York: Philomel Books. [ P/I ]

Bunting, Eve (1991). *Fly away home.* Illus. by Ronald Himler. Boston: Clarion. [ P/I ]

Bunting, Eve (1994). *Smoky night.* Illus. by David Diaz. San Diego: Harcourt Brace. [ P/I ]

Bunting, Eve (1996). *Train to somewhere.* San Diego: Harcourt Brace. [ I ]

Curtis, Gavin (1998). *The bat boy and his violin.* Illus. by E. B. Lewis. New York: Simon & Schuster. [ P/I ]

Fox, Mem (1985). *Wilfred Gordon McDonald Partridge.* Illus. by Julie Vivas. LaJolla, CA: Kane Miller. [ P/I ]

Mitchell, Margeree King (1993). *Uncle Jed's barber shop.* Illus. by James Ransome. New York: Simon & Schuster. [ P/I ]

Mochizuki, Ken (1997). *Passage to freedom: The Sugihara story.* Illus. by Dom Lee. New York: Lee & Low Books. [ I/M ]

Say, Allen (1993). *Grandfather's journey.* Boston: Houghton Mifflin. [ P/I ]

Shange, Ntozake (1997). *Whitewash.* Illus. by Michael Sporn. New York: Walker. [ I/M ]

Shannon, George (1993). *Climbing Kansas mountains.* Illus. by Thomas B. Allen. Bradbury. [ P ]

Turner, Ann (1997). *Mississippi mud: Three prairie journals.* Illus. by Robert Blake. New York: Harper-Collins. [ I ]

Yolen, Jane (1994). *Granddad Bill's song.* Illus. by Melissa Bay Mathis. New York: Philomel Books. [ P/I ]

### Chapter Books

DeFelice, Cynthia (1992). *Devil's bridge.* New York: Macmillan. [ I ]

Fox, Paula (1997). *Radiance descending.* New York: DK Publishing, Inc. [ I ]

Gardiner, John (1980). *Stone fox.* New York: Harper Trophy. [ P/I ]

George, Jean Craghead (1959). *My side of the mountain.* New York: Dutton. [ I ]

George, Jean Craighead (1990). *On the far side of the mountain.* New York: Dutton. [ I ]

Henkes, Kevin (1997). *Sun and spoon.* New York: Greenwillow. [ I ]

Hesse, Karen. (1994). *Sable.* New York: Henry Holt. [ P/I ]

Lowry, Lois. (1989). *Number the stars.* Boston: Houghton Mifflin. [ I ]

MacLachlan, Patricia (1991). *Journey.* New York: Delacorte. [ I ]

MacLachlan, Patricia (1985). *Sarah, plain and tall.* New York: HarperCollins. [ P/I ]

MacLachlan, Patricia (1994). *Skylark.* New York: HarperCollins. [ P/I ]

Naylor, Phyllis R. (1991). *Shiloh.* New York: Macmillan. [ I ]

Naylor, Phyllis R. (1994). *The fear place.* New York: Atheneum. [ I ]

Naylor, Phyllis R. (1996). *Shiloh's season.* New York: Atheneum. [ I ]

Park, Barbara (1995). *Mick Harte was here.* New York: Random House. [ I ]

Wells, Rosemary (1998). *Mary on horseback:* Three mountain stories. New York: Dial. [ I ]

---

ter by chapter, or each student reads the selected book independently. At the end of selected chapters, students are asked to respond to a teacher-constructed prompt. The teacher prepares these prompts by appropriately selecting from all four avenues of reader interaction. The events of particular chapters naturally lend themselves to any one of four prompt types, as discussed next.

***Experiential prompts.***    These are response prompts that elicit prior knowledge, prior personal experience (text-to-life connections), and prior reading (text-to-text connections). They focus on what the reader brings to the reading experience.

- How do you relate this chapter to your own life?
- How does (*name a character*) remind you of someone you know?
- How does (*name a character*) remind you of some other character you've met in a book?

***Aesthetic prompts.***    These are response prompts that elicit feelings, empathy, and character identification. They promote emotional interactions with the text, moving response beyond efferent plot summary.

- How does this chapter make you feel?
- How would you feel if you were (*name a character*) in this situation?
- How would you feel if you were (*name another character*)?

***Cognitive prompts.***    These are response prompts that encourage solving problems, making predictions, and making inferences about characters and plot development. They require readers to think, brainstorm, create, and construct outcomes.

- What do you think will happen to (*name a character*)?
- If you were (*name a character*), what would you do in this situation?
- What advice would you give (*name a character*) at this point in the story?

***Interpretive prompts.***    These are response prompts that elicit personal consideration of meaning or message, morals or values, and personal judgment of characters and situations. They call for a degree of higher level reasoning by requiring an explanation that is often difficult to put into words.

- What meaning or message does this chapter have for you?
- Why do you believe (*name of character*) did or did not make the right choice?
- What do you think the following words mean? (*Quote text*)
- What kind of person do you think (*name of character*) is? How do you know?

These prompts worked particularly well in a study designed and conducted by Hancock (1994, 1995) with children in Ireland and the United States. *Under the Hawthorn Tree* by Marita Conlon-McKenna is set in Ireland in the late 1840s during the height of the Great Famine. Three homeless children (Michael, Eily, and Peggy) escape the workhouse and begin a journey beset with hunger and danger in an attempt to locate their only living relatives in a distant Irish village. The prompt categories formed the framework for this reader response study, which encouraged a multiple perspective on response. The study also explored the ability of children's literature to transcend cultural differences and build humanistic empathy, trust, and understanding while enriching a global perspective of our world.

Figure 10.2 gives a complete overview of the experiential, aesthetic, cognitive, and interpretive prompts designed for varying chapters of *Under the Hawthorn Tree*. Note that the prompts delve into four perspectives of response: (1) background experience, (2) feelings, (3) predictions and problem solving, and (4) personal interpretation and judgment. While

*From* Under the Hawthorn Tree
*by Marita Conlon-McKenna.*
*Illustrated by Donald Teskey.*
*Copyright © 1990. Reprinted by*
*permission of Holiday House.*

they vary from chapter to chapter, they integrate the four response perspectives throughout the entire book. Sample authentic responses from each category of response from Irish and American children reveal the potential effectiveness of these well-designed, open-ended prompts with this book title. The Irish students, while having experience with literature in their reading program, had never experienced open-ended prompts previously. Yet the power of the literature, the thought-provoking prompts, the openness of the teachers, and the honesty of the readers combined to provide authentic testimony to capturing written thoughts on paper. The following samples illustrate this point.

***Experiential prompt (prereading/chapter 1).*** *What do you know about the Great Famine in Ireland or what do you think it was?* Ronan, who lives in County Cork in a small town that still bear the scars of the Great Famine, responded:

> The famine years were 1845, 1846 and 1847. Ireland's population decreased by over two
> million. Over half of those emigrated to other countries. . . . Because of their poverty, most of

**FIGURE 10.2**    Response prompts: *Under the Hawthorn Tree*

### Experiential Prompts

*Response prompts that elicit prior knowledge, life connections, and connections to prior reading*
What do you know about the Great Famine in Ireland or what do you think it was? (Prereading)
Of what other book or story that you have read do the events of this story remind you? (Chapter 5)
What does this chapter remind you of from your own life? (Chapter 9)
Although this story takes place a long time ago, why does it still seem so real as we read it today?
    (Chapter 11)
What does this chapter remind you of from your own life? (Chapter 12)

### Aesthetic Prompts

*Response prompts that elicit feelings, emotional reactions, empathy, and character identification*
How do you feel about what is happening to the O'Driscoll family? (Chapter 1)
What would you say to Michael, Eily, and Peggy to ease the pain they feel inside over the death of
    their baby sister, Bridget? (Chapter 2)
*"We're Irishmen, and our food is being sent away, grown in Irish soil to feed English bellies, while ours
    are empty and our people starve and die."* How do these words make you feel? (Chapter 10)
How would you feel if you were Michael in his desperate search for help? (Chapter 14)
How did you react to the children's attempts to use any kind of nourishment, even cow's blood, to
    keep them going? (Chapter 15)

### Cognitive Prompts

*Response prompts that encourage solving problems, making predictions, and making inferences
    about characters and plot*
What do you think about the children's plans to escape the workhouse? (Chapter 4)
What advice would you give Michael and Eily as they struggle to help their sick little sister, Peggy?
    (Chapter 13)
What do you predict will happen now that the children have finally reached Castletaggart? (Chapter 16)
Why do you think this author titled this book *Under the Hawthorn Tree?* (Chapter 17)

### Interpretive Prompts

*Response prompts that elicit personal consideration of meaning or message, morals or values, and
    personal judgment of characters and situations*
What kind of mother does Mrs. O'Driscoll seem to be? (Chapter 3)
What event will you remember most from this chapter? (Chapter 6)
What special meaning or message does this chapter have for you? (Chapter 7)
*"We're still alive. We're tired and hungry and on our own, but we still have each other. . . ."* What do
    Eily's words mean to you? (Chapter 8)
*"Those that emigrated to America and Canada brought with them their strength and their courage and
    hope. Those that were left behind struggled to survive and worked to build a country where such
    a disaster could never happen again."* What special meaning do these words have for you?
    (Postreading)

2nd March happened in Ireland it The Great Famine 1993
The great famine was about potatoes. The people were so lazy, they wouldn't grow anything but potatoes. But the blight came. The blight is a disease. A potato disease. The leaves devoled brown spots, and the potato rotted away. Thousands of people died. And it gave of a realy bad smell. The Americans brought Maize, but The Irish people did not no how to cooking it,.

A Sickley Smell

**FIGURE 10.3** Response to *Under the Hawthorn Tree*, Chapter 1, by Sophie from Ireland

the Irish people depended on potatoes for food. Irelands potatoe failure was caused by a plant disease called blight. . . . People used to call the people donkey eaters . . . because they ate donkey flesh. . . . My house is three famine cottages put together. . . .

Sophie, also from County Cork, responded with both words and a drawing (see Figure 10.3) to illustrate the experiential schema she brought to the book.
Another child quoted a famine poem in Gaelic,

| | |
|---|---|
| *Pr'tai ar naidin, pra'tai um noin* | (Potatoes in the morning, potatoes at midday, |
| *Agus da' n-eireoinn i nean-oiche,* | And if we got up at midnight, |
| *Pra'tai gheobhainn* | We could get potatoes again.) |

while another related a long tale of mistaken famine death at a local cemetery. The variety of responses to a simple experiential prompt serves as testimony to the individuality of reader response.

***Aesthetic prompt (Chapter 10).*** *"We're Irishmen, and our food is being sent away, grown in Irish soil to feed English bellies, while ours are empty and our people starve and die."*

*12/5/93* CHAPTER 13 Peggy's fever

I would give them a choice of my suggestions. They could just wait a while until Peggy is better, or maybe (if possible) make some sort of seat which they could carry her on. A sort of criss-cross shape. Example → (Michael + Eily carry it by holding these sticks either side) (Peggy sits here) sticks DUMB PICTURE

I certainly would not advise them to turn back to the workhouse now. They've come a long way and not just to waist it, I hope.

**FIGURE 10.4**   Response to *Under the Hawthorn Tree*, Chapter 13, by Matthew from Ireland

*How do these words make you feel?* Charlotte from Dublin revealed anger at the English and used a "we–they" identification as she responded:

> I feel jealous about this. The English taking all our food when we are starving to death. We are dieing and they are probably very healthy, wealthy, and well off. We are about to die and they litrualy have us as slaves so that they don't die.

Noteworthy here is that Irish children do not study the famine formally until their fifth–sixth class. A movement in Irish textbooks and by teachers has arisen to avoid portraying the English as "bad guys," and to instead put the famine in the context of international happenings and to explain the political, social, and cultural attitudes of the time. Children often bring their personal biases to the actions in the literature.

***Cognitive prompt (Chapter 13).***   *What advice would you give Michael and Eily as they struggle to help their sick little sister, Peggy?* Irish responses suggested treating the fever with cold compresses, herbal remedies, and suggestions and even drawings (see Figure 10.4) of carrying devices such as Matthew's from County Cork. In contrast to this stands American children's responses, which tended to choose today's remedies to cure the ills of the famine by sharing:

> Go get tilinole [Tylenol] or . . . let one of them go to the closest store to get some medicine.

***Interpretive prompt (postreading).***   *"Those that emigrated to America and Canada brought with them their strength and their courage and hope. Those that were left behind struggled to survive and worked to build a country. . . ."* What special meaning do these words have for you? American children developed empathy for the Irish, as Sharon from the United States shares:

> These words make me feel very thankful for what I have and make me feel very sorry for the people in Ireland that didn't survive the famine. It is hard to believe such a horrible disaster happened to such wonderful people.

Stephen from Dublin records a final reflection that projects the religious sentiment that pervades many Irish responses:

> . . . and I'm sad to say that there was so many people who saved our lives by giving their own. I pray that God will enter this country and be with us as we are his children and I know he loved the people in the famine the exzact same way he does now.

These responses inform practitioners of the variety and depth of responses collected from all four avenues of response: experiential, aesthetic, cognitive, and interpretive. These prompts have no right or wrong preconceived answers. Their value lies in personal honesty and a willingness to share innermost thoughts through the written response mode.

Not all books lend themselves to these varied response options, so it is important for the teacher to locate an appropriate book and to design worthwhile prompts. Although *Under the Hawthorn Tree* linked a prompt to each book chapter, it is not necessary to introduce a prompt for all chapters. Be certain the prompts are meaningfully designed and will elicit thoughts worthy of written response. Those who achieve success with this title might be interested to know that there are two sequels: *Wildflower Girl,* which continues the saga of the youngest child who journeys alone to America to start a new life in Boston, and *Fields of Home,* which completes the trilogy.

The potential of prompts to elicit written responses to literature through active reflection and thought should not be underestimated. The prompt categories and related prompts provide a framework or model for many titles. These prompts ask readers to think, to feel, to express, to connect, to predict, to interpret, to relate, to become. The prompts compel the reader to focus on the characters, the dilemmas, the causes, the outcomes, and the implications. While some may view prompts as restrictive, they exist to serve as facilitators of understanding, feeling, and engagement in literature.

# THE LITERATURE RESPONSE JOURNAL

As students become familiar with the kinds of responses that can be shared in a written format, they will require fewer prompts and gain more independence and trust in sharing their thoughts, opinions, and viewpoints in a journal. Developmentally, the time is ripe for children to express their individual responses. They've been read to, responded to prompts orally, read independently, and responded to teacher-constructed prompts through writing. The next logical step is to introduce the freedom of the unstructured literature response journal.

The literature response journal is the primary vehicle through which students capture their personal written responses to the literature they read (Hancock, 1993c; Wollman-Bonilla, 1989, 1991). The literature response journal is described as "a sourcebook, a repository for wanderings and wonderings, speculations, questionings . . . a place to explore thoughts, discover reactions, let the mind ramble . . . a place to make room for the unexpected" (Flitterman-King, 1988).

The final stage of written response involves independent reading and spontaneous recording of thoughts. While a natural first step in the response process is to write at the end of each chapter, capable students should be encouraged to respond at any point in the book at which a response enters their mind. This freedom elicits the fullest, richest range of responses. For others who may still have difficulty with such an open-ended request, the guidelines in Figure 10.5 provide direction, focus, and options for sharing written responses through a literature journal. They reflect the openness and freedom of the journal and encourage risk taking and trust. The guidelines provide impetus, but do not limit response options.

**FIGURE 10.5**    Guidelines for literature response journals

*From Hancock, M. R. (1993). Exploring and extending personal response through literature journals. The Reading Teacher, 46(6), 472. Copyright © 1993 by the International Reading Association. All rights reserved.*

---

### Guidelines for literature response journals

- *Feel free to write* your innermost feelings, opinions, thoughts, likes, and dislikes. This is your journal. Feel the freedom to express yourself and your personal responses to reading through it.
- *Take the time to write* down anything that you are thinking while you read. The journal is a way of recording those fleeting thoughts that pass through your mind as you interact with the book. Keep your journal close by and stop to write often, whenever a thought strikes you.
- *Don't worry* about the accuracy of spelling and mechanics in the journal. The content and expression of your personal thoughts should be your primary concern. The journal will not be evaluated for a grade. Relax and share.
- *Record the page number* on which you were reading when you wrote your response. Although it may seem unimportant, you might want to look back to verify your thoughts.
- *One side only* of your spiral notebook paper, please. Expect to read occasional, interested comments from your teacher. These comments will not be intended to judge or criticize your reactions, but will create an opportunity for us to "converse" about your thoughts.
- *Relate the book* to your own experiences and share similar moments from your life or from books you have read in the past.
- *Ask questions* while reading to help you make sense of the characters and the unraveling plot. Don't hesitate to wonder why, indicate surprise, or admit confusion. These responses often lead to an emerging understanding of the book.
- *Make predictions* about what you think will happen as the plot unfolds. Validate, invalidate or change those predictions as you proceed in the text. Don't worry about being wrong.
- *Talk to the characters* as you begin to know them. Give them advice to help them. Put yourself in their place and share how you would act in a similar situation. Approve or disapprove of their values, actions, or behavior. Try to figure out what makes them react the way they do.
- *Praise or criticize* the book, the author, or the literary style. Your personal tastes in literature are important and need to be shared.
- *There is no limit* to the types of responses you may write. Your honesty in capturing your thoughts throughout the book is your most valuable contribution to the journal. These guidelines are meant to trigger, not limit, the kinds of things you write. Be yourself and share your personal responses to literature through your journal.

# EXPLORING RESPONSE OPTIONS

What kinds of responses can teachers expect students to produce in literature response journals when complete freedom of expression is granted the reader? Several classroom studies have provided information about the types of responses children exhibit to quality literature when reading and responding in a literature journal or reading log. Knowing the response capabilities of varying ages of children assists in teacher expectations of response options. In the studies discussed in the following subsections, the suggested categories must not be considered all inclusive. Children should always be encouraged to explore their own ideas and response styles, even those responses that do not fit these categories. Teachers are encouraged to use these categories as a framework for response options, not a limitation on them.

## Primary-Grade Responses

Julie Wollman-Bonilla and Barbara Werchadlo (1995) noted two qualitatively different kinds of responses from a yearlong study of first graders which originated with whole class journals and narrowed to a research focus on a small group.

- Text-centered responses (what is happening in the book)
  1. *Retelling.* Recounts text events.
  2. *Understanding characters.* Expresses understanding of characters' thoughts or feelings, either stated or implied in the text.
  3. *Question.* Questions or expresses curiosity about plot or characters' actions.
  4. *Prediction.* Predicts plot or characters' actions.
- Reader-centered responses (readers' thoughts and feelings about the book and the experience of reading the book)
  1. *Personal reaction.* Expresses students' thoughts or feelings about the text.
  2. *Relating to experience.* Relates text to students' own experiences.
  3. *Self in story.* Expresses students' sense of being in the story or desire to be participating in the story events (pp. 564–565).

The researchers reported the majority of responses to *James and the Giant Peach* in the first 2 months of school as 83% text centered and 17% reader centered. A small group of four girls continued with the project and a dramatic shift from text centered (29%) to reader centered (71%) occurred during November through May for the case study participants. The study articulates the importance of discussion prior to writing for emergent readers and writers, the challenge involved with some children recording written thoughts even with the encouragement of constructive spelling, and the growth in response quantity and diverse categories over time. The study presents an initial working framework for the potential responses of primary-age children and serves as a guide for classroom teachers.

Through teacher action research, Mary Dekker (1991) reported results of a 2-year study of the use of self-selected texts, silent reading, and reading logs as part of her second- and third-grade reading program. Student responses at this age/grade level fell into six categories:

1. *Retelling.* Students tells all or parts of the story they read.
2. *Simple evaluation.* Students write that they liked or disliked the book, but did not provide textual information.

3. *Elaborated evaluation.* Students write why they liked the book and provided one or more incidents from the text to describe what they liked.

4. *Personal experience.* Students relate the events in the book to events in their own lives.

5. *Character response.* Students tell what they liked or disliked about particular characters.

6. *Record questions.* Students ask questions about the book itself or ideas the text explored.

Dekker (1991) found that describing response was only one part of her role as response facilitator. She also used her knowledge of types of response to help the students create richer and more varied responses. By valuing book talk and continually demonstrating connections between oral and written response, Dekker's students grew to love literature and appreciate options for response. This practitioner study reflects longitudinal growth of a teacher and her students in the realm of primary-grade reader response. The results validate an earlier study by Diane Barone (1990) about the potential of primary-level students to move beyond comprehension toward aesthetic response. Dekker's categories serve as catalysts for teachers who want to begin, but need to set some expectations for themselves while building an awareness of the response potentials of their primary students.

## Intermediate/Middle-Level Responses

An extensive case study of written responses of intermediate-level students (Hancock, 1991, 1993c) revealed a variety of rich options of which practitioners need to be made aware. Teachers need to be cognizant of the possible avenues of response before they can assist their students in extending response in personal literature response journals.

The following "categories of response" originated from a study of sixth-grade subjects' responses to realistic fiction (Hancock, 1991). They have been adapted and supplemented to include a wider range of students (grades 4–8) via a continuing study of reader response through written journals (Hancock, 1993a, 1995). An exploration of these categories and sample responses in each category alert the teacher to the possibilities, not the probabilities, of response.

The categories of response are organized into three response stances of the reader: (1) immersion, (2) self-involvement, and (3) detachment. Each major category and accompanying subcategories are supplemented by examples from authentic journals for Gary Paulsen's *Hatchet,* Katherine Paterson's *The Great Gilly Hopkins,* or Paula Fox's *One-Eyed Cat.*

***Immersion categories.***    Indicates reader immersion in the text in an attempt to make sense of emerging character and plot.

1. *Understanding.* Responses indicate the reader's current understanding of both character and plot. Responses move beyond summary to reflect a personal interpretation or they may reflect sudden discovery of meaning.

   *Brian is having trouble taking the death of the pilot.*
   *W. E. doesn't want Gilly to leave that's for sure.*
   *These past few pages show how one lie can lead to a whole series of lies.*

2. *Character introspection.* Responses indicate the reader's effort to make introspective insights into the feelings, thoughts, and motives for behavior of the characters. Responses reflect a sense of understanding through reasoning but indicate a degree of uncertainty

on the part of the reader. They often begin with tentative statements [i.e., "It sounds like . . .," "He must be . . .," "She probably . . .," "I think (*character's name*) . . ."].

*I think Brian is having trouble forgetting the divorce.*
*Trotter is probably ignoring Gilly to get her mad.*
*It sounds like Ned doesn't like where he lives.1*

3. *Predicting events.* Responses reflect reader speculation about what will emerge as the text proceeds. These statements often begin with "I bet . . .," "I guess . . .," "I think . . .," "If . . . then." Also included are response statements that validate or invalidate both stated and unstated predictions, serving as a link between prediction and understanding.

*If he keeps eating the berries, he will die.*
*I bet Brian will get his parents together. They will probably work together to find him.*
*The parent's didn't get together. (invalidates earlier prediction)*
*I didn't think she'd steal the money.*

4. *Questioning.* Responses reflect a lack of complete understanding or a questioning of text. They may reflect puzzlement indicated by "I wonder why . . .," "I can't tell." Questions may reflect confusion. Statements which begin "I can't believe . . .," "I'm surprised . . .," "I didn't know . . .," may reflect doubt or disbelief in the reader's attempt to comprehend the text.

*I wonder if the pilot is all eaten up by now.*
*This is weird. What does Brian have the flu? You don't normally throw up water.*
*What do they mean by "When the ax dropped"?*

***Self-involvement categories.***     Reflects responses that exhibit personal involvement with character and plot in which the reader vicariously becomes the character, becomes part of the plot or setting, or puts him- or herself in place of the character in the book's action.

5. *Character identification.* Responses show the reader has achieved a sense of personal identification with the character through statements like, "If I were . . .," "I probably would/wouldn't . . ." Empathetic identification such as, "I know how he feels . . .," "I feel sorry for . . ." or sharing a related experience from the reader's life may also occur. Directly addressing the character or giving advice also indicates involvement.

*For Pete's sake, Brian, tell me what you know.*
*If I were Ned, I'd get that thought out of my head.*
*Poor Gilly. I gues that's the way it is if your a foster child.*
*I experience the same, lawyers, yelling, and fighting.*

6. *Character assessment.* Responses indicate the reader's judgment of the actions and values of the character measured against his or her own personal standards of behavior. Evaluative terms such as traits of the character (i.e., smart, dumb, nice, mean) and distinctive expression of likes or dislikes may appear. Responses may also reflect perception of growth or change such as, "She's starting to . . .," "He's beginning to . . ."

*Brian is very unintelligent he ate the berries with the pits and now he's sick serves him right.*

*I like Gilly. She says what she thinks.*
*Brian is starting to change for the good. He is very responsible at times.*

7.  *Story involvement.* Responses indicate the reader's personal involvement in the story and resulting reaction to setting, theme, actions, or sensory aspects of the story. Evaluative terms (i.e., "disgusting," "cool," "weird") often reflect this interaction. Responses may reflect personal satisfaction or dissatisfaction with the unfolding events of the story. Active or passive anticipation of reading might be shared by "I can't wait . . .," "Do I have to go on?"

    *I just lost my appetite. Brian eating turtle eggs. Raw eggs at that.*
    *It would be nice to live on a hill with a view in a big old house.*
    *I can't wait to get to the part where he shoots the cat.*
    *Disgusting. Absolutely disgustingly chilling. Gross! Gross! Gross!*

**Detachment categories.**     Responses indicate that the reader detaches from the book in order to make a statement regarding evaluation of the literature or to contemplate his/her perspective on reading/writing.

8.  *Literary evaluation.* Responses indicate the reader's evaluation of all or part of the book. They may indicate praise or criticism of the author, writing style, literary genre, or ability to maintain reader interest. Responses may compare or contrast the book, author, or genre to others known to the reader. (Includes text-to-text connections.)

    *These were boring pages because all they talked about was fish.*
    *I don't think the author should have Gilly use swear words.*
    *This is so realistic. I love it.*

9.  *Reader/writer digressions.* Responses indicate the wanderings of the reader's mind while he or she interacts with the text, often showing thoughts outside the context of the book. They may include references to the act of reading, the literature response journal, the nature of the reading/writing environment, or simply digressive statements. (Includes text-to-life connections.)

    *I think I'd like to go backpacking. My mom did with her sister when she was younger.*
    *I know people say you can't hear a book, but I sort of can. Like you can hear almost anything that is said.*
    *I have found something out about the responses. I write the most when there is some kind of action in the story.*
    *I'm sick of writing right now. I'll write again at the end of the chapter.*

Teacher knowledge of response categories provides an informative framework for encouraging all that response can offer. Be aware that not all children will be comfortable with or capable of all types of response. The goal should not be to include all types of response, but to expand the number and kinds of individual response options over time. Continuous, encouraging feedback with some directive, but not demanding, comments helps lead children to fulfill their own unique response potential and develop a characteristic response style.

# EXTENDING RESPONSE THROUGH WRITTEN FEEDBACK

Perhaps the most powerful component of the literature response journal is the written feedback that a teacher provides on an intermittent basis to each student (Hancock, 1993b). Written feedback sustains the journal writing process through comments valuing personal response to a book. Eager students anticipate the daily/weekly return of their journals savoring the rich, personal comments of the teacher. Particularly early in the literature response journal experience, students need to know that they are on the "right track," that their honest responses are valued, and that responses deserve to be shared. The teacher needs to react to the literature response journal as often as possible—at least three times per week at first. Writing in the margins of the journal works for some teachers, while others believe sticky notes keep the journal in the handwritten control of the reader.

A common pitfall of response journals is that students become limited by the type of response they are willing to try. While unaware of the multiplicity of response options to literature, they take the safe road and continue what has worked for them in the past. A talented, informed teacher, however, can skillfully identify some options that might be open to each reader. These categories of response then become options for possible exploration by a student.

During the early stages of response journal writing, teacher comments tend to be reinforcing, nondirective, and encouraging. They inspire the reader to reflect, to connect, and to continue to share innermost thoughts and feelings. Subtly, those comments may even model the kinds of responses to which the reader may aspire. For example, an excellent choice for a literature response journal is Sharon Creech's *Chasing Redbird*. Written in short chapters, the format lends itself to intermittent writing as it concerns the character of 13-year-old Zinny Taylor and her struggle to deal with her aunt's death and to find her own identity. In response to a student response journal entry, the teacher may respond:

> You really have put yourself into Zinny's situation. You seem to be on the verge of reacting to her decision to clear the trail on her own. What do you think of that decision? Is it what you would do if these circumstances of a loved one's death surrounded your life? Just what is it Zinny is trying to accomplish anyway? I worry about her out there alone, especially if she stays away from home for days at a time. You've really grasped Zinny's adventurous spirit, perhaps because she is really a lot like you, Jennifer.

While Jennifer is not required to answer the teacher's questions, teacher feedback does make her think more deeply and encourages her to further identify with the main character. Her responses are likely to reflect a value judgment on Zinny's decision and perhaps a personal connection to the loss of a special person in her life. Teacher encouragement, not directives, provides powerful momentum to think deeper, share more honestly, and connect story events to one's own life.

Figure 10.6 shares excerpts from an ongoing response journal to Gary Paulsen's *The Haymeadow* by a sixth-grade student. Note the parallel ongoing comments from the teacher that motivate the student to persist, grow, and stretch through response. The development of a comfortable response style begins during the first journal and usually continues to blossom through subsequent journals. Take the time to read the student responses (cursive) and the teacher comments (manuscript) to confirm the difference teacher encouragement made in maintaining the momentum and increasing the depth of response.

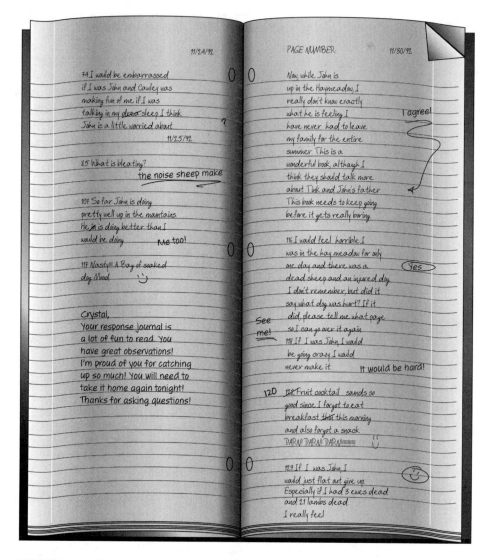

**FIGURE 10.6**   Literature response journal of a sixth grader to Gary Paulsen's *The Haymeadow*. Note teacher feedback.

Following an initial period of teacher–student confidence building, response partners take on an important role in the feedback process. Self-selected partners may exchange journals at the end of reading workshop to react to partner comments. If this is uncomfortable for specific children, it is important to continue teacher feedback with those individuals. Teachers should always be certain to provide their own feedback once a week, even when the literature response journal process is well in place.

Response provides a unique mode of expression, and a teacher demanding responses in a particular mode may negate the freedom of response. At the same time, well-directed

FIGURE 10.6 *(Continued)*

suggestions may lead the student to explore any otherwise unexplored options. A teacher wields powerful influence over a student's initiative to explore and expand response. Students must feel the freedom to accept or reject suggestions offered. The literature response journal is primarily a vehicle for personal expression. When that expression becomes stagnant, however, it is the teacher's responsibility to provide additional ideas for varying the natural response categories. As students in a trusting environment acquire more experience with response, they must feel free to accept or reject suggestions and only internalize response options that feel comfortable to their style of responding (Hancock, 1993b).

**FIGURE 10.7    In the Words of a Teacher: Reflections on Response Journals**

Because I believe you have to sometimes bait students to read and respond, I always try to get them motivated before any instruction or learning takes place. I also feel it is best if you can model to the students what you want them to do. For these reasons I initiated the response journey by reading *Toughboy and Sister* orally to my sixth-grade class. I had my students respond informally to Bleich's prompts: What did you notice in the story? How did the story make you feel? What does this story remind you of in your own life? During dramatic moments in the story, I asked the students to predict in their journals what happened to the father, what would happen to the children, and what they would do if their father died in the wilderness.

Next, we had an author study about Gary Paulsen to prepare them for their own response journals without using teacher-prescribed prompts. Following a two-day author study and discussion, I explained my expectations for a response journal. When I first suggested journals, several students groaned having already been saturated with response-type journals in previous grades. They were surprised and delighted, however, as I outlined my expectations.

1. I reassured them that they could write whatever they were thinking.
2. I encouraged them to write as they read. "Write as you read!" was my motto.
3. I emphasized complete ideas versus complete sentences.
4. I asked that they record any fleeting thought: deviations, frustrations, response to a tense or touching moment, anything that grossed them out or made them laugh, any connection to the book that made them think of another book or event in their own lives. In other words, be an active reader by making predictions, putting themselves in the character's place or giving the character advice.

By now the students were honestly grabbing at the three stacks of Gary Paulsen books I had next to me. I briefly summarized *Hatchet, The River,* and *The Haymeadow,* the three books from which they could choose. Within several minutes, the students had divided themselves into three groups, picked up a journal and asked if they could start. They were hooked!

It was interesting that several of the students started directly to me the first day. They asked about the meaning of certain words or phrases or asked questions about certain things they did not understand. Each day as I wrote comments or questions about their responses, they could hardly wait to pick them up to read. Our room was hushed each day as 23 children read and scribbled feverishly trying to record their thoughts.

Another interesting thing I observed from the onset was the variety of styles students demonstrated. Several students struggled to simply summarize each chapter. Not surprisingly, these were the students who struggled with reading comprehension and seldom read for pleasure. As I continued to encourage them to tell me how they were feeling, I began seeing these "nonreaders" make connections to the book by predicting and giving advice.

There were a few students who simply resisted the effort of putting down their thoughts. Even as I shared excellent examples of responses, divided the students into partners or groups to share, and encouraged them through written comments to write about the book, these mostly "verbal" students had difficulty with the written log of their thoughts. Perhaps these students would be better served with a tape recorder nearby. Ultimately, though, they still grew from the process. One thing I had not anticipated was the continued enthusiasm of many students who finished much quicker than anticipated and eagerly asked if they could read another Gary Paulsen book and write another response journal. And the entries in these response journals were just as detailed and involved.

Upon the conclusion of the response journals, I divided the students into their original groups and had them discuss their books. I had guide sheets for the group leader to facilitate questions, but all three groups were able to discuss the book without relying on the sheets. This was just another way of indicating just how much deeper their comprehension was through this mode of response journals.

Overall, I feel response journals were an overwhelming success. My students became active readers with higher comprehension and appreciation for the books they read. Through the response journals, my class learned to give life to their books and thus find meaning.    —Rene Maule

**FIGURE 10.8** Books that invite literature response journals

Avi (1990). *The true confessions of Charlotte Doyle.* New York: Orchard Books. [ I/M ]
Avi (1996). *Beyond the western sea. Book One: The escape from home.* New York: Orchard
  Books. [ I/M ]
Avi (1996). *Beyond the western sea. Book Two: Lord Kirkle's money.* New York: Orchard Books. [ I/M ]
Conlon-McKenna, Marita (1990). *Under the hawthorn tree.* New York: Holiday House. [ I ]
Conlon-McKenna, Marita (1991). *Wildflower girl.* New York: Holiday House. [ I ]
Conlon-McKenna, Marita (1997). *Fields of home.* New York: Holiday House. [ I ]
Conly, Jane Leslie (1995). *Trout summer.* New York: Henry Holt. [ I ]
Cushman, Karen (1994). *Catherine, called Birdy.* Boston: Clarion. [ M ]
Dorris, Michael (1997). *The window.* New York: Hyperion. [ M ]
Fenner, Carolyn (1995). *Yolanda's genius.* New York: McElderry Books. [ I ]
Fleischman, Paul (1997). *Seedfolks.* New York: HarperCollins. [ M ]
Fletcher, Ralph (1995). *Fig pudding.* Boston: Houghton Mifflin. [ I ]
George, Jean Craighead (1994). *Julie.* New York: HarperCollins. [ M ]
Hesse, Karen (1992). *Letters from Rifka.* New York: Holt. [ I ]
Holt, Kimberly Willis (1998). *My Louisiana sky.* New York: Henry Holt. [ I/M ]
Hurwitz, Johanna (1998). *Faraway summer.* New York: Morrow. [ I ]
Lowry, Lois (1995). *The giver.* Boston: Houghton Mifflin. [ M ]
Paterson, Katherine (1994). *Flip-flop girl.* New York: Lodestar. [ I ]
Paulsen, Gary (1987). *Hatchet.* New York: Delacorte. [ I ]
Salisbury, Graham (1994). *Under the blood-red sun.* New York: Delacorte. [ I ]
Staples, Suzanne Fisher (1989). *Shabanu: Daughter of the wind.* New York: Knopf. [ M ]
Staples, Suzanne Fisher (1996). *Dangerous skies.* New York: Farrar, Straus and Giroux. [ M ]
Taylor, Theodore (1993). *Timothy of the cay.* San Diego: Harcourt Brace. [ I ]

Figure 10.7 shares the voice of a sixth-grade teacher who incorporated literature response journals into her reading/writing program. Her honesty in describing teacher effort and student reactions to written response reconfirms the value of recording spontaneous response to literature. In addition, Figure 10.8 lists several books that work well with literature response journals because of dramatic episodes, memorable characters, and presentation of moral dilemmas. The selection of motivating reading is the first step toward success with response journals.

# THE CHARACTER JOURNAL

A steady flow of literature response journals with every book read in a literature-based program is not advised. Just as students turn off to routine worksheets, they can easily tire of the same format of response journal writing. This text introduces several other response modes that provide a change from written response. If response journals prove popular with students, however, another type of response journal, the character journal, provides a viable format that truly engages the reader in the reading process through a first-person writing stance.

A character journal is a written diary kept by the reader as he or she assumes the role of a character as a book is read. The reader actually becomes the character and keeps an ongoing journal by writing about prominent episodes that occur during specific chapters of a book. The reader writes in the first-person voice of the character sharing his or her thoughts, feelings, trepidations, and responses to the unfolding events of the book. Note the first-person journal entries in the role of *Lyddie* that open this chapter. A character journal compels the reader to climb under the character's skin, to walk in the character's shoes, and to realize the character's joys and frustrations. Simultaneously, the character journal encourages reflection as the reader thinks, judges, and weighs the actions, emotions, and reaction of the character against his or her own standards and behavior (Hancock, 1993a).

Purposefully, the character journal serves as a mode for recording the interactive process of reading and writing and promoting character involvement during the reading of literature. Because the journal is written from a character's point of view, the reader becomes the character and vicariously lives through the experiences and emotions of the story. Specific benefits of the journal include the following:

- Attain a high level of involvement with the literature read. The character journal sustains a personalized reading transaction enhanced by taking on the persona of the character, discouraging a distanced reading stance.
- Sustain a personal interest in the outcome of the story. With a greater stake in the unraveling plot, the events not only happen to the character, but to the reader as well.
- Experience growth as an interactive reader by becoming a part of the book. As both an active participant in reading and an engaged spectator, the reader realizes that an inside stance in reading enhances the literature experience itself.
- Gain a deeper sense of story and appreciation for literature. Deeper immersion in reading through character stance may contribute to the reader's levels of understanding and enjoyment.
- Attain a deeper understanding of characters of different cultures, genders, ages, and times. Sharing the fate of characters encourages the reader to challenge or clarify his or her own beliefs and choices resulting in insights into one's own self.

Not all book titles and genres work with the character journal format of response. Careful selection can make the difference between outstanding responses and mediocre response. Several criteria assist in choosing a book to partner with the character journal.

- The age of the main character must be similar to the age of the readers. The closer the age, the greater the level of involvement. Stated simply, 12-year-olds want to read about and identify with 12- to 14-year-olds. They want to walk in the shoes of a character similar to their immediate or approaching age.
- The main character must be strongly portrayed and evidence growing maturity as the book unfolds. The same principles for defining a strongly portrayed character can be applied here. If readers are indeed to grow in an understanding of themselves, the character must continuously question, likely falter, but ultimately move ahead and learn from an experience.
- The plot must unfold through a series of highly emotional events compelling the reader to become involved. A balance of character introspection and action events blended with anticipation and momentum result in stronger reader participation.

- The text must be written in the third person so that conversion to the first-person response as character retains originality. First-person accounts of first-person texts usually result in repetition and summary. First-person responses to third-person writing, however, cultivate original entries filled with honesty and emotion.

Figure 10.9 highlights literature that invites first-person response through a character journal. These books reflect the criteria listed and invite the reader to step into the shoes of the character and project his or her narrative voice.

A study by Hancock (1993a) was instrumental in exploring, defining, and stylizing the journal as part of a literature-based reading program. Two books that fit the criteria given earlier include Will Hobbs's *Bearstone* and Katherine Paterson's *Lyddie*. *Bearstone* is a coming of age story of a lonely 14-year-old Native American foster child in search of his own identity, who learns to love and be loved by an aging Colorado rancher.

To see how the first-person voice of the writer enters third-person context of the writing, evidence Beth's response to Cloyd's irresponsible, but emotional revenge on his foster parent:

> Well, I showed him. I took that saw . . . and cut every stupid, monster like, precious peach tree of his. Everyone I cut I thought of the sweet revenge I was getting . . . I wanted the death of those trees to be slow and painful not just for the trees but for Walter too. I want Walter to pay for the hurt he caused me . . . I want him to watch the trees die and know it's his fault. . . .

*Lyddie* is historical fiction about the harsh life and adult responsibilities of a 13-year-old factory girl in Lowell, Massachusetts, in 1843 as she struggles to earn money to save her family farm. The harassing attentions of the boss at the mill toward Lyddie were expressed by Justin, who was empathetically able to identify with Lyddie's distress:

> That day was hot. I started feeling sick. I couldn't wait to go to bed. My head hurt. But Mr. Marden told me to wait when all the girls left. I was with him all alone. I was to disy to understand anything. He put his hands on me. He was saying something but I couldn't understand him. I didn't know what he was trying to do. What ever it was I wasn't going to put up with it. I stomped on his foot and ran out of there.

Getting into the character is hard work; it can, in fact, be emotionally draining. Yet the strong characterization of these titles brought the students back to this level of intensity repeatedly throughout their reading.

The guidelines in Figure 10.10 assist students as they embark on character journals for the first time. Involvement in the life of a literary character provides an opportunity for readers to respond to the lives of others and an invitation to reflect on their own emerging identities.

## Responding to Character Journals

To sustain the motivation needed to maintain the intense involvement expressed in the character journal, the teacher (or peer) needs to respond intermittently in writing to character journal entries. The comments serve two purposes: (1) to ensure the reader that he or she is responding as the character and (2) to address the reader as the main character as complete character involvement and identification evolve. Although the need for encouragement declines, students anticipate teacher/peer comments each day before continuing the reading and responding process. As with all journals, the enthusiasm and effort for the

**FIGURE 10.9**   Books that invite character journal response

---

Bauer, Marion Dane (1994). *A question of trust.* New York: Scholastic. [ I ]
DeFelice, Cynthia (1998). *The ghost of fossil glen.* New York: Farrar, Straus and Giroux. [ I ]
Dygard, Thomas J. (1998). *River danger.* New York: Morrow. [ I/M ]
Fenner, Carol (1991). *Randall's wall.* New York: Macmillan. [ I/M ]
Fox, Paula (1991). *Monkey island.* New York: Orchard Books. [ I/M ]
Hahn, Mary Downing (1991). *Stepping on the cracks.* Boston: Clarion. [ I/M ]
Hill, Kirkpatrick (1990). *Toughboy and Sister.* New York: Macmillan. [ I ]
Hobbs, Will (1989). *Bearstone.* New York: Atheneum. [ I ]
Houston, Gloria (1997). *Littlejim's dream.* San Diego: Harcourt Brace. [ I ]
Meyer, Carolyn (1996). *Gideon's people.* San Diego: Gulliver Books/Harcourt Brace. [ M ]
Mikaelsen, Ben (1993). *Sparrow hawk red.* New York: Hyperion. [ I ]
Paterson, Katherine (1991). *Lyddie.* New York: Lodestar. [ M ]
Paulsen, Gary (1992). *The Haymeadow.* New York: Delacorte. [ I/M ]
Spinelli, Jerry (1990). *Maniac Magee.* New York: HarperCollins. [ I ]

---

**FIGURE 10.10**   Student guidelines for a character journal
*From Hancock, M. R. (1993). Character journals: Initiating involvement and identification through literature.* Journal of Reading, *37, 45. Copyright © 1993 by the International Reading Association. All rights reserved.*

---

- Become the main character and record your thoughts, feelings, and reflections in your journal through the character's voice.
- Write the chapter number to which your journal entry refers in the left margin.
- Choose one episode from each chapter to relive in your written journal entry.
- Write on only the front side of each page in your journal. Your teacher (or partner) will comment back to you as you become the main character.
- There are no right or wrong entries for the character journal. Your journal will be unique. Find a style of first-person writing that feels comfortable to you.
- Don't be concerned about spelling/mechanics. Expressing your thoughts in the voice of the character through involvement in the book is your main objective.
- Feel free to write whatever you are thinking as you become the character. One of the unique features of the journal is the freedom it allows. You may say the things you feel in the role of the character.
- Use parenthesis (   ) following your character entry to express your own personal thoughts on the actions, motives, decisions, or feelings of the character. Use this option as a means of being and expressing yourself.
- Remember: Write the thoughts and feelings of the character as you live through the episodes of the book with him/her. Put yourself in the mind and heart of that character and write what you, as the main character, think and feel.

character journal is sustained when the readers/responders know an awareness of and appreciation for a high level of involvement is recognized.

Note these comments constructed as teacher feedback to a reader/responder. Notice how the student is addressed as herself, and subsequently addressed as the main character as reader involvement becomes ever apparent in response entries.

> Carrie,                                                                                                    (Chapter 1)
>
> You have already become Lyddie as you take charge of the bear incident. Already you are showing your empathetic nature when you refer to your mama's "condition" at the end of the entry. You'll have no trouble becoming Lyddie. You are already feeling and thinking like her.

> Lyddie:                                                                                                    (Chapter 8)
>
> You've been through so many changes. Now a new job! You express your fear of failing so intensely. It's not bad enough to have to learn the tricks of the trade in the factory, but now you have that unending noise to bear. Running the loom is a real challenge. But think of all you've been through and how far you've come. You're a factory girl now!

As with all journals, the enthusiasm and effort for the character journal can be sustained when the respondents know that someone cares about and appreciates their level of involvement.

Reading in the guise of a literary character, feeling his or her emotions, joys and fears, and reflecting on one's own identity provide a meaningful experience unavailable in a traditional reading program. Not only do character journals result in well-written, emotionally packed entries, but the first-person response process results in a level of involvement previously unknown to many readers.

# CLOSING THOUGHTS

Written response to literature provides an excellent means to record those transient thoughts that flow through the mind of the reader during the act of reading. They provide documentation of the personal transaction between reader and text as a permanent record of a journey through literature. Readers who have completed several literature response journals over time claim that the response journal process stays in their heads even when reading independently. Children report more continuous reflective reading throughout a book as a result of engagement in this process.

Of all the benefits of written responses to literature, perhaps the long-term one that stands out the most is that written response causes the child to become a more reflective reader. Forcing oneself to stop reading, to capture a thought on paper, and to reenter the text with a personal commitment creates lifelong readers. The conversation that results between the reader and the journal writing continues on in the reader's mind even after the pencil leaves the paper. Meaning making is enhanced through the power of the written response. The written response mode is time consuming and requires commitment and feedback if it is to succeed. Yet the treasure of reading and revisiting the documented flow of thoughts captured during the reading event makes this a response mode to inspire and appreciate in readers.

# REFERENCES

Barone, D. (1990). The written response of young children: Beyond comprehension to story understanding. *The New Advocate, 3,* 49–56.

Dekker, M. M. (1991). Books, reading, and response: A teacher-researcher tells a story. *The New Advocate, 4,* 37–46.

Flitterman-King, S. (1988). The role of the response journal in active reading. *The Quarterly of the National Writing Project and the Center for the Study of Writing, 10,* 4–11.

Hancock, M. R. (1991). A case study investigation of the process and content of sixth-grade literature response journals. Doctoral dissertation, Northern Illinois University.

Hancock, M. R. (1992). Literature response journals: Insights beyond the printed page. *Language Arts, 69,* 36–42.

Hancock, M. R. (1993a). Character journals: Initiating involvement and identification through literature. *Journal of Reading, 37,* 42–50.

Hancock, M. R. (1993b). Exploring and extending personal response through literature journals. *The Reading Teacher, 46,* 466–474.

Hancock, M. R. (1993c). Exploring the meaning-making process through the content of literature response journals: A case study investigation. *Research in the Teaching of English, 27,* 335–368.

Hancock, M. R. (1994). Reader response across the sea: Irish and American children respond to literature. Presented at the 39th Annual Convention of the International Reading Association, Toronto, Canada.

Hancock, M. R. (1995). Discovering common bonds: Linking Ireland and America through literature. *Children's Books in Ireland (Journal of the Children's Literature Association of Ireland),* 12, 17–18.

Wollman-Bonilla, J. E. (1989). Reading journals: Invitations to participate in literature. *The Reading Teacher, 43,* 112–120.

Wollman-Bonilla, J. E. (1991). *Response journals: Inviting students to think and write about literature.* New York: Scholastic.

Wollman-Bonilla, J. E., & Werchadlo, B. (1995). Literature response journals in a first-grade classroom. *Language Arts, 72,* 562–570.

# CHILDREN'S BOOKS CITED [ P ] = K–2; [ I ] = 3–5; [ M ] = 6–8

Conlon-McKenna, Marita (1990). *Under the hawthorn tree.* New York: Holiday House. [ I ]

Conlon-McKenna, Marita (1991). *Wildflower girl.* New York: Holiday House. [ I ]

Conlon-McKenna, Marita (1997). *Fields of home.* New York: Holiday House. [ I ]

Creech, Sharon (1997). *Chasing redbird.* New York: HarperCollins. [ I ]

Dahl, Roald (1961). *James and the giant peach.* Illus. by Nancy Ekholm Burkert. New York: Knopf. [ P/I ]

Fox, Paula (1984). *One-eyed cat.* New York: Bradbury. [ I ]

Hobbs, Will (1989). *Bearstone.* New York: Atheneum. [ M ]

Paterson, Katherine (1978). *The great Gilly Hopkins.* New York: Crowell. [ I/M ]

Paterson, Katherine (1991). *Lyddie.* New York: Lodestar. [ M ]

Paulsen, Gary (1987). *Hatchet.* New York: Bradbury. [ I/M ]

Paulsen, Gary (1992). *The haymeadow.* New York: Delacorte. [ I/M ]

## Chapter 11

# Literature as a Model for Writing

## *Apprenticing the Author's Craft*

**I BELONG**

When I tend to my flourishing garden,
Everything vanishes except for the rows
Of Prairie land
and me.
Time strolls by, and
Unknowingly, I work away
In the midst of
Nature's creations.
I turn my eyes toward the harvest.
And swell with pride, knowing that
I belong,
In the breathtaking beauty and quiet
of the Earth.
As the familiar Night drops its dark veil,
I stop to rest,
With a lantern shining on me,
And the fragrance of pines and roses
Float in the air.

A solitary crow circles the sky
Then two, then three,
Cawing encouragement and praise
While a cool breeze
Caresses my face.
I gaze into a sunflower,
Seeing its seeds start to whiten.
I think,
"If I help the Earth,
It will help me."
And I hasten to finish
before the fog rolls in.

Fifth-Grade Student*

The relationship between readers and writers becomes increasingly apparent as children read more literature and write more often in their classrooms. The more one reads, the better one writes. The more exposure to quality literature, the better the model for one's own writing efforts (Dressel, 1990; Eckhoff, 1983; Hansen, 1987). The student poem that opens the chapter, for example, indicates a writer with a potentially rich literature background. This chapter's intent is to connect readers and writers through exposure to quality literature and invited opportunities to extend literature experiences through writing as a mode of response. Literature serves as a model of literary genres, literary elements, writing styles, and formats for writing. One of the many responses to quality literature is to note the writing craft that is incorporated in literature and apply that craft to one's own writing. Reading literature for enjoyment is always a priority, but looking beyond the personal meaning of the words to uncover an author's writing skill impacts a reader's own writing efforts (Walmsley & Walp, 1990).

From the time parents first read to a child, a sense of story begins to develop. A sense of standard openings (*Once upon a time...*) and optimistic endings (*... and they lived happily ever after*) forms the parameters of a child's internalization of story structure. A familiarity with characters—what they look like, how they act, what they say—provides the young child with the critical role of character in story. The setting (*... in a deep, dark forest at the edge of the kingdom*) also invites young children into the secrecy and intrigue of literature. These repeated, initial exposures to books provide a schema through which future readers will comprehend story in their minds, create story in their imaginations, and even eventually write stories of their own (Applebee, 1980; Golden, 1984). The natural tendency to incorporate literary elements and techniques into their own writing—"literary borrowing" (Lancia, 1997)—is a cumulative response to the reading of literature in which children have engaged during many early years of their lives.

*From "Younger Kansas Writers" issue of *Kansas English, 80*(5). Reprinted by permission of the Kansas Association of Teachers of English.

This chapter covers several areas in which literature is celebrated as a model for writing. The earliest writing of predictable text based on patterned books provides a first experience of literature as a model for writing. Using quality literature for extended writing activities forms the typical core of most school literature-writing connections. Moving beyond these initial experiences, however, children can become true apprentices of the author's craft through both author studies and recognition of writing traits within the titles of their favorite authors. Literature as a model for writing provides high standards as budding writers attempt to share their personal and creative stories through the written response of composition. A child's imaginative or informative writing is a long-term response to literature built on multiple episodes of reading aloud, independent reading, and numerous writing experiences. The cumulative effect of writing calls into play what one knows about the writing craft and blends that knowledge with what one has discovered through a lifetime of encounters with quality literature.

# PREDICTABLE BOOKS: AN EFFECTIVE BEGINNING

The youngest children may get their first opportunity at being authors as they collaboratively play a role in writing their own version of a predictable/pattern book (Heald-Taylor, 1987; Rhodes, 1981). A predictable/pattern book is based on a simple idea and enhanced through repetition or patterned elements making it effective for learning to read as well as for first attempts at story writing. The most well known classic of this type is Bill Martin's *Brown Bear, Brown Bear What Do You See?* The title phrase is followed by "I see a red bird looking at me." Subsequent passages utilize different colored animals, but predictably follow the question, "Color/animal, color/animal what do you see?" Children are eager to "write" new phrases, including "I see a black and white panda looking at me" or "I see a green dinosaur looking at me." These early attempts at writing within the framework of a patterned book are delightful experiences that build a feeling of confidence and success in writing. At the same time, children are learning to read their own writing. Not only do predictable/pattern books create authors, they reinforce emerging readers. Books like *The Very Hungry Caterpillar, Goodnight Moon,* and *In the Tall, Tall Grass* provide important early models for emergent literacy.

As children gain confidence in simple pattern books, they move toward those that are a bit more complicated and often take collaboration and planning. A trip across America on *My Sister's Rusty Bike* by Jim Aylesworth provides short, energetic accounts of quirky people and real places across the country. For example,

> I rode to <u>Massachusetts</u>
> On my sister's rusty bike,
> And found just <u>south</u> of <u>Marblehead</u>
> A place I think you'll like.
> A <u>gal</u> lives there named <u>Pat McDuff.</u>
> <u>Her cats have purple fur.</u>
> <u>They love to pile up in Pat's lap,</u>
> <u>And as she pets, they purr.</u>*

*From *My Sister's Rusty Bike*. Text copyright © 1996 by Jim Aylesworth. Reprinted by permission of Atheneum Books for Young Readers.

**FIGURE 11.1**     Predictable/patterned texts

Appelt, Kathi (1993). *Elephants aloft.* Illus. by Keith Baker. San Diego: Harcourt Brace. [ P ]
Aylesworth, Jim (1994). *My son John.* Illus. by David Frampton. New York: Holt. [ P/I ]
Bayer, Jane (1984). *A, my name is Alice.* Illus. by Stephen Kellogg. New York: Dial. [ P/I ]
Blos, Joan (1992). *A seed, a flower, a minute, and hour.* New York: Simon & Schuster. [ P ]
Charlip, Remy (1964). *Fortunately.* New York: Parents Magazine Press. [ P/I ]
Fleming, Denise (1992). *Lunch.* New York: Holt. [ P ]
Fleming, Denise (1993). *In the small, small pond.* New York: Holt. [ P ]
Gag, Wanda (1929). *Millions of cats.* New York: Coward-McCann. [ P ]
Goldstone, Bruce (1998). *The beastly feast.* Illus. by Blair Lent. New York: Holt.
Hutchins, Pat (1986). *The doorbell rang.* New York: Greenwillow. [ P ]
Martin, Jr., Bill (1991). *Polar bear, polar bear, what do you hear?* Illus. by Eric Carle. New York: Holt. [ P ]
Peek, Merle (1985). *Mary wore her red dress.* Boston: Clarion. [ P ]
Purviance, Susan & O'Shell, Marcia (1988). *Alphabet Annie announces an all American album.*
     Boston: Houghton Mifflin. [ I ]
Scheer, J., & Bileck, M. (1964). *Rain makes applesauce.* New York: Holiday House. [ P ]
Slate, Josephy (1998). *Miss Bindergarten celebrates the 100th day of kindergarten.* Illus. by Ashley
     Wolff. New York: Dutton. [ P ]
Van Laan, Nancy (1998). *Little fish, lost.* Illus. by Jane Conteh-Morgan. New York: Atheneum. [ P ]
Van Laan, Nancy (1998). *So say the little monkeys.* Illus. by Yami Heo. New York: Atheneum. [ P ]
Williams, Sue (1990). *I went walking.* Illus. by Julie Vivas. San Diego: Harcourt Brace. [ P ]
Williams, Sue (1998). *Let's go visiting.* Illus. by Julie Vivas. San Diego: Harcourt Brace. [ P ]
Yolen, Jane (1993). *Mouse's birthday.* New York: Putnam. [ P ]

The underlining indicates the sections children will create with their own rhyme and imaginations. An entire class can follow a route across the entire country creating a host of unusual characters and incidents.

Predictable/pattern books abound across age levels, so there is no shortage of possibilities for including them in the primary reading–writing literacy program. Many of these titles are classics as they have proven themselves over time to be children's favorites. See Figure 11.1 for additional titles that invite patterned writing and accompanying illustrations as response to their formats.

# LITERATURE AS A SPRINGBOARD FOR WRITING

Some quality books actually serve as a model for writing and beg for written extensions that allow the form or format to be used for the written response. Savoring them first as literature is important. The experience of reading immersion must always precede the actual writing experience. Weaving literature into the writing workshop fosters the reading–writing connection in the literacy classroom (Harwayne, 1992).

## Wordless Books

Wordless picture books provide a sound source for group writing in the primary grades. Tomie de Paola's *Pancakes for Breakfast* is a favorite of young children. For this book, a teacher adds children's dictated words to a story chart as the class creates a story to accompany the colorful illustrations. Wordless picture books are indeed a natural resource for imaginative writing, especially for older children who can share their texts with their younger peers. Action-packed illustrations and artistic character portrayals provide the seed for plot and character development. Books like Lynd Ward's *The Silver Pony* can result in worthy texts composed in groups or with the dedication of an individual writer. David Wiesner's Caldecott award-winning *Tuesday* generates unusual ideas in young writers as they develop words for the memorable illustrations or write a sequel for the impending invasion of pigs. With ample opportunity to peruse the books prior to and during writing, imaginative response generates the words of the child's evolving text. The variety and ingenuity that results once again documents the diversity of response. See additional listings in Chapter 3 for wordless picture books that invite writing.

## Journal Writing

Teachers who desire students to keep personal journals to capture informal writing experiences need only look to literature models to inspire the journaling process. Opal Whiteley, a foster child living in the lumber camps of the Northwest at the turn of the century, poignantly shares her love of nature through excerpts from the diary she kept when she was 5 and 6 years old.

> A note from Jane Boulton at the end of the book shares Opal's prowess and persistence at keeping a diary. The reader learns that Opal kept the diary in constructed spelling on the back of envelopes. She spent many years as a foster child in nineteen different lumber camps following the tragic death of her parents. Although Opal hid her treasured diary, a stepsister found it and tore it into "a million pieces," which Opal preserved. When she was 20-years-old, Opal met a book publisher who suggested she reproduce her diary in its original form for publication. Opal painstakingly pasted all the scraps of paper together so her eloquent diary could be shared in book form. The selector then issues the following invitation to captivated readers:
>      "And now you may want to start a diary of your own."

This informational note, the text of *Only Opal: The Diary of a Young Girl,* and the gentle paintings of Barbara Cooney truly invite children to respond by recording their daily experiences in a journal format.

Similarly, Deborah Hopkinson's *Birdie's Lighthouse* diary format reflects the courageous voice of true-to-life lighthouse heroines of the 1800s through the fictional character of Birdie Holland. The strong first-person voice of children finds it way naturally into personal journal writing, and these titles model the importance of recording personal experience and feelings. Additional journal and diary titles are listed in Figure 11.2.

## Letter/Postcard Writing

Personal written communication is a standard requirement of the elementary writing curriculum. Books that include letters, postcards, and other forms of written communication serve as models for children's authentic writing experiences. When *The Jolly Postman* was published in 1986, teachers warmed to the innovative idea of literature/writing links. *Stringbean's Trip to the Shining Sea* chronicled Stringbean Coe's cross-country trip through postcards and snapshots while inspiring children to respond by writing and designing their own picture postcards. Books continue to hold the letter writing model that encourages response in this format.

*Dear Mr. Henshaw* touches readers as a link to letter writing to authors while *Dear Great American Writers Club* brims with a series of letters to a writing school that actually turned Bobby Lee Pomeroy into a bright and aspiring author. *The Magic Cornfield* takes the reader on an imaginative journey via postcards as Tottem's car breaks down on his way to his cousin Bottom's 100th birthday party in Minneapolis. Literature models abound to model the form and the expectations for responding through written communication formats. Additional titles in which letters/postcards convey the story can be found in Figure 11.2.

## Fairy-Tale Variants

Since the appearance of Jon Scieszka's *The True Story of the Three Little Pigs*, an explosion of fairy-tale variants have appeared both in children's book publishing and in classrooms. The point-of-view shift to the perspective of A. Wolf served as an inspiration and model for children to write their own fairy-tale variants. Titles such as *The Stinky Cheese Man, The Frog Prince Continued, Somebody and the Three Blairs,* and *The Three Little Javelinas* have further fed the imaginations of children to write their own versions of popular fairy tales. Transforming traditional stories, enjoying modern variants, and creating their own versions reflect enthusiastic responses to literature. Sipe (1993) lists a variety of ways to transform stories. In Figure 11.3 his suggestions allow children individually or as a group to decide how they want to alter the original traditional tale.

The *Cowboy and the Black-Eyed Pea* mirrors the *Princess and the Pea* with a Western motif. Farethee Well's test of a single pea hidden under a saddle blanket challenges a cast of perspective cowboys. *The Bootmaker and the Elves* transforms this traditional tale into one with a modern Western motif. Children's imaginations soar as they respond by renaming characters, twisting the plot, or adding humor to these often familiar tales. Teachers, however, need to recognize that not all children have the original tale in their literary schema, so it is just as important to share an original version alongside the usually humorous variant. The reading–writing connection is apparent and natural in traditional tale transformations as children respond to literature by learning more about the elements of this genre through their own creative writing efforts. Additional fairy-tale variant models can be found in Figure 11.2.

**FIGURE 11.2** Additional titles as springboards to writing

**Journal Writing**

Blos, Joan (1979). *A gathering of days: A New England girl's journal.* New York: Scribner's. [ I/M ]

Cushman, Karen (1994). *Catherine, called Birdy.* Boston: Clarion. [ M ]

George, Jean Craighead (1988/1959). *My side of the mountain.* New York: Dutton. [ I ]

Heinrich, Bernd (1990). *An owl in the house: A naturalist's diary.* Adapted by Alice Calaprice. New York: Joy Street/Little, Brown, [ I ]

Hest, Amy (1995). *Private notebooks of Katie Roberts.* Illus. by S. Lamut. Cambridge, MA: Candlewick Press. [ I ]

Lyons, Mary E. (1995). *Keeping secrets: The girlhood diaries of seven women writers.* New York: Holt. [ M ]

Moss, Marisa (1996). *Amelia writes again.* Berkeley, CA: Tricycle Press. [ I ]

Moss, Marisa (1998). *Rachel's journal: The story of a pioneer girl.* San Diego: Silver Whistle/Harcourt Brace. [ I ]

Rocklin, Joanne (1997). *For your eyes only! (FYEO).* New York: Scholastic. [ M ]

Turner, Ann (1997). *Mississippi mud: Three prairie journals.* Illus. by Robert Blake. New York: Harper-Collins. [ I ]

Williams, Vera B. (1981). *Three days on a river in a red canoe.* New York: Greenwillow. [ P/I ]

**Letter/Postcard Formats**

Ada, Alma Flor (1994). *Dear Peter Rabbit.* Illus. by Leslie Tryon. New York: Atheneum. [ P ]

Ada, Alma Flor (1998). *Yours truly, Goldilocks.* Illus. by Leslie Tryon. New York: Atheneum. [ P/I ]

Avi (1991). *Nothing but the truth.* New York: Orchard Books. [ M ]

Cleary, Beverly (1991). *Strider.* New York: Morrow. [ I ]

Cushman, Karen (1996). *The ballad of Lucy Whipple.* Boston: Clarion. [ I/M ]

Hesse, Karen (1992). *Letters from Rifka.* New York: Holt. [ I/M ]

MacLachlan, Patricia (1985). *Sarah, plain and tall.* New York: Harper & Row. [ P/I ]

Stewart, Sarah (1997). *The gardener.* Illus. by David Small. New York: Farrar, Straus and Giroux. [ P ]

**Fairy-Tale Variants**

Cole, B. (1989). *Prince Cinders.* London: Collins. [ I ]

Egielski, Richard (1997). *The gingerbread boy.* New York: HarperCollins. [ P/I ]

Ernst, Lisa Campbell (1995). *Little Red Riding Hood: A newfangled prairie tale.* New York: Simon & Schuster. [ P/I ]

Gwynne, Fred (1990). *Pondlarker.* New York: Simon & Schuster. [ P/I ]

Kellogg, Steven (1997). *The three little pigs.* New York: Morrow. [ P/I ]

Ketteman, Helen (1997). *Bubba the cowboy prince: A fractured Texas tale.* Illus. by James Warhola. New York: Scholastic. [ I ]

Petach, Heidi (1995). *Goldilocks and the three hares.* New York: Putnam. [ P/I ]

**FIGURE 11.3**   Class chart for ways to transform stories

---

**How can we change a story?**

1. We can change the style, from old-fashioned to modern language.
2. We can change or add to the details in the plot (*Somebody and the Three Blairs*).
3. We can change a few of the main events in the plot (Stephen Kellogg's *Chicken Little*).
4. We can keep a few of the main events but change most of the plot (*Sleeping Ugly*).
5. We can change the setting (time and place). If the setting is changed, there will probably need to be many more changes in characters and detail (*Snow White in New York; Ugh*).
6. We can change the point of view (*The True Story of the Three Little Pigs,* told by the wolf).
7. We can change the characters in the story by
   —changing their occupation (*The Principal's New Clothes*)
   —changing their gender (*Prince Cinders*)
   —reversing their roles in the story (*Somebody and the Three Blairs*).
8. We can write a sequel to the original story (*The Frog Prince Continued*).
9. We can keep the words of the original story but change the illustrations (Anthony Browne's *Hansel and Gretel*).

From Sipe, L. R. (1993). Using transformations of traditional stories: Making the reading–writing connection. *The Reading Teacher, 47*(1), 22. Reprinted by permission of the International Reading Association.

---

## Special Invitations to Write

Occasionally, a book invites children to participate in the writing process by writing a sequel, continuing an unfinished story, or naturally updating a format. The premier example of this writing connection is Chris Van Allsburg's *The Mysteries of Harris Burdick*. The story introduction, read convincingly aloud, motivates children to write imaginative stories to accompany the 14 mysterious black-and-white illustrations. The brief, but interesting captions serve as a stimulus for creative writing. Even reluctant writers are invigorated by the opportunity to respond to these unique visual invitations. The beautiful language of Owl Moon provides opportunities for extended writing for primary children (Egawa, 1990). Another direct and meaningful writing extension emerges from reading Judith Viorst's title poem from *If I Were in Charge of the World and Other Worries*. Children long to update and personalize the poem based on its original format and message.

A genuine writing invitation from Thomas Locker and Candace Christiansen's *Home: A Journey Through America* is issued directly to the reader. "It is my hope that this book will present a vision of our varied and special land, and that *Home* will inspire readers to celebrate the special places they call home" (Introduction). Writing about and perhaps illustrating one's own home—state, terrain, building—form a natural connection to literature.

A caution is in order so that writing extensions remain natural responses to literature. Too often well-intentioned teachers warp literature or insist on repeated writing extensions with every literature sharing. The writing connection should flow naturally from the literature. If the desired activity is not authentic and strays away from the literary model, perhaps the literature should merely be enjoyed for its own merits. Preserve the writing experience

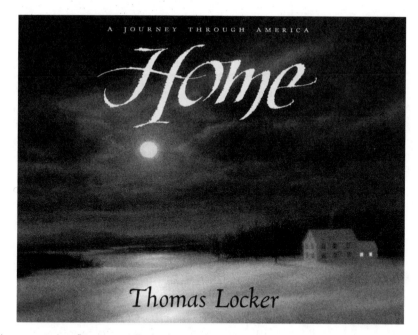

A writing connection flows naturally from special titles and ensures authenticity of response. *From* Home: A Journey Through America. *Illustrations copyright © 1998 by Thomas Locker. Reprinted by permission of Silver Whistle/Harcourt Brace.*

exclusively for those books with inherent connections to writing since they foster rather than tamper with authentic response.

# AUTHOR STUDIES

The most powerful way to introduce students to the writing craft and foster a commitment to writing is to introduce them to the flesh-and-blood authors behind their favorite books. Ideally, a visit to a school by an author would answer typical queries about how he got started, where she gets her ideas, and how long it takes to write a book. While author visits are becoming more common and easier to arrange and facilitate (Jacobs & Tunnel, 1996), they still remain a dream for most children. But a teacher can, so to speak, bring an author to the classroom through an author study (Peck & Hendershot, 1997). An author study blends biographical information on an author with an intensive exposure to his or her published books. Immersion in background information coupled with familiarity of many works by a single author provide much speculation and inspiration about the writing craft.

Reader response to author studies exhibit themselves in several ways. Children are invited to explore via these tasks:

- Locate and read more books by the author.
- Research further biographical information on the author.
- E-mail an author.
- Create an author brochure with biographical information and annotations of selected books.

- List similar writing techniques of the author across books.
- Incorporate writing techniques of the author into own writing.
- Compare/contrast author's writing style to other known authors through discussion.

Reading a biography/autobiography of an author alongside the author's work incorporates an added dimension to an author study and enhances a student perspective on the connection between an author's life and his or her work. For example, a teacher read-aloud of Marion Dane Bauer's *A Writer's Story: From Life to Fiction* coupled with a literature group reading of *A Question of Trust* and *On My Honor* build connections between the author's life experiences, personal emotions, and the stories she writes. This idea presents a powerful combination for aspiring writers as they blend the author's life and writing craft with the product of his or her efforts. Suggestions for author biography/autobiography and creative works to be read side by side include:

Bauer, Marion Dane (1986). *On my honor.* Boston: Houghton Mifflin.
Bauer, Marion Dane (1994). *A question of trust.* Boston: Houghton Mifflin.
Bauer, Marion Dane (1995). *A writer's story: From life to fiction.* Boston: Houghton Mifflin.

Byars, Betsy (1985). *Cracker Jackson.* New York: Viking.
Byars, Betsy (1991). *The moon and I.* New York: Morrow.
Byars, Betsy (1996). *Tornado.* New York: HarperCollins.

Cleary, Beverly (1984). *Ramona forever.* New York: Morrow.
Cleary, Beverly (1988). *A girl from Yamhill: A memoir.* New York: Morrow.
Cleary, Beverly (1991). *Strider.* New York: Morrow.

Naylor, Phyllis Reynolds (1987). *How I came to be a writer.* New York: Simon & Schuster.
Naylor, Phyllis Reynolds (1991). *Shiloh.* New York: Atheneum.
Naylor, Phyllis Reynolds (1996). *Shiloh season.* New York: Atheneum.

Spinelli, Jerry (1989). *Maniac Magee.* Boston: Little, Brown.
Spinelli, Jerry (1997). *Wringer.* New York: HarperCollins.
Spinelli, Jerry (1998). *Knots in my yo-yo string: The autobiography of a kid.* New York: Knopf.

# APPRENTICING THE AUTHOR'S CRAFT

In *Author: A True Story,* Helen Lester, author of popular children's books, shares her struggles with writing both as a child and a successful author. She humorously shares the hurdles that are a part of writing:

> Sometimes writing stories is so HARD for me!
> I can't come up with a single idea,
> and my stories get stuck in the middle,
> and I can't think of a title,
> and I have trouble making the changes my
> editor wants me to make,
> and I lose my pencils,
> and I wonder why I'm doing this,
> and I get very very VERY frustrated.*

Authors share their personal struggles and successes with writing through biographies that serve as models of the author's craft.
*From* AUTHOR: A True Story *by Helen Lester. Copyright © 1997 by Helen Lester. Reprinted by permission of Houghton Mifflin Company. All rights reserved.*

Writing is hard work, but the reward lies in the accomplishments of bringing ideas of the imagination to the page as written words. Learning the author's craft takes time and multiple models of strong writing. That's why literature plays such a crucial role in helping young writers by providing models that reflect various aspects of the craft of writing.

If response to literature is to include improved student writing, the teacher must guide young writers in an awareness of the craft of writing within the context of quality children's/ young adult literature. The six-trait analytic model of writing (Spandel & Stiggins,1996) provides a framework for discussion of the author's craft. Although intended for analytic assessment of writing, the six traits can also be viewed as areas addressed by effective writers. The six writing traits include ideas and content development, organization, voice, word choice, sentence fluency, and writing conventions. By understanding these traits and seeing their use modeled in authentic, published works, student response to literature may be enriched by the use of these traits in their own writing. For example, a student who is aware of Gary Paulsen's use of ellipses in *The Haymeadow* may effectively incorporate this writing convention into her or his own survival story. The notion of an opening phrase repeatedly used for dramatic effect like Cynthia Rylant's *When I Was Young in the Mountains* might come to mind when writing one's own personal narrative. Literature provides the models that make readers first, then writers.

An elaboration of each trait will assist us in understanding the relationship between the trait and a young author's response by the application of each trait in one's own writing. The following discussion defines each writing trait, makes suggestions for exposure to and application of the trait, and includes a list of literature that effectively models and reflects use of the trait. Children need to become familiar with the terminology of writing. As literature is discussed following its enjoyment (or alongside it in the case of chapter books), these writing traits might be identified and analyzed as components of the writing craft.

## Ideas and Content Development

Ideas are the seeds of writing and grow by developing content into story. Young authors always wonder where authors get their ideas and how they turn them into stories. Reading authentic literature and discussing a core idea and its development are essential to understanding this trait. Perhaps idea development is most easily detected in a picture book, such as *Too Many Tamales* (Soto, 1993), in which a traditional Hispanic Christmas Eve is interrupted by a supposed missing wedding ring. From simple ideas, based on personal experiences, stories grow.

Many authors report they keep a small notebook handy for writing down ideas and young authors should be encouraged to do the same. Experiences give rise to ideas that can be developed into stories. Eve Bunting was inspired to write *Fly Away Home* upon witnessing the homeless in a large airport. Because writers seem to write best within the context of familiar settings, children should be allowed to choose their own writing topics based on personal experiences. Patricia Polacco uses her husband's familiar open-air restaurant in Oakland, California, as a setting for *In Enzo's Splendid Garden*. Writers develop stories from small bits and pieces of their own lives. Sharing as many literary connections as possible to demonstrate the seed of an idea will help young writers plant their own seeds for writing.

A graphic organizer or story web also shows how an idea can expand into a story. By having young writers make a web of a favorite book, they can visualize the seed idea and monitor its growth through character and plot development (Bromley, 1996). An event sequence web for Zinnea Taylor's clearing of the Bybanks-Chocton trail in Sharon Creech's *Chasing Redbird* provides visual evidence of how an author stages events as part of plot development. Webs can naturally become a rehearsal outline for a child's own story. David Williams's *Grandma Essie's Covered Wagon* follows the author's grandmother's journey from Missouri to Kansas to Oklahoma, highlighting all the joys and disasters along the way. A graphic organizer of this literary journey would indicate beginning, conflicts, highpoints, roadblocks, and eventual resolutions.

Robert Blake's *The Perfect Spot* provides a model for a web for a young author's own perfect spot. Envision the seed for writing as the name of the place forms the core of the web and descriptions of the sights, sounds, tastes, and feelings surround it with details. The web as a framework for story in both reading and writing illustrates to the young author the importance of a key idea and its development in the creation of story.

## Organization

Organization can be described as a well-marked trail that winds its way through a piece of writing so the reader can find the way toward meaning. This trait must be exhibited successfully in both narrative and expository writing if story plot or informational facts are to be delivered in a meaningful, sequential fashion.

***Narrative writing.***   In exploring the structure of narrative writing, it is crucial to read aloud literature that develops the beginning/middle/end concept of story. Read, for example, *Where Does the Trail Lead?* to verbally and visually experience the beginning, middle, and end of the trail at the beach. *To Climb a Waterfall* through both illustration and text leads the reader from the base to the top of an Adirondack waterfall. Children should also be encouraged to engage in oral, written, or artistic retellings of stories to establish a model for sequence. Sharing authentic literature that delivers a story in sequential order provides additional models to acquire this sense of organization. David Cunningham monitors *A Crow's Journey* seeking an answer to the crow's inquiry:

> A wandering crow
> was curious to know:
> Where does it go,
> this mountain snow,
> each spring?

Through the eyes of the crow, the reader follows the crisp snow as it melts into a stream, over a waterfall, through a meadow, and past a village, until it meets the sea. In teaching the trait of organization, this book provides a precisely articulated, poetic map of words and paintings that leads to an answer to the original query.

> Here the river
> mouth spreads wide
> and finally meets the ocean tide.

> And now the crow is satisfied.*

Application of this sense of organization results in a related response through a child's own application in his or her writing so the reading audience can follow the same type of organized trail.

In addressing organization, literature also models effective leads and conclusions as young writers learn the value of capturing the reader's attention and leading toward a sense of resolution. Examine the opening paragraphs of *The Shakespeare Stealer* by Gary Blackwood to illustrate a strong lead that entices the reader toward continued reading. This strong opening invites even the most reluctant reader to learn more about the orphan, Widge.

> I never knew my mother or my father. As reliably as I can learn, my mother died the same year I was born, the year of our Lord 1587, the twenty-ninth of Queen Elizabeth's reign.
> The name I carried with me throughout my youth was attached to me, more or less accidentally, by Mistress MacGregor of the orphanage. I was placed in her care by some

*From *A Crow's Journey* by David Cunningham. Copyright © 1996 by David Cunningham. Reprinted by permission of Albert Whitman & Co.

neighbor. When she saw how small and frail I was, she exclaimed, "Och, the poor little pigwidgeon!" From that unfortunate expression came the appellation of Widge, which stuck to me for years, like pitch. It might have been worse, of course. They might have called me Pig. (p. 3)

As the author seeks closure for his character and the reader, he concludes his historical novel with these words:

For every *ken* and *wis* and *aye* I had dropped from my vocabulary, I had picked up a dozen new and useful terms. Some were fencing terms, some were peculiar to London, some were the jargon of the players' trade. But the ones that had made the most difference to me were the words I had heard before and never fully understood their import-words such as honesty and trust, loyalty and friendship.
And family.
And home. (pp. 215–216)[*]

Teach children to appreciate the last lines of books that bring resolution, satisfaction, and closure to the reader. Making the last sentence count leaves the reader with something about which to think. This type of model brings high standards to the young writer, but supplies varied techniques for responding to those expectations in his or her own writing.

***Expository writing.***     Informational books reflect the internal structure and organization of a second type of writing—expository writing (Freeman, 1991). Modeling begins with read-alouds and independent reading of informational books. Noting how information is organized through graphic organizers or outlines provides a visual framework for the delivery of information to the reader. A graphic organizer for Loretta Krupinski's *Into the Woods: A Woodland Scrapbook,* for example, begins with the topic of forest animals but radiates outward to include packages of information on forest birds, trees and seeds, wildflowers and mushrooms, and woodlore. Providing graphic organizers or data charts to assemble information obtained through expository reading prepares students for the research process and key organization of expository writing. Researching a topic and organizing details into tables, charts, or webs parallels preparing an outline for a writer as information is transmitted to the reader. Perhaps the trait of organization is the most important aspect of expository writing. Locating books that describe, sequence, compare and contrast, relate cause and effect, and propose problems and solutions are ideal candidates for models of quality expository writing.

Effective leads and concluding sentences carry the same importance in expository as in narrative writing. Seymour Simon begins and ends *The Heart: Our Circulatory System* with this opening and conclusion.

Make a fist. This is about the size of your heart. Sixty to one hundred times every minute your heart muscles squeeze together and push blood around your body through tubes called blood vessels. . . . The heart works hard when we relax or sleep and even harder when we work or exercise. It never stops for work or repair. The heart is a most incredible pump.

*From *The Shakespeare Stealer* by Gary Blackwood. Copyright © 1998. Reprinted by permission of Dutton Children's Books, a division of Penguin Putnam.

> Within each of us flows a river unlike any river on planet Earth. This river of blood flows past every part of the body on an incredible sixty-thousand mile voyage, enough to travel two and a half times around the world. It is as strange and wonderful as any journey to the stars.*

Other expository models to which student might respond through modeled writing include Carol Carrick's *Whaling Days* (problem–solution), Lynne Cherry's *A River Ran Wild* (cause–effect), Jean Craighead George's *Everglades* (description), and Laurence Pringle's *Fire in the Forest: A Cycle of Growth and Renewal* (sequence).

Pointing out organizational skills and strategies in both narrative and expository writing in the context of literature students have read and respect serves to inspire their own writing. The visual example and the application in the context of literature supplies the momentum for budding authors as they try their hands at the art of writing. A natural written response to immersion in quality literature with a focus on the writing craft is the utilization of the best techniques of honored children's authors in one's own writing.

## Voice

Voice is best described as the trait that leaves an the imprint of the author on a piece. As writers compose, they leave their distinctive fingerprints on their work through a commanding voice projected through their words. The read-aloud or independent reading model of locating literary examples exhibiting a strong element of voice is the most effective way of introducing this writing trait to perspective young authors. Personal voice is best practiced and identified through journal writing (i.e., literature response journals, character journals, personal journals). As young writers hear their own voices in their written words, they begin to carry that voice through to more formal writing assignments.

Locating the author's voice in quality literature is a simple task. If one is fortunate enough to have heard an author speak in person, you can almost hear that author's voice loud and clear as the words propel through your mind. Michael Dorris portrays nearsighted Walnut, who must compensate for his poor eyesight by developing an inner vision. Recognition of his special talent results in the awarding of the name *Sees Behind Trees*. Hear the character's and the author's voice reveling in this honor:

> Overnight I went from being myself to being a person who was expected to know things. I could feel people watching me, their glances like soft grass I walked through. I couldn't be sure, but I thought they were talking about me as well, about my special sight that was better than ordinary eyes, about how amazingly I had identified Gray Fire and how quickly I had found Diver's needle. I notice a difference in the way I was treated . . . how older cousins didn't laugh anymore when I greeted them by the wrong names until they got closer to me or when I stumbled on a log or bumped into a yard pole.*

*From *The Heart: Our Circulatory System* (n.p.). Text copyright © 1996 by Seymour Simon. Reprinted by permission of Morrow Junior Books.

*From *Sees Behind Trees* (p. 21) by Michael Dorris. Copyright © 1996. Reprinted by permission of Hyperion Books for Children.

Clarification of voice in informational writing becomes a simple task when comparing an encyclopedia entry on the Chicago fire with an opening excerpt from Jim Murphy's Newbery Honor book, *The Great Fire.*

> A shed attached to the barn was already engulfed in flames. . . . Fire ran along the dry grass and leaves, and took hold of a neighbor's fence. The heat from the burning barn, shed, and fence was so hot that the O'Leary's house, forty feet away, began to smolder. Neighbors rushed from their homes, many carrying buckets or pots of water. The sound of music and merrymaking stopped abruptly, replaced by the shout of "FIRE!" It would be a warning cry heard thousands of times during the next thirty-one hours.*

Although both examples would contain facts, dates, and details, the Murphy writing contains the author's voice filled with an overwhelming sense of the power and tenacity of this fire. The writing is lively, confident, honest, powerful, knowledgeable, and places the reader at the scene. The author's voice speaks directly to the audience, giving the reader an eyewitness account. The author's voice comes through in every word and the writing sounds different from the way anyone else would depict the event. Other titles in which authors' voices ring loud and clear include Avi's *The True Confessions of Charlotte Doyle* (first-person historical fiction), Robert Burleigh's *Flight: The Journey of Charles Lindbergh* (third person narrative), and Paul Fleischman's *Bull Run* (first-person historical fiction/multiple characters).

## Word Choice

Word choice can be described as the author's selection of precise words that clarify the message and paint pictures in the mind of the reader. Word choice is rich, sharp, vivid vocabulary that uses brisk, fresh adjectives, and sharp, energetic verbs to add momentum to the writing. While word choices increase the power of the author, they must remain natural, sensible, and meaningful. They are the words that make the reader say, "Aaah, that was a good way to say it!"

Teachers can naturally teach the art of word choice by pointing out exquisite examples ever present in literature read-alouds. Students can also be asked to be aware of effective word choice in their independent reading and take note in a writing notebook of "aaah" words collected from literature. Kevin Henkes presents a masterful example of simple, but effective word choice in his tale of a confident mouse who goes off to her first day of school. *Chrysanthemum* is ridiculed by her mouse peers because of her unusual name. As Victoria taunts her with demeaning statements, the author states "Chrysanthemum wilted." Aaah! As the story continues and her beautiful name is even considered for the music teacher's offspring, Henkes writes "She blushed. She beamed. She bloomed." Aaah! This simple example points out the power of the perfect word in one's writing.

Poetry and alphabet books, in particular, place an emphasis on word choice. *Listen to the Rain* (Martin & Archambault 1988) is a poem picture book which sets the stage for

---

*From *The Great Fire* (p. 15). Copyright © 1995 by Jim Murphy. Reprinted by permission of Scholastic, Inc.

the approaching and fleeting rainstorm. Listen to the word choice that captures this natural occurrence:

> Listen to the rain,
> the whisper of the rain,
> the slow soft sprinkle,
> the drip-drop tinkle,
> the first wet whisper of rain . . .
> Listen to the quietude,
> the silence and the solitude
> of after-rain,
> the dripping, dripping, dropping,
> the slowly, slowly stopping
> the fresh
>     wet
>        silent
>           after-time
>              of rain.*

Explore and savor the word choice and language that reminds the reader of the power of words. Not only are vocabularies enriched, but an awareness of the power of words is renewed.

Jerry Spinelli provides an example of snapshot writing in *Maniac Magee* that highlights the importance of detailed words in transmitting a description to the reader. Savor the rich word choices in this description of the infested kitchen.

> [He] had seen some amazing things in his lifetime, but nothing as amazing as that house. . . . Cans and bottles lay all over, along with crusts, peelings, cores, scraps, rinds, wrappers—everything you would normally find in a garbage can, and everywhere there were raisins. . . .
>
> Nothing could be worse than the living and dining rooms, yet the kitchen was. A jar of peanut butter had crashed to the floor; someone had gotten a running start, jumped into it, and skied a brown, one-footed track to the stove. On the table were what appeared to be the remains of an autopsy performed on a large bird, possibly a crow. The refrigerator contained two food groups: mustard and beer. The raisins here were even more abundant. He spotted several of them moving. They weren't raisins; They were roaches.*

Models like these provide excellent examples and inspire young writers to incorporate strong word choices as they compose. Perfect word choice doesn't just happen, particularly in a picture book where words are at a minimum. Nor does it happen in chapter books just because words are more plentiful. Word choice should be noted, valued, and applauded using quality literature as a model. Students will respond to this writing trait by using "aaah" words in their own writing. In fact, this is probably the trait to which they most easily respond and that most quickly flows into their own written work. A focus on word choice in a humorous format can be found in Cathi Hepworth's *ANTics* and *Bug Off!*

*From *Listen to the Rain*. Text copyright © 1988 by Bill Martin, Jr., and John Archambault. Reprinted by permission of Henry Holt.

*From *Maniac Magee*. Text copyright © 1990 by Jerry Spinelli. Reprinted by permission of Little, Brown and Company.

## Sentence Fluency

When writing is read aloud, sentence fluency becomes evident. Sentence fluency is the smooth rhythm and effortless flow of the words as they leap off the page into the mind of the reader. Sentence fluency evidences itself through variation in sentence length and the use of transitions between paragraphs, pages, or chapters. Sentence fluency clarifies, energizes, and condenses thoughts into a natural flow of ideas. When we say some titles like Avi's *Poppy* are meant to be read aloud, we are probably bringing the writing element of sentence fluency into focus.

Sentence length can vary from long and stretchy to short and snappy. Variety brings a read-aloud flow to writing. Gloria Houston uses this technique in *My Great Aunt Arizona* as she repetitively describes her dedicated teacher/aunt.

> Every year Arizona
> had a Christmas tree
> growing in a pot.
> The girls and boys made
> paper decorations
> to brighten up the tree.
> Then they planted their tree
> at the edge of the school yard,
> year after year,
> until the entire playground
> was lined with
> living Christmas trees,
> like soldiers guarding the room
> where Arizona taught,
> with her long gray braids
> wound 'round her head,
> with her long full dress,
> and pretty white apron,
> with her high-button shoes,
> and many petticoats, too.*

This title creates a joyful read-aloud. Response to this writing trait is often seen in young writer's attempts to vary sentence length. While their initial flow may be a bit awkward, they soon realize that sentence length variation takes planning to be an effective literary device.

Other aspects of sentence fluency might be varying sentence order and repetition of particular sentences. Smooth transitions between paragraphs is exemplified in Cherie Mason's *Wild Fox: A True Story*. The rhythm of writing forms an aspect of writing that can be identified in works by children's literature authors and applied in one's own writing. Once again, the literary model extends into the response mode as young authors incorporate these ideas into their own writing.

## Writing Conventions

Writing conventions include all of the things writers add to polish a piece of writing so the other five traits can be appreciated by the reader. In actuality, it is often editors who apply these finishing touches to a literary work. These include spelling, punctuation, mechanics, paragraphing, formatting, and printing. Examining a published page from a child's favorite book is an effective way for that child to realize how important these conventions are to the reader. While we take correctness for granted as readers, as writers we must work so conventions help clarify the writer's message. Once again, by looking to literature to model conventions, a young writer sees the importance of correctness and, in return, responds by polishing his or her own writing with professional conventions. Literature should not be used as drill and practice for inserting conventions in a page of a book. Pointing out and appreciating the use of punctuation in Chris Raschka's *Yo! Yes?*, for example, makes emergent writers more aware of conventions as a function of writing.

The more authentic literature that surrounds readers, the more writers will respond by applying new techniques and traits to their own quality writing. Teachers who point out the six traits in writing of children's authors and who focus on the author's craft alongside book discussion are likely to encourage stronger writing in their own young authors.

# CLOSING THOUGHTS

Response to literature can be evidenced in the impact of the literary craft on a child's own writing. Surrounding young authors with quality literature is probably the best way to help teach them the art of writing. Whether they hear literature through a read-aloud or experience it in their minds during independent reading, emergent writers, with the guidance of an aware teacher, note literary techniques and slowly emulate them in their own creative works. Young writers internalize writing through literature. Therefore, a child's own writing can be considered a cumulative response to the well-written literature that has surrounded him or her during a childhood of quality reading.

Only selected literature titles are meant to create authentic writing extensions. An overdose of writing extensions weakens the literary response and dishonors the literature. Used selectively and judiciously, well-planned writing extensions can be meaningful and create special literature memories. A growing awareness of children's literature and quality writing assist the teacher in making decisions that assist the young writer, rather than imposing restrictions on him or her.

Children's authors serve as role models for writing. Through biographies and autobiographies they share how ideas emerge, how their childhoods influenced their writing, and how hard work surrounds writing. Young authors begin to view writers as their friends as they familiarize themselves not only with their books, but also with characteristics of their writing.

Finally, providing writing models through literature reinforces the reading–writing connection. Because the processes of reading and writing exhibit many parallels, it is only reasonable to place literature at the center of both literary processes. While quality literature can motivate reading, it can also impact writing (Barksdale-Ladd & Nedeff, 1997). Children respond to literature by reading more, writing with more spirit and interest, and feeling growing pride in the impact of literacy in their lives.

# REFERENCES

Applebee, A. (1980). Children's narratives: New directions. *The Reading Teacher, 34,* 137–142.

Barksdale-Ladd, M. A., & Nedeff, A. R. (1997). The worlds of a reader's mind: Students as authors. *The Reading Teacher, 50,* 564–573.

Bromley, K. D. (1996). *Webbing with literature: Creating story maps with children's books.* Boston: Allyn & Bacon.

Dressel, J. H. (1990). The effects of listening to and discussing different qualities of literature on the narrative writing of fifth graders. *Research in the Teaching of English, 24,* 397–414.

Eckhoff, B. (1983). How reading affects children's writing. *Language Arts, 60,* 607–616.

Egawa, K. (1990). Harnessing the power of language: First graders' literature engagement with "Owl Moon". *Language Arts, 67,* 582–588.

Freeman, E. B. (1991). Informational books: Models for student report writing. *Language Arts, 68,* 470–473.

Golden, J. M. (1984). Children's concept of story in reading and writing. *The Reading Teacher, 37,* 578–584.

Hansen, J. (1987). *When writers read.* Portsmouth, NH: Heinemann.

Harwayne, S. (1992). *Lasting impressions: Weaving literature into the writing workshop.* Portsmouth, NH: Heinemann.

Heald-Taylor, G. (1987). How to use predictable books for K–2 language arts instruction. *The Reading Teacher, 40,* 656–661.

Jacobs, J. S., & Tunnel, M. O. (1996). *Children's literature, briefly.* Englewood Cliffs, NJ: Merrill/Prentice Hall.

Lancia, P. J. (1997). Literary borrowing: The effects of literature on children's writing. *The Reading Teacher, 50,* 470–475.

Peck, J., & Hendershot, J. (1997). Meet Officer Buckle and Gloria through their creator's own story. *The Reading Teacher, 50,* 404–408.

Rhodes, L. K. (1981). I can read! Predictable books as resources for reading and writing instruction. *The Reading Teacher, 34,* 511–518.

Sipe, L. R. (1993). Using transformations of traditional stories: Making the reading–writing connection. *The Reading Teacher, 47,* 18–26.

Spandel, V., & Stiggins, R. J. (1996). *Creating writers: Linking writing assessment and instruction* (2nd ed.). White Plains, NY: Longman.

Walmsley, S. A., & Walp, T. P. (1990). Integrating literature and composing into the language arts curriculum: Philosophy and practice. *The Elementary School Journal, 90,* 251–274.

# CHILDREN'S BOOKS CITED      [ P ] = K–2; [ I ] = 3–5; [ M ] = 6–8

Ahlberg, Janet, & Ahlberg, Allan (1986). *The jolly postman, or other people's letters.* Boston: Little, Brown. [ P/I ]

Albert, Burton (1993). *Where does the trail lead?* Illus. by Brian Pinkney. New York: Simon & Schuster. [ P/I ]

Avi (1990). *The true confessions of Charlotte Doyle.* New York: Orchard Books. [ M ]

Avi (1996). *Poppy.* New York: Orchard Books. [ I ]

Aylesworth, Jim (1996). *My sister's rusty bike.* Illus. by Richard Hull. New York: Atheneum. [ P/I ]

Bauer, Marion Dane (1986). *On my honor.* Boston: Houghton Mifflin. [ I ]

Bauer, Marion Dane (1994). *A question of trust.* Boston: Houghton Mifflin. [ I ]

Bauer, Marion Dane (1995). *A writer's story: From life to fiction.* Boston: Houghton Mifflin. [ I/M ]

Blackwood, Gary (1998). *The Shakespeare stealer*. New York: Dutton.

Blake, Robert (1993). *The perfect spot*. New York: Philomel Books. [ P/I ]

Boulton, Jane (Adapter) (1994). *Only Opal: The diary of a young girl*. Illus. by Barbara Cooney. New York: Philomel Books. [ I ]

Brown, Marcia (1947). *Goodnight moon*. New York: Harper & Row. [ P ]

Bunin, Sherry (1995). *Dear Great American Writers School*. Boston: Houghton Mifflin. [ M ]

Bunting, Eve (1991). *Fly away home*. Illus. by Ron Himler. Boston: Clarion. [ I ]

Burleigh, Robert (1991). *Flight: The journey of Charles Lindbergh*. Illus. by Mike Wimmer. New York: Philomel Books. [ I ]

Carle, Eric (1971). *The very hungry caterpillar*. New York: Crowell. [ P ]

Carrick, Carol (1993). *Whaling days*. Woodcuts by D. Frampton. Boston: Clarion. [ I ]

Cherry, Lynne (1992). *A river ran wild: An environmental history*. San Diego: Harcourt Brace. [ I/M ]

Cleary, Beverly (1983). *Dear Mr. Henshaw*. New York: Morrow. [ I ]

Creech, Sharon (1997). *Chasing redbird*. New York: HarperCollins. [ I ]

Cunningham, David (1996). *A Crow's journey*. Morton Grove, IL: Albert Whitman. [ P/I ]

de Paola, Tomie (1978). *Pancakes for breakfast*. San Diego: Harcourt Brace. [ P ]

Dorris, Michael (1996). *Sees behind trees*. New York: Hyperion. [ I/M ]

Fleischman, Paul (1993). *Bull run*. Woodcuts by David Frampton. New York: HarperCollins. [ I ]

Fleming, Denise (1991). *In the tall, tall grass*. New York: Holt. [ P ]

George, Jean Craighead (1995). *Everglades*. Illus. by Wendell Minor. New York: HarperCollins. [ I ]

George, Jean Craignead (1995). *To climb a waterfall*. Illus. by Thomas Locker. New York: Philomel Books. [ P/I ]

Henkes, Kevin (1992). *Chrysanthemum*. New York: Greenwillow. [ P ]

Hepworth, Cathi (1992). *ANTics! An alphabetical anthology*. New York: Putnam. [ I ]

Hepworth, Cathi (1998). *Bug off!* New York: Putnam. [ I ]

Hopkinson, Deborah (1997). *Birdie's lighthouse*. Illus. by Kimberly B. Root. New York: Atheneum. [ I ]

Houston, Gloria (1992). *My great Aunt Arizona*. Illus. by Susan Conde Lamb. New York: HarperCollins. [ I ]

Johnston, Tony (1992). *The cowboy and the black-eyed pea*. Illus. by Warren Ludwig. New York: Putnam. [ I ]

Krupinski, Loretta (1997). *Into the woods: A woodland scrapbook*. New York: HarperCollins. [ P/I ]

Lester, Helen (1997). *Author: A true story*. Boston: Houghton Mifflin. [ P/I ]

Locker, Thomas, & Christiansen, Candace (1998). *Home: A journey through America*. Illus. by Thomas Locker. San Diego: Silver Whistle/Harcourt Brace. [ I/M ]

Lowell, Susan (1992). *The three little javelinas*. Illus. by Jim Harris. New York: Scholastic. [ P/I ]

Lowell, Susan (1997). *The bootmaker and the elves*. Illus. by Tom Curry. New York: Orchard Books. [ P/I ]

Martin, Jr., Bill (1983). *Brown bear, brown bear, what do you see?* Illus. by Eric Carle. New York: Holt. [ P ]

Martin, Jr., Bill, & Archambault, John (1988). *Listen to the rain*. Illus. by J. Endicott. New York: Holt. [ P/I ]

Mason, Cherie (1993). *Wild fox: A true story*. Illus. by J. McAllister Stammen. Camden, ME: Down East. [ I ]

Murphy, Jim (1995). *The great fire*. New York: Scholastic. [ I/M ]

Paulsen, Gary (1992). *The haymeadow*. New York: Delacorte. [ I/M ]

Polacco, Patricia (1997). *In Enzo's splendid garden*. New York: Putnam. [ I ]

Pringle, Laurence (1995). *Fire in the forest: A cycle of growth and renewal*. Paintings by Bob Marstall. New York: Atheneum. [ I/M ]

Raschka, Chris (1993). *Yo! Yes?* New York: Orchard Books. [ P/I ]

Rylant, Cynthia (1982). *When I was young in the mountains*. Illus. by Diane Goode. New York: Dutton. [ I ]

Scieszka, Jon (1989). *The true story of the three little pigs*. Illus. by Lane Smith. New York: Viking. [ P/I ]

Scieszka, Jon (1991). *The frog prince continued*. Illus. by Lane Smith. New York: Viking. [ I ]

Scieszka, Jon (1992). *The stinky cheese man and other fairly stupid tales*. Illus. by Lane Smith. New York: Viking. [ I ]

Simon, Seymour (1996). *The heart: Our circulatory system*. New York: Morrow Junior Books. [ I ]

Soto, Gary (1993). *Too many tamales*. Illus. by J. Martinez. New York: Putnam. [ P/I ]

Spinelli, Jerry (1990). *Maniac Magee*. Boston: Little, Brown. [ I ]

Tollhurst, M. (1990). *Somebody and the three Blairs.* New York: Orchard Books. [ P/I ]

Van Allsburg, Chris (1984). *The mysteries of Harris Burdick.* Boston: Houghton Mifflin. [ I/M ]

Viorst, Judith (1981). *If I were in charge of the world and other worries.* New York: Atheneum. [ I ]

Ward, Lynd (1973). *The silver pony.* Boston: Houghton Mifflin. [ I ]

Wiesner, David (1991). *Tuesday.* Boston: Clarion. [ I ]

Willard, Nancy (1997). *The magic cornfield.* San Diego: Harcourt Brace. [ I ]

Williams, David (1993). *Grandma Essie's covered wagon.* Illus. by Wiktor Sadowski. New York: Knopf. [ I ]

Williams, Vera B., & Williams, Jennifer (1988). *Stringbean's trip to the shining sea.* New York: Greenwillow. [ I ]

Yolen, Jane (1987). *Owl moon.* Illus. by Jon Schoenherr. New York: Philomel Books. [ P ]

## Chapter 12

# Drama, Art, and Music
## *Expressive Arts as Response to Literature*

*F*irebird, *a story based on Igor Stravinsky's ballet, draws the reader into a mystical land of brilliant beauty and fairy tale romance. I fell in love with the illustrations. Across the room the book called to me from my seat to the chalkboard where you had placed it among other picture books. The cover illustration filled me with excitement, longing, familiarity, and regret all at once. As far back as I can remember I have always wanted to dance ballet. I pursued it for awhile and was even asked to study at a private school of arts. Lack of finances and courage kept me from going any further. Anything that has to do with the ballet sends me dreaming, remembering, spinning.*

*I was surprised when I read that the author was a former ballerina. The first time I read through the book, I read it silently to myself. It seemed like the text was outweighed by the impact of the illustrations. The second time I read the story, I added music in the background and read it aloud. Isadora's illustrations were so vibrant that they made me not only read the story, but their life and radiance made me dance the dance.*

Preservice Teacher's Response to
*Firebird* by Rachel Isadora

Dramatic, artistic, and musical responses to literature have often been reserved for enrichment and, hence, unfortunately experienced by only the most academically talented students. The ability to express oneself through dramatic presentation, artistic media, or musical prowess, however, is the preferred mode of response for many children. Integrating the expressive arts into the lives of all children through response to children's literature should be considered a natural part of the culture of childhood. Although the oral and written response to literature dominate research and practice in the area of literature-based instruction, the expressive modes of response offer endless possibilities for sharing personal response to children's books (Booth, 1985; Busching, 1981; Lamme, 1990). Drama, art, and music have just begun to be more extensively explored as channels and outlets for creative response to literature. As teachers of children with varied learning styles and expressive styles, we must keep our minds open to the stimulating possibilities of children's books that encourage personal response through the expressive arts.

# DRAMATIC RESPONSE

Dramatic response to literature emerges as performance and emotion blend into personal expression (McCaslin, 1990). This mode of response displays itself through dramatic movement, choral readings, readers' theater, puppetry, and plays. Children's literature must be read, listened to, and savored before any form of dramatic response can result. A child must feel a familiarity with the text, establish a kinship with characters, internalize the plot sequence, and develop a joy in the language and style before they can be expected to respond expressively. The lived through experience of repeated readings of the text prepares the performer for the task at hand. Literature of all genres inspires dramatic response but requires immersion, freedom to be oneself, and a growing sense of confidence before the dramatic response is shared. For younger children, dramatic response is spontaneous and unencumbered. A group of first graders spontaneously performed *Goldilocks and the Three Bears* following a reading of several versions of the classic tale. Older children prefer some time for informal rehearsal for collaborative efforts, but expression, not perfection, is always the priority of dramatic response.

## Movement and Dance as Dramatic Response

Preschool children possess a natural tendency to move in response to the invitations afforded by literature. Movement as response was identified by Hickman (1983) as a spontaneous response to read-alouds. Young listeners will find it hard to resist Jean Marzollo's invitation to become cats, bees, squirrels, or seals in *Pretend You're a Cat*. Each two-page spread reveals a rollicking verse and lively illustrations that feature a targeted animal and one or more children imitating it. Michael Rosen's *We're Going on a Bear Hunt* brings an old favorite to life as the sound of language demands movement to "swishy-swashy" and "splash-splosh." Ball bouncing, jump roping, swinging, and hide-and-seek games provide an international play experience through Jane Yolen's collection of *Street Rhymes Around the World*. A piece of colored string enhanced by an imagination changes Carole Schaefer's *The Squiggle* into a dragon, an acrobat, and a full moon through movement. This natural invitation and celebration of literature through movement builds a foundation for expanding dramatic response as the child grows in reading and performance ability.

Dance is a form of movement that may exhibit itself as response to literature. *Song and Dance,* a selection of poems by Lee Bennett Hopkins, invites young children to do-si-do to Beverly McLoughland's "Birds' Square Dance" and tap their toes to "From Lines Written for Gene Kelly to Dance To" by Carl Sandburg. Poems like "What is Jazz?" by Mary O'Neill and "Harlem Night Song" by Langston Hughes should be accompanied by the sound of music and dance. Older children skilled in dance may choose movement as a response to literature for *Let's Dance,* George Ancona's cultural tribute to dance.

Margot Fonteyn's *Coppelia* includes a copious endnote describing the original ballet that inspired her story. Music from the ballet by Leo Delibes might accompany a performance by talented dancers in the classroom or community. Dance needs to be included as an option for dramatic response, particularly for those children who find it a comfortable means of individual expression.

## Choral Reading

A simple, but effective outlet for dramatic response exists through the performance medium of choral reading (McCauley & McCauley, 1992). Poetry is the genre that naturally lends itself to this oral sharing of language, expression, and rhythm through dramatic response. Young children have a comfortable affinity toward verse, rhyme, riddles, and songs while older readers revel in the well-chosen language, varied moods, and succinctness of poetry. Just as each child responds to a poem in a unique way, so too does he or she share that unique response through the art of choral reading.

The choral reading response can be delivered in several ways. Choral reading can be orchestrated as individual performance, partner presentations, in small groups, or as a whole class. Stewig's (1981) suggested choral reading formats are discussed next.

***Echo reading.*** The leader reads each line and the group repeats it. This requires a simple, quiet poem where repetition breeds reflection. "Forest Secrets" from Constance Levy's *A Tree Place and Other Poems* lends itself to echo reading.

> The forest talks, /
> The forest sings, /
> Snapping twigs /
> Brushing wings. /
> Doves are cooing. /
> Owls are whooing. /
> But I can't see
> who's doing things. /
>
> The forest talks, /
> The forest sings. /
> The underbrush is
> Rustling
> from some small creature's feet, /

> Each line is read by a leader
> and echoed by the group.

I'm sure, /
But I can't find
The rustle-er. /

Secrets make good listening /
When forests talk, /
When forests sing. / *

***Paired reading.***    This mode of choral reading became particularly popular through Paul Fleischman's books, *I Am Phoenix* and *Joyful Noise: Poems for Two Voices,* which invite side-by-side reading by two readers. Children learn to appreciate the sounds, feelings, joy, and magic of poetry through this planned vocal expression experience. An excerpt from "Whirligig Beetles" reflects the magic of dual voices resounding the text.

| | |
|---|---|
| We're whirligig beetles | |
| we're swimming in circles, | We're whirligig beetles |
| black backs by the hundred. | we're swimming in circles, |
| | black backs by the hundred. |
| | We're spinning and swerving |
| We're spinning and swerving | as if we were on a |
| as if we were on a | mad merry-go-round. |
| mad merry-go-round. | |
| We never get dizzy | |
| from whirling and weaving | We never get dizzy |
| and wheeling and swirling. | from whirling and weaving |
| | and wheeling and swirling. . .* |

***Small group reading.***    The class divides and each group or individual within a group reads part of the poem. The repetition and simplicity of "Can I, Can I Catch the Wind" from Pat Mora's *Confetti* lends itself to this type of reading. Envision a group of seven students, each attaining ownership of a single line with all joining on the final answer to the repeated query.

Can I, can I catch the wind, in the morning, catch the wind?
Can I, can I catch the wind, in my two hands, catch the wind?
Can I, can I catch the wind, in my basket, catch the wind?
Can I, can I catch the wind, in my clay pot, catch the wind?
Can I, can I catch the wind, in my tin box, catch the wind?
Can I, can I catch the wind, in my straw hat, catch the wind?
Can I, can I catch the wind, in my bird cage, catch the wind?
Wind, Wind, run and spin, dance and spin, run and spin.*

***Cumulative reading.***     One student or group reads the first line or stanza as other students or groups join in with additional lines or stanzas. An entire class presentation can emerge from Rebecca Kai Dotlich's collection *Sweet Dreams of the Wild*. Each of 16 poems begins with a simple question that can be read by the whole group. The answer to the question can be prepared for presentation by an individual reader. The final line of each poem is the same and can be read by the entire group again. For example:

| | |
|---|---|
| Hummingbird, | Whole group |
| hummingbird, | |
| where do you sleep? | |
| | |
| I rest near the ivy | Individual reader |
| that hugs the wall, | |
| in a teacup-sized nest | |
| because I'm so small. | |
| High in a tree | |
| I weave a warm bed, | |
| with cattail fluff | |
| and cobweb threads. | |
| I cuddle up tight | Small group |
| with sweet dreams of the wild, | |
| and THAT's where I sleep, | |
| sleepy child!* | |

An opening and closing rhyme in this poetry collection enclose this special blend of read-aloud poems, which beg for choral performance by the entire class.

Children naturally warm to the humorous poetry of Shel Silverstein or Jack Prelutsky (Kutiper & Wilson, 1993). Their rhymed nonsense focuses on topics of children's everyday existence to create both personal interest and a need to share. Hear the voices and envision the expression of three students who each claim alternate lines of "Monday's Troll," the title poem from Prelutsky's collection of the same name. Listen to the last two lines as they all three voices join force in a final exclamation of humorous distaste:

> Monday's troll is mean and rotten,
> Tuesday's troll is misbegotten.
> Wednesday's troll is extra smelly,
> Thursday's has a baggy belly.
> Friday's troll is great and grimy,
> Saturday's is short and slimy—
> But Sunday's troll is crabby, cross,
> And full of sour applesauce.*

While humor is a welcome springboard for choral reading, other poetry warrants read-aloud response as well. Interdisciplinary units can address their themes through poetry as

*From *Sweet Dreams of the Wild*. Text copyright © 1996 by Rebecca Dotlich. Reprinted by permission of Wordsong/Boyds Mills Press.

choral reading journeys across the curriculum. For example, choral readings of poems about creatures of the ocean from Douglas Florian's *In the Swim* and Jane Yolen's *Sea Watch* might effectively be shared by partners to introduce research on sharks, seahorses, whales, or jellyfish.

Poetry provides the core of the material for choral reading as an isolated or integrated dramatic response activity. Easy to locate and fun for students to arrange and rehearse for presentation, poetry contributes a wealth of material for use in choral reading events. Chapter 5 contains a wealth of quality poetry books to enhance choral reading in the classroom. Not only will students improve oral expression, but their attitude toward the poetry genre is likely to grow stronger through positive group sharing.

## Readers' Theater

Readers' theater as a dramatic response mode provides an effective means to communicate the language of literature and the joy of reading. Readers' theater defines a presentation of text that is expressively and dramatically read aloud by two or more readers. While the primary emphasis is on reading aloud (as opposed to memorization, action, props, or costumes), the intent is for the readers to read expressively so that they paint an image of the events and actions in the minds of the audience (Bauer, 1987). While the words come from literature, the expressive response comes from inside the heart of the reader as he or she internalizes both characters and situation. A second-grade performance of Martin Waddell's *Owl Babies,* for example, yields concern, fear, and relief from a trio of baby owls as a mother owl leaves the nest to seek food for her growing family.

While intended to benefit the reader through smoother reading fluency, increased sight vocabulary, and improved comprehension, readers' theater as response to literature focuses on other outcomes as well (Laughlin & Latrobe, 1989). Expressiveness of oral reading and individual interpretation of text constitutes the core of personal response. Delivery, tone, pitch, and volume become components of expression as the reader strives to share the emotion of the text. Personal interpretation results in individual response as the meaning one derives from the text gives rise to the emotional effort behind the oral interpretation of text (Wolf, 1994).

Teacher-generated scripts provide a preliminary experience for initial efforts at readers' theater with personal expression emphasized as a response mode. A simple starting point for whole class response is Amy MacDonald's *Cousin Ruth's Tooth.* This humorous story follows the Fister family and friends as they seek a solution for the latest family crisis—a lost tooth. The search efforts of relatives, neighbors, and friends move at a rapid pace to the solution offered by the wise Queen. The text easily adapts into a script with minimal roles for about 20 students. The crisp, brief, and fast-paced text abounds with humorous characters and should be introduced as a read-aloud and reread and savored several times before a response performance. Characters are likely to match distinct classroom personalities to bring a read-aloud to life through readers' theater response. The opening portion of the adapted

*From "Monday's Troll" in *Monday's Troll* (p. 23). Text copyright © 1996 by Jack Prelutsky. Reprinted by permission of Greenwillow.

**FIGURE 12.1**   A readers' theater script

---

**Cousin Ruth's Tooth**

**Amy McDonald**
**Illus. by Marjorie Priceman**
**Houghton Mifflin, 1996**

**Adapted for a Readers' Theater**

| | |
|---|---|
| MRS. FISTER: | Rachel Fister, get your sister! |
| NARRATOR: | Mrs. Fister spread the word. |
| MRS. FISTER: | Cousin Ruth has lost a tooth! O, careless youth! It's too absurd. |
| RACHEL: | Never mind it! We shall find it! |
| | We will search both low and high. |
| RUTH: | Well . . . to tell the truth, I ............ |
| MRS. FISTER: | Hush, now darling, don't you cry |
| MR. FISTER: | Find your cousins,—several dozens— |
| | Get your uncles and your aunts. |
| RACHEL: | Bess! Matilda! . . . Olga! Zelda! . . . Mary Lee and Uncle Lance! |
| MR. FISTER: | Uncle Walter! Never falter. |
| | Search the cellar, check the roof. |
| MRS. FISTER: | Norma Jean and Aunt Bodine |
| | Go check the attic for the tooth. |
| BESS: | Search the yard and search the garden. |
| UNCLE LANCE: | Check the engine of the car. |
| MATILDA: | Check the hatbox. Check the catbox. |
| OLGA: | Look inside the VCR! |
| ZELDA: | Faster! Harder! Check the larder. |
| MARY LEE: | Check the pocket of your pants! |
| AUNT BEA: | Harder! Faster! Quelle disaster! |
| NARRATOR: | Said Aunt Bea, who'd been to France. |
| NARRATOR: | Though they searched in ways most ruthless, after days they still were . . . |
| ALL: | TOOTHLESS! |

*Consult the original book to continue text adaptation into Readers' Theater Script.
Text adaptation from *Cousin Ruth's Tooth* by Amy McDonald. Copyright © 1996. Adapted version reprinted with permission of Houghton Mifflin.

---

text for this rollicking readers' theater can be found in Figure 12.1. A similar romp might be created with MacDonald's earlier title, *Rachel Fister's Blister*.

Success in early ventures into readers theater are built on selection of quality literature that easily translate into script format. Characteristics of books that work with readers theater response include these:

- Books that are short in length so they can be shared in their entirety
- Books that follow a simple story line

- Books that have three or four main characters
- Books that contain ample dialogue.

*A Beautiful Feast for a Big King Cat* (Archambault & Martin, 1994) provides another scriptable text for a small group readers' theater response. A mischievous, bold mouse shielded by his protective mother challenges an arrogant cat. Mouse finds himself in the cat's clutches, but plays on the cat's ego to get released and return home safely. The portrayals of the teasing mouse, the arrogant cat, and the protective mother mouse provide for individual response through oral expression. Written entirely in rhymed text, repeated lines also lend the text to small group performance. Varied voices, rhyming text, and interesting characters make this a delightful avenue for response to a children's book.

Older children are capable of adapting books into scripts themselves. In this case, written script combines with expressive response through readers' theater. Picture books may provide a beginning resource at this level with performances shared with younger students. Shakespeare's *The Tempest* retold in picture book format by Ann Beneduce contains dialogue that easily transforms into a written script to present to upper grade audiences. After this simple scriptwriting modeling, students should be challenged to script specific portions of chapter books into a readers' theater format. The clever language and action of *The Whipping Boy* (Fleischman, 1986) provides several episodes for script adaptation. Because of its motivational value, readers' theater leads to more reading as the audience is inspired to read the original title while the performers seek other books by the same author.

The dramatic verbal portrayal through readers' theater aids comprehension and this seems to be particularly true through historical connections (Fennessey, 1995; Hancock, 1997). An adapted script of Ann Turner's *Katie's Trunk* is an outstanding example of helping children grasp the emotional upheaval of war. While Katie hides in her mother's trunk, her home is invaded by revolutionists. A former neighbor, now a part of the revolutionary mob, manages to turn the attention of his comrades away from the trunk as he announces the approaching Tories. The episode shared in the literature breathes life and reality into the divisions, opposing positions, and changes imposed by war. Paul Fleischman's *Bull Run* provides short first-person accounts of the first battle of the Civil War from the changing points of view of eager boys, a worried sister, a general, and a physician. Read aloud selectively and emotionally, the voices of the readers reflect the glory, horror, thrill, and disillusionment of war. This text provides a moving performance that enhances the depth and appreciation of the human perspective of this historical period.

Young and Vardell (1993) also suggest weaving readers' theater and the informational genre into the curriculum. While the response mode highlights readers' theater, the genre focus is nonfiction. Suggested titles include the Magic School Bus series, photo essays of Joan Anderson, and even science books by Seymour Simon. Because this material needs to be rescripted for readers' theater, much of the response lies in the creative, collaborative adaption of expository information to script format.

Primary students will savor the script of Robert Kalan's *Moving Day*, which shares the saga of a hermit crab's quest to find the perfect home. Even emergent readers will find the simple text to be quite readable achieving not only science concepts but reading confidence as well. A simple, readable script may also be created from Jez Alborough's *Watch Out! Big Bro's Coming* with dialogue well characterized in the context of the book itself. Intermediate students might choose a lighter prepared script from Suzy Kline's *Herbie Jones Readers Theater*. A more dramatic journey would include writing a script for Robert Burleigh's *Flight* for biographical insights into the young Charles Lindbergh's life. The informational genre invites creative challenges across the curriculum that can be met through dramatic response through readers' theater.

In any genre, literature must be the primary focus of the readers' theater response. Children must read the book or have it read aloud to them initially. Immersion in the story and personal interpretation of dialogue is mandatory if the readers' theater is built on genuine response. While scripting, assignment of roles, rehearsal, and staging are all important facets of readers' theater, its true success as response lies in the interpretive oral reading of literature. Within the freedom to express oneself through the character's words lies the repetitive strength of readers' theater as dramatic response to literature.

## Puppetry and Plays

Informal use of puppets in a retelling dramatization of literature provides another means of dramatic response to literature. Puppets provide a means for the inexperienced performer to restate a character's words and let his or her voice portray character traits (Flower & Fortney, 1983). The literature that fits so naturally with puppetry usually contains animal characters who can easily be portrayed through animal puppets. Whether the puppets are purchased furry delights or made from socks or cereal boxes, they provide a medium for dramatic oral response.

Martin Waddell's *Farmer Duck* (1991) provides ample animal characters for a story reenactment. Envision a lazy farmer surrounded by a hardworking duck supported by a cast of a cow, hens, and a sheep. A read-aloud of the story with children responding through the interaction and words of their puppets forms a unique response to literature. Verna Aardema's *Traveling to Tondo: A Tale of the Nkundo of Zaire* is well suited for paper plate masks or stick puppets as animal travelers en route to a wedding are delayed by a series of silly circumstances.

Any retellings of traditional tales, such as those by Paul Galdone, contain similar characters and stories that some children already know. Familiarity builds confidence through puppetry. Although children tell the story in their own words, some sense of story aids in their ability to articulate their thoughts in the guise of a puppet. Ed Young's *The Lost Horse* is actually a book and puppet set with intricate, jointed cut paper puppets of Sai, his son, and his horse. This simple story begs retelling with these magical puppets. Carlo Collodi's *Pinocchio* has been represented by Ed Young and formatted in theater scenes making it near ready for an intermediate-level student puppet performance.

Although a minimal number of quality plays have been published during the 1990s, a written play script provides a literary base for response (Manna, 1984). Dominic Catalano's *Frog Went A-Courting: A Musical Play in Six Acts* provides a familiar tale for performance. A brilliant cast of characters including Frog, Miss Mouse, Reverend Bug, and Madam Moth and brief, memorizable lines are accompanied by music to the well-

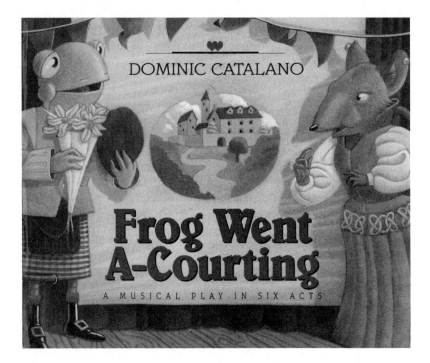

Dramatic and musical performance blend through Dominic Catalano's *Frog Went A-Courting*. *Illustration copyright © 1998 by* Dominic Catalano from *Frog Went A-Courting; A Musical Play in Six Acts by Dominic Catalano. Published by Boyds Mills Press, Inc. Reprinted by permission.*

known song. The dramatic/musical response combination would provide a commendable parent night performance.

The publishing of Gary Soto's *Navajo Boy* (1997) may rejuvenate an interest in play performances from literature for older students. This lighthearted play about the mixed joy and sorrow of young love in the Mexican American community will spark the response of middle-level students. Ann Hayes's *Onstage & Backstage at the Night Owl Theater* offers a behind-the-scenes look into the world of theater. Sources of quality literature in play format provide a solid option for dramatic response to literature.

Drama provides a valid avenue for response, particularly for students with whom oral performance is a comfortable response mode. Young children delight in movement response. Ranging from choral reading and readers' theater to puppet and play performances, children of all ages are invited to express their individuality in the guise of animal or human characters emerging from literature. At the core of these dramatic response modes lies quality literature that supplies the words, emotions, characters, and situations that call for this unique interaction with literature.

# ARTISTIC RESPONSE TO LITERATURE

Art provides an interesting means for readers to respond to the books they read (Hickman, 1983). Art as response can also spring from illustrator studies, art extensions from literature, and the relationship of art elements to children's book illustrations. The responder does not need to be artistically talented to use art as a means of expression. The artistic response to literature may arise as a response to text, to illustrations, to a poem, or even to an art element such as line, space, or color. While interdisciplinary in nature, the artistic response provides variety in response modes to readers who feel and express themselves through pictures as comfortably as others do through words.

## Extending Response Through Art

The primary means to utilize the artistic mode of response in the classroom lies in art enhancement activities suggested by the teacher. These activities must lie within the literature itself rather than being artificially attached to a book. For example, Diana Pomeroy's *One Potato* and *Wildflower ABC* books illustrate various colorful quantities of vegetables and wildflowers with potato prints. A natural, yet authentic extension includes potato prints presented in counting patterns or ABC shapes. The final two pages of the books actually inform adults about how Pomeroy's prints were completed, suggesting the same procedure for children. Another example is Molly Bang's illustrations in *Red Dragonfly on My Shoulder* with three-dimensional collage enhancing a book of translated haiku. Screws, safety pins, feathers, keys, clothespins, and chocolate-covered almonds provide inspiration for a related art activity. Art extensions are misused in the classroom context if they are distanced from the book itself. The artistic mode of response appears undervalued because of its overuse in unnatural connections to literature. Many titles provide valid art enhancements that extend the message and memory of the reading experience.

In classrooms in which choice is a foundation of response, art can be a medium for extending response to literature. Murals, dioramas, collages, and related art formats can provide a means of expression as response to information, plot, or character. A prairie diorama of *Sarah, Plain and Tall*, a mural of the journey West recorded in response to the journal entries of Amelia Knight in *The Way West*, or a series of character sketches for Pam Conrad's *Prairie Songs* are all appropriate and valued choices for response. It is important to remember that when the medium of art is the student's choice for a response mode, the authentic self-selected response is typically more meaningful than a teacher-assigned art extension.

Recent research points to the value of artistic response for young children (Hubbard, 1996; Madura, 1995). Although written expression is difficult for emerging readers and writers, children can readily share personal connections through drawings. Visual representation as a language art has been reinforced by professional standards (National Council of Teachers of English, 1996) and should be encouraged and respected as a mode of response for children of any age.

## Connecting Art Elements and Response

The high quality of artwork represented by the works of children's book illustrators deserves and demands attention and response. Art teachers are beginning to turn toward award-winning illustrators to teach art elements. As studies of an illustrator's works are displayed and their stories read to the children, elements of art are showcased and discussed. A directed response to the illustration as a valued component of literature can be designed to incorporate the art element in a student-created work. The illustrator's work of art serves as a model for response through a child's own application of an element of art. The following examples from an art teacher's lesson plans point out the connection between art elements and artistic response across grade levels.

An elementary art teacher analyzed the media, techniques, and styles of a variety of illustrators for children's books and developed an art lesson for each illustrator selected. Selection of illustrators was based on the unique and diverse characteristics of his or her work. Lessons were developed that allowed each child to identify an illustrator's use of basic art concepts. Students were asked to create their own piece of artwork in response to the characteristics and treatment of art concepts as the illustrator being studied. Figure 12.2 lists illustrators and art concepts across grade levels. These art element connections provide masters of children's illustration as models for artistic response. Several books from each illustrator should be read and revisited to further reinforce the model. Viewing videos of artists' techniques (Eric Carle, Patricia Polacco) can further enhance the art value of these lessons.

These art element connections invite reading of text and studying of illustrations before artistic response is expressed. The effective connections between literature, illustrations, and artistic response are evident in these examples. Illustrator studies enhanced by a focus on specific art characteristics bring an awareness of the power of art to the picture book. The artistic response to the art of the picture book brings individual interpretation of art forms to life. Children learn more about observation of art and become keener in their encounters with illustration.

## Response to Books About Art and Artists

Language and art intertwine as response modes as children explore books in which art is creatively shared. The oral response to art is natural as children browse through books like *A Child's Book of Play in Art, Horses: Looking at Paintings,* and the many titles from Rizzoli Publications including *Who Has Seen the Wind?,* a blend of art chosen as response to poetry. These books are meant to be visually cherished and the natural verbal response of the child to the artwork should be noted. Individualized responses resulting from small group encounters with these titles foster particularly rich comments and insights.

Children's books also encourage budding artists. Tomie de Paola's *The Art Lesson* (1989) humorously reveals the famed illustrator's own dreams and aspirations of being an artist during his early school experiences. In *Regina's Big Mistake* (Moss, 1990) a misplaced mark on one piece of paper becomes a creative and original drawing. Yang Wani, a Chinese girl who started painting at age three, stands as an inspiration in *A Young Painter* (Zhensun & Low, 1991). Even in *Bonjour, Mr. Satie* (de Paola, 1991) a world traveling cat brings home

**FIGURE 12.2** Art elements and response

---

### Grade 1: Leo Lionni

Lesson focus: Lionni's mice collage
Media: Torn/cut paper
Art Concepts: Collage; overlapping; paper techniques and usage
Illustrator Models:

> Lionni, Leo (1967). *Frederick.* New York: Pantheon.
> Lionni, Leo (1969). *Alexander and the wind-up mouse.* New York: Pantheon.
> Lionni, Leo (1971). *Theodore and the talking mushroom.* New York: Pantheon.
> Lionni, Leo (1981). *Mouse days.* New York: Pantheon.
> Lionni, Leo (1992). *Mr. McMouse.* New York: Knopf.

### Grade 2: Eric Carle

Lesson focus: Carle's animal train using simple shapes
Media: Painted paper/tissue paper
Art concepts: Mixed media; using shapes to create form; texture
Illustrator models:

> Carle, Eric (1968). *1, 2, 3, to the zoo.* New York: Philomel Books.
> Carle, Eric (1971). *Do you want to be my friend?* New York: Crowell/HarperCollins.
> Carle, Eric (1987). *Have you seen my cat?* New York: Picture Book Studio/Simon & Schuster.
> Carle, Eric (1989). *Animals, animals.* New York: Philomel Books.

### Grade 3: Paul Goble

Lesson focus: Goble's Native American teepee with skies showing value
Media: Crayons/watercolors
Art concepts: Color value; tint and shade; patterns
Illustrator models:

> Goble, Paul (1983). *Star boy.* New York: Bradbury Press.
> Goble, Paul (1988). *Her seven brothers.* New York: Bradbury Press.
> Goble, Paul (1990). *Dream wolf.* New York: Bradbury Press.
> Goble, Paul (1992). *Love flute.* New York: Bradbury Press.

### Grade 4: Peter Parnall

Lesson focus: Parnall's trees
Media: Pencil/colored pencil
Art concepts: Lines; linear quality; contour; restricted palette
Illustrator models:

> Baylor, Bird (1986). *I'm in charge of celebrations.* Illus. by Peter Parnall. New York: Scribner's.
> Parnall, Peter (1988). *Apple tree.* New York: Macmillan.
> Parnall, Peter (1990). *Woodpile.* New York: Macmillan.
> Parnall, Peter (1991). *The rock.* New York: Macmillan.

**FIGURE 12.2**   Art elements and response *(continued)*

---

**Grade 5: Patricia Polacco**

Lesson focus: Polacco's people
Media: Pencil/colored pencil/marker
Art concepts: Contrasting elements; facial proportions; pattern repetition
Illustrator models:
    Polacco, Patricia (1988). *Rechenka's eggs.* New York: Philomel Books.
    Polacco, Patricia (1990). *Babushka's doll.* New York: Simon & Schuster.
    Polacco, Patricia (1990). *Thunder cake.* New York: Philomel Books.
    Polacco, Patricia (1992). *Mrs. Katz and Tush.* New York: Philomel Books.

**Grades 6/7/8: Jerry Pinkney**

Lesson focus: Pinkney's watercolor flowers
Media: Watercolor
Art concepts: Watercolor techniques—transparent overlays; light to dark
Illustrator models:
    Carlstrom, Nancy (1987). *Wild wild sunflower child Anna.* Illus. by Jerry Pinkney. New York: Macmillan.
    Lester, Julius (1988). *More tales of Uncle Remus.* Illus. by Jerry Pinkney. New York: Dial Books.
    McKissack, Patricia (1988). *Mirandy and Brother Wind.* Illus. by Jerry Pinkney. New York: Knopf.
    Pinkney, Gloria (1992). *Back home.* Illus. by Jerry Pinkney. New York: Dial Books.

---

art supplies to his niece and nephew who proudly draw pictures built on their uncle's tales of Pablo and Henri.

Furthermore, children can meet the artists through series books on masters of the art world. The First Impression series offers the success of Rembrandt, Chagall, and da Vinci while the Getting to Know the World's Greatest Artists series traces the lives of Monet, van Gogh, and Picasso. Imagine spending time with Auguste Renoir accompanying him on a walk down the Seine, on a ride to the French countryside, and lunching in a riverside town. *A Weekend with Renoir* and other titles in this first-person artist series brings the masters to life by virtually having the artist talk to the reader.

Artistic fantasy focuses imaginatively on the world of art. Journey with *Linnea in Monet's Garden* as illustrations, photographs, and reprints of authentic Monet paintings guide us through the garden at Giverny. Reproductions of Bosch's original works will enhance Nancy Willard's *Pish, Posh Said Hieronymus Bosch*, the tale of a housekeeper driven wild by this 15th-century artist. Take a stroll through the National Gallery of Art in Washington, D.C., as *The Girl with a Watering Can* exits her famed Renoir frame and mischievously creates unexpected trouble with 10 famous paintings in the museum collection. Verbal links between the stories and reproduction of paintings of the masters encourage interesting response links between literature and art.

Children's books do foster the artistic response in a variety of ways and play a special role in encouraging this mode of response. Whether the response is creating art, the appreciation of world-renowned art, or the reaction to artists and their work, art is a treasured medium of response for children of all ages and talents. Georgia O'Keefe stated, "I found I could say things with color and shapes that I couldn't say in any other way—things I had no words for". Teachers are encouraged to value and honor the artistic response to literature because it may provide the most expressive means of reader response for many children.

# MUSIC AS A RESPONSE TO LITERATURE

Musical response to literature exhibits itself in a variety of guises. Musical response may include singing the lyrics/text of a book, accompanying the reading of a book with musical instruments, selecting music as background for a read-aloud, or celebrating the life of musicians by listening to and appreciating their music. Music tends to be an interdisciplinary response across literary genres as related topics range from showtunes to spirituals, from mountain music to childhood songs, from Mozart to a homemade string band. Exploring these musical avenues for response opens a new venue of books and response activities to children and teachers.

## Sing a Song

A wealth of picture books utilize song lyrics as text (Lamme, 1979, 1990). The rhyming lyrics tell delightful stories and naturally invite reader response through song. Musical response, however, needn't be reserved for music time since music serves as a mode of expression that can be shared across the curriculum. Response is natural, but not perfect, so a few flat notes shouldn't discourage a teacher from encouraging children to break out in song. *A Real Nice Clambake* captures the music of Richard Rogers and the lyrics of Oscar Hammerstein II as family and friends gather on a New England beach to savor the wonderful clambake foods. "Our hearts are warm/Our bellies are full/And we are feelin' prime. This was a real nice clambake/and we all had a real good time." The musical score is included, but the words are meant for singing either on or off key.

On a more serious note, Jeanette Winter's *Follow the Drinking Gourd* provides a connection to the subject of slavery and the underground railroad. The lyrics of the simple folk song, sung by slaves, carries the directions north to freedom. While the words powerfully stand alone, the slow drone of the music tells of the long, tired struggle of the slaves for freedom. Accompanying the book is the music that begs to be played and sung for an even richer understanding of the plight of slavery. The words and music appear on the endpapers of Floyd Cooper's *Cumbayah* while the inspired art of Chris Raschka and musical accompaniment represents the Shaker hymn, *Simple Gifts*. Most music teachers welcome an opportunity to integrate lessons with the classroom teacher, so teachers should take the initiative to communicate their requests.

Integrating books like these into the curriculum and planning for musical response can only enhance a topic of study. Other titles stand alone as sound literature with the natural response link to music. A literature-based music teacher will be alert to these titles and be ready to collaborate with the classroom teacher. But the classroom teacher does not need to wait for a music teacher to elicit musical response. Opening this avenue of response to literature reaches a special group of talented students who may resist other response modes while welcoming music.

## Surround Literature With Music

Several books beg to be accompanied by music. Imagine Rimski-Korsakov's "The Flight of the Bumblebee" playing quietly behind the read-aloud of Jan Brett's *Berlioz the Bear*. Listen to the overture from Rossini's opera to accompany Leonard Everett Fisher's *William Tell*. Hear Beethoven's *Rondo in C* echo behind the words of Paul Fleischman's book of the same name. Revel in Madam Butterfly as the opera accompanies *The Bear Who Loved Puccini*. The musical mode of reader response exhibits itself not through musical performance, but through the thoughts inspired by the blend of text and music. Whether those thoughts are kept private or shared orally, they often result in the desire to listen to the musical work repeatedly, to learn more about a musician's life, or to recognize or introduce classical music.

Fictionalized biographies of musicians call for an introduction to their creations through their music. Accompanying the reading of these books with the well-known music of the composers connects literature and music effectively. Mozart, for example, may be introduced through *Mozart: Scenes from the Childhood of a Great Composer* or *Wolferl*, which covers the first 6 years of Mozart's life. Handel's Messiah may accompany Bryna Stevens' *Handel and the Famous Sword Swallower of Halle*, while the tones of opera radiate against the backdrop of Leontyne Price's *Aida*.

Children also are profoundly talented at selecting music to accompany books they may be reading. A media specialist helped children locate music to supplement *The Maestro Plays* by Bill Martin, Jr., as the sounds were recorded on CD-ROM to blend with the text of this piece of children's literature. Bill Martin and John Archambault's love of language emerges in *Barn Dance!*, which invites children to add the sound effects of a square dance music background and sing refrains. Anne Hayes's *Meet the Orchestra* has animals introducing various instruments as the orchestra warms up for a performance led by the king of the jungle. Older students could easily identify and play appropriate music to highlight each instrument and select a symphonic melody for the jungle performance. Insert the sounds of instruments throughout Lionel Le Neouanic's *Long live music!*, the tale of a giant who plans to stop all music from playing. Musical sounds strategically placed will bring this unusual history of music to life. Some popular chapter books might deserve musical background during some of their most intense moments. Just as movies are backed by well-composed scores, read-alouds might be enhanced by locating appropriate music to accompany dramatic episodes in favorite chapter books.

Another option for musical response to literature is to place the instruments, handmade or homemade, into the hands of the children as they respond in accompaniment to the story. Besides the Birdseyes' sharing of a new version of an old favorite in *She'll Be Comin' Round the Mountain*, this book invites musical participation with instruments suggested by the illustrations. Fiddles, spoons, guitars, and banjos provide the background sounds to turn this participatory read-aloud into a memorable musical response experience. The same instruments can accompany *Granny Will Your Dog Bite and Other Mountain Rhymes*. The African American spiritual is showcased in *All Night, All Day* by Ashley Bryan and in *Shake It to the One That You Love the Best* by Cheryl Mattox, which both contain musical accompaniments. You can almost hear Art Flowers' *Cleveland Lee's Beale Street Band* and the jazz of Alan Schroeders' *Satchmo's Blues* as instruments reveal the music of Memphis and New Orleans jazz. Music as an accompaniment for literature provides another illustration of how music, literature, and response form a complementary blend in exposing and motivating children through the music that carries an expressive language of its own.

# CLOSING THOUGHTS

The expressive modes of response through dramatic, artistic, and musical performance can be easily overshadowed by the consistent use of oral language and writing as the dominant reader response modes. To attain a balance in reader response to literature and to address the needs of all types of learners, the dramatic, artistic, and musical response must be invited, offered, and celebrated as a valuable response option. Just as emotions are captured through words for some learners, others find expression in the performance media. A classroom that encourages choice and exploration of a variety of response modes is more likely to create lifelong readers.

To reach children with varying expressive talents, teachers need to design literature experiences that open the door to performance response through drama, art, and music. Those who feel less talented in these areas should enlist the help of art, music, or drama teachers to build confidence and comfort in the joy these responses bring to children. Taking advantage of the wealth of books that naturally extend themselves into these response modes will assist in reaching all children in a cross-curricular context. Teachers are encouraged to open their minds to the unlimited possibilities of children's books that celebrate involvement in literature through the fine arts.

# REFERENCES

Bauer, C. (1987). *Presenting readers theater.* New York: Wilson.

Booth, D. (1985). "Imaginary gardens with real toads?": Reading and drama in education. *Theory Into Practice, 24,* 193–198.

Busching, B. A. (1981). Readers theatre: An education for language and life. *Language Arts, 58,* 330–338.

Fennessey, S. (1995). Living history through drama and literature. *The Reading Teacher, 49,* 16–19.

Flower, C., & Fortney, A. (1983). *Puppets—methods and materials.* New York: Davis.

Hancock, M. R. (1997). Another time, another place: Bringing social studies to life through literature. In P. J. Farris & S. Cooper (Eds.), *Elementary and middle school social studies: A whole language approach* (2nd ed., pp. 121–150). Madison, WI: Brown-Benchmark.

Hickman, J. (1983). Everything considered: Response to literature in an elementary school setting. *Journal of Research and Development in Education, 16,* 8–13.

Hubbard, R. S. (1996). Visual responses to literature: Imagination through images. *The New Advocate, 9,* 309–323.

Kutiper, K., & Wilson, P. (1993). Updating poetry preferences: A look at the poetry children really like. *The Reading Teacher, 47,* 28–35.

Lamme, L. L. (1979). Song picture books: A maturing genre of children's literature. *Language Arts, 56,* 400–407.

Lamme, L. L. (1990). Exploring the world of music through picture books. *The Reading Teacher, 44,* 294–300.

Laughlin, M. K., & Latrobe, K. H. (1989). *Readers theatre for children: Scripts and script development.* Englewood, CO: Libraries Unlimited.

Madura, S. (1995). The line and texture of aesthetic response: Primary children study authors and illustrators. *The Reading Teacher, 49,* 110–118.

Manna, A. (1984). Making language come alive through reading plays. *The Reading Teacher, 37,* 712–717.

McCaslin, N. (1990). *Creative drama in the classroom* (5th ed.). New York: Longman.

McCauley, J. K., & McCauley, D. S. (1992). Using choral reading to promote language learning for ESL students. *The Reading Teacher, 45,* 526–533.

National Council of Teachers of English and International Reading Association. (1996). *Standards for the English language arts* (p. 25). Urbana, IL, and Newark, DE: Author.

Stewig, J. (1981). Choral speaking: Who has the time? Why take the time? *Childhood Education, 57,* 25–29.

Wolf, S. A. (1994). Learning to act/acting to learn: Children as actors, critics, and characters in classroom theatre. *Research in the Teaching of English, 28,* 7–44.

Young, T. A., & Vardell, S. (1993). Weaving readers theatre and nonfiction into the curriculum. *The Reading Teacher, 46,* 396–406.

# CHILDREN'S BOOKS CITED   [ P ] = K–2; [ I ] = 3–5; [ M ] = 6–8

Aardema, Verna (1991). *Traveling to Tondo: A tale of the Nkundo of Zaire.* Illus. by Will Hillenbrand. New York: Knopf. [ P/I ]

Alborough, Jez (1997). *Watch out! Big Bro's coming!* Cambridge, MA: Candlewick Press. [ P ]

Ancona, George (1998). *Let's dance.* New York: Morrow. [ P/I ]

Archambault, John, & Martin, Jr., Bill (1994). *A beautiful feast for a big king cat.* Illus. by Bruce Degen. New York: HarperCollins. [ P ]

Beneduce, Ann Keay (Reteller) (1996). *William Shakespeare The Tempest.* Illus. by Gennady Spirin. New York: Philomel Books. [ I/M ]

Birdseye, Tom, & Birdseye, Debbie (1994). *She'll be comin' round the mountain.* Illus. by Andrew Glass. New York: Holiday House. [ P/I ]

Bjork, Christina (1987). *Linnea in Monet's garden.* Illus. by Lena Anderson. New York: R & S Books. [ I ]

Brett, Jan (1991). *Berlioz the bear.* New York: Putnam. [ P ]

Brighton, Catherine (1990). *Mozart: Scenes from the childhood of a great composer.* New York: Doubleday. [ P/I ]

Bryan, Ashley (1991). *All night, all day: A child's first book of African-American spirituals.* Musical arrangement by David Manning Thomas. New York: Atheneum. [ P/I ]

Burleigh, Robert (1991). *Flight: The journey of Charles Lindbergh.* Illus. by Mike Wimmer. New York: Philomel Books. [ I/M ]

Cassedy, Sylvia, & Suetake, Kunihiro (1992). *Red dragonfly on my shoulder.* Illus. by Molly Bang. New York: HarperCollins. [ I/M ]

Catalano, Dominic (1998). *Frog went a-courting: A musical play in six acts.* Honesdale, PA: Boyds Mills Press. [ P ]

Collodi, C. (1996). *Pinocchio.* Adapted and illustrated by Ed Young. New York: Philomel Books. [ I/M ]

Conrad, Pam (1985). *Prairie songs.* New York: HarperCollins. [ I ]

Cooper, Floyd (1998). *Cumbayah.* New York: Morrow. [ P/I ]

de Paola, Tomie (1989). *The art lesson.* New York: Putnam. [ P ]

de Paola, Tomie (1991). *Bonjour, Mr. Satie.* New York: Putnam. [ I/M ]

Dotlich, Rebecca K. (1996). *Sweet dreams of the wild.* Honesdale, PA: Wordsong/Boyds Mills Press. [ P ]

Fisher, Leonard Everett (1996). *William Tell.* New York: Farrar, Straus and Giroux. [ I ]

Fleischman, Paul (1993). *Bull run.* Woodcuts by David Frampton. New York: HarperCollins. [ I/M ]

Fleischman, Paul (1985). *I am Phoenix: Poems for two voices.* Illus. by K. Nutt. New York: Harper & Row. [ I/M ]

Fleischman, Paul (1988). *Joyful noise: Poems for two voices.* Illus. by E. Beddows. New York: Harper & Row. [ I/M ]

Fleischman, Paul (1988). *Rondo in C.* Illus. by Janet Wentworth. New York: Harper & Row. [ P/I ]

Fleischman, Sid (1986). *The whipping boy.* Illus. by Peter Sis. New York: Greenwillow. [ I ]

Florian, Douglas (1997). *In the swim.* Paintings by Doug Florian. San Diego: Harcourt Brace. [ I/M ]

Flowers, Art (1996). *Cleveland Lee's Beale Street band.* Illus. by Anna Rich. Mahwah, NJ: Bridge Water Books. [ P ]

Fonteyn, Margot (1998). *Coppelia.* Paintings by Steve Johnson & Lou Fancher. San Diego: Gulliver Books/Harcourt Brace. [ I ]

Hayes, Anne (1991). *Meet the orchestra.* Illus. by Karmen Thompson. San Diego: Harcourt Brace. [ P ]

Hayes, Ann (1997). *Onstage & backstage at the Night Owl Theater.* Illus. by Karmen Thompson. San Diego: Harcourt Brace. [ I ]

Hopkins, Lee Bennett (1997). *Song and dance.* New York: Simon & Schuster. [ P ]

Isadora, Rachel (1994). *Firebird.* New York: Putnam. [ P/I ]

Kalan, Robert (1996). *Moving day.* Illus. by Y. Abolafia. New York: Greenwillow. [ P ]

Kline, Suzy (1992). *Herbie Jones readers theater.* New York: Putnam. [ I ]

Knight, Amelia Stewart (1993). *The way west.* Illus. by Michael McCurdy. New York: Simon & Schuster. [ I ]

Levy, Constance (1994). *A tree place and other poems.* Illus. by Robert Sabuda. New York: McElderry Books. [ I ]

MacDonald, Amy (1996). *Cousin Ruth's tooth.* Illus. by M. Priceman. Boston: Houghton Mifflin. [ I ]

MacDonald, Amy (1990). *Rachel Fister's blister.* Illus. by Marjorie Priceman. Boston: Houghton Mifflin. [ I ]

MacLachlan, Patricia (1985). *Sarah, plain and tall.* New York: Harper. [ P/I ]

Martin, Jr., Bill, & John Archambault (1986). *Barn dance!* Illus. by Ted Rand. New York: Holt. [ P/I ]

Marzollo, Jean (1990). *Pretend you're a cat.* Illus. by J. Pinkney. New York: Dial. [ P ]

Mattox, Cheryl Warren (1989). *Shake it to the one that you love the best: Play songs and lullabies from black musical traditions.* Nashville, TN: JTG. [ P/I ]

Micklethwait, Lucy (1996). *A child's book of play in art.* New York: Dorling Kindersley. [ P/I ]

Milnes, Gerald (1990). *Granny will your dog bite and other mountain rhymes.* Illus. by K. B. Root. New York: Knopf. [ P/I ]

Mora, Pat (1996). *Confetti: Poems for children.* Illus. by Enrique O. Sanchez. New York: Lee & Low Books. [ P/I ]

Moss, Marisa (1990). *Regina's big mistake.* Boston: Houghton Mifflin. [ P ]

Pomeroy, Diane (1996). *One potato.* San Diego: Harcourt Brace. [ P ]

Pomeroy, Diane (1997). *Wildflower ABC.* San Diego: Harcourt Brace. [ P ]

Prelutsky, Jack (1996). *Monday's troll.* Illus. by Peter Sis. New York: Greenwillow. [ P/I ]

Price, Leontyne (1990). *Aida.* Illus. by Leo & Diane Dillon. San Diego: Harcourt Brace. [ I/M ]

Raschka, Chris (1998). *Simple gifts.* New York: Holt. [ P/I ]

Roalf, Peggy (1992). *Horses: Looking at paintings.* (Looking at Paintings series). New York: Hyperion. [ I/M ]

Rosen, Michael (1989). *We're going on a bear hunt.* Illus. by Helen Oxenbury. New York: McElderry Books. [ P ]

Schaefer, Carole Lexa (1996). *The squiggle.* Illus. by Pierre Morgan. New York: Crown. [ P ]

Schroeder, Alan (1996). Satchmo's blues. Illus. by Floyd Cooper. New York: Doubleday. [ I ]

Schwartz, Gary (1992). *Rembrandt.* (First Impression series). New York: Abrams. [ I/M ]

Skira-Venturi, Rosabianca (1990). *A weekend with Renoir.* (A Weekend with Artists series). Boston: Rizzoli. [ I/M ]

Soto, Gary (1997). *Navajo boy: A play.* San Diego: Harcourt Brace. [ M ]

Stevens, Bryna (1990). *Handel and the famous sword swallower of Halle.* Illus. by Ruth Councell. New York: Philomel Books. [ I ]

Sungaard, Arnold (1992). *The bear who loved Puccini.* Illus. by D. Catalano. New York: Putnam. [ P/I ]

Turner, Ann (1992). *Katie's trunk.* Illus. by Ron Himler. New York: Macmillan. [ I ]

Turner, Robyn M. (1991). *Georgia O'Keefe* (Portrait of Women Artists for Children series). Boston: Little, Brown. [ I/M ]

Venezia, Mike (1990). *Monet* (Getting to Know the World's Greatest Artists series). Danbury, CT: Children's Press. [ I/M ]

Waddell, Martin (1991). *Farmer duck.* New York: Candlewick Press. [ P ]

Waddell, Martin (1992). *Owl babies.* Illus. by Patrick Benson. New York: Candlewick Press. [ P ]

Weil, Lisl (1991). *Wolferl: The first six years in the life of Wolfgang Amadeus Mozart, 1756–1762.* New York: Holiday House. [ P/I ]

Westcott, Nadine Bernard (1992). *A real nice clambake.* Boston: Little, Brown. [ P/I ]

*Who has seen the wind?* (1990). An illustrated collection of poetry for young people. Boston: Rizolli. [ P/I ]

Willard, Nancy (1991). *Pish, posh, said Hieronymus Bosch.* Illus. by Leo & Diane Dillon. San Diego: Harcourt Brace. [ I/M ]

Winter, Jeanette (1988). *Follow the drinking gourd.* New York: Knopf. [ I/M ]

Yolen, Jane (1996). *Sea watch: A book of poetry.* Illus. by Ted Lewin. New York: Philomel Books. [ I ]

Yolen, Jane (1992). *Street rhymes around the world.* Illus. by 17 international artists. Honesdale, PA: Boyds Mills Press. [ P ]

Young, Ed (1998). *The lost horse: A Chinese folktale.* San Diego: Silver Whistle/Harcourt Brace. [ P/I ]

Zadrzynska, Ewa (1990). *The girl with a watering can.* New York: Chamelon. [ I ]

Zhensun, Zheng, & Low, Alice (1991). *A young painter: The life and paintings of Yang Wani—China's extraordinary young artist.* New York: Scholastic. [ I/M ]

## Chapter 13

# Response to Nonfiction

## *Blending Efferent Reading and Aesthetic Response*

*I think that the way Langston spent a lot of his early years alone dreaming and wondering at the things around him reminds me of myself. . . . I kind of explore things and notice the smells and sounds and way things look around me, and also dream that it is all from a different time or place, like maybe Langston did when he was alone and remembered the old stories his Grandma would tell him.*

Sixth-Grade Response to *Coming Home: From the Life of Langston Hughes*

On the shelves of elementary/middle-level library media centers lies a dormant literary genre longing to be rescued from decades of restricted use. Nonfiction books, including informational books and biography, often limited as a research tool in the past, have experienced a resurgence as the demands for this genre have nurtured its growth beyond its former role. Teachers browse the shelves to locate an informational read-aloud, children scan nonfiction choices for independent reading, and aesthetic response to informational titles becomes a reality in the classroom. The informational picture book or picture book biography, in particular, has echoed the reverberations of the expanding publication of children's nonfiction

273

literature in the past few years. The appeal of the picture book format and the ability of quality text to transfer our ever-growing body of knowledge to children supports the blossoming growth of this genre. Teachers and media specialists are challenged to create a new vision for the informational book by exploring afresh, moving it beyond a traditional research tool, and considering its potential as a valid option for reading and responding.

Children's literature advocates and researchers have collectively explored the complexities of selection and the countless possibilities of utilizing nonfiction in the elementary curriculum (Bamford & Kristo, 1998; Freeman & Person, 1992) and documented the diverse options of response to nonfiction (McClure & Zitlow, 1991; Vardell, 1996; Vardell & Copeland, 1992). The potential for including nonfiction read-alouds as part of a balanced read-aloud program (Doiron, 1994; Moss, 1991) and the recognition that primary children can process exploratory texts (Duthie, 1994; Pappas, 1991; Robb, 1994) point to expanded use in the school program. As the role of the informational book in the classroom expands, the expectations for quality informational books also heighten. The quantity of informational books has expanded in the past five years and the quality has paralleled this growth. The availability of quality informational books for children of both elementary and middle-level programs makes it a natural choice for inclusion within the reading program and in interdisciplinary instruction.

This chapter takes an innovative look at response options for the informational book in a literature-based classroom. From read-alouds to independent reading, from author studies to authentic accounts, from personal connections to biography to aesthetic response to nonfiction, informational books provide a fresh tool for integrated instruction. Reader response to informational books is the major focus of this chapter. To illustrate that reader response can move beyond its typical embedded fictional stature, authentic written responses of sixth-grade students to selected informational titles (Hancock, 1994) are interspersed throughout the chapter as support for aesthetic response to nonfiction.

# INFORMATIONAL BOOKS

A children's informational book is a factual representation of information in a well-written, often illustrated or photographed, format. The text and visual images both play an important role in contributing to the understanding of a topic. Books in this genre are further enhanced and documented by accurate glossaries, time line chronologies, extended bibliographies, informative captions, related maps, useful indexes, and the expert credentials of authors, illustrators, and photographers. The breadth of the informational genre spans the curriculum and integrates traditional areas. Before the reader's eyes unfolds a visual world of color and a textual world of well-documented information. See Chapter 7 for an overview of biography and informational genres as an introduction to nonfiction.

Although informational books are typically located in the nonfiction section of the school or public library, a large number find their way to the picture book shelves because they are identified by format rather than content. This particular type will be referred to as an informational picture book, a special type of informational book whose inviting format and well-written text appeals to younger students. Both traditional informational books and informational picture books will be shared with respect to their potential use for response-based activities.

## Read-Aloud Informational Books

To a great degree, teachers have almost exclusively chosen fictional chapter and picture book titles for class read-alouds. Although their students savored their read-aloud voices and the imaginary happenings of the stories, they were unknowingly being sheltered from a literary genre that has great appeal to readers of all ages. Teachers who select informational books as read-alouds take the first step in informing the reader of the respectability and acceptability of these books as a choice for independent reading. Although many children eventually become adult readers of nonfiction, this genre has been unexplored as a read-aloud option in many classrooms. The natural curiosity of primary students fosters a sense of inquiry through nonfiction titles especially geared to younger children (Moss, 1991; Roop, 1992). If our goal is to create lifelong readers, it is wise to open wide this previously guarded research genre for variety in read-alouds and personal reading choices.

In an effort to overcome the stereotype of informational books as boring and mundane, Doiron (1994) suggests several criteria for a suitable nonfiction read-aloud selection:

- Identify quality authors who share their subjects with clarity, authority, and whose writing style speaks directly to the reader.
- Look for an inviting presentation that attracts the reader's initial curiosity, but gradually leads to independent thinking and the generation of additional inquiry.
- Focus on the language of fact presented in a memorable voice that will motivate and hold the reader's attention.

Reading for information can be an enjoyable experience that touches both the efferent needs of the mind and the aesthetic realms of the heart.

The same recommendations for reading aloud quality fiction also apply to reading aloud quality informational books. Specific tips related to nonfiction adapted from suggestions by Doiron (1994) include these:

- Provide background information on the book topic prior to the read-aloud by sharing an artifact, conducting an experiment, or discussing the subject.
- Take advantage of the ability of the genre to generate interest and inquiry by allowing children to become active participants through questions and explanations.
- Focus on the author and illustrator pointing out documentation of factual accuracy, publication date, format style, and speculating on research procedures for acquiring information.
- Select an appropriate chapter, a small section, or important excerpts from longer chapter books. Not all informational books are meant to be read in their entirety. Provide access to the book for students' further independent reading.
- Choose informational books on a variety of topics to reflect a wide range of appeal to readers.
- Use informational picture books to bridge the reading of fiction and nonfiction as narrative language transmits informative facts.

Many informational books are written in narrative and capture student interest during read-alouds. *From* An Extraordinary Life: The Story of a Monarch Butterfly. *Paintings by Bob Marstall. Copyright © 1997. Reprinted by permission of Orchard Books.*

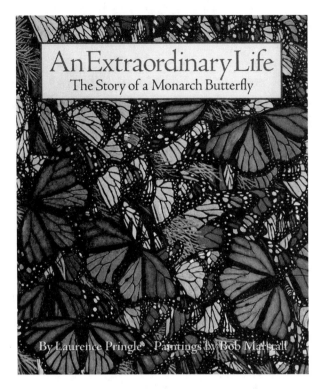

An exemplary read-aloud for young children that fits these criteria is Joanne Ryder's *Jaguar in the Rain Forest.* Written in the second person, the author engages children in becoming the main character—the jaguar—as you, as this powerful cat, climb your favorite tree with nature's camouflage making you invisible, then stalk and grasp an armadillo in your powerful jaws. The strength of the use of "you" in the text transforms the reader into the animal role and reader response lies in experiencing the day in the guise of a rain forest predator. This book is a part of the Just for a Day series, which transforms readers into a polar bear, a Canada goose, a chameleon, a humpback whale, and a sea otter. Expressing response in the guise of the animal creates empathy for endangered animals and their plight to survive.

An outstanding example of an informational picture book read-aloud for older children is Laurence Pringle's *An Extraordinary Life: The Story of a Monarch Butterfly.* This title won the Orbis Pictus Award for 1998 as the best nonfiction book for children of the year. Written in narrative, this fact-based tale follows the amazing journey of Danaus, a monarch butterfly, from her emergence as a caterpillar in a Massachusetts hayfield, through her metamorphosis into a butterfly, and culminates in her flight south, her mating, and her return migration in spring. Weighing only one-fifteenth of an ounce, Danaus flies more than 2,500 miles surrounded by dangers from weather, predators, and humans. Written as four chapters, the book allows for daily read-alouds culminating in a final day of active response as the class sets up an environment for raising monarch butterflies guided by information in the book.

FIGURE 13.1 Nonfiction books to read aloud

---

## Picture/Photograph Books

Brandenburg, Jim (1996). *Scruffy: A wolf finds his place in the pack.* New York: Walker. [ P/I ]

Cherry, Lynne (1997). *Flute's journey: The life of a woodthrush.* San Diego: Gulliver Books/Harcourt Brace. [ I ]

Fisher, Leonard Everett (1997). *Anasazi.* New York: Atheneum. [ I ]

George, Jean Craighead (1997). *Look to the north: A wolf pup diary.* Illus. by Lucia Washburn. New York: HarperCollins. [ P/I ]

Gibbons, Gail (1997). *The honey makers.* New York: Morrow. [ P/I ]

Guiberson, Brenda Z. (1995). *Winter wheat.* Illus. by Megan Lloyd. New York: Holt. [ P/I ]

Kramer, Stephen (1997). *Eye of the storm: Chasing storms with Warren Faidley.* Photographs by Warren Faidley. New York: Putnam. [ I ]

Markle, Sandra (1996). *Outside and inside sharks.* New York: Atheneum. [ I ]

Miller, Debbie S. (1997). *Disappearing lake: Nature's magic in Denali National Park.* Illus. by Jon Van Zyle. New York: Walker. [ I ]

Pringle, Laurence (1997). *An extraordinary life: The story of a monarch butterfly.* Paintings by Bob Marstall. New York: Orchard Books. [ I/M ]

Ryder, Joanne (1996). *Jaguar in the rain forest* (A Just for a Day Book series). Illus. by Michael Rothman. New York: Morrow. [ P/I ]

## Chapter Books

Blumberg, Rhoda (1990). *The great American gold rush.* New York: Bradbury. [ I/M ]

Freedman, Russell (1994). *Kids at work: Lewis Hine and the crusade against child labor.* Photos by Lewis Hine. Boston: Clarion. [ I/M ]

Hampton, Wilborn (1997). *Kennedy assassinated! The world mourns: A reporter's story.* Cambridge, MA: Candlewick Press. [ I/M ]

Hopcraft, Xan, & Hopcraft, Carol Canthra (1997). *How it was with Dooms: A true story from Africa.* New York: McElderry Books. [ I ]

Lauber, Patricia (1990). *The news about dinosaurs.* New York: Bradbury. [ I ]

Murphy, Jim (1994). *Across America on an emigrant train.* Boston: Clarion. [ M ]

Murphy, Jim (1995). *The great fire.* New York: Scholastic. [ I/M ]

Myers, Walter Dean (1992). *Now is your time: The African-American struggle for freedom.* New York: HarperCollins. [ I/ M ]

Stanley, Jerry (1993). *Children of the Dust Bowl: The true story of the school at Weedpatch Camp.* New York: Crown. [ I/M ]

Tunnell, Michael O., & Chilcoat, George W. (1996). *The children of Topaz: The story of a Japanese-American internment camp.* New York: Holiday House. [ I/M ]

---

Figure 13.1 provides a list of read-aloud informational books that epitomizes the quality and quantity of books available to capture student reading interest through the informational genre. By reading these titles aloud and probing response through appropriate prompts, students begin to respond to informational text aesthetically. Rather than limiting response to efferent information, they actually interact personally with the text, eliciting personal feelings, reactions, and opinions about a topic.

## Informational Author/Illustrator Studies

Just as literature-based instruction supports students becoming informed about the real lives of authors, so too does it challenge the investigative capabilities of those who compile, write, and illustrate informational books. The insatiable quest for information lures individuals from professional careers and sends them to the far reaches of the earth to acquire knowledge to share with children through words, illustrations, or photographs. The spirit of discovery and research that motivates these authors and artists sparks interest in their books and models the inquiry process for students' own quests for answers.

A noteworthy example of a subject for an informational author/illustrator study is Diane Stanley, who, often accompanied by her husband, Peter Vennema, has painstakingly traveled, researched, and illustrated superb picture book biographies of *Joan of Arc* (1998), *Leonardo da Vinci* (1996), *Cleopatra* (1994), *Charles Dickens* (1993), *The Bard of Avon: The Story of William Shakespeare* (1992), and *Good Queen Bess* (1991). Stanley, a former medical illustrator, found her artistic strength in realism as she portrays authentic moments from the lives of her subjects. With the historical expertise of her husband, she is able to share interesting biographical information acquired via extensive travel and library research through both elegant language and revealing illustrations.

Students may be inspired by Joanna's Cole's development since her first informational book on *Cockroaches* (1971) to her latest journey into a beehive in the Magic School Bus series. Readers will be informed by Gail Gibbon's *Wolves,* one of her 70 nonfiction masterpieces, or awed by the intricate writing and detailed illustrations of Aliki in *Communication.* Becoming acquainted with the authors as researchers is as important as knowing and responding to them as writers and illustrators. Responding to the research expertise and techniques of informational authors provides a valid model for personal research. Other informational author/illustrators for focused study include Leonard Everett Fisher, Russell Freedman, Jean Craighead George, Diane Hoyt-Goldsmith, Kathryn Lasky, Patricia Lauber, Sandra Markle, Laurence Pringle, and Seymour Simon. While teachers may prepare and share these author studies, students are also encouraged to research, compile, and present their own informational author studies as a viable response to literature. See Appendix B for a variety of professional resources for accessing information on authors and illustrators. The blending of biographical information, authentic nonfiction literature, and student response to process and content creates an interesting response format.

# READER RESPONSE TO INFORMATIONAL BOOKS

Response stands at the threshold of informational books just as it does with narrative titles. While it might be expected that efferent response would predominate natural reactions to informational books, documentation indicates that readers do respond aesthetically to nonfiction (Vardell & Copeland, 1992). The same rich mixture of responses is available for the reader's transaction with nonfiction. Particularly with texts that lie midway on the continuum of aesthetic and efferent, readers may choose a stance that fluctuates between these two realms of response.

## Response to Informational Picture Books

An example of the aesthetic response to an informational picture book includes *America the Beautiful* (Bates, 1993). The text provides an opportunity to revisit the simple but stately words that portray our great land while acquiring information about our natural treasures. Each eloquent line is matched to a majestic illustration of one of America's natural wonders, enhanced at the book's end by identification and additional information on each sight. After a teacher read-aloud, Martha selected an important phrase and explained its significance.

> *"For amber waves of grain." That phrase reminds me of where I live, the great plains. Kansas' nickname is the breadbasket of America. It is like the wide wonderful pastures of wheat we have in Kansas. When the wind blows the wheat, it looks like long waves from the ocean. . . .*

The quality of writing in informational books has improved dramatically in the past few years and contributes to the quality of reader response. No longer is informational text dominated by the encyclopedic delivery of dull, factual information. The presentation has been heightened by quality authors whose flow of language to the reader's ear greatly enhances the conveyance of knowledge. Moving from strained expository text to riveting portrayal of factual events nudges the reader toward the aesthetic side of the response continuum. An outstanding example is Robert Burleigh's *Flight* (1991), which shares the portrayal of Lindbergh's struggle to stay awake during his cross-Atlantic flight by textually placing the reader in the cockpit with this American hero. Savor this excerpt based on Lindbergh's journal during his 33½-hour flight from New York to Paris:

> To sleep is to die!
> These are some of the things he does to stay awake:
> He leans his face near the open window to feel the cold air.
> He holds his eyelids up with his fingers to keep them from closing.
> He remembers growing up on a farm in Minnesota.
> He remembers being a trick pilot, and walking out on a plane's wings.
> He remembers the people in St. Louis who paid for this plane.
> Sometimes he takes a sip of water from his canteen.
> He also has five chicken sandwiches with him. That is all the food he has brought.
> But he eats nothing. It is easier to stay awake on an empty stomach.*

Following the reading of this book, Heather responds to this aesthetic blend of text and illustrations:

> *It . . . really makes you feel as though you were in that cramped cockpit with no sleep. The pictures really tell you how he feels, like when the illustrator uses dark colors, he's tired or there's bad weather. The words made it very colorful though. You can tell how he feels: sad, tired, lonely, happy, worried— everything. It was very descriptive.*

*From FLIGHT: THE JOURNEY OF CHARLES LINDBERGH (pp. 16–17) by Robert Burleigh. Copyright © 1991 by Robert Burleigh, text. Copyright © 1991 by Mike Wimmer, illustrations. Used by permission of Philomel Books, a division of Penguin Putnam Inc.

Examples of other texts that weave language and illustrations in an informational context include *The Moon of the Fox Pups* (George, 1992), *A River Ran Wild* (Cherry, 1992) and *Christmas in the Bighouse, Christmas in the Quarters* (McKissack & McKissack, 1994). These titles not only read aloud exceedingly well, but also suggest informational books as a valid reader response option for students.

## Responding to Biography

Biographies have advanced far beyond the carbon-copy accounts of presidents and explorers traditionally formatted in dull, serialized chapter books. Today's well-written visual accounts of impressive individuals cover figures from the worlds of science, literature, politics, and history. These books become viable options for reader response as the reader soars beyond facts to an identification and understanding of personal and professional traits of the subject. The blend of dynamic text and, in many cases, vivid visual interpretation adds a new dimension to these biographies.

For example, Cindy read *Michael the Angel* (Fischetto, 1993), a picture book biography of the great sculptor Michelangelo as a defiant child. She was asked to reflect on what part of Michelangelo's personality reminded her of herself. She maturely proclaimed:

> *No part of Michelangelo's personality reminds me of myself. Michelangelo wouldn't study in school. He would only draw, but I study in school and don't goof off. He wouldn't obey his father, but I obey my parents. . . . He quit being a painter because he wanted to be famous . . . but I don't give up or care if I will be famous. I just be the best I can be. Michelangelo never liked where he was, and always wanted to be better, but I just do the best I can, and I except that.*

Open-ended prompts that might be used to assist children in responding to biographies allude to connections between portrayal and personality, greatest accomplishments and disappointments of the subject, and emulation of personality traits in one's own life.

- What did you notice about (*name subject of biography*)?
- What part of (*name subject*) personality remind you of yourself?
- What part of (*name subject*) life do you find to be an accomplishment?
- What part of (*name subject*) life do you find to be a disappointment?
- What part of (*name subject*) personality would you like to emulate in your own life?

These prompts invite a connected dimension between the life of the reader and the subject of the biography.

Another response option for biography includes responding to the biographical subject by writing a bio-poem (Danielson, 1989; Hancock, 1997). The format of the poem includes the following structure and response:

| | |
|---|---|
| Line 1: | First name of biographical subject |
| Line 2: | Four adjectives or phrases describing the subject |
| Line 3: | Husband/wife/sibling/child of . . . |
| Line 4: | Lover of . . . (three things or people) |
| Line 5: | Who feels . . . (three emotions) |
| Line 6: | Who fears . . . (three things) |

Aesthetic response to biography includes a bio-poem sharing facts and feelings about the subject. *From ELEANOR by Barbara Cooney. Copyright © 1996 by Barbara Cooney. Used by permission of Viking Penguin, a division of Penguin Putnam Inc.*

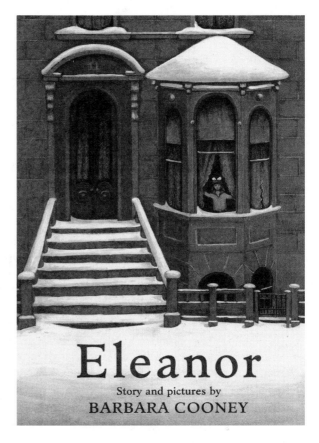

Eleanor

Story and pictures by
BARBARA COONEY

Line 7:        Who would like to . . . (three things)
Line 8:        Resident of . . . (city/state/country)
Line 9:        Last name of biographical subject

After reading Barbara Cooney's *Eleanor*, the following bio-poem was written in response to the personality and childhood of Eleanor Roosevelt.

Anna Eleanor
A disappointment to her mother, "a miracle from
        heaven" to her father, withdrawn and alone, an
        ugly duckling.
Sister of Ellie and Brudie, her little brothers.
Lover of her father, summertime at Tivoli, her father's
        letters, and Mlle. Souvestre
Who feels unattractive, eager to please, capable of
        thinking for herself, and finally prepared for
        her future.

Who fears being an orphan after her mother and father
    die, going to a boarding school in Europe, being a
    coward, and crossing the ocean by ship.
Who would like her family's approval, the affection of
    friends, to be poised and confident, and to marry
    a president.
Resident of East 38th Street in New York City.
Roosevelt.

This poetic form provides an interesting format as a child reads and responds to the life, personality, values, and contributions of historical and current biographical subjects.

## Responding to Authentic Accounts

One trend in informational books is to present authentic words, accounts, and documentation of actual people and places in history. The first-person voice of these books brings the individual and the event to life as words and pictures become reality in the reader's mind. *Grandma Essie's Covered Wagon* (Williams, 1993) presents an oral history of a family's settling in the Great Plains. When Amber read the book, she responded to a parallel in her own life:

> *It's the same because I live in the country. When I look up into the pasture I see tall grass all the way up the hill, and whenever I'm in a new pasture I like to run in them . . . when we hear of a bad thunderstorm in the area we all go into our back room. It's real dark back there and we're all scared so we sit close together, just like Grandma Essie and her family did in the cellar.*

Amelia Stewart Knight's authentic diary shared in *The Way West: Journal of a Pioneer Woman* elicited emotions in Heather. She reports reactions to the blend of real words and scratchboard illustrations:

> *It made you feel like you were right there, riding in the wagon beside them. The characters seemed real, not just names on a piece of paper. The most descriptive parts were: the long winding trail, the dust rising off the trail as the wind came up, causing you to choke until your chest hurt. . . . The hardships were told like someone would tell, not an encyclopedia.*

Gripping accounts of discovery and expeditions are also brought to life through extraordinarily researched informational books. These books transport readers to another time and place and offer them the thrill of becoming an active, involved member of a team of explorers in search of a new world, an ancient civilization, or a sunken ship. The Time Quest Books series includes several titles that accompany the reader on an arctic expedition, into a mummy's tomb, on board the *Titanic,* or into the depths of Vesuvius. The Living History series carries the reader along on the voyages of Columbus, on the knightly quests of the Middle Ages, and aboard Viking ships through first-person text and authentically costumed and photographed historical characters. The Brown Paper School series includes firsthand accounts, diary entries, letters, speeches, and activities that place the reader in the middle of decisions that have affected our country's history. *Stephen Biesty's Cross-Sections: Man of War* carries the reader to the deck of an 18th-century warship to deliver information. Heather commented on the blend of authentic information and intricate, detailed drawings in this book:

> *It showed the reality of it all. It didn't just tell you about the good things. Instead of just showing the good guys winning, it showed things like: men getting smashed by loose cannons, how the admiral took only one bath a week, sailors getting carried to the nurses with only one leg, or men getting hit by huge splinters of wood, and men being whipped for stealing or gambling. . . . Like I said, it's the reality of it all that really kept me listening.*

Note the use of Heather's word "listening." Although she read this text independently, she "heard" the words through the authenticity of the text and detailed drawings.

Response to these first-person accounts might also be in the form of a first-person dramatization as an eyewitness to a piece of history. Since the first-person voice is a strong one for both writing and oral sharing, students enjoy assuming the role of an observer of history. These authentic accounts provide an amazing motivation to both reluctant and avid readers as they share the voice of history as it unfolds.

## Responding to Nature Through Photographic Essays

The complexities of science become easier to visualize and understand with informational books that explain and extend our knowledge of life itself. Microscopic photographs that magnify the tiniest creatures and plants or satellite photos that capture the far reaches of outer space serve to motivate further reading and understanding. Barrett and Marantz (1989) suggest that photographs as an illustrative medium be honored with respect and admiration in informational contexts. When provided classroom access to various photographed titles, sixth-grade students readily chose them for independent reading (Hancock, 1994). They responded to prompts that focused their attention on the research and preparation that goes into the making of a photographed informational book, including the following:

- How would this book be different if written ten years sooner?
- How would this book be different if written ten years later?
- Which photographs do you wish you had taken yourself? Why?
- Compare this book with another book on the same topic that uses drawings rather than photography. Which is better and why?
- What process would the author/photographer use to gather and present this information?
- If you interviewed the author/photographer, what questions would you ask?
- What did you learn from the photographs that you didn't learn from the text?
- What is the most important word in the text to you? Why?

These prompts open unexplored territory to readers of informational books who might never have thought about these ideas. Thinking about the process of writing/photographing an informational book gives the reader an added dimension of response. Responding to how a book is composed gives insights into the research process itself.

After reading Seymour Simon's *Venus* (1992), students were asked to determine what steps the author/photographer took to gather and present the information and photographs:

> *I think he contacted NASA and ask if they would give him pictures of different parts of Venus . . . so he could . . . make the story good to the reader.*   (Nick)
> *. . . He probably researched the planets too and went to the library. He probably interviewed top scientists and astronauts. Then he wrote a book about the planets.*   (Martha)

A sequential, photographic study of *Jack-in-the-Pulpit* (Wexler, 1993) elicited this response from Cindy:

> *To get all of this information it would take a few years. . . . A photographer would have to spend alot of time to take pictures of the plants as they grow through the years. First they'd have to start with the plant's birth, to its death, and after death. An author would have to do the same. They'd have to keep a close eye on it to get every single piece of information as possible.*

The value of both text and photographs as supporting tools for acquiring knowledge should be emphasized. While reading Patricia Lauber's spectacular *Summer of Fire: Yellowstone 1988*, Scott was asked to contemplate what he gleaned from the photographs that he didn't learn from the text. He responded:

> *I remember more pictures than I do facts. Yellowstone's prettier than it sounds. . . . Sometimes a picture can tell more than the words, like on page 15 or 17, where you can actually see and feel the fire.*

Students might exhibit response by actually blending photography and research in preparing their own photographic essay on topics such as wildflowers, insects, or a history of their community. Photography and text as either the inspiration for response or as a response to sharing information on a topic provides the visual support that appeals to many readers of informational books.

## Critical Response to Related Informational Texts

Older students can respond to informational texts on the same topic by critically comparing and contrasting the information shared in each of several texts (Hoffman, 1992). Locating several books on a topic and comparing their contents and student response to presentation, style, and information blends critical thinking with reader response. For example, the following picture books on the topic of the first Thanksgiving bring different informational perspectives to a topic that remains a mainstay of the social studies curriculum:

George, Jean Craighead (1993). *The first Thanksgiving.* New York: Putnam.
Harness, Cheryl (1992). *Three young pilgrims.* New York: Bradbury.
San Souci, Robert (1991). *N. C. Wyeth's Pilgrims.* San Francisco, CA: Chronicle Books.
Waters, Kate (1989). *Sarah Morton's day.* New York: Scholastic.
Waters, Kate (1993). *Samuel Eaton's day.* New York: Scholastic.

Individual readers can respond to each selected title as books are circulated among group members. Responses can be recorded on a chart and may address predetermined prompts such as these: What is your impression of the Pilgrims after you read this book? With what hardship did you most identify? What feelings did this portrayal of Thanksgiving inspire in you? Which book do you prefer as the "best" choice for sharing the Thanksgiving story? Charts can be recorded by group members or a whole class comparison/contrast table may be prepared. The major outcome of the activity is to help readers of information realize that (1) presentation style and point of view can affect the delivery of information to the reader, (2) facts may vary from book to book depending on resources and documentation used for accuracy, and (3) preferences for informational presentation vary from reader to reader.

Integrated thematic teaching demands the location of related book titles on a common topic for individual enjoyment as well as comparison/contrast of themes, moral dilemmas, or factual encounters. A study of endangered species might blend Molly Cone's *Come Back Salmon,* Caroline Arnold's *On the Brink of Extinction,* and Dorothy Henshaw Patent's *Ospreys,* which all provide valuable information and vivid photographs of genuine struggles to preserve native wildlife. When studying Native Americans, Russell Freedman's *An Indian Winter* and George Ella Lyon's *Dreamplace* return the reader to the past, while Diane Hoyt-Goldsmith's *Cherokee Summer* and George Anacona's *Powwow* bring the culture of today to reader attention. Varied perspectives on the ocean might be gleaned from a combination of an historical view of life on the high seas through *Whaling Days* (Carrick, 1993), a humorous, but accurate view of undersea life from *The Magic School Bus on the Ocean Floor* (Cole, 1992), and the wondrous emergence of an island in *Surtsey: The Newest Place on Earth* (Lasky, 1992). Related titles on varying subjects abound with fresh data, a taste of history, an appreciation of nature, or an unbiased view of cultures. Thinking in terms of clusters of books, rather than a single literature resource, allows for expanding the breadth and depth of a topic. Relating books and the information they share shapes the critical comparative aspects of reader response.

Thinking about the inquiry and presentation process in a book sharpens a student's own research presentation tools. Note that informational books are transmitting more than facts—they reflect the complexity of the inquiry process and the art of accurately and effectively presenting information. Student responses reveal that research takes time, focuses on attention to details, and requires planning. Sharing these books as format and stylistic models for their own future research builds an effective means of sharing inquiry-related findings across the curriculum. Refer back to the section in Chapter 11 on formats for expository writing to further reinforce the connection between informational literature as a model for student sharing of individual research.

# CLOSING THOUGHTS

Informational books foster both a literacy and a learning experience. The pleasures of factual literature are obtained both by information gathering and savoring the creative manner in which information is shared through this genre. As teachers naturally select special fiction to share with readers, they must also show selectivity in the informational books they choose to share. Quality nonfiction can hook and motivate children to read just as fiction inspires them. Reading aloud informational books helps balance expository and narrative text as children broaden their sense of sharing information alongside their developing sense of story. Read-aloud nonfiction solicits reader response at both the efferent and aesthetic levels. Spontaneous interaction is frequently the basis of response as questions, speculations, related personal experiences, and natural inquiry takes hold during oral discussion.

Vardell and Copeland (1992) refer to "the great gift of the genre"—to develop critical thinking so that readers become actively involved in processing information and less accepting of the written word. Literary quality, variety, and appeal are the hallmark of the new informational book, while reader response ranges from spontaneous response to modeling the style of literature for presenting research, to inquiry-based discussions. The gift of the genre lies in both the literary and stylistic quality that now graces informational books as well as its power to incite the thinking abilities and curiosity of the reader. The natural desire to respond to new information, to relate it to prior knowledge, and the need to formulate new inquiries bridges informational books and reader response.

# REFERENCES

Bamford, R. A., & Kristo, J. V. (Eds.) (1998). *Making facts come alive: Choosing quality nonfiction literature K–8.* Norwood, MA: Christopher-Gordon.

Barrett, T., & Marantz, K. (1989). Photographs as illustrations. *The New Advocate, 2,* 227–238.

Danielson, K. (1989). Helping history come alive with literature. *Social Studies, 80,* 65–68.

Doiron, R. (1994). Using nonfiction in a read-aloud program: Letting the facts speak for themselves. *The Reading Teacher, 47,* 616–624.

Duthie, C. (1994). Nonfiction: A genre study for the primary classroom. *Language Arts, 71,* 588–595.

Freeman, E. B., & Person, D. G. (Eds.) (1992). *Using nonfiction trade books in the elementary classroom: From ants to zeppelins.* Urbana, IL: National Council of Teachers of English.

Hancock, M. R. (1994). *The 3Rs of informational picture books: Responding, reflecting, and researching.* Paper presented at the National Council of Teachers of English Spring Conference, Portland, OR.

Hancock, M. R. (1997). Another time, another place: Bringing social studies to life through literature. In P. J. Farris & S. Cooper (Eds.), *Elementary and middle school social studies: A whole language approach* (2nd ed., pp. 121–150). Madison, WI: Brown & Benchmark.

Hoffman, J. V. (1992). Critical reading/thinking across the curriculum: Using I-charts to support learning. *Language Arts, 69,* 121–127.

McClure, A. A., & Zitlow, C. S. (1991). Not just the facts: Aesthetic response in elementary content area studies. *Language Arts, 68,* 27–33.

Moss, B. (1991). Children's nonfiction trade books: A complement to content area textbooks. *The Reading Teacher, 45,* 26–35.

Pappas, C. C. (1991). Fostering full access to literacy by including information books. *Language Arts, 68,* 449–462.

Robb, L. (1994). Second graders read nonfiction: Investigating natural phenomena and disasters. *The New Advocate, 7,* 239–252.

Roop, P. (1992). Nonfiction books in the primary classroom: Soaring with the swans. In E. B. Freeman & D. G. Person (Eds.), *Using nonfiction trade books in the elementary classroom: From ants to zeppelins* (pp. 106–112). Urbana, IL: National Council of Teachers of English.

Vardell, S. M. (1996). The language of facts: Using nonfiction books to support language growth. In A. A. McClure & J. V. Kristo (Eds.), *Books that invite talk, wonder, and play* (pp. 59–77). Urbana, IL: National Council of Teachers of English.

Vardell, S. M., & Copeland, K. A. (1992). Reading aloud and responding to nonfiction: Let's talk about it. In E. B. Freeman & D. G. Person (Eds.), *Using nonfiction trade books in the elementary classroom: From ants to zepellins* (pp. 76–85). Urbana, IL: National Council of Teachers of English.

# CHILDREN'S BOOKS CITED    [ P ] = K–2; [ I ] = 3–5; [ M ] = 6–8

Aliki (1993). *Communication.* New York: Greenwillow.

Anacona, George (1993). *Powwow.* San Diego: Harcourt Brace. [ I ]

Arnold, Caroline (1993). *On the brink of extinction: The California condor.* Photographs by Michael Walker. San Diego: Gulliver Books/Harcourt Brace. [ I ]

Bates, Katherine L. (1993). *America the beautiful.* Illus. by N. Waldman. New York: Atheneum. [ P/I ]

Burleigh, Robert (1991). *Flight: The journey of Charles Lindbergh.* Illus. by Mike Wimmer. New York: Philomel Books. [ I/M ]

Carrick, Carol (1993). *Whaling days.* Woodcuts by David Frampton. Boston: Clarion. [ I ]

Cherry, Lynne (1992). *A river ran wild: An environmental history.* San Diego: Harcourt Brace. [ I ]

Clare, John D. (1992). *The voyages of Christopher Columbus* (Living History series). San Diego: Gulliver Books/Harcourt Brace. [ I/M ]

Cole, Joanna (1971). Cockroaches. New York: Morrow. [ I ]

Cole, Joanna (1992). *The magic school bus on the ocean floor.* Illus. by Bruce Degen. New York: Scholastic. [ I ]

Cone, Molly (1992). *Come back salmon: How a group of dedicated kids adopted Pigeon Creek and brought it back to life.* Photographs by Sidnee Wheelwright. San Francisco, CA: Sierra Club. [ I/M ]

Cooney, Barbara (1996). *Eleanor.* New York: Viking. [ I ]

Cooper, Floyd (1994). *Coming home: From the life of Langston Hughes.* New York: Philomel Books. [ P/I ]

Fischetto, Galli (1993). Michael the angel. New York: Doubleday. [ P/I ]

Freedman, Russell (1992). *An Indian winter.* Paintings and drawings by Karl Bodmer. New York: Holiday House. [ M ]

George, Jean Craighead (1992). *The moon of the fox pups* (Thirteen Moon series). San Diego: Harcourt Brace. [ I ]

Gibbons, Gail (1994). *Wolves.* New York: Holiday House. [ P/I ]

Hoyt-Goldsmith, Diane (1993). *Cherokee summer.* Photographs by Lawrence Migdale. New York: Holiday House. [ I ]

Knight, Amelia Stewart (1993). *The way west: Journal of a pioneer woman.* Illus. by Michael McCurdy. (Adapted by Lillian Schlissel from an 1853 diary.) New York: Simon & Schuster. [ I ]

Krull, Kathleen (1997). *Lives of the athletes: Thrills, spills (and what the neighbors thought).* Illus. by Kathryn Hewitt. San Diego: Harcourt Brace. [ I/M ]

Lasky, Kathryn (1992). *Surtsey: The newest place on earth.* Photographs by Christopher Knight. New York: Hyperion. [ I/M ]

Lauber, Patricia (1991). *Summer of fire: Yellowstone 1988.* New York: Orchard Books. [ I ]

Leiner, Katherine (1996). *First children: Growing up in the White House.* Portraits by Katie Keller. New York: Tambourine Books. [ I/M ]

Lindbergh, Reeve (1996). *Nobody owns the sky: The story of brave Bessie Coleman.* Illus. by Pamela Paparone. Cambridge, MA: Candlewick Press. [ I ]

Lyon, George Ella (1993). *Dreamplace.* Illus. by Peter Catalano. New York: Orchard Books. [ P ]

McKissack, Patricia C., & McKissack, Frederick L. (1994). *Christmas in the big house, Christmas in the quarters.* Illus. by John Thompson. New York: Scholastic. [ I/M ]

Osofsky, Audrey (1996). *Free to dream. The making of a poet: Langston Hughes.* New York: Lothrop, Lee & Shepard. [ M ]

Patent, Dorothy Henshaw (1993). *Ospreys.* Photographs by William Munoz. Boston: Clarion. [ I ]

Platt, R. (1993). *Stephen Beisty's cross-sections: Man of war.* Illus. by Stephen Beisty. New York: Dorling Kindersley/Knopf. [ I/M ]

Pringle, Laurence (1997). *An extraordinary life: The story of a monarch butterfly.* Illus. by Bob Marstall. New York: Orchard Books. [ I/M ]

Ryder, Joanne & Rothman, Michael (1996). *Jaguar in the Rain Forest.* New York: Morrow [ P/I ]

Simon, Seymour (1992). *Venus.* New York: Morrow. [ P/I ]

Stanley, Diane (1996). *Leonardo da Vinci.* New York: Morrow. [ I/M ]

Stanley, Diane (1998). *Joan of Arc.* New York: Morrow. [ I/M ]

Stanley, Diane, & Vennema, Peter (1991). *Good Queen Bess: The story of Elizabeth I of England.* New York: Four Winds/Simon & Schuster. [ I/M ]

Stanley, Diane, & Vennema, Peter (1992). *The Bard of Avon: The story of William Shakespeare.* New York: Morrow.

Stanley, Diane, & Vennema, Peter (1993). *Charles Dickens: The man who had great expectations.* New York: Morrow. [ I/M ]

Stanley, Diane, & Vennema, Peter (1994). *Cleopatra.* New York: Morrow. [ I/M ]

Wexler, Jerome (1993). *Jack-in-the-pulpit.* New York: Dutton. [ P/I ]

Williams, David (1993). *Grandma Essie's covered wagon.* Illus. by Wiktor Sadowski. New York: Knopf. [ P/I ]

**PART IV**

# Celebrating Interdisciplinary Connections

Response-based links to children's literature through oral response, written journals, and drama/art/music activities provide continuously satisfying reader response connections to literature. Yet, perhaps one of the most gratifying appeals of children's literature for teachers and a most meaningful connection for children, moves beyond response to individual books. The creative blending of multiple titles of children's literature around a single theme, both across literary genres and academic disciplines, provides literature-based connections that make learning relevant to the real world.

Once teachers and readers become adept at varied response options to literature, the challenge exists to plan and implement interdisciplinary, response-based units built on quality children's books. Part IV of *A Celebration of Literature and Response* focuses on the planning, implementation, and response to both literature clusters (a selective collection of books across genres and disciplines related to a single theme) and theme explorations (a vast offering of books across genres and disciplines related to a single higher-level concept or theme through interconnected subthemes). Teachers' increasing knowledge of literature and students' growing confidence with reader response enable them to move beyond isolated response activities to experience the natural, thematic nature of higher level inquiry as a result of the creative blending of children's books through an interdisciplinary focus.

Chapter 14 supportively guides preservice and inservice teachers through the process of creating literature clusters and theme explorations by sharing tips on selecting a topic, locating literature, utilizing professional resources, designing response-based instruction, and implementing an interdisciplinary blend of literature-based activities in the classroom.

Lists and graphic organizers of literature clusters and theme explorations enhance this chapter while providing a model for individually planned thematic, interdisciplinary instruction. In particular, detailed reflections and advice during each stage of the planning process serve to authenticate the challenge and satisfaction of effectively blending literature across genres and disciplines. Examples of whole class, small group, and individualized response-based connections provide further guidance for creating unique literature-based, interdisciplinary instruction.

Throughout the implementation of a brief literature cluster or a long term theme exploration, children respond to literature in ways that help them make connections to the real world. Indeed, the challenge of connecting literature and responses through interdisciplinary connections may result in some of the most meaningful literature-based teaching and response-based inquiry and learning that occurs in a literature-based classroom.

# Literature Clusters and Theme Explorations:

## *Response Through Interdisciplinary Study*

*I sat on my office floor and piled high the literature offerings. I don't remember how the hours flew by as I absorbed myself in reading, appreciating, viewing, and perusing the varied genres I had collected related to my theme. I began to group the books in piles which were eventually to become subthemes. While a few titles were difficult to categorize, most of them immediately belonged and connected to other related titles. After manipulating, assigning, and rethinking literature placement, I had eight piles of books towering at my feet. It was then that I paused and realized that the reading, the touching, the turning, and the shifting were actually my response to the literature I had collected. The organization and the designation of subthemes was, in reality, a personal response to the books I was planning to share with children.*

Author's Reflections on Planning Her First
Theme Exploration on Immigration

Sharing children's literature in a classroom one quality book at a time effectively supports literacy and content area instruction. Inviting children to respond to isolated titles encourages varying modes of response often suggested by the book itself. Yet literature has the power to contribute even more to the broader scope of a child's learning. Creatively blending pieces of literature across genres, authors, and related disciplines enhances the connectedness of literature and content knowledge. Designing classroom instruction based on related titles and planning an array of response-based literature activities associated with them provides a solid base for effective teaching (Pappas, Kiefer, & Levstik, 1996).

This chapter introduces a sequential means to blend literature across genres for interdisciplinary instruction. The process of locating, balancing, and blending related literature for thematic teaching is presented in two stages. First, literature clusters (Hancock, 1997) form a first step in integrating a variety of book titles on a single theme. Books from all literary genres keyed to a single topic provide the basis for instruction of facts and meaningful response-based activities. Second, theme explorations (Weaver, Chaston, & Peterson, 1993) form a longer range view of instruction as a broad-based theme encompasses several subthemes in the form of literature clusters. Together the subthemes and quality children's books blend, connect, relate, and combine into an integrated instructional mode for effective literacy and interdisciplinary instruction. Figure 14.1 characterizes the instructional models of literature clusters and theme explorations. The listing will assist in pointing out similarities and differences between these two literature-based, response-oriented modes of instruction.

To aid in modeling the process of planning and teaching through literature clusters and theme explorations, the chapter contains several graphic organizers, annotated bibliographies, and lists of literature-based response activities as the core of interdisciplinary instruction. These examples and the accompanying procedures for creating them serve as models for planning and implementing thematic interdisciplinary teaching at the primary,

**FIGURE 14.1**     Comparison/contrast of literature clusters and theme explorations

| **Literature Clusters** | **Theme Explorations** |
| --- | --- |
| Eight to 12 titles that support a curricular topic | Twenty-five or more titles related to a broad-based theme that is interdisciplinary in nature |
| Blends narrative, expository, and poetic voices of literature | Blends narrative, expository, and poetic voices of literature |
| Includes books selected from several literary genres | Includes books from virtually all literary genres |
| Basis for aesthetic and efferent response | Basis for aesthetic and efferent response |
| Planned for read-aloud and whole group response-based activities | Planned for whole group, small group, and individual response-based activities |
| Shared during a 1- to 2-week period during content area scheduled time | Shared across language arts/curricular scheduled time for 2 to 6 weeks (often an entire quarter or school year) |
| Used in a single-classroom configuration | Used in multiage settings or through collaborative teaching/planning |
| Building block of a theme exploration | Composed of four to six related literature clusters |
| Enhances response-based instruction and literature-based learning | Enhances response-based instruction, integration of content, inquiry learning, and literature-based learning |

intermediate, and middle levels of instruction. Effectively blended and balanced "whole literature" across all genres provides the essential connections between the narrative, expository, and poetic voices that cause real learning to occur (Crook & Lehman, 1991).

# CREATING LITERATURE CLUSTERS

As teachers attempt to include literature across the curriculum, it is crucial to realize that all genres of literature can contribute to conceptual understanding. Confining a science unit to informational books on weather can limit a child's curiosity for and understanding of meteorological concepts. Expanding the literary coverage on weather to include folktales explaining weather phenomenon, picture storybooks set in differing weather conditions, and poetry that captures the natural wonder of weather phenomena entices children to learn. Learners relate weather to their own lives, enhance their knowledge base and depth of understanding, and broaden their perceptions beyond factual information.

The means for reaching this depth of conceptual development is literature. The literature must be grouped into meaningful clusters of books that allow children to see the connections between factual, fictional, and poetic perspectives on a topic. A literature cluster is defined as a blend of quality children's trade books chosen from a variety of literary genres that contain narrative, expository, and poetic perspectives on a concept or theme. The goal of a literature cluster is to blend trade books across genres through varying perspectives that address a single topic in an effort to enhance both instruction and learning (Hancock, 1997).

A science/social studies focused example best illustrates the creation and relevance of a literature cluster on the desert. While this topic is often covered in intermediate science units, the topic begs to be stretched beyond factual information. Examine the list of related titles shown in Figure 14.2, note their specific genre, and sense the creative blend of varied

**FIGURE 14.2**    Model of literature selections for a literature cluster on deserts

Baylor, Byrd (1986). *I'm in charge of celebrations.* Illus. by Peter Parnell. New York: Scribners.
Dunphy, Madeline (1995). *Here is the southwestern desert.* Illus. by Anne Coe. New York: Hyperion.
Guiberson, Brenda Z. (1991). *Cactus hotel.* Illus. by Megan Lloyd. New York: Holt.
Johnston, Tony (1994). *The tale of rabbit and coyote.* Illus. by T. de Paola. New York: Putnam.
Johnston, Tony (1995). *Alice Nizzy Nazzy: The witch of Santa Fe.* Illus. by T. de Paola. New York: Putnam.
Kessler, Cristina (1995). *One night: A story from the desert.* Illus. by Ian Schoenherr. New York: Philomel Books.
Lesser, Carolyn (1997). *Storm on the desert.* Illus. by Ted Rand. San Diego: Harcourt Brace.
Mora, Pat (1994). *Listen to the desert/Oye al desierto.* Illus. by F. Mora. Boston: Clarion.
Pallotta, Jerry (1994). *The desert alphabet book.* Illus. by M. Astrella. Watertown, MA: Charlesbridge.
Wallace, Marianne D. (1996). *America's deserts: Guide to plants and animals.* Golden, CO: Fulcrum.
Wright-Frierson, Virginia (1996). *A desert scrapbook: dawn to dusk in the Sonoran Desert.* New York: Simon & Schuster.
Yolen, Jane (1996). *Welcome to the sea of sand.* Illus. by Laura Regan. New York: Putnam.

perspectives on the topic of deserts to be used with children from second through fourth grades. This list of 12 books contains two multicultural titles, three informational picture books, two poem picture book, two folktale variants, an ABC book, a cumulative tale, and a literature classic. Besides exposing children to the vast array of genres focused on a single topic, the varied perspectives on desert information provide the learner with a multitude of information.

The poetic perspective of literature often provides the impetus for a themed study. Jane Yolen's *Welcome to the Sea of Sand* or Carolyn Lesser's *Storm on the Desert* provides an opening read-aloud with sensory descriptions of the "sea of sand." These descriptions enhance visual images and inspire connections and inquiries in the learner. The cumulative pattern nature of *Here Is the Southwestern Desert* opens the door to a choral reading performance with voices added as additional information is introduced. Not only are the students learning facts, they are also gaining an understanding of the interrelatedness of desert inhabitants. The desert speaks in the language of its creatures and natural surroundings in *Listen to the Desert/Oye al Desierto* in which desert sounds are shared in both English and Spanish. Set in the southwestern desert, *I'm in Charge of Celebrations* illuminates the wonders of the desert as a triple rainbow, an encounter with a coyote, and a view of falling stars inspire the author's poetic response to this unique ecosystem.

Factual information and the roots of research can be delivered through interesting book formats. *A Desert Scrapbook, Cactus Hotel,* and *The Desert Alphabet Book* are informational titles that provide a format for drawing, labeling, organizing, and describing desert flora and fauna. A multitude of other information titles displayed in the classroom become resources for individual animal, plant, or geographic reports.

For a connected, light fictional touch, read-alouds of *Alice Nizzy Nazzy,* a southwestern version of the Russian Baba Yaga tale and *The Tale of Rabbit and Coyote* may initiate a discussion on the role of the desert in the tales, the factual foundations in each tale, and the location of other world folktales set in a desert environment. The narrative voice of literature and a world perspective emerge from Kessler's *One Night* in which a young Tuareg nomadic boy, Mohammed, faces an adventure while watching a grazing herd of goats one night on the Sahara Desert. The beauty and the mystery of the desert of this multicultural selection moves the reader beyond the limited perspective of the American southwestern desert to a global sense of arid regions around the world.

A literature cluster can be implemented as an isolated unit or used as an enhancement to textbook instruction. The books can be shared through read-alouds by the teacher or multiple copies may be made available to groups of students for independent reading. The cluster may be shared during content area instructional time or woven into a reading/language arts block so as to address both literacy and knowledge. The most important aspect of a literature cluster is its ability to blend literary genre through narrative, expository, and poetic voices with the student absorbing multiple perspectives—aesthetic and efferent—on a topic. Beyond the informational focus of traditional units lies the importance of connecting facts to feelings, appreciation, and insights that personalize and enhance learning.

## Benefits of Literature Clusters

The desert model clarifies the importance of blending literary genres in a content area lesson in order to relate the narrative, expository, and poetic voices of literature on a single topic.

The range of literature takes the unit far from the traditional content area base to an inter-disciplinary approach steeped in language. Consider the benefits of such an approach to literature-based instruction in the content areas.

- **Children are exposed to all literary genres.** Their exposure to narrative, expository, and poetic voices not only varies informational perspectives, but provides models for reading and writing in these three modes. Literature clusters are in and of themselves interdisciplinary in nature; they are contrived to extend content area learning into the language arts.
- **Literature clusters contain multiage possibilities.** Because cluster selections make the literary experience, rather than a grade-level match, a priority, literature clusters appeal to a wide range of age and ability levels. In fact, they provide a sound base for interdis-ciplinary instruction in multiage configurations.
- **Literature clusters provide a broader vision of a topic.** Unlike traditional textbook instruction, children are encouraged to connect learning within a cluster as they detect relationships, compare factual and fictional perspectives, and revel in the language arts/literature enhancement of the informational base. As learners accumulate a medley of literature clusters throughout the school year, they even begin to connect learning between clusters. While their exposure to and familiarity with literature increases, children begin to create connections between clusters. For example, a science-based cluster on deserts might later connect to a social studies-based cluster on Egypt.
- **Literature clusters naturally connect fact and fiction for both enjoyment and learning.** Their greatest strength lies in their ability to create lifelong readers. Through exposure to all literary genres, readers find comfort and satisfaction in a wide variety of books. In addition to building content area knowledge, they are immersed in a multi-plicity of books, which fosters their desire to read and contributes to their future as lifelong readers.
- **Literature clusters create natural opportunities for reader response.** As books across genres are shared, response-based activities meaningfully match specific titles. Readers' theater, extended writing, graphic organizers, choral reading, and literature response journals extend the themed literature into varied response modes.

## Creating a Literature Cluster

What resources can be used for creating literature clusters? What steps does a teacher take to intentionally blend books from all literary genres? Several suggestions and sequential steps make the process challenging, fulfilling, and functional.

- **Determining a theme.** A theme for a literature cluster finds its roots in the curriculum guide or it can be generated from the interests of the students. It can build from a topic currently being studied, focus on one aspect of a topic under study, or be an original, freshly conceived topic that has never been investigated before. It can be broad if the intent is to pursue it in depth through further clusters, or it can be narrow and limit it-self to a short survey of a topic.
- **Locating a core book.** As a teacher begins to view literature on the designated topic, he or she can usually locate a book that truly appeals to one's taste, sparks imagination,

and relates to the topic at hand. This title might be considered the core book. Read it to get an introduction to the topic and to activate the flow of related literature titles. Plan a potential opening activity for your theme based on this book. Although no other literature may have been collected at this point, the core book serves as an inspiration for finding, accessing, and linking related literature to the topic. For example, Levine's *The Tree that Would Not Die* sparks interest in an exploration of trees because of its potential to inspire the reader/listener to appreciate the value and longevity of trees in our environment. Or Janet Stevens's *Tops and Bottoms* might be just what it takes to get primary students enthused about a "How Does Your Garden Grow?" theme. Often a children's literature title might actually be creative enough to generate the theme for an entire cluster. Avi's *Poppy,* for example, serves as a powerful fantasy read-aloud to initiate a theme on "Fine Feathered Friends." A core book naturally generates enthusiasm in the teacher for the possibilities of the literature, the framework of the theme, and the related activities that will accompany the literature cluster.

- **Conduct a library search.** Use general subject descriptors to access related book titles in your school or public library. The verso page of your core book provides additional subject descriptors that might result in further titles. The importance of these descriptors in stretching the literature search cannot be underestimated. With most libraries on-line—and often linked with other schools, the public library, and a university children's collection—this process is invigorating as well as challenging.
- **Brainstorm with teachers and media specialists.** Two minds are better than one when you attempt to brainstorm literature that might be related to a potential theme. Locate those professionals who know children's literature well. It is amazing what can be derived from a 10-minute session with people who appreciate and know children's books. Literature clusters taught in multiaged classrooms already have a team of professionals in place for this brainstorming session. Keep in mind the breadth of all literary genres throughout your brainstorming. A common tendency is to readily locate informational texts with little thought given to a possible fantasy connection, a multicultural focus, and the importance of biography to almost every topic.
- **Access professional resources.** Teachers are often surprised by how much of the brainstorming has already been done for them by professional experts in children's literature. Two helpful resources for creating literature clusters are *Book Links,* a journal of the American Library Association that focuses on thematically related titles across genres, and *The Reading Teacher,* a journal of the International Reading Association that consistently has a monthly column, "Children's Books" which reviews children's literature in an interdisciplinary mode by focusing on a single topic (Freeman, Lehman, & Scharer, 1996-1999). These sources often guide the teacher to not only titles that relate well to a theme, but also to the highest quality literature. See Appendix B for additional resources to use in locating literature for the cluster.
- **Design response-based instruction to accompany the literature.** Determine which books will be shared through read-alouds, which will be available as multiple copies for independent reading, and which will be resources for research. Review reader response modes to plan varied response activities or to allow for student-selected response-based projects.

- **Implement the literature cluster as the basis of instruction.** Typically housed in a content area time slot or woven into reading/writing blocks, the literature cluster should relate to the topic and strive for connectedness between books and information. Blending aesthetic and efferent response to a theme results in a higher level learning experience.

Literature clusters provide the perfect balance of fiction and nonfiction, imaginative and informative, narrative and expository, matter-of-fact and poetic. They challenge readers to sample all literary genres and synthesize them into a meaningful and memorable understanding of a topic. Clusters of related literature broaden the scope of study, immerse the learner, and evoke natural curiosity and further inquiry. Although these clusters stand alone as an introduction to a topic, they also form the foundation of theme explorations, which are discussed next in this chapter. The art of creating literature clusters establishes a model for blending literature clusters into the larger scope of a theme exploration. In a special way, the creation of literature clusters encompasses an educator's response to the literature she or he knows will open a new level of inquiry to the learner. Literature clusters form an intertextual link that challenges teachers to absorb children's literature, relate titles to each other, and take a first step toward understanding the interdisciplinary ramifications of children's books across the curriculum.

## Sample Literature Clusters

The next few pages of this chapter contain several models of literature clusters built on the open-ended topics of trees, journeys, and Japan. While the bases of these clusters lie in the language arts, science, and social studies, the literature itself blends varied voices and genres into a meaningful introduction to each topic. These clusters serve as models and are meant to inspire the creation of literature clusters on topics for your curriculum.

Examine each sample cluster for (1) quality literature, (2) a genre blend, (3) an interdisciplinary focus, and (4) narrative, expository, and poetic perspectives. Determine a core book with personal appeal that will initiate interest in the topic. Distinguish between teacher read-alouds and independent reading titles. Connect appropriate books to both spontaneous and teacher-initiated response-based activities. Supplement additional titles that instinctively come to mind. Appreciate the high- quality literature and the blended perspective of the literature cluster itself. Imagine and match reader response to individual titles as well as to the total package of literature. Consider teacher enthusiasm in sharing these titles as an introduction to a curricular theme. Finally, celebrate the connectedness of learning created by quality literature across literary genres that captures blended voices on a topic.

The three literature clusters included in this chapter provide a model for blending literature on a single theme across literary genres. Spreading the topic of trees across disciplines is the goal of "The Life and Legend of Trees" (Figure 14.3). At a more abstract level, "Journeys Within and Apart" (Figure 14.4) creatively explores a broad view of journeys of animals, people, and those that occur within ourselves. A cultural study of "Japan and Japanese Americans" (Figure 14.5) focuses on the history of the Japanese in America during World War II as well as touching on their artistic contributions. These sample clusters should generate fresh ideas for blending books across genres on a single topic.

**FIGURE 14.3**   Literature cluster: The life and legend of trees

Arnosky, Jim (1992). *Crinkleroot's guide to knowing the trees.* New York: Bradbury. INFORMATIONAL
Crinkleroot teaches the reader to identify trees, determine their age, and respect them as homes for animals.

Bannerman, Helen (1899/1996). *The story of little Babaji.* Illus. by Fred Marcellino. New York: HarperCollins.
This new edition of "Little Black Sambo" takes place in India with Babaji, Mamaji, and Papaji. The high-spirited illustrations of tigers melting into butter at the foot of the palm tree give new life to a classic tale. FOLKTALE

Behn, Harry (1992/1949). *Trees.* Illus. by James Endicott. New York: Holt. POEM PICTURE
*Trees are the kindest things I know, They do no harm, they simply grow.* Printed on recycled paper.

Fleming, Denise (1996). *Where once there was a wood.* New York: Holt. INFORMATIONAL
The wooded area near the author's home, now a housing development, inspired her story. So as not to forget the former woodland, she inspires children to turn their backyards into homes for wildlife.

Lester, Julius (1996). *Sam and the tigers.* Illus. by Jerry Pinkney. New York: Dial. FOLKTALE
This new retelling of the controversial "Little Black Sambo" brings new life to Sam, making this tale accessible to a new generation of readers. The tigers prowl off the page and chase each other around the tree until they melt into butter "as golden as a dream come true."

Levine, Ellen (1995). *The tree that would not die.* Illus. by Ted Rand. New York: Scholastic. HISTORICAL FICTION
The Treaty Oak of Austin, Texas, tells America's history through its own voice during its 400-year life span.

Levy, Constance (1994). *A tree place and other poems.* Illus. by R. Sabuda. New York: McElderry Books. POETRY
Forty small poems celebrate nature from inchworms and cicadas to forests and volcanoes.

Locker, Thomas, & Candace Christiansen (1995). *Sky tree: Seeing science through art.* Illus. by T. Locker. New York: HarperCollins. PICTURE BOOK
Locker's luminous paintings ask readers to consider a tree's seasonal changes from an artist's perspective.

Lyon, George Ella (1989). *A B Cedar: An alphabet of trees.* Illus. by Tom Parker. New York: Orchard Books. ABC CLASSIC
Alphabet book introducing leaves and tree identification and classification.

Orr, Richard (1995). *Richard Orr's nature cross sections.* New York: Dorling Kindersley. INFORMATIONAL
View the cross-section of a northern woodland setting and a majestic oak tree for deeper understanding.

Pringle, Laurence (1994). *Fire in the forest: A cycle of growth and renewal.* Paintings by B. Marstall. Atheneum. INFORMATIONAL
Fire is a friend to the forest as it recycles organic matter, provides new food sources for wildlife, and clears the way for a new generation of trees and plants. View a forested landscape before, during, and after a fire.

_____ (1993). *Trees and forests* (Voyages of Discovery Series). New York: Scholastic. INFORMATIONAL
An interactive blend of information, visual images, and literary connections.

**FIGURE 14.3**   Literature cluster: The life and legend of trees *(continued)*

Wood, Audrey (1996). *The Bunyans*. Illus. by David Shannon. New York: Blue Sky/Scholastic.
FOLKTALE
You may know the tale of Paul Bunyan, taller than a redwood tree and smarter than a library full
of books, and his great blue ox named Babe. But you may not know that Paul was married and
had two children!

Yarbrough, Camille (1996). *The little tree growin' in the shade*. Illus. by T. Geter. New York: Putnam.
MULTICULTURAL
The Tree of Life grew in Africa, but a branch was broken off when millions of Africans were
captured and brought as slaves to America. That branch took root and grew into a little tree
nourished by the richness of the culture the people had brought with them. Spirituals and oral
tradition brings this culture to the reader.

**FIGURE 14.4**   Literature cluster: Journeys within and apart

Balgassi, Haemi (1996). *Peacebound trains*. Illus. by Chris K. Soentpiet. Boston: Clarion. HISTOR-
ICAL FICTION/MULTICULTURAL
Poetic language and exquisite paintings evoke the people who fled Korea and a special grand-
mother and granddaughter relationship.

Bunting, Eve (1996). *Going home*. Illus. by David Diaz. New York: HarperCollins. MULTICULTURAL
Carlos and his family are going home to Mexico for Christmas. To Carlos, Mexico does not seem
like home, but as the family drives through villages and across landscapes, Carlos and his
sisters discover magic in their roots.

Bunting, Eve (1996). *Train to somewhere*. Illus. by Ron Himler. Boston: Clarion. HISTORICAL
FICTION
The story of the Orphan Train told by Marianne, one of a group of 14 children journeying from
New York across the Midwest in 1878. Marianne is the one nobody wants, but is finally adopted
by an elderly couple.

Conrad, Pam (1995). *Call me Ahnightito*. Illus. by Richard Egielski. New York: HarperCollins.
INFORMATIONAL/PICTURE
Narrative personification in first-person voice of a meteor's journey from outer space to
Greenland to its place in New York's American Museum of Natural History.

Cooney, Barbara (1996). *Eleanor*. New York: Viking. BIOGRAPHY
A journey through the childhood of Eleanor Roosevelt and the shaping of her indomitable spirit
that would make her one of the most beloved first ladies. Meticulously researched illustrations of
late 19th century.

Coy, John (1996). *Night driving*. Illus. by Peter McCarthy. New York: Holt. PICTURE BOOK
A father and son journey into the night on a trip to the mountains. Staying awake, stopping at
truck stops, viewing the sunrise are highlights that capture the warmth and nostalgia of a road
trip.

**FIGURE 14.4**    Literature cluster: Journeys within and apart *(continueed)*

Cunningham, David (1996). *A crow's journey.* Morton Grove, IL: Albert Whitman. POETRY
Where does the mountain snow go in spring? Through the journey of a crow, we follow the melted water from stream to waterfall, through a trout pool and a meadow, until it meets the sea.

Fisher Staples, Suzanne (1996). *Dangerous skies.* New York: Farrar, Strauss and Giroux. REALISTIC FICTION
This journey of friendship between a white boy and a black girl leads to murder, betrayal, and breaks the reader's heart as it confronts issues of racism and hypocrisy that continue to plague our country.

Fleischman, Paul (1996). *Dateline: Troy.* Collages by G. Frankfeldt and G. Morrow. Cambridge, MA: Candlewick Press. INFORMATIONAL
The author juxtaposes his compelling retelling of the Trojan War with newspaper clippings of modern events from World War I to the Gulf War. *The Trojan War is still being fought. Simply open a newspaper. . . .*

Hunt, Jonathan (1996). *Leif's saga: A viking tale.* New York: Simon & Schuster. FOLKTALE
Based on the Icelandic oral histories of Leif Ericksson, this tale tells of gripping challenges, lost dreams, and renewed hope. Illustrations are filled with historical detail, costumes, geography, and architecture.

Kehret, Peg (1996). *Small steps: The year I got polio.* Morton Grove, IL: Albert Whitman. AUTOBIOGRAPHY
The popular author of scary stories tells of her own battle with polio during the 1950s and her struggle to overcome its effects as a 12-/13-year-old.

Kharms, Daniil (1996). *First, second.* Translated from Russian by R. Pevear. Illus. by M. Rosenthal. Farrar, Strauss and Giroux. PICTURE BOOK/FANTASY/COUNTING
The short journey of four companions proves hilariously complicated. Only with collaborative problem solving can these friends overcome the obstacles. Wit, whimsy, and comic artistic style entertain the reader.

Sorenson, Henri (1995). *New Hope.* New York: Lothrop, Lee & Shepard. HISTORICAL FICTION
A chance broken axle on a journey west establishes the future town of New Hope, Minnesota.

Stanley, Diane (1996). *Elena.* New York: Hyperion. HISTORICAL FICTION
Elena, so different from her sisters, longs to visit distant places, learn to read books, and master the magic of numbers. The Mexican Revolution forces her to leave her country on an unforgettable journey to freedom.

**FIGURE 14.5**    Literature cluster: Cultural study: Japan and Japanese Americans

Coerr, Eleanore (1994). *Sadako.* New York: Putnam. HISTORICAL FICTION
A picture book dramatization of the aftermath of the atomic bomb on Japan. The hope of folding a thousand paper cranes inspires severely injured Sadako.

Kroll, Virginia (1994). *Pink paper swans.* Illus. by N. Clouse. Grand Rapids, MI: Eerdmans. PICTURE BOOK
Mrs. Tsujimoto teaches Janetta the art of origami and becomes her hands when Mrs. Tsujimoto's arthritis makes it difficult for her to continue. Includes instruction for a pink paper folded swan.

**FIGURE 14.5** Literature cluster: Cultural study: Japan and Japanese Americans *(continued)*

Levine, Ellen (1995). *A fence away from freedom: Japanese Americans and World War II.* New York: Putnam. AUTOBIOGRAPHY
The Japanese Americans imprisoned in internment camps as children and young adults tell their stories today. These stories tell of pain, hurtful discrimination, extraordinary courage, and unexpected kindnesses. A strong first-person voice speaks to the reader.
Lewis, J. Patrick (1995). *Black swan/white crow.* Woodcuts by C. Manson. New York: Atheneum. POETRY
One of the simplest forms of poetry came from the Japanese—haiku. The best haiku make you think and wonder about nature for longer than it takes to say them.
Little, Mimi Otey (1996). *Yoshiko and the foreigner.* New York: Farrar, Strauss and Giroux. PICTURE BOOK
Japanese girls are not to speak to foreign strangers, but Yoshiko changes her life forever by helping a young American Air Force officer on a crowded Tokyo train. A true story bridging two worlds.
Martin, Rafe (1996). *Mysterious tales of Japan.* Illus. by T. Kiuchi. New York: Putnam. TRADITIONAL TALES
This collection of traditional Japanese tales is haunting, evocative, ghostly, and serene. All of the tales possess an elegant beauty that leads them toward conclusions that mirror the realities of our own lives.
Mochizuki, Ken (1993). *Baseball saved us.* Illus. by Dom Lee. New York: Lee & Low Books. HISTORICAL FICTION
A Japanese American boy learns to play baseball when he and his family are forced to live in an internment camp during WWII. His ability to play helps him after the war is over.
Salisbury, Graham (1994). *Under the blood red sun.* New York: Delacorte Press. HISTORICAL FICTION
From a treetop on Oahu, Tomi Nakaji, 13, and his *haole*/white best friend witness in disbelief the bombing of Pearl Harbor. Tomi's father and grandfather are arrested while Tomi assumes responsibility for the family honor. Racial tension is subtly presented but escalates following the Japanese attack.
Say, Allen (1994). *Grandfather's journey.* Boston: Houghton Mifflin. PICTURE BOOK CLASSIC
A grandfather's love of two countries, Japan and America, is portrayed through this Caldecott award-winning book.
Stanley, Jerry (1994). *I am an American: A true story of Japanese internment.* Illus. with photos. New York: Crown. INFORMATIONAL
The bombing of Pearl Harbor results in the forced imprisonment of 120,000 Japanese, two thirds of whom were U.S. citizens. Their only crime—Japanese ancestry. Focuses on the internment of Shiro Nomura whose future is shattered by racial prejudice and war.
Tunnell, Michael O., & Chilcoat, G. W. (1996). *The children of Topaz: The story of a Japanese-American internment camp.* New York: Holiday House. DIARY
Daily life in a relocation camp is captured through 20 diary entries of children in a third grade.
Uchida, Yoshiko (1994). *The bracelet.* Illus. by J. Yardley. New York: Philomel Books. HISTORICAL FICTION/PICTURE
A Japanese girl is interned in a California camp during WWII with only a bracelet to remember a special friendship.
Yep, Laurence (1996). *Hiroshima: A novella.* New York: Scholastic. HISTORICAL FICTION
On the morning of August 6, 1945, the *Enola Gay* roars toward Hiroshima, Japan. Its cargo is an atom bomb. The same morning, 12-year-old Sachi and her sister walk to school. Their country is at war. Sachi will never see her sister again. Based on true-life accounts written by survivors of the Hiroshima bombing.

# BUILDING THEME EXPLORATIONS: A RESPONSE-BASED PROCESS

One of the most effective literature-based techniques for integrating the elementary/middle-level curriculum is through theme explorations. Theme exploration describes a means of organizing instruction around a broad-based theme and connected subthemes rather than around content areas. By teaching through theme exploration, it is possible to integrate instruction, utilize quality children's literature, and implement response-based activities in a meaningful way across curricular areas.

Theme explorations have gained popularity as the amount of knowledge we seek to disseminate as teachers has become overwhelming. No longer can we teach the entire content curriculum. It appears far more productive to teach the process of exploring quality themes rather than delivering quantified, superficial content area information. Theme explorations are motivating to both teachers and students because they encourage the pursuit of ideas more thoroughly to develop a deeper, rather than a broader, understanding. Their connectedness results in students developing an awareness of relationships among, between, and across ideas. The relevance of the relationship of learning across disciplines offers an added dimension to learning (Shanahan, Robinson, & Schneider, 1995).

The term "theme exploration" (Weaver et al., 1993) must be differentiated from the more traditional meaning of "thematic units." Theme explorations move beyond topic coverage to dynamic ideals. For example, food may be a topic, but the role of food as a contributor to quality of life in our global society is a theme. With traditional primary-level topics (penguins, bears, apples, friendship) the curriculum is unnaturally stretched to allow content area activities related to each content area. In doing so, content areas that do not realistically connect are forced to work. Theme explorations, however, allow for a deeper examination of ideas and ideals through quality literature that encourages response and thinking at higher levels. For example, the adaptation of animals to climate is a broader based theme that encompasses penguins and polar bears.

Theme explorations even raise the possibility of new ideas being introduced to students that are not even considered in a traditional isolated subject curriculum. If content areas don't fit, there is no mandate to include them as part of the theme exploration. Arrangements can be made for pursuing them independently of the theme. In teachers' zeal to pull all content areas together, we often overdo and create more irrelevant connections than intellectual gain. Theme exploration provides the flexibility and freedom to bring more intellectually stimulating ideas, meaningful literature, and related response-based activities to interdisciplinary instruction.

The process of constructing a theme exploration consists of five major steps:

1. Choosing a broad-based theme;
2. Brainstorming related children's literature;
3. Locating additional children's literature;
4. Creating a graphic web reflecting connectedness between main theme and related subthemes;
5. Planning literature-based response activities designed for whole class, small group, and individual learning; and
6. Sharing the theme exploration in the classroom.

Looking at each step in detail assists us in the design, planning, and implementation of classroom theme explorations. Personal reflections during the evolution of the author's theme exploration should assist readers with insights into the theme exploration process as well as the final instructional product. "Tracing the Fabric of Our Nation Through Story," interspersed throughout the following discussion, provides a model theme exploration. Refer to the graphic organizer (Figure 14.6), the bibliography (Figure 14.7) and the response-based activities (Figure 14.8) as you internalize the process of creating an interdisciplinary themed exploration.

## Choosing a Theme

Choosing a theme is the first, and unquestionably the most important step in theme exploration. Choosing a broad theme, an innovative question, or a motivating issue can make the difference between a mediocre and a powerful theme exploration. The theme must be broad enough to incorporate several trade book genres and response-based activities, but not so broad as to lose the connectedness between elements or subthemes. Because choice is considered an aspect of response, teachers must open possibilities for choosing themes to students. Their apparent interest and motivation can influence the selection and direction the theme exploration takes. Theme explorations may spring from curricular topics, but are handled in a more creative mode than textbook delivery of instruction. A few examples of theme exploration titles such as "That Was Then/This Is Now: Exploring Change," "It's a Jungle Out There," "The Road to Freedom," and "Making a Difference" provide sound examples of the various types of thematic journeys on which students and teachers might embark.

*The reading of Karen Hesse's* Letters from Rifka *brought back nostalgic recollections of my own grandparents who came to America from Czechoslovakia and Germany through Ellis Island. Thoughts of a theme exploration on immigration grew, but were limited by my own narrow perspective on European immigration. As I began to talk to colleagues and children and explore existing literature about this theme, broadening possibilities came to mind. What about the new wave of immigrants? What about the unwelcomed reaction to Japanese immigrants during World War II? What about those immigrants who journeyed across the prairies of America to the West? My narrow focus of immigration began to grow and I felt energized as the prospect of locating literature and designing instruction from that literature seemed possible. After countless attempts at theme titles, "Tracing the Fabric of Our Nation Through Story" was born as a theme exploration title that inspired, directed, connected, and broadened the topic of immigration.*

## Brainstorming and Locating Literature

Literature is a major factor in the direction and scope of the theme. This step is often the most invigorating part of the planning stage for the theme exploration because it does involve the heartbeat of the theme exploration—children's literature. The goal is to locate literature across all literary genres: picture books, traditional/folktales, informational books, historical fiction, biography/autobiography, poetry, realistic fiction, fantasy, and multicultural literature. Although connections to some genres dominate, time and persistence will allow meaningful books from almost all genres to be highlighted for the theme. Don't be too discerning when choosing a preliminary selection of related books. Brainstorm as many titles as you can.

Meet with a multiage group of teachers and get input from titles they deem appropriate. Consult with the library/media center director. Ask the children what books come to mind. This initial brainstorming opens the mind to possibilities for connected subthemes and also honors related literature. The initial inclusion of a particular book title or a series of books may actually shape the theme.

This stage must be open minded and open ended. Too often we limit our scope by following traditional connections to themes. Avoid going to the card catalog, the bookshelves, or the computer subject guide initially. Let the collaborative effort of colleagues and children stretch the possibilities that energize the theme exploration.

*I began with those titles that were foremost in my mind—titles I had just read, recently seen in bookstores, or read reviews about. I looked to old favorites that had always provided the core of study on this topic. I was reinspired by Emma Lazarus's poetic inscription on the Statue of Liberty and shed a tear as I really looked at photographs in Russell Freedman's* Immigrant Kids *for the first time. The local librarian suggested Jerry Stanley's* I Am an American *and a colleague shared a copy of Eve Bunting's* A Day's Work. *Suddenly the theme exploration was bigger than European immigration; it expanded to include Japanese Americans and the new wave of immigrants from Mexico and Southeast Asia. I was overwhelmed by where this simple theme could take us, but comforted by the fact that the literature was plentiful, of high quality, and accessible.*

## Locating Additional Literature

After the initial bookstorming session, library and literature resources should be consulted to extend the related theme literature. Expand the scope and criteria to include both new books as well as classic titles that might contain related information and a desirable style of delivery. Consult the following resources as your literary repertoire continues to grow:

School district on-line catalog
Public library on-line catalog
*Subject Guide to Books in Print* (use subject descriptors suggested in other books on the topic)
*Book Links* (American Library Association).

See Appendix B for more information about these and additional resources for accessing literature. Continue to keep in mind the priority of locating a blend of all literary genres. Surprisingly, poetry does exist on the designated theme and biographies span the disciplines. Continue to search until the possibilities slow and connections become stretched instead of meaningful. At this point, the theme exploration collection might number between 50 and 100 books. While all of these may not provide a primary focus for your theme, many can be used for related independent research and reading by your students.

*Time flew by as I sat in front of the library computer screen plugging in descriptors from books I had located. New entries brought new titles and new possibilities for subthemes. I pulled up titles related to grandparents and westward movement. The orphan trains and Japanese concentration camps elicited many new titles. Several issues of* Book Links *provided additional listings of related literature. I was amazed that biography, poetry, and picture books had effectively invaded a theme I was sure was dominated by historical fiction. I located, recalled, and eventually handled over seventy books which showed promise for read- alouds, independent reading selections, research, and response.*

## Absorbing the Literature

Read, enjoy, savor, learn, connect, grow, and design your theme exploration from the literature itself. Although reading all of the books is impossible, begin to identify books by genre, to locate possible read-alouds, to devise tentative response-based activities, and to sort and clarify the direction of the theme. Inherent connections between and among titles will become apparent. Spread the books out on a table or floor and begin to organize them in a meaningful way. Move them around, eliminate some, add others, but remain open minded and let the literature direct thought and evolving subthemes. Do a quick check of literary genres. Don't force books to fit the theme, but attempt to include at least six genres in your theme exploration. In this preliminary immersion stage, the teacher is actually responding to literature by creatively linking and extending the theme to related subthemes. Connecting book titles, planning innovative response activities, and reading the literature are all fertile soil for teachers' personal responses.

Reread this chapter's opening reflection to recapture the process of organizing the literature into meaningful subthemes. Focus on the immigration bibliography to internalize this process (see Figure 14.7).

## Creating a Visual Image of the Theme Exploration

With all of the literature surrounding the theme, the need for organization through a graphic organizer is apparent. To get the webbing process started, sort the literature into four to six related subthemes. Bring in a colleague or a few students to prevent you from being locked into traditional modes. As connections become apparent, books will be linked in related subtheme categories and new connections will begin to emerge.

As the graphic organizer begins to take shape, focus more definitely on potential response-based activities with particular books. Designate a core book and related activity as a springboard for the exploration. Consider a class set of a chapter book title for a reading workshop. Note the potential of informational titles for independent research topics and presentations. Identify possible titles for drama, art, and musical extensions.

The graphic organizer is intended to be an extended theme exploration lesson plan. When complete, it will contain the creative title of the theme exploration, motivating titles of four to six meaningfully related subthemes, lists of literature related to those subthemes, and response-based activities related to particular pieces of literature. In viewing the graphic organizer, innovative organization, motivating presentation, quality literature, and meaningful literature-based activities are apparent (see Figure 14.6). Books span at least six literary genres so fictional, factual, and poetic perspectives on the theme are present. Interdisciplinary presentation of the thematic focus becomes clearer and teacher confidence in the planning is evidenced. Teachers might choose to share the graphic organizer with each student (bulletin board or handout) so they can visualize the connectedness of subthemes to the main theme. Many teachers also like to include students in the theme planning at this stage. Children see the connections in learning differently than adults and often provide important input at this point in the theme exploration planning.

*This next step seemed to flow naturally from the piles that lay before me. The books themselves formed a graphic web. My task was simply to transfer the breadth of this theme to a graphic*

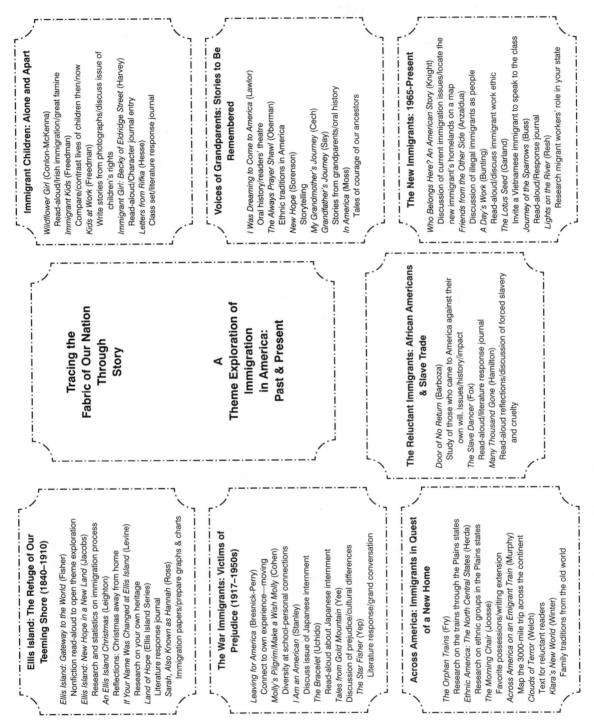

**Immigrant Children: Alone and Apart**

*Wildflower Girl* (Conlon-McKenna)
 Read-aloud/Irish immigration/great famine
*Immigrant Kids* (Freedman)
 Compare/contrast lives of children then/now
*Kids at Work* (Freedman)
 Write stories from photographs/discuss issue of children's rights
*Immigrant Girl: Becky of Eldridge Street* (Harvey)
 Read-aloud/Character journal entry
*Letters from Rifka* (Hesse)
 Class set/literature response journal

**Voices of Grandparents: Stories to Be Remembered**

*I Was Dreaming to Come to America* (Lawlor)
 Oral history/readers' theatre
*The Always Prayer Shawl* (Oberman)
 Ethnic traditions in America
*New Hope* (Sorenson)
 Storytelling
*My Grandmother's Journey* (Cech)
*Grandfather's Journey* (Say)
 Stories from grandparents/oral history
*In America* (Moss)
 Tales of courage of our ancestors

**The New Immigrants: 1965–Present**

*Who Belongs Here? An American Story* (Knight)
 Discussion of current immigration issues/locate the new immigrant's homelands on a map
*Friends from the Other Side* (Anzaldua)
 Discussion of illegal immigrants as people
*A Day's Work* (Bunting)
 Read-aloud/discuss immigrant work ethic
*The Lotus Seed* (Garland)
 Invite a Vietnamese immigrant to speak to the class
*Journey of the Sparrows* (Buss)
 Read-aloud/Response journal
*Lights on the River* (Resh)
 Research migrant workers' role in your state

**Tracing the Fabric of Our Nation Through Story**

**A Theme Exploration of Immigration in America: Past & Present**

**The Reluctant Immigrants: African Americans & Slave Trade**

*Door of No Return* (Barboza)
 Study of those who came to America against their own will. Issues/history/impact
*The Slave Dancer* (Fox)
 Read-aloud/literature response journal
*Many Thousand Gone* (Hamilton)
 Read-aloud reflections/discussion of forced slavery and cruelty

**Ellis Island: The Refuge of Our Teeming Shore (1840–1910)**

*Ellis Island: Gateway to the World* (Fisher)
 Nonfiction read-aloud to open theme exploration
*Ellis Island: New Hope in a New Land* (Jacobs)
 Research and statistics on immigration process
*An Ellis Island Christmas* (Leighton)
 Reflections: Christmas away from home
*If Your Name Was Changed at Ellis Island* (Levine)
 Research on your own heritage
*Land of Hope* (Ellis Island Series)
 Literature response journal
*Sarah, Also Known as Hannah* (Ross)
 Immigration papers/prepare graphs & charts

**The War Immigrants: Victims of Prejudice (1917–1950s)**

*Leaving for America* (Bresnick-Perry)
 Connect to own experience—moving
*Molly's Pilgrim/Make a Wish Molly* (Cohen)
 Diversity at school-personal connections
*I Am an American* (Stanley)
 Discuss issue of Japanese internment
*The Bracelet* (Uchido)
 Read-aloud about Japanese internment
*Tales from Gold Mountain* (Yee)
 Discussion of prejudice/cultural differences
*The Star Fisher* (Yep)
 Literature response/grand conversation

**Across America: Immigrants in Quest of a New Home**

*The Orphan Trains* (Fry)
 Research on the trains through the Plains states
*Ethnic America: The North Central States* (Herda)
 Research on ethnic groups in the Plains states
*The Morning Chair* (Joosse)
 Favorite possessions/writing extension
*Across America on an Emigrant Train* (Murphy)
 Map the 3000-mile trip across the continent
*Clouds of Terror* (Welch)
 Text for reluctant readers
*Klara's New World* (Winter)
 Family traditions from the old world

**FIGURE 14.6** Theme exploration graphic organizer

**FIGURE 14.7**   Theme exploration bibliography

**A bibliography of children's books**
**Tracing the Fabric of Our Nation Through Story**

### Ellis Island: The Refuge of our Teeming Shore (1840–1910)

Bartone, Elisa (1993). *Peppe the lamplighter.* Illus. by Ted Lewin. New York: Lothrop, Lee & Shepard. [ P/I ]

Fisher, Leonard Everett (1986). *Ellis Island: Gateway to the New World.* New York: Holiday House. [ I/M ]

Gross, Virginia (1990). *It's only good-bye* (Once Upon America series.) New York: Viking. [ I ]

Jacobs, William Jay (1990). *Ellis Island: New hope in a new land.* New York: Charles Scribner's Sons. [ I ]

Leighton, Maxinne Rhea (1992). *An Ellis Island Christmas.* Illus. by Dennis Nolan. New York: Viking. [ P/I ]

Levine, Ellen (1992). *If your name was changed at Ellis Island.* Illus. by W. Parmenter. New York: Scholastic. [ I ]

Levitin, Sonia (1992). *Silver days.* New York: Atheneum. [ I/M ]

Nixon, Joan Lowery (1994). *Land of dreams.* (Ellis Island series). New York: Delacorte Press. [ I/M ]
Also see: *Land of promise* (Irish) and *Land of hope* (Russian)

Ross, Lillian Hammer (1994). *Sarah, also known as Hannah.* Illus. by H. Cogancherry. Morton Grove, IL: Whitman. [ I ]

### Across America: Immigrants in Quest of a New Home

Fry, Annette R. (1994). *The orphan trains* (American Event series). New York: Macmillan. [ I/M ]

Herda, D. J. (1991). *Ethnic America: The North Central States.* Brookfield, CT: Millbrook. [ I/M ]

Joosse, Barbara M. (1995). *The morning chair.* Illus. by M. Sewall. Boston: Clarion. [ P ]

Murphy, Jim (1993). *Across America on an emigrant train.* Boston: Clarion. [ I/M ]

Sandler, Martin W. (1995). *Immigrants: A Library of Congress book.* Photos. New York: HarperCollins. [ I/M ]

Welch, Catherine A. (1994). *Clouds of terror.* Illus. by L. K. Johnson. Minneapolis, MN: Carolrhoda. Carolrhoda 'On My Own' Books. [ I ]

Winter, Jeanette (1992). *Klara's new world.* New York: Knopf. [ P/I ]

### Immigrant Children: Alone and Apart

Conlon-McKenna, Marita (1992). *Wildflower girl.* New York: Holiday House. [ I/M ] Sequel to *Under the hawthorn tree* (1991). [ I/M ]

Freedman, Russell (1980). *Immigrant kids.* Illus. with photographs. New York: E. P. Dutton. [ I/M ]

Freedman, Russell (1994). *Kids at work: Lewis Hine and the crusade against child labor.* Boston: Clarion. [ I/M ]

Harvey, Brett (1987). *Immigrant girl: Becky of Eldridge Street.* Illus. by D. Kogan Ray. New York: Holiday House. [ P/I ]

Hesse, Karen (1992). *Letters from Rifka.* New York: Holt. [ I/M ]

### Voices of Our Grandparents: Stories to Be Remembered

Cech, John (1991). *My grandmother's journey.* Illus. by S. McGinley-Nally. New York: Bradbury. [ P/I ]

Lawlor, Veronica (1995). *I was dreaming to come to America.* New York: Viking. [ I/M ]

FIGURE 14.7 Theme exploration bibliography *(continued)*

Levinson, Riki (1985). *Watch the stars come out.* Illus. by Diane Goode. New York: Dutton. [ P/I ]

Moss, Marisa (1994). *In America.* New York: Dutton. [ P ]

Oberman, Sheldon (1994). *The always prayer shawl.* Illus. by Ted Lewin. Honesdale, PA: Boyds Mills Press. [ P/I ]

Say, Allen (1993). *Grandfather's journey.* Boston: Houghton Mifflin. Caldecott Medal 1994. [ P/I ]

Sorenson, Henri (1995). *New Hope.* Illus. by Ted Lewin. New York: Lothrop, Lee & Shepard. [ P/I ]

### The War Immigrants: Victims of Prejudice (1917–1950s)

Bresnick-Perry, Roslyn (1992). *Leaving for America.* Illus. by Mira Reisberg. Emeryville, CA: Children's Book Press. [ P/I ]

Cohen, Barbara (1983). *Molly's pilgrim.* Illus. by M. Deraney. New York: Lothrop, Lee & Shepard. [ P ]

Cohen, Barbara (1994). *Make a wish, Molly.* Illus. by Jan Naimo Jones. New York: Doubleday. [ P ]

Stanley, Jerry (1994). *I am an American: A true story of Japanese internment.* Illus. with photos. New York: Crown. [ I/M ]

Uchida, Yoshiko (1994). *The bracelet.* New York: Putnam. [ I ]

Yee, Paul (1989). *Tales from Gold Mountain: Stories of the Chinese in the New World.* New York: Macmillan [ I/M ]

### The New Immigrants: Southeast Asia, Mexico, Central America, the Caribbean, S. Korea, & China (1965–Present)

Anzaldua, Gloria (1993). *Friends from the other side.* Illus. by Consuelo Mendez. Emeryville, CA: Children's Book Press. [ I ]

Brown, Tricia (1991). *Lee Ann: The story of a Vietnamese-American girl.* New York: Putnam. [ P/I ]

Bunting, Eve (1988). *How many days to America? A Thanksgiving story.* Boston: Clarion. [ P/I ]

Bunting, Eve (1994). *A day's work.* Illus. by R. Himler. Boston: Clarion. [ P/I ]

Buss, Fran Leeper (1991). *Journey of the sparrows.* New York: Lodestar. [ I/M ]

Carlson, Lori M (Ed.) (1994). *Cool salsa: Bilingual poems on growing up Latino in the United States.* New York: Fawcett. [ M ]

Garland, Sherry (1993). *The lotus seed.* Illus. by Tatsuro Kiuchi. San Diego: Harcourt Brace. [ P/I ]

Graff, Nancy Price (1993). *Where the river runs.* Photo essay. Boston: Little, Brown. [ I/M ]

Knight, Margie Burns (1993). *Who belongs here? An American story.* Illus. by A. O'Brien. Gardiner, ME: Tilbury House. [ I/M ]

Poynter, Margaret (1992). *The uncertain journey: Stories of illegal aliens in El Norte.* New York: Atheneum. [ I/M ]

Resh, Jane (1994). *Lights on the river.* Illus. by M. Dooling. New York: Hyperion. [ P/I ]

### The Reluctant Immigrants: African Americans and the Slave Trade

Barboza, Steven (1994). *Door of no return: The legend of Goree Island.* Photos. New York: Cobble-hill/Dutton. [ I/M ]

Fox, Paula (1973). *The slave dancer.* New York: Bradbury. [ I/M ]

Hamilton, Virginia (1993). *Many thousand gone: African Americans from slavery to freedom.* New York: Knopf. [ I/M ]

### Celebrating the Fabric of our Nation: Reflective Thoughts

Ashabranner, Brent (1993). *Still a nation of immigrants.* Photos by J. Aschabranner. New York: Cobblehill/Dutton. [ I/M ]

**FIGURE 14.7**    Theme exploration bibliography *(continued)*

Hamanaka, Sheila (1994). *All the colors of the earth.* New York: Morrow. [ P ]
Hopkins, Lee Bennett (Compiler) (1994). *Hand in hand: An American history through poetry.* Illus. by Peter Fiore. New York: Simon & Schuster. [ P/I/M ]
Panzer, Nora (Ed.) (1994). *Celebrate America in poetry and art.* Published in association with the National Museum. New York: Hyperion. [ P/I/M ]
Whipple, Laura (Compiler) (1994). *Celebrating America: A collection of poems and images of the American spirit.* In association with the Art Institute of Chicago. New York: Philomel Books. [ P/I/M ]

*representation on paper. The titling of subthemes came surprisingly swiftly and a reaffirmation of books across many literary genres was reassuring. Stirrings of response-based connections soared in my mind and it was difficult to pick up a book without thinking of a meaningful response connection. Many informational titles begged to be researched and a few promised dramatic presentation. While a lack of personal adeptness with the word processor slowed the visual image of the web, the relatedness of the literature to the theme and the connectedness of the subthemes were continuously and emphatically present.*

## Response-Based Connections to Literature

Finalizing the response-based connections to literature is an important part of the process. Although gathering and organizing the literature is crucial to the success of the theme exploration, the response-based connections will provide the literacy base to this unique delivery of instruction. A mixture of whole class, small group, and individual response activities should be devised (see Figure 14.8). The response modes should be varied and include some listening to read-alouds, some oral prompting or free discussion, personal written response, and some interactive art, music, or performance activities. Special attention should be given to the opening literature and response because it provides the motivation and inquiry for the entire theme exploration. The culminating activity and final sharing of literature is of equal import because it serves to synthesize, connect, and evaluate the thinking and learning as a result of the theme exploration. This response-based focus to the theme exploration can include research, the writing of mathematical problems, hands-on science, or oral history interviews. The interdisciplinary strength of the theme exploration must be utilized and the response possibilities across disciplines must be explored.

*Aside from reveling in the literature, I admit to thoroughly enjoying planning the response-based connections to literature. Mandatory was a literature response journal to* Letters from Rifka. *Hadn't that book enthralled me as I completed it in a single reading session? A grand conversation on* Who Belongs Here? An American Study *was likely to initiate personal connections and experiences for students.* Ellis Island: Gateway to the New World *presented an informational read-aloud with facts and photos to open our minds and hearts to immigrants. A dramatic reenactment of* New Hope *and a readers' theatre from the words of immigrants and their families in* I Was Dreaming to Come to America *inspired me and the evolving exploration. They were not stretches; they were meaningful response options created by themed literature. They would aesthetically connect the students in a relevant way to the message and ideals of this theme exploration.*

**FIGURE 14.8**   Theme exploration response-based activities

---

### Suggested Activities: Tracing the Fabric of Our Nation through Story

#### Individual

Keep a literature response journal as you read one of the many chapter books on immigrants (i.e., *Letters from Rifka,* Ellis Island series). Share your innermost thoughts and feelings about leaving a homeland, family, and friends to come to a new life in America.

Keep a character journal—a first-person account of coming to America—while reading *Wildflower Girl.* Write from the point-of-view of Peggy as she leaves Ireland, travels on a coffin ship, arrives alone in Boston, and obtains a job as a domestic helper. Include the feelings and thoughts going through her/your mind as her tale unfolds.

Collect photographs from your own family history. Interview family members about the photos and tape record the interview. Use your notes in compiling a fact-based story to accompany the photograph.

Write a poem that reflects the feelings and thoughts of immigrants about leaving their homeland and coming to a strange, new world in America—either in the past or today.

#### Small Group

Use oral storytelling to present books told through the voices of grandparents who tell their stories of immigration and finding a home in America, i.e., *New Hope, In America, The Always Prayer Shawl.*

Use a readers' theater format to present dramatic readings from *I Was Dreaming to Come to America.* Let the book spark an interest in oral history and the worthy task of documenting history through first-hand accounts.

Read *Friends from the Other Side* in both English and Spanish. Discuss the issue of illegal immigration.

Research one of the many European ethnic groups that came to America through Ellis Island (i.e., Irish, German, Russians, Scandinavians). Discover why they left, when they came, where they settled, and what their ethnic group has added to the fabric of our nation. Record any statistics you might find on a class chart.

Research the plight of immigrant children, both in the cities and those who traveled west on the orphan trains. Compare/contrast life of children today with life of early immigrant children.

Research one of the "new immigrants" from Vietnam, Cambodia, Korea, Mexico, or the Caribbean. Discover why they left, when they came, where they settled, and what their ethnic group adds to the fabric of our nation.

Investigate immigration laws from 1840–1910 and compare them with today's immigration laws. What changes have taken place? Why? Why do we have so many "illegal aliens" today? What should we do in our country to address this issue?

Research migrant workers' role in America. Read *A Day's Work* and *Lights on the River* to demonstrate the work ethic of the new immigrant.

Conduct a "grand conversation" on the books you have been reading about immigration. What are some consistent facts that keep reappearing? What have you learned that you didn't know before? What questions still need to be answered?

**FIGURE 14.8**   Theme exploration response-based activities *(continued)*

---

**Whole Class**

Read *Who Belongs Here? An American Story* as an introduction to the issues surrounding immigration. Use the questions in the text to spark discussion.

Invite a person from the community to the classroom to discuss their own (or their parents') immigration to America. Brainstorm a list of questions prior to their presentation. Write a thank- you note for their time and sharing.

Compile and laminate a class scrapbook of immigration photographs and written stories from members of the class.

Celebrate an ethnic cooking day with food from your own culture— German, Hispanic, English, Irish, Scandinavian, etc. Share group reports on each ethnic group and share the wonderful culinary delights as a culminating theme activity.

Make a "quilt" that depicts the many pieces of America that are bound together by the common thread of immigration— America is the land of opportunity and an appreciation of the cultures that make up the fabric of our nation.

---

## Sharing the Theme Exploration With Children

The apex of gathering, reading, inventing, and planning is the actual implementation of the theme exploration in the classroom. While theme explorations can be pursued throughout the entire school day, they are most often shared in half-day formats with the other half-day being used for supplemental instruction that does not meaningfully fit the theme. Mini-portfolios to house theme-related projects, research, and response are useful. While initial theme explorations may span a 2-week period, many experienced teachers see them stretching across a 9-week quarter or, in a few cases, across the entire school year. While this type of authentic instruction requires time for planning and accessing materials, the quality of learning justifies the investment (Bergeron & Rudenga, 1996). Many school districts provide a day a month for collaborative thematic planning. The joy of this type of teaching comes in the delivery of meaningful instruction through which responses to literature include both an efferent and an aesthetic understanding of a theme or concept.

## Benefits of Theme Explorations

Literature-based, response-centered theme explorations benefit both teachers and learners as they revitalize instruction and energize the classroom. This interdisciplinary style of teaching and learning scores tremendous advantages over traditional instruction.

- Teachers are challenged by the opportunity to creatively plan and teach through literature collected on a broad-based theme.
- Teachers gain confidence in teaching the required curriculum through a unique interdisciplinary approach to learning.

- Teachers personally respond to literature through their own creative selection and blending of quality titles related to a broad-based theme.
- Students realize a natural connectedness to learning rather than viewing content as being related to isolated topics.
- Students experience a wide range of literature across genres that connects the factual, fictional, and poetic perspectives on a theme.
- Students experienced genuine, meaningful response-based activities centralized on a theme.
- Students accept the challenge of higher level thinking and initiate research inquiry into related aspects of the theme.
- Teachers and students become immersed in quality literature across genres which piques their motivation to read, to learn, and to respond.

Figures 14.9 through 14.12 illustrate several models that provide visual and literature cues for creating theme explorations. The graphic organizers contain ideas for theme titles and subthemes and a visual blend of literature across genres and are grouped developmentally for sharing with students.

"Under a Blanket of Darkness" (Figure 14.9) explores the mystery of the night in a multiage primary setting. A typical third/fourth-grade solar system science theme is enhanced in "Beyond the Heavens" (Figure 14.10) as the sun, stars, planets, and moon become the topic for fictional and factual exploration. Fifth graders take a literacy journey across our country on the "Read Across America" (Figure 14.11). Sixth, seventh, and eighth graders delight in "The Lives and Legends of Medieval Times" (Figure 14.12) as the age of knights, castles, and King Arthur comes to life. These graphic organizers and related literature are the authentic efforts of classroom teachers who felt invigorated and challenged by an integrated, literature-based means for delivering interdisciplinary instruction. These examples serve as inspiration, not limitation on the power of literature to create effective interdisciplinary instruction through theme explorations.

**FIGURE 14.9** Theme exploration graphic organizer

**Under a Blanket of Darkness: A Thematic Unit Surrounding the Night**

**Core Literature:** *Moonhorse* **by Mary Pope Osborne**

### Looking on the World with Nighttime Eyes: A Description of the Night

*A Visit to Sleep's House* by Mary Pope Osborne
  FANTASY
*The Sun's Asleep Behind the Hill* by Mirra Ginsburg
  PICTURE BOOK
*The Moon's the North Wind's Cooky* by Susan Russo
  POETRY
*Still as a Star* by Lee Bennett Hopkins
  POETRY
*The Night of the Whippoorwill* by Nancy Larrick
  POETRY

### Pull Up the Covers, Turn Out the Lights: Getting Ready for Bed

*In the Middle of the Night* by Kathy Henderson
  POETRY
*The Summer Night* by Charlotte Zolotow
  PICTURE BOOK
*To Sleep* by James Sage
  PICTURE BOOK
*Animals Don't Wear Pajamas* by Eve B. Feldman
  INFORMATIONAL BOOK
*Nine O'Clock Lullaby* by Marilyn Singer
  MULTICULTURAL BOOK

### Illuminating the Darkness: Heavenly Bodies

*Stargazers* by Gail Gibbons
  INFORMATIONAL BOOK
*The Moon Was At a Fiesta* by Matthew Gollub
  MULTICULTURAL BOOK
*Is It Dark? Is It Light?* by Mary D. Lankford
  MULTICULTURAL BOOK
*How Night Came From the Sea* by Mary Joan Gerson
  MULTICULTURAL BOOK

### Creatures of the Darkness: Animals of the Night

*Stellaluna* by Janell Cannon
  PICTURE BOOK
*Salt Hands* by Jane Chelsea Aragon
  PICTURE BOOK
*Hidden by Darkness* by Kim Taylor
  INFORMATIONAL BOOK
*Midnight Animals* by Christopher Tunney
  INFORMATIONAL BOOK
*Creatures of the Night* by Judith E. Rinard
  INFORMATIONAL BOOK

### Braving a Strange World: Adventures of the Night

*This Is the Bear and the Scary Night* by Sarah Hayes
  PICTURE BOOK
*Bunny's Night Out* by Roni Schotter
  PICTURE BOOK
*Night Ride* by Bernie and Mati Karlin
  PICTURE BOOK
*Moonlight on the River* by Deborah Kovacs
  PICTURE BOOK
*When Sheep Cannot Sleep* by Satoshi Kitamura
  COUNTING BOOK

**FIGURE 14.10**   Theme exploration graphic organizer

### The Great Ball of Fire

*Grandmother Spider Brings the Sun* (G. Keams, 1995)
*How the Sun Was Brought Back to the Sky* (M. Ginsburg, 1975)
*The Miser Who Wanted the Sun* (J. Obrist, 1984)
*The Mouse Who Owned the Sun* (S. Derby, 1993)
*Sunpainters* (B. Whitethorne, 1994)
*Welcome Back Sun* (M. Emberley, 1993)

### The Sky's Diamonds

*Coyote Places the Stars* (H. Taylor, 1993)
*Galileo* (L. Fisher, 1992)
*The Lost Children* (P. Goble, 1993)
*The Sky Is Not so Far Away* (M. Hillert, 1996)
*Still as a Star* (L. Hopkins, 1989)
*Twinkle, Twinkle, Little Star* (J. Taylor, 1992)

### Midnight Pearl

*Moon Soup* (L. Desimini, 1993)
*The Moon Was at a Fiesta* (M. Gollub, 1994)
*The Night of the Whippoorwill* (N. Larrick, 1992)
*Rabbit Moon* (J. Rowe, 1992)
*Ricky, Rocky, and Ringo Go to the Moon* (M. Kunnas, 1986)
*The Unicorn and the Moon* (T. dePaola, 1995)
*What Rhymes with Moon?* (J. Yolen, 1993)

### The Sky's Rhinestones

*The Magic School Bus* (J. Cole, 1990)
*Planetarium* (B. Brenner, 1993)
*Pluto* (G. Vogt, 1994)
*Pluto: A Double Planet?* (I. Asimov, 1990)
*Stars and Planets* (D. Lambert, 1994)
*Venus* (S. Simon, 1992)

**FIGURE 14.11** Theme exploration graphic organizer

# READ ACROSS AMERICA

### The Peaceful Pacific States
*Grandfather's Journey* (A. Say, 1993)
MULTICULTURAL
*Alaska's Three Bears* (S. Gill, 1990)
INFORMATIONAL
*Smoky Night* (E. Bunting, 1994)
MULTICULTURAL
*Raven* (G. McDermott, 1993)
FOLKTALE
*Anno's U.S.A.* (A. Mitsumasa, 1983)
PICTURE BOOK

### The Rambling Rocky Mountain States
*All the Places to Love* (P. MacLachlan, 1994)
PICTURE BOOK
*Dinosaur Mountain* (C. Arnold, 1989)
INFORMATIONAL
*Jack Creek Cowboy* (N. Johnson, 1993)
BIOGRAPHY
*Snowed In* (B. Lucas, 1993)
HISTORICAL FICTION
*Sierra* (D. Siebert, 1991)
POETRY

### The Sizzling Southwest States
*Roxaboxen* (A. McLerran, 1991)
PICTURE BOOK
*Alice Nizzy Nazzy, the Witch of Santa Fe* (T. Johnston, 1995)
FOLKTALE
*Pueblo Boy* (M. Keegan, 1991)
MULTICULTURAL BIOGRAPHY
*The Legend of the Bluebonnet* (T. dePaola, 1983)
FOLKTALE
*When Clay Sings* (B. Baylor, 1972)
INFORMATIONAL

### The Glorious Great Plains States
*In the Tall, Tall Grass* (D. Fleming, 1991)
PICTURE BOOK
*Moles Hill: A Woodlands Tale* (L. Ehlert, 1994)
FOLKTALE
*Heartland* (D. Siebert, 1989)
POETRY
*Log Cabin in the Woods* (J. Henry, 1988)
BIOGRAPHY
*The Legend of the Indian Paintbrush* (T. dePaola, 1988)
FOLKTALE

### The Notorious New England States
*Make Way for Ducklings* (R. McCloskey, 1969)
PICTURE BOOK
*Miss Rumphius* (B. Cooney, 1982)
FOLKTALE
*The Bear That Heard Crying* (N. Kinsey-Warnock, 1993)
HISTORICAL FICTION
*New England Scrapbook* (L. Krupinski, 1994)
POETRY
*Waiting for the Evening Star* (R. Wells, 1993)
HISTORICAL FICTION

### The Magnificent Middle Atlantic States
*If You Want to Find Golden* (E. Spinelli, 1993)
PICTURE BOOK
*Tar Beach* (F. Ringold, 1991)
PICTURE BOOK
*The Statue of Liberty* (J. Haskins, 1986)
INFORMATIONAL
*Growing up Amish* (R. Ammon, 1989)
MULTICULTURAL
*How Pizza Came to Queens* (K. Dayal Kaur, 1989)
PICTURE BOOK

### The Spectacular Southeast States
*Bigmama's* (D. Crews, 1991)
PICTURE BOOK
*Georgia Music* (H. Griffith, 1986)
PICTURE BOOK
*The Story of the White House* (K. Waters, 1991)
INFORMATIONAL
*My Great Aunt Arizona* (G. Houston, 1992)
BIOGRAPHY
*Swamp Angel* (A. Isaacs, 1994)
FOLKTALE

**FIGURE 14.12**    Theme exploration graphic organizer

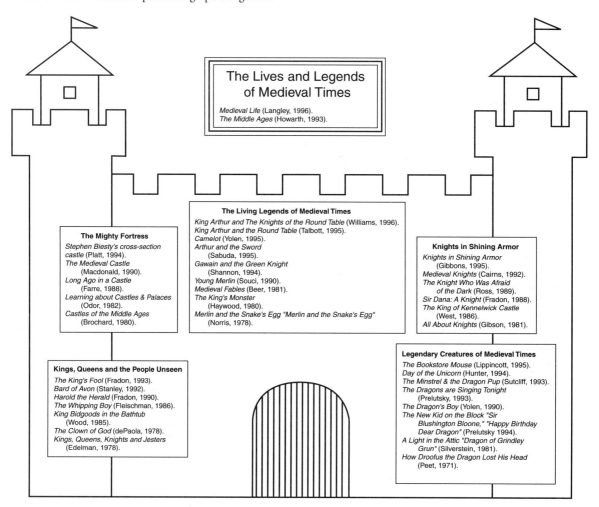

The following text appears within the figure:

**The Lives and Legends of Medieval Times**
*Medieval Life* (Langley, 1996).
*The Middle Ages* (Howarth, 1993).

**The Living Legends of Medieval Times**
*King Arthur and The Knights of the Round Table* (Williams, 1996).
*King Arthur and the Round Table* (Talbott, 1995).
*Camelot* (Yolen, 1995).
*Arthur and the Sword*
    (Sabuda, 1995).
*Gawain and the Green Knight*
    (Shannon, 1994).
*Young Merlin* (Souci, 1990).
*Medieval Fables* (Beer, 1981).
*The King's Monster*
    (Haywood, 1980).
*Merlin and the Snake's Egg "Merlin and the Snake's Egg"*
    (Norris, 1978).

**The Mighty Fortress**
*Stephen Biesty's cross-section castle* (Platt, 1994).
*The Medieval Castle*
    (Macdonald, 1990).
*Long Ago in a Castle*
    (Farre, 1988).
*Learning about Castles & Palaces*
    (Odor, 1982).
*Castles of the Middle Ages*
    (Brochard, 1980).

**Knights in Shining Armor**
*Knights in Shining Armor*
    (Gibbons, 1995).
*Medieval Knights* (Cairns, 1992).
*The Knight Who Was Afraid of the Dark* (Ross, 1989).
*Sir Dana: A Knight* (Fradon, 1988).
*The King of Kennelwick Castle*
    (West, 1986).
*All About Knights* (Gibson, 1981).

**Kings, Queens and the People Unseen**
*The King's Fool* (Fradon, 1993).
*Bard of Avon* (Stanley, 1992).
*Harold the Herald* (Fradon, 1990).
*The Whipping Boy* (Fleischman, 1986).
*King Bidgoods in the Bathtub*
    (Wood, 1985).
*The Clown of God* (dePaola, 1978).
*Kings, Queens, Knights and Jesters*
    (Edelman, 1978).

**Legendary Creatures of Medieval Times**
*The Bookstore Mouse* (Lippincott, 1995).
*Day of the Unicorn* (Hunter, 1994).
*The Minstrel & the Dragon Pup* (Sutcliff, 1993).
*The Dragons are Singing Tonight*
    (Prelutsky, 1993).
*The Dragon's Boy* (Yolen, 1990).
*The New Kid on the Block "Sir Blushington Bloone," "Happy Birthday Dear Dragon"* (Prelutsky 1994).
*A Light in the Attic "Dragon of Grindley Grun"* (Silverstein, 1981).
*How Droofus the Dragon Lost His Head*
    (Peet, 1971).

# CLOSING THOUGHTS

Initially, the possibilities for literature clusters and theme explorations may seem restricted by the school curriculum, but literature as the basis of sound teaching actually allows traditional topics to be covered in a creative, interrelated manner. In some cases, literature clusters and theme explorations are limited only by the creativity of teachers and the accessibility of titles. Whereas some teachers will be ready to take the plunge and voice total commitment to this type of instruction, others might want to work progressively with literature clusters, building some degree of success and affirmation before moving on to more comprehensive theme explorations.

These types of literature-based interdisciplinary instruction provide diverse opportunities for reader response to quality literature. The challenge of reading across genres in conjunction with the gaining of an understanding of broad conceptual ideas makes this type of instruction highly valuable to both the professional educator of children and the recipients of lifelong literacy and learning.

# REFERENCES

Bergeron, B. S., & Rudenga, E. A. (1996). Seeking authenticity: What is "real" about thematic literacy instruction? *The Reading Teacher, 49,* 544–551.

Crook, P. R., & Lehman, B. (1991). Themes for two voices: Children's fiction and nonfiction as "whole literature." *Language Arts, 68,* 34–41.

Freeman, E. B., Lehman, B. A., & Scharer, P. L. (Eds.) (1996–1999). Children's books. *The Reading Teacher, 49–50.* Volumes 49–52.

Hancock, M. R. *(1997). Literature clusters: Balancing narrative, expository, and poetic voices for effective interdisciplinary learning.* Paper presented at the 42nd Annual Convention of the International Reading Association.

Pappas, C. C., Kiefer, B. Z., & Levstik, L. S. (1996). *An integrated language perspective in the elementary school: Theory into action* (2nd ed.). New York: Longman.

Shanahan, T., Robinson, B., & Schneider, M. (1995). Integrating curriculum: Avoiding some of the pitfalls of thematic units. *The Reading Teacher, 48,* 718–719.

Weaver, C., Chaston, J., & Peterson, S. (1993). *Theme exploration: A voyage of discovery.* Portsmouth, NH: Heinemann.

# CHILDREN'S BOOKS CITED

All children's books cited in this chapter are referenced in the literature clusters and theme explorations interspersed throughout.

# PART V

# Celebrating Response Through Assessment

Throughout *A Celebration of Literature and Response*, each chapter has shared the genuine joy and promise of literature-based, response-filled classrooms. Yet the documentation of the craft of reading and personal, related response remains a vital issue in literature-based instruction. The ongoing collection of reading accomplishments and response connections in a literature-based classroom attains importance in a society that demands accountability. While our hearts warm to literature and our faces smile at the spontaneous words of a child's response, assessment must indicate that a response-based classroom contributes to both the art and the craft of lifelong reading.

Part V of *A Celebration of Literature and Response* focuses on authentic documentation of reader response to literature. Authentic assessment is that which builds on the authentic happenings in the classroom—reading and responding to literature. Because response does not and cannot equate into a number or letter grade, there must be justifiable assessment alternatives that indicate the evolving nature of the reading process and the quality of reader response over time.

Chapter 15 overflows with sample instruments and assessment tools for documenting reader response to literature including checklists, rubrics, and response categorization schemes. Multiple perspectives on assessing literature response journals and literature circles provide assessment alternatives to be shared with students and parents. Elements of a response portfolio become visible evidence of growth in breadth of response options and quality of response as students collect, select, and reflect on their ongoing literary readings and responses.

Teachers must address the needs of assessment within a literature-based classroom. Since students deserve to celebrate their response successes, authentic assessment provides a means to keep account of reading achievements and response connections. These assessment tools produce convincing shortterm evidence for parents, administrators, and readers themselves. They also support reader transactions with literature as an optimal goal of creating lifelong readers who read and respond on both aesthetic and efferent levels each time they pick up a book and make it their own through response.

As this textbook draws to a close, it seems critical to address the often neglected aspect of response-based assessment in a literature-rich classroom. The numerous and multifaceted authentic assessment options presented in this chapter collectively and convincingly reflect the strength of literature in enhancing literacy instruction and the power of response to capture the uniqueness of the individual reader.

## Chapter 15

# Documenting Response to Literature:

## *Authentic Perspectives*

*I*love teaching with literature. I have never felt more convinced that I am creating lifelong readers as I do when I incorporate literature, response journals, and literature discussion in my classroom. I see students reading more, talking about books inside and outside the classroom, and actually checking out more books from the library. They have grown in their confidence to respond through writing and in discussions with peers.

My major concern is that I have to convince my principal and my parents that their children are learning. Many of the fine responses they make don't equate into a number or a letter grade. There is no place on my report card for what is happening in my classroom, except the tiny narrative comment space. If I don't come up with something soon on paper, I may be forced to go back to textbook teaching where unit tests give numerical results. That would a tragedy for me, but more so for my students. How do I keep the quality of literature-based instruction and still come up with the evidence of learning?

Fifth-Grade Teacher's Conversation in Author's
Office, December 3, 1997

Active involvement in response-based literature activities in an elementary/middle-level classroom provides a rich experience for students, but an assessment challenge for teachers. Although many books, research-based articles, and teacher-action research reports applaud the benefits of literature-based instruction and reader response activities, few address the important issue of assessment of response. If confident teachers align their literature-based philosophies with response-based expressions of personal interactions with books, they must also align meaningful assessment with that focus and allow their teaching to be informed by that assessment. This chapter strives to share an assortment of assessment standards and tools designed for reader response-based activities at a variety of age levels. They range from observations to accountability logs, from rubrics to checklists, from self-evaluation to peer evaluation, and from portfolio documentation to program evaluation.

# PRINCIPLES OF ASSESSMENT

In focusing on assessment of response-based literature interactions, basic principles of assessment should be introduced and connected to a response-based philosophy of learning. Support for response-based assessment is grounded in a framework based on several basic principles of assessment (Tierney, Carter, & Desai, 1991).

1. **Assessment should be centered in the classroom.** While reading and responding to literature occur both inside and outside the school setting, assessment should be focused on what occurs in the academic setting. Personal transactions with literature are genuinely influenced by experiences outside the classroom; however, assessment should be on literature shared and responses made in the academic setting.
2. **Assessment should be consistent with curricular goals.** Because aesthetic teaching and response-based learning are grounded in a teaching philosophy that values literature and the unique response of each individual, curricular goals are most likely to focus on individual choice, interests, and performance. If the goals focus on creating lifelong readers and learners through literature, there is likely to be a valid connection between curriculum and assessment.
3. **Assessment must be consistent with what is known about human learning.** The uniqueness of the individual learner, the importance of growth over time, the measurement of an individual against his or her own progress, and the importance of choice in learning are essential building blocks of literature-based and response-based learning. The individuality of the learner is respected and individual growth is monitored and celebrated over time.
4. **Assessment must be comprehensive and balanced.** Response-based activities must expand to include literature from across all literary genres and to include all modes of response. Limiting a response experience to a teacher's favorite genre and a comfortable mode of responding does little to enhance and broaden learning. A comprehensive diet of literature across genres shared across the curriculum and rotating suggestions of varied response-based activities will provide the comprehensive balance suggested by this principle.

5. **Literature and response-based experiences must be numerous and multifaceted, leading to profiles of growth over time.** Assessments must be qualitative as well as quantitative. In other words, keeping track of numbers of books and kinds of responses is important, but this must be supplemented by data on quality and depth of response and the various literature experiences. Response assessment must be reflective of the constructive nature of meaning making so that comprehension is reflected within the personal transaction with literature. Assessment may be accomplished through individual or collaborative means. Most important, perhaps, is that assessment be noncompetitive and that each respondent to literature be assessed on her or his own growth, exploration of response options, and special talents in interactions with trade books.

6. **Assessment guides and improves instruction and learning.** Our role as teachers is to document the evolving development of response and to identify a student's strengths and weaknesses in response to literature. Assessment guides and improves instruction. Our role as teachers is to empower students with the freedom to respond, to model response mechanisms, and to sharpen our own observations of response and increase our confidence in them. Assessment monitors the outcomes of a response-based literature program. Our role as teachers is to assemble documentation about a student as reader and respondent to literature to share with others while determining program strengths and weaknesses for further instructional planning.

# ASSESSMENT OF RESPONSE-BASED ACTIVITIES

The International Reading Association and National Council of Teachers of English Joint Task Force on Assessment (IRA/NCTE, 1994) prepared a list of standards for the assessment of reading and writing. Drawing from these standards with literary response as a basis for assessment, the following standards should guide assessment of response-based celebrations of literature.

***The literature tastes and response-based preferences of students are paramount in assessment.*** Assessment needs to address what students *do* read and how they *do* respond, rather than what they do *not* accomplish. Immediate teacher feedback is critical to response modes. Specific comments need to be delivered in a timely fashion. Because individual response is not suited to standardized assessment, "the most powerful assessments of students are likely to be those that occur in the daily activity of the classroom" (IRA/NCTE, 1994, p. 15). Allowing reflection on the reader's own literature choices and related response, planning for evaluation of their own growth in reading and response, and setting goals for future literary experiences and response to that literature are mandatory, ongoing portions of response-based reading assessment.

***The primary purpose of response-based assessment is to improve teaching and learning.*** The central function of assessment is not to prove whether teaching and learning have occurred, but to improve the quality of the literacy experience for the learner and to increase the likelihood that the learner will become a lifelong reader who naturally views literature as an aesthetic experience. The teacher assumes a facilitator role in a response-based classroom and must be certain that a blend of literary genres, a variety of response modes, and ample opportunity for response are provided. On the other hand, the teacher must document the ways in which the student is growing in appreciation of literature, attitude toward reading, and personal interaction with literature. If our goals are to create lifelong literate individuals, both our program and our students' response progress must be monitored and reflected on continuously by both teacher and reader.

***Response-based assessments must recognize and reflect the intellectual and social complexity of literacy and the role of school, home, and society in literacy development.***    Reader response captures the experiences of the reader in the broader sense of a literate community since it is the product and culmination of experiences in life and literacy that bring the unique transaction to books. The interactive roles of school, home, and society are honored in a response-based classroom because aesthetic teaching philosophy acknowledges and respects learning beyond the classroom walls.

***Response-based assessment must be fair and equitable.***    Response must be judged on an individual basis free of gender, cultural, ethnic, religious, linguistic, physical, and socioeconomic bias. It is indeed the mixture of these factors that makes each child a unique reader and respondent. Because the common denominator of reader response is the individual reader, inequitable judgment is less likely to occur in response-based assessment because each reader's thoughts and reactions are individually valued.

***The teacher is the most important agent of response-based assessment.***    In the past, society valued and invested in testing and devalued the information that teachers gained daily about student learning. Professionals have gained in stature as society begins to come to terms with the knowledge each teacher holds about each child. For teachers to become more effective agents of response-based assessment, they must read and respond themselves. They must discuss the books they read, write their own reflective responses, and share their thoughts and feelings. Only through an understanding of their own response mechanisms can they assess the literary response of their students.

***The response-based assessment process should involve multiple perspectives and sources of data.***    Limiting reader response assessment to a singular response product shortchanges the reader. Teachers need to triangulate sources of response by acquiring products of various modes of response (written, oral, artistic) and validating them through informal interviews and formal observations. The reliability of response-based assessment will improve when there are multiple opportunities to observe and discuss response to varied literary selections.

***Parents must be involved as active, essential participants in a response-based assessment process.***    Parent involvement might include:

- Becoming knowledgeable about reader response and its relationship to literature across the curriculum,

- Actively participating in the assessment process by commenting on response-based performance,
- Contributing knowledge of their children as readers and responders in the home environment, and
- Seeking ways in which to become more encouraging of their child's development as a reader and responder to literature.

Ongoing communication and reporting procedures between school and home should enable parents to talk in productive ways about their children and their literature and response experiences.

While these standards are adapted from broader perspectives on reading and writing, they do provide a parallel framework for meeting the new challenge of creating and implementing response-based assessments. The instruments, checklists, and suggestions in this chapter evolve from the considerations given about assessment.

# TOOLS FOR DOCUMENTING READER RESPONSE

The purpose of this section of the chapter is to address the needs of practitioners who support a response-based literature program in their classrooms. The need to assess and document response as a means of literacy development is likely in most schools. Elaborating on the lifelong implication of reader response to literature may be enough for those who encompass its philosophy, but the reality of assessment retains a strong presence in our educational institutions.

This section suggests a variety of formats—checklists, anecdotal records, graphs, categories, hierarchies—with which to assess multiple dimensions of response. From oral response to written response, from self-assessment to program evaluation, these suggestions provide a much requested component to round out the capabilities of reader response as a reflection of learning.

## Response Checklists: Monitoring the Program and the Individual

A response-based literature program should be built on outcomes of engaging in reading and response. Two forms provide checklists of both programs and individual student performance. Response-based literature program opportunities (Figure 15.1) can be utilized by a teacher to assess response activity offerings within a program context. Updating and monitoring of the checklist encourage a mix of response modes as part of the total literature program. As a teacher notes limited response options in a particular area, a conscious effort may be made to improve instruction through the provision of broader response options.

The student engagement profile (Figure 15.2), on the other hand, is used to monitor an individual student's level of involvement in response modes. Dependent on response offerings, the teacher documents indications of respondent performance across several response modes. A small area for comments allows minimal space for professional notes or book titles.

**FIGURE 15.1** Form for monitoring response program

| Teacher Documentation of Response-Based Literature Program Opportunities | | | |
|---|---|---|---|
| Teacher _____ Grade/Age _____ | | | |
| Assessment Period _____ | | | |
| | Date  Book Title | Date  Book Title | Date  Book Title |
| **Listening Behavior**<br><br>   Physical response<br>   Spontaneous response<br>   Participatory response | | | |
| **Contact with Books**<br><br>   Browsing and choosing<br>   Attention to books<br>   Proximity to books | | | |
| **Impulse to Share**<br><br>   Reading together<br>   Telling about a book<br>   Sharing a discovery<br>   Sharing connections to other<br>     books<br>   Sharing connections to own<br>     experiences | | | |
| **Actions and Drama**<br><br>   Echoing the action<br>   Dramatic play<br>   Readïers' theater | | | |
| **Art, Music, and Constructed Products**<br><br>   Visual representation (drawing)<br>   Constructions<br>   Culinary response<br>   Musical response | | | |
| **Oral Response**<br><br>   Retelling/storytelling<br>   Literature conversations<br>   Prompted response | | | |
| **Written Response**<br><br>   Literature response journals<br>   Literature as a model for writing | | | |

Categories based on: Hickman, J. (1981). A new perspective on response to literature: Research in an elementary classroom setting. *Research in the Teaching of English, 15*, 343–354.

**FIGURE 15.2**   Form for monitoring student response involvement

| Student Engagement Profile: Response-Based Literature Program | | |
|---|---|---|
| Student name _____ | Grade/Age _____ | |
| | Date(s) observed | Teacher Comment |
| **Listening Behavior**<br><br>Physical response<br>Spontaneous response<br>Participatory response | | |
| **Contact With Books**<br><br>Browsing and choosing<br>Attention to books<br>Proximity to books | | |
| **Impulse to Share**<br><br>Reading together<br>Telling about a book<br>Sharing a discovery<br>Sharing connections to other books<br>Sharing connections to own experiences | | |
| **Actions and Drama**<br><br>Echoing the action<br>Dramatic play<br>Readers' theater | | |
| **Art, Music, and Constructed Products**<br><br>Visual representation (drawing)<br>Constructions<br>Culinary response<br>Musical response | | |
| **Oral Response**<br><br>Retelling/storytelling<br>Literature conversations<br>Prompted response | | |
| **Written Response**<br><br>Literature response journals<br>Literature as a model for writing | | |

Categories based on: Hickman, J. (1981). A new perspective on response to literature: Research in an elementary classroom setting. *Research in the Teaching of English, 15,* 343–354.

A checklist of reader responses to teacher-generated prompts (Figure 15.3) focuses on the development of both oral and written responses to literature. Applicable to both primary and intermediate students, the checklist monitors progress and growth in communicating thoughts and feelings to read-alouds or independently read literature. The checklist implies developmental levels of response to aesthetic, experiential, interpretive, and cognitive prompts. The checklist can be used over a designated period of time by dating and recording the observed growth in response of an individual student. At the same time, teachers can monitor their use of prompt types and the individual's performance over time through the response continuum—emerging, developing, maturing. Teachers may determine how effectively they are addressing variety in prompts to stimulate continuous response development.

## Teacher Anecdotal Records

Each teacher needs to keep a notebook containing anecdotal records acquired from his or her observational perspective. This becomes particularly important with primary children where teacher written records of spontaneous response document valuable evidence of daily response growth. Dated mailing labels are suggested as teachers or participant observers (student teachers, paraprofessionals, inclusion teachers) record daily anecdotal notes on read-aloud responses, sharing time comments, literature circles, etc. These events could be audio- or videotaped, but then the tapes require transcription for individual students. That task can easily become backlogged and overwhelming, so on-the-spot anecdotal records seem to be more effective. The mailing labels should be transferred daily to the teacher notebook containing observational sheets for each child. As they are accumulated by date, a sequential account of growing response may become evident. These records, as a necessary supplement to the student response portfolio (discussed later in this chapter), provide strong support for response documentation.

## Daily Reading Logs and Literature Response Files

As early primary-level children (grades K–2) read individual picture books, informational picture books, or transitional chapter books, they should be asked to record a brief list of the books they read (Hill & Ruptic, 1994) (Figure 15.4). For older students (grades 3–6), the daily reading log shown in Figure 15.5 (Hill & Ruptic, 1994), provides for a brief response on a daily basis.

For many teachers, a response file could be dated, handwritten on index cards, or entered into a computer file. Not only does this file serve as a series of written responses to literature, but it keeps track of the number of books and genres of literature being explored. Teachers might model sample responses of their own or share other children's former responses on overhead transparencies. Subjective guidelines used for ongoing response assessment include these:

- Depth, honesty, sincerity, and personal voice in response
- Level of personal involvement with text

**FIGURE 15.3**   Form for assessing student responses to prompts

## Reader Responses to Teacher-Generated Prompts

Name _____   Grade/Age _____

Book Title(s) _____   Oral _____   Written _____

E = Emerging Response
   Response minimally connects text to focus of prompt.
   Response reflects slight degree of honesty or emotional impact.

D = Developing Response
   Response adequately connects text to focus of prompt.
   Response reflects some degree of honesty and emotional impact.

M = Maturing Response
   Response substantially connects text to focus of the prompt.
   Response reflects complete honesty and emotional impact.

| | Date(s) of Evidence | Quality | | |
|---|---|---|---|---|
| | | E | D | M |
| **AESTHETIC PROMPTS** | | | | |
| How does this book make you feel? | | E | D | M |
| How would you feel if you were (*character*)? | | E | D | M |
| **EXPERIENTIAL PROMPTS** | | | | |
| How does this book remind you of your own life? | | E | D | M |
| How does (*character*) remind you of someone you know? | | E | D | M |
| How does (*character's*) actions remind you of another book? | | E | D | M |
| **INTERPRETIVE PROMPTS** | | | | |
| What did you notice in this book? | | E | D | M |
| What meaning or message does the book have for you? | | E | D | M |
| What do these words mean to you? | | E | D | M |
| What kind of person do you think (*character*) is? | | E | D | M |
| **COGNITIVE PROMPTS** | | | | |
| What do you think will happen to (*character*)? | | E | D | M |
| If you were (*character*), what would you do? | | E | D | M |
| What advice would you give (*character*)? | | E | D | M |

**FIGURE 15.4**   Reading log for grades K–2

| 📖 📖 📖 📖 📖 📖 📖   READING LOG   📖 📖 📖 📖 📖 📖 📖 | | |
|---|---|---|
| Name _____ | | Term _____ |
| Date Completed | Title of Book | Author |
|  |  |  |
|  |  |  |
|  |  |  |
|  |  |  |
|  |  |  |
|  |  |  |
|  |  |  |
|  |  |  |
|  |  |  |
|  |  |  |
|  |  |  |
|  |  |  |

*Source: From* Practical Aspects of Authentic Assessment: Putting the Pieces Together *by Bonnie Campbell Hill and Cynthia Ruptic. Reprinted by permission of Christopher-Gordon Publishers, Inc.*

- Willingness to explore and expand new response options
- Willingness to share authentic thoughts and feelings through writing
- Growth of response over a significant period of time.

Responses should be submitted on an ongoing basis throughout an assessment period. Teacher comments would affirm, suggest, or attempt to stretch (but not force) the kinds and quality of response. Model responses can also be shared during whole class mini-lessons on enhancing response. The entire file is submitted at the end of the assessment period with a main criteria of growth and development of response style over the assigned time. A narrative evaluation is the key assessment and could be attached to a rubric or point system if a mandated score or grade is necessary.

**FIGURE 15.5**  Daily reading log for grades 3–6

DAILY READING LOG

| Name | | | | Title | |

Date Started      Date Finished                                    Author

| Date | Pages Read | Event(s) | Response/Prediction |
|------|-----------|----------|---------------------|
|      |           |          |                     |
|      |           |          |                     |
|      |           |          |                     |
|      |           |          |                     |
|      |           |          |                     |
|      |           |          |                     |
|      |           |          |                     |
|      |           |          |                     |
|      |           |          |                     |
|      |           |          |                     |
|      |           |          |                     |
|      |           |          |                     |

*Source: From* Practical Aspects of Authentic Assessment: Putting the Pieces Together *by Bonnie Campbell Hill and Cynthia Ruptic. Reprinted by permission of Christopher-Gordon Publishers, Inc.*

# ASSESSING LITERATURE RESPONSE JOURNALS

As intermediate-level readers (grades 3–5) and middle-level students (grades 6–8) respond to longer chapter books across genres, it is important that their journals capture responses throughout the entire active reading process. This means not only capturing thoughts at the book's conclusion, but, more importantly, recording ongoing response throughout the entire reading process. Therefore, the response base will be much longer and in-depth than the brief, authentic response to a picture book from a younger child. This facilitates the need for a more intricate assessment tool to determine growth of response of higher quality and perhaps greater quantity.

## Self-Assessment and Teacher Feedback

The first vehicle for achieving, sustaining, and providing impetus to the power of written response to literature is the teacher comment. It is vital that student response be recognized, encouraged, and expanded on a periodic basis. To ensure both teacher and peer comments to literature response journals, a simple system of colored circle stickers (red/blue/green/yellow/orange) is suggested. The teacher designs a schema for labeling various response perspectives. Students label several responses according to this scheme. A sample system might include:

Blue sticker(s) = a response that captures your deepest interaction with the text; teacher will read and respond to it.

Yellow sticker(s) = another powerful response; a peer or reading partner will respond to it.

Green sticker(s) = a response that reflects a text-to-life connection (usually a newly introduced response category is the focus).

Orange sticker(s) = a response that reflects a prediction or anticipation of the unfolding text (or any other category for a secondary focus).

Red sticker(s) = a response that reflects reader involvement with a character.

By applying the stickers, the students are actually rereading and self-assessing while categorizing their responses. The teacher's (or peer's) task is tapered to reading and responding to targeted responses. This allows time to share a few significant responses rather than numerous, brief, often less meaningful ones. Figure 15.6 reveals several excerpts from a preservice teacher's journal in response to *Letters from Rifka* by Karen Hesse. Read the entries, note the colored stickers that categorize responses, and focus on teacher feedback in this context.

This system can be adapted for readers from upper primary grades through middle-level grades. The color code can be used over two or three literature books or changed with the reading of each book. Older readers can even devise their own coded system for teacher/peer comments. The benefits to the reader include periodic quality feedback and the opportunity to reread and self-evaluate one's own responses. The benefits to peer readers is the opportunity to read another student's response for variety and extension of one's own response style. Finally, the benefits to the teacher include an opportunity to engage in ongoing assessment of response with an emphasis on quality, not quantity feedback.

## Literature Response Journal Rubric

Another form of authentic assessment is a rubric designed for literature response journals. The rubric differentiates response performance by listing characteristics of respondents at each stage of evolving response—novice, emerging, maturing, and self-directed responder. As noted in Figure 15.7, the rubric is built on an evolving continuum associated more with response experience than with age or ability.

The rubric is intended for use with readers from fourth through eighth grade who engage in the literature response journal process (aligned with Chapter 10 of this text) primarily with realistic fiction or historical fiction books. Four stages of response should discourage the use of a letter grade for each developing stage. Letter grades are never suggested for use with response journals, but growth over time from one developmental category to the next is to be expected.

Well-written strong interaction with the text.

Letters from Rifka : Responses

PAGE NO. 1

PREPARED BY

DATE

YELLOW

Do you think 5th graders will react in a similar way? How will adolescents view this scene?

**September 2, 1919**

Russia: This entry made me feel both angry and sorry for Rifka. It is hard for me to believe that Rifka's parents put so much responsibility and danger on her. I know that they are trying to save their son but in so doing, they are putting their only daughter's life on the line. Why did the son leave the army anyway? Didn't he know what would happen to his family if he was caught? Later in the entry I felt scared for Rifka. The way the guards were looking at her and touching her hair made me feel almost disgusted inside. This is just a little girl!

GREEN

Excellent text to-life connection that builds empathy toward this character.

**September 2, 1919**

Russia: At the end of this entry when Rifka is saying good-bye to her home, to her family, and to her past life I could really relate to her. I have moved many times and can remember the way I felt on moving day. One time that really sticks out in my mind was when I was only five years old. My family was moving from Barstow CA to Rowland Heights, CA because my dad had gotten transferred. I remember being very upset and thinking that all of my things were going to be left behind with the house. I of course was not placed in a dangerous position like Rifka and her family but I was still scared because I wasn't sure what lay ahead for me.

Would this be a point to bring up with your students? Today's society is so mobile.

**November 27, 1919**

I wanted to warn Rifka. Kindness is great, but it backfires on her here.

en route to Warsaw: The events in this entry made me cringe. The thought of touching someone's hair that hasn't been washed for such a long time and seeing all of these scabs on her head is awful. What is wrong with this girl? Is she going to die? What will become of her baby? I can't imagine being as strong as Rifka. Even after seeing this girl's scalp Rifka still fixed her hair. It makes me worry about the type of person I am. If I had been in her place I would have somehow excused myself rather than touch this sick girl. How did Rifka become so honorable?

**FIGURE 15.6** Literature response journal: self-assessment and teacher feedback

A *novice responder* is just beginning to experiment with the response process. He or she can be a younger student or a student who has never been challenged to respond to literature before. While responses may verge on retelling or plot summary, responses are typically brief and tend to occur at the end of, rather than intermittently throughout the chapter. Most literature response journal candidates begin their development at this level, but noteworthy, encouraging comments from teachers and gradual developmental stances assuredly move them up the rubric.

The *emerging responder* holds promise and gradual growth is present in his or her journal. Although commitment to the response process is still questionable, the responder might be better guided by teacher-initiated response prompts rather than the free response

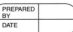

PAGE NO. 2

PREPARED BY

DATE

ORANGE

Predictions are crucial to meaning making. Share this entry as a model with your students.

September 14, 1920

Antwerp, Belgium: Things are finally looking up for Rifka. I am hoping that all of her problems are finally over but I know they can't be. Something else has to happen to her because the book is only half over. Maybe once she gets to America she won't be able to find her family. What if after all of this trouble to finally get to America and there is no one waiting there for her. If this happens, could Rifka survive on her own? She can't possibly return to Russia. I predict that Rifka gets to New York and has to wander around, being in the streets searching for her family. She, after going through many ordeals, finally finds her family.

BLUE

Can you relate Rifka to other strong, female characters in children's lit?

October 7, 1920

Ellis Island: The words quoted by Pushkin at the opening of this entry must mean a lot to Rifka. This book of poetry has helped her all of her journey but this particular poem is very important. It gives Rifka added energy. She is a survivor and this poem reinforces this fact. Even though she has been through such turmoil, Rifka wants to continue to live. Even if that living includes more suffering and possibly never seeing her family again. She may even get sent back to Russia but Rifka is strong. No matter what happens, she will continue wanting to live.

All these poems relate so well to her ordeals. Her book gives her strength to endure.

RED

October 7, 1920

Ellis Island: If I were Rifka in this situation, I would be a basket-case! I would be so scared that I would never see my family again, and even though Rifka says Ellis Island is not so bad she has to be scared. I would not be able to help others if I had so many worries on my mind. What is going to happen? I would not be able to think of anything but my problems, although this is not helping anyone. I would feel so lost and alone and worried about my future. I think, if I were Rifka, I would stay in my room and cry all the time. I would write some of my feelings down in the Pushkin book, but I don't think that I would have much hope left.

I can't believe that I am looking up to a twelve year old girl. She has a lot of admirable qualities and I wish that there were more people like her.

Putting yourself in the role of the character causes you to self-assess your own strengths and weaknesses

In the midst of all her hardships, she reaches out to help others. She deserves her freedom & and opportunities our country will provide her.

**FIGURE 15.6** Literature response journal: self-assessment and teacher feedback (*continued*)

process. Given time and encouragement, the emerging responder will grow, stretch, and explore response options while indicating a stronger involvement with character and story.

The *maturing responder* is characterized by a willingness to explore response options and to increase engagement in reading. Responses become more varied, often lengthier, genuinely spontaneous, and more deeply emotional. The reader indicates involvement with the characters and even indicates a stake in the outcome of the book. Meaning making becomes evident as predictions and queries lead to a fuller understanding of the text. Although responses may

**FIGURE 15.7**   Response rubric for literature response journals

## Self-Directed Responder

The responder expresses unique personal interactions with the text which indicates the development of an individual response style.

The responder evidences deep involvement with the text and incorporates powerful writing to share his/her personal opinions/emotions/thoughts.

The responder judges and assesses characters against his/her own personal standards, often sharing advice, criticism, empathy, or disparity.

The responder reacts to the text as a literary work and addresses both literary elements and the language/writing techniques used in the text.

The responder compares the text to other texts of the same genre, by the same author, or addressing a similar theme.

The responder exhibits other response characteristics in the Maturing Responder category.

## Maturing Responder

The responder expresses his/her personal interactions with the text, although they are similar to what other responders may share.

The responder shows a willingness to use writing to share personal opinions/emotions/thoughts.

The responder evidences involvement with the main character by talking to them, giving them advice, or telling how he/she might behave in the same circumstance.

The responder makes sound predictions based on information from the text and validates or refutes those predictions in later responses.

The responder shows a willingness to try new response options suggested by instructor comments or growing knowledge of response.

The responder exhibits other response characteristics from the Emerging Responder category.

## Emerging Responder

The responder attempts to share spontaneously, but he/she might be better suited to a transitional response prompt format.

The responder makes reasonable predictions using information from the text.

The responder shares reactions through writing, but the entries maintain a detached commitment or connection to the text.

The responder poses many questions, either to make sense of the story or to avoid confusion.

The responder shows detached insights into the character(s), maintaining a distance from deeper character involvement.

The responder exhibits other response characteristics from the Novice Responder category.

## Novice Responder

The responder writes briefly, but seems better able to communicate thoughts and feelings through oral response.

The responder writes a number of brief responses which merely fulfills an assignment, rather than sharing a commitment to the text and characters.

The responder summarizes, mostly retelling the story, rather than interacting with it.

The responder indicates a sense of comprehension, but rarely exhibits or indicates personal involvement in the text.

The responder expresses frustration with the reading/writing format of the response journal.

parallel those of other readers of the same response stature, they are beginning to reflect individuality of thought and someone who is on the verge of becoming a self-directed responder.

The *self-directed responder* expresses highly unique, emotional responses to characters and situations in literature. This independent level is characterized by reading and responding aesthetically across literary genres and becoming adept at intertextual connections as a broader scope of reading is reached. Personal opinions and character assessment against personal standards are common, while an identifiable individual response style emerges. At this level of response accomplishment, the reader continues to respond in her or his mind even if the thoughts are not recorded in a journal. The response process has become completely comfortable and the response process becomes internalized as part of the active process involved in full reading engagement. Readers/responders who reach this level are likely to develop into lifelong readers who continue to respond to literature in their minds and hearts as adults.

This rubric should be adjusted to better suit the developmental levels of readers in a particular classroom. Simplification of the rubric stretches its use to younger children, while still maintaining the prime characteristics of respondents to literature.

## Categorizing Response to Literature

Teachers and students in upper intermediate/middle-level grades can serve as monitors of evolving response styles in written journals by categorizing response entries. By coding and graphing written responses to literature, a teacher/student can determine which response options dominate a journal, which response options are being explored, and which response options likely need introduction, modeling, or encouragement. While the process is time consuming, its advantage is that it provides a visual presentation of written response showing most shared and least attempted response options to a particular book. The purpose is not to obtain an even graph across columns, for to expect that is to distort the individuality of response. The purpose is to verify differences of responses to books of different literary genres, to designate primary response categories over several books, and to determine categories that need yet to be explored.

The categories of response to literature shown in Figure 15.8 are adapted from Hancock (1993) whose research was based on intermediate/middle-level journals in response to realistic fiction. (See Chapter 11 as a reminder of those categories and rich responses that exemplify each.) Note the description for additional response options—it encourages unique response options rather than limiting them to the list. Expect and encourage those to be added to the table and the graph. As students reread their journal entries, they code the type of response they have made. In cases of longer entries, more than one type of response may be applied. The accuracy does not come in placing one's entry into the "correct" category. The usefulness comes in the coder/student being consistent with the placement within categories. After coding, the coded categories are transferred to a graph and filled in (Figure 15.9). The visual representation allows for an overview of categories of written response to literature. While there is value in the visual image itself, its application to future response is the true benefit of implementing this assessment procedure. Two examples, accompanied by narrative overviews, assist in justifying the value of this assessment procedure.

**FIGURE 15.8**   Categories of response to literature

**UNDERSTANDING**

Responses indicate the reader's current understanding of character or plot. While bordering on summary, the response may reflect a personal interpretation of the story.

**CHARACTER INTROSPECTION**

Responses indicate the reader's effort to project insight into the feelings, thoughts, and motives for behavior of the character. (It sounds like. . . . He must be. . . . She probably. . . .)

**PREDICTING EVENTS**

Responses reflect the reader's speculations about what will emerge as the text proceeds. This type of response includes validation or invalidation of previous predictions. (I bet. . . . I think. . . . If. . . . then. . . .)

**QUESTIONING**

Responses reflect a lack of complete understanding of what is evolving in the text. (I wonder why. . . . I can't tell. . . .)

**CHARACTER IDENTIFICATION**

Responses indicate the reader has achieved a sense of kinship with the character by putting him/herself in the character's role. (If I were. . . . I would. . . .)

**TEXT-TO-LIFE CONNECTIONS**

Responses share a connection between the plot or character and the reader's own life.

**CHARACTER ASSESSMENT**

Responses indicate the reader's judgment of the actions or values of the character measured against his/her own personal values or standards of behavior.

**STORY INVOLVEMENT**

Responses indicate the reader's personal reactions to the setting, theme, events, or sensory aspects of the text.

**LITERARY ELEMENTS**

Responses reflect a knowledge of literary elements which are weighed against other authors, other texts, or other reading/writing experiences.

**TEXT-TO-TEXT CONNECTIONS**

Responses share a connection between the current text and one or more texts which are a part of the reader's literary repertoire.

**READER/WRITER DIGRESSIONS**

Responses indicate the wanderings of the respondent's mind while he/she interacts with the text.

**ADDITIONAL RESPONSE OPTIONS**

Response options must not be limited by the categories listed above. Respondents must be encouraged and allowed to expand these categories through natural response modes.

Categories adapted from Hancock, M. R. (1993). Exploring the meaning-making process through the content of literature response journals. *Research in the Teaching of English, 27,* 335–368.

**FIGURE 15.9**   Graph for
categorization responses

**Categorization of Responses**

Name _____ Date _____
Title _____
Author _____ Genre _____

UNDERSTANDING

CHARACTER INTROSPECTION

PREDICTING EVENTS

QUESTIONING

CHARACTER IDENTIFICATION

TEXT-TO-LIFE CONNECTIONS

CHARACTER ASSESSMENT

STORY INVOLVEMENT

LITERARY ELEMENTS

TEXT-TO-TEXT CONNECTIONS

READER/WRITER DIGRESSIONS

ADDITIONAL OPTIONS

As a seventh grader, Lori's categorized and graphed responses to Lois Lowry's *The Giver* (Figure 15.10) show intense immersion in the text with predictions and questioning as critical components of this science fiction response. Lori, however, does not attempt to judge, support, or refute Jonas's decisions or his relationship to Gabriel, a foster child. For the most part, Lori bypasses the opportunity to make connections between Jonas's fate and decisions in her own life. Her involvement with plot may have caused her to forego response to Lowry's literary elements of a setting devoid of color or characters devoid of free choice.

FIGURE 15.10 Visual Representation of Response to *The Giver:* Lori

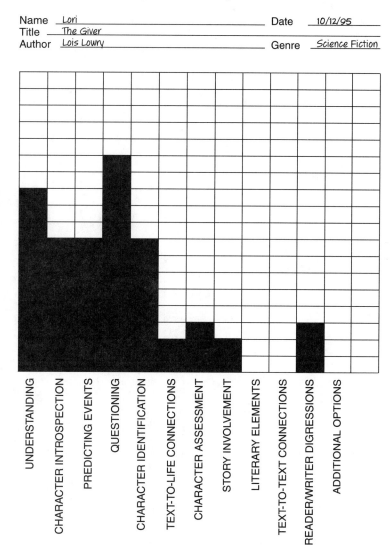

**Categorization of Responses**

Name   Lori                                          Date   10/12/95
Title   The Giver
Author   Lois Lowry                                  Genre   Science Fiction

Lori, like so many students, has had little experience with the science fiction genre, perhaps explaining a lack of text-to-text connections.

Daniel's graphic representation (Figure 15.11) indicates a difference in response patterns. While he questions his way through the book, he avoids predictions. As with many readers, he doesn't want those predictions to be wrong, so he avoids putting them in print. Daniel is quick to judge, support, and encourage Jonas in his decisions, but rarely identifies with him or speculates on his feelings or thoughts. Although a science fiction character, Jonas carries qualities of

**FIGURE 15.11** Visual representation of response to *The Giver:* Daniel

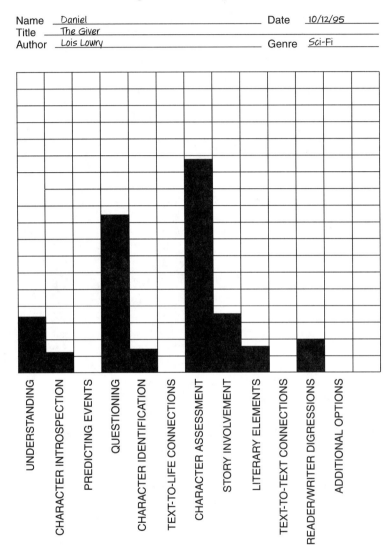

**Categorization of Responses**

Name ___Daniel___ Date ___10/12/95___
Title ___The Giver___
Author ___Lois Lowry___ Genre ___Sci-Fi___

UNDERSTANDING
CHARACTER INTROSPECTION
PREDICTING EVENTS
QUESTIONING
CHARACTER IDENTIFICATION
TEXT-TO-LIFE CONNECTIONS
CHARACTER ASSESSMENT
STORY INVOLVEMENT
LITERARY ELEMENTS
TEXT-TO-TEXT CONNECTIONS
READER/WRITER DIGRESSIONS
ADDITIONAL OPTIONS

most early adolescents and readers might be expected to identify with those traits. A consistent lack of text-to-text connections reveals a classroom void of experience with this genre.

Because it would be impossible to conduct this process on every response journal for every reader, it is to the teacher's advantage to model the procedure to students using one of his or her own response journals on an overhead projector. In addition, the modeling might continue by utilizing a volunteer's response journal. Debating categorical placement is not an issue. As long as the coder is consistent in designating categories, the overall purpose will be fulfilled. Students may keep these graphs in portfolios as part of assessment and can even be presented to the teacher (and parents) for self-evaluation during a conference. The importance of categorizing and graphing of responses becomes apparent in assessing response over time. Four graphs, dated and displayed side by side, show expansion of response and familiarity with literature. The visual imaging of response through categorical placement is time consuming, but is an option that should be considered if response variation and exploration are valued, encouraged, and respected.

## Hierarchy of Reader Response (Grades 4–8)

Sebesta, Monson, and Senn (1995) developed, refined, and researched a taxonomy of aesthetic response for assessing and interpreting developmental response in grades 4–10. Figure 15.12 developmentally presents four stages of aesthetic response and allows the assessor to determine the degree (minimal, moderate, complete) to which the reader expresses each category. Note the realistic inclusion of an efferent stage, which merely reflects summary or repetition of the story, not an emotional interaction with the text.

Stage 1, *Evocation,* focuses on reliving the experience of the text or imagining or picturing literary elements (character, setting, plot events). Stage 2, *Alternatives,* exhibits itself through text-to-life connections, text-to-text connections, and exploration of personal and interpersonal perspectives on the text. Stage 3 rises to the application level of *Reflective Thinking,* which highlights personal interpretation of the text. Stage 4, *Evaluation,* forms the pinnacle of aesthetic response as the reader assesses the text within his or her own transaction and evaluates the quality of the work reflective of one's own preset criteria for quality literature.

The researchers found that students in the lower grades "tended to respond more often at the evocation and alternative levels, while the majority of the reflective thinking and evaluation responses came from students in the upper grades" (Sebesta et al., 1995, p. 449). This suggests that response tends to be developmental and provides a tool for the assessment of aesthetic response over time and across grade levels. It also provides a scope and sequence for expanding the response horizons of individual readers/responders over time.

This suggested hierarchy documents individual and class development in reader response and focuses teachers on instruction. The researchers, however, caution teachers to avoid strong dependence on the categories for creating response prompts or comprehension-like questions. "Aesthetic stance . . . is more fluid and emergent than this, and perhaps more holistic than categorical" (Sebesta et al., 1995, p. 450). Those who utilize the taxonomy for categorization should not expect every response to fit in a distinct category. Response-based teachers must not lose sight of seeking the totally original response that defies categorization. That, indeed, exemplifies the premise of aesthetic response.

# ASSESSING LITERATURE CONVERSATIONS

If literature conversations are reader response centered, then an authentic assessment of this oral response sharing format must also be response centered, rather than text centered. Teachers who weave conversations into their classrooms find a need to assess reading attitudes, reading preparation, levels of response, and amount and range of reading.

**FIGURE 15.12** A taxonomy of aesthetic response

| | Minimal | Moderate | Complete |
|---|---|---|---|

0. Efferent response.
   Example: "The main characters in the story are the talking mule, the talking dog, the boy, and his father."

**Stage 1: Evocation**

1. Relive the experience: reexperience what happened as you read; includes acting out, telling, rereading a part that you, the reader, choose to reread.
   Example: "When the mule spoke it was a surprise. I was thinking it was going to be a magical or in some way a special mule."

2. Imagine or picture characters, setting, or events from the selection; elaborate on the basic idea.
   Example: "The son was so scared that he almost had a heart attack. He screamed as loud as he could. Then he ran as far as he could."

**Stage 2: Alternatives (comparing, contrasting the original evocation)**

3. *Apply own experience:* reconsider response by relating self.
   Example: "This is a picture of all the people telling Bill what to do and where to go because it reminds me of my brother and everyone telling him what to do and him telling them NO!"

4. *Apply other reading or media to the work:* e.g., comparing folk tales.
   Example: "This story reminds me of a story I was told when I was little about a King who had a chair that talked and nobody would believe him. . . ."

5. *Apply other readers' views (as in book discussions) or reexamine your own views.*
   Example: "I really liked the story. It was unpredictable and humorous. . . . It was surprising when the dog started talking, too. . . . It would be great to be able to talk to animals and have them talk back."

6. *Reexamine text from other perspectives:* including hypothesizing, considering another point of view, extrapolating.
   Example: "I wonder why the mule hadn't talked before now? Why did he wait so long to say he was sick of being yelled at?"

**Stage 3: Reflective Thinking (thematic level, requiring generalization and application)**

7. *Interpretation:* generalize about the meaning of the literary experience, with application to the reader's own life, hence extending #3 to application.
   Example: "Finding out what animals thought would change the world. There may not be anymore eating beef or poultry. Yikes! I love a good leg of chicken."

**FIGURE 15.12**    A taxonomy of aesthetic response *(continued)*

---

**Stage 4: Evaluation (classified only as aesthetic if the above categories have been met)**

8. *Evaluating what you got from the transaction.*
   Example:  "If I were the boy I wouldn't trip out. I would go and talk
   to the animals. What harm can talking to a mule do?
   Most people chat with their pets anyways. It wouldn't
   make much difference if the pet talked back. It would
   actually be nice."

9. *Evaluating the "goodness" of the work itself:* In regard to
   criteria set by the reader.
   Example:  "I think this story really does not have any other point
   beside the fact that things are not always what they
   seem. Writing about this donkey might be a lot easier if
   the story was longer and more thought provoking."

---

Source: From Sebesta, S. L., Monson, D. L., & Senn, H. D. (1995). A hierarchy to assess reader response. *Journal of Reading, 38(6),* 446–447. Reprinted by permission of the International Reading Association.

For primary-grade literature conversations, Hill (1995) suggests a simple self-evaluation that allows young children to assess preliminary responsibilities as a member of a literature circle (Figure 15.13). As children enter early intermediate grades, a literature self-reflection (Hill, 1995), Figure 15.14, is more appropriate because it requires written self-evaluations. Figure 15.15 is an adaptation of a form utilized by Hill and Ruptic (1994) in attempting to monitor literature conversations at the grade 6–8 levels. The form not only assesses the quality and types of response generated during discussion, but also allows for both self- and peer evaluation.

The emphasis in literature conversation assessment is self-reflection, which meshes well with the philosophy on reader response. Each individual provides the most thorough understanding of their group responsibilities, response capabilities, and contributions to discussion. Just as a reader is responsible for sharing unique responses through reflection, so too does self-reflection play an important role in assessment.

# A READER RESPONSE PORTFOLIO

A portfolio is defined as a collection of student's work, in different stages of development, which reveals strengths and weaknesses, and allows both the student and the teacher to evaluate progress (Tierney et. al, 1991). A reader response portfolio, on a narrower scope, is defined as a collection of a student's responses to literature across literary genres and through varying modes of response that reveals a unique and developing response style allowing for both student reflection and teacher narrative assessment.

The reader response portfolio is built on the guiding principles of a portfolio approach to literacy assessment. First, a response portfolio is anchored in *authenticity.* Real evidence or real

**FIGURE 15.13**   Literature circle self-evaluation: Primary grades (K–2)

---

**LITERATURE CIRCLE SELF-EVALUATION**

**Name** _____   **Date** _____

**Title** _____

| | | |
|---|---|---|
| 1. I read my book | yes | no |
| 2. I marked places in my book | yes | no |
| 3. I brought my book on Monday | yes | no |
| 4. I shared my book with others | yes | no |
| 5. I thought this book was: | | |

              Not So Good           O.K.           Very Good

---

*Source: From "Literature Circles: Assessment and Evaluation" by Bonnie Campbell Hill. In* Literature Circles and Response *by Bonnie Campbell Hill, Nancy J. Johnson, & Katherine L. Schlick Noe. Copyright © 1995. Reprinted by permission of Christopher-Gordon Publishers, Inc.*

**FIGURE 15.14**   Literature circle self-reflection: Intermediate grades (3–5)

---

**LITERATURE CIRCLE SELF-EVALUATION**

**Name** _____   **Date** _____

**Title** _____

    What did I do well today during our literature circle meeting? (asked good questions, listened actively, responded to others, reread, took a risk, compared the book to my experiences, compared the book to another book)

_____
_____
_____
_____
_____
_____
_____

    What do I still need to work on during literature circle meetings?

_____
_____
_____
_____
_____
_____
_____
_____

---

*Source: From "Literature Circles: Assessment and Evaluation" by Bonnie Campbell Hill. In* Literature Circles and Response *by Bonnie Campbell Hill, Nancy J. Johnson, & Katherine L. Schlick Noe. Copyright © 1995. Reprinted by permission of Christopher-Gordon Publishers, Inc.*

**FIGURE 15.15**   Peer-assessment of a grand conversation/literature circle: Middle level (6–8)

**Peer-Assessment of a Grand Conversation/Literature Circle**

**Book Title** _____   **Date** _____

**Author** _____   **Focus** _____

*

**Names of Participants**

**Preparation**

    Read the assigned chapter book
    Prepared literature response journal entries
    Noted book excerpts to share
    Prepared critical thinking questions for discussion

**Participation**

    Read-aloud response entries from journal
    Posed challenging questions to the group
    Used text to support/clarify
    Made inferences from the text
    Referred to the author's craft
    Shared intertextual connections
    Shared text-to-life connections
    Elicited responses from other group members
    Kept an open mind to the contributions of others
    Maintained a professional conversational demeanor

*Denotes person completing form.

*Source: Adapted from* Practical Aspects of Authentic Assessment: Putting the Pieces Together *by Bonnie Campbell Hill and Cynthia Ruptic. Reprinted by permission of Christopher-Gordon Publishers, Inc.*

response is reflected in the portfolio content. All artifacts arise in the aesthetic classroom setting and are products of interactions with authentic children's literature. Second, reader response assessment is a *continuous, ongoing process.* Because response styles are constantly growing and changing, portfolio documentation forms a dated record of evolving response to a variety of literary genres through a variety of response modes. Third, reader response assessment within a portfolio is *multidimensional.* Because response modes encompass oral and written response as well as dramatic and artistic response, the portfolio artifacts are likely to include a variety of formats beyond literature response journals. Finally, portfolio assessment for response must provide for *interactive reflection* by both reader and teacher so personal goals may be set. The consistent nature of teacher feedback, readers' narrative evaluations of their own response, and a response conference support these criteria.

No single observation of literature discussion, no single entry from a response journal, no single art form, no single written product built on a literature model can capture the overall authentic, continuous, multidimensional, interactive nature of sound portfolio assessment. The fit between reader response and portfolio documentation is a natural one that supports the uniqueness of the individual learner yet monitors aspects of growth and refinement of reading material choice and response style.

## Elements of a Reader Response Portfolio

The multiplicity of items that might be placed in a reader response portfolio is only limited by the assignments of the teacher and the ingenuity and creativity of the responder. These are the two overlying criteria for each artifact: (1) response is based on authentic children's literature; and (2) response reflects a genuine, unique, personal perspective on that literature.

The form that the response documentation may take could include the following:

- **Literature response file.** Selected brief entries from the reading of picture books, transitional chapter books, or chapter books.
- **Literature response journal.** A notebook or photocopied entries from individual journals.
- **Audiotape.** Recorded conversations (or transcripts) from read-alouds or literature conversations highlighting the individual's oral response and/or interactions with other readers.
- **Videotape.** Performance documentation of response to literature that is likely to include a play, a readers' theater presentation, movement, or musical performance.
- **Photographs.** Documentation of constructions, three-dimensional projects, murals, or presentations resulting from a response to literature.
- **Artwork.** Any original artistic response to literature including drawing, painting, sculpture, or book illustration.
- **Book list.** A list of books read and responded to including date, author, title, illustrator (if applicable), publisher, genre, and response mode chosen for response to each title.
- **Book graph.** A bar graph that records books read and responded to organized by literary genre.
- **Response checklist.** A list that records modes of literary response to literature (i.e., oral, written journals, written product, artistic, music, cooking, sharing)
- **Categorized graphs.** Graphs of response journal entries over several books.

This list is not inclusive, but it does provide an idea of the many options for portfolio inclusion. Although it might be adjusted depending on classroom response options at various age/grade levels, it does show the value of accumulating a variety of artifacts as documentation of response growth and future potential.

## Stages of Response Portfolio Development

The four stages of *collection, selection, reflection,* and *projection* that apply to general academic portfolios should be applied to the response-based portfolio as well. Readers can collect all of their responses over a period of time and include them in the portfolio in their different forms.

At scheduled intervals, the selection process causes students to apply self-evaluative techniques to determine which response documentation will remain in the portfolio and which will be excluded. This can be determined by two factors: predetermined standards or numerical criteria with self-selection as a primary factor. Guidelines set by the teacher may require evidence of the following:

- Written response to literature that best reflects growing response style
- Oral response to literature that reflects your ability to contribute to group discussions on literature
- Art or musical or dramatic response documentation through a performance product
- Responder's favorite response
- Responder's choice.

Numerical choice simply involves students including a designated number of responses, but student choice is paramount in either selection process.

Whether requirements are imposed or choice is dominant, the third aspect of portfolio assessment is reflection. The reader/responder must include a written reflection on each selection including the following:

1. Why he or she chose the response artifact
2. How the response artifact reflects the literature read
3. What the artifact indicates about his or her growing confidence to respond to literature.

The personal reflection is most important and should never be eliminated from the portfolio assessment process. Self-reflection reveals personal insights into growth in appreciation of literature and in one's own response to what is read.

The final aspect of portfolio assessment is projection or goal setting. This is jointly managed by the teacher and the student through a portfolio conference. Readers should focus on three areas of concern:

1. Am I reading books across a variety of genres?
2. Am I responding to books through a variety of response modes?
3. Am I growing in depth and breadth in response to literature?

Goals can be set in all of these areas. Reading across genres can be addressed by stating which literary genres need to be encountered through future reading. The goal is not for readers to forsake their favorite kinds of books, but to ensure exposure to all genres to some degree. Response modes can be addressed by looking for voids in type of response. If a reader is only responding through writing, a goal should be set to explore other options that might otherwise be avoided or dismissed. The purpose once again is not to forsake a favorite mode of response, but to ensure exposure to various modes of response. Goals set can enhance response in a favored mode, but also reach toward new options as well. The goals must be jointly set, but those sincerely set by the reader are most likely to be realized.

The reader response portfolio should be shared at a parent–teacher–student conference because it indicates growth in reading, appreciation of literature, and the ability to share personal interactions with books read. Providing an extended view of the reading process, it documents the individuality rather than standardization of the child as reader and responder. The list of books, the graph of genres, and the graph of response modes visually show parents the amount and types of books read and the variety of response modes experienced as an extension of the reading experience. Sharing of individual oral, written, dramatic, or artistic responses reflects the multiple talents of students in communicating personal thoughts and innermost feelings. The reader response portfolio moves assessment far beyond the reading test battery scores in comprehension, vocabulary, and decoding skills. The response portfolio reflects the potential of a reader to become involved in a lifetime of rich literary encounters long after the school experience concludes. Reading as a matter of choice rather than to fulfill a requirement is a valid measure of the growth of a child as a reader.

## CLOSING THOUGHTS

Because accountability is a reality in a response-based literature program, teachers must meet the challenge of assessment and documentation of reader response to literature. Perhaps the single most important concern of inservice teachers is literature-based assessment. They feel pressure from administrators and parents to "prove" that children are really learning through literature. This chapter provides a variety of tools to assist the teacher and the reader in documenting response that reflects growth over time. The principles of authentic assessment provide the foundation for checklists, categories of response, a hierarchy of response, and reader response portfolios. Other tools provide a means for assessment to inform instruction through checklists of prompts, response activities, and insightful anecdotal records.

If a response-based view of literature is to be legitimized as part of a balanced reading program, the necessity of meaningful assessment must be addressed. While most Rosenblatt advocates believe that lifelong reading is an intangible outcome of reader response to literature in the elementary school, they must show documented evidence of short-term gains and provide specific examples that indicate meaning making and personal reflection are taking place. Although this type of assessment is certainly more time consuming to collect and assimilate than traditional types of assessment, it should be part of a balanced literacy assessment program for K–8 students. This chapter's offerings attempt to supply educators with those tools to assist with this challenging task. These assessment suggestions produce convincing evidence to support what we instinctively know happens to children when they are given the freedom to read and are encouraged in their personal transactions with literature.

## REFERENCES

Hancock, M. R. (1993). Exploring the meaning-making process through the content of literature response journals: A case study investigation. *Research in the Teaching of English, 27*, 335–368.

Hill, B. C. (1995). Literature circles: Assessment and evaluation. In B. C. Hill, N. J. Johnson, & K. L. Schlick Noe (Eds.), *Literature circles and response* (pp. 167–198). Norwood, MA: Christopher-Gordon.

Hill, B. C., & Ruptic, C. (1994). *Practical aspects of authentic assessment: Putting the pieces together.* Norwood, MA: Christopher-Gordon.

International Reading Association and the National Council of Teachers of English. (1994). *Standards for the assessment of reading and writing.* Newark, DE & Urbana, IL: Author.

Sebesta, S. L., Monson, D. L., & Senn H. D. (1995). A hierarchy to assess reader response. *Journal of Reading, 38,* 444–450.

Tierney, R., Carter, M., & Desai, L. (1991). *Portfolio assessment in the reading-writing classroom.* Norwood, MA: Christopher-Gordon.

## CHILDREN'S BOOKS CITED     [P] = K–2; [I] = 3–5; [M] = 6–8

Hesse, Karen (1992). *Letters from Rifka.* New York: Holt. [ I ]

Lowry, Lois (1993). *The giver.* Boston: Houghton Mifflin. [ M ]

# Epilogue
## *Continuing the Celebration*

*I am not under the illusion that the schools alone can change society. However, I can reaffirm the belief uttered so many years ago: We teachers of language and literature have a crucial role to play as educators and citizens. We phrase our goals as fostering the growth of the capacity for personally meaningful, self-critical literary experience. The educational process that achieves this aim most effectively will serve a broader purpose, the nurturing of men and women capable of building a fully democratic society. The prospect is invigorating!*

Louise M. Rosenblatt, "Retrospect" in
*Transactions with Literature: A Fifty-Year
Perspective* (1990), p. 107

Throughout your journey through *A Celebration of Literature and Response,* you have been immersed in an enormous amount of information about children's literature and children as readers and respondents to literature. You have been introduced to a philosophy of literature-based instruction with reader response at its core. By reading and responding to some of the quality literature shared throughout these pages and by actively becoming involved in some of the response-based activities suggested throughout the text, you have grown in your knowledge of both books and readers. But the celebration has only just begun as you take your expertise to real readers in real classrooms with real literature as the focus of learning.

Whether you go forth as a preservice teacher, a student intern, a first-year teacher, or an experienced practitioner, you have much to celebrate as you carry this information to children in a classroom setting. How have you enriched your response-based, literature expertise to ensure the celebration will continue with children? With judicious reading and response to this text, you have likely assumed the following knowledge base:

- Understanding of Louise Rosenblatt's transactional theory of reader response, efferent and aesthetic response, and short- and long-term impact of literature and response on children as readers and critical thinkers.
- Knowledge of the varied response options across developmental levels and the need to nurture response potential in your classroom.
- Recognition of an aesthetic teaching philosophy and its focus, acceptance, and encouragement of the expression of unique interactions with literature by and among individual readers.
- Knowledge of hundreds of children's books and literary genres to enhance literacy experiences throughout the school day and across an entire elementary K–8 spectrum.
- Familiarity with oral response to literature including spontaneous read-aloud response, the use of prompts to elicit unique response, and the enhancement of oral response through literature conversations.
- Confidence in the power of the written response to literature, both through literature response journals and through literature as a model for writing.
- Appreciation for responses built on the fine arts of drama, art, and music as an option for sharing responses to literature.
- Ability to connect and blend literature across genres into an effective knowledge base for interdisciplinary instruction.
- Understanding of authentic assessment tools as a means to monitor and document growth in reader response to literature over time.
- Ability to articulate the connection between reader response theory, children's literature, and the critical role of the reader in creating lifelong learners and critical thinking citizens in a democratic society.

You are invited to begin your own celebration of literature and response with children as you focus on the application of philosophy, literature, and response in an instructional setting. Open your eyes to all the ways in which readers respond to literature in your classroom and build from that foundation. Take these quality children's books and share them with children throughout the day and across the curriculum. Try developmentally appropriate response-based activities with children hungry for an opportunity to express their reactions to literature. Vary your menu of response activities to capture the interest and abilities of diverse learners. Add a component to your assessment package that focuses on documentation of growth of response. Make connections between your own state standards and the literature-based activities you have experienced through this text. Only when the contents and spirit of this book are carried to real children in real classrooms can the genuine celebration of literature and response begin.

As you move beyond this text into the world of children, literature, and teaching, your professional growth must continue. What can you do to continue your growth in children's literature and reader response to literature?

- Read children's literature. Build a wide repertoire of books to sustain interest and excitement in literature-based teaching. Read across genres, across authors, and include multicultural books.
- Be aware of book awards and lists (see Appendix A), anticipate their announcement, and add them to your media center collection.
- Read professional review journals (see Appendix B) to constantly update your knowledge of new books for children.
- Read professional journals in reading, language arts, and children's literature (see Appendix B) for continued research-based connections to the classroom.
- Access up-to-date information on children's authors and newly published titles on the Internet (see Appendix C). Explore cyberspace for new ways to connect children and books.
- Attend professional meetings with a focus on literature in the classroom.
- Conduct teacher action research in your own classroom on response-based activities or children's responses to particular genres or titles.
- Share books, response, and excitement with other teaching professionals. Spread the enjoyment of literature and response throughout your school.

As you move beyond *A Celebration of Literature and Response,* take with you a passion for quality children's literature, the power of response, and the impact of teaching children. You can't create lifelong readers if you lack a genuine enthusiasm for children's literature. You can't expect responses to grow if you are not open to risk taking and a belief in the uniqueness of the individual reader. And you can't impact children as readers if you don't bring energy, commitment, and dedication to the classroom. When these essentials are in place, you are ready to move on with quality literature, unique response, and enthusiastic readers as the foundation of your teaching.

Cause the celebration of literature and response to continue. . . .

Rosenblatt, L. M. (1990). Retrospect. In Farrell, E. J., & Squire, J. R. (Eds.) *Transactions with literature: A fifty-year perspective* (pp. 97–107). Urbana, IL: National Council of Teachers of English.

# Children's Book Awards and Recognition

## The Caldecott Medal

Named in honor of the 19th-century English illustrator, Randolph Caldecott, this medal is presented annually to the illustrator of the most distinguished American picture book for children published during the preceding year. A number of honor books may also be named by the selection committee. Sponsored by the Association for Library Service to Children, a division of the American Library Association, eligibility for this award is limited to U.S. citizens and residents.

**1999**   *Snowflake Bentley* by Jacqueline Briggs Martin. Illus. by Mary Azarian. Houghton Mifflin.

**Honor Books:** *Duke Ellington* by Andrea Davis Pinkney. Illus. by Brian Pinkney. Hyperion. *No, David!* by David Shannon. Blue Sky/Scholastic. *Snow* by Uri Shulevitz. Farrar, Straus and Giroux. *Tibet: Through the Red Box* by Peter Sis. Farrar, Straus and Giroux.

**1998**   *Rapunzel* by Paul O. Zelinsky. Dutton

**Honor Books:** *The Gardener* by Sarah Stewart. Illus. by David Small. Farrar, Straus and Giroux. *Harlem* by Walter Dean Myers. Illus. by Christopher Myers. Scholastic. *There Was an Old Lady Who Swallowed a Fly* by Simms Taback. Viking.

**1997**   *Golem* by David Wisniewski. Clarion

**Honor Books:** *Hush! A Thai Lullaby* by Minfong Ho. Illus. by Holly Meade. Orchard. *The Graphic Alphabet* by Neal Porter. Illus. by David Pelletier. Orchard. *The Paperboy* by Dave Pilkey. Orchard. *Starry Messenger: Galileo Galilei* by Peter Sis. Farrar, Straus and Giroux.

**1996**    *Officer Buckle and Gloria* by Peggy Rathmann. Putnam.

**Honor Books:** *Alphabet City* by Stephen Johnson. Viking. *Zin! Zin! Zin! a Violin* by Lloyd Moss. Illus. by Marjorie Priceman. Simon. *The Faithful Friend* by Robert D. San Souci. Illus. by Brian Pinkney. Simon. *Tops and Bottoms* by Janet Stevens. Harcourt.

**1995**    *Smoky Night* by Eve Bunting. Illus. by David Diaz. Harcourt.

**Honor Books:** *Swamp Angel* by Anne Isaacs. Illus. by Paul O. Zelinsky. Dutton. *John Henry* by Julius Lester. Illus. by Jerry Pinkney. Dial. *Time Flies* by Eric Rohmann. Crown.

**1994**    *Grandfather's Journey* by Allen Say. Houghton Mifflin.

**Honor Books:** *Peppe the Lamplighter* by Elisa Barone. Illus. by Ted Lewin. Lothrop. *In the Small, Small Pond* by Denise Fleming. Holt. *Owen* by Kevin Henkes. Greenwillow. *Raven: A Trickster Tale from the Pacific Northwest* by Gerald McDermott. Harcourt. *Yo! Yes?* by Chris Raschka. Orchard.

**1993**    *Mirette on the High Wire* by Emily Arnold McCully. Putnam.

**Honor Books:** *Seven Blind Mice* by Ed Young. Philomel. *The Stinky Cheese Man and other Fairly Stupid Tales* by Jon Scieszka. Illus. by Lane Smith. Viking. *Working Cotton* by Sherley Anne Williams. Illus. by Carole Byard. Harcourt.

**1992**    *Tuesday* by David Weisner. Clarion.

**Honor Book:** *Tar Beach* by Faith Ringgold. Crown.

**1991**    *Black and White* by David McCaulay. Houghton Mifflin.

**Honor Books:** *Puss 'n Boots* by Charles Perrault. Illus. by Fred Marcellino. Farrar. *"More, More, More," Said the Baby: 3 Love Stories* by Vera B. Williams. Greenwillow.

**1990**    *Lon Po Po: A Red Riding Hood Tale from China* translated and illustrated by Ed Young. Philomel.

**Honor Books:** *Hershel and the Hanukkah Goblins* by Eric Kimmel. Illus. by Trina Schart Hyman. Holiday House. *The Talking Eggs* adapted by Robert D. San Souci. Illus. by Jerry Pinkney. Dial. *Bill Peet: An Autobiography* by Bill Peet. Houghton Mifflin. *Color Zoo* by Lois Ehlert. Lippincott.

**1989**    *Song and Dance Man* by Karen Ackerman. Illus. by Stephen Gammell. Knopf.

**Honor Books:** *Free Fall* by David Wiesner. Lothrop. *Goldilocks and the Three Bears* retold and illustrated by James Marshall. Dial. *Mirandy and Brother Wind* by Patricia McKissack. Illus. by Jerry Pinkney. Knopf. *The Boy of the Three-Year Nap* by Diane Snyder. Illus. by Allen Say. Houghton Mifflin.

**1988**    *Owl Moon* by Jane Yolen. Illus. by John Schoenherr. Philomel.

**Honor Books:** *Mufaro's Beautiful Daughters* retold by John Steptoe. Lothrop.

**1987**    *Hey, Al* by Arthur Yorinks. Illus. by Richard Egielski. Farrar.

**Honor Books:** *The Village of Round and Square Houses* by Ann Grifalconi. Little, Brown. *Alphabatics* by Suse MacDonald. Bradbury. *Rumpelstiltskin* retold and illustrated by Paul O. Zelinsky. Dutton.

**1986**    *The Polar Express* by Chris Van Allsburg. Houghton Mifflin.

**Honor Books:** *The Relatives Came* by Cynthia Rylant. Illus. by Stephen Gammell. Bradbury. *King Bidgood's in the Bathtub* by Audrey Wood. Illus. by Don Wood. Harcourt.

**1985** *Saint George and the Dragon* adapted by Margaret Hodges. Illus. by Trina Schart Hyman. Little, Brown.

**Honor Books:** *Hansel and Gretel* adapted by Rika Lesser. Illus. by Paul O. Zelinsky. Dodd. *The Story of Jumping Mouse* retold and illustrated by John Steptoe. Lothrop. *Have You Seen My Duckling?* by Nancy Tafuri. Greenwillow.

**1984** *The Glorious Flight: Across the Channel with Louis Blériot,* by Alice and Martin Provensen. Viking.

**Honor Books:** *Ten, Nine, Eight* by Molly Bang. Greenwillow. *Little Red Riding Hood* by the Brothers Grimm. Retold and illustrated by Trina Schart Hyman. Holiday House.

**1983** *Shadow* by Blaise Cendrars. Translated and illustrated by Marcia Brown. Scribner's.

**Honor Books:** *When I Was Young in the Mountains* by Cynthia Rylant. Illus. by Diane Goode. Dutton. *A Chair for My Mother* by Vera B. Williams. Greenwillow.

**1982** *Jumanji* by Chris Van Allsburg. Houghton Mifflin.

**Honor Books:** *A Visit to William Blake's Inn: Poems for Innocent and Experienced Travelers* by Nancy Willard. Illus. by Alice and Martin Provensen. Harcourt. *Where the Buffaloes Begin* by Olaf Baker. Illustrated by Stephen Gammell. Warne. *On Market Street* by Arnold Lobel. Illus. by Anita Lobel. Greenwillow. *Outside Over There* by Maurice Sendak. Harper.

**1981** *Fables* by Arnold Lobel. Harper.

**Honor Books:** *The Bremen-Town Musicians* retold and illustrated by Ilse Plume. Doubleday. *The Grey Lady and the Strawberry Snatcher* by Molly Bang. Four Winds. *Mice Twice* by Joseph Low. Atheneum. *Truck* by Donald Crews. Greenwillow.

**1980** *Ox-Cart Man* by Donald Hall. Illus. by Barbara Cooney. Viking.

**Honor Books:** *Ben's Trumpet* by Rachel Isadora. Greenwillow. *The Treasure* by Uri Schulevitz. Farrar. *The Garden of Abdul Gasazi* by Chris Van Allsburg. Houghton Mifflin.

**1979** *The Girl Who Loved Wild Horses* by Paul Goble. Bradbury.

**Honor Books:** *Freight Train* by Donald Crews. Greenwillow. *The Way to Start a Day* by Byrd Baylor. Illus. by Peter Parnall. Scribner's.

**1978** *Noah's Ark* by Peter Spier. Doubleday.

**Honor Books:** *Castle* by David McCaulay. Houghton Mifflin. *It Could Always Be Worse* retold and illustrated by Margot Zemach. Farrar.

**1977** *Ashanti to Zulu: African Traditions* by Margaret Musgrove. Illus. by Leo and Diane Dillon. Dial.

**Honor Books:** *The Amazing Bone* by William Steig. Farrar. *The Contest* by Nonny Hogrogian. Greenwillow. *Fish for Supper* by M. B. Goffstein. Dial. *The Golem: A Jewish Legend* retold and illus. by Beverly Brodsky McDermott. Lippincott. *Hawk, I'm Your Brother* by Byrd Baylor. Illus. by Peter Parnall. Scribner's.

**1976** *Why Mosquitoes Buzz in People's Ears* retold by Verna Aardema. Illus. by Leo and Diane Dillon. Dial.

**Honor Books:** *The Desert Is Theirs* by Byrd Baylor. Illus. by Peter Parnall. Scribner's. *Strega Nona* retold and illustrated by Tomie dePaola. Prentice Hall.

**1975**    *Arrow to the Sun* adapted and illustrated by Gerald McDermott. Viking.

   **Honor Book:** *Jambo Means Hello: Swahili Alphabet Book* by Muriel Feelings. Illus. by Tom Feelings. Dial.

**1974**    *Duffy and the Devil* retold by Harve Zemach. Illus. by Margot Zemach. Farrar.

   **Honor Books:** *Three Jovial Huntsmen* adapted and illustrated by Susan Jeffers. Bradbury. *Cathedral: The Story of Its Construction* by David McCaulay. Houghton Mifflin.

**1973**    *The Funny Little Woman* retold by Arlene Mosel. Illus. by Blair Lent. Dutton.

   **Honor Books:** *Hosie's Alphabet* by Hosea Baskin, Tobias Baskin, and Lisa Baskin. Illus. by Leonard Baskin. Viking. *When Clay Sings* by Byrd Baylor. Illus. by Tom Bahti. Scribner's. *Snow-White and the Seven Dwarfs* by the Brothers Grimm. Translated by Randall Jarrell. Illus. by Nancy Ekholm Burkert. Farrar. *Anansi the Spider: A Tale from the Ashanti* adapted and illustrated by Gerald McDermott. Holt.

**1972**    *One Fine Day* by Nonny Hogrogian. Macmillian.

   **Honor Books:** *If All the Seas Were One Sea* by Janina Domanska. Macmillan. *Moja Means One: Swahili Counting Book* by Muriel Feelings. Illus. by Tom Feelings. Dial. *Hildilid's Night* by Cheli Duran Ryan. Illus. by Arnold Lobel. Macmillan.

**1971**    *A Story, a Story: An African Tale* by Gail E. Haley. Atheneum.

   **Honor Books:** *The Angry Moon* retold by William Sleator. Illus. by Blair Lent. Atlantic/Little, Brown. *Frog and Toad Are Friends* by Arnold Lobel. Harper. *In the Night Kitchen* by Maurice Sendak. Harper.

**1970**    *Sylvester and the Magic Pebble* by William Steig. Windmill.

   **Honor Books:** *Goggles!* by Ezra Jack Keats. Macmillan. *Alexander and the Wind-Up Mouse* by Leo Lionni. Pantheon. *Pop Corn and Ma Goodness* by Edna Mitchell Preston. Illus. by Robert Andrew Parker. Viking. *Thy Friend, Obadiah* by Brinton Turkle. Viking. *The Judge: An Untrue Tale* by Harve Zemach. Illus. by Margot Zemach. Farrar.

**1969**    *The Fool of the World and the Flying Ship: A Russian Tale* by Arthur Ransome. Illus. by Uri Schulevitz, Farrar.

   **Honor Book:**    *Why the Sun and the Moon Live in the Sky: An African Folktale* by Elphinstone Dayrell. Illus. by Blair Lent. Houghton Mifflin.

**1968**    *Drummer Hoff* adapted by Barbara Emberley. Illus. by Ed Emberley. Prentice Hall.

   **Honor Books:** *Frederick* by Leo Lionni. Pantheon. *Seashore Story* by Taro Yashima. Viking. *The Emperor and the Kite* by Jane Yolen. Illus. by Ed Young. World.

**1967**    *Sam, Bangs and Moonshine* by Evaline Ness. Holt.

   **Honor Book:** *One Wide River to Cross* adapted by Barbara Emberley. Illus. by Ed Emberley. Prentice Hall.

**1966**    *Always Room for One More* by Sorche Nic Leodhas (pseud. for Leclaire Alger). Illus. by Nonny Hogrogian. Holt.

   **Honor Books:** *Hide and Seek Fog* by Alvin Tresselt. Illus. by Roger Duvoisin. Lothrop. *Just Me* by Marie Hall Ets. Viking. *Tom Tit Tot* adapted by Joseph Jacobs. Illus. by Evaline Ness. Scribner's.

**1965**      *May I Bring a Friend?* by Beatrice Schenk de Regniers. Illus. by Beni Montresor. Atheneum.

**Honor Books:** *Rain Makes Applesauce* by Julian Scheer. Illus. by Marvin Bileck. Holiday House. *The Wave* by Margaret Hodges. Illus. by Blair Lent. Houghton Mifflin. *A Pocketful of Cricket* by Rebecca Caudill. Illus. by Evaline Ness. Holt.

**1964**      *Where the Wild Things Are* by Maurice Sendak. Harper.

**Honor Books:** *Swimmy* by Leo Lionni. Pantheon. *All in the Morning Early* by Sorche Nic Leodhas (pseud. for Leclaire Alger). Illus. by Evaline Ness. Holt. *Mother Goose and Nursery Rhymes* by Philip Reed. Atheneum.

**1963**      *The Snowy Day* by Ezra Jack Keats. Viking.

**Honor Books:** *The Sun Is a Golden Earring* by Natalia Belting. Illus. by Bernarda Bryson. Holt. *Mr. Rabbit and the Lovely Present* by Charlotte Zolotow. Illus. by Maurice Sendak. Harper.

**1962**      *Once a Mouse* retold by Marcia Brown. Scribner's.

**Honor Books:** *The Fox Went Out on a Chilly Night: An Old Song* by Peter Spier. Doubleday. *Little Bear's Visit* by Else Minarik. Illus. by Maurice Sendak. Harper. *The Day We Saw the Sun Come Up* by Alice Goudey. Illus. by Adrienne Adams. Scribner's.

**1961**      *Baboushka and the Three Kings* by Ruth Robbins. Illus. by Nicolas Sidjakov. Parnassus.

**Honor Book:** *Inch by Inch* by Leo Lionni. Obolensky.

**1960**      *Nine Days to Christmas* by Marie Hall Ets and Aurora Labastida. Illus. by Marie Hall Ets. Viking.

**Honor Books:** *Houses from the Sea* by Alice E. Goudey. Illus. by Adrienne Adams. Scribner's. *The Moon Jumpers* by Janice May Udry. Illus. by Maurice Sendak. Harper.

**1959**      *Chanticleer and the Fox* by Chaucer. Adapted and illustrated by Barbara Cooney. Crowell.

**Honor Books:** *The House That Jack Built ("La Maison Que Jacques a Bâtie"): A Picture Book in Two Languages* by Antonio Frasconi. Harcourt. *What Do You Say, Dear? A Book of Manners for All Occasions* by Sesyle Joslin. Illus. by Maurice Sendak. Scott. *Umbrella* by Taro Yashima. Viking.

**1958**      *Time of Wonder* by Robert McCloskey. Viking.

**Honor Books:** *Fly High, Fly Low* by Don Freeman. Viking. *Anatole and the Cat* by Eve Titus. Illus. by Paul Galdone. McGraw.

**1957**      *A Tree Is Nice* by Janice May Udry. Illus. by Marc Simont. Harper.

**Honor Books:** *Mr. Penny's Race Horse* by Marie Hall Ets. Viking. *1 Is One* by Tasha Tudor. Walck. *Anatole* by Eve Titus. Illus. by Paul Galdone. McGraw. *Gillespie and the Guards* by Benjamin Elkin. Illus. by James Daugherty. Viking. *Lion* by William Pène du Bois. Viking.

**1956**      *Frog Went A-Courtin'* retold by John Langstaff. Illus. by Feodor Rojankovsky. Harcourt.

**Honor Books:** *Play With Me* by Marie Hall Ets. Viking. *Crow Boy* by Taro Yashima. Viking.

**1955**   *Cinderella, or the Little Glass Slipper* by Charles Perrault. Translated and illustrated by Marcia Brown. Scribner's.

 **Honor Books:** *Book of Nursery and Mother Goose Rhymes* compiled and illustrated by Marguerite de Angeli. Doubleday. *Wheel on the Chimney* by Margaret Wise Brown. Illus. by Tibor Gergely. Lippincott. *The Thanksgiving Story* by Alice Dalgliesh. Illus. by Helen Sewell. Scribner's.

**1954**   *Madeline's Rescue* by Ludwig Bemelmans. Viking.

 **Honor Books:** *Journey Cake, Ho!* by Ruth Sawyer. Illus. by Robert McCloskey. Viking. *When Will the World Be Mine?* by Miriam Schlein. Illus. by Jean Charlot. Scott. *The Steadfast Tin Soldier* by Hans Christian Andersen. Translated by M. R. James. Illus. by Marcia Brown. Scribner's. *A Very Special House* by Ruth Krauss. Illus. by Maurice Sendak. Harper. *Green Eyes* by Abe Birnbaum. Capitol.

**1953**   *The Biggest Bear* by Lynd Ward. Houghton Mifflin.

 **Honor Books:** *Puss in Boots.* Translated and illustrated by Marcia Brown. Scribner's. *One Morning in Maine* by Robert McCloskey. Viking. *Ape in a Cape: An Alphabet of Odd Animals* by Fritz Eichenberg. Harcourt. *The Storm Book* by Charlotte Zolotow. Illus. by Margaret Bloy Graham. Harper. *Five Little Monkeys* by Juliet Kepes. Houghton Mifflin.

**1952**   *Finders Keepers* by Will (pseud. for William Lipkind). Illus. by Nicolas (pseud. for Nicolas Mordvinoff). Harcourt.

 **Honor Books:** *Mr. T. W. Anthony Woo* by Marie Hall Ets. Viking. *Skipper John's Cook* by Marcia Brown. Scribner's. *All Falling Down* by Gene Zion. Illus. by Margaret Bloy Graham. Harper. *Bear Party* by William Pène du Bois. Viking. *Feather Mountain* by Elizabeth Olds. Houghton Mifflin.

**1951**   *The Egg Tree* by Katherine Milhous. Scribner's.

 **Honor Books:** *Dick Whittington and His Cat.* Translated and illustrated by Marcia Brown. Scribner's. *The Two Reds* by Will (pseud. for William Lipkind). Illus. by Nicolas (pseud. for Nicolas Mordvinoff). Harcourt. *If I Ran the Zoo* by Dr. Seuss (pseud. for Theodor Geisel). Random. *T-Bone, the Baby-Sitter* by Clare Turlay Newberry. Harper. *The Most Wonderful Doll in the World* by Phyllis McGinley. Illus. by Helen Stone. Lippincott.

**1950**   *Song of the Swallows* by Leo Politi. Scribner's.

 **Honor Books:** *America's Ethan Allen* by Stewart Holbrook. Illus. by Lynd Ward. Houghton Mifflin. *The Wild Birthday Cake* by Lavinia R. Davis. Illus. by Hildegard Woodward. Doubleday. *The Happy Day* by Ruth Krauss. Illus. by Marc Simont. Harper. *Henry-Fisherman* by Marcia Brown. Scribner's. *Bartholomew and the Oobleck* by Dr. Seuss (pseud. for Theodor Geisel). Random.

**1949**   *The Big Snow* by Berta and Elmer Hader. Macmillan.

 **Honor Books:** *Blueberries for Sal* by Robert McCloskey. Viking. *All Around Town* by Phyllis McGinley. Illus. by Helen Stone. Lippincott. *Juanita* by Leo Politi. Scribner's. *Fish in the Air* by Kurt Wiese. Viking.

**1948**   *White Snow, Bright Snow* by Alvin Tresselt. Illus. by Roger Duvoisin. Lothrop.

 **Honor Books:** *Stone Soup: An Old Tale* by Marcia Brown. Scribner's. *McElligot's Pool* by Dr. Seuss (pseud. for Theodor Geisel). Random. *Bambino the Clown* by George Schreiber. Viking. *Roger and the Fox* by Lavinia Davis. Illus. by Hildegard Woodward. Doubleday. *Song of Robin Hood* edited by Anne Malcolmson. Illus. by Virginia Lee Burton. Houghton Mifflin.

**1947**   *The Little Island* by Golden MacDonald. Illus. by Leonard Weisgard. Doubleday.

**Honor Books:** *Rain Drop Splash* by Alvin Tresselt. Illus. by Leonard Weisgard. Lothrop. *Boats on the River* by Marjorie Flack. Illus. by Jay Hyde Barnum. Viking. *Timothy Turtle* by Al Graham. Illustrated by Tony Palazzo. Viking. *Pedro, the Angel of Olvera Street* by Leo Politi. Scribner's. *Sing in Praise: A Collection of the Best Loved Hymns* by Opal Wheeler. Illus. by Marjorie Torrey. Dutton.

**1946**   *The Rooster Crows* selected and illustrated by Maud and Miska Petersham. Macmillan.

**Honor Books:** *Little Lost Lamb* by Golden MacDonald. Illus. by Leonard Weisgard. Doubleday. *Sing Mother Goose* by Opal Wheeler. Illus. by Marjorie Torrey. Dutton. *My Mother Is the Most Beautiful Woman in the World* retold by Becky Reyher. Illus. by Ruth Gannett. Lothrop. *You Can Write Chinese* by Kurt Wiese. Viking.

**1945**   *Prayer for a Child* by Rachel Field. Illus. by Elizabeth Orton Jones. Macmillan.

**Honor Books:** *Mother Goose: Seventy-Seven Verses With Pictures.* Illus. by Tasha Tudor. Walck. *In the Forest* by Marie Hall Ets. Viking. *Yonie Wondernose* by Marguerite de Angeli. Doubleday. *The Christmas Anna Angel* by Ruth Sawyer. Illus. by Kate Seredy. Viking.

**1944**   *Many Moons* by James Thurber. Illus. by Louis Slobodkin. Harcourt.

**Honor Books:** *Small Rain: Verses from the Bible.* Text arranged from the Bible by Jessie Orton Jones. Illus. by Elizabeth Orton Jones. Viking. *Pierre Pigeon* by Lee Kingman. Illus. by Arnold Edwin Bare. Houghton Mifflin. *The Mighty Hunter* by Berta and Elmer Hader. Macmillan. *A Child's Good Night Book* by Margaret Wise Brown. Illus. by Jean Charlot. Scott. *Good Luck Horse* by Chih-Yi Chan. Illus. by Plato Chan. Whittlesey.

**1943**   *The Little House* by Virginia Lee Burton. Houghton Mifflin.

**Honor Books:** *Dash and Dart* by Mary and Conrad Buff. Viking. *Marshmallow* by Clare Turlay Newberry. Harper.

**1942**   *Make Way for Ducklings* by Robert McCloskey. Viking.

**Honor Books:** *An American ABC* by Maud and Miska Petersham. Macmillan. *In My Mother's House* by Ann Nolan Clark. Illus. by Velino Herrera. Viking. *Paddle-to-the-Sea* by Holling Clancy Holling. Houghton Mifflin. *Nothing at All* by Wanda Gág. Coward-McCann.

**1941**   *They Were Strong and Good* by Robert Lawson. Viking.

**Honor Book:** *April's Kittens* by Clare Turlay Newberry. Harper.

**1940**   *Abraham Lincoln* by Ingri d'Aulaire and Edgar Parin d'Aulaire. Doubleday.

**Honor Books:** *Cock-a-Doodle-Doo* by Berta and Elmer Hader. Macmillan. *Madeline* by Ludwig Bemelmans. Viking. *The Ageless Story* by Lauren Ford. Dodd.

**1939**   *Mei Li* by Thomas Handforth. Doubleday.

**Honor Books:** *The Forest Pool* by Laura Adams Armer. McKay/Longmans. *Wee Gillis* by Munro Leaf. Illus. by Robert Lawson. Viking. *Snow White and the Seven Dwarfs.* Translated and illustrated by Wanda Gág. Coward-McCann. *Barkis* by Clare Turlay Newberry. Harper. *Andy and the Lion* by James Daugherty. Viking.

**1938**    *Animals of the Bible, a Picture Book.* Text selected from the King James *Bible* by Helen Dean Fish. Illus. by Dorothy P. Lathrop. Lippincott.

  **Honor Books:** *Seven Simeons: A Russian Tale* by Boris Artzybasheff. Viking. *Four and Twenty Blackbirds* compiled by Helen Dean Fish. Illus. by Robert Lawson. Stokes/Lippincott.

# The Newbery Medal

Named for 18th-century British bookseller, John Newbery, this medal is presented annually to the author of the most distinguished contribution to American literature for children published in the preceding year. A number of honor books may also be named by the selection committee. Sponsored by the Association for Library Service to Children, a division of the American Library Association, eligibility is limited to U.S. citizens and residents.

**1999**    Holes by Louis Sachar. Farrar, Straus and Giroux.

  **Honor Book:** *A Long Way from Chicago* by Richard Peck. Dial Books for Young Readers.

**1998**    *Out of the Dust* by Karen Hesse. Scholastic.

  **Honor Books:** *Ella Enchanted* by Gail Carson Levine. HarperCollins. *Lily's Crossing* by Patricia Reilly Giff. Delacorte. *Wringer* by Jerry Spinelli. HarperCollins.

**1997**    *The View from Saturday* by E. L. Konigsburg. Atheneum.

  **Honor Books:** *A Girl Named Disaster* by Nancy Farmer. Orchard. *Moorchild* by Eloise McGraw. McElderry. *The Thief* by Megan Whalen Turner. Greenwillow. *Belle Prater's Boy* by Ruth White. Farrar, Straus and Giroux.

**1996**    *The Midwife's Apprentice* by Karen Cushman. Clarion.

  **Honor Books:** *What Jamie Saw* by Carolyn Coman. Front Street. *The Watsons Go to Birmingham—1963* by Christopher Paul Curtis. Delacorte. *Yolanda's Genius* by Carol Fenner. McElderry. *The Great Fire* by Jim Murphy. Scholastic.

**1995**    *Walk Two Moons* by Sharon Creech. HarperCollins.

  **Honor Books:** *Catherine, Called Birdy* by Karen Cushman. Clarion. *The Ear, the Eye and the Arm* by Nancy Farmer. Orchard.

**1994**    *The Giver* by Lois Lowry. Houghton Mifflin.

  **Honor Books:** *Crazy Lady* by Jane Leslie Conly. HarperCollins. *Dragon's Gate* by Laurence Yep. HarperCollins. *Eleanor Roosevelt: A Life of Discovery* by Russell Freedman. Clarion.

**1993**    *Missing May* by Cynthia Rylant. Orchard.

  **Honor Books:** *The Dark-Thirty: Southern Tales of the Supernatural* by Patricia McKissack. Knopf. *Somewhere in the Darkness* by Walter Dean Myers. Scholastic. *What Hearts* by Bruce Brooks. HarperCollins.

**1992**    *Shiloh* by Phyllis Reynolds Naylor. Atheneum.

  **Honor Books:** *Nothing But the Truth* by Avi. Orchard. *The Wright Brothers: How They Invented the Airplane* by Russell Freedman. Holiday House.

**1991**  *Maniac Magee* by Jerry Spinelli. Little, Brown.

**Honor Books:** *The True Confessions of Charlotte Doyle* by Avi. Orchard.

**1990**  *Number the Stars* by Lois Lowry. Houghton Mifflin.

**Honor Books:** *Afternoon of the Elves* by Janet Taylor Lisle. Orchard. *Shabanu: Daughter of the Wind* by Suzanne Fisher Staples. Knopf.

**1989**  *Joyful Noise: Poems for Two Voices* by Paul Fleischman. Harper.

**Honor Books:** *In the Beginning: Creation Stories from Around the World* by Virginia Hamilton. Harcourt. *Scorpions* by Walter Dean Myers. Harper.

**1988**  *Lincoln: A Photobiography* by Russell Freedman. Clarion.

**Honor Books:** *After the Rain* by Norma Fox Mazer. Morrow. *Hatchet* by Gary Paulsen. Bradbury.

**1987**  *The Whipping Boy* by Sid Fleischman. Greenwillow.

**Honor Books:** *On My Honor* by Marion Dane Bauer. Clarion. *Volcano: The Eruption and Healing of Mount St. Helens* by Patricia Lauber. Bradbury. *A Fine White Dust* by Cynthia Rylant. Bradbury.

**1986**  *Sarah, Plain and Tall* by Patricia MacLachlan. Harper.

**Honor Books:** *Commodore Perry in the Land of the Shogun* by Rhoda Blumberg. Lothrop. *Dogsong* by Gary Paulsen. Bradbury.

**1985**  *The Hero and the Crown* by Robin McKinley. Greenwillow.

**Honor Books:** *Like Jake and Me* by Mavis Jukes. Illus. by Lloyd Bloom. Knopf. *The Moves Make the Man* by Bruce Brooks. Harper. *One-Eyed Cat* by Paula Fox. Bradbury.

**1984**  *Dear Mr. Henshaw* by Beverly Cleary. Morrow.

**Honor Books:** *The Sign of the Beaver* by Elizabeth George Speare. Houghton Mifflin. *A Solitary Blue* by Cynthia Voigt. Atheneum. *Sugaring Time* by Kathryn Lasky. Photographs by Christopher Knight. Macmillan. *The Wish Giver* by Bill Brittain. Harper.

**1983**  *Dicey's Song* by Cynthia Voigt. Atheneum.

**Honor Books:** *The Blue Sword* by Robin McKinley. Greenwillow. *Dr. DeSoto* by William Steig. Farrar. *Graven Images* by Paul Fleischman. Harper. *Homesick: My Own Story* by Jean Fritz. Putnam. *Sweet Whispers, Brother Rush* by Virginia Hamilton. Philomel.

**1982**  *A Visit to William Blake's Inn: Poems for Innocent and Experienced Travelers* by Nancy Willard. Illus. by Alice and Martin Provensen. Harcourt.

**Honor Books:** *Ramona Quimby, Age 8* by Beverly Cleary. Morrow. *Upon the Head of the Goat: A Childhood in Hungary, 1939–1944* by Aranka Siegal. Farrar.

**1981**  *Jacob Have I Loved* by Katherine Paterson. Crowell.

**Honor Books:** *The Fledgling* by Jane Langton. Harper. *A Ring of Endless Light* by Madeleine L'Engle. Farrar.

1980     *A Gathering of Days: A New England Girl's Journal, 1830–32* by Joan Blos. Scribner's.

**Honor Book:** *The Road from Home: The Story of an Armenian Girl* by David Kherdian. Greenwillow.

1979     *The Westing Game* by Ellen Raskin. Dutton.

**Honor Book:** *The Great Gilly Hopkins* by Katherine Paterson. Crowell.

1978     *Bridge to Terabithia* by Katherine Paterson. Crowell.

**Honor Books:** *Anpao: An American Indian Odyssey* by Jamake Highwater. Lippincott. *Ramona and Her Father* by Beverly Cleary. Morrow.

1977     *Roll of Thunder, Hear My Cry* by Mildred D. Taylor. Dial.

**Honor Books:** *Abel's Island* by William Steig. Farrar. *A String in the Harp* by Nancy Bond. Atheneum/McElderry.

1976     *The Grey King* by Susan Cooper. Atheneum/McElderry.

**Honor Books:** *The Hundred Penny Box* by Sharon Bell Mathis. Viking. *Dragonwings* by Lawrence Yep. Harper.

1975     *M. C. Higgins, the Great* by Virginia Hamilton. Macmillan.

**Honor Books:** *Figgs & Phantoms* by Ellen Raskin. Dutton. *My Brother Sam Is Dead* by James Lincoln Collier and Christopher Collier. Four Winds. *The Perilous Gard* by Elizabeth Marie Pope. Houghton Mifflin. *Philip Hall Likes Me, I Reckon Maybe* by Bette Greene. Dial.

1974     *The Slave Dancer* by Paula Fox. Bradbury.

**Honor Book:** *The Dark Is Rising* by Susan Cooper. Atheneum/McElderry.

1973     *Julie of the Wolves* by Jean Craighead George. Harper.

**Honor Books:** *Frog and Toad Together* by Arnold Lobel. Harper. *The Upstairs Room* by Johanna Reiss. Crowell. *The Witches of Worm* by Zilpha Keatley Snyder. Atheneum.

1972     *Mrs. Frisby and the Rats of NIMH* by Robert C. O'Brien. Atheneum.

**Honor Books:** *Incident at Hawk's Hill* by Allan W. Eckert. Little, Brown. *The Planet of Junior Brown* by Virginia Hamilton. Macmillan. *The Tombs of Atuan* by Ursula K. LeGuin. Atheneum. *Annie and the Old One* by Miska Miles. Little, Brown. *The Headless Cupid* by Zilpha Keatley Snyder. Atheneum.

1971     *Summer of the Swans* by Betsy Byars. Viking.

**Honor Books:** *Kneeknock Rise* by Natalie Babbitt. Farrar. *Enchantress from the Stars* by Sylvia Louise Engdahl. Atheneum. *Sing Down the Moon* by Scott O'Dell. Houghton Mifflin.

1970     *Sounder* by William H. Armstrong. Harper.

**Honor Books:** *Our Eddie* by Sulamith Ish-Kishor. Pantheon. *The Many Ways of Seeing: An Introduction to the Pleasure of Art* by Janet Gaylord Moore. World. *Journey Outside* by Mary Q. Steele. Viking.

1969     *The High King* by Lloyd Alexander. Holt.

**Honor Books:** *To Be a Slave* by Julius Lester. Dial. *When Shlemiel Went to Warsaw and Other Stories* by Isaac Bashevis Singer. Farrar.

**1968**  *From the Mixed-Up Files of Mrs. Basil E. Frankweiler* by E. L. Konigsburg. Atheneum.

**Honor Books:** *Jennifer, Hecate, Macbeth, William McKinley, and Me, Elizabeth* by E. L. Konigsburg. Atheneum. *The Black Pearl* by Scott O'Dell. Houghton Mifflin. *The Fearsome Inn* by Isaac Bashevis Singer. Scribner's. *The Egypt Game* by Zilpha Keatley Snyder. Atheneum.

**1967**  *Up a Road Slowly* by Irene Hunt. Follett.

**Honor Books:** *The King's Fifth* by Scott O'Dell. Houghton Mifflin. *Zlateh the Goat and Other Stories* by Isaac Bashevis Singer. Harper. *The Jazz Man* by Mary H. Weik. Atheneum.

**1966**  *I, Juan de Pareja* by Elizabeth Borten de Treviño. Farrar.

**Honor Books:** *The Black Cauldron* by Lloyd Alexander. Holt. *The Animal Family* by Randall Jarrell. Pantheon. *The Noonday Friends* by Mary Stolz. Harper.

**1965**  *Shadow of a Bull* by Maia Wojciechowska. Atheneum.

**Honor Books:** *Across Five Aprils* by Irene Hunt. Follett.

**1964**  *It's Like This, Cat* by Emily Cheney Neville. Harper.

**Honor Books:** *Rascal* by Sterling North. Dutton. *The Loner* by Esther Wier. McKay/Longmans.

**1963**  *A Wrinkle in Time* by Madeleine L'Engle. Farrar.

**Honor Books:** *Thistle and Thyme* by Sorche Nic Leodhas (pseud. for Leclaire Alger). Holt. *Men of Athens* by Olivia Coolidge. Houghton Mifflin.

**1962**  *The Bronze Bow* by Elizabeth George Speare. Houghton Mifflin.

**Honor Books:** *Frontier Living* by Edwin Tunis. World. *The Golden Goblet* by Eloise J. McGraw. Coward. *Belling the Tiger* by Mary Stolz. Harper.

**1961**  *Island of the Blue Dolphins* by Scott O'Dell. Houghton Mifflin.

**Honor Books:** *America Moves Forward* by Gerald Johnson. Morrow. *Old Ramon* by Jack Schaefer. Houghton Mifflin. *The Cricket in Times Square* by George Selden. Farrar.

**1960**  *Onion John* by Joseph Krumgold. Illus. by Symeon Shimin. Crowell.

**Honor Books:** *My Side of the Mountain* by Jean George. Dutton. *America Is Born* by Gerald Johnson. Morrow. *The Gammage Cup* by Carol Kendall. Harcourt.

**1959**  *The Witch of Blackbird Pond* by Elizabeth George Speare. Houghton Mifflin.

**Honor Books:** *The Family Under the Bridge* by Natalie S. Carlson. Harper. *Along Came a Dog* by Meindert DeJong. Harper. *Chucaro: Wild Pony of the Pampa* by Francis Kalnay. Harcourt. *The Perilous Road* by William O. Steele. Harcourt.

**1958**  *Rifles for Watie* by Harold Keith. Illus. by Peter Burchard. Crowell.

**Honor Books:** *The Horsecatcher* by Mari Sandoz. Westminster. *Gone-Away Lake* by Elizabeth Enright. Harcourt. *The Great Wheel* by Robert Lawson. Viking. *Tom Paine, Freedom's Apostle* by Leo Gurko. Crowell.

**1957**  *Miracles on Maple Hill* by Virginia Sorensen. Illus. by Beth and Joe Krush. Harcourt.

**Honor Books:** *Old Yeller* by Fred Gipson. Harper. *The House of Sixty Fathers* by Meindert DeJong. Harper. *Mr. Justice Holmes* by Clara I. Judson. Follett. *The*

*Corn Grows Ripe* by Dorothy Rhoads. Viking. *The Black Fox of Lorne* by Marguerite de Angeli. Doubleday.

**1956**    *Carry on, Mr. Bowditch* by Jean Lee Latham. Houghton Mifflin.

**Honor Books:** *The Golden Name Day* by Jennie D. Lindquist. Harper. *The Secret River* by Marjorie Kinnan Rawlings. Scribner's. *Men, Microscopes and Living Things* by Katherine B. Shippen. Viking.

**1955**    *The Wheel on the School* by Meindert DeJong. Illus. by Maurice Sendak. Harper.

**Honor Books:** *The Courage of Sarah Noble* by Alice Dalgliesh. Scribner's. *Banner in the Sky* by James Ramsey Ullman. Lippincott.

**1954**    *And Now Miguel* by Joseph Krumgold. Illus. by Jean Charlot. Crowell.

**Honor Books:** *All Alone* by Claire Huchet Bishop. Viking. *Shadrach* by Meindert DeJong. Harper. *Hurry Home, Candy* by Meindert DeJong. Harper. *Theodore Roosevelt, Fighting Patriot* by Clara I. Judson. Follett. *Magic Maize* by Mary and Conrad Buff. Houghton Mifflin.

**1953**    *Secret of the Andes* by Ann Nolan Clark. Illus. by Jean Charlot. Viking.

**Honor Books:** *Charlotte's Web* by E. B. White. Harper. *Moccasin Trail* by Eloise J. McGraw. Coward-McCann. *Red Sails to Capri* by Ann Weil. Viking. *The Bears on Hemlock Mountain* by Alice Dalgliesh. Scribner's. *Birthdays of Freedom, Vol. 1* by Genevieve Foster. Scribner's.

**1952**    *Ginger Pye* by Eleanor Estes. Harcourt.

**Honor Books:** *Americans Before Columbus* by Elizabeth Chesley Baity. Viking. *Minn of the Mississippi* by Holling Clancy Holling. Houghton Mifflin. *The Defender* by Nicholas Kalashnikoff. Scribner's. *The Light at Tern Rock* by Julia L. Sauer. Viking. *The Apple and the Arrow* by Mary and Conrad Buff. Houghton Mifflin.

**1951**    *Amos Fortune, Free Man* by Elizabeth Yates. Illus. by Nora Unwin. Dutton.

**Honor Books:** *Better Known as Johnny Appleseed* by Mabel Leigh Hunt. Lippincott. *Gandhi, Fighter Without a Sword* by Jeanette Eaton. Morrow. *Abraham Lincoln, Friend of the People* by Clara I. Judson. Follett. *The Story of Appleby Capple* by Anne Parrish. Harper.

**1950**    *The Door in the Wall* by Marguerite de Angeli. Doubleday.

**Honor Books:** *Tree of Freedom* by Rebecca Caudill. Viking. *The Blue Cat of Castle Town* by Catherine Coblentz. McKay/Longmans. *Kildee House* by Rutherford Montgomery. Doubleday. *George Washington* by Genevieve Foster. Scribner's. *Song of the Pines* by Walter and Marion Havighurst. Holt.

**1949**    *King of the Wind* by Marguerite Henry. Illus. by Wesley Dennis. Rand.

**Honor Books:** *Seabird* by Holling Clancy Holling. Houghton Mifflin. *Daughter of the Mountains* by Louise Rankin. Viking. *My Father's Dragon* by Ruth S. Gannett. Random. *Story of the Negro* by Arna Bontemps. Knopf.

**1948**    *The Twenty-One Balloons* by William Pène du Bois. Lothrop.

**Honor Books:** *Pancakes-Paris* by Claire Huchet Bishop. Viking. *Li Lun, Lad of Courage* by Carolyn Treffinger. Abingdon. *The Quaint and Curious Quest of Johnny Longfoot, The Shoe-King's Son* by Catherine Besterman. Bobbs-Merrill. *The Cow-Tail Switch, and Other West African Stories* by Harold Courlander and

George Herzog. Holt. *Misty of Chincoteague* by Marguerite Henry. Illus. by Wesley Dennis. Rand.

**1947** *Miss Hickory* by Carolyn Sherwin Bailey. Illus. by Ruth Gannett. Viking.

**Honor Books:** *The Wonderful Year* by Nancy Barnes. Messner. *The Big Tree* by Mary and Conrad Buff. Viking. *The Heavenly Tenants* by William Maxwell. Harper. *The Avion My Uncle Flew* by Cyrus Fisher. Appleton. *The Hidden Treasure of Glaston* by Eleanore M. Jewett. Viking.

**1946** *Strawberry Girl* by Lois Lenski. Lippincott.

**Honor Books:** *Justin Morgan Had a Horse* by Marguerite Henry. Follett. *The Moved-Outers* by Florence Crannell Means. Houghton Mifflin. *Bhimsa, the Dancing Bear* by Christine Weston. Scribner's. *New Found World* by Katherine B. Shippen. Viking.

**1945** *Rabbit Hill* by Robert Lawson. Viking.

**Honor Books:** *The Hundred Dresses* by Eleanor Estes. Harcourt. *The Silver Pencil* by Alice Dalgliesh. Scribner's. *Abraham Lincoln's World* by Genevieve Foster. Scribner's. *Lone Journey: The Life of Roger Williams* by Jeanette Eaton. Illus. by Woodi Ishmael. Harcourt.

**1944** *Johnny Tremain* by Esther Forbes. Illus. by Lynd Ward. Houghton Mifflin.

**Honor Books:** *These Happy Golden Years* by Laura Ingalls Wilder. Harper. *Fog Magic* by Julia L. Sauer. Viking. *Rufus M.* by Eleanor Estes. Harcourt. *Mountain Born* by Elizabeth Yates. Coward-McCann.

**1943** *Adam of the Road* by Elizabeth Janet Gray. Illus. by Robert Lawson. Viking.

**Honor Books:** *The Middle Moffat* by Eleanor Estes. Harcourt. *"Have You Seen Tom Thumb?"* by Mabel Leigh Hunt. Lippincott.

**1942** *The Matchlock Gun* by Walter D. Edmonds. Illus. by Paul Lantz. Dodd.

**Honor Books:** *Little Town on the Prairie* by Laura Ingalls Wilder. Harper. *George Washington's World* by Genevieve Foster. Scribner's. *Indian Captive: The Story of Mary Jemison* by Lois Lenski. Lippincott. *Down Ryton Water* by Eva Roe Gaggin. Illus. by Elmer Hader. Viking.

**1941** *Call It Courage* by Armstrong Sperry. Macmillan.

**Honor Books:** *Blue Willow* by Doris Gates. Viking. *Young Mac of Fort Vancouver* by Mary Jane Carr. Crowell. *The Long Winter* by Laura Ingalls Wilder. Harper. *Nansen* by Anna Gertrude Hall. Viking.

**1940** *Daniel Boone* by James H. Daugherty. Viking.

**Honor Books:** *The Singing Tree* by Kate Seredy. Viking. *Runner of the Mountain Tops* by Mabel L. Robinson. Random. *By the Shores of Silver Lake* by Laura Ingalls Wilder. Harper. *Boy with a Pack* by Stephen W. Meader. Harcourt.

**1939** *Thimble Summer* by Elizabeth Enright. Holt.

**Honor Books:** *Leader by Destiny: George Washington, Man and Patriot* by Jeanette Eaton. Harcourt. *Penn* by Elizabeth Janet Gray. Viking. *Nino* by Valenti Angelo. Viking. *"Hello, the Boat!"* by Phyllis Crawford. Holt. *Mr. Popper's Penguins* by Richard and Florence Atwater. Little, Brown.

**1938**   *The White Stag* by Kate Seredy. Viking.

   **Honor Books:** *Bright Island* by Mabel L. Robinson. Random. *Pecos Bill* by James Cloyd Bowman. Little, Brown. *On the Banks of Plum Creek* by Laura Ingalls Wilder. Harper.

**1937**   *Roller Skates* by Ruth Sawyer. Illus. by Valenti Angelo. Viking.

   **Honor Books:** *Phoebe Fairchild: Her Book* by Lois Lenski. Lippincott. *Whistler's Van* by Idwal Jones. Viking. *The Golden Basket* by Ludwig Bemelmans. Viking. *Winterbound* by Margery Bianco. Viking. *Audubon* by Constance Rourke. Harcourt. *The Codfish Musket* by Agnes D. Hewes. Doubleday.

**1936**   *Caddie Woodlawn* by Carol Ryrie Brink. Illus. by Kate Seredy. Macmillan.

   **Honor Books:** *Honk: The Moose* by Phil Strong. Illus. by Kurt Wiese. Dodd. *The Good Master* by Kate Seredy. Viking. *Young Walter Scott* by Elizabeth Janet Gray. Viking. *All Sail Set* by Armstrong Sperry. Winston.

**1935**   *Dobry* by Monica Shannon. Illus. by Atanas Katchamakoff. Viking.

   **Honor Books:** *The Pageant of Chinese History* by Elizabeth Seeger. McKay/Longmans. *Davy Crockett* by Constance Rourke. Harcourt. *A Day on Skates: The Story of a Dutch Picnic* by Hilda Van Stockum. Harper.

**1934**   *Invincible Louisa: The Story of the Author of "Little Women"* by Cornelia Meigs. Little, Brown.

   **Honor Books:** *The Forgotten Daughter* by Caroline Dale Snedeker. Doubleday. *Swords of Steel* by Elsie Singmaster. Houghton Mifflin. *ABC Bunny* by Wanda Gág. Coward-McCann. *Winged Girl of Knossos* by Erick Berry. Appleton. *New Land* by Sarah L. Schmidt. McBride. *The Apprentice of Florence* by Anne Kyle. Houghton Mifflin. *The Big Tree of Bunlahy: Stories of My Own Countryside* by Padraic Colum. Illus. by Jack Yeats. Macmillan. *Glory of the Seas* by Agnes D. Hewes. Illus. by N.C. Wyeth. Knopf.

**1933**   *Young Fu of the Upper Yangtze* by Elizabeth Foreman Lewis. Illus. by Kurt Wiese. Holt.

   **Honor Books:** *Swift Rivers* by Cornelia Meigs. Little, Brown. *The Railroad to Freedom* by Hildegarde Swift. Harcourt. *Children of the Soil* by Nora Burglon. Doubleday.

**1932**   *Waterless Mountain* by Laura Adams Armer. Illus. by Sidney Armer and Laura Adams Armer. McKay/Longmans.

   **Honor Books:** *The Fairy Circus* by Dorothy Lathrop. Macmillan. *Calico Bush* by Rachel Field. Macmillan. *Boy of the South Seas* by Eunice Tietjens. Coward-McCann. *Out of the Flame* by Eloise Lownsbery. McKay/Longmans. *Jane's Island* by Marjorie Hill Alee. Houghton Mifflin. *The Truce of the Wolf and Other Tales of Old Italy* by Mary Gould Davis. Harcourt.

**1931**   *The Cat Who Went to Heaven* by Elizabeth Coatsworth. Illus. by Lynd Ward. Macmillan.

   **Honor Books:** *Floating Island* by Anne Parrish. Harper. *The Dark Star of Itza* by Alida Malkus. Harcourt. *Queer Person* by Ralph Hubbard. Doubleday. *Moun-*

*tains Are Free* by Julia Davis Adams. Dutton. *Spice and the Devil's Cave* by Agnes D. Hewes. Knopf. *Meggy McIntosh* by Elizabeth Janet Gray. Doubleday. *Garram the Hunter: A Boy of the Hill Tribes* by Herbert Best. Illus. by Allena Best (Erick Berry). Doubleday. *Ood-Le-Uk, The Wanderer* by Alice Lide and Margaret Johansen. Illus. by Raymond Lufkin. Little, Brown.

**1930**   *Hitty: Her First Hundred Years* by Rachel Field. Illus. by Dorothy P. Lathrop. Macmillan.

**Honor Books:** *The Tangle-Coated Horse and Other Tales: Episodes from the Fionn Saga* by Ella Young. Illus. by Vera Brock. Longmans. *Vaino: A Boy of New Finland* by Julia Davis Adams. Illus. by Lempi Ostman. Dutton. *Pran of Albania* by Elizabeth C. Miller. Doubleday. *The Jumping-Off Place* by Marian Hurd McNeely. McKay/Longmans. *A Daughter of the Seine* by Jeanette Eaton. Harper. *Little Blacknose* by Hildegarde Hoyt Swift. Illus. by Lynd Ward. Harcourt.

**1929**   *The Trumpeter of Krakow* by Eric P. Kelly. Illus. by Angela Pruszynska. Macmillan.

**Honor Books:** *The Pigtail of Ah Lee Ben Loo* by John Bennett. McKay/Longmans. *Millions of Cats* by Wanda Gág. Coward-McCann. *The Boy Who Was* by Grace T. Hallock. Dutton. *Clearing Weather* by Cornelia Meigs. Little, Brown. *The Runaway Papoose* by Grace P. Moon. Doubleday. *Tod of the Fens* by Eleanor Whitney. Macmillan.

**1928**   *Gay-Neck, The Story of a Pigeon* by Dhan Gopal Mukerji. Illustrated by Boris Artzybasheff. Dutton.

**Honor Books:** *The Wonder Smith and His Son* by Ella Young. McKay/Longmans. *Downright Dencey* by Caroline Dale Snedeker. Doubleday.

**1927**   *Smoky, the Cowhorse* by Will James. Scribner's. (No record of the runners-up.)

**1926**   *Shen of the Sea* by Arthur Bowie Chrisman. Illus. by Else Hasselriis. Dutton.
**Honor Book:** *The Voyagers* by Padraic Colum. Macmillan.

**1925**   *Tales from Silver Lands* by Charles J. Finger. Illus. by Paul Honoré. Doubleday.
**Honor Books:** *Nicholas* by Anne Carroll Moore. Putnam. *Dream Coach* by Anne and Dillwyn Parrish. Macmillan.

**1924**   *The Dark Frigate* by Charles Boardman Hawes. Little, Brown. (No record of the honor books.)

**1923**   *The Voyages of Doctor Dolittle* by Hugh Lofting. Lippincott. (No record of the honor books.)

**1922**   *The Story of Mankind* by Hendrik Willem Van Loon. Liveright.
**Honor Books:** *The Great Quest* by Charles Boardman Hawes. Little, Brown. *Cedric the Forester* by Bernard G. Marshall. Appleton. *The Old Tobacco Shop* by William Bowen. Macmillan. *The Golden Fleece and the Heroes Who Lived Before Achilles* by Padraic Colum. Macmillan. *Windy Hill* by Cornelia Meigs. Macmillan.

## Coretta Scott King Awards

The award commemorates Dr. Martin Luther King, Jr., and his wife, Coretta Scott King, for their work in promoting world peace and brotherhood. Since 1974, one African American author and one African American illustrator have been honored for outstanding inspirational and educational contributions to children's literature and young people for books published during the previous year. The awards are sponsored by the Social Responsibilities Roundtable of the American Library Association.

**1999**     Author: *Heaven* by Angela Johnson. Simon & Schuster.
Illustrator: *i see the rhythm* by Toyomi Igus. Illus. by Michele Wood. Children's Book Press.

**1998**     Author: *Forged by Fire* by Sharon M. Draper. Atheneum.
Illustrator: *In Daddy's Arms I Am Tall* by Javaka Steptoe. Lee & Low.

**1997**     Author: *Slam!* by Walter Dean Myers. Scholastic.
Illustrator: *Minty: A Story of Young Harriet Tubman* by Alan Schroeder. Illus. by Jerry Pinkney. Dial.

**1996**     Author: *Her Stories: African American Folktales* by Virginia Hamilton. Illus. by Leo & Diane Dillon. Blue Sky/Scholastic.
Illustrator: *The Middle Passage: White Ships Black Cargo* by Tom Feelings. Dial.

**1995**     Author: *Christmas in the Big House, Christmas in the Quarters* by Patricia McKissack and Frederick McKissack. Illus. by John Thompson. Scholastic.
Illustrator: *The Creation* by James Weldon Johnson. Illus. by James Ransome. Holiday.

**1994**     Author: *Toning the Sweep* by Angela Johnson. Orchard.
Illustrator: *Soul Looks Back in Wonder* compiled and illustrated by Tom Feelings. Dial.

**1993**     Author: *The Dark-Thirty: Southern Tales of the Supernatural* by Patricia McKissack. Knopf.
Illustrator: *Origins of Life on Earth: An African American Creation Myth* by David A. Anderson. Illus. by Kathleen Atkins Smith. Sight Productions.

**1992**     Author: *Now Is Your Time! The African-American Struggle for Freedom* by Walter Dean Myers. HarperCollins.
Illustrator: *Tar Beach* by Faith Ringgold. Crown.

**1991**     Author: *Road to Memphis* by Mildred D. Taylor. Dial.
Illustrator: *Aida* retold by Leontyne Price. Illus. by Leo and Diane Dillon. Harcourt.

**1990**     Author: *A Long Hard Journey* by Patricia and Frederick McKissack. Walker.
Illustrator: *Nathaniel Talking* by Eloise Greenfield. Illus. by Jan Spivey Gilchrist. Black Butterfly Press.

**1989**     Author: *Fallen Angels* by Walter D. Myers. Scholastic.
Illustrator: *Mirandy and Brother Wind* by Patricia McKissack. Illus. by Jerry Pinkney.

**1988**     Author: *The Friendship* by Mildred D. Taylor. Illus. by Max Ginsberg. Dial.
Illustrator: *Mufaro's Beautiful Daughters: An African Tale* retold and illustrated by John Steptoe. Lothrop.

**1987** Author: *Justin and the Best Biscuits in the World* by Mildred Pitts Walter. Lothrop.
Illustrator: *Half Moon and One Whole Star* by Crescent Dragonwagon. Illus. by Jerry Pinkney. Macmillan.

**1986** Author: *The People Could Fly: American Black Folktales* by Virginia Hamilton. Knopf.
Illustrator: *Patchwork Quilt* by Valerie Flournoy. Illus. by Jerry Pinkney. Dial.

**1985** Author: *Motown and Didi* by Walter Dean Myers. Viking.
Illustrator: No award.

**1984** Author: *Everett Anderson's Good-Bye* by Lucille Clifton. Holt.
Illustrator: *My Mama Needs Me* by Mildred Pitts Walter. Illus. by Pat Cummings. Lothrop.

**1983** Author: *Sweet Whispers, Brother Rush* by Virginia Hamilton. Philomel.
Illustrator: *Black Child* by Peter Mugabane. Knopf.

**1982** Author: *Let the Circle Be Unbroken* by Mildred D. Taylor. Dial.
Illustrator: *Mother Crocodile: An Uncle Amadou Tale from Senegal* adapted by Rosa Guy. Illus. by John Steptoe. Delacorte.

**1981** Author: *This Life* by Sidney Poitier. Knopf.
Illustrator: *Beat the Story-Drum, Pum-Pum* by Ashley Bryan. Atheneum.

**1980** Author: *The Young Landlords* by Walter Dean Myers. Viking.
Illustrator: *Cornrows* by Camille Yarbrough. Illus. by Carole Bayard. Coward.

**1979** Author: *Escape to Freedom* by Ossie Davis. Viking.
Illustrator: *Something on My Mind* by Nikki Grimes. Illus. by Tom Feelings. Dial.

**1978** Author: *Africa Dream* by Eloise Greenfield. Day/Crowell.
Illustrator: The same title, illustrated by Carole Bayard.

**1977** Author: *The Story of Stevie Wonder* by James Haskins. Lothrop.
Illustrator: No award.

**1976** Author: *Duey's Tale* by Pearl Bailey. Harcourt.
Illustrator: No award.

**1975** Author: *The Legend of Africana* by Dorothy Robinson. Johnson.
Illustrator: The same title, illustrated by Herbert Temple.

**1974** Author: *Ray Charles* by Sharon Bell Mathis. Crowell.
Illustrator: The same title, illustrated by George Ford.

**1973** *I Never Had It Made* by Jackie Robinson as told to Alfred Duckett. Putnam.

**1972** *17 Black Artists* by Elton C. Fax. Dodd.

**1971** *Black Troubador: Langston Hughes* by Charlemae Rollins. Rand.

**1970** *Martin Luther King, Jr.: Man of Peace* by Lillie Patterson. Garrard.

# Pura Belpé Award

Given biennially, this award is presented to a Latino/Latina writer and illustrator whose work best portrays, affirms, and celebrates the Latino cultural experience in an outstanding work of literature for children and youth. The award is cosponsored by the Association of Library Services to Children, a division of the American Library Association (ALA), and the National Association to Promote Library Service to the Spanish Speaking, an ALA affiliate. The award is named for Pura Belpé, the first Latina librarian from the New York Public Library.

**1998**    Narrative: *Parrot in the Oven: Mi Vida* by Victor Martinez. HarperCollins, 1996.

**Honor Books:** *Laughing Tomatoes and Other Spring Poems* by Francisco X. Alarcón. Illus. by Maya Christina Gonzales. Children's Book Press, 1997. *Spirits of the High Mesa* by Floyd Martinez. Houston, TX: Arte Público Press. (Jitomates Risueños y Otros Poemas de Primavera).

Illustrated: *Snapshots from the Wedding* by Gary Soto. Illus. by Stephanie Garcia. Putnam, 1997.

**Honor Books:** *In My Family/En Mi Familia* by Carmen Lomas Garza. Childrens Press, 1996. *The Golden Flower: A Taino Myth From Puerto Rico* by Nina Jaffe. Illus. by Enrique O. Sánchez. Simon & Schuster, 1996. *Gathering the Sun: An Alphabet in Spanish and English* by Alma Flor Ada. Illus. by Simón Silva. Lothrop, 1997.

**1996**    Narrative: *An Island Like You: Stories of the Barrio* by Judith Ortiz Cofer. Orchard, 1995.

**Honor Book:** *Baseball in April and Other Stories* by Gary Soto. Harcourt Brace, 1990.

Illustrated: *Chato's Kitchen* by Gary Soto. Illus. by Susan Guevara. Putnam, 1995.

**Honor Books:** *The Bossy Gallito: A Traditional Cuban Folktale.* Retold by Lucia M. Gonzalez. Illus. by Lulu Delacre. Scholastic, 1994. *Pablo Remembers: The Fiesta of the Day of the Dead* written and photographed by George Ancona. Lothrop, 1993. *Family Pictures/Cuadros de Familia* by Carmen Lomas Garza. Children's Book Press, 1990.

# Orbis Pictus Award for Outstanding Nonfiction for Children

The Orbis Pictus Award was established by the National Council of Teachers of English in 1989 to promote and recognize excellence in nonfiction writing for children. The name, Orbis Pictus, commemorates the work of Johannes Amos Comenius, Orbis Pictus—The World in Pictures (1657), considered to be the first book actually planned for children. Each year, one award book and up to five honor books are named. Criteria for selection include accuracy, content, style, organization, illustration, and format. An annotated list of the winner, honor books, and other outstanding works of nonfiction is published in the November issue of *Language Arts* (NCTE) each year.

**1999**    *Shipwreck at the Bottom of the World: The extraordinary true story of Shackleton and the Endurance* by Jennifer Armstrong. Crown.

**Honor Books:** *Black Whiteness: Admiral Byrd alone in the Antarctic* by Robert Burleigh. Illus. by Walter Lyon Krudop. Atheneum. *Fossil Feud: The rivalry of the first American dinosaur hunters* by Thom Holmes. Messner. *Hottest, Coldest, Highest, Deepest* by Steve Jenkins. Houghton Mifflin. *No Pretty Pictures: A Child of War* by Anita Lobel. Greenwillow.

**1998** *An Extraordinary Life: The Story of a Monarch Butterfly* by Laurence Pringle. Illus. by Bob Marstall. Orchard.

**Honor Books:** *A Drop of Water: A Book of Science and Wonder* by Walter Wick. Scholastic. *A Tree Is Growing* by Arthur Dorros. Illus. by S. D. Schindler. Scholastic. *Digger: The Tragic Fate of the California Indians from the Missions to the Gold Rush* by Jerry Stanley. Crown. *Charles A. Lindbergh: A Human Hero* by James Cross Giblin. Clarion. *Kennedy Assassinated! The World Mourns: A Reporter's Story* by Wilborn Hampton. Candlewick.

**1997** *Leonardo da Vinci* by Diane Stanley. Morrow.

**Honor Books:** *Full Steam Ahead: The Race to Build a Transcontinental Railroad* by Rhonda Blumberg. National Geographic Society. *The Life and Death of Crazy Horse* by Russell Freedman. Holiday House. *One World, Many Religions: The Ways We Worship* by Mary Pope Osborne. Knopf.

**1996** *The Great Fire* by Jim Murphy. Scholastic.

**Honor Books:** *Rosie the Riveter: Women Working on the Home Front in World War II.* by Penny Colman. Crown. *Dolphin Man: Exploring the World of Dolphins.* by Laurence Pringle. Atheneum.

**1995** *Safari Beneath the Sea: The Wonder of the North Pacific Coast* by Diane Swanson. Sierra Club Books.

**Honor Books:** *Wildlife Rescue: The Work of Dr. Kathleen Ramsey* by Jennifer Owings Dewey. Boyds Mills Press. *Kids at Work: Lewis Hine and the Crusade Against Child Labor* by Russell Freedman. Clarion. *Christmas in the Big House, Christmas in the Quarters* by Patricia McKissack and Frederick McKissack. Scholastic.

**1994** *Across America on an Emigrant Train* by Jim Murphy. Clarion.

**Honor Books:** *To the Top of the World: Adventures with Arctic Wolves* by Jim Branderburg. Walker. *Making Sense: Animal Perception and Communication* by Bruce Brooks. Farrar, Straus and Giroux.

**1993** *Children of the Dust Bowl: The True Story of the School at Weedpatch Camp* by Jerry Stanley. Crown.

**Honor Books:** *Talking With Artists* by Pat Cummings. Bradbury Press. *Come Back, Salmon* by Molly Cone. Sierra Club Books.

**1992** *Flight: The Journey of Charles Lindbergh* by Robert Burleigh. Illus. by Mike Wimmer. Philomel Books.

**Honor Books:** *Now Is Your Time! The African American Struggle for Freedom* by Walter Dean Myers. HarperCollins. *Prairie Vision: The Life and Times of Solomon Butcher* by Pam Conrad. HarperCollins.

**1991** *Franklin Delano Roosevelt* by Russell Freedman. Clarion.

**Honor Books:** *Arctic Memories* by Normee Ekoomiak. Holt. *Seeing Earth From Space* by Patricia Lauber. Orchard.

**1990** *The Great Little Madison* by Jean Fritz. Putnam.

**Honor Books:** *The Great American Gold Rush* by Rhoda Blumberg. Bradbury Press. *The News About Dinosaurs* by Patricia Lauber. Bradbury Press.

## Other Children's Literature Awards in the United States

### Boston Globe/Horn Book Awards.

These awards are presented annually to the creators of three outstanding children's books—an excellent work of fiction, a picture book with outstanding illustrations, and an exceptional work of nonfiction. Jointly sponsored by the Boston Globe and the Horn Book magazine, these awards are published on the Fanfare pages of the January/February issue of *Horn Book.*

### Edgar Allen Poe Award—Best Juvenile Novel.

This award is presented to the author of a mystery novel intended for children. Given annually since 1961, it is sponsored by the Mystery Writers of America.

### International Reading Association Children's Book Award.

This award honors a children's book by a new author who "shows unusual promise in the children's book field." Given since 1975, it is sponsored by the Institute for Reading Research and administered by the International Reading Association.

### Laura Ingalls Wilder Medal.

Named after the author of the Little House series, this medal is presented every 3 years (originally every 5 years) by the American Library Association (Children's Book Division) to an author or illustrator whose books have made a lasting contribution to children's literature. Established in 1954, the selection is restricted to books published in the United States. Winners include Russell Freedman (1998), Virginia Hamilton (1995), Marsha Brown (1992), Elizabeth George Speare (1989), Jean Fritz (1986), Maurice Sendak (1983), Theodor Geisel (Dr. Seuss) (1980), Beverly Cleary (1975), E. B. White (1970), Ruth Sawyer (1965), Clara Ingram Judson (1960), and Laura Ingalls Wilder (1954).

### Mildred L. Batchelder Award.

This award is given to the publisher of a children's book that has been translated into English in the previous year and that originally appeared in a country other than the United States. Given annually since 1968, it is sponsored by the Association for Library Service to Children of the American Library Association.

### NCTE Excellence in Poetry for Children Award.

Established in 1977 by the National Council of Teachers of English, this award honors living U.S. poets whose poetry has contributed substantially to the lives of children. Currently awarded every 3 years, the recognition is given to a poet for the entire body of writing for children ages 3 through 13. Winners include Eloise Greenfield (1997), Barbara Juster Esbensen (1994), Valerie Worth (1991), Arnold Adoff (1988), Lilian Moore (1985), John Ciardi (1982), Eve Merriam (1981), Myra Cohn Livingston (1980), Karla Kuskin (1979), Aileen Fisher (1978), and David McCord (1977).

### Scott O'Dell Award for Historical Fiction.

This award is given to the author of a distinguished work of historical fiction for children or young adults set in the New World and published in English by a U.S. publisher. The award originated with celebrated author Scott O'Dell and is administered and selected by an advisory board chaired by Zena Sutherland. Recent winners include *Under the Blood-Red Sun* by Graham Salisbury (1995), *Bull Run* by Paul Fleischman (1994), *Morning Girl* by Michael Dorris (1993), and *Stepping on the Cracks* by Mary Downing Hahn (1992). Other authors include Carolyn Reeder, Patricia Beatty, Scott O'Dell, Patricia MacLachlan, Avi, and Elizabeth George Speare.

## Phoenix Award.

Since 1985, the Phoenix Award has been given annually to the author (or the estate of the author) of a children's book that was published in English 20 years earlier that did not win a major award at the time of its original publication. The selectors may also name one or more honor books. The award is sponsored by the Children's Literature Association.

## State Children's Choice Award Programs

| STATE | Title of Award [ Grade levels/Categories ] Year award founded. |
|---|---|
| ALABAMA | Emphasis on Reading Award [ K–2; 3–5; 6–8 ] 1980 |
| ARIZONA | Arizona Young Reader's Award [ Picture; Chapter; M/YA ] 1977 |
| ARKANSAS | Charlie May Simon Children's Book Award [ 4–6 ] 1970 |
| CALIFORNIA | California Young Readers Medal [ Primary; Interm; MS/JH; YA ] 1975 |
| COLORADO | Colorado Children's Book Award [ Picture Bk; Junior Novel ] 1976<br>Colorado Blue Spruce Young Adult Book Award [ Young Adult ] 1985 |
| CONNECTICUT | Nutmeg Children's Book Award [ 4–6 ]; 1993 |
| FLORIDA | Sunshine State Young Reader's Award [ 3–5; 6–8 ] 1983 |
| GEORGIA | Georgia Picture Storybook Award [ K–4 ] 1976<br>Georgia Children's Book Award [ 4–8 ] 1968 |
| HAWAII | Nene Award [ 4–6 ] 1964 |
| ILLINOIS | Rebecca Caudill Young Reader's Book Award [ 4–8 ] 1988 |
| INDIANA | Young Hoosier Book Award [ K–3; 4–6; 6–8 ] 1972 |
| IOWA | Iowa Children's Choice Award [ 3–6 ] 1980<br>Iowa Teen Award [ 6–9 ] 1985 |
| KANSAS | William Allen White Children's Book Award [ 4–8 ] 1953 |
| KENTUCKY | The Bluegrass Award [ K–3; 4–8 ] 1983 |
| MARYLAND | Maryland Children's Book Award 1988 |
| MASSACHUSETTS | Massachusetts Children's Book Award [ 4–6 ] 1976 |
| MINNESOTA | Maud Hart Lovelace Book Award [ 3–8 ] 1980 |
| MISSOURI | Mark Twain Award [ 4–8] 1972 |
| MONTANA | Treasure State Award [ K–3 ] 1991 |
| NEBRASKA | Golden Sower Award [ K–3; 4–6; Young Adult ] 1981 |
| NEVADA | Nevada Young Reader's Award [ K–2; 3–5; 6–8; 9–12 ] 1988 |
| NEW HAMPSHIRE | Great Stone Face Children's Book Award [ 4–6 ] 1980 |

| | |
|---|---|
| NEW JERSEY | Garden State Children's Book Award [ Easy to Read; Younger Nonfiction; Younger Nonfiction ] 1977 |
| NEW MEXICO | Land of Enchantment Children's Book Award [ 4–8 ] 1981 |
| NORTH CAROLINA | North Carolina Children's Book Award [ Picture Bk K–3; Jr. Bk 4–6 ] 1992 |
| NORTH DAKOTA | Flicker Tale Book Award [ Picture Bk PreK–3; Juvenile 4–61 + 1978 |
| OHIO | Buckeye Children's Book Award [ K–2; 3–5 ] 1981 |
| OKLAHOMA | Sequoyah Children's Book Award [ 3–6 ] 1959 <br> Sequoyah Young Adult Book Award [ 7–9 ] 1987 |
| RHODE ISLAND | Rhode Island Children's Book Award [ 3–6 ] 1991 |
| SOUTH CAROLINA | South Carolina Children's Book Award [ 3–6 ] 1975 <br> South Carolina Junior Book Award [ 6–9 ] 1992 <br> South Carolina Young Adult Book Award [ 9–12 ] 1979 |
| SOUTH DAKOTA | Prairie Pasque Book Award [ 4–6 ] 1987 |
| TENNESSEE | Volunteer State Book Award [ K–3; 4–6; 7–9YA ] 1978 |
| TEXAS | Texas Bluebonnet Award [ 3–6 ] 1981 |
| UTAH | Utah Children's Book Award [ 3–6 ] 1980 <br> Utah Children's Informational Book Award [ 3–6 ] 1986 <br> Utah Young Adult Book Award [ 7–12 ] 1991 <br> Utah Children's Picture Book Award [ K–3 ] 1996 |
| VERMONT | Dorothy Canfield Fisher Children's Book Award [ 4–8 ] 1957 |
| VIRGINIA | Virginia Young Readers Program [ Primary; Elem; MS; HS ] 1982 |
| WASHINGTON | Washington Children's Choice Picture Book Award [ K–3 ] 1982 |
| WEST VIRGINIA | West Virginia Children's Book Award [ 3–6 ] 1985 |
| WISCONSIN | Golder Archer Award [ 4–8 ] 1974 <br> Little Archer Award [ K–3 ] |
| WYOMING | Indian Paintbrush Award [ 4–6 ] 1986 <br> Soaring Eagle Book Award [ 7–12 ] 1989 |
| ALASKA <br> IDAHO <br> MONTANA <br> OREGON <br> WASHINGTON <br> ALBERTA/B.C. | Northwest Pacific Young Reader's Choice Award [ Youth 4–8 ] 1940 <br> Northwest Pacific Young Reader's Choice Award [ Senior 9–12 ] 1990 |

# Other Notable Children's Book Recognitions

## Notable Books for a Global Society.

The Children's Literature and Reading Special Interest Group of the International Reading Association identifies a yearly list of quality literature published during the previous year and written for grades K–12 that enhances student understanding of people and cultures throughout the world. Criteria focus on titles that are culturally authentic and rich in cultural details and that celebrate both diversity and the common bonds of humanity. An annotated list of the notable titles are published in the December/January issue of *The Reading Teacher* (IRA) and an extended list including teaching suggestions and related books is available in the fall issue of *The Dragon Lode*.

## Notable Children's Books.

This annual American Library Association list is compiled by the Association of Library Service to Children at the midwinter meeting of the ALA. The unannotated titles appear in the March issue of *School Library Journal* and also in the March 15 issue of *Booklist*.

## Notable Children's Books in the Language Arts K–8.

Sponsored by the Children's Literature Assembly (CLA) of the National Council of Teachers of English (NCTE), this recognition is given to works of fiction, nonfiction, and poetry published during the previous year that meet specific criteria. The books must deal explicitly with language, such as plays on words, word origins, or history of language; demonstrate uniqueness in the use of language or style; or invite child response or participation. An annotated list is published annually in the November issue of *Language Arts* and a list with extended annotations and related titles is published in the fall issue of the *Journal of Children's Literature* (CLA).

## Notable Children's Trade Books in the Field of Social Studies.

The National Council for the Social Studies (NCSS) in cooperation with the Children's Book Council (CBC) selects notable children's trade books in the field of social studies published during the previous year and primarily written for grades K–8. Criteria for selection include books that emphasize human relations, represent a diversity of groups and are sensitive to a broad range of cultural experiences, present an original theme or fresh slant on a traditional topic, are easily readable and of high literary quality, and have a pleasing format, and, when appropriate, illustrations that enrich text. Organized by thematic strands, the annotated list is published in the March/April issue of *Social Education* and can be found on the NCSS web site: http://ncss.org.resources/notable/home/html.

## Outstanding Science Trade Books for Children.

The National Science Teachers Association (NSTA) in cooperation with the Children's Book Council (CBC) selects outstanding science trade books published during the previous year. Criteria for selection include specific guidelines on both content and presentation. An annotated list is published annually in the March issue of *Science and Children*. Additional information available on these web sites: http://nsta.org and http://cbcbooks.org.

## Teachers' Choices.

Each year the International Reading Association's Teachers' Choices project has identified outstanding U.S. trade books published for children and adolescents that teachers find to be exceptional in curriculum use. Criteria for selection include books that reflect high literary qualities; books that might not be discovered or fully appreciated by children without an introduction by a knowledgeable educator or adult; or books that have potential for use across the curriculum. An annotated list (K–2; 3–5; 6–8) including curriculum connections has been published annually since 1989 in the November issue of *The Reading Teacher* (IRA).

## Young Adult Choices.

Funded by a grant to the International Reading Association (IRA) and supervised by the association's Literature for Adolescents Committee, this project makes teens (grades 7–12) aware of new literature for young adults and allows them to voice their opinions about books being written for them. Young Adult Choices are published in an annotated bibliography in the November issue of the *Journal of Adolescent & Adult Literacy* (IRA).

# Children's Literature Awards Given in other Countries

## Amelia Frances Howard-Gibbon Medal (Canada).

This award is given to the illustrator of an outstanding picture book first published in Canada during the preceding year. Sponsored by the Canadian Library Association since 1971, eligibility is limited to Canadian citizens.

## Canadian Library Association Book of the Year for Children (Canada).

This award is given to the author of an outstanding children's book first published in Canada during the preceding year. Given annually since 1947, eligibility for this award is limited to Canadian citizens. Occasionally, a second award is given to an outstanding children's book written in French.

## Carnegie Medal (Great Britain).

This award is given to the author of an outstanding children's book first published in the United Kingdom during the preceding year. Given annually since 1937, the Carnegie Medal is sponsored by the British Library Association.

## Hans Christian Andersen Prize.

This award is given to a living author and, since 1966, to a living illustrator whose works have made significant international contributions to children's literature. Sponsored by the International Board on Books for Young People (IBBY), the award has been given every 2 years since 1956. Winners from the United States include Katherine Paterson (1998), Virginia Hamilton (1992), Paul Fox (1978), Scott O'Dell (1972), Maurice Sendak (1970), and Meindert DeJong (1962).

## Kate Greenaway Medal (Great Britain).

This award is given to the illustrator of an outstanding picture book first published in the United Kingdom during the preceding year. Given annually since 1957, it is sponsored by the British Library Association.

# Appendix B

# Professional Resources

The following list of professional resources proves most useful to preservice teachers planning practicum and student teaching lessons, inservice teachers seeking to enhance their literature-based teaching and response-based perspectives of students, and librarians/media center directors striving to support teachers by acquiring the best literature to suit a reader response perspective on literature in the classroom. The professional resources have been organized to meaningfully access materials for author/illustrator studies, reader response enrichments, literature clusters, and theme explorations.

## Author and Illustrator Information

———— (1971–present). *Something about the author*. Detroit, MI: Gale Research. (Volumes 1–97 and comprehensive indexes)

Aimed at a general audience, this series provides readers with a personal introduction to authors, illustrators, and poets. Every volume contains information on more than 100 creators. Special features include biographical information, addresses, career overview, awards and honors, chronological bibliography of books written or illustrated, and quotations from interviews. Cumulative indexes at the back of every volume and special volume indexes help access specific names in one or more volumes. With four volumes per year, this resource tends to be the most up-to-date resource on authors, including those new to the realm of children's literature.

———— (1986–present). *Something about the author: Autobiography series*. Detroit, MI: Gale Research.

Longer entries written by the authors and illustrators themselves range from formal accounts to personal essays to childhood reflections. Entries typically include photographs and visual offerings. While there is a limited number of authors, this is an excellent resource for reading the author's own thoughts on his or her career and accomplishments.

Copeland, J. (1993). *Speaking with poets: Interviews with poets who write for children and young adults.* Urbana, IL: National Council of Teachers of English.

This book opens the window on poet studies in the classroom through well-designed interviews that reveal insights into the composing processes and poetic visions of 16 popular poets/anthologists including Arnold Adoff, Myra Cohn Livingston, Eloise Greenfield, Lee Bennett Hopkins, and Eve Merriam.

Cummings, Pat (1992). *Talking with artists.* New York: Simon & Schuster.
Cummings, Pat (1995). *Talking with artists* (Vol. 2). New York: Simon & Schuster.

These excellent biographical essays share the lives and talents of children's book illustrators. A series of questions often asked by children elicit illustrator responses from 24 well-known illustrators. Highlights include early artistic work and sample illustrations from children's books.

Holtze, Sally H. (Ed.) (1996). *Seventh book of junior authors and illustrators.* New York: The H. W. Wilson Company.

This most recent volume, seventh in a series that began with the first edition in 1934, is filled with more than 200 entries on authors and illustrators. The earlier editions are valuable when researching children's literature creators from the past decades.

Hopkins, Lee Bennett (1995). *Pauses: Autobiographical reflections of 101 creators of children's books.* New York: HarperCollins.

This volume contains reflective thoughts—pauses—expressed by 101 authors, author-illustrators, illustrators, and poets who use their talents to enrich children's lives. Reminiscences spark interest in young readers as they view these artists in a new human light.

Silvey, Anita (Ed.). (1995). *Children's books and their creators.* Boston, MA: Houghton Mifflin.

This comprehensive biographical dictionary includes 800 entries that focus primarily on individual authors and illustrators. Emphasizing books and creators from the past 50 years, entries also cover genre, history, and issues. Interspersed throughout the text, 75 "Voices of the Creators" essays capture first-person perspectives of authors and artists on the creative process.

## Award-Winning Books

Gillespie, J. T., & Naden, C. J. (1996). *The Newbery companion: Booktalk and related materials for Newbery medal and honor books.* Englewood, CO: Libraries Unlimited.

Each Newbery medal entry includes author background, plot summary, related themes and subjects, incidents for booktalking, related titles, and abbreviated annotations for honor books. A useful introduction includes a profile of John Newbery, background on the creation of the medal, and the guidelines for selection.

Mahmoud, Lisa V. (1996). *Children's books: Awards and prizes* (10th ed.). New York: Children's Book Council.

This authoritative listing of book awards and recognitions includes U.S. awards selected by adults; U.S. awards selected by young readers; awards of Australia, Canada, New Zealand, and the United Kingdom; and selected international and multinational awards.

Smith, H. M. (1994). *The Coretta Scott King awards book: From vision to reality.* Chicago, IL: American Library Association/Coretta Scott King Task Force.

Listed chronologically from 1970 (author) and 1974 (illustrator) through 1993, each entry provides an extensive summary of each African American award winner. Photographs and biographical information, history of the award, and some full-color illustrations are included.

# Genre/Format Specific Resources

## Picture Books

Ammon, B. D., & Sherman, G. W. (1996). *Worth a thousand words: An annotated guide to picture books for older readers.* Englewood, CO: Libraries Unlimited.

This special focus on picture books for grades 4 through college includes brief annotations for 645 titles. Icons identify curricular links, classroom activities, and related reading. Margins provide alphabetic lists of subject connections for each entry. The scope is extensive and formats include all genres.

Kiefer, B. (1995). *The potential of picturebooks: From visual literacy to aesthetic understanding.* Upper Saddle River, NJ: Merrill/Prentice Hall.

Besides sharing a fresh look at the art of the picture book, this text contains its own chapters on "Children's Responses to Picturebooks" and "Developing a Context for Response to Picturebooks." Links to the classroom and excellent appendixes enhance knowledge of and appreciation for picture book art.

Lima, Carolyn W., & John A. *(1998). A to zoo: Subject access to children's picture books* (5th ed.). New York: R. R. Bowker.

Organized around 800 subject headings, this resource guides the user to more than 14,000 picture books for K–2 students. The configuration readily provides numerous book titles for literature clusters or theme explorations.

Stewig, John W. (1995). *Looking at picture books.* Fort Atkinson, WI: Highsmith Press.

Encouraging the adult to become a more discerning consumer of picture books, this text enhances appreciation of picture books through information. Discussions of pictorial elements, composition, media, book design elements, and artistic styles lead the reader to share knowledge of and an enthusiasm for the wonder of the picture book with children.

## Traditional Literature/Fantasy

Bosma, Betty (1992). *Fairy tales, fables, legends, and myths: Using folk literature in your classroom* (2nd ed.). New York: Teachers College Press.

Highlighting classroom activities for exploring this genre with children, this practical text shares a wealth of related language arts connections. Activities for responding to literature through puppetry, art, drama, and music assist in including traditional tales across the curriculum.

Helbig, Alethea K., & Perkins Agnes R. (Eds.) (1997). *Myths and hero tales: A cross-cultural guide to literature for children and young adults.* Westport, CT: Greenwood Press.

This selection guide to recent retellings focuses on stories from North America, Asia, Africa, the Middle East, Central and South America, and Oceania. Annotations of 189 books published from 1985–1996 include title, author, illustrator, culture, story type, and grade level. A bibliography of standard works in the genre is included.

Nadelman Lynn, Ruth (1995). *Fantasy literature for children and young adults: An annotated bibliography* (4th ed.). New Providence, NJ: R. R. Bowker.

Dividing the fantasy realm into 10 subgenres, this comprehensive bibliography includes both classic and contemporary fantasy. Opening essay and educational bibliography adds professionalism to this resource.

## Poetry

Blackburn, G. M. (1994). *Index to poetry for children and young people 1988–1992.* New York: H. W. Wilson Company.

A title, subject, author, and first-line index to poetry in collections for children. See also volumes by Blackburn (1982–1987); Brewton, Blackburn, and Blackburn (1976–1981 and 1970–1975);

and Brewton, Brewton, and Blackburn (1964–1969 and 1957–1975) for accessing older children's poetry.

Chatton, Barbara (1993). *Using poetry across the curriculum: A whole language approach.* Phoenix: Oryx Press.

Chapters link poetry to content area curriculum through subtopics, providing lists and bibliographical information to locate poems. Indexing by poets, poems, and topics assists in locating well-remembered and content appropriate poetry.

Cullinan, Beatrice, Scala, Marilyn C., & Schroeder, Virginia C. (1995). *Three voices: An invitation to poetry across the curriculum.* York, ME: Stenhouse.

Thirty-three strategies and 300 suggestions for using poetry with children overflow these pages. Teacher descriptions and student work help the reader envision classroom connections.

Hopkins, Lee Bennett (1987). *Pass the poetry, please* (rev. ed.). New York: Harper & Row.

A plethora of ideas for bringing poetry to life in the classroom, suggestions for creating interest and for writing poetry form the core of the book. Interviews with 20 poets bring this genre to life.

## Realistic and Historical Fiction

Adamson, Lynda G. (1994). *Recreating the past: A guide to American and world historical fiction for children and young adults.* Westport, CT: Greenwood Press.

This resource is especially useful to those who desire to integrate literature with particular periods in history. Plot summaries of well-written historical fiction abound while providing information about reading/interest levels as well as setting dates and locales of each title.

Bernstein, Joanne E., & Rudman, Masha K. (1988). *Books to help children cope with separation and loss* (3rd ed.). New York: R. R. Bowker.

Summaries of 600 fiction (and nonfiction) titles grouped by meaningful topics including divorce, mental illness, moving, loss, and disabilities help adults connect children with the titles they need to deal with personal problems in contemporary life.

Dreyer, Sharon S. (1989). *The bookfinder: A guide to children's literature about the needs and problems of youth aged 2–15.* Circle Pines, MN: American Guidance Service.

Excellent literary connections to children's understanding of contemporary problems are indexed and annotated effectively. Responsibility, parental absence, friendship, and others help link readers and the books that they need for growing up.

Tunnell, M. O., & Ammon, R. (Eds.) (1993). *The story of ourselves: Teaching history though children's literature.* Portsmouth, NH: Heinemann.

This collection of essays that link literature, history, and social studies includes perspectives of well-known authors of historical fiction and practical classroom connections. An annotated bibliography of American historical fiction highlights this teacher-oriented text.

## Nonfiction: Biography/Informational

Bamford, Rosemary A., & Kristo, Janice F. (Eds.) (1998). *Making facts come alive: Choosing quality nonfiction literature K–8.* Norwood, MA: Christopher-Gordon.

Sixteen educators write about all aspects of selecting and sharing the best in nonfiction with students. Selection criteria, content specific titles, classroom connections, and response guides to Orbis Pictus award books form the framework of this valuable resource. Annotated bibliography of Orbis Pictus award and honor books and extensive list of nonfiction books cited make this increasingly useful.

Freeman, Evelyn B., & Person, Diane G. (1992). *Using nonfiction trade books in the elementary classroom*. Urbana, IL: National Council of Teachers of English.

This collection of essays focuses on trends and issues in informational books and practical suggestions for integrating informational books across the curriculum.

Kobrin, Beverly (1995). *Eyeopeners II: Children's books to answer children's questions about the world around them*. New York: Scholastic.

This review of 500 nonfiction books for children includes teaching connections. Specific titles are linked to specific activities and the convenient format makes this a reference tool across the curriculum.

Wyatt, Flora, Coggins, Margaret, & Imber, Jane H. (1998). *Popular nonfiction authors for children: A biographical and thematic guide*. Englewood, CO: Library Unlimited.

Each entry for an informational children's author includes birth date, address, photo, substantive background, a message to students from the author, and a selected bibliography of author's nonfiction titles.

Zarnowski, Myra (1990). *Learning about biographies: A reading-and-writing approach for children*. Urbana, IL: National Council of Teachers of English and the National Council on Social Studies.

The author shares the tasks and responsibilities of a biographer for an audience of upper elementary/middle school students. Discussion of the biography genre, guides for biography in the classroom, and a pertinent bibliography are included.

## Multicultural Children's Literature

Berrera, R. B., Thompson, V. D., & Dressman, M. (Eds.) (1997). *Kaleidoscope: A multicultural booklist for grades K–8* (2nd ed.). Urbana, IL: National Council of Teachers of English.

Annotations of nearly 400 books published between 1993 and 1995 focus on children's books that reflect the diversity of American children. Chapters are grouped by genre and theme rather than cultural group.

Bishop, R. S. (Ed.) (1994). *Kaleidoscope: A multicultural booklist for grades K–8*. Urbana, IL: National Council of Teachers of English.

Annotations of nearly 400 books published between 1990 and 1992 focus on people of color. Literature about or set in other countries is also included as a source of understanding of cultural heritage. Chapters grouped by genre and theme rather than cultural group.

Day, F. A. (Ed.) (1994). *Multicultural voices in contemporary literature: A resource for teachers*. Portsmouth, NH: Heinemann.

Celebrates the lives and works of 39 authors and illustrators of children's books from 20 different cultures. Noted authors include Virginia Hamilton (African American), Shoto Begay (Navajo), Johanna Frank Hurwitz (Jewish American), Yoshiko Uchida (Japanese American), and Laurence Yep (Chinese American). Guidelines for evaluating books and excellent appendixes are included.

Day, F. A. (Ed.) (1997). *Latina and Latino voices in literature for children and teenagers*. Portsmouth, NH: Heinemann.

Focused on authors, each entry includes a photo, birth date, address, and quote; bibliography of author's work; 2-page article on background; bibliography of articles for further author information. Includes Alma Flor Ada, Lulu Delacre, Carmen Garza, Pat Moro, Gary Soto, and others. Useful appendixes and resources make this a rich, culturally specific resource.

Harris, V. H. (1997). *Using multiethnic literature in the K–8 classroom*. Norwood, MA: Christopher-Gordon.

Essays by multicultural experts who share selection criteria and focus on children's literature depicting blacks, Puerto Ricans, Asian Pacific Americans, Mexican Americans, and Native Americans. Up-to-date lists of quality multiethnic titles.

Helbig, Alethea, & Perkins, Agnes (1994). *This land is our land: A guide to multicultural literature for children and young adults*. Westport, CT: Greenwood Press.

Organized around four ethnic groups—African American, Asian American, Hispanic American, and Native American Indian—this single volume provides annotations for 559 books published from 1985–1993. The titles include novels, traditional literature collections, and poetry.

Kruse, G. M., Horning, K. T., & Schliesman, M. (1997). *Multicultural literature for children and young adults, Volume 2: 1991–1996*. Madison, WI: Cooperative Children's Book Center.

This selected listing of books by and about people of color contains more than 350 multicultural titles with author, illustrator, ethnicity, and full subject index. See also previous volume (Kruse & Horning, 1991), which lists multicultural titles published from 1980–1990.

Muse, Daphne (Ed.) (1997). *The New Press guide to multicultural resources for young readers*. New York: New Press (distributed by W. W. Norton).

Containing 1,000 annotations for K–8 literature, each entry includes title, author, cultural connection, and a 250- to 500-word review. Meaningfully organized by themes including community, family, social justice, and building cross-cultural bridges, each chapter is further organized by K–3, 4–6, and 7–8 grade levels. Friendly layout invites frequent use.

## Children's Literature Selection

*Children's books in print* (published annually). New York: R. R. Bowker.

Title, author, and subject indexes to all children's books in print giving necessary bibliographic information for creating bibliographies or ordering books. The subject index, in particular, assists in locating titles for literature clusters and theme explorations.

*The elementary school library collection: A guide to books and other media* (20th ed.). (1996). Williamsport, PA: Brodart.

An arrangement presents entries in card catalog format that provide descriptive annotations as well as priority acquisition information. Books are indexed by author, title, subject, and illustrator with a revised edition available biennially.

Horning, Kathleen T. (1997). *From cover to cover: Evaluating and reviewing children's books*. New York: HarperCollins.

The author demonstrates how to think about and critically evaluate different genres of children's books. The importance of different parts of a book and criteria for each genre lead professionals toward a more discerning look at books selected for children. Particularly excellent for the writer of reviews.

Lehr, Susan (Ed.) (1995). *Battling dragons: Issues and controversy in children's literature*. Portsmouth, NH: Heinemann.

Twenty essays by scholars and authors focus on the issue of censorship and include children's books that have been the target of discussion. With the increased use of literature in the classroom, censorship issues become more relevant and this text envisions current and potential roadblocks to literary freedom.

Odean, K. (1997). *Great books for girls: More than 600 books to inspire today's girls and tomorrow's women*. New York: Ballantine.

Books with strong female heroines and role models encourage girls to read. Strong annotations serve as motivation to read both new and familiar titles.

Odean, K. (1998). *Great books for boys: More than 600 books for boys 2 to 14*. New York: Ballantine.

Challenged by the reality that young boys often give up their love of reading, the author stages a campaign to share plenty of ideas and book titles to encourage boys to read. Lively, informative annotations act as bait to hook boys who might otherwise lose their zest for reading due to cultural expectations.

Price, Anne, & Yaakov, Juliette (Eds.) (1996). *The children's catalog* (17th ed.). New York: H. W. Wilson.

Published every 5 years, this comprehensive listing of books and magazines recommended for preschool through sixth grade is arranged by Dewey decimal system nonfiction, fiction, collections, and easy books. An alphabetical, comprehensive key includes author, titles, subject, and analytical listings.

Samuels, B. G., & Beers, G. K. (Ed.) (1996). *Your reading: An annotated booklist for middle school and junior high.* Urbana, IL: National Council of Teachers of English.

Introduces more than 1,200 selected young adult book titles published between 1993–1995 through informative annotations in meaningfully organized chapters. Detailed indexes aid in locating books for curricular areas. See former editions for a wealth of quality titles from earlier years.

Sutton, W. K. (Ed.) (1997). *Adventuring with books: A booklist for Pre-K–Grade 6* (11th ed.). Urbana, IL: National Council of Teachers of English.

This title does not replace earlier editions, but updates the selections with books of literary merit published in 1993–1995. Organized by genres and themes, annotations include plot summary, description of illustrations, and classroom connections.

West, Mark I. (1997). *Everyone's guide to children's literature.* Fort Atkinson, WI: Highsmith Press.

This general resource about children's literature includes annotated lists of resources, awards, children's literature collections, organizations, journals, etc., connected to children's books. A great place to begin a search or an inquiry or to find most general information about resources related to children's literature.

## Professional Books Supporting Response to Literature

Almasi, J., & Gambrell, L. (1996). *Lively discussions! Fostering engaged reading.* Newark, DE: International Reading Association.

A powerful tool for encouraging oral response to literature in the classroom, this book focuses on helping students develop discussion skills necessary to explore the world of literature and literacy.

Bauer, C. F. (1993). *New handbook for storytellers with stories, poems, magic, and more.* Illus. by L. Bredeson. Chicago: American Library Association.

Updated version of a 1977 classic to assist in getting started, selecting stories, and planning storytelling programs that elicit oral response.

Bromley, K. D. (1996). *Webbing with literature: Creating story maps with children's books (2nd ed.).* Boston: Allyn and Bacon.

A valuable resource for 125 webs and annotations for more than 200 children's books by genre. Chapter 5 focuses on responding to literature with a strong section on dramatic response.

Egroff, Sheila, Stubbs, G. T., & Ashley, L. F. (1996). *Only connect: Readings on children's literature* (3rd ed.). Toronto: Oxford University Press.

An anthology of articles by noted authors and respected children's literature experts. Intended to expand the view of the literary realm through scholarship and thought-provoking essays, the collection connects teachers, authors, students, parents, and others with literature and each other as advocates of children's books.

Goforth, Frances, & Spillman, Carolyn (1994). *Using folk literature in the classroom: Encouraging children to read and write.* Phoenix: Oryx Press.

Built on a response-based approach to folk literature in the classroom, six instructional units are shared through themes. Teaching connections, extensive lists of folk literature, and outstanding appendixes makes this an excellent resource for eliciting response to and appreciation for folk literature.

Hill, B. C., Johnson, N. J., & Noe, C. L. S. (Eds.) (1995). *Literature circles and response.* Norwood, MA: Christopher-Gordon.

Provides specific information for integrating literature circles into a reading program as an outlet for oral response and an aid to meaning construction. An annotated bibliography of 500 books for use in literature circles provides a valuable resource.

Holland, K., Hungerford, R., & Ernst, S. (Eds.) (1993). *Journeying: Children responding to literature.* Portsmouth, NH: Heinemann.

Teacher-researcher studies explore the verbal, artistic, dramatic, and written responses of children to books in classroom settings. Organized developmentally, the articles explore strategies for using children's literature, teachers' influences on response, contexts for response, and response to all literary genres. Transcripts of book conversations and children's response complement the text.

Huck, C. S., Hepler, S., Hickman, J., & Kiefer, B. Z. (1997). *Children's literature in the elementary school* (6th ed.). Dubuque, IA: Brown & Benchmark.

Since 1961 this classic, comprehensive, respected text has focused on connecting children's literature, readers, and school literature programs. Noteworthy are Chapter 2 on "Understanding Children's Responses to Literature" and Part 3 on "Developing a Literature Program."

Jody, M., & Saccardi, M. (1996). *Computer conversations: Readers and books online.* Urbana, IL: National Council of Teachers of English.

Powerful response connections exist between books and readers via the internet. A BookRead project details e-mail conversations about books. Also presented are details of author chats and a reader response workshop on-line, encouraging the sharing of response in cyberspace.

McClure, A. A., & Kristo, J. V. (Eds.) (1994). *Inviting children's responses to literature: Guides to 57 notable books.* Urbana, IL: National Council of Teachers of English.

Provides a reader response perspective on the use of quality literature PreK–8. Each guide contains plot summary, teaching suggestions, and a list of 12 to 15 related titles. Especially valuable encouraging integrated use of language arts, comparisons of stories, and connections to personal experience.

McClure, A. A., & Kristo, J. V. (Eds.). (1996). *Books that invite talk, wonder, and play.* Urbana, IL: National Council of Teachers of English.

Essays by Children's Literature Assembly members energize literature-based programs with "notable" books and a blend of classroom activities to stimulate in-depth response to books that make children think and wonder. Final section of essays by 38 authors reflects the art of wordcrafting.

Meinlach, A. M., Rothlein, L., & Fredericks, A. D. (1995). *The complete guide to thematic units: Creating the integrated curriculum.* Norwood, MA: Christopher-Gordon.

Provides valuable guidelines for using children's literature to develop self-generated thematic units. Planning forms facilitate creation, organization, and implementation. See also *More thematic units for creating the integrated curriculum* by the same authors.

Norton, D. E. (1999). *Through the eyes of a child: An introduction to children's literature* (5th ed.). Upper Saddle River, NJ: Merrill/Prentice Hall.

This classic and well-organized comprehensive text effectively links children's literature and classroom practice. Following each genre chapter is a related one titled "Involving Children in. . ." incorporating meaningful suggestions for the genre's use with children. Outstanding annotated bibliographies follow each chapter and a CD-ROM disk accompanies the text for increased curricular access.

Roser, N. L., & Martinez, M. G. (Eds.) (1995). *Book talk and beyond: Children and teachers respond to literature.* Newark, DE: International Reading Association.

New ideas for encouraging children to talk about books and to learn from the value and direction of that talk. Prominent authors share steps for encouraging aesthetic response, using the tools of story talk, guiding book talk, and fostering dramatic, artistic, and journal responses.

Short, K. G. (1995). *Research and professional resources in children's literature: Piecing a patchwork quilt.* Newark, DE: International Reading Association.

This comprehensive title provides publication information and brief annotations for articles and books about children's literature, including recent research completed in response to literature. An outstanding resource for those seeking a research base on literature response, those conducting teacher action or dissertation research, or those linking theory and research into classroom practice.

Sorenson, M., & Lehman, B. (Eds.) (1995). *Teaching with children's books: Paths to literature-based instruction.* Urbana, IL: National Council of Teachers of English.

Twenty-seven essays share practical experiences in understanding, considering, preparing, modeling, teaching, collaborating, assessing, and supporting literature-based programs. Charts, figures, and lists of children's books provide plentiful ideas for response-based instruction.

Whitin, Phyllis (1996). *Sketching stories, stretching minds: Responding visually to literature.* Portsmouth, NH: Heinemann.

Sketching as a response to literature facilitates inquiry, extends thinking, and provides a window into that thinking. Numerous drafts of student sketches helps envision potential of the artistic response to literature and its use as a bridge to writing about literature.

## Professional Journals

*Book Links: Connecting Books, Libraries, and Classrooms.* Chicago, IL: American Library Association.

Published six times per year, this publication links books, classrooms, and libraries. Features include articles on authors and illustrators and book themes with plentiful bibliographies.

*Children's Literature in Education: An International Quarterly.* New York: Human Sciences Press.

Scholarly articles include interviews of authors and illustrators, practitioner connections, evaluation of literature, and discussions on social issues reflected in children's books.

*The Dragon Lode.* Children's Literature and Reading Special Interest Group of the International Reading Association.

Intended primarily for teachers, two issues per year contain articles on utilizing children's literature in the elementary curriculum, reviews of children's books, professional reviews, and annotated bibliographies of themed books.

*Journal of Children's Literature.* Urbana, IL: Children's Literature Assembly of the National Council of Teachers of English.

Two issues per year contain articles and features on multiple aspects of children's literature. Useful to university professors, classroom teachers, and anyone who appreciates children's books, the journal often features articles focusing on response of children to literature. Themed issues provide a focus, but not a limit to the kinds of articles and information shared.

*Language Arts.* Urbana, IL: National Council of Teachers of English.

This journal includes themed issues on topics related to the teaching of language arts. Special features include a special book review section as well as practical applications of literature in the classroom.

*The New Advocate.* Norwood, MA: Christopher-Gordon.

Published quarterly, this highly professional journal is intended for "those involved with young people and their literature." Features include a focus on the creative process and concepts and themes with reviews of children's books and professional resources.

*The Reading Teacher.* Newark, DE: International Reading Association.

Published eight times per year, articles focus on theory-into-practice with a high focus on literature-based instruction. Features also include reviews of children's books with classroom connections.

# Professional Review Journals

*Booklist.* Chicago: American Library Association.

Published twice monthly (except for July and August), *Booklist* carries recommended reviews worthy of consideration for purchase by public and school libraries. Children's books are presented by age and grade level with special bibliographies commonly published on a specific subject.

*The Bulletin for the Center for Children's Books.* Urbana, IL: University of Illinois Press.

Published monthly from September to July, reviews of children's books stress curricular connections and literary merit. Both negative and positive reviews are included.

*The Horn Book Guide to Children's and Young Adult Books.* Boston: Horn Book, Inc.

Published in March and September since 1990, this guide contains brief reviews of all hardcover books published in the United States during the previous 6 months. Excellent support for selection or ordering information on the newest children's books.

*Horn Book Magazine.* Boston: Horn Book, Inc.

Includes literature-focused articles and detailed reviews of positively reviewed children's books. Founded in 1924, this is the oldest children's literature journal in the United States. The acceptance speeches of the Newbery author and Caldecott illustrator are published here, and "The Hunt Breakfast" features announcements of conferences, awards, and various items of interest to children's literature enthusiasts.

*School Library Journal: For Children's, Young Adult, and School Librarians.* New York: R. R. Bowker.

Librarians write these positive and negative reviews of most children's books published. The December issue features an index and a "Best Books" listing.

# Children's Literature Internet Sites

The following web sites are of particular interest to those interested in children's literature. They provide users with a wealth of information and options for using literature in the classroom. A vast body of knowledge about children's books can easily be accessed to assist in updated information in the field.

## Literature-Based Sites

American Library Association

<http://www.ala.org>

Home page of the national association representing public, school, state, and special libraries. Contains ALA news, ALA library, ALA events, and links to other web sites including Notable Children's web sites and author web site of the month.

Association for Library Service to Children (ALSC)

<http://www.ala.org/alsc/>

This division of the American Library Association includes the Newbery Medal home page, the Caldecott Medal home page, and the Coretta Scott King Award Site. Announcements of winners are available immediately following their presentation at the American Library Association winter meeting in January.

Carol Hurst's Children's Literature Site

<http://www.carolhurst.com>

An author/language arts consultant (Carol Hurst) and an author/computer consultant (Rebecca Otis) provide book reviews, curriculum connections, themes, and professional topics of interest.

The Children's Book Council

<http://www.cbcbooks.org/>

This association of book publishers sponsors Children's Book Week in November. The site includes an on-line catalog of materials and articles of interest written by literature specialists and intended for publishers, booksellers, parents, and teachers/librarians.

Children's Literature: Beyond Basals

<http://www.beyondbasals.com/>

Created and maintained by Gale W. Sherman and Bette D. Ammon (see *Book Links,* March 1998), this site features links to in-depth book guides useful for K–12 literature-based curriculum planning.

The Children's Literature Web Guide

<http://acs.ucalgary.ca/~dkbrown/index.html>

The most comprehensive general children's literature site created by David K. Brown from the Doucette Library at the University of Calgary in Canada. From this site, quick access is available to author information, lists of recommended books, lesson plans, book reviews, children's book awards, and resources for teachers, parents, storytellers, and writers. Direct links to numerous sites on the World Wide Web are listed.

Cooperative Children's Book Center (CCBC)

<http://www.soemadison.wisc.edu/ccbc/>

Maintained by the School of Education at the University of Wisconsin, this source provides an excellent reference for the holdings of the noncirculating children's literature collection.

Kay Vandergrift's Children's Literature Page

<http://www.scils.rutgers.edu/special/kay/childlit.html>

Interesting site maintained by a children's literature professor and author at Rutgers University. Categories with links include children's literature and literature/learning connections.

amazon.com (largest online bookstore) and barnesandnoble.com

<http://www.amazon.com>or <http://www.barnesandnoble.com>

These virtual bookstores extend beyond the holdings of the local library and bookstores. Extensive search options easily access related books for theme explorations and bibliographies of books in print. Books can be ordered at a discount with efficient delivery. In addition, book reviews can be written and posted on-line at this site. The "Write an online review" option of amazon.com can be used by students as well as adults as they respond to quality children's  books.

## Children's Author/Illustrator Information

Author's Pen

<http://www.books.com/scripts/authors.exe/>

This site includes information for more than 1000 children's and adult authors and is updated frequently. "Book Stacks" is a comprehensive resource for locating authors on the web. Searching can be accomplished by author's name or by scrolling through the alphabetized list. Direct links to many author home pages are provided.

Fairrosa Cyber Library/Authors and Illustrators

<http://www.interport.net/~fairrosa/cl.authors.html>

Extensive direct links to author/illustrator websites.

Internet School Library Media Center's Index to Author and Illustrator Internet Sites

<http://falcon.jmu.edu/ramseyil/biochildhome.htm>

This extensive site provides easy access to Teacher Resource Files and curriculum-related Web resources for teachers, school librarians, parents, and students.

Kay Vandergrift's Learning About the Author and Illustrator Pages

<http://www.scils.rutgers.edu/special/kay/author.html>

Links to more than 500 author webpages. Also includes lists of author biographies and autobiographies and a list of author videos.

The Scoop's Interviews of Authors and Illustrators

<http://www.friend.ly.net/scoop/biographies/>

Famous book creators are featured in this online magazine.

Examples of Specific Author Sites:

| | |
|---|---|
| Avi | <http://www.avi-writer.com> |
| Jan Brett | <http://www.janbrett.com> |
| Marc Brown | <http://www.mbrown.com> |
| Eric Carle | <http://eric-carle.com> |
| Tomie dePaola | <http://tomie.com> |
| Leo & Diane Dillon | <http://www.best.com/~libros/dillon> |
| Virginia Hamilton | <http://www.virginiahamilton.com> |
| Brian Jacques | <http://www.redwall.org/dave/jacques.html> |
| Dave Pilkey | <http://www.pilkey.com> |
| Beatrix Potter | <http://www.peterrabbit.co.uk/index2.html> |
| Cynthia Rylant | <http://rylant.com> |
| Seymour Simon | <http://seymoursimon.com> |
| Janet Stevens | <http://www.janetstevens.com> |
| Colin Thompson | <http://www.ozemail.com.au/~colinet/> |
| Audrey Wood | <http://www.AudreyWood.com> |

Children's Book Publishers

| | |
|---|---|
| Avon Books | <http://www.avonbooks.com> |
| Bantam Doubleday Dell | <http://www.bdd.com/kids> |
| DK Publishing, Inc. | <http://dk.com> |
| Harcourt Brace | <http://harcourtbooks.com> |
| HarperCollins | <http://www.harperchildrens.com> |
| Lee & Low | <http://leeandlow.com> |
| Morrow | <http://www.williammorrow.com> |
| Penguin Putnam | <http://www.penguinputnam.com> |
| Random House | <http://www.randomhouse.com/kids/catalog> |
| Scholastic | <http://scholastic.com> |
| Simon & Schuster | <http://www.SimonSaysKids.com> |

# Children's Literature Listservs

CCBC-Net    <listserv@ccbc.soemadison.wisc.edu>

The Cooperative Children's Book Center at the University of Wisconsin focuses on a monthly theme, author, subject, or issue.

Child_Lit    <listserv@email.rutgers.edu>

This Children's Literature Criticism and Theory group is the most academic of the listservs. This discussion group fosters the sharing of ideas by researchers engaged in scholarship on any topic.

Kidlit-Lit    <listserv@bingvmb.cc.binghamton.edu>

Children's literature supporters discuss teaching, innovative ideas, and current research and share ideas, questions, and stories with the group.

# Other Literature-Related Sites for Teachers

Aaron Shepard's Reader's Theater Editions

<http://www.aaronshep.com/rt/RTE.html>

Stories including humor, fantasy, and retold tales from different cultures are adapted into readers' theater scripts for third grade and above.

AskERIC Home Page

<http://ericir.syr.edu>
Literature-based lesson plans, virtual libraries, full texts of fairy tales and fables, bibliographies, and links to other web sites are available through this home page.

Banned Books Online

<http://www.cs.cmu.edu/Web/People/spok/banned-books.html>
An overview of books once considered controversial and links to many texts. An update of books challenged in schools, including a list of "The Most Frequently Banned Books in the 1990s."

BDD Books for Young Readers

<http://bdd.com/teachers>
The Teachers Resource Center shares teaching tools to bring quality literature to life for young readers.

Booklist

<http://www.ala.org/booklist/>
*Booklist* magazine's on-line site includes selected reviews, articles, and a cumulative index of the journal.

Education World

<http://www.education-world.com/>
A search engine that grades over 100,000 Internet sites of interest to educators. New sites added continuously.

HornBook Magazine

<http://hbook.com>
The web site of a premier review journal of children's books.

Internet Public Library

<http://www.ipl.org>
Resources are arranged in graphical rooms that represent a library offering browser access to Reference Room, Youth, Teens, and more.

Kid's Web

<http://www.npac.syr.edu/textbook/kidsweb/literature.html>
This site includes on-line books, creative writing, fairy tales, and lots of literature links.

Library of Congress Online

<http://www.loc.gov>
General server for the nation's library includes special exhibits, documents, photos, and rare books and objects.

Scholastic Network

<http://scholasticnetwork.com/index.htm>
On on-line network for children and teachers.

# Subject and Author Index

# Title/Author/Illustrator Index

*Chato's Kitchen* (Soto), 67, 75, 175
*Cherokee Summer* (Hoyt-
    Goldsmith), 160, 285, 287
Cherry, Lynne, 48, 59, 73, 114, 118,
    154, 164, 245, 251, 277, 280,
    287
Chessare, Michele, 114
*Chicka Chicka ABC* (Martin &
    Archambault), 51, 53, 54
*Chicka Chicka Boom Boom*
    (Martin & Archambault),
    53, 74, 191, 205
*Chicken Little* (Kellogg), 238
*Chicken Sunday* (Polacco), 201
Chilcoat, George W., 277, 301
*Children of Lir, The* (MacGill-
    Callahan), 81
*Children of the Dustbowl: The True
    Story of the School at
    Weedpatch Camp* (Stanley),
    161, 277
*Children of Topaz, The: The Story
    of a Japanese-American
    Internment Camp* (Tunnell),
    277, 301
Children's Book Council (CBC),
    164
*Child's Book of Play in Art, A*
    (Micklethwait), 264, 271
*Child's Garden of Verses, The*
    (Stevenson), 106, 118
Chocolate, Debbi, 172, 184
Chorao, Kay, 205
Christiansen, Candice, 68–69, 74,
    298
Christie, Gregory, 183
*Christmas in the Big House,
    Christmas in the Quarters*
    (McKissack & McKissack),
    59, 66, 74, 183, 184, 186,
    280, 287
Christopher, John, 94, 98
*Chronicles of Narnia, The* (Lewis).
    *See* Narnia Chronicles
Chronicles of Prydian
    (Alexander), 88
*Chrysanthemum* (Henkes), 6, 22,
    30, 42, 47, 68, 74, 201, 246,
    251

Ciardi, John, 110, 114
*Cinderella or the Little Glass
    Slipper* (Brown), 178
*Circle of Seasons* (Livingston), 18,
    114
*Circles and Squares Everywhere!*
    (Grover), 55
*City in Winter, A* (Helprin), 59
*Clap Your Hands* (Cauley), 30, 42
Clapp, John, 98
Clare, John D., 287
Clark, Emma Chichester, 55
*Class Clown* (Hurwitz), 129
*Class President* (Hurwitz), 129
*Clay Boy* (Ginsberg), 36, 42
*Clay Marble, The* (Ho), 139, 142
Clay, Wil, 43, 205
*Clean House* (Haas), 60
Cleary, Beverly, 19, 87, 123, 141,
    237, 240, 251
Clements, Andrew, 141
*Cleopatra* (Stanley & Vennema),
    278, 287
Clerk, Jessica, 205
*Cleveland Lee's Beale Street Band*
    (Flowers), 268, 271
*Climbing Kansas Mountains*
    (Shannon), 69, 75, 209
Climo, Shirley, 178
*Close, Closer, Closest* (Rotner), 56, 75
*Cloudland* (Burningham), 95, 98
*Clouds of Terror* (Welch), 305
Clouse, Nancy, 42, 300
*Clown* (Blake). 56, 73
*Cock-a-doodle-doo: A Farmyard
    Counting Book* (Lavis), 55
*Cockroaches* (Cole), 278, 287
*Cody* (Brooks), 128
Coe, Anne, 293
Coerr, Eleanor, 35, 42, 182, 300
Cofer, Judith Ortiz, 181
Cohen, Barbara, 306
*Cold and Hot Winter, The*
    (Hurwitz), 129
Cole, B., 237
Cole, Brock, 98
Cole, Henry, 42, 205
Cole, Joanna, 60, 159, 163, 278,
    285, 287

Cole, William, 114
Coleman, Evelyn, 172, 175, 185
Collier, Christopher, 143
Collier, James Lincoln, 143
Collodi, Carlo, 261, 270
Colon, R., 82
*Come Back, Salmon: How a Group
    of Dedicated Kids Adopted
    Pigeon Creek and Brought It
    Back to Life* (Cone), 159,
    285
*Comet's Nine Lives* (Brett), 65, 73
*Coming Home: From the Life of
    Langston Hughes* (Cooper),
    183, 273, 287
*Communication* (Aliki), 278, 286
*Comus* (Milton, adapted by
    Hodges), 79, 97
Condon, Ken, 118
Cone, Molly, 159, 285, 287
*Confetti: Poems for Children*
    (Mora), 178, 180, 186, 256,
    257, 271
Conlon-McKenna, Marita, 210,
    211, 225, 230, 305
Conly, Jane Leslie, 5, 22, 122, 201,
    226
Conrad, Pam, 93, 98, 263, 270, 299
Conteh-Morgan, Jane, 234
*Cool Salsa: Growing Up Latino in
    the United States* (Carlson,
    ed), 114, 180, 306
Cooney, Barbara, 42, 62, 73, 74,
    147, 163, 235, 251, 281, 287,
    299
Cooper, Floyd, 122, 164, 175, 180,
    183, 186, 267, 270, 287
Cooper, Susan, 88, 92, 98, 201
*Coppelia* (Fonteyn), 255, 271
Coretta Scott King Award and
    Honor Book Artists, 185
Councell, Ruth, 272
*Counting Crocodiles* (Sierra), 55
*Counting on the Woods: A Poem*
    (Lyon), 55
*Count Silvernose* (Kimmel), 48, 74,
    80
*Count Your Way Through Ireland,*
    (Haskins & Benson), 55